Work-Life Balance in the Modern Workplace

Bulletin of Comparative Labour Relations

VOLUME 98

Founding Editor

The series started in 1970 under the dynamic editorship of Professor Roger Blanpain (Belgium), former President of the International Industrial Relations Association. Professor Blanpain, Professor Emeritus of Labour Law, Universities of Leuven and Tilburg, was also General Editor of the International Encyclopedia of Laws (with more than 1,600 collaborators worldwide) and President of the Association of Educative and Scientific Authors Authors. He passed away in October 2016.

General Editor

In 2015 Frank Hendrickx, Professor of labour law at the Faculty of Law of the University of Leuven (Belgium) joined as a co-Editor. Frank Hendrickx has published numerous articles and books and regularly advises governments, international institutions and private organisations in the area of labour law as well as in sports law. He is the Editor-in-Chief of the European Labour Law Journal and General Editor of the International Encyclopaedia of Laws.

Introduction

The Bulletins constitute a unique source of information and thought-provoking discussion, laying the groundwork for studies of employment relations in the 21st century, involving among much else the effects of globalization, new technologies, migration, and the greying of the population.

Contents/Subjects

Amongst other subjects the Bulletins frequently include the proceedings of international or regional conferences; reports from comparative projects devoted to salient issues in industrial relations, human resources management, and/or labour law; and specific issues underlying the multicultural aspects of our industrial societies.

Objective

The Bulletins offer a platform of expression and discussion on labour relations to scholars and practitioners worldwide, often featuring special guest editors.

The titles published in this series are listed at the end of this volume.

BULLETIN OF COMPARATIVE LABOUR RELATIONS – 98

Work-Life Balance in the Modern Workplace

Interdisciplinary Perspectives from Work-Family Research, Law and Policy

Editor

Sarah De Groof

Contributors

Alberto Barrio
Sonja Bekker
Stephanie Bernstein
Robert J. Blomme
Amy K. Brown
Jorge Cabrita
Sarah De Groof
Harun Demirkaya
Daantje Derks
Katherine S. Drake
Nimet Eryiğit
Émilie Genin
Lonnie Golden
Lena Hipp
Jaeseung Kim
Barbara Kresal
Janine Leschke
Annick Masselot
Ifat Matzner-Heruti
Lourdes Mella Méndez
Friederike Molitor
Gürol Özcüre
Agnès Parent-Thirion
Pascale Peters
Amanda Reilly
Niklas Selberg
Mathilde Valentini
Anne van Heertum
Greet Vermeylen
Tracey Warren
Mathijn Wilkens
Ania Zbyszewska
Nuna Zekić

General Editor

Frank Hendrickx

Founding Editor

Roger Blanpain

Wolters Kluwer

Published by:
Kluwer Law International B.V.
PO Box 316
2400 AH Alphen aan den Rijn
The Netherlands
Website: www.wolterskluwerlr.com

Sold and distributed in North, Central and South America by:
Wolters Kluwer Legal & Regulatory U.S.
7201 McKinney Circle
Frederick, MD 21704
United States of America
Email: customer.service@wolterskluwer.com

Sold and distributed in all other countries by:
Quadrant
Rockwood House
Haywards Heath
West Sussex
RH16 3DH
United Kingdom
Email: international-customerservice@wolterskluwer.com

Printed on acid-free paper.

ISBN 978-90-411-8630-0

e-Book: ISBN 978-90-411-8648-5
web-PDF: ISBN 978-90-411-8649-2

Printed in the United Kingdom.

Notes on Contributors

Alberto Barrio is a Ph.D. researcher at the Department of Labour Law and Social Policy at Tilburg University, Netherlands.

Dr **Sonja Bekker** is an Associate professor European Social Policy, ReflecT, Tilburg University, Netherlands.

Dr **Stephanie Bernstein** is a professor of labour and employment law at the Law Department of the Université du Québec à Montréal, and a member of CINBIOSE (www.cinbiose.uqam.ca) and CRIMT (www.crimt.org).

Dr **Robert J. Blomme** is a Professor of Organization Behaviour at Nyenrode Business Universiteit and a Professor Management and Organization at Open Universiteit, Netherlands.

Amy K. Brown is a human resources consultant working in Minneapolis/St. Paul, Minnesota. She holds an M.A. in Human Resources and Industrial Relations from the Carlson School of Management at the University of Minnesota and an A.B. from Mount Holyoke College.

Jorge Cabrita is research manager in the Working life unit at the European Foundation for the Improvement of Living and Working Conditions, Ireland.

Dr **Sarah De Groof** recently obtained her Ph.D. in law from KU Leuven, Belgium, where she still works as a research and teaching assistant. She is also a certified lawyer.

Dr **Harun Demirkaya** is a full professor and works at the Kocaeli University Faculty of Economics and Administrative Sciences, Department of Business Administration, Turkey.

Dr **Daantje Derks** is an Associate Professor Work & Organizational Psychology at the Centre of Excellence for Positive Organizational Psychology, Erasmus University Rotterdam, Netherlands.

Dr. Katherine S. Drake is an independent consultant. She earned her M.A. and Ph.D. in Educational Psychology (Measurement and Program Evaluation) at the University of Minnesota.

Dr **Nimet Eryiğit** works for the Ordu University, Ünye Faculty of Economics and Administrative Sciences, Department of Business Administration in Turkey as a research assistant since 2004, July.

Dr **Émilie Genin** is an Associate Professor at the school of Industrial Relations of University of Montréal, Canada. She received her Ph.D. from HEC Paris in 2007.

Dr **Lonnie Golden** is a Professor of Economics and Labor Studies at Penn State University, Abington College, USA and Senior Research Analyst at University of Illinois at Urbana-Champaign.

Dr **Lena Hipp** is Head of the Research Group Work and Care, Social Science Research Centre, Berlin, Germany.

Dr **Jaeseung Kim** is a lecturer at the University of Chicago.

Dr **Barbara Kresal** is Professor of Labour Law and Social Security at the University of Ljubljana, Faculty of Social Work and the Institute for Labour Law at the Faculty of Law, Slovenia.

Dr **Janine Leschke** is Associate Professor, Department of Business and Politics, Copenhagen Business School (CBS), Denmark.

Dr **Annick Masselot** is an Associate Professor in law at the University of Canterbury, New Zealand.

Dr **Ifat Matzner-Heruti** is a lecturer at the Faculty of Society and Culture in Beit-Berl College; at the LLM programme in Tel-Aviv University Law School; and at the M.A. programme in Women and Gender Studies in Haifa University, Israel. She received her Ph.D. in law (JSD) from UC Berkeley, California.

Dr **Lourdes Mella Méndez** is a Senior Lecturer (Professor Accredited) in Labour Law and Social Security of the University of Santiago de Compostela. Spain.

Friederike Molitor is doctoral student in the doctoral programme 'Good Work', Social Science Research Centre, Berlin, Germany.

Dr **Gürol Özcüre** is an Associate professor and head of department at the Ordu University, Faculty of Economics and Administrative Sciences, Department of Labour Economics and Industrial Relations, Turkey.

Agnès Parent-Thirion is senior research manager in the Working life unit at the European Foundation for the Improvement of Living and Working Conditions, Ireland.

Dr **Pascale Peters** is an Associate Professor Strategic Human Resource Management (SHRM) and Chair of the Alumni board at the Department of Business Administration at the Faculty of Management Sciences, Radboud University in Nijmegen, Netherlands.

Dr **Amanda Reilly** is a Senior lecturer at the University of Victoria in Wellington, New Zealand.

Niklas Selberg, LL.M., is a doctoral candidate in private law, particularly labour law, at the Faculty of Law, Lund University, Sweden.

Mathilde Valentini is a lawyer and a Master of Law student at the Université du Québec à Montréal, Canada.

Anne van Heertum, Msc is an Alumnus of the master specialization Strategic Human Resource Management (SHRM) of the Department of Business Administration, Faculty of Management Sciences, Radboud University in Nijmegen, Netherlands.

Greet Vermeylen is senior research manager in the Working life unit at the European Foundation for the Improvement of Living and Working Conditions, Ireland.

Dr **Tracey Warren** is a professor of sociology at the University of Nottingham, UK.

Mathijn Wilkens is researcher in the Working life unit at the European Foundation for the Improvement of Living and Working Conditions, Ireland.

Dr **Ania Zbyszewska** is an Assistant Professor at the University of Warwick School of Law, United Kingdom.

Dr **Nuna Zekić** is an assistant Professor in Labour Law at the Department of Social Law and Social Policy at Tilburg University, Netherlands.

Summary of Contents

Table of Contents

Foreword

Work-life balance has always been a complex field of study, and it involves researchers from many different disciplines. It is hard enough even to get agreement on the correct term to use, much less how to apply it in practice. Although the term 'work-life balance' is widely used in both academic circles and policy discussions, there are many other terms in use as well. For example, some scholars feel that work-life balance is an unattainable state of being, and thus prefer 'work-life integration', 'work-life fit', or some similar construction. Other authors don't use the term 'life' at all, but rather prefer to focus on the 'family', as in the terms 'work-family balance', 'work and family reconciliation', and similar constructs. Still others prefer more negative terms, such as work-life or work-family 'conflict', 'interference', and 'spillover', among others. Regardless of the terminology used, however, most scholars are still talking about the same fundamental phenomenon – the relationship between paid work in all of its various forms and personal life, which includes family but is not limited to it. And of course, gender permeates nearly every aspect of research in this wide-ranging field.

Traditionally, work-life balance research has tended to focus on time – and with good reason. A large body of research form many different disciplines has shown that excessively long hours of work have negative effects on work-life balance, work-family conflict, and even more fundamentally, human health, well-being, and even life itself – such as *karōshi*, which is the Japanese word for death from overwork. Clearly, however, there are other important issues as well. One need look no further than the rise of various forms of 'marginal' part-time work with very short working hours and 'on call' work, such as 'zero-hours' contracts, that have no guaranteed hours at all. These developments have reinforced and expanded longstanding concerns regarding the adequacy of workers' earnings – including those working in various forms of casual work and in the informal economies of many developing countries – and they have obvious implications for their ability to achieve any kind of meaningful work-life balance. On top of that, we have also seen a rise in highly variable and unpredictable work schedules, so-called 'just-in-time scheduling', in many developed countries. Such schedules obviously wreak havoc on workers' ability to plan even the most basic aspects of their personal lives.

As if work-life balance wasn't already complex enough, the boundary between paid work and personal life is becoming more and more blurred. New Information and Communications Technologies (New ICTs), such as smartphones and tablet computers, have revolutionized everyday work and life in the twenty-first century. On the one hand, they enable constant connection with friends and family, as well as with work colleagues and supervisors; on the other hand, paid work may increasingly intrude into the time periods and physical spaces normally reserved for personal life. Crucial to this development is the detachment of work from traditional office spaces. Twenty-first century work is often supported by internet connections, and thus can be done from basically anywhere and at any time. This new independence of work from place changes the role of technology in the work environment dramatically. Scholars are increasingly concerned with the advantages and disadvantages of New ICTs for a variety of different aspects of working conditions, including work-life balance.

Work-life balance is also a complex domain for policymaking as well. Of course, as with many areas of research, most policymakers simply don't have the time to get up to speed regarding the latest developments in work-life balance research. Also, many researchers don't have the inclination to focus very much on the policy implications of their research. And even if policymakers are inclined towards legal and regulatory solutions – which are increasingly difficult to enact in a world dominated by a neoliberal discourse – there are many aspects of work-life balance policies that simply can't be addressed through national legislation. For example, one can enact a law providing paid leave, but such a law can't require colleagues to be supportive of workers taking such leave. Rather, effective work-life balance policies may require social dialogue at national, sectoral and enterprise levels to provide frameworks for action, and then polices at the workplace level to create concrete actions that are adapted to the needs and preferences of workers and the particular circumstances of each organization.

This volume brings together a wide range of scholars from a number of different academic disciplines, presenting their research findings regarding various aspects of work-life balance and the implications of those findings for policies at all levels (national, sectoral, enterprise, workplace) to improve the balance between paid work and personal life. It is my sincere hope that it can make an important contribution to a better work-life balance for workers in various jobs and occupations and with different personal circumstances, needs, and preferences.

*Jon C. Messenger**
International Labour Office
Geneva

* The opinions shared in this foreword represent the personal views of the author and does not constitute an endorsement of these opinions by the ILO.

CHAPTER 1

Introduction

Sarah De Groof

§1.01 GENERAL BACKGROUND

The world of work is changing. Technological, demographical, societal and individual changes cause many individuals to reconsider the way we work, what role work plays in our lives and how we can reconcile work and family or private life. A major challenge is that the boundary between work and private life is blurring, a challenge that can be both a potential and a threat. In academic scholarship, the debate on these issues is very lively. This is, for example, demonstrated by the more than 700 academics from 45 different countries attending the Work and Family Researchers Network Conference in June 2016 in Washington DC. But often, academic insights are not translated into policy.

In part because policy makers serve several or other goals than the reconciliation of work and private life. In part also because, although many scientific contributions on work and family formulate policy recommendations regarding for example the fit of careers and care, they rarely specify what policy should exactly look like. For example, if it is demonstrated that support at the workplace correlates to a lower work-life conflict, how then can policy encourage the supervisor's and colleagues' support? In part also because policy makers are not aware of the impressive body of literature on work and private life research.

This book project seeks to close the gap between research and policy by bringing together the academic findings from several disciplines together in one book.

§1.02 OVERVIEW OF THE CONTRIBUTIONS

Alberto Barrio and **Nuna Zekic** highlight a crucial phenomenon of the 'Modern Workplace', namely crowd-work. They define crowd-work as the on-demand performance of tasks by persons selected remotely through online platforms from a large pool of potential and generic workers. According to Alberto and Nuna, several features of crowd-work may have an impact on work-life balance, such as the possibility to perform work on distance, flexible working hours and having multiple jobs. Furthermore, the lack of clarity on the (employment) status of persons performing crowd-work hinders its possible regulation. They highlight the argument that has been put forward before that crowd-work and other forms of casual employment often seek to remove slack times from work to have employers or customers pay only for productive working times or results. As a result, workers are often forced to work long hours to achieve sufficient income, often performing multiple jobs, and rarely able to work as much as they would desire. But even when the technology used in crowd-work is new, Alberto and Nuna point out that the most essential characteristics of what work entails might remain the same. Therefore, they suggest a return to the basic aims of labour and social security law in protecting crowd-workers against, among others, negative effects of this new way of working on their work-life balance. Finally and most importantly, Alberto and Nuna invite us to think of the specific case of crowd-workers when studying for example telework.

Sonja Bekker, Lena Hipp, Janine Leschke and **Friederike Molitor** discuss the differences and similarities between men and women and particularly between mothers and fathers in their choices to work part-time. By analysing part-time work in Germany, Sweden, Ireland and the Netherlands in 2014 using individual level data from the European Labour Force Survey they show that for men a lower earning capacity compared to their partner or family responsibilities do not seem to lead to higher part-time shares, which is the opposite of what they find for women. They suggest that the differences they find may be attributed to the welfare state regimes, institutions such as childcare, income taxation, right to work part-time and the gender values prevalent in the different countries.

Sarah De Groof reflects on how work-life balance literature can be used to evaluate working time law and even to formulate recommendations. Based on the criteria she deducts from work-life balance literature, she demonstrates that European working time law focuses a lot on the limitation of working time, and not as much on, for example, the predictability of working hours. The law also does not strengthen the worker's position to set his own working hours. She suggests a modern working time law should reflect a qualitative time dimension, which would mean taking into account the constraints one life sphere puts on the other.

According to **Katherine Drake** and **Amy Brown** changes in workforce demographics require work redesign that prioritizes work-life integration. They give us successful examples from companies in the United States (US) suggesting that a paradigm shift will benefit both workers and employers. In absence of a federal mandate, paid parental leave for example is an opportunity for companies in the US to attract and retain talented workers, increase staff diversity and avoid the expense of hiring and training new employees. But Katherine and Amy realize things don't change based on knowledge only. They therefore provide a useful approach to implement these changes, namely the 3A-model: Accommodate – Accept – Adapt.

Émilie Genin explores the phenomenon of a 'Third Shift'. To deal with the heavy pressure from work and from home, research shows especially professional women tend to frequently resume work from home in the evening, at night or during weekends. Émilie uses a Canadian and French sample to suggest that men and women work at home for different reasons. Thus, the Third Shift phenomenon appears to be embedded in gendered and organizational dynamics such as the dematerialization of work through technological intermediation and the intensification of work pressures. Such developments challenge according to Émilie existing patterns of work regulation but do not really seem to challenge the gendered organization of the professional and personal spheres.

Lonnie Golden and **Jaeseung Kim** explore the consequences of irregular work scheduling. Their empirical analysis demonstrates that work-family conflict is worsened not only by longer weekly hours of work, but also by having irregular shift work. Working on rotating shift times exacerbates work-family conflict, although slightly less than does working irregular/on-call shifts and split-shift arrangements. The analysis finds that the adverse effect of irregular and on-call shifts can be quite moderated or mitigated by workers having schedule flexibility – ability to alter their starting and ending times and especially, to take time off during work. Lonnie and Jeaseung then explore which policies might prove most effective at mitigating work-family conflict, given this empirical evidence. According to them, policy should aim at reducing the incidence or severity of shift time irregularity over a workweek. An alternative aim for policy should be to offset the impact of irregular work schedules by providing workers more choice to refuses shifts, change shifts or request shift. An example of this is the 'right to request', that is for example part of Vermont law. They mainly focus on US policies, but also give examples from Canada, the United Kingdom (UK) and France. Lonnie and Jeaseung conclude that there is a movement in the US not so much at Federal level, but at state and local levels to address the underlying sources of the work-family consequences observed in the empirical results, particularly regarding work schedules that are on-call, unstable and cancelled on very short notice.

Barbara Kresal and **Ania Zbyszewska** scrutinize the current legal frameworks for reconciliation of work and family life in two EU Member States, Slovenia and the UK. They are, from a comparative perspective, particularly interested in the extent to which the existing national frameworks enable employees to take advantage of their entitlements, and especially the degree to which they also support redistribution of unpaid work between men and women. They also consider how robust the two frameworks have remained during the crisis. In their comparison, they look beyond the obvious. For example, when they consider which system is more employee friendly, they point out that the income replacement is not only much higher in Slovenia, but also that the administration of it is centralized. In the UK, individual employers remain responsible for covering the partial replacement costs, which they can then claim back from the state. The extent to which employers perceive management of this process to be a 'burden', may have – according to Barbara and Ania – implications for how they will be predisposed of workers who seek to draw on their statutory leave rights. As for how egalitarian the national legislative framework is, Barbara and Ania demonstrate both systems establish more or less equal entitlements for mothers and fathers, or women and men. But Barbara and Ania nonetheless suggest the structure of the Slovenian framework renders it overall more likely to de facto support combining parental responsibilities between the parents. According to them, enabling transfer of leaves between parents is unlikely to facilitate their take up by fathers.

Ifat Matzner-Heruti explores why fathers in the US and Israel lack of involvement in caregiving and housework. She shows that men in both countries are subject to masculine imperatives, according to which being breadwinners is their primary role as fathers, requiring them to invest most of their time and energy at work. According to her this exemplifies the interconnection between masculinity and breadwinning, as those who deviate from their traditional gendered roles not only jeopardize their work status but also their manly façade. She advocates for the deconstruction of the ideal worker norm and does so by using masculinities theory's core principles. Furthermore, she connects between masculinities and neo-institutionalism theories for the purpose of evaluating the role of organizations in holding back or bolstering fathers' usage of work-family arrangements.

Lourdes Mella Méndez uses a comparative method to study teleworking in Spain and Portugal to highlight positive and negative effects of this way of working on the ability to combine work and family life. She positively assesses the Portuguese system as it has according to her an approach clearly aimed at protecting the personal and family lives of workers and facilitates their professional development. The Spanish system does not have an individual right of the worker based on personal circumstances, comparable to what Portugal has. But Lourdes also highlights the potential threat of teleworking on the blurring of boundaries between working life and private life. She makes the case that even with teleworkers, the employer has the obligation to control and limit the working time.

Gürol Özcüre, Nimet Eryiğit and **Harun Demirkaya** discuss the Turkish situation. After giving us some general background information, they discuss a survey they conducted to compare it with the sixth European Working Conditions Survey. They conclude by pointing out that care services used to be provided within the family in Turkey, but this solution is no longer an option today. Partly because of this, women are forced in Turkey to choose between participating in employment or having a child.

Pascale Peters, Rob Blomme, Anne van Heertum and **Daantje Derks** elaborate on the management concept of 'New Ways of Working' (NWW) and what they call the 'boundary control paradox'. But first, they give us an interesting historical backdrop of the modernization process that has led to the boundary control paradox and introduce to us the increasingly popular Boundary Theory in order to familiarize us with the specific field of the work-life literature on how individuals manage the boundaries between the work and non-work domains. They then demonstrate that enabling autonomous work behaviour in a NWW context, stressing job autonomy, time-spatial flexibility and team work, can contribute to more congruence between individuals' enacted and preferred boundary management strategies, possibly enhancing work-life balance. However, the presence of an organizational culture signalling the need to be available for supervisors may diminish this effect. Moreover, enacted integration by co-workers may also lead to (too much) loss of perceived control affecting work-life conflict through more work-life integration. In order to achieve a better fit between individuals' preferred and enacted boundary management strategies in NWW context, not only work practices, but also organizational and team cultures and associated leadership styles should be adjusted to workers' needs.

Amanda Reilly and **Annick Masselot** explore whether New Zealand's legal framework is fit for the purpose of supporting precarious workers in work-family reconciliation. New Zealand workers have the right to request flexible working arrangements. Technically, this right is now available to all employees, whether they have care obligations, or they simply want to enjoy a better work-life balance. This right is available to all employees including those in non-standard work, and it can be exercised from the beginning of employment. But the enforcement mechanisms are weak and the penalties for non-compliance by employers are token. Amanda and Annick further discuss the regulation of working time in New Zealand and how it supports precarious workers. They correctly point out that in addition to long working hours and irregular and uncertain hours, insufficient hours are also an issue for precarious workers. They therefore find it a positive development that New Zealand law since 2016 effectively prohibits the use of 'zero hour' contracts. Finally, they discuss and stress the important role of trade unions. Notwithstanding the positive legal developments they have discussed, according to them unions remain the best hope for precarious workers to improve their ability to reconcile work and family needs.

Niklas Selberg explores work-life balance – particularly related to working time – in a Swedish context. But before giving the Swedish example, he rightly points out that work-life balance is and has always been a classical concern for labour law. Although Sweden is perhaps best known for its long leave periods to take care of young children, Niklas demonstrates that there are in fact a lot more rules contributing to employees' work-life balance in Sweden related to working time. Interestingly, this legislation is not thanks to international labour standards. Quite on the contrary: Swedish stance towards international labour standards regarding working time is characterized by a certain amount of disinterests according to Niklas. Niklas discusses legislation regarding part-time work, full-time work, overtime, work intensity, and so on and highlights the important role trade unions play in Sweden. Collective agreements are according to me an important source of inspiration on how to deal with work-life balance issues. For example, Niklas points out the existence of framework agreements in collective agreement in which a time frame within which the employer is free to schedule work is defined. Going outside of the frames set by the agreement presupposes consent from the plant level trade union. Another notion from these collective agreements is collective self-scheduling, where the employer determines the number of workers needed per shift, but the employees then distribute the night- and day shifts and weekends among themselves. But Niklas also stresses that although Sweden has been in the forefront of women's labour market participation, even in Sweden the gendered division of labour persists in paid as well as unpaid work, as women still taken about 75% of the parental leave benefit days. More in general, statistics show that women spend less time in paid work and more time in unpaid work than men.

Mathilde Valentini and **Stéphanie Bernstein** give us the example of Canadian anti-discrimination laws that prohibit practices in employment that have an adverse impact on workers because of their family situation. Recent case law developments have established that when such discrimination occurs, employers have an obligation to accommodate their employees if their working arrangements present a significant obstacle to fulfilling their family responsibilities and they have demonstrated that they have failed in their attempts to fulfil these obligations without accommodation. Although this duty to accommodate allows employees to gain some control over their working time, Mathilde and Stéphanie demonstrate with case law that it is in practice still limited in comparison to the extent of an employer's duty in the case of other types of discrimination. They conclude by highlighting the limits of the individual duty to accommodate which does not promote a rethinking of work organization at a broader level, nor necessarily promote institutional change. Moreover, this duty does not take into account the gendered nature of the distribution of family responsibilities.

Greet Vermeylen, **Agnès Parent-Thirion**, **Jorge Cabrita** and **Mathijn Wilkens** are researchers at Eurofound. Eurofound plays a role that cannot be underestimated in the European work-life balance debate because of the questions directly related to work-life balance in the European Working Conditions Survey. Eurofound sees reconciliation of work and private life as a key element for sustainable work throughout the life course for men and women. Greet, Agnès, Jorge and Mathijn give us an overview of the latest findings in what was already the 6th European Working Conditions Survey. They recall that reconciliation measures consist of a mix of different possible solutions consisting in care infrastructure, family leaves, working time options and working time arrangements, being able to adapt your working hours to your private needs including flexitime, predictable hours, being able to take time off at short notice. According to them, it is the combination of the different facilities which enhance the capabilities for work-life balance. Also, workers have different needs at different times. They therefore suggest that not a 'one fits all solution', but a wide range of working time arrangements, options and leaves could enhance the worker's capabilities for reconciling work and private life and sustainable work.

Tracey Warren makes a very important point, an insight that is often neglected in literature. She shows how time trumps money in dominant understandings of what 'work-life' means and in what parts of our lives are presumed to be in need of balance. Working 'too many' hours is seen to be the major challenge for achieving a work-life balance. Having enough time is indeed core to a balanced work-life. Yet it is not the only ingredient and nor is it one that dominates the narratives of the working class, for whom financial hardship is a serious threat to work-life balancing. According to Tracey, if we are to take the work-life needs of working class workers seriously too, it is essential to widen out our understanding of work-life balance in academic debate and policy formulation. It is time for researchers, employers, worker representatives and policy makers to co-produce a more holistic and inclusive work-life balance agenda.

§1.03 WHAT THEY HAVE IN COMMON

I did not ask the contributors why they are interested in work-life balance literature or why we should care about work-life balance. I can think of several reasons: because work-life conflict is associated with negative health outcomes, because it causes gender inequalities, because women should have the possibility to participate in paid work and men should have the possibility to participate in family life, because it is interesting from an economical point of view that women participate in paid work, and many more reasons. But what all contributors probably have in common is that they want to deepen their understanding: what does work-life balance literature say, what does it not say, how should the law respond to that, what are the caveats of such laws, ... They wanted to add something to the academic debate, and have in my truly view succeeded in doing so.

By adding to the academic debate, many contributions have looked beyond the obvious. Instead of the traditional focus on work and family conflict because of time constraints mothers experience because of too much time spent working in a traditional indefinite and fulltime employment relationship, the contributions explore how work-life imbalance could come from too little working time, too little pay, too irregular work or work-life imbalance of fathers. They all kept the modern workplace in mind, where single or both parents work, where workers face many work-life balance constraints for example because of domestic violence, where workers are bound with many short-term contracts and where worker's needs change over the life course. But what is truly new according to me, is that this book brought scholars from many different disciplines including legal scholars on work-life balance. Because what connects these scholars, is that they all reflect on what policy – be it at a supranational, national or organizational level – should look like in light of work-life balance insights.

CHAPTER 2

Connecting Crowd-Work with Work-Life Balance: Mission Impossible?

Alberto Barrio & Nuna Zekić

§2.01 INTRODUCTION

Even though it is a fairly new phenomenon, the literature on 'crowd-work' or 'the sharing economy' is growing vastly. Dictionaries often define 'crowd-work' as the process of obtaining needed services, ideas, or content by soliciting contributions from a large group of people, especially an online community, rather than from employees or suppliers. It is a timely topic in economic, business, computer-science, sociological, and legal research. Even though crowd-work might still be in its infancy, it has the potential to affect the 'world of work' greatly. For now, it challenges some of the basic principles and definitions of that field, such as the employment contract.

Currently, it has been observed that this model might offer 'job opportunities' to people who are bound to stay at home, or give the chance to top-up income for persons already in employment.[1] In that respect, some of the advantages of crowd-work have been identified – easy access, quick turnaround, flexible scheduling, etc.[2] – but so have its disadvantages or 'challenges'.[3] The impact of crowd-work on work-life balance can be found among both the advantages and disadvantages, as discussed in the literature. On first sight, that might not be surprising, since it is precisely in these work arrangements that boundaries between private time and working time become blurred.

1. J. Berg, 'Income Security in the On-Demand Economy: Findings and Policy Lessons from a Survey of Crowdworkers', *Comparative Labor Law & Policy Journal* 2016 Vol. 37 No. 3, pp. 543–576.
2. M.A. Cherry, 'Beyond Misclassification: The Digital Transformation of Work', *Comparative Labor Law & Policy Journal* 2016 Vol. 37 No. 3, p. 599.
3. *See* for example, I. Mandl, 'Working Conditions in Crowd Employment and ICT-Based Mobile Work' *The Digital Economy and the Single Market. Employment Prospects and Working Conditions in Europe*, FEPS – Foundation for European Progressive Studies 2016, pp. 111–138.

However, this is not the only reason why it is difficult to pinpoint exactly whether crowd-work has a positive or negative impact on work-life balance. Different types of crowd-work may produce different results, while the group of workers active on platforms may also be very diverse.

Our main argument is that the complexity of crowd-work should be integrated in the current discussion. A correct appraisal of the different features of crowd-work is fundamental in a moment when attempts of regulating it at national and transnational level are being performed. This study aims to bring together and highlight some main aspects of the discussions on crowd-work in relation to work-life balance. One can find that, within the literature on crowd-work, its potential impact on work-life balance is not elaborated in much detail. Further details on crowd-work and the existing assumptions and arguments in the literature (especially, but not limited to research in the labour and social security law area) on its impact on work-life balance must be brought together in order to take into account the combined effects of all features of crowd-work on this particular topic.

Section §2.02 gives a detailed explanation of crowd-work. It outlines the essential features of crowd-work, describing (diversity of) the platforms, the providers and the consumers together with the process. In addition, it is explained why terminology is important when this topic is discussed. Section §2.03 discusses the main legal challenges crowd-work is posing today. Section §2.04 further zooms in on the relation between crowd-work and work-life balance, while section §2.05 contains some concluding remarks.

§2.02 WHAT IS CROWD-WORK?

The concept of crowd-work has been broadly used, to a point of covering in occasions almost any productive activity performed in connection to the Internet. In this context, achieving an integrated concept of crowd-work – without leaving out important forms of work that have been included in this term – is a significant challenge. Nevertheless, in this chapter we will attempt to both note the diversity among forms of crowd-work while at the same time highlighting the common threads between them, as we believe in those two aspects reside the importance of a proper discussion about crowd-work and work-life balance.

In order to do so, we will draft a wide definition of crowd-work, from which we will develop a typology of crowd-work that will address relevant features in greater detail. This classification does not attempt to be exhaustive, but instead to exemplify the complexity of crowd-work, adding to the legal debate on the issue.

Finally, some remarks concerning terminology must be done before delving further into the topic. Being a fairly new development, there is no consensus yet on the designation, definition and forms of work, which may be covered by what we refer in this chapter as 'crowd-work'. In fact, the terminological academic debate, which is common concerning new developments, is even more complex than usual due to the parallel legal discussion on the employment status of the persons providing services or products through crowd-work platforms. As a result, when trying to rely on one term or another, particularly to design those persons providing services, there is the risk of seeming to take a part in this discussion (whether the term user – favoured by platforms – is the one chosen, or instead the term worker is preferred – used by advocates of considering them in an employment relationship). In order to avoid such conundrum, we have opted to use the term 'providers' (i.e., providers of services or products) to refer to these persons. The receivers of such services or products are referred to as 'consumers', while the internet-based structure which links both (as well as the organisation or individual who owns the platforms and/or controls them) is referred to as 'platform'.

[A] Definition of Crowd-Work

In this chapter, we define crowd-work as the on-demand performance of tasks by persons selected remotely through online platforms from a large pool of potential and generic workers. Other terms have been used to refer to forms of work that we understand to be encompassed by the concept 'crowd-work': crowdsourcing, gig economy, sharing economy, on-demand economy, participatory economy, collaborative economy, peer-to-peer economy, digital economy, ICT-based mobile work or peer production. We select the term 'crowd' in order to emphasise both the scale and the undefined[4] character of the mass of workers on whose contributions crowd-work is based.

[B] Essential Features of Crowd-Work

We divide the features of crowd-work among those referred to the providers, the receivers, the platforms and the process itself.[5,6]

4. In this regard, we base our work on the concept 'crowdsourcing' as established by Howe (*see* Howe, 'Crowdsourcing: A Definition', June 02, 2006, Retrieved on 31 January 2017 at http://crowdsourcing.typepad.com/cs/2006/06/crowdsourcing_a.html).
5. This last group of features draws from Information System literature, such as D. Geiger, et al., 'Managing the Crowd: Towards a Taxonomy of Crowdsourcing Processes', *Proceedings of the Seventeenth Americas Conference Systems*, Detroit, August 2011.
6. For further information on typologies of crowd work (and particularly in relation to crowdsourcing) *see*, inter alia, E. Estellés-Arolas and F. González-Ladrón-de-Guevara, 'Towards an Integrated Crowdsourcing Definition', *Journal of Information Science* 2012 Vol. 38 No. 2, pp. 189–200; E. Estellés-Arolas, R. Navarro-Giner, and F. González-Ladrón-de-Guevara, 'Crowdsourcing Fundamentals: Definition and Typology', in F. J. Garrigos-Simon, I. Gil-Pechuán and S. Estelles-Miguel (eds.), *Advances in Crowdsourcing*, New York: Springer International Publishing, 2015, pp. 33–48; D. Geiger, M. Rosemann, and E. Fielt. 'Crowdsourcing Information Systems: A Systems Theory Perspective', *Proceedings of the 22nd Australasian Conference on Information Systems* 2011; A.C. Rouse, 'A Preliminary Taxonomy of Crowdsourcing', *Proceedings of the 21st Australasian Conference on Information Systems* 2010; D. Geiger, et al, 'Managing the Crowd: Towards a Taxonomy of Crowdsourcing Processes', *American Conference on Information Systems 2011* 2011.

[1] Platforms

In all the different variants of crowd-work, platforms are website-based structures. Furthermore, and as far as we are aware, the platform is owned by others than the providers. This is a key aspect, as platforms are the ones who define most of the elements that will be addressed below. In a similar line of thought, platforms may be divided between those in which the providers cannot participate in its governance and configuration and those which allow some form of participation (an example of the latter is *Wikipedia*[7]). Furthermore, crowd-work forms of work may be divided between those that seek a profit for the owner of the platform (which is the general rule), and those that are non-profit (such as, again, *Wikipedia*[8]).

[2] Process

By process, we refer to the set of characteristics of the crowd-work that determines how work is performed and monitored. In this regard, all forms of crowd-work are characterised for providing flexibility for both parties (being based on the *demand*[9] of both the provider - who may choose when she wants to work - and the consumer) and linking them *remotely*[10] with the intervention of an *algorithm*.

Also, the capability of crowd-work platforms to motivate providers to participate is an essential element of crowd-work itself, as it is this significant power of summoning a large group of potential workers that is one of the main aspects that makes crowd-work platforms attractive for consumers. This motivation boils down to a form of *compensation* for providers, which may materialise in many forms (in most cases, platforms will provide different forms of compensation simultaneously): Payment (whether in cash,[11] product or service - e.g., access to the platform), feeling of

7. Wikipedia is part of the non-profit organisation 'Wikimedia Foundation'. The Wikimedia Foundation is governed by a Board of Trustees, which is composed by the founder of the platform (Jimmy Wales), two representatives of the regional Wikimedia chapters, three users voted in biannual elections at the Wikimania, and four experts selected by the rest of the Board. *See* Wikimedia Foundation Meta-Wiki, 'Wikimedia Foundation Board of Trustees', Retrieved on 31 January 2017 at https://meta.wikimedia.org/wiki/Wikimedia_Foundation_Board_of_Trustees.
8. *See* Wikimedia Foundation Meta-Wiki, 'Frequently asked questions', Retrieved on 31 January 2017 at https://wikimediafoundation.org/wiki/FAQ/en#How_is_the_Wikimedia_Foundation_run.3F.
9. A. Kittur et al., 'The Future of Crowd-Work', *Proceedings of the 2013 Conference on Computer Supported Cooperative Work*, pp. 1301–1318.
10. P. Heymann and H. Garcia-Molina, 'Turkalytics: Analytics for Human Computation', *Proceedings of the 20th International Conference on World Wide Web*, New York, 2011, p. 477.
11. O. Tokarchuk, R. Cuel and M. Zamarian, 'Analyzing Crowd Labor and Designing Incentives for Humans in the Loop', *IEEE Internet Computing* 2012 Vol. 16 No. 5, pp. 45–51.

altruism[12] (i.e., contribution to a greater social goal), social status,[13] self-marketing,[14] entertainment value[15] or personal achievement and learning.[16]

Furthermore, crowd-work platforms may differentiate themselves from the way they supervise the quality of the work performed by the providers. In almost all platforms, the control is done based on results and not (as it was the case in some traditional forms of work) on the process. In this regard, providers in crowd-work have greater freedom on determining how to perform their task. However, the way this supervision is performed varies among platforms. In some cases, the platform relies on ratings done by consumers,[17] while in others consumers are given the choice of selecting the outcome they consider the best among those offered by different providers, or otherwise the platform uses a more complex set of algorithms for the monitoring aspect.

Finally, crowd-work will differ on whether the form of crowd-work is or is not *location-dependent* (with some platforms linking providers and consumers in a world-wide or nationwide scale – as is the case for most platforms who offer work online, such as Amazon Mechanical Turk[18] –, while others connecting consumers to only those providers who are near them), which will also reflect on the way the work is performed (whether online or offline).

[3] Providers

As mentioned above, crowd-work is characterised by the fact that the providers are part of a generic pool of workers to which receivers have access through the platform. By generic we refer to the fact that the relationship between the provider and the receiver are generally *sporadic and non- permanent,*[19] as well as to the fact (developed further below) that in most cases anybody may register in the platform and be a potential provider. There is nonetheless space for diversity among the characteristics of the crowd targeted by different crowd-work platforms.

---

12. *Idem.*
13. A.C. Rouse, 'A Preliminary Taxonomy of Crowdsourcing', *21st Australasian Conference on Information Systems*, Brisbane, 2010, p. 6.
14. J. Leimester et al., 'Leverage Crowdsourcing: Activation-Supporting Components for IT-based Ideas Competitions', *Journal of Management Information Systems* 2009 Vol. 26 No. 1, p. 205.
15. G. Kazai, J. Kamps and N. Milic-Frayling, 'An Analysis of Human Factors and Label Accuracy in Crowdsourcing Relevance Judgements', *Inform Retrieval* 2013 Vol. 16 No. 2, pp. 138–178.
16. J. Leimester et al., 'Leverage Crowdsourcing: Activation-Supporting Components for IT-based Ideas Competitions', *Journal of Management Information Systems* 2009 Vol. 26 No. 1, p. 206.
17. This is often done through so-called rating or scoring systems, in which the parties may rate their satisfaction with the transaction. Often, the platform deactivates accounts with low ratings, particularly concerning providers (*see*, for example, concerning Uber in the US, Uber, *Legal. Uber community guidelines,* Retrieved on 24 January 2017 at https://www.uber.com/legal/community-guidelines/us-en/).
18. *See* Amazon Mechanical Turk, 'FAQ', Retrieved on 31 January 2017 at https://www.mturk.com/mturk/help?helpPage=overview.
19. *See* A. Felstiner, 'Working the Crowd: Employment and Labor Law in the Crowdsourcing Industry', *Berkeley Journal of Employment & Labor Law* 2011 Vol. 32 No. 1, p. 194.

In this regard, crowd-work may differ depending on the *features of the work* that the platform requires from the crowd. Some platforms are focused on providers perceived as consumers (whose perspective as such is valuable for the company in order to improve the product[20]); while others reach for persons that provide a professional service that the receiver would not perform by himself (whether for lack of the necessary expertise or to reduce costs). Even in the latter case, the form of crowd-work varies depending on the different levels of skill requested from providers by the platform, from almost no expertise to those focused on skilled[21] or highly skilled providers.[22] Most platforms provide an open-call, meaning they let any provider (with possible limitations concerning location, which we already mentioned) apply, although some platforms seeking very specialised work make a previous selection of the persons allow to present their candidacy.[23] When the platform focuses on skilled workers, there are differences in crowd-work depending on the duration and complexity of the tasks required by the platform. Finally, crowd-work varies depending on the degree of freedom in deciding how to perform the task allowed to the provider.

[4] Consumers

Finally, there is also diversity in which kind of consumers the platforms target, whether they are companies looking to outsource part of its activity or individual consumers trying to access certain services. Furthermore, depending on the platform, the consumers may or may not have to make some sort of payment to the platform and/or the provider in order to access the service or product.

20. M. Hossain and I. Kauranen, 'Crowdsourcing: A Comprehensive Literature Review', *Strategic Outsourcing: An International Journal* 2015 Vol. 8 No. 1, p. 3. An example of platform used to improve the product through the input of consumers may be the case of 'Lego Ideas', a website created by Lego that allows users to propose ideas for new Lego products, *see* Lego Ideas, *Discover*, Retrieved on 30 January 2017 at https://ideas.lego.com/howitworks.
21. An example is the case of TaskRabbit, who advertise itself with the slogan 'we are skilled specialists', *see* TaskRabbit, 'Homepage', Retrieved on 24 January 2016, at https://www.taskrabbit.com/.
22. Examples may be the case of the design of parts of the 787 Streamliner (which Boing opened to the contributions of 100 of its regular providers through crowdsourcing, *see* CBS, 'For Boing, it Takes a Village to Build a New Airplane', *CBS News*, Jun 17, 2008, Retrieved on 31 January 2017 at http://www.cbsnews.com/news/for-boeing-it-takes-a-village-to-build-a-new-airplane/) or, closer to a definition of crowdsourcing, the open competitions for the design of spaceflight software created by the US Government and its contractors (for an example of the functioning of such a competition, *see* S. Nag, *Collaborative Competition for Crowdsourcing Spaceflight Software and STEM Education Using SPHERES Zero Robotics*, Space System Laboratory of the Massachusetts Institute for Technology, 2012.
23. This was the case in the abovementioned call for contributions on the design of the 787 Streamliner, which was open to only 100 companies which have previous collaborated with Boing, *see* CBS, 'For Boing, it Takes a Village to Build a New Airplane', *CBS News*, Jun 17, 2008, Retrieved on 31 January 2017 at http://www.cbsnews.com/news/for-boeing-it-takes-a-village-to-build-a-new-airplane/.

[C] Other Features of Crowd-Work

Besides the features that define the nature of the crowd-work platform, there are other elements that define the nature of the relationship between providers, receivers and platforms. The most prominent is the assumed casualty of the work performed (i.e., it is generally assumed that this activity does not constitute the main professional activity of the performer).[24] Furthermore, the role that crowd-work plays in the overall life of the provider must be taken into consideration when differentiating crowd-work situations. Depending on whether it is the provider's main occupation or not,[25] or whether she is part of a family unit in which one of its members is in (full-time) standard employment, performing crowd-work will produce very different situations.

§2.03 LEGAL CHALLENGES CROWD-WORK POSES

[A] Employment Status

When we focus on the relationship between the platforms and the providers of work or services, in this early stage of crowd-work, the main question at this point is whether this relationship is an employment relationship. Most of legal debate on the topic of crowd-work relates to this question. Are the providers employees of the platforms, are they independent contractors (self-employed), or do they form a whole new category?[26] As *Aloisi* explains, platforms challenge traditional business models, but they also tend to undermine the common structure of the 'employer-employee' scheme.[27] Most platforms regard the providers not as employees (or workers) but as independent contractors. Consequently, this business model can become a means to circumvent labour and social security laws. The European Commission has issued a (non-binding) guidance on how existing European Union (EU) law should be applied to – what the Commission calls – the collaborative economy.[28] The Commission firstly notes that the working arrangements in the collaborative economy are part of a more structural shift where there are increasingly blurred boundaries between the self-employed and the workers. For this bigger problem, the Commission refers to the consultation it issued in

24. N. Raval and P. Dourish, 'Standing Out from the Crowd: Emotional Labor, Body Labor, and Temporal Labor in Ridesharing', *Proceedings of the 19th ACM Conference on Computer-Supported Cooperative Work & Social Computing*, San Francisco, 2016, p. 97.
25. J. Berg, 'Income Security in the On-Demand Economy: Findings and Policy Lessons from a Survey of Crowdworkers', *Comparative Labor Law & Policy Journal* 2016 Vol. 37 No. 3, pp. 543–576.
26. Some jurisdictions have border concepts for economically dependent workers: the English law acknowledges 'workers' besides 'employees', the German law 'Arbeitnehmerähnliches' besides 'Arbeitnehmers', and the Spanish law recognised the form of the 'Trabajador autónomo económicamente dependiente'.
27. A. Aloisi, 'Commoditized Workers: Case Study Research on Labor Law Issues Arising from a Set of on-Demand/Gig Economy Platforms', *Comparative Labor Law & Policy Journal* 2016 Vol. 37 No. 3, p. 655.
28. European Commission, 'A European agenda for the collaborative economy', *Communication from the commission to the European Parliament, the Council, the European Economic and Social Committee and the Committee of the Regions* COM (2016) 356, 2016.

2016 on a European Pillar of Social Rights.[29] Since the definition of the employment contract and most of labour law fall under national competence,[30] the Commission calls on the Member States to 'provide guidance on the applicability of their national employment rules in light of labour patterns in the collaborative economy'.[31] In most cases, this will have to be determined on the basis of a case-by-case assessment, looking cumulatively in particular at the well-known three essential criteria for an employment relationship,[32] but also considering all the relevant facts and circumstances characterising the relationship between the platform and the underlying service provider, and the performance of the related tasks.[33] More or less the same legal test is applied also outside the EU.[34] Furthermore, it is also worth noting that it is often the case in crowd-work that the traditional employer functions (e.g., supervision, remuneration, providing of the tools) are distributed among different parties to the employment relationship (often between the platform and the consumer). In this regard, suggestions have been made to assign the duties and obligations of the employer depending on who assumes which functions.[35]

When assessing whether a worker is indeed an employee or an independent contractor, one of the most relevant factors is that the business model described seems to imply a lack of dependence or subordination of the worker.[36] In most cases the provider is able to choose when and how long to work. She even seems to enjoy a considerable freedom in the way the work is being performed. The factor 'remuneration' can, however, also play an important role. The English Employment Tribunal in London ruled in 2016 that claimants - Uber drivers - can be classified as workers.[37] One of the arguments used by the judges is that under London's Uber Policy, it was not

---

29. European Commission, 'Launching a consultation on a European Pillar of Social Rights', *Communication from the commission to the European Parliament, the Council, the European Economic and Social Committee and the Committee of the Regions* COM (2016) 127, 2016.
30. At EU level the Court of Justice (CJEU) has defined the concept of worker for the purpose of applying EU law: 'the essential feature of an employment relationship is that for a certain period of time a person performs services for and under the direction of another person in return for which he receives remuneration'. European Commission, 'Reaffirming the free movement of workers: rights and major developments' *Communication from the commission to the European Parliament, the Council, the European Economic and Social Committee and the Committee of the Regions* COM (2010) 373, 2010.
31. European Commission, 'A European agenda for the collaborative economy', *Communication from the commission to the European Parliament, the Council, the European Economic and Social Committee and the Committee of the Regions* COM (2016) 356, 2016, p. 13.
32. International Labour Office and European Labour Law Network, *Regulating the Employment Relationship in Europe: A Guide to Recommendation No. 198*, Geneva: International Labour Office, 2013.
33. *Idem*, p. 12.
34. A. Felstiner, 'Working the Crowd: Employment and Labor Law in the Crowdsourcing Industry', *Berkeley Journal of Employment & Labor Law* 2011 Vol. 32 No. 1, pp. 143-204.
35. Referred to as the 'functional concept of the employer', *see* J. Prassl, and M. Risak, 'Uber, TaskRabbit, and Co.: Platforms as Employers? Rethinking the Legal Analysis of Crowdwork', *Comparative Labor Law & Policy Journal* 2016 Vol. 37 No. 3, pp. 646-649.
36. A. Todolí Signes, 'The End of the Subordinate Worker: Sharing Economy, On-demand Economy, Crowdsourcing, Uber Economy and Other Ways of Outsourcing', *SSRN Electronic Journal*, 2015, p. 11.
37. Employment Tribunals, *Aslam, Farrar and others versus Uber B.V., Uber London Ltd, Uber Britannia Ltd*, 28 October 2016, Case Nos: 2202550/2015.

possible for the drivers to negotiate with passengers for a higher fee than the standard fee that Uber sets and passes to the passenger as an estimated fee for every ride. A lower fee is possible, but this is not advantageous, since Uber's commission remains based on that standard fee.

This discussion about employment status classification is fundamental, as when the providers are treated as independent contractors, they usually do not enjoy any of the labour law protection granted to employees, such as the payment of a minimum wage. In most cases, they may be partly or fully excluded from certain social insurance schemes, like unemployment benefits.[38] There is usually no (investment in) training involved. For these reasons, some authors have already labelled this type of work as precarious work.[39]

Some authors have argued that the service provided on platforms 'represent a genuinely novel form of work, deserving of its own legal status and regulatory apparatus?'[40] In such proposals, such third category – intermediate between employee and self-employed or independent contractor – would qualify for some benefits and protections that employees receive, but not all. For example, in the United States (US) it has been suggested that service providers should fall under the protection of antidiscrimination laws, but not under the protection of minimum wage or unemployment benefits.[41]

The question of employment status is also relevant in the context of collective bargaining. The Court of Justice of the EU (CJEU) has ruled that an organisation, which carries out negotiations acting in the name and on behalf of self-employed persons who are its members, 'it does not act as a trade union association and therefore as a social partner, but, in reality, acts as an association of undertakings'.[42] The EU law prohibits agreements between undertakings that limit competition in the EU market (Article 101 Treaty on the Functioning of the European Union, TFEU). Setting minimum fees for the self-employed in collective agreements is thus not allowed under EU competition law.[43] Where the CJEU has found in other cases[44] that collective agreements are excluded

38. While significant progress has been made worldwide during the last twenty years concerning the social security coverage of the self-employed (particularly regarding pensions), there is still an important gap concerning schemes such as unemployment benefits, *see* ILO, *World Employment and Social Outlook – The changing nature of jobs*, 2015, p. 79. *See also*, inter alia, W. Eichhorst et al., *Social Protection Rights of Economically Dependent Self-employed Workers*, Luxembourg: European Parliament, 2013. Even if they are included in social insurance schemes, often they may receive a very limited benefit as a result of having chosen a low contributory base, *see Ibid*, p. 42.
39. M.A. Cherry, 'Beyond Misclassification: The Digital Transformation of Work', *Comparative Labor Law & Policy Journal* 2016 Vol. 37 No. 3, pp. 598–602.
40. S.D. Harris and A.B. Krueger, 'A Proposal for Modernizing Labor Laws for Twenty-First-Century Work: The "Independent Worker"', *The Hamilton Project* Discussion Paper 2015-10, 2015.
41. *Idem.*
42. *FNV Kiem*, CJEU 4 December 2014, C-413/13, para. 28.
43. In general, the same applies in the United State under federal antitrust law.
44. *Albany International BV v Stichting Bedrijfspensioenfonds Textielindustrie*, CJEU 21 December 1999, C-67/96; *Brentjens' Handelsonderneming BV v Stichting Bedrijfspensioenfonds voor de Handel in Bouwmaterialen*, CJEU 21 September 1999, C-115/97-117/97; *Maatschappij Drijvende Bokken BV v Stichting Pensioenfonds voor de Vervoer- en Havenbedrijven*, CJEU 21 September 1999, C-219/97.

from the prohibition of Article 101(1) TFEU if certain broad conditions are fulfilled, this is not the case where it concerns collective agreements on minimum fees for the self-employed. The agreements may, however, be regarded as the result of collective bargaining and therefore, they may be covered by the collective bargaining exception only if the service providers, in the name and on behalf of whom the trade union negotiated, are in fact 'false self-employed'.[45] 'False self-employed' are, according to CJEU, service providers who are in a situation comparable to that of employees, i.e., a subordinated relationship. Whether the workers are indeed 'false self-employed' is left to the referring court to determine.

It is unclear whether – by introducing false self-employment – the CJEU intended to create a new category of economic actors as discussed above, or did the Court instead only meant to prevent abusive misclassification. Several authors believe the latter is true and they praise the Court for taking 'a realist mode of interpretation'.[46]

The debate on false or bogus self-employment has not reached a final conclusion, nor has the discussion on the employment status of crowd-workers. The case law is still under development. The final judgment in the Uber-cases is unknown at the time of this writing, since the London Uber is appealing against the decision of the Employment Tribunal and in the US a high-profile case, *O'Connor v. Uber*, was settled out of court.[47] Moreover, it is difficult to produce any general conclusions on the possible outcomes of applying the conventional legal test of determining the employment relationship to platform work in general, since the platforms can differ greatly, as was illustrated in the second section of this chapter. The relevant conclusion for our purposes is that the providers of work or services on platforms *could be* determined to be workers or employees, but that for the time being most of them are treated as independent contractors.

[B] Differences Within Employment Status

If the providers are in fact considered employees, another important issue remains to be resolved. In *which form* of employment are they performing work? Are they trainees or workers, in temporary or open-ended labour contracts, on full-time or part-time basis and, in case of the latter, which percentage of reduction on their working time do they have and how is this working time distributed –in a daily, weekly, monthly or even annually basis, whether they are on-call or not, or whether there is a third intermediate party or not? In this regard, the characteristics of the employment relationship may have very significant consequences on whether the person may effectively access the rights to which in theory she may be entitled. Nonetheless, the legal discussion on crowd-work has left this important aspect mostly unattended.

45. *Idem*, para. 31.
46. E. Grosheide and M. Barenberg, 'Minimum Fees for the Self-Employed: A European Response to the "Uber-ized" Economy?' *Columbia Journal of European Law* 2016 Vol. 22 No. 2, p. 224.
47. M.A. Cherry, 'Beyond Misclassification: The Digital Transformation of Work', *Comparative Labor Law & Policy Journal* 2016 Vol. 37 No. 3, p. 583.

In this regard, it is worth noting that the comparison to temporary agency workers has not been made very often, while the triangular relationship between the provider (or worker), the platform and the consumer resembles the relationship between the agency worker, the agency and the user firm. In addition, the role of the platforms resembles the intermediate role of the agencies in matching the offers of and the applicants for paid work. One of the main differences is, however, the fact that duration of the relationship between agency workers and user companies usually tends to be (much) longer compared to the relationship between the providers and consumers. Moreover, the agency workers perform work under the supervision and direction of the user company,[48] while in crowd-work control is mostly exercised by the platforms, if it is exercised at all.

[C] New Forms of Subordination

We have seen above that the element of subordination is relevant for the question whether the crowd-worker is an employee. However, whether the crowd-worker is subordinated to the platform and in what form are questions that have relevance on their own. They can pose different (legal) problems. In this case, the question of subordination comes to the forefront when we consider how the crowd-workers are managed or controlled by the platforms. Many platforms use some sort of a rating system as a form of quality control. The consumers can rate the providers. In some respects, that means less control than is normally exercised by the employer, because the platforms do not monitor the workers themselves. On the other hand, it can mean more effective control, because the platform has at its disposal a wealth of information that allows for automatically determining the ideal outcome per task on an individualised basis.[49] Such internal rating system has an impact on the successive hiring. It can put a worker into 'an endless probation period'.[50] Moreover, it is not enough to have high ratings, as Cherry explains, 'their scores are ranked, ordered, and the workers are expected to out-achieve each other'.[51] The ranking system also ties them to a specific platform, even though this might not be different from the dependency of some employees on their employer. However, when the rating system is dependent solely on customers' ratings as opposed to evaluation by a (trained) manager, it is more prone to racial or religious bias, whether conscious or unconscious.[52]

---

48. Directive 2008/104/EC of the European Parliament and of the Council of 19 November 2008 on temporary agency work.
49. S. O'Çonnor, 'When Your Boss Is an Algorithm', *Financial Times*, 8 September 2016, Retrieved on 31 January 2017 at https://www.ft.com/content/88fdc58e-754f-11e6-b60a-de4532d5ea35.
50. A. Aloisi, 'Commoditized Workers: Case Study Research on Labor Law Issues Arising from a Set of On-Demand/Gig Economy Platforms', *Comparative Labor Law & Policy Journal* 2016 Vol. 37, No. 3, p. 671.
51. M.A. Cherry, 'Beyond Misclassification: The Digital Transformation of Work', *Comparative Labor Law & Policy Journal* 2016 Vol. 37, No. 3, p. 601.
52. *Ibid*, p. 597; N. Zatz, 'Beyond Misclassification: Gig Economy Discrimination Outside Employment Law', *On Labor*, January 19, 2016, Retrieved on 31 January 2017 at https://onlabor.org/

[D] Collective Representation

The increase of the number of crowd-workers can pose (additional) challenges for trade unions and collective bargaining. Irrespective of the classification, an important feature of platform work is that work is strongly individualised. Providers of services (or crowd-workers) are not 'centralised', work is not performed at one physical workplace as it usually the case in for example manufacturing sectors, and it usually does not take place within a bounded geographic area. All of this makes it more difficult to organise compared to the typical working organisations where workers work at one or more employer's premises. Even though this is not a problem specific to crowd-work, since it is acknowledged that the increase in all kinds of 'atypical' or precarious forms of work has created one of the major challenges trade unions are facing today.[53] It is nevertheless important to stress, that this seems to be even truer for crowd-work. As a result, the providers may be left without a collective representation as a countervailing power to the primacy of platforms.

When platforms operate on a global scale – in cases when there is no requirement of local execution –, it becomes even more difficult to organise. In that case, these emerging markets can 'give people in poor countries access to buyers in rich countries'.[54] This is obviously beneficial for workers in developing countries, but is can also be seen as a disadvantage for workers, since it puts them in a greater competition with one another. It can even cause protective laws of all countries in the world to compete with each other.[55]

§2.04 ATTENTION PAID TO WORK-LIFE BALANCE

To our knowledge, no research has been conducted on the relationship between crowd-work and work-life balance. However, several studies on crowd-work hint (explicitly or implicitly) to its possible impact on work-life balance.[56] More often, the literature on crowd-work highlights features of this form of work which might have an impact on work-life balance, but without analysing this possible impact directly. For example, the results from a survey undertaken in 2015 by the *ILO* of crowd-workers on the *Amazon Mechanical Turk* and *Crowdflower* platforms show that one of the main

2016/01/19/beyond-misclassification-gig-economy-discrimination-outside-employment-law/; R. Brisben, 'The Social Costs of Uber', *The University of Chicago Law Review Dialogue*, 2015 Vol. 82, p. 95.

53. R. Gumbrell-McCormick, 'European Trade Unions and "Atypical" Workers', *Industrial Relations Journal* 2011 Vol. 42 No. 3, pp. 293–310.
54. A. Aloisi, 'Commoditized Workers: Case Study Research on Labor Law Issues Arising from a Set of On-Demand/Gig Economy Platforms', *Comparative Labor Law & Policy Journal* 2016 Vol. 37, No. 3, p. 658.
55. A. Todolí Signes, 'The End of the Subordinate Worker: Sharing Economy, On-Demand Economy, Crowdsourcing, Uber Economy and Other Ways of Outsourcing', *SSRN Electronic Journal* 2015, p. 6.
56. *See* G. Valenduc and P. Vendramin, 'Work in the Digital Economy: Sorting the Old from the New', Working Paper 2016.03, Brussels: Etui, 2016; W. Wobbe, E. Bova, C. Dragomirescu-Gaina (eds.), *The Digital Economy and the Single Market. Employment Prospects and Working Conditions in Europe*, Brussels: FEPS, 2016.

reasons for crowd-working is the fact that the respondents prefer to work from home.[57] This finding might imply that crowd-work has a positive impact on work-life balance, since this type of work allows the workers to reconcile the work with their other responsibilities or to have more free time, but the chapter does not investigate this assumption.

Based on a review of the literature, we have identified several features that are present in most forms of crowd-work (although to a different degree) and that may have an impact on work-life balance.

[A] Possibility to Perform Work on Distance

The element of telework (i.e., work performed independent of a location, often from home, and particularly present in those forms of crowd-work where work is performed online) is probably the one feature that has received the greatest attention from the literature. In this regard, research has been conducted on the impact of 'virtual work' on work-life balance.[58] Even though telework is a much broader concept and the research in question is usually concerned with *employees* who perform telework, the results may nevertheless be transferred to some forms of crowd-work.

However, the results on telework are mixed: most (highly educated) workers find that virtual technology makes the reconciliation of work and family life easier, but also more complicated 'as it is more difficult to be off from work, even on vacation',[59] reducing the opportunities to recover.[60] In a similar line of thought, the opportunity to (continue to) work from home due to digital technology tends to blur the boundaries between work and private (or family) life. While many workers may appreciate the blurring boundaries between work and family life up to a point, they also acknowledge the challenges of this development.[61]

[B] Flexibility on Working Time

Arguably, in crowd-work the providers enjoy more flexibility to decide *whether and when* to work, what has been equalised by some authors with greater work-life balance.[62] In a broader perspective, social scientists have different theories about the relationship between job autonomy (of which flexibility arguable is one element) and

57. J. Berg, 'Income Security in the On-Demand Economy: Findings and Policy Lessons from a Survey of Crowdworkers', *Comparative Labor Law & Policy Journal* 2016 Vol. 37 No. 3, p. 552.
58. For example, G.L. Rafnsdóttir and A.S. Stefánsson, 'Virtual Work and Work-Life Balance for Managers', *International Journal of Business and Management* 2014 Vol. 9 No. 11, pp. 1-12.
59. G.L. Rafnsdóttir and A.S. Stefánsson, 'Virtual Work and Work-Life Balance for Managers', *International Journal of Business and Management* 2014 Vol. 9 No. 11, pp. 1-12.
60. J. Popma, *The Janus Face of the 'New Ways of Work'. Rise, Risks and Regulation of Nomadic Work*, ETUI, Working Paper, Brussels. 2013.
61. *Idem. See also* European Commission, *The increasing use of portable computing and communication devices and its impact on the heath of EU workers*, Publications Office of the European Union, Luxembourg 2010.
62. *See*, for example, W. Wobe et al., *The Digital Economy and the Single Market*, Brussels: FEPS, 2016, p. 128, 134, 145.

work-family conflict for employees and the self-employed. In short, a high level of job autonomy in self-employment does not necessarily lead to greater work-family balance.[63] Transferred to our crowd-work-case: the fact that crowd-workers may enjoy more autonomy does not necessarily mean they experience more work-life balance.

Aloisi argues that a contradictory idea of flexibility exists in the context of crowd-work.[64] Although providers have the possibility to decide when to 'log in' and be available to perform work, the time they spend on the platform impacts their daily compensation (and their internal ranking). Because in most cases the payment is low[65] – below minimum wage – providers might have to work more hours every day than a 'standard' worker in order to earn a significant amount of money. This is particularly important, of course, concerning those workers for whom crowd-work is their main source of income, a group that in Europe constitutes a small but important minority, [66] and the in the US amount to one third of all workers. [67]

Furthermore, in order to find tasks to perform, providers in crowd platforms often have to spend long hours online just searching for paid tasks (a time that is not remunerated).[68] As *Berg* indicates, this 'pressure to be on-line to find work appears to erode the flexibility that is so coveted in the job'.[69]

Moreover, the theoretical flexibility to decide *when* to work might be eroded as a result of the demand-driven character of the relationship, as providers will often need to work in rush hours in order to obtain work.[70]

[C] Holding Multiple Jobs

Another consequence of the low compensation per task in crowd-work mentioned above is that, in most cases, such work cannot replace a 'normal' full-time job in terms of income security. Often, such workers may need an extra job. Arguably, having multiple jobs is not beneficial for work-life balance. It can even become questionable whether the workers have enough 'free time'. However, in case of platform work, this possible effect has not yet been investigated fully.

---

63. S. Drobnič and A.M. Guillén Rodríguez, 'Tensions Between Work and Home: Job Quality and Working Conditions in the Institutional Contexts of Germany and Spain' *Social Politics* 2011 Vol. 18 No. 2, pp. 232–268.
64. A. Aloisi, 'Commoditized Workers: Case Study Research on Labor Law Issues Arising from a Set of On-Demand/Gig Economy Platforms', *Comparative Labor Law & Policy Journal* 2016 Vol. 37, No. 3, p. 662.
65. J. Berg, 'Income Security in the On-Demand Economy: Findings and Policy Lessons from a Survey of Crowdworkers', *Comparative Labor Law & Policy Journal* 2016 Vol. 37 No. 3, p. 557.
66. U. Huws, N.H. Spencer and S. Joyce, *Crowd-Work in Europe. Preliminary Results from a Survey in the UK, Sweden, Germany, Austria and the Netherlands*, FEPS Studies December 2016.
67. J. Berg, 'Income Security in the On-Demand Economy: Findings and Policy Lessons from a Survey of Crowdworkers', *Comparative Labor Law & Policy Journal* 2016 Vol. 37 No. 3, p. 554.
68. As *Berg* reports, for every hour of paid work, AMT workers spent eighteen minutes searching and doing unpaid preparatory work. Idem, pp. 543–576.
69. *Idem*, p. 561.
70. In addition, due to the often global character of the platform, providers may even have to work at 'unsocial hours'. *See* V. De Stefano, 'The Rise of the "Just-In-Time Workforce": On-Demand Work, Crowdwork, and Labor Protection in the "Gig-Economy"', *Comparative Labor Law & Policy Journal* 2016 Vol. 37 No. 3, p. 480.

While, for example, an author will acknowledge that 'having a second job means that the scheduling may get a worker fired from the first' and therefore, puts the worker 'in a trap',[71] the issue of work-life balance is left untouched. This is despite the fact that most persons in crowd-work use it to complement their main occupation.[72] In fact, it has been noted that those workers who rely on crowd-work as their primary source of income are in a significantly insecure position (both financially and concerning their labour market and social security situation).[73]

§2.05 CONCLUSIONS

Through this chapter, we have identified two potential issues that crowd-work presents for a well-protected work-life: one drawing from the still generally unclear legal nature of crowd-work, and another originating from the potential threads that apparently common features among forms of crowd-work may present to work-life balance.

It is difficult (if not impossible) to regulate something that is unknown or undefined. It seems therefore understandable that most legal discussions on crowd-work surround the basic issue of its employment status. Currently, arguments move between considering persons providing services or products through crowd-work platforms as self-employed, employees or members of a third category with some features of both. At the moment of writing this chapter, the outcome seems unclear, with most platforms considering persons who provide services or products through them as self-employed, while some judicial decisions have forced them to grant providers some minimum labour rights. A decision in one or other direction will obviously have significant implications, mostly concerning the possibility to apply the already existing legislation on work-life balance for employees. However, it is quite likely that we are heading towards a system with different individual decisions depending on the features of each platform or contract rather than towards a general and all-encompassing regulation for all crowd-work. Furthermore, the discussion may become even more complex if taken into account the fact that, sometimes, one and the same person can have the status of consumer and provider of services simultaneously. Consider, for example a person that writes a review after receiving a service or product, and that review being a service itself that helps other users and the platform to monitor quality;[74] or a person that must perform a micro-task in order to access a service.[75]

71. M.A. Cherry, 'Beyond Misclassification: The Digital Transformation of Work', *Comparative Labor Law & Policy Journal* 2016 Vol. 37 No. 3, p. 598.
72. J. Berg, 'Income Security in the On-Demand Economy: Findings and Policy Lessons from a Survey of Crowdworkers', *Comparative Labor Law & Policy Journal* 2016 Vol. 37 No. 3, p. 554.
73. *Idem.*
74. For example, the website 'Yelp' exists for the purpose of rating everything commercial. The reviews written by consumers form the main value of the site. While Yelp does not pay for reviews, it does encourage loyalty among its most active and well- respected reviewers by awarding them 'Elite' status along with certain perks. *See* concerning this issue M.A. Cherry, 'Beyond Misclassification: The Digital Transformation of Work', *Comparative Labor Law & Policy Journal* 2016 Vol. 37 No. 3, p. 589.
75. This was the case in *Gabriela Rojas-Lazano v Google Inc.* In this case, the plaintiff challenged the use by Google of CAPTCHAs (small sections of text embedded in images that sometimes must be

While this issue has not yet been fully introduced into the bigger debate of status classification, when (and if) it does, it may have disruptive effects for the traditional regulation of work.

Even if we accept the broad and generally undefined nature of crowd-work, it is still possible to determine a set of essential features of crowd-work. Through this chapter, we have highlighted the importance of some of these features, such as the online character of work or the fact that it addresses an undefined pool of workers. However, it is no less important to also acknowledge the current form in which crowd-work is present in the labour market, and the nature of the platforms: Highly flexible, with a low remuneration, and complementing income from other occupations.

If there is one key concept that defines crowd-work, that may be flexibility, with some authors even referring to crowd-work as 'hyperflexible'.[76] This is in fact a feature shared by all of the so-called 'new forms of work' or non-standard work, which answers to a demand for greater flexibility from employers, employees or both.[77] However, it is important to not confuse flexibility with a displacement of the costs of production. As *Holtgrewe* explains, crowd-work and other forms of casual employment have 'the aim to comprehensively remove slack times from work and to have employers or customers pay for active working times or immediate results only'.[78] This is particularly significant if combined with the low and diverse compensation received by workers, as analysed above. As a result, workers are often forced to work long hours to achieve sufficient income, often performing multiple jobs (whether with different platforms, and/or combining crowd-work with another form of work), and rarely achieving to work as much as they would desire.[79] These issues, together, often provoke an insecure situation for those in crowd-work, due to its casual and unstable nature.

In this regard, we must beware of arguments on crowd-work that present it as a completely new phenomenon, one that escapes from the traditional discussion on labour and social security rights. While some of the features of crowd-work may be unique, the most essential of them (casualisation, flexible character, third party

recognised and written by the user of Google products in order to prove that the person is a human being and not an algorithm producing fake traffic) to transcript books for Google, something about which the users where not informed. The Court, however, considered that the fact that Google profited did not necessarily mean that there was any damage to the user, dismissing the claim due to the small amount of effort from the user that filling the CAPTCHA required. *See* further United States District Court N.D. California, *Gabriela Rojas-Lazano v Google Inc*, February 3, 2016, Case No. 15-Cv-03751/JSC.

76. Eurofound, *New Forms of Employment*, Publications Office of the European Union, Luxembourg 2015, p. 135.
77. *Idem.*
78. U. Holtgrewe, 'Working in the Low-Paid Service Sector: What Is to Be Learned from the Analogue World?' *The Digital Economy and the Single Market. Employment Prospects and Working Conditions in Europe*, FEPS – Foundation for European Progressive Studies 2016, p. 101.
79. As noted from a survey performed by the *ILO*, 90% of the respondents say they would like to do more crowdwork than they are currently doing, *see* J. Berg, 'Income Security in the On-Demand Economy: Findings and Policy Lessons from a Survey of Crowdworkers', *Comparative Labor Law & Policy Journal* 2016 Vol. 37 No. 3, p. 560.

employment relationship) have been present for decades if not centuries.[80] It is important to not let technology or new terms disguise old issues, and to return to the basic aims of labour and social security law (such as security or solidarity) when possible. At the same time, it is also undeniable that the combination of features presented in crowd-work sometimes originates new challenges, particularly so for work-life balance. In this regard, the wealth of literature on telework and work-life balance may need some adaptations in order to integrate the interaction between this element of work on distance and others such as casualisation, divergent methods of monitoring, lesser accountability and more complex methods for the resolution of individual conflicts.

80. *Finkin* shows that models such as the Amazon Mechanical Turk uses are in fact similar to home-based contract work that has been used for most of history. M.W. Finkin, 'Beclouded Work, Beclouded Workers in Historical Perspective', *Comparative Labor Law & Policy Journal* 2016 Vol. 37 No. 3, pp. 603–618.

CHAPTER 3

Part-Time Fathers and Mothers? Comparing Part-Time Employment in Germany, Sweden, Ireland and the Netherlands

Sonja Bekker, Lena Hipp, Janine Leschke & Friederike Molitor

§3.01 INTRODUCTION

The idea of reduced working hours has gained prominence in current debates on combining work and care and reducing gender inequality in the labour market. In theory, part-time work allows both fathers as well as mothers to combine paid and unpaid work, thus calming down the 'rush hour of life' by allowing them to adapt the work to the changes in family life (e.g., Bittman and Wajcman 2000, Lothaller 2009, Bertram et al. 2011, Bujard and Panova 2014). But while there are benefits of part-time employment, such as better work and care combinations, there are also disadvantages compared to full-time employment, including lower earnings, lower career prospects, and lower social security entitlements (Folk and Beller 1993, Walsh 1999, Warren 2004, Román 2006, Vlasblom and Schippers 2006, Hinz 2008, Webber and Williams 2008, Trischler and Kistler 2011, Korpi et al. 2013, Yerkes 2013, Allmendinger et al. 2013). Although there are more and more men working less than full-time (Allmendinger et al. 2013, Brenke 2011, Hobler et al. 2016), part-time work is still a predominantly 'female' phenomenon (Hipp et al. 2015). This is also reflected in the academic literature.

Many studies have examined the conditions under which women and particularly mothers work reduced hours (e.g., Kitterød et al. 2013, Korpi et al. 2013, Yerkes 2013, Gash 2008, Vlasblom and Schippers 2006), while little is known about what determines men's and fathers' part-time work (see Hipp et al. 2017). Such knowledge is, however, vital if governments want to help fathers to combine work and care responsibilities via part-time work arrangements. Various studies have considered the effects of more recent 'family friendly' policies and institutions such as earmarked parental leave that are supposed to support young fathers (Bünning and Pollmann-Schult 2016, Bünning 2015, Pollmann-Schult and Wagner 2014, Trappe 2013, Eggebeen and Knoester 2001). However, there are few analyses on the extent to which fathers change their working hours due to care responsibilities. Moreover, the findings are often based on the experiences in a single country, meaning that the relationship between different welfare state institutions and policies and the likelihood of working part-time is not explored in a comparative setting. In addition, studies do not always include the household context when explaining the working hours of fathers. Thus, we still know little about what encourages fathers to reduce their working hours including the question whether the same factors play a role as are found to matter for women.

By analysing individual-level data from the European Labour Force Survey (LFS) from the year 2014, we aim to close this gap in the existing literature. We examine the part-time work of fathers and mothers in four European countries: Germany, Sweden, Ireland, and the Netherlands. We compare part-time employment of parents with those of men and women who do not have children. Inspired by theories of family and household economics, including social exchange theories (SET), we also show differences in part-time employment across gender and country by partners' earnings capacity and according to marital status. Married couples experience tax advantages in some countries, which in turn might impact the working hours' distribution in couples, including the take up of part-time employment. Even though our data and research design does not allow us to directly link institutions to part-time outcomes, differences across countries by household characteristics will give us a hint regarding the role of institutions such as childcare provisions, leave policies, right to work part-time, and income taxation. The four countries have been chosen based on the different welfare state regime types they represent. Moreover, the country choice includes the largest 'part-time economy': the Netherlands. Section §3.02 briefly introduces welfare state typologies in order to justify our choice of countries and lays out SET with a focus on the household. In section §3.03, we review the literature on part-time employment with respect to individual and household explanations for men's part-time employment, and then discuss the role of institutions in facilitating part-time work in section §3.04. Section §3.05 presents and discusses the results of our descriptive analysis of part-time employment for men and women with regard to parental status and household characteristics. The paper concludes with a summary and a discussion of the main findings.

§3.02 WELFARE STATE TYPOLOGIES AND SET

The four countries selected for this study represent different types of welfare state regimes following Esping-Andersen's typology (1990). These ideal regime types have been clustered according to the notion that 'in the relationship between state and economy a complex of legal and organizational features are systematically interwoven' (*ibid.*: 2; Ferrera 1996). Different regime clusters correspond to different welfare state arrangements and social rights. The original work of Esping-Andersen (1990) distinguishes three ideal welfare state regimes: the liberal, the conservative-corporatist, and the social-democratic welfare state. The liberal welfare state model is characterised by means-tested social assistance, modest universal transfers, and modest social insurance. Benefits usually cater to low-income groups and the welfare state development is influenced by traditional, liberal work-ethic norms. In our case selection, Ireland represents this regime type. Within the conservative-corporatist regime type, the logic of the market is not thought to have exerted much influence on the development of social rights. Such rights were instead connected to status and class. The influence of religion is also relevant for our investigation, as religion sets out to preserve traditional views on family life, reflected in family benefits that promote motherhood and provide childcare facilities. Germany represents the conservative-corporatist welfare state in our study, although through the introduction of more modern social policies it has begun to move away from familialistic values in the last decade (*see* section §3.04). The social-democratic regime type, in our study represented by Sweden, follows an egalitarian policy approach, including both high childcare coverage, individualisation of taxes and benefits alongside modern gender values. A high degree of public spending on families including childcare and other services both supports and necessitates comprehensive participation in employment of both men and women. The Netherlands is included because it represents the world's first 'part-time economy' and has an unusually high amount of workers in part-time employment (Visser 2002). Moreover, this country is characterised as a hybrid regime type, which mixes characteristics of both conservative-corporatist and social-democratic regime types. In spite of acknowledging that the welfare state regimes are ideal types and that countries in practice do not conform fully to these in their institutional configurations, we still assume that we will find different types of institutional arrangements that either support or do not support mothers and fathers in combining work and care. We thus expect that the case selection will allow for a maximum distribution of different rules and regulations related to parenthood that can explain why mothers and fathers choose or have to work part-time.

We build on SET to justify the household context to frame our analyses. The notion of exchange can refer both to the macro-level, i.e., to the performance of work in exchange for money (Tsui et al. 1997, Shore et al. 2009), and to the micro-level, i.e., to interpersonal exchanges of paid and unpaid work between household members (Miller and Bermudez 2004). At the micro-level, social exchange relationships and resource bargaining in couples (Blossfeld and Drobnic 2001, Bernasco et al. 1998, Thébaud 2010, Hipp and Leuze 2015) are characterised by a long-term orientation with important emphasis on mutual trust, reciprocity, commitment, and attachment (Blau 1964, Shore et al. 2009). The rules of exchange at the micro-level vary systematically for different types of transactions in interpersonal relationships. Foa and Foa (1974, 2012) distinguish six different classes of resources exchanged in interpersonal encounters: love, status, information, money, goods (i.e., tangible products, objects, or materials), and services (which involve activities that affect the body or belongings of a person and often constitute labour for another).

For the purpose of our study, the exchange of money or goods and services within households are the most relevant, as these reflect the division of work and care tasks.

Some of such divisions can be closely linked to the traditional male breadwinner/female carer model, where the male breadwinner provides money or goods for the family, while the female carer provides services in the form of care and household chores (Crompton 1999, Lewis 2001). These traditional patterns of distribution of wage and non-wage work in couples have been substantially challenged by recent changes in life-course patterns, including higher labour market participation among women, increasing individualisation – not least of social benefits – and less stable partnerships (OECD 2011). Applying SET concepts to our research, we can define reduced working time due to care and household commitments (services) as costs. Having a spouse means that within a household these costs can be compensated or rewarded through money or goods provided through wage work. It is important to also take the welfare state conditions and broader economic circumstances into account, which will impact on the exchange relationships both with regard to the micro- and macro-level.

Distinct family, state, and market interrelations are deeply enshrined in the different welfare state models and go hand in hand with specific sets of institutions and social policies (e.g., Esping-Andersen 1990, Ferrera 1996). Institutions and social policies are motivated by different objectives, such as coping with the challenges of demographic change and improving horizontal redistribution, poverty alleviation, or gender equality (Daly 2010). Together with societal gender orientations, they differentially affect gender equality in couples with regard to the distribution of wage and nonwage work. Of the regime types represented in this chapter, conservative-corporatist welfare state regimes are rooted in the so-called male-bread winner/female (part-time) carer model. This was traditionally supported by, among other things, joint income taxation and derived benefits for nonworking partners and characterised by institutional designs (e.g., the existence of parental leave and childcare policies). This in turn supported home-making or (predominantly female) part-time work rather than externalising of care. The welfare regimes thus go hand in hand with different institutional configurations and gender orientations, which have been shown to impact women's labour force participation and working hours. However, much less is known about the determinants of fathers' part-time work, particularly in a cross-country perspective and a focus on to the household level. Women's working hours and countries' institutional settings, are likely to determine also male part-time employment at least to some degree. Moreover, they are likely to influence individuals' bargaining positions within couples.

§3.03 PART-TIME EMPLOYMENT: INDIVIDUAL AND HOUSEHOLD CHARACTERISTICS

Besides education or training related part-time work, which usually takes place early in an individual's employment career, and part-time employment in combination with gradual early retirement, there are four main motives to work part-time: private and family reasons, economic constraints and health reasons. Part-time employment is a way to combine paid employment with care responsibilities for children or other people, either voluntarily or due to the absence of full-time, quality, and affordable care institutions. Moreover, part-time employment offers some income when full-time employment is not available, for instance, due to bad economic circumstances, or when full-time employment is not possible due to psychological or physical constraints (compare for example Hipp et al. 2015; Hobler et al. 2013; Keller and Haustein 2014; OECD 2010). Having a part-time job due to bad economic circumstances could point to underemployment or involuntary part-time work. This involuntary part-time employment increased in most countries during the crisis, with a particularly sharp increase in Ireland where the share of involuntary part-time workers (those who stated that an inability to find a full-time job was their main reason for working part-time) rose from 10.9% in 2007 to 43.1% in 2013 (Horemans et al. 2016). The substantial increase in involuntary part-time employment seen recently in Southern European countries and Ireland, all countries strongly affected by the economic crisis, support the economic argument.

There are relatively few studies about part-time employment of men. Buddelmeyer et al. (2004) for example, show for a number of EU countries that economic factors impact on middle-aged male part-time employment whereas the authors do not find a relationship for women (for similar results on the US see Leppel and Clain 1988). Also, employment in the services sector goes hand in hand with higher rates of (involuntary) part-time employment for both men and women (Leppel and Clain 1988, Delsen 2002, Kitterød and Rønsen 2012).

Additionally some studies show that an individual's family situation, such as the age and number of children, do play some role for part-time employment among men (*see* Delsen 2002 for a comprehensive discussion). However, the impact of family characteristics on part-time work of men seems to be lower than for women, or has the opposite effect compared to the effect for women. For instance, a number of studies show that fathers of small children usually work more hours than fathers with older children and men without children (OECD 2001, Eggebeen and Knoester 2001 for the US). For Great Britain, Dermott (2006) does not find a significant impact of fatherhood on working time. For Norway, Dommermuth and Kitterød (2009) show that contractual working hours of men are not significantly impacted by parenthood; yet real working time goes down for example through fewer over-time hours when small children are present. Kjeldstad and Nymoen (2012) conclude also for Norway that children have no significant impact on fathers' probabilities of working part-time.

In spite of the limited and often contradictory empirical evidence of a relationship between parenthood and working-time reduction among fathers, the couple and household level does seem to be the adequate frame of analysis for part-time motives of men. Theories on household economics argue that the division of household tasks and paid employment is the outcome of gender specialisation (Becker 1981, 1985) or of negotiations between partners (Blood and Wolfe 1960, Lundberg and Pollak 1996). Both approaches have a similar starting-point, this being that the contribution of a partner to paid work and household tasks depends on their resources, most notably their income (*see also* section §3.02); both are in principle gender neutral. According to the first approach, the partner with the highest earning capacities specialises in paid work and leaves the unpaid tasks for his or her partner. This maximises the total household utility function, meaning that given the care and paid work tasks, the distribution of tasks between the spouses maximises their revenues from work (Becker 1985, Bernasco et al. 1998, Hendrickx et al. 2001, Sorensen 1983). In theory, it does not matter whether the male or female partner specialises in gainful employment. In the second approach, the partner with the highest earning capacity uses this advantage to spend more hours in paid employment than his or her spouse (Blood and Wolfe 1960, Lundberg and Pollak 1996). This should also in principle happen in a gender neutral way.

For the purpose of this study we assume that fathers – similar to what has been shown for mothers in the past (e.g., Hipp et al. 2015 for an overview) – are more inclined to accept a part-time job if their earning capacity is lower than that of their partner. We expect that this will in particular be the case if there are more care responsibilities (i.e., a higher number of children in the household). Some countries provide tax advantages to married couples, which in turn might impact the working hours' distribution in couples including male part-time employment. In particular, we assume that married men with lower earnings capacities than their female partners are more inclined to work part-time compared to unmarried men in countries with joint income taxation. Our data and research design does not allow us to directly test the link between institutions, such as childcare, leave policies, right to work part-time and income taxation, and differences in part-time outcomes across gender and countries; institutional information will however help us to contextualise our results.

§3.04 PART-TIME WORK AND NATIONAL INSTITUTIONS

Apart from individual and household characteristics, the national institutional context is also likely to impact on fathers' part-time work, at least to some degree, similar to what has been shown extensively for mothers (Gash 2008; Hipp et al. 2015; Vlasblom and Schippers 2006; Walsh 1999). In multi-country comparative studies on mothers' part-time work, the role of working-time regulations (especially the right to work part-time), income taxation, the economic situation and childcare coverage have been identified as factors impacting part-time employment (compare Hipp et al. 2015). There are a few single country studies looking at the impact of national institutional context factors for male part-time work. Several studies show that cyclical trends matter (Leppel and Clain 1988, European Commission 2016, Buddelmeyer et al. 2004) whereas family and social policy seem to play a lesser role. For example, Bünning (2015) finds that fathers in Germany who have used parental leave subsequently reduce their working hours somewhat. In the US however, a country where there is little institutional support, men rarely adjust their working hours and professional obligations to deal with household obligations, which is quite the opposite case for women (Maume 2006). According to Sanchez and Thomson (1997) compared to fathers with one child, fathers with several children have more working hours per week in the US. In their review article Hegewisch and Gornick (2011) show that fathers use family policy options less often than mothers (*see also* O'Brien et al. 2007). Given this finding it is not surprising that, in their comparison of eleven European countries,

Buddelmeyer et al. (2005) find a significant relationship between country-specific context factors and the part-time probability for women but not for men. Importantly, the predominant gender norms, which differ across welfare state regimes (*see* section §3.02), are also likely to impact on the willingness of fathers to reduce their working-time temporarily.

Table 3.1 illustrates the use of part-time work and other central labour market characteristics for our four countries and also compares the institutional characteristics which can impact on part-time work.

Table 3.1 Overview Country Characteristics, 2014 (or Latest Available Data)

Land	*DE*	*NL*	*IE*	*SE*
% men in part-time[1)]	9.1%	19.4%	12.5%	10.5%
% women in part-time[1)]	37.5%	60.6%	35.4%	18.3%
% involuntary part-time men[2)]	22.3	15.2[(u)]	59.5	31.8[(u)]
% involuntary part-time women[2)]	12.8	9.4[(u)]	33.6	29.1
Employment rate of men[3)]	78%	78.2%	66.9%	76.5%
Employment rate of women[3)]	69.5%	68.1%	56.7%	73.1%
Unemployment rate[4)]	5.0%	7.4%	11.3%	8.0%
Right to work part-time (when employed)[5)]	yes	Yes	no	yes
Statutory parental leave	Bundeselterngeld- und Elternzeitgesetz (BEEG)	Ouder-schapsverlof	Parental Leave Act	Föräldra-ledighetslagen
Childcare coverage (< 3 years)[6)]	29.3%	54.6%	30.2%	47.3%
Income taxation[7)]	joint	individual	joint	individual
Participation tax rate for second earners[8)]	45.6%–46.5%	35.9%–39.7%	42.1%–49.2%	23.4%–26.8%
Gender norms[9)]	65.7%	81.6%	78.1%	86.2%

Data sources: (1) (Wo-)men working part-time as a percentage of all employed (wo-)men. Part-time employment is defined as people in employment (employees or self-employed) aged 15 and over who work less than thirty hours/week in their main job (OECD Data 2014b); (2) Involuntary part-time employment as percentage of the total part-time employment. Persons working on an involuntary part-time basis are those who declare that they work part-time because they are unable to find full-time work (Eurostat 2014); (3) Employed (wo-)men as share of all working age population of the respective gender (OECD Data 2014a); (4) Unemployed persons as percentage of the labour force (OECD Data 2014c); (5) Right to work part-time (Eurofound 2011); (6) Use of childcare facilities of 0 to 2 year olds (OECD Family Database 2013); (7) Legal rule on joint or individual taxation of the income of married couples (Rastrigina and Verashchagina 2015, Citizens Information Board 2016b); (8) Participation tax rates for an individual entering employment with gross earnings equal to 50% to 100% of average earnings (OECD 2016). (9) Information on gender norms is taken from the European Social Survey (ESS) Round 5 in 2010 (relevant data from the latest Round 8 (2016) not yet available). We used the proportion of people (strongly) disagreeing to the statement 'When jobs are scarce, men should have more right to a job than women.' (u) Low reliability.

From the four countries that we explore, Germany has the second highest part-time employment rate for women and the lowest for men. The proportion of part-time workers who does so involuntarily (because they are not able to find a full-time job)[1] is relatively low compared to Ireland and Sweden, but higher than in the Netherlands. The growth of part-time employment in Germany has been supported by the institutional setting, notably by the implementation of the European part-time directive in 2001 (*Teilzeit- und Befristungsgesetz, TzBfG)* which gives employees who work in companies with more than fifteen employees the right to reduce their weekly working hours (BMAS 2016). In addition, joint income taxation promotes part-time work (or non-employment) of one of the partners if the couple is married (z.B. Bach et al. 2011). In recent years, both spouses have been encouraged to take up a paid job (both part-time and full-time) via a boost in childcare coverage (*Kinderförderungs-gesetzes, KiföG, 2008)* and by the introduction of earnings-related parental leave. The 2007 parental leave Act (*Bundeselterngeld- und Elternzeitgesetz, BEEG)* entitles parents to take leave from work. Currently, there is the option to get in total twelve months plus two months. Paid parental leave can be shared equally between the parents, the maximum of paid parental leave that one of the partners can take amounts to twelve months. For parents to receive the maximum of fourteen months of paid parental leave, the partner not taking the bulk of the leave has to take at least two months. Irrespective of how long their leave is, both parents are eligible to take parental leave in a part-time construction (up to thirty hours per week) (BMFSFJ 2015). Since 1 August 2013 parents have a right to a place in childcare for children aged over one year (BMFSFJ 2014). Since 2006, the percentage of children under the age of three in childcare has more than doubled, amounting to 32.2% in 2015 (BMFSFJ 2016). A higher rate of accessible

1. The authors are aware that this commonly used definition of involuntary part-time is problematic in so far as part-time employment can also be involuntary in light of institutional constrains and in particular the absence of comprehensive childcare.

childcare helps parents with young children to be in paid employment (including in part-time jobs).

In the Netherlands, the part-time employment rate of women amounts to almost 61 %, and it is uncommon for women within this group to be involuntarily in part-time work because they could not find a full-time job. Men work part-time here more often than in the other three countries. Among Dutch part-time working men there is a comparatively small group that is in this position involuntarily due to a lack of full-time options. Facilitated by the Working Hour Adjustment Act *(Wet op de aanpassing van de arbeidsduur, WWA)* and the Flexible Work Act *(Wet flexibel werken)*, employees can ask for an adjustment of their working hours, if they work in companies with more than ten employees (Jacobs and Schmidt 2001). In spite of the individual income taxation of married couples, the Income Taxes Act (*Wet inkomstenbelasting)* of 2001 gives married couples the option to shift their tax free allowance to their partner, thus jointly generating a lower taxation rate (Eurostat 2015). The Netherlands also has parental leave provisions (*Ouderschapsverlof*) which were implemented in 1997. It gives both parents the right to take up parental leave amounting to twenty-six times their weekly working hours per child. This entitlement expires as soon as the child is eight years old. Parental leave is unpaid, however, in some collective labour agreements the social partners have managed to secure paid parental leave up to a certain percentage of the wage. In 2013, 57% of mothers entitled to parental leave used this arrangement, while 23 % of fathers made use of parental leave (den Dulk 2016). And whereas the 2005 Act on childcare *Wet op de kinderopvang* sets national-level standards for childcare quality and funding, there is no guaranteed access to childcare (Tyroller 2005). Still, around 45% of children aged below three were in formal childcare in 2014, and about 23 % of this age group are cared for solely by their parents (Vandewiele and Di Meglio 2016).

In Ireland women have a part-time employment rate of 35.4% compared to 12.5% for men. What is remarkable is that quite a large group of these part-time working women and men say that they work part-time because they could not find a fulltime job (33.6% for women with a part-time job and 59.5% for men with a part-time job). Although the 2001 *Protection of Employees (Part-Time Work) Act*, in line with the EU part-time work directive, has introduced equal treatment for part-time workers, Ireland does not have a universal right to request part-time work (Citizens Information Board 2015). In Ireland, married couples also benefit from joint income taxation, particularly if one spouse works part-time (Citizens Information Board 2016b).

The 1998 *Parental Leave Act* entitles fathers and mothers to unpaid parental leave, which cannot be transferred, until their child is eight years old. In 2013, this leave period increased from fourteen to eighteen weeks for each parent per child. After an employee has returned to work and has used up his/her parental leave he/she can request a change in working hours (Citizens Information Board 2016a). The comparatively low rates of care of small children in public or publicly funded institutions – in 2014 51 % of children under 3 were cared for exclusively by their parents (Vandewiele and Di Meglio 2016) and only 28% attended a formal childcare facility – could also lead to higher part-time employment rates among parents with young children.

Sweden is the country with the lowest share of women in part-time employment (18.3%) in our study and the part-time employment rate for men is also comparably low with 10.5%. In contrast, involuntary part-time work in our limited definition (those who could not find a full-time job) is relatively high for both men and women, though not as high as in Ireland. Part-time work is encouraged by various institutional arrangements. The Swedish Working Hours Act 1982 *(Arbetstidslagen)* and the 2002 Prohibition of Discrimination of Employees Working Part Time and Employees with Fixed-term Employment Act *(2002:293)* enable flexible working hours while demanding equal treatment. The 1995 Parental Leave Act *(Föräldraledighetslagen)* gives parents the right to work part-time (Arbetsförmedlingen 2015). Up until their child is eight years old, parents can request a reduction of their regular working time by a maximum of 25% (Försäkringskassan 2016). Unlike Germany the income of Swedish couples (either married or not) is subject to individual taxation (Eurostat 2015). This is offset by generous parental leave rights. Parents may have a fulltime break from work until their child is 18 months old. Each parent has 240 days of parental leave that can be transferred to their spouse; 90 days are reserved for the father and cannot be transferred. In the first 195 days of their parental leave, parents receive 80% of their wages, and for the remaining 45 days there is a flat rate (Haas et al. 2016, Fegert et al. 2011). Sweden has the highest percentage of fathers taking up parental leave in the EU (Schulze and Gergoric 2015). In 2014, 45% of all parental leave recipients were men and 55% were women, while mothers took, on average, 94 days and fathers 39 days that year (Haas et al. 2016). Childcare facilities are also well established in Sweden. In 2014 more than half of children aged between 0 and 2 attended formal childcare (56%) and 42% were cared for solely by their parents (Vandewiele and Di Meglio 2016).

§3.05 DESCRIPTIVE ANALYSIS: PART-TIME EMPLOYMENT AND HOUSEHOLD CONTEXT

We use individual level data for 2014 from the European LFS for our analysis. Our total sample includes 259,360 employed respondents (134,912 of which are men, including 65,531 fathers) aged between 25 and 54 years in Germany, the Netherlands, Ireland and Sweden. This age restriction is aimed at excluding those persons who are working part-time as part of their education or who are working part-time as part of early retirement schemes. The observations per country range from 12,422 survey respondents in Sweden to 159,183 in Germany. We define and operationalise part-time employment in line with international classifications as dependent employment or self-employment with an average weekly working time of thirty hours or less (OECD 2010).

Table 3.2 *Overview of Variables*

part-time	1 – weekly working time of thirty hours or less, 0 – weekly working time of more than thirty hours
occupational status difference	1 – occupational status of the man is higher than of his female partner (ISEI Score difference of + 5 or more), 0 – occupational status of the man is lower than or equal to the female partner's
number of children in the household	no children (reference), one child, two children, three children or more
small child in the household	1 – child up to 5 years in the household, 0 – no small child in the household
marital status	1 – married, 0 – not married

In order to determine the earnings potential of both partners we use the difference in occupational status, which we derive from the international socio-economic index classification (ISEI) and Ganzeboom's (2010) coding scheme (*see* Hipp und Leuze 2015 for details). This variable is coded with the value '0' if the male partner has a job with lower or equal status and with '1' if he has a job with higher status (> 5 ISEI Score) than his female spouse or cohabiting partner. Further relevant variables are marital status, the number of children and the presence of a small child in the household (Table 3.2).

Figure 3.1 Proportion of Men and Women Having a Part-Time Job, Aged 25–54, by Parental Status (2014)

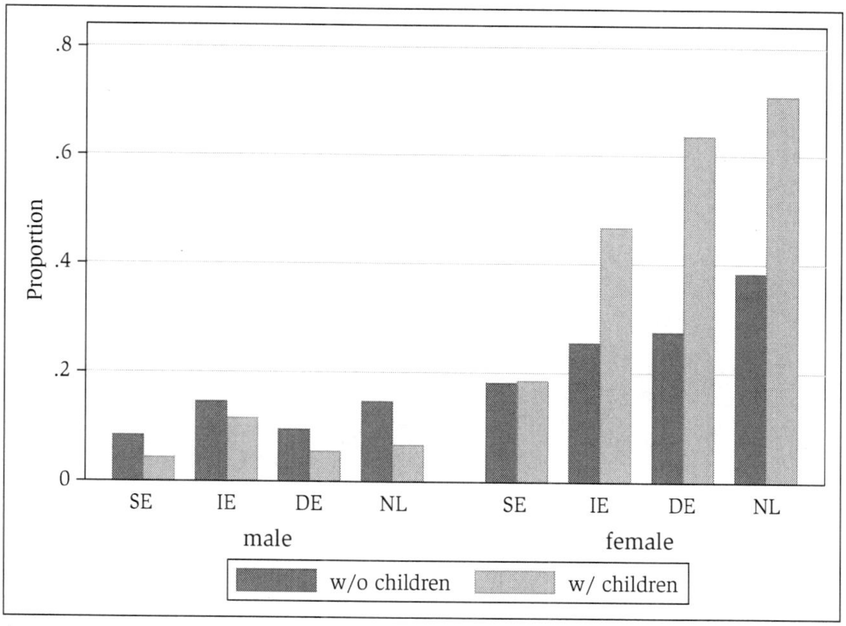

Source: EU LFS2014, weighted results, N (men) = 11,734, N (women) = 55,480, N (fathers) = 5,027, N (mothers) = 40,357.

Figure 3.1 shows the proportion of part-time workers among men without children and fathers, and, respectively, women without children and mothers – the focus here is on prime age persons (25–54 years). Apart from the well-known large gender difference in the incidence of part-time employment, it is particularly interesting that the proportion of mothers working part-time is substantially higher compared to childless women in Ireland, Germany and the Netherlands but not in Sweden. For fathers we see the inverse trend in all four countries with the lowest differences in Ireland where 15% of childless men and 12% of fathers work part-time. Ireland and the Netherlands are the countries with the highest share of prime age male part-time workers (15%), while the share of part-time working fathers is more than 5 percentage points higher in Ireland (12%) than in the Netherlands (6.7%). The high rate of involuntary part-time work among men in Ireland due to not being able to find a full-time job – with substantial increases during the economic crisis – suggests that in this country economic factors play a large role when it comes to reduced working hours. This is also supported by higher unemployment rates in Ireland than in the other three countries. Conversely, in the Netherlands the rate of involuntary part-time work among men is relatively low.

As is well known, the Netherlands has the highest share of female part-time workers for both women without and with children (38% and 71%, respectively). Sweden has by far the lowest share of female part-time employment (18%), which is in line with its generous institutions and more progressive gender values. This is supported by the fact that in Sweden, there is practically no difference in part-time employment rates between women with and without children. In the other three countries by contrast, much higher shares of mothers work part-time than childless women, especially in Germany, where the share of part-time employed mothers (64%) is more than twice that of childless women.

We have argued before that, following our discussion of SET, we assume that parents with lower earnings potentials than their partners tend to work part-time. Figure 3.2 shows the proportion of part-time working parents by occupational status differences within couples. Irrespective of status differences within couples we again find substantially higher part-time rates for mothers compared to fathers in all four countries: Sweden exhibits, as expected based on the literature on the welfare state regime types, the lowest gender differences in part-time employment with respect to status differences (yet it is still at about 4% for fathers and 16% or 22% respectively for mothers).

Figure 3.2 Proportion of Parents Working Part-Time by Differences in Occupational Status Within Couples

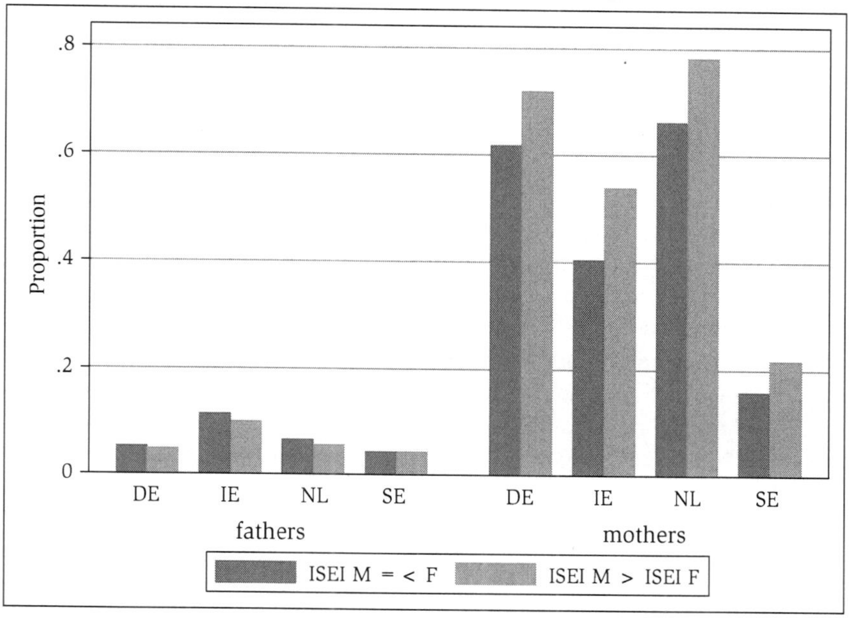

Source: EU LFS2014, weighted results, N (fathers) = 4,444, N (mothers) = 34,152.

For fathers we find almost no differences in part-time rates between fathers with lower occupational statuses and fathers with higher occupational statuses than their female partner in any of the four countries. For Ireland and the Netherlands we see a 1 percentage point difference across status differences for fathers: those with lower earnings potentials than their partners are somewhat more often in part-time employment compared to fathers with higher statuses than their partner. The difference between the part-time rates of fathers with higher and those with lower status than their female partners in Germany and Sweden is even smaller. Our SET assumptions do not seem to apply in these two countries. The findings might rather be attributed to the different welfare state setups and gender norms.

The findings for mothers, by contrast, are in line with our expectations based on SET, since the share of mothers working part-time is considerably higher for those with equal or lower earnings potentials than their male partners than for those with higher earnings potentials– in all four countries. The Netherlands shows the highest share of mothers with a lower occupational status than their partner working part-time (78%), followed by Germany with 72%. Different part-time rates by status differences for mothers are largest in the Netherlands, the hybrid welfare state and 'part-time economy', with a difference of 12 percentage points for mothers with equal or lower compared to those with higher statuses than their partners; this is closely followed by the conservative-corporatist welfare state Germany with a difference of 10 percentage points between mothers with equal or lower and mothers with higher statuses than their partners. The difference is less pronounced in the social-democratic Sweden. The gender differences in the applicability of assumptions from SET at the household level points to the t impact of gender values, gender expectations and stereotypes, an issue we do not have room to further address here.

In order to get a sense of the potential impact of income taxation on part-time employment among married couples with children, figure 3.3 shows the proportion of parents working part-time by occupational status difference and marital status. Theoretically, joint income taxation systems, as compared to individual ones, set higher incentives to work part-time (or to be non-employed) rather than to work full-time in married couples for the partner with lower earnings potential. Germany has a classical joint income taxation system. The Netherlands, though in principle using individual taxation, also encourages part-time work, for instance, if a partner with a comparatively high income lives in a household with a person who has a relatively low income (*see also* Table 3.1, participation tax rate for second earner). In practice, this might have a similar effect on the prevalence of part-time work as the German income taxation system. Ireland's income taxation system for married couples also encourages (substantial) part-time work of one spouse. For these three countries we thus expect higher part-time rates among married partners with lower earnings potentials (whether male or female) as compared to unmarried ones. For Sweden with its individualised taxation system we do not expect to find this relationship. In Germany, Ireland and the Netherlands married mothers with lower earnings potential than their spouse have considerably higher part-time shares than cohabiting mothers. In Germany, the Netherlands and in Ireland this also holds for married mothers with higher earnings potential. Their specific taxation systems – albeit following a different logic and motivation – all seem to encourage part-time work of one of the spouses. In line with our expectations, part-time rates in Sweden among married and cohabiting mothers are relatively similar – married mothers with higher earnings potential have even somewhat lower part-time shares, similar to the Irish case.

For men, the expectations of an impact of joint taxation on part-time behaviour does not hold for our chosen cases – emphasising again that gender values, expectations and stereotypes (breadwinner) as well as economic factors might play a more prominent role among men than women. In Sweden with an individual taxation system and a welfare regime supporting institutions and more modern gender values, again, there are hardly any differences between married and cohabiting fathers across occupational status differences. In Germany and Ireland with their de facto tax advantages for a part-time earner, married fathers, independent of their earnings potential vis-à-vis their partner have lower part-time rates than cohabiting ones emphasising the traditional breadwinner model.

Figure 3.3 Proportion of Parents Working Part-Time by Differences in Occupational Status Within Couples and Marital Status

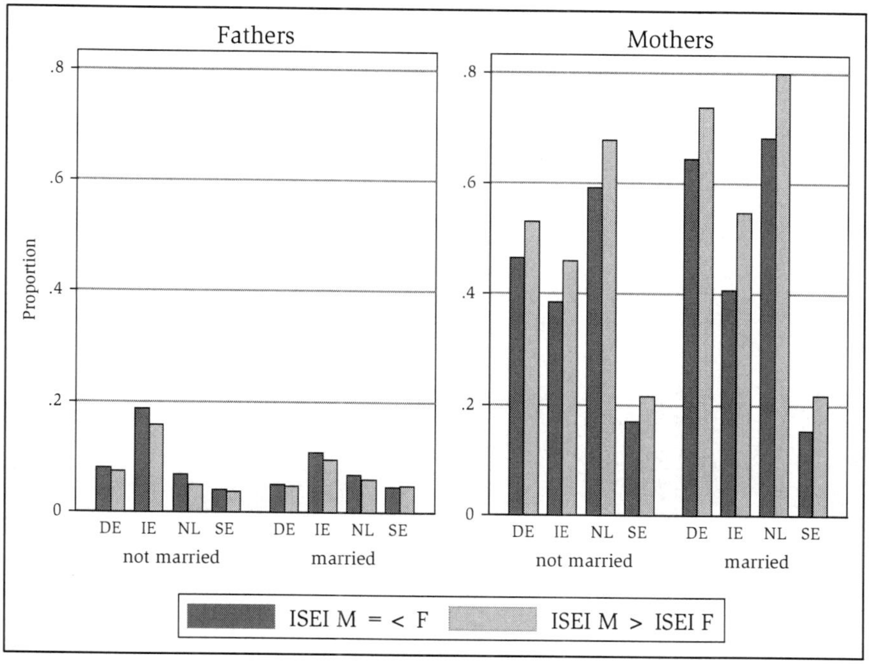

Source: EU LFS 2014, weighted results, N (fathers) = 4,444, N (mothers) = 34,152.

No clear pattern emerges regarding the proportion of part-time working men by number of children and status differences (figure 3.4). Childless men with lower occupational status than their partner have the highest proportions of part-time work in all four countries compared to men with children. This difference is most pronounced in the Netherlands and least pronounced in Ireland. In the Netherlands, part-time employment shares gradually decrease with the number of children, independent of occupational status differences. Men's part-time rates drop substantially from 12% down to 6.1% (men with an equal or lower status) or from about 10% down to 4.3% (men with a higher status) when having three children. The proportion of part-time working men in Germany is somewhat higher for men with three children, as compared to one or two children – and higher for men with a higher occupational status and three children than for those with an equal or lower status than their partner. In Sweden, the part-time rate for men with a higher status increases with the number of children and is almost equal to childless men (at 5.7% and 5.6% respectively). For Ireland we see practically no differences in the part-time shares of men with an equal or lower occupational status (steady at 11% to 12%); the part-time rate increases for men with a higher status to 12% when having three children (as compared to one or two). There is no clear trend across countries and the number of children regarding the occupational status differences in the household. These results seem to hint at a complicated interaction of individual, household, economic and institutional factors as well as gender norms at play here.

Figure 3.4 Proportion of Men Working Part-Time by the Number of Children in the Household and Occupational Status Differences Within Couples

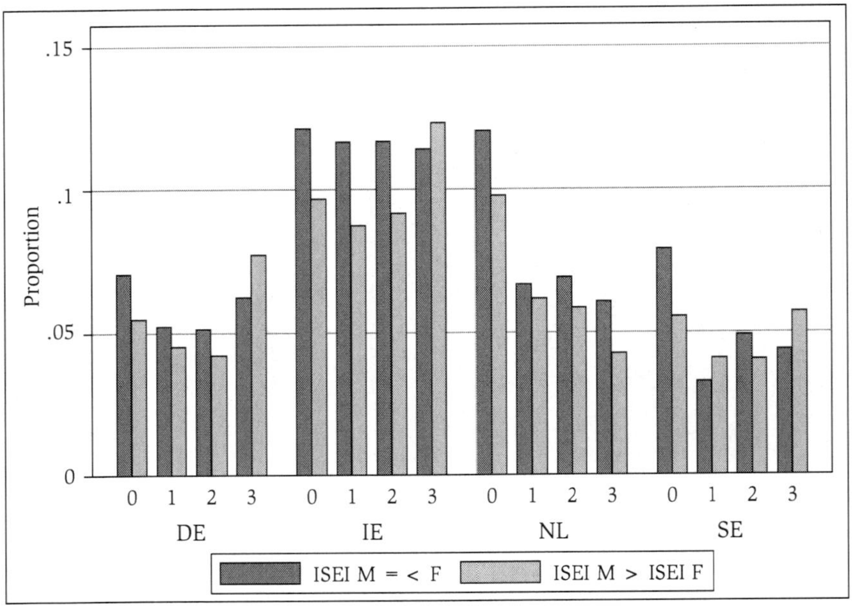

Source: EU LFS 2014, weighted results, N (men) = 6,468, N (women) =43,338.

In contrast, figure 3.5 shows a clear-cut trend in the part-time rates of women by number of children and occupational status in Germany, Ireland and the Netherlands: The part-time rates of women with lower and with a higher occupational status than their partner steadily increase with the number of children living in the household; childless cohabiting women have the lowest part-time rates. In Germany the proportion of women in part-time work increases from 26% or 41% (childless women) to more than 70% when having three children or more, and the findings for the Netherlands are again similar: the rate increases from 34% or 51% (childless women) up to 81% when the number of children increase. The part-time rates substantially increase when women have an equal or lower occupational status than their partners. The overall rates in Ireland are again somewhat lower than in Germany and the Netherlands, but they still increase with the number of children. In Sweden there are hardly any differences between women without children and mothers of one child (irrespective of status), somewhat lower proportions for mothers with two children and a higher occupational status than their partner and higher proportions for mothers with three children and an equal or lower occupational status than their partner. These results point to the incentives and institutional support in Sweden (e.g., comparatively high childcare coverage with generous parental leave rules) that allow both mothers and fathers to work full-time, whereas in the other countries this seems to be less the case, especially when there is more than one child. Again a complex interaction with gender values, norms and expectations shaped by the welfare regime type should be stressed here.

Figure 3.5 Proportion of Women Working Part-Time by the Number of Children in the Household and Occupational Status Differences Within Couples

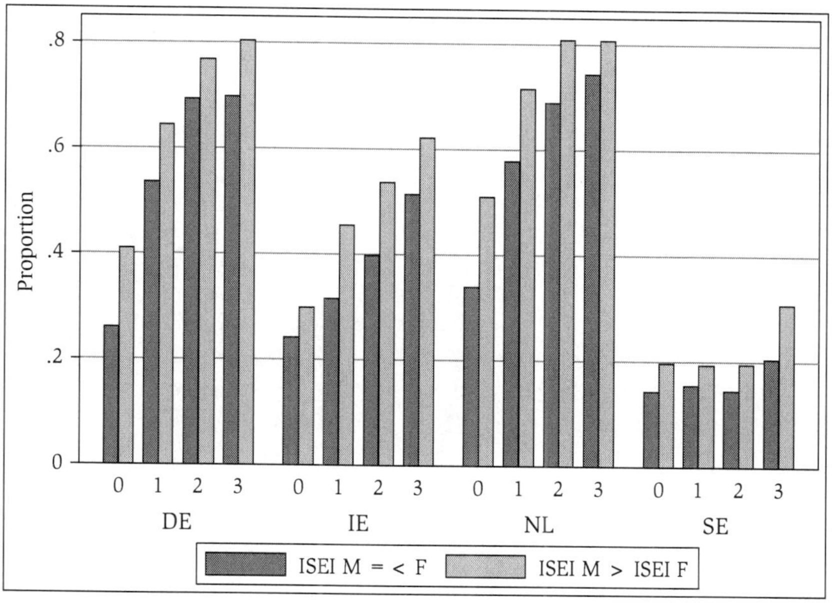

Source: EU LFS 2014, weighted results, N (men) = 6,468, N (women) = 43,338.

§3.06 CONCLUSION

The research aim was to highlight the differences between men and women, most notably mothers and fathers, in their choices to work part-time, given a particular household and welfare state context. Part-time employment allows people to combine paid work with care responsibilities within families, and moreover could support couples in creating an egalitarian labour division, particularly in the absence of sufficient institutions to support full-time work for both partners. However, traditionally, part-time employment has been seen as a 'female affair'. On the backdrop of SET and welfare regime typologies and the institutional configurations we compared part-time employment among men and women in Germany, Ireland, the Netherlands and Sweden. We tried to find out whether men and fathers make similar choices to work part-time as women and mothers, and what differences may be found concerning in particular household characteristics such as earnings potential of the partner and number of children in the four different welfare state contexts.

Our analysis of the individual level European LFS 2014 data supports earlier findings that in all four countries part-time work is highly gendered. This is least evident in Sweden. Regardless of the household and institutional context, women always tend to work part-time more often than their male peers, and this is regardless of having children, having a higher occupational status than their partner or having access to particular welfare state arrangements. Actually, in all four countries, fathers work part-time less often than men without children. Sweden confirms the expectations of the relatively egalitarian welfare state regime with institutions including individual taxation supporting full-time employment of both mothers and fathers. Here, part-time employment rates are lowest for women and mothers, the difference between mothers and fathers and men and women is the smallest and the household impact is lowest.

There are some interesting patterns when comparing fathers and mothers in the different household and welfare state settings. Our findings suggest that for women the logic of specialisation within couples regarding wage work and household work based on the difference in earnings potential is prevalent with the exception of Sweden. For men this logic is of little relevance. It is particularly Germany and the Netherlands, countries with conservative-corporatist regime traits, which show traditional characteristics of gendered household specialisation. Our results for Ireland indicate that particularly for men and fathers but potentially also for women and mothers – and especially those with higher earning potential than their partner – there is also an important economic component in the choice for or against part-time employment. Our findings also tell us something about the prevalence of gender values, norms, stereotypes and expectations, which are particularly traditional in countries that are close to the conservative-corporatist regimes. Thus, particularly in Germany and the Netherlands, married couples with children seem to be incentivised by the institutional, economic and cultural framework, to engage often in a specialisation in either family or work responsibilities. This could be the result of maximising the joint family resources, or stem from the 'bargaining' processes on the division of care and work responsibilities which outcome is strengthened by the logic and incentive of the framework.

Within the framework of our study we cannot directly ascribe the observed differences between countries to specific differences in the institutional rules and regulations. However, the detailed descriptions we have given of each of the countries suggest that the system of income taxation of married couples, the presence or accessibility of childcare facilities, and a right to work part-time influence the working time choices of women and mothers much more than that of men. This is probably due to the complex interaction of these rights with gender values, norms and stereotypes. Only Sweden seems to have considerably more egalitarian values, showing relatively small differences in part-time employment rates between men and women across household types and occupational status differences. In the other countries the differences are more pronounced and having more children means a higher chance of working part-time for mothers and a lower chance of working part-time for fathers. This is even more pronounced if the male partner has a higher occupational status. Future research could build on our findings by trying to link the welfare state arrangements and household context more systematically to the choices in working hours. Moreover, given previous findings and our findings particularly on Ireland, economic factors should be taken into account more systematically in order to explain part-time employment of men.

REFERENCES

Allmendinger, J., Hipp, L. & Stuth, S. (2013). Atypical employment in Europe 1996–2011. WZB Discussion Paper.

Arbetsförmedlingen (2015). Living and working in Sweden.

Bach, S., Geyer, J., Haan, P. & Wrohlich, K. (2011). Reform des Ehegattensplittings: Nur eine reine Individualbesteuerung erhöht die Erwerbsanreize deutlich. *DIW Wochenbericht,* 78, 13–19.

Becker, G. S. (1981). Altruism in the family and selfishness in the market place. *Economica,* 48, 1–15.

Becker, G. S. (1985). Human capital, effort, and the sexual division of labor. *Journal of Labor Economics,* 3, S33–S58.

Bernasco, W., de Graaf, P. M. & Ultee, W. C. (1998). Coupled careers: Effects of spouse's resources on occupational attainment in the Netherlands. *European Sociological Review,* 14, 15–31.

Bertram, H., Bujard, M. & Rösler, W. (2011). Rush-hour des Lebens: Geburtenaufschub, Einkommensverläufe und familienpolitische Perspektiven. *Journal für Reproduktionsmedizin und Endokrinologie-Journal of Reproductive Medicine and Endocrinology,* 8, 91–99.

Bittman, M. & Wajcman, J. (2000). The rush hour: The character of leisure time and gender equity. *Social Forces,* 79, 165–189.

Blau, P. M. (1964). *Exchange and Power in Social Life,* Transaction Publishers.

Blood, R. O. & Wolfe, D. M. (1960). *Husbands and Wives: The Dynamics of Family Living,* Oxford: Free Press.

Blossfeld, H.-P. & Drobnic, S. (2001). *Careers of Couples in Contemporary Societies: From Male Breadwinner to Dual Earner Families,* Oxford: Oxford University Press.

BMAS (2016). Teilzeit- und Befristungsgesetz. Gesetz über Teilzeitarbeit und befristete Arbeitsverträge.

BMFSFJ (2014). Gesetzliche Grundlagen für den Ausbau der Kinderbetreuung.

BMFSFJ (2015). Bundeselterngeld- und Elternzeitgesetz.

BMFSFJ (2016). Gute Kinderbetreuung.

Brenke, K. (2011). Anhaltender Strukturwandel zur Teilzeitbeschäftigung. *DIW Wochenbericht,* 78, 2–12.

Buddelmeyer, H., Mourre, G. & Ward-Warmedinger, M. E. (2004). The determinants of part-time work in EU countries: Empirical investigations with macro-panel data. *IZA DP.*

Buddelmeyer, H., Mourre, G. & Ward-Warmedinger, M. E. (2005). Part-time work in EU countries: Labour market mobility, entry and exit. *ECB Working Paper,* 460.

Bujard, M. & Panova, R. (2014). Rushhour des Lebens. *Dossier Familienpolitik.* Bundeszentrale für politische Bildung (bpb).

Bünning, M. (2015). What happens after the 'Daddy Months'? Fathers' involvement in paid work, Child care, and housework after taking parental leave in Germany. *European Sociological Review,* jcv072v071.

Bünning, M. & Pollmann-Schult, M. (2016). Family policies and fathers' working hours: Cross-national differences in the paternal labour supply. *Work, Employment & Society,* 30, 256–274.

Citizens Information Board (2015). Working part-time.

Citizens Information Board (2016a). Parental leave.

Citizens Information Board (2016b). Taxation of married people and civil partners.

Crompton, R. (1999). Discussion and conclusion. In R. Crompton (Ed.), *Restructuring Gender Relations and Employment: The Decline of the Male Breadwinner* (pp. 201–214), Oxford: Oxford University Press.

Daly, M. (2010). Families versus state and market. In F. Castles, S. Leibfried, J. Lewis & H. Obinger (Eds.), *The Oxford Handbook of the Welfare State,* Oxford: Oxford University Press.

Delsen, L. (2002). When do men work part-time? In J. O'Reilly & C. Fagan (Eds.), *Part-Time Prospects: An International Comparison of Part-Time Work in Europe, North America and the Pacific Rim.* London: Routledge.

den Dulk, L. (2016). Netherlands country note. In A. Koslowski, S. Blum & P. Moss (Eds.), *International Review of Leave Policies and Research* Vienna: The international network on leave policies and research, (pp. 240–249).

Dermott, E. (2006). What's parenthood got to do with it? Men's hours of paid work. *The British Journal of Sociology,* 57, 619–634.

Dommermuth, L. & Kitterød, R. H. (2009). Fathers' employment in a fatherfriendly welfare state: Does fatherhood affect men's working hours. *Community, Work and Family,* 12, 417–436.

Eggebeen, D. J. & Knoester, C. (2001). Does fatherhood matter for men? *Journal of Marriage and Family,* 63, 381–393.

Esping-Andersen, G. (1990). *The Three Worlds of Welfare Capitalism,* Princeton, NJ: Princeton University Press.

Eurofound (2011). *Part-Time Work in Europe. European Company Survey 2009.* Luxemburg: Publications Office of the European Union.

European Commission (2016). Part-time work: A divided Europe. News item, date 04/05/2016, available at http://ec.europa.eu/social/main.jsp?langId = en&catId = 1196&newsId = 2535&furtherNews = yes, last accessed 24 April 2017.

Eurostat (2014). Involuntary part-time employment as percentage of the total part-time employment, by sex and age (%). *Eurostat Statistical Books.*

Eurostat (2015). Taxation trends in the European Union - Data for the EU Member States, Iceland and Norway. *Eurostat Statistical Books.*

Fegert, J. M., Liebhardt, H., Althammer, J., Baronsky, A., Becker-Stoll, F., Besier, T., Dette-Hagenmeyer, D., Eickhorst, A., Gerlach, I., Gloger-Tippelt, G., Kindler, H., Leyendecker, B., Limmer, R., Merkle, T., Reichle, B., Walter, H., Wöckel, A., von Bresinski, B. & Ziegenhain, U. (2011). *Vaterschaft und Elternzeit - Eine interdisziplinäre Literaturstudie zur Frage der Bedeutung der Vater-Kind-Beziehung für eine gedeihliche Entwicklung der Kinder sowie den Zusammenhalt in der Familie,* Berlin: Bundesministerium für Familie, Senioren, Frauen und Jugend.

Ferrera, M. (1996). The 'Southern model' of welfare in social Europe. *Journal of European Social Policy,* 1, 17–37.

Foa, E. B. & Foa, U. G. (2012). Resource theory of social exchange. In K. Törnblom & A. Kazemi (Eds.), *Handbook of Social Resource Theory. Theoretical Extensions, Empirical Insights, and Social Applications.* (pp. 15–32): Springer.

Foa, U. G. & Foa, E. B. (1974). *Societal Structures of the Mind,* Springfields: Charles C. Thomas.

Folk, K. F. & Beller, A. H. (1993). Part-time work and child care choices for mothers of preschool children. *Journal of Marriage and the Family,* 55, 146–157.

Försäkringskassan (2016) Employees and parental leave.

Ganzeboom, H. B. G. (2010) A new International Socio-Economic Index (ISEI) of occupational status for the International Standard Classification of Occupation 2008 (ISCO-08) constructed with data from the ISSP 2002–2007. *Annual Conference of International Social Survey Programme.* Lissabon.

Gash, V. (2008). Preference or constraint? Part-time workers' transitions in Denmark, France and the United Kingdom. *Work, Employment & Society,* 22, 655–674.

Haas, L., Duvander, A.-Z. & Hwang, C. P. (2016). Sweden country note. In K. Alison, B. Sonja & M. Peter (Eds.), *12th International Review of Leave Policies and Related Research 2016.* (pp. 340–348).

Hegewisch, A. & Gornick, J. C. (2011). The impact of work-family policies on women's employment: A review of research from OECD countries. *Community, Work & Family,* 14, 119–138.

Hendrickx, J., Bernasco, W. & De Graaf, P. M. (2001). *Couples' Labour-Market Participation in the Netherlands,* Oxford: Oxford University Press.

Hinz, S. K. (2008). *Teilzeitarbeit-Chance oder Risiko?* Uelvesbüll: Der Andere Verlag.

Hipp, L., Bernhardt, J. & Allmendinger, J. (2015). Institutions and the prevalence of nonstandard employment. *Socio-Economic Review,* 13, 351–377.

Hipp, L. & Leuze, K. (2015). Institutionelle Determinanten einer partnerschaftlichen Aufteilung von Erwerbsarbeit in Europa und den USA. *Kölner Zeitschrift für Soziologie und Sozialpsychologie,* 67(4), 659-684.

Hipp, L., Molitor, F., Leschke, J., & Bekker, S. (2017). Teilzeitväter? Deutschland, Schweden, Irland und die Niederlande im Vergleich. *Zeitschrift für Familienforschung/Journal of Family Research,* 29 (1), *forthcoming.*Hobler, D., Pfahl, S. & Weeber, S. (2016). Arbeitszeiten. Abstand der Teilzeitquoten von Frauen und Männern wird größer. *WSi GenderDatenportal.*

Hobler, D., Pfahl, S., Weeber, S. & Oerder, L. (2013). Gründe für Teilzeittätigkeit nach Elternschaft 2013. In W. GenderDatenPortal (Ed.). WSI.

Horemans, J., Marx, I. & Nolan, B. (2016). Hanging in, but only just: Part-time employment and in-work poverty throughout the crisis. *IZA Journal of European Labor Studies,* 5.

Jacobs, A. & Schmidt, M. (2001). The right to part-time work: The Netherlands and Germany compared. *International Journal of Comparative Labour Law and Industrial Relations,* 17, 371–384.

Keller, M. & Haustein, T. (2014). Vereinbarkeit von Familie und Beruf. Ergebnisse des Mikrozensus 2013. *Wirtschaft und Statistik,* 12, 733–753.

Kitterød, R. H. & Rønsen, M. (2012). Non-traditional dual earners in Norway: When does she work at least as much as he? *Work, Employment and Society,* 26, 657–675.

Kitterød, R. H., Rønsen, M. & Seierstad, A. (2013). Mobilizing female labour market reserves. What promotes women's transitions between part-time and full-time work? *Acta Sociologica,* 56, 155–171.

Kjeldstad, R. & Nymoen, E. H. (2012). Part-time work and gender: Worker versus job explanations. *International Labour Review,* 151, 85–107.

Korpi, W., Ferrarini, T. & Englund, S. (2013). Women's opportunities under different family policy constellations: Gender, class, and inequality tradeoffs in western countries re-examined. *Social Politics: International Studies in Gender, State & Society,* 20, 1–40.

Leppel, K. & Clain, S. H. (1988). The growth in involuntary part-time employment of men and women. *Applied Economics,* 20, 1155–1166.

Lewis, J. (2001). The decline of the male breadwinner model: Implications for work and care. *Social Politics: International Studies in Gender, State & Society,* 8, 152–169.

Lothaller, H. (2009). Die 'rush hour' des Lebens und die Bedeutung der Familienarbeit und ihrer Aufteilung. *Journal für Generationengerechtigkeit,* 9, 52–56.

Lundberg, S. & Pollak, R. A. (1996). Bargaining and distribution in marriage. *The Journal of Economic Perspectives,* 10, 139–158.

Maume, D. J. (2006). Gender differences in restricting work efforts because of family responsibilities. *Journal of Marriage and Family,* 68, 859–869.

Miller, M. M. & Bermudez, J. M. (2004). Intersecting gender and social exchange theory in family therapy. *Journal of Feminist Family Therapy,* 16, 25–42.

O'Brien, M., Brandth, B. & Kvande, E. (2007). Fathers, work and family life: Global perspectives and new insights. *Community, Work and Family,* 10, 375–386.

OECD (2001). Balancing work and family life: Helping parents into paid employment. *OECD Employment Outlook.*

OECD (2010). OECD employment outlook 2010: Moving beyond the jobs crisis. Paris: OECD.

OECD (2011). The future of families to 2030. Projections, policy challenges, and policy options. A synthesis report. Paris: OECD.

OECD (2016). Tax and benefit systems: OECD indicators.

OECD Data (2014a). Employment rate.

OECD Data (2014b). Part-time employment rate.

OECD Data (2014c). Unemployment rate.

OECD Family Database (2013).

Pollmann-Schult, M. & Wagner, M. (2014). Vaterschaft im Kontext. Wie die Familiengründung die Erwerbstätigkeit von Männern beeinflusst. *Heft, WZB Mitteilungen,* 134.

Rastrigina, O. & Verashchagina, A. (2015). Secondary earners and fiscal policies in Europe. Europäische Kommission.

Román, A. A. (2006). *Deviating from the Standard: Effects on Labor Continuity and Career Patterns,* Utrecht: Utrecht University.

Sanchez, L. & Thomson, E. (1997). Becoming mothers and fathers parenthood, gender, and the division of labor. *Gender & Society,* 11, 747–772.

Schulze, E. & Gergoric, M. (2015). *Maternity, Paternity and Parental Leave: Data Related to Duration and Compensation Rates in the European Union.* European Parliament Policy Department C: Citizens' Rights and Constitutional Affairs.

Shore, L. M., Chung-Herrera, B. G., Dean, M. A., Ehrhart, K. H., Jung, D. I., Randel, A. E. & Singh, G. (2009). Diversity in organizations: Where are we now and where are we going? *Human Resource Management Review,* 19, 117–133.

Sorensen, A. (1983). Women's employment patterns after marriage. *Journal of Marriage and Family,* 45, 311–321.

Survey, E. S. (2010). ESS Round 5: European Social Survey Round 5. Data file edition 3.3. In N. D. A. a. d. o. E. d. f. E. E. NSD - Norwegian Centre for Research Data (Ed.).

Thébaud, S. (2010). Masculinity, bargaining, and breadwinning: Understanding men's housework in the cultural context of paid work. *Gender & Society,* 24, 330–354.

Trappe, H. (2013). Väter mit Elterngeldbezug: Nichts als ökonomisches Kalkül? / Fathers who claim parental leave benefits: Only a matter of economic considerations? *Zeitschrift für Soziologie,* 42, 28–51.

Trischler, F. & Kistler, E. (2011). Arbeitspapier 5: Erwerbsverläufe und Alterseinkünfte im Paar-und Haushaltskontext.

Tsui, A. S., Pearce, J. L., Porter, L. W. & Tripoli, A. M. (1997). Alternative approaches to the employee-organization relationship: Does investment in employees pay off? *Academy of Management Journal,* 40, 1089–1121.

Tyroller, S. (2005). Kinderbetreuung in den Niederlanden.

Vandewiele, T. & Di Meglio, E. (2016). Die Hälfte der unter 3-Jährigen wurde 2014 in der EU ausschließlich von den Eltern betreut. In Eurostat (Ed.).

Visser, J. (2002). The first part-time economy in the world: A model to be followed? *Journal of European Social Policy,* 12, 23–42.

Vlasblom, J. D. & Schippers, J. (2006). Changing dynamics in female employment around childbirth evidence from Germany, the Netherlands and the UK. *Work, Employment & Society,* 20, 329–347.

Walsh, J. (1999). Myths and counter-myths: An analysis of part-time female employees and their orientations to work and working hours. *Work, Employment & Society,* 13, 179–203.

Warren, T. (2004). Working part-time: Achieving a successful 'work-life' balance? *The British Journal of Sociology,* 55, 99–122.
Webber, G. & Williams, C. (2008). Mothers in 'good' and 'bad' part-time jobs different problems, same results. *Gender & Society,* 22, 752–777.
Yerkes, M. (2013). Choice or constraint? Women's weekly working hours in comparative perspective. *Sociologia, Problemas e Práticas*, 9–30.

CHAPTER 4

How Can Labour Law Contribute to Work-Life Balance? Recommendations for a Modern Working Time Law

Sarah De Groof

§4.01 INTRODUCTION

Let me start in an unusual way this academic contribution, namely with a few confessions: I went to law school to make the world a little better. I was interested in labour law because this branch of law had to do with 'real persons'. And I became passionate about labour law because Professor Frank Hendrickx took me as a student to the International Labour Organisation where over one week we heard lectures on how decent work for all is necessary for world peace. So after I worked as a lawyer for a few years (and to be honest, not really making the world much better), it was with a clear normative goal that I wanted to do research. I wanted to make the law a little – or to be completely honest a lot – better, and by doing so make the world better.

In my view, a good way of making the law better, was by looking at work-life balance literature. So many scientists have a clear idea on what circumstances are beneficial or detrimental to one's work-life balance outcomes, why not use these insights to check whether the law positively or negatively influences these circumstances from being reality. But I soon discovered that although many scientific contributions on work and family formulate policy recommendations regarding the fit of careers and care, they rarely specify what policy should exactly look like. So in this paper, I seek to close this gap: I will build on the impressive body of literature in the work and family research, and more precisely on work-life conflict, and will investigate how labour legislation and more particularly working time law can respond to the recommendations or normative claims deriving thereof. For this, first, I needed to read and understand work-life balance literature in order to deduct criteria that I could, second, use to evaluate the law and formulate recommendations. Let me guide you through this experience.

§4.02 WORK-LIFE BALANCE 'CRITERIA'

Research on work and family started in the 70' and 80', to really expand as from the 90'. With contributions from sociology, psychology, economy and management, it is a multi- or interdisciplinary academic field of expertise with its own journals and professional organisations. As from the 90', research began to focus on work aspects that could be changed to influence work-life balance outcomes of workers.[1]

Most research on work and family focused on work-family conflict.[2] The level of conflict is mostly measured through self-assessed reports by individuals of subjective measures of well-being, like the degree of 'fit' that they consider existing between their working time and their personal time or the extent of work-life balance they feel they have.[3] Research then shows that work-family conflict has an influence on outcomes like psychological distress, job satisfaction, dedication to the organisation, turnover and life satisfaction.[4] The first definition of work-family conflict stems from GREENHAUS and BEUTELL in 1985: 'a form of interrole conflict in which the role pressures from the work and family domains are mutually incompatible in some respect. That is, participation in the work (family) role is made more difficult by virtue of participation in the family (work) role'.[5] This definition is still widely used.[6] Role pressures can be time-based, strain-based or behaviour-based.[7] FRONE and colleagues then empirically

1. K.A. French en R.C. Johnson, 'A Retrospective Timeline of the Evolution of Work-Family Research' in T.D. Allen en L.T. Eby (eds.), *The Oxford Handbook of Work and Family*, Oxford, Oxford University Press, 2016, (9) 15.
2. S.M. Macdermid, '(Re)Considering Conflict Between Work and Family' in E.E. kosseK en S.J. Lambert (eds.), *Work and Life Integration*, New Jersey, Lawrence Erlbaum Associates Inc., 2005, (19) 19; C. Thompson, L.L. Beauvais en T.D. Allen, 'Work and Family from an Industrial/Organization Psychology Perspective' in M. Pitt-Catsouphes, E.E. Kossek en S. Sweet (eds.), *The Work and Family Handbook*, East Sussex, Psychology Press, 2008, (283) 284.
3. C. Fagan, C. Lyonette, M. Smith en A. Saldaña-Tejeda, *The Influence of Working Time Arrangements on Work-Life Integration or 'Balance': A Review of the International Evidence*, Geneva, International Labour Office, 2012, 4; S.M. Macdermid, '(Re)Considering Conflict Between Work and Family' in E.E. Kossek en S.J. Lambert (eds.), *Work and Life Integration*, New Jersey, Lawrence Erlbaum Associates Inc., 2005, (19) 25.
4. D.S. Carlson, K.M. Kacmar en L.J. Williams, 'Construction and Initial Validation of a Multidimensional Measure of Work-Family Conflict', *Journal of Vocational Behavior* 2000, vol. 56, (249) 249.
5. J.H. Greenhaus en N.J. Beutell, 'Sources of Conflict Beween Work and Family Roles', *Academy of Management Review* 1985, vol. 10, (76) 77.
6. K.A. French en R.C. Johnson, 'A Retrospective Timeline of the Evolution of Work-Family Research' in T.D. Allen en L.T. Eby (eds.), *The Oxford Handbook of Work and Family*, Oxford, Oxford university press, 2016, (9) 12.
7. J.H. Greenhaus en N.J. Beutell, 'Sources of Conflict Between Work and Family Roles', *Academy of Management Review* 1985, vol. 10, (76) 76-88; D.S. Carlson, K.M. Kacmar en L.J. Williams, 'Construction and Initial Validation of a Multidimensional Measure of Work-Family Conflict', *Journal of Vocational Behavior* 2000, vol. 56, (249) 250.

established the bidirectional nature of work-family conflict.[8] A parent might experience family-to-work conflict when it is necessary to take time off from work to stay home with a sick child, and work-to family conflict when late work hours make it difficult to cook healthy family meals.[9] Empirical evidence demonstrates each direction has its own antecedents.[10] The most recent research tries to also understand the positive effect of work on family life and vice versa.[11] GREENHAUS calls this work-life integration which occurs 'when attitudes in one role positively spill over into another role, or when experiences in one role serve as resources that enrich another role in one's life'.[12] FRONE calls this work-family facilitation, namely 'the extent to which participation at work (or home) is made easier by virtue of experiences, skills and opportunities gained or developed at home (or work)'.[13] Other terms used for this idea are work-family spill-over, compensation, enhancement and facilitation.[14] This research, however, is far less developed then research on work-family conflict.[15]

Work-life balance outcomes have many antecedents, such as job insecurity, social infrastructure (such as child care) or personal characteristics.[16] For example,

8. K.A. French en R.C. Johnson, 'A Retrospective Timeline of the Evolution of Work-Family Research' in T.D. Allen en L.T. Eby (eds.), *The Oxford Handbook of Work and Family*, Oxford, Oxford University Press, 2016, (9) 14.
9. G.M. Bellavia en M.R. Frone, 'Work-Family Conflict' in J. Barling, K.E. Kelloway en M.R. Frone (eds.), *Handbook of Work Stress*, Thousand Oaks CA, Sage Publications, 2005, (113) 115; M.R. Frone, Y.K. Yardley en K.S. Markel, 'Developing and Testing an Integrative Model of the Work-Family Interface', *Journal of Vocational Behavior* 1997, vol. 50, (145) 145–167.
10. K. Byron, 'A Meta-Analytical Review of Work-Family Conflict and its Antecedents', *Journal of Vocational Behavior* 2005, afl. 67, (169) 194.
11. C. Thompson, L.L. Beauvais en T.D. Allen, 'Work and Family from an Industrial/Organization Psychology Perspective' in M. Pitt-Catsouphes, E.E. Kossek en S. Sweet (eds.), *The Work and Family Handbook*, East Sussex, Psychology Press, 2008, (283) 284; G.M. Bellavia en M.R. Frone, 'Work-Family Conflict' in J. Barling, K.E. Kelloway en M.R. Frone (eds.), *Handbook of Work Stress*, Thousand Oaks CA, Sage Publications, 2005, (113) 136.
12. J.H. Greenhaus en S. Parasuraman, 'Reseach on Work, Family and Gender: Current Status and Future Directions.' in G.N. Powell (ed.), *Handbook of Gender & Work*, Newbury Park, Sage Publications, 1999, (391) 391–412.
13. G.M. Bellavia en M.R. Frone, 'Work-Family Conflict' in J. Barling, K.E. Kelloway en M.R. Frone (eds.), *Handbook of Work Stress*, Thousand Oaks CA, Sage Publications, 2005, (113) 136.
14. M. O'driscoll, P. Brough en T. Kalliath, 'Work-Family Conflict and Facilitation' in F. Jones, R.J. Burke en M. Westman (eds.), *Work-Life Balance. A Psychological Perspective*, New York, Psychology Press, 2006, (117) 134.
15. G.M. Bellavia en M.R. Frone, 'Work-Family Conflict' in J. Barling, K.E. Kelloway en M.R. Frone (eds.), *Handbook of Work Stress*, Thousand Oaks CA, Sage Publications, 2005, (113) 136. Eurofound only added a question on work-family enrichment in its latest survey. 48% of the respondents state that they get on better with their children because they have a job. The results indicate wide differences between countries. In Italy for example, only 26% of workers feel that having a job improves their relationship with their children (Eurofound, *Sixth European Working Conditions Survey*, Luxembourg, Publications Office of the European Union, 2016, 117).
16. C. Fagan, C. Lyonette, M. Smith en A. Saldaña-Tejeda, *The Influence of Working Time Arrangements on Work-Life Integration or 'Balance': A Review of the International Evidence*, Geneva, International Labour Office, 2012, 5–6; E.E. Kossek, B.A. Lautsch en S.C. Eaton, 'Flexibility Enactment Theory: Implications of Flexibility Type, Control, and Boundary Management for Work-Family Effectiveness' in E.E. Kossek en S.J. Lambert (eds.), *Work and Life Integration*, New Jersey, Lawrence Erlbaum Associates Inc., 2005, (243) 254; E.E. Kossek, B.A. Lautsch en S.C. Eaton, 'Telecommuting, Control, and Boundary Management: Correlates of Policy Use and Practice, Job Control, and Work-Family Effectiveness', *Journal of Vocational*

workers with many children, larger families or dependent parents are more likely to report work-life conflict.[17] However, research shows that when workers report work-life conflict, this is more often caused by negative effects from work to life instead of the other way around.[18] Research also shows that working time organisation or working time quality plays a crucial role in work-life conflict outcomes and has a significant effect, even when they control for other job characteristics.[19] The rest of this chapter will therefore focus on work-life balance criteria related to working time. I will point out eight work-life balance criteria related to working time.

[A] Number of Working Hours

A first consistent finding from studies is the negative impact of long working hours on work-life balance outcomes. The proportion of men and women who report incompatibility, tension or time pressure between employment, family and social life rises with the number of hours they worked:[20] 38% of the respondents who work forty-eight hours per week or more report work-life conflict, compared to 18% on average.[21] Limiting long working hours as such will, however, not solve everything. When the average working time in France was limited to thirty-five hours per week, half of those working on atypical hours stated this did not make it easier for them to realise work-life balance, compared to 36% of the workers working on usual business hours.[22] Also, in

Behavior 2006, vol. 68, (347) 350; G.M. Bellavia en M.R. Frone, 'Work-Family Conflict' in J. Barling, K.E. Kelloway en M.R. Frone (eds.), *Handbook of Work Stress*, Thousand Oaks CA, Sage Publications, 2005, (113) 121.

17. C. Thompson, L.L. Beauvais en T.D. Allen, 'Work and Family from an Industrial/Organization Psychology Perspective' in M. Pitt-Catsouphes, E.E. Kossek en S. Sweet (eds.), *The Work and Family Handbook*, East Sussex, Psychology Press, 2008, (283) 285; M. O'driscoll, P. Brough en T. Kalliath, 'Work-Family Conflict and Facilitation' in F. Jones, R.J. Burke en M. Westman (eds.), *Work-Life Balance. A Psychological Perspective*, New York, Psychology Press, 2006, (117) 125; Eurofound, *Third European Quality of Life Survey – Quality of Life in Europe: Impacts of the Crisis*, Luxemburg, Publications Office of the European Union, 2012, 62–63.
18. P. Blyton, 'Working Time and Work-Life Balance' in P. Blyton, E. Heery, N.A. Bacon en J. Fiorito (eds.), *The SAGE Handbook of Industrial Relations*, Thousand Oaks CA, SAGE Publications USA, 2009, (513) 523; Eurofound, *Sixth European Working Conditions Survey*, Luxembourg, Publications Office of the European Union, 2016, 118.
19. C. Fagan, C. Lyonette, M. Smith en A. Saldaña-Tejeda, *The Influence of Working Time Arrangements on Work-Life Integration or 'Balance': A Review of the International Evidence*, Geneva, International Labour Office, 2012, 5–6; Eurofound, *Sixth European Working Conditions Survey*, Luxembourg, Publications Office of the European Union, 2016, 115.
20. C. Fagan, C. Lyonette, M. Smith en A. Saldaña-Tejeda, *The Influence of Working Time Arrangements on Work-Life Integration or 'Balance': A Review of the International Evidence*, Geneva, International Labour Office, 2012, 27; M. O'driscoll, P. Brough en T. Kalliath, 'Work-Family Conflict and Facilitation' in F. Jones, R.J. Burke en M. Westman (eds.), *Work-Life Balance. A Psychological Perspective*, New York, Psychology Press, 2006, (117) 122–123; C. Thompson, L.L. Beauvais en T.D. Allen, 'Work and Family from an Industrial/Organization Psychology Perspective' in M. Pitt-Catsouphes, E.E. Kossek en S. Sweet (eds.), *The Work and Family Handbook*, East Sussex, Psychology Press, 2008, (283) 286.
21. Eurofound, *Fifth European Working Conditions Survey*, Luxembourg, Publications Office of the European Union, 2012, 91.
22. C. Lyonette, 'Atypical Working in Europe and the Impact on Work-Family Reconciliation' in N. Busby en G. James (eds.), *Families, Care-Giving and Paid Work*, Cheltenham, Edward Elgar

some cases research also demonstrates that long working hours can have a lower work-life conflict as a result.[23]

Research has focused much less on the effect of holiday periods and longer careers breaks on work-life balance, which is said to be a lacunae in the research.[24] However, longer time off periods are often used in companies to enable workers to take care of their children or solve other work-life balance issues.[25]

[B] Non-standard Working Hours

Another important criterion useful to predict work-life conflict, are non-standard working hours. Non-standard work schedules are associated with increased work-family conflict and stress and reduced satisfaction with the amount of time available to spend as a couple and with children.[26] Sometimes research demonstrates a significant difference but, when other factors are corrected for, their negative effect is not as strong as other working time features.[27] The negative effect is especially apparent when non-standard working hours are combined with long working hours.[28]

[C] Working Time Regularity and Predictable Working Hours

Research also shows that the regularity and predictability of work schedules play an important role in work-life balance outcomes: when work schedules are irregular and/or unpredictable, workers experience higher work-family conflict.[29] 13% of

---

Publishing Limited, 2011, (31) 45. *See also* J. Fagnani en M.-T. Letablier, 'Work and Family Balance: The Impact of the 35-Hour Laws in France', *Work Employment Society* 2004, vol. 18, afl. 3, (551) 551–572.

23. E.E. KOSSEK, B.A. LAUTSCH en S.C. EATON, 'Telecommuting, control, and boundary management: Correlates of policy use and practice, job control, and work-family effectiveness', *Journal of Vocational Behavior* 2006, vol. 68, (347) 353.
24. E.L. Kelly, E.E. Kossel, L.B. Hammer, M. Durham, J. Bray, K. Chermack, L.A. Murphy en D. Kaskubar, '7 Getting There from Here: Research on the Effects of Work-Family Initiatives on Work-Family Conflict and Business Outcomes', *The Academy of Management Annals* 2008, vol. 2, afl. 1 (305) 323.
25. P. Blyton, 'Working Time and Work-Life Balance' in P. Blyton, E. Heery, N.A. Bacon en J. Fiorito (eds.), *The SAGE Handbook of Industrial Relations*, Thousand Oaks CA, SAGE Publications USA, 2009, (513) 524.
26. L. Lembrechts, V. Dekocker, P. Zanoni en V. Pulignano, 'A Study of the Determinants of Work-to-Family Conflict Among Hospital Nurses in Belgium', *Journal of Nursing Management* 2014, (898) 898–909; C. Fagan, C. Lyonette, M. Smith en A. Saldaña-Tejeda, *The Influence of Working Time Arrangements on Work-Life Integration or 'Balance': A Review of the International Evidence*, Geneva, International Labour Office, 2012, 39; C. Lyonette, 'Atypical Working in Europe and the Impact on Work-Family Reconciliation' in N. Busby en G. James (eds.), *Families, Care-giving and Paid Work*, Cheltenham, Edward Elgar Publishing Limited, 2011, (31) 39.
27. Eurofound, *Fifth European Working Conditions Survey*, Luxembourg, Publications Office of the European Union, 2012, 92.
28. C. Fagan, C. Lyonette, M. Smith en A. Saldaña-Tejeda, *The Influence of Working Time Arrangements on Work-Life Integration or 'Balance': A Review of the International Evidence*, Geneva, International Labour Office, 2012, 39.
29. E.E. Kossek, B.A. Lautsch en S.C. Eaton, 'Flexibility Enactment Theory: Implications of Flexibility Type, Control, and Boundary Management for Work-Family Effectiveness' in E.E.

workers with very regular schemes have problems with the balance between work and private live, compared with 28 % of workers with no regularity in their working time.[30] Shift work in general leads to a higher work-life conflict, but the effect is stronger for those on alternating or rotating shifts. 30 % of the respondents on alternating or rotating shifts report work-life conflict, compared to 26% of the respondents on permanent shifts, but both outcomes are above average.[31] Changes to the work schedules also lead to difficulties. Only 14% of workers with no changes indicate having problems with work-life balance, compared to 35 % who know about these changes the same day or 21 % who know about them several weeks in advance.[32]

[D] Little Overtime and Extra Working Hours

Overtime and extra time - by which we mean all hours worked outside of the normal work schedules - are also associated with more work-family conflict, especially when these hours worked are unexpected or involuntary.[33]

[E] Emergency Leave

45 % of the workers and independent workers believe the possibility to take a day off at short notice when needed, would help them to balance work and private life.[34] And they seem to be right about this: 31 % of those who could, report to have a very good fit between working hours and family commitments, compared to only 18 % of those not able to do this.[35] Having the possibility to take time off during working hours at short notice for private reasons nearly triples the likelihood of having a good work-life balance.[36]

Kossek en S.J. Lambert (eds.), *Work and Life Integration*, New Jersey, Lawrence Erlbaum Associates Inc., 2005, (243) 253; C. Thompson, L.L. Beauvais en T.D. Allen, 'Work and Family from an Industrial/Organization Psychology Perspective' in M. Pitt-Catsouphes, E.E. Kossek en S. Sweet (eds.), *The Work and Family Handbook*, East Sussex, Psychology Press, 2008, (283) 286.

30. Eurofound, *Fifth European Working Conditions Survey*, Luxembourg, Publications Office of the European Union, 2012, 91.
31. *Ibid.*
32. *Ibid.*, 92.
33. E.L. Kelly, E.E. Kossel, L.B. Hammer, M. Durham, J. Bray, K. Chermack, L.A. Murphy en D. Kaskubar, '7 Getting There from Here: Research on the Effects of Work-Family Initiatives on Work-Family Conflict and Business Outcomes', *The Academy of Management Annals* 2008, vol. 2, afl. 1, (305) 320; C. Thompson, L.L. Beauvais en T.D. Allen, 'Work and Family from an Industrial/Organization Psychology Perspective' in M. Pitt-Catsouphes, E.E. Kossek en S. Sweet (eds.), *The Work and Family Handbook*, East Sussex, Psychology Press, 2008, (283) 286.
34. Eurofound, *Third European Quality of Life Survey - Quality of Life in Europe: Impacts of the Crisis*, Luxemburg, Publications Office of the European Union, 2012, 59–60.
35. Eurofound, *Third European Quality of Life Survey - Quality of Life in Europe: Impacts of the Crisis*, Luxemburg, Publications Office of the European Union, 2012, 60.
36. Eurofound, *Fifth European Working Conditions Survey*, Luxembourg, Publications Office of the European Union, 2012, 92.

[F] Control over Start and Finish Times

Having more control over start and finish times of work would enable workers to avoid traffic jams and thus longer travel periods.[37] Research then shows that this kind of flexible scheduling indeed lowers work-life conflict outcomes.[38] Among workers able to vary their start and finish times, 3% reported their working hours and family commitments fitted 'very well' compared with only 21% of workers without this option.[39] The mere possibility to accumulate working hours were less impressive (30% reports a very good fit between work and family and social responsibilities, but also 28% of those who do not have this possibility report a very good fit).[40]

[G] Intensity of Work

When thinking of working time, one should also be thinking of the amount of work that is done within one hour. Next to working time volume and working time organisation, work intensity also plays a role in work-life balance outcomes. According to MILLIKEN and DUNN-JENSEN, managers and higher staff experience three types of time pressure: the pressure to get tasks done faster, the pressure to work longer hours, and the pressure to work 24/7.[41]

Workers experience higher work-life conflict when they experience more work pressure, work demands or work intensity.[42] If a job combines high demands, such as a heavy workload, intense pace of work, emotionally demanding tasks, complex

37. SERV, *Wat als we Nieuw gaan Werken?* Brussel, Stichting Innovatie & Arbeid, 2014, www.serv.be/sites/default/files/documenten/HNW_Informatiedossier_watalswenieuwgaanwerken_def_0.pdf (consultatie 12 juli 2016), 239.
38. C. Thompson, L.L. Beauvais en T.D. Allen, 'Work and Family from an Industrial/Organization Psychology Perspective' in M. Pitt-Catsouphes, E.E. Kossek en S. Sweet (eds.), *The Work and Family Handbook*, East Sussex, Psychology Press, 2008, (283) 286.
39. Eurofound, *Third European Quality of Life Survey – Quality of Life in Europe: Impacts of the Crisis*, Luxemburg, Publications Office of the European Union, 2012, 60.
40. *Ibid.*, 60.
41. F.J. Milliken en L.M. Dunn-Jensen, 'The Changing Time Demands of Managerial and Professional Work: Implications for Managing the Work-Life Boundary' in E.E. Kossek en S.J. Lambert (eds.), *Work and Life Integration*, New Jersey, Lawrence Erlbaum Associates Inc., 2005, (43) 46.
42. E.L. Kelly, E.E. Kossel, L.B. Hammer, M. Durham, J. Bray, K. Chermack, L.A. Murphy en D. Kaskubar, '7 Getting There from Here: Research on the Effects of Work-Family Initiatives on Work-Family Conflict and Business Outcomes', *The Academy of Management Annals* 2008, vol. 2, afl. 1, (305) 320; K. Byron, 'A Meta-analytical Review of Work-Family Conflict and its Antecedents', *Journal of Vocational Behavior* 2005, afl. 67, (169) 190; G.M. Bellavia en M.R. Frone, 'Work-Family Conflict' in J. Barling, K.E. Kelloway en M.R. Frone (eds.), *Handbook of Work Stress*, Thousand Oaks CA, Sage Publications, 2005, (113) 126; L. Lembrechts, V. Dekocker, P. Zanoni en V. Pulignano, 'Werk-privémaatregelen, een oplossing om het beroep van verpleegkundige aantrekkelijker te maken?', *Over.Werk* 2014, afl. 3, (17) 22; C. Lyonette, 'Atypical Working in Europe and the Impact on Work-Family Reconciliation' in N. Busby en G. James (eds.), *Families, Care-Giving and Paid Work*, Cheltenham, Edward Elgar Publishing Limited, 2011, (31) 42; F.J. Milliken en L.M. Dunn-Jensen, 'The Changing Time Demands of Managerial and Professional Work: Implications for Managing the Work-Life Boundary' in E.E. Kossek en S.J. Lambert (eds.), *Work and Life Integration*, New Jersey, Lawrence Erlbaum Associates Inc., 2005, (43) 44; N.A. Bowling, G.M. Alarcon, C.B. Bragg en M.J. Hartman, 'A Meta-analytic Examination of the Potential Correleates and Consequences of Workload', *Work*

problem solving and insufficient resources to get the job done, with a lack of control or decision-making autonomy, this generates job strain which is related to negative impacts on work-life balance.[43] Higher work pressure is also related to longer working hours and overtime and extra time, which in turn lead to higher work-life conflict outcomes.[44]

[H] Autonomy over Working Time

Research shows less work-family conflict is reported when one has more control over when and how much he works, compared to those who have their working hours set by the company.[45] But the available evidence also suggests that the positive effect of autonomy and control over work schedules or the scope to choose particular hours of work has a rather modest effect and is insufficient to counteract the negative effects of long hours or unsocial schedules.[46] Golden also points out that having scheduling control may be a double-edged sword where it can go hand in hand with longer working hours or the feeling that work is never done.[47]

& Stress: An International Journal of Work, Health & Organisations 2015, vol. 29, afl. 2, (95) 110; Eurofound, *Sixth European Working Conditions Survey*, Luxembourg, Publications Office of the European Union, 2016, 115.

43. C. Fagan, C. Lyonette, M. Smith en A. Saldaña-Tejeda, *The Influence of Working Time Arrangements on Work-Life Integration or 'Balance': A Review of the International Evidence*, Geneva, International Labour Office, 2012, 5.
44. E.L. Kelly, E.E. Kossel, L.B. Hammer, M. Durham, J. Bray, K. Chermack, L.A. Murphy en D. Kaskubar, '7 Getting There from Here: Research on the Effects of Work-Family Initiatives on Work-Family Conflict and Business Outcomes', *The Academy of Management Annals* 2008, vol. 2, afl. 1, (305) 320.
45. E.L. Kelly, E.E. Kossel, L.B. Hammer, M. Durham, J. Bray, K. Chermack, L.A. Murphy en D. Kaskubar, '7 Getting There from Here: Research on the Effects of Work-Family Initiatives on Work-Family Conflict and Business Outcomes', *The Academy of Management Annals* 2008, vol. 2, afl. 1, (305) 318; E.E. Kossek, B.A. Lautsch en S.C. Eaton, 'Telecommuting, Control, and Boundary Management: Correlates of Policy Use and Practice, Job Control, and Work-Family Effectiveness', *Journal of Vocational Behavior* 2006, vol. 68, (347) 361; C. Lyonette, 'Atypical Working in Europe and the Impact on Work-Family Reconciliation' in N. Busby en G. James (eds.), *Families, Care-giving and Paid Work*, Cheltenham, Edward Elgar Publishing Limited, 2011, (31) 48; Eurofound, *Fifth European Working Conditions Survey*, Luxembourg, Publications Office of the European Union, 2012, 92; L. Golden, B. Wiens-Tuers, S.J. Lambert en J.R. Henly, 'Working Time in the Employment Relationship: Working Time, Perceived Control and Work-Life Balance' in K. Townsend en A. Wilkinson (eds.), *Research Handbook on the Future of Work and Employment Relations*, Cheltenham, Edward Elgar Publishing, 2011, (188) 203.
46. C. Fagan, C. Lyonette, M. Smith en A. Saldaña-Tejeda, *The Influence of Working Time Arrangements on Work-Life Integration or 'Balance': A Review of the International Evidence*, Geneva, International Labour Office, 2012, 39. *See also* Eurofound, *Sixth European Working Conditions Survey*, Luxembourg, Publications Office of the European Union, 2016, 115.
47. L. Golden, B. Wiens-Tuers, S.J. Lambert en J.R. Henly, 'Working Time in the Employment Relationship: Working Time, Perceived Control and Work-Life Balance' in K. Townsend en A. Wilkinson (eds.), *Research Handbook on the Future of Work and Employment Relations*, Cheltenham, Edward Elgar Publishing, 2011, (188) 191. *See also* B.-J. Krings, L. Nierling, M. Pedaci en M. Piersanti, *Working Time, Gender and Work-Life Balance*, Leuven, Higher institute of labour studies (KU Leuven), 2009, 67.

§4.03 A WORK-LIFE BALANCE EVALUATION

These criteria can then be used to evaluate working time law. For this contribution, working time law is that part of labour law that determines the worker's availability for his employer, including maximum hours of work, rest periods, holiday, maternity leave,.... At a European level, we can think of the European Working Time Directive,[48] the Maternity Leave Directive,[49] the Parental Leave Directive,[50] and the Part-time Work Directive.[51] European Union (EU) Member States have to translate these directives into national law, but can go further than these minimum requirements.

[A] Some Work-Life Balance Criteria Are Positively or Negatively Influenced

[1] Number of Working Hours

I will start with the limitation of working hours. The Working Time Directive limits working hours to forty-eight hours per week.[52] Next to this, the European Working Time Directive imposes rest periods of eleven hours per twenty-four-hour period and thirty-five hours per seven-day period.[53] Longer leave periods are also provided at a European level. The Working Time Directive provides a four weeks paid annual leave.[54] The Maternity Leave Directive grants a continuous period of at least fourteen weeks before or after confinement for pregnant workers, workers who have recently given birth and workers who are breastfeeding. Two weeks of these fourteen weeks are compulsory and are allocated before and/or after confinement.[55] The worker on maternity leave is entitled to pay or to an adequate allowance.[56] And the Parental Leave Directive entitles men and women workers to at least four weeks parental leave each

48. Directive 2003/88/EC of the European Parliament and of the Council of 4 November 2003 concerning certain aspects of the organisation of working time, OJ L 299, 18 November 2003, http://data.europa.eu/eli/dir/2003/88/oj.
49. Council Directive 92/85/EEC of 19 October 1992 on the introduction of measures to encourage improvements in the safety and health at work of pregnant workers and workers who have recently given birth or are breastfeeding (tenth individual Directive within the meaning of Article 16(1) of Directive 89/391/EEC), OJ L 348, 28 November 1992, http://data.europa.eu/eli/dir/1992/85/oj.
50. Council Directive 2010/18/EU of 8 March 2010 implementing the revised Framework Agreement on parental leave concluded by BUSINESSEUROPE, UEAPME, CEEP and ETUC and repealing Directive 96/34/EC (Text with EEA relevance), OJ L 68, 8 March 2010, http://data.europa.eu/eli/dir/2010/18/oj.
51. Council Directive 97/81/EC of 15 December 1997 concerning the Framework Agreement on part-time work concluded by UNICE, CEEP and the ETUC – Annex: Framework agreement on part-time work, OJ L 14, 20 January 1998, http://data.europa.eu/eli/dir/1997/81/oj.
52. Article 6 Directive 2003/88/EC.
53. Articles 3, 4 and 6 Directive 2003/88/EC.
54. Article 7 Directive 2003/88/EC
55. Article 8 Directive 92/85/EEC.
56. Article 11 Directive 92/85/EEC.

on the grounds of the birth or adoption of a child to take care of that child until a given age up to eight years.[57] Maintenance of payment or allowance is not obligatory.

In general, a large part of the EU's working time law deals with the work-life balance criterion 'number of working hours'.[58] But the simple and at first sight generous rules just described are in fact not so easy to apply and allow for many derogations.[59] Let me give you the example of the forty-eight hours per week working time limit. This limit, first, can actually be calculated on average over a four months period, thus allowing much more working hours in a certain period.[60]

Second, for some workers exceptions or derogations are provided in the Working Time Directive, such as for managing executives or other persons with autonomous decision-taking powers or family workers.[61] The most (in)famous derogation is the so called 'opt-out'.[62] If certain conditions are fulfilled, the employer and worker can agree not to apply the forty-eight-hour working week limit. The worker must give his individual consent to do so.[63] Although the opt-out was at first only part of the Working Time Directive to convince the United Kingdom (UK) not to oppose against the directive, it is now more and more used in all Member States as it is regarded to be the most convenient and effective mechanism for avoiding the forty-eight-hour limit which is hindering for Member States given the large definition of working time by the Court of Justice of the EU (CJEU).[64] This increasing popularity of the opt-out is problematic. It is said that it undermines both the market-making as the market-correcting rationale of the directive.[65] Moreover, the opt-out has insulated employers from the need to consider whether organisational changes are necessary to reduce the length of the

57. Clause 2 Framework agreement on Parental Leave, annex to Directive 2010/18/EU.
58. This was also an outcome of my study of Belgian working time legislation. For my Ph.D. thesis, defended in December 2016 and to be published in Dutch by die Keure in May 2017, I analysed the European Working Time Directive, national (Belgian) legislation and the agreements at sectorial level and company level. *See* S. De Groof, F. Hendrickx (sup.) (2016). *Arbeidstijd en vrije tijd in het arbeidsrecht: een juridisch onderzoek naar work-life balance*, Brugge, die Keure, 2017, 367 p.
59. Article 17 and further Directive 2003/88/EC.
60. Article 16 Directive 2003/88/EC.
61. Article 17 Directive 2003/88/EC.
62. C. Barnard, 'EU "Social" Policy: From Employment Law to Labour Market Freedom' in P. Craig en G. de Búrca (eds.), *The Evolution of EU Law*, Oxford, Oxford University Press, 2011, (641), 652.
63. Article 22, 1 (a) Directive 2003/88/EC; CJEU 3 October 2000, C-303/98, *Sindicato de Médicos de Asistencia Pública (Simap) v Conselleria de Sanidad y Consumo de la Generalidad Valenciana*, *ECR* 2000, I, 7963, section 73; CJEU 5 October 2004, C-397/01 until C-403/01, *Pfeiffer*, *ECR* 2004, I, 8835, section 86.
64. Communication from the Commission 30 December 2003, *to the Council, the European Parliament, the European Economic and Social Committee and the Committee of the Regions concerning the re-exam of Directive 93/104/EC concerning certain aspects of the organization of working time*, (COM)843, 16; C. Barnard, *EC Employment Law. Third Edition*, Oxford, Oxford University Press, 2006, 590–591; C. Barnard, S. Deakin and R. Hobbs, 'Opting Out of the 48-Hour Week: Employer Necessity or Individual Choice? An Emperical Study of the Operation of Article 18(1)(b) of the Working time Directive in the UK', *Industrial Law Journal*, vol. 32, no. 4, (223) 224.
65. C. Barnard, 'EU "Social" Policy: From Employment Law to Labour Market Freedom' in P. Craig and G. de Búrca (eds.), *The Evolution of EU Law*, Oxford, Oxford University Press, 2011, (641), 652.

working week and improve productivity.[66] In general, the (increasing) popularity of the opt-out demonstrates the (increasing) failure of the directive, pushing more and more Member States to run for the security blanket the opt-out provides, even if they do not actually need it.[67] The real problem then is not that workers agree to work more than the forty-eight-hour limit, but really the widespread use of it making it impossible for a worker to refuse to sign the opt-out before he even has an employment contract, by fear of missing out on the contract.[68]

Third, the working time limit can be calculated per contract, instead of per head. In other words: one could work 24/7 without infringing the directive, as long as he works for different employers.[69]

Fourth, it is not even clear which time should be taken into account as working time to check whether the legal limits are respected. According to the directive, working time means (1) any period during which the worker is working; (2) at the employer's disposal; and (3) carrying out his activity or duty, in accordance with national laws and/or practice. Rest period means any period which is not working time.[70] Given the jurisprudence of the CJEU, the three conditions of the definition of working time are cumulative.[71] But the difference between the first and third condition is not quite clear. However, in the Spanish, French and Italian version of the directive the first condition is '*whether the worker is at the work place*'.[72] The CJEU seems to

66. C. Barnard, *EC Employment Law. Third Edition*, Oxford, Oxford University Press, 2006, 598.
67. *Cf.* above, C. Barnard, *EC Employment Law. Third Edition*, Oxford, Oxford University Press, 2006, 598.
68. The European Commission questioned the generalization in the presentation of the opt-out agreement when the work contract is signed (Communication from the Commission 30 December 2003, *to the Council, the European Parliament, the European Economic and Social Committee and the Committee of the Regions concerning the re-exam of Directive 93/104/EC concerning certain aspects of the organization of working time*, (COM)843, 9–10).
69. According to the European Commission (as already stated in its 2000 Report on application of the Working Time Directive, COM (2000) 787, at point 14.2) the limits of the Directive should in view of the health and safety objectives of the Directive, as far as possible, be applied per worker (and not per contract) in the case of any worker who works concurrently under two or more employment relationships. However, the Commission noticed there is a considerable variation in the approaches followed by the Member States in that respect. The Commission therefore considered that the inclusion of this issue in the revision of the working time directive would make it nearly impossible to reach agreement in Council and therefore rejected an amendment of the Council (Opinion of the Commission pursuant to Article 251(2), third subparagraph, point (c) of the EC Treaty on the European Parliament's amendments to the Council's common position regarding the proposal for a Directive of the European Parliament and of the Council amending Directive 2003/88/EC concerning certain aspects of the organisation of working time amending the proposal of the Commission pursuant to Article 250(2) of the EC Treaty, COM(2009) 57 final, 11).
70. Article 2, § 1 and 2 Directive 2003/88/EC; CJEU 3 October 2000, C-303/98, *Sindicato de Médicos de Asistencia Pública (Simap) v Conselleria de Sanidad y Consumo de la Generalidad Valenciana, ECR* 2000, I, 7963, section 47.
71. J. Fairhurst, 'SIMAP – Interpreting the Working Time Directive', *Industrial Law Journal* 2001, vol. 30, no. 2, (236), 242; L. Rodgers, 'The Notion of Working Time', *Industrial Law Journal-Journal* 2008, vol. 38, no. 1, (80), 82.
72. The entire definition in Spanish is '*tiempo de trabajo: todo período durante el cual el trabajador permanezca en el trabajo, a disposición del empresario y en ejercicio de su actividad o de sus funciones, de conformidad con las legislaciones y/o prácticas nacionales*', in French it is '*temps de travail: toute période durant laquelle le travailleur est au travail, à la disposition de*

interpret the first condition accordingly.[73] In sum, because of this definition, the CJEU holds that when a doctor is obliged to be in the hospital to respond to emergency situations, all the time spent in the hospital is working time even when the doctor is actually sleeping. On the contrary, when the doctor has to respond to any emergency call and be able to be in the hospital even within five minutes, all this time 'on-call' is not working time since the first criterion interpreted in the French version is not fulfilled... Whether the doctor can rest or sleep during the on-call time spent at the health care centre, is in no way material according to the CJEU.[74] Indeed, the intensity of the work done by the worker and his output are not among the characteristic elements of the concept of 'working time' within the meaning of the directive, according to the CJEU.[75] This definition of working time is of course problematic in the modern workplace and may lead to controversy in other particular situations, such as lunch breaks, travelling or training time, zero hours contracts, the right to time off work for trade union activities, health- and safety responsibilities, public duties and work-related activities.[76] In a recent case the CJEU was less strict on the condition of workplace. The question asked before the CJEU was whether the time the technicians spent travelling from their homes to their first customers was working time. Although the time spent travelling to work is usually not working time, the CJEU ruled otherwise in this case. The technician was at the disposal of the employer while driving to his first customer and he was carrying out his activities or duties. Finally, he was also 'at the workplace', according to the CJEU, 'given that travelling is an integral part of being a worker without a fixed or habitual place of work, the place of work of such workers cannot be reduced to the physical areas of their work on the premises of their employer's customers'.[77] But other situations are not adequately solved yet. For example, when someone voluntarily restarts working in the evening – called the third shift by Genin in this Bulletin – this time spent working will not be working time for the calculation of the legal limits.

---

l'employeur et dans l'exercice de son activité ou de ses fonctions, conformément aux législations et/ou pratiques nationales' and in Italian is: *'orario di lavoro: qualsiasi periodo in cui il lavoratore sia al lavoro, a disposizione del datore di lavoro e nell'esercizio della sua attività o delle sue funzioni, conformemente alle legislazioni e/o prassi nazionali'.*

73. CJEU 3 October 2000, C-303/98, *Sindicato de Médicos de Asistencia Pública (Simap) v Conselleria de Sanidad y Consumo de la Generalidad Valenciana, ECR* 2000, I, 7963, section 48 and 52; CJEU 9 September 2003, C-151/02, *Landeshauptstadt Kiel v. Norbert Jaeger, ECR* 2003, I, 8389, section 63; CJEU 3 July 2001, C-241/99, *Confederación Intersindical Galega (CIG) v Servicio Galego de Saúde (Sergas), ECR*, I, 5139, section 33. *See also* the opinion of the advocate-general in the Jaeger-case.
74. CJEU 9 September 2003, C-151/02, *Landeshauptstadt Kiel v. Norbert Jaeger, ECR* 2003, I, 8389, section 60.
75. CJEU 1 December 2005, C-14/04, *Abdelkader Dellas et al. v Premier ministre and Ministre des Affaires sociales, du Travail et de la Solidarité, ECR* 2005, I, 10253, section 43.
76. S. Hardy, 'Harmonising European Working Time in an Enlarged EU: A Case of Failed "Humanisation"?', *International Journal of Comparative Labour Law And Industrial Relations* 2006, vol. 22, no 4, (563), 567.
77. CJEU 10 September 2015, C-266/14, ECLI:EU:C:2015:578, *Federación de Servicios Privados del sindicato Comisiones obreras (CC.OO.)/Tyco Integrated Security SL en Tyco Integrated Fire & Security Corporation Servicios SA*, section no. 43.

In sum, although there is a clear limitation of working time in the European Working Time Directive, this limitation may in practice not really contribute to the work-life balance criterion 'limited working time' because the working time is calculated on average, because there are many exceptions and derogations, because the working time limits are calculated per contract instead of per head, and because not even all time spent working is calculated as working time. All of these reasons also explain why working conditions surveys do not reflect the legal norm in a given country.

[2] Non-standard Working Hours

As regards non-standard working hours, only very non-standard working hours are limited at a European level.[78] To be precise, the Working Time Directive only provides stricter provisions for 'night workers', not for any kind of work outside of typical business hours like evening work or weekend work.

The Working Time Directive limits night work by imposing that the normal hours of work of night workers should be limited to eight hours in any twenty-four-hour period. Night workers whose work involves special hazards or heavy physical or mental strain should not work more than eight hours in any period of twenty-four hours during which they perform night work.[79] Member States must also take measures to ensure that night workers suffering from health problems related to their night work are transferred, whenever possible, to day work.[80] But, again, there are many derogations and exceptions.[81] Moreover, who is a night worker is rather strictly defined: to be a night worker, one must on a daily basis usually work for at least three hours at night, and on an annual basis for at least a sufficient proportion of one's work must be at night time. Night time is then any period of not less than seven hours as defined by national law and which must include, in any case, the period between midnight.[82]

Next to night work, the directive first did prohibit Sunday work, but – thanks to UK-opposition – this prohibition was annulled by the CJEU. According to the Court, the European Council failed to explain why Sunday, as a weekly rest day, is more closely connected with the health and safety of workers than any other day of the week, which

78. This was also an outcome of my study of Belgian working time legislation, *see* S. De Groof, F. Hendrickx (sup.) (2016). *Arbeidstijd en vrije tijd in het arbeidsrecht: een juridisch onderzoek naar work-life balance*, 367 pp, to be published in May 2017 by die Keure.
79. Article 8 Directive 2003/88/EC.
80. Articles 8–13 Directive 2003/88/EC. *See also* Art. 7 Directive 92/85/EEC. Pregnant workers, workers who have recently given birth or workers who are breastfeeding are entitled to a transfer to daytime work or leave from work or extension of maternity leave where such a transfer is not technically and/or objectively feasible or cannot reasonably be required on duly substantiated grounds.
81. Articles 17–21 Directive 2003/88/EC.
82. Article 2, § 4 Directive 2003/88/EC.

was necessary because the legal EU-basis for this directive allowing the EU to intervene was a health and safety provision in the European Treaty.[83]

Thus, the Working Time Directive does not encourage Member States or companies to set their work schedules at normal business hours. An employer can just as easily set working schedules from six to fourteen or from fourteen to twenty-two, instead of the typical nine to seventeen. And even schedules from twenty-two to six are not so difficult, given the rather strict definition of a night worker and – yet again – the many derogations hereto. Therefore, although the EU legislation does contribute in some way to the work-life balance criterion, a lot more could be done to encourage employers to schedule at normal business hours.

[3] Emergency Leave

The Parental Leave Directive explicitly provides – 'in order to promote better reconciliation' – that Member States and/or social partners shall take the necessary measures to entitle workers to time off from work on grounds of force majeure for urgent family reasons in cases of sickness or accident making the immediate presence of the worker indispensable. But of course: not in all circumstances. First, they must only take these measures 'in accordance with national legislation, collective agreements and/or practice'. Moreover, Member States and/or social partners may specify the conditions of access and detailed rules for applying this right and limit the right to a certain amount of time per year and/or per case.[84] But all in all, we could say this legal rule has a positive influence on the work-life balance criterion.

[4] Intensity of Work

As already discussed, the CJEU has held that the intensity of the work done by the worker and his output are not among the characteristic elements of the concept of 'working time' within the meaning of the directive, according to the CJEU.[85] To calculate whether the legal limits have been respected, it neither matters whether the worker was sleeping or working really hard at the workplace (this time will be working time), nor does it matter whether he had half a day to return to the workplace after receiving an emergency call from his employer or whether he had to stay really close by the workplace to restart working in case of an emergency call within five minutes (this time will not be working time).

83. HvJ 12 november 1996, nr. C-84/94, ECLI:EU:C:1996:431, Verenigd Koninkrijk/Commissie, para. 37.
84. Clause 7 Framework Agreement on Parental Leave (Revised), 18 June 2009. In Belgium, for example, I demonstrated in my Ph.D. thesis that the emergency leave is too narrowly constructed to really contribute to the work-life balance criterion, *see* S. De Groof, F. Hendrickx (sup.) (2016). *Arbeidstijd en vrije tijd in het arbeidsrecht: een juridisch onderzoek naar work-life balance*, 367 pp, to be published in May 2017 by die Keure.
85. CJEU 1 December 2005, C-14/04, *Abdelkader Dellas et al. v Premier ministre and Ministre des Affaires sociales, du Travail et de la Solidarité, ECR* 2005, I, 10253, section 43.

But the EU's working time law is not entirely silent on the intensity of work. For example, the Working Time Directive does provide breaks should be provided at least every six hours.[86] A break can obviously lower the general work intensity. Also, sometimes stricter rules are provided taking into account the burden of the work that is done. For example, normal hours of work for night workers are limited to an average of eight hours in any twenty-four-hour period and night workers whose work involves special hazards or heavy physical or mental strain may not work more than eight hours in any period of twenty-four hours during which they perform night work.[87] Finally, Article 13 of the Working Time Directive provides more in general that Member States 'shall take the measures necessary to ensure that an employer who intends to organise work according to a certain pattern takes account of the general principle of adapting work to the worker, with a view, in particular, to alleviating monotonous work and work at a predetermined work-rate, depending on the type of activity, and of safety and health requirements, especially as regards breaks during working time'. However, it remains unclear whether this largely defined requirement has any influence on national legislation.

Generally speaking, EU law conceives time as an objective reference or a numerical unit without considering what is done during that hour, or how heavy the burden of that hour of work is for the worker. Different scholars challenge this point of view. SUPIOT calls for a personal and subjective dimension of time, a shift from working time to worker time.[88] GENIN suggests the concept of 'time porosity' to capture the time in between personal time and working time, a conceptual framework that integrates objective and subjective time.[89] I have already suggested that modern working time law must acknowledge that the regulation of availability can no longer be measured through a 'quantitative time' dimension only. A solely quantitative dimension means that 'an hour is always an hour', and that no distinction is made with regard to what is done during that time. A qualitative dimension on the other hand could come from taking into account the constraints that one's life sphere places on the other.[90]

[5] Autonomy over Working Time

Regarding the criterion of having autonomy over working time, I will make a distinction between having a say in how much you work, and when you work.

A worker can of course influence *how much* he works when he enters into the employment relationship, by accepting a contract for twenty, thirty or forty hours per week. He can also change the number of hours worked during the employment

86. Article 4 Directive 2003/88/EC.
87. Article 8 Directive 2003/88/EC.
88. A. SUPIOT, *Beyond Employment. Changes in Work and the Future of Labour Law in Europe*, Oxford, Oxford University Press, 2001, 60 and 84.
89. E. Genin, 'Proposal for a Theoretical Framework for the Analysis of Time Porosity', *International Journal of Comparative Labour Law and Industrial Relations* 2016, (280), 280–300.
90. S. De Groof, 'Working Time in Modern Law' in L. Mella Méndez en L. Serrani (eds.), *Work-life Balance and the Economic Crisis*, Cambridge, Cambridge Scholars Publishing, 2015, (172) 184–185.

contract when the employer agrees. Apart from this, EU law gives the workers some tools to change the number of hours they work. The Part Time Work Directive for example provides that Member States 'should identify and review obstacles of a legal or administrative nature which may limit the opportunities for part-time work and, where appropriate, eliminate them'. As far as possible, employers should give consideration to: (a) requests by workers to transfer from full-time to part-time work that becomes available in the establishment; (b) requests by workers to transfer from part-time to full-time work or to increase their working time should the opportunity arise; (c) the provision of timely information on the availability of part-time and full-time positions in the establishment in order to facilitate transfers from full-time to part-time or vice versa; (d) measures to facilitate access to part-time work at all levels of the enterprise, including skilled and managerial positions, and where appropriate, to facilitate access by part-time workers to vocational training to enhance career opportunities and occupational mobility; (e) the provision of appropriate information to existing bodies representing workers about part-time working in the enterprise. [91] Of course, the existence of maternity leave and parental leave and the rights protecting these leaves also allow a worker to – for a certain time period – influence how much he works. Member States are also free to determine whether parental leave can be taken on a part-time basis.[92]

Regarding the autonomy to decide on *when* the worker works, there is a lot less EU law that positively influences the criterion. The Parental Leave Directive does provide that, in order to promote better reconciliation, Member States and/or social partners shall take the necessary measures to ensure that workers, when returning from parental leave, may request changes to their working hours and/or patterns for a set period of time. Employers shall consider and respond to such requests, taking into account both employers' and workers' needs.[93] And night workers suffering from health problems recognised as being connected with the fact that they perform night work must be transferred whenever possible to day work to which they are suited.[94]

91. Clause 5 of Annex: Framework agreement on part-time work, OJ L 14, 20 January 1998, http://data.europa.eu/eli/dir/1997/81/oj of Council Directive 97/81/EC of 15 December 1997 concerning the Framework Agreement on part-time work concluded by UNICE, CEEP and the ETUC.
92. Clause 3 of Annex: Framework agreement on part-time work, OJ L 14, 20 January 1998, http://data.europa.eu/eli/dir/1997/81/oj of Council Directive 97/81/EC of 15 December 1997 concerning the Framework Agreement on part-time work concluded by UNICE, CEEP and the ETUC.
93. Clause 6 of Annex: Framework agreement on part-time work, OJ L 14, 20 January 1998, http://data.europa.eu/eli/dir/1997/81/oj of Council Directive 97/81/EC of 15 December 1997 concerning the Framework Agreement on part-time work concluded by UNICE, CEEP and the ETUC.
94. Article 9 Directive 2003/88/EC. *See also* Art. 7 Directive 92/85/EEC. Pregnant workers, workers who have recently given birth or workers who are breastfeeding are entitled to a transfer to daytime work or leave from work or extension of maternity leave where such a transfer is not technically and/or objectively feasible or cannot reasonably be required on duly substantiated grounds.

[B] On Some Work-Life Balance Criteria There is No Influence

What is more striking, however, is what EU law does not provide. There are no minimum rules on how long workers should know their working schedules in advance, and thus no legislation contributing to the criterion 'working time regularity and predictability'. The Working Time Directive also does not even say working schedules should be respected in the first place, and thus does not limit overtime and extra-time. There is also nothing on whether it is the employer or the worker that decides on when to start and finish work, so there is no impact on the work-life balance criterion 'control over start and finish times'.

[C] Limitations to a Work-Life Balance Evaluation

The approach used to evaluate European Working Time law has many limitations. Some of these limitations are related to the limitations of work-life balance studies as such. A critique that is often heard is that most research only studies conflict between work and family, thus limited to families which is moreover receives a rather traditional meaning and does not cover modern relationships.[95] Obviously, not only family roles can conflict with work, people also have hobbies, or are active in community life and so on.[96] Another critique is that of causal relations. Most work-life balance studies take one situation and determine how much work-life conflict is reported. Only very few research is experimental and actually measures the effect of changing for example the criterion long working hours and its impact on work-life conflict outcomes.[97] It is also often said that a lot more research needs to be done on work-life enrichment or the positive effect of life on work and vice versa.[98]

95. K.A. French en R.C. Johnson, 'A Retrospective Timeline of the Evolution of Work-Family Research' in T.D. Allen en L.T. Eby (eds.), *The Oxford Handbook of Work and Family*, Oxford, Oxford University Press, 2016, (9) 19.
96. G.M. Bellavia en M.R. Frone, 'Work-Family Conflict' in J. Barling, K.E. Kelloway en M.R. Frone (eds.), *Handbook of Work Stress*, Thousand Oaks CA, Sage Publications, 2005, (113) 136–137; M. Pitt-Catsouphes, E.E. Kossek en S. Sweet, 'Charting New Territory: Advancing Multi-Disciplinary Perspectives, Methods, and Approaches in the Study of Work and Family' in M. Pitt-Catsouphes, E.E. Kossek en S. Sweet (eds.), *The Work and Family Handbook*, East Sussex, Psychology Press, 2008, (1) 8–9.
97. E.L. Kelly, P. Moen, M. Oakes, W. Fan, C. Okechukwu, K.D. Davis, L.B. Hammer, E.E. Kossel, R.B. King, G.C. Hanson, F. Mierzwa en L.M. Casper, 'Changing Work and Work-Family Conflict: Evidence from the Work, Family, and Health Network', *American Sociological Review* 2014, afl. 79, (485) 487; E.L. Kelly, E.E. Kossel, L.B. Hammer, M. Durham, J. Bray, K. Chermack, L.A. Murphy en D. Kaskubar, '7 Getting There from Here: Research on the Effects of Work-Family Initiatives on Work-Family Conflict and Business Outcomes', *The Academy of Management Annals* 2008, vol. 2, afl. 1, (305) 321; S.M. Macdermid, '(Re)Considering Conflict Between Work and Family' in E.E. Kossek en S.J. Lambert (eds.), *Work and Life Integration*, New Jersey, Lawrence Erlbaum Associates Inc., 2005, (19) 31; K.A. French en R.C. Johnson, 'A Retrospective Timeline of the Evolution of Work-Family Research' in T.D. Allen en L.T. Eby (eds.), *The Oxford Handbook of Work and Family*, Oxford, Oxford University Press, 2016, (9) 18.
98. C. Thompson, L.L. Beauvais en T.D. Allen, 'Work and Family from an Industrial/Organization Psychology Perspective' in M. Pitt-Catsouphes, E.E. Kossek en S. Sweet (eds.), *The Work and Family Handbook*, East Sussex, Psychology Press, 2008, (283) 284–287; G.M. Bellavia en M.R. Frone, 'Work-Family Conflict' in J. Barling, K.E. Kelloway en M.R. Frone (eds.), *Handbook of*

Also, the use of work-life balance literature to deduct criteria to evaluate and even more to formulate recommendations is not without danger. For example, if it is demonstrated that working less hours correlates with a lower work-life conflict, does this mean the law should in general limit the number of hours that one is allowed to work? Also, some recommendations do not seem to be transposable into law. For example, if it is demonstrated that support at the workplace correlates to a lower work-life conflict, how can law than encourage the supervisor's and colleagues' support? Finally, recommendations can also conflict with labour law's own functions. For example, if it were demonstrated that working part-time correlates with a lower work-life conflict, labour law must perhaps not simply and only encourage part-time work if this is usually taken up by women and thus makes the actual pay gap between man and woman bigger, which conflicts with labour law's non-discrimination function. All these examples should not restrain legal scholars from using the work-life balance literature and deduce criteria therefrom, as long as they are clear on these limitations. The advantage of explicitly using work-life balance criteria is that it renders the debate more honest, allowing a real debate on the validity of the criteria, or the way they are used to evaluate the law, or the way they are used to formulate recommendations, and so on. Making the debate more honest is necessary, because work-life balance is already often used to claim that the law should be changed in this or that direction.[99]

The most obvious and yet most important limitation in using work-life balance literature to evaluate the law, is that this will not tell us anything on individual work-life outcomes. We cannot with certainty say that a legal system that seems to positively influence work-life balance criteria, will also lead to less work-life conflict of individual workers. This should restrain us from evaluating the law with these criteria since being able to predict individual work-life outcomes was not our intention in the first place, but must just be kept in mind as a limitation to the evaluation.

§4.04 RECOMMENDATIONS FOR A MODERN WORKING TIME LAW

The evaluation showed that working time law pays a lot of attention to the criterion limited 'number of working hours', but as we have demonstrated may in practice not really have an important positive influence on the criterion given the many exceptions and derogations and even the concept of working time as such. Non-standard working hours are only limited when they are very atypical, namely in the case of night work.

Work Stress, Thousand Oaks CA, Sage Publications, 2005, (113) 136; J.H. Greenhaus en S. Parasuraman, 'Reseach on Work, Family and Gender: Current Status and Future Directions.' in G.N. Powell (ed.), *Handbook of Gender & Work*, Newbury Park, Sage Publications, 1999, (391) 391–412; M. O'driscoll, P. Brough en T. Kalliath, 'Work-Family Conflict and Facilitation' in F. Jones, R.J. Burke en M. Westman (eds.), *Work-Life Balance. A Psychological Perspective*, New York, Psychology Press, 2006, (117) 134 and R.C. Barnett en K.C. Gareis, 'Role Theory Perspectives on Work and Family' in M. Pitt-Catsouphes, E.E. Kossek en S. Sweet (eds.), *The Work and Family Handbook*, East Sussex, Psychology Press, 2008, (209) 213.

99. S. Fleetwood, 'Why Work-Life Balance Now?', The *International Journal of Human Resource Management* 2007, vol. 18, afl. 3, (387) 396.

European law does provide for emergency leave. Regarding the intensity of work, however, the legislation departs from time as a quantitative dimension and does not take into account the quality of time. The legislation also hardly puts workers in control over how much and when they work or when to start and end work. The European legislation also does not provide that the worker must know his schedule in advance, or even that work schedules must be respected, thus not contributing to the criteria 'working time regularity or predictable working hours' and 'little overtime and extra time'.

Recommendations for a modern working time law that would have a more positive influence on the work-life balance criteria, can be sought in national legislation or practice. Regarding the number of working hours, it is for example interesting to note that Dutch legislations limits the number of times the worker has to be available for the employer, referred to as on-call periods.[100] Another positive example is what SELBERG describes in this Bulletin. Collective agreements in Sweden sometimes determine a time space is defined during which the employer is free to schedule. Going outside of the frames set by the agreement presupposes consent from the plant level trade union. This obviously positively influences the criterion 'non-standard working hours' and 'working time regularity and predictable working hours'. Another positive example is the right for individuals to adapt their working hours or schedules can be seen as an example of legislation that contributes to the criterion 'autonomy over working time'. According to GOLDEN, expanding rights to request and rights to refuse would be more likely to facilitate work-life balance among workers than a one-size-fits-all standard working week length.[101] COLLINS distinguishes three models: an obligation to bargain in good faith, a possible rejection on objective grounds, or an obligation for reasonable accommodation.[102] In this Bulletin, REILLY and MASSELOT reflect on the right to request in New Zealand and VALENTINI and BERNSTEIN reflect on the duty to accommodate following Canadian anti-discrimination laws. Other examples are the right to request in the UK: a qualifying employee can ask for a change in their number of worker hours, can ask for a different work schedule or can ask to work from home.[103] The employer can refuse the request, for example because he

100. Article 5: 9 Arbeidstijdenwet, http://wetten.overheid.nl/BWBR0007671/2016-01-01/0/#Hoofdstuk5_Paragraaf5.2_Sub-paragraaf_8_Artikel5:11; J. Van Drongelen (ed.), *Arbeidsomstandighedenrecht. Deel 2 Arbeidstijden gebundeld. Over misverstanden, onbegrip en de uitleg van de Arbeidstijdenrichtlijn 2003 en andere internationale verplichtingen*, Zutphen, Paris, 2011, 42; J. Van Drongelen en W.J.P.M. Fase, *Individueel arbeidsrecht. Deel 1 De overeenkomsten tot het verrichten van arbeid. Vakantie en verlof*, Zutphen, Paris, 2011, 227; X., *De Arbeidstijdenwet. Informatie voor werkgevers en werknemers*, Ministerie van Sociale Zaken en Werkgelegenheid, 2010, file:///C:/Users/u0064813/Downloads/brochure-de-arbeidstijdenwet%20(1).pdf, 8.

101. L. Golden, B. Wiens-Tuers, S.J. Lambert en J.R. Henly, 'Working Time in the Employment Relationship: Working Time, Perceived Control and Work-Life Balance' in K. Townsend en A. Wilkinson (eds.), *Research Handbook on the Future of Work and Employment Relations*, Cheltenham, Edward Elgar Publishing, 2011, (188) 206–207.

102. H. Collins, 'The Right to Flexibility' in J. Conaghan en K. Rittich (eds.), *Labour Law, Work, and Family. Critical and Comparative Perspectives*, Oxford, Oxford University Press, 2005, (99) 117.

103. Article 80F Employment Rights Act.

considers there is a detrimental effect on the ability to meet customer demands.[104] The Netherlands also have a right to request that is even stronger, as the reasons the employer can refuse are more narrowly constructed than in the UK. Finally, Belgian legislation provides strict rules on overtime and extra time. The normal working time limit is thirty-eight hours per week on average, but if an employee works more than forty hours in a given week these hours must be paid at (at least) 150%, which contributes to the criterion 'little overtime and extra time'.[105] A part-time employee working with a variable schedule must be given notice at least five days in advance of his schedule, which contributes to the criterion 'working time regularity and predictability'.[106] And new legislation will give companies the possibility to allow their employees to start and finish their work as they please, provided they respect certain maximum and minimum limits. An employee can then choose to start work for example between 8 and 10 AM and end between 4 and 6 PM.[107]

Apart from these very concrete recommendations based on national legislation and practice, we can use work-life balance literature to more in general think of what modern working time law should look like. As I have described above, the work-life balance literature evolved from work-life conflict, to work-to life and life-to-work conflict, and more recently work-life enrichment. The underlying idea is that what happens in one life sphere has an effect on the other: if work is very consuming, one might feel exhausted after work hours and perhaps experience work-to-life conflict. If work on the other hand is something the employee really enjoys, he might be able to cope better with the terrible-two phase every toddler goes through... As already mentioned, I have suggested before that a modern working time law must acknowledge that the regulation of availability can no longer be measured through a 'quantitative time' dimension only.[108] A solely quantitative dimension means that 'an hour is always an hour', that no distinction is made with regard to what is done during that time. However, doubts have been cast on the conception of time as an objective reference that could be used to regulate labour relations. Calls have been made for new perspectives on labour law in which time is perceived in a personal and subjective dimension.[109] Therefore, it is proposed that the new provisions on working time must encompass a qualitative dimension. I suggest that this qualitative dimension could come – with thanks to work-life balance literature – from taking into account the constraints that one's life sphere places on the other. For example, under the European Working Time Directive 2003/88/EC, the time a doctor spends sleeping at the workplace while being on-call or the time he spends performing complicated surgery, are both counted as one hour of work. However, in the first case, the doctor returns home and feels able to play with his children or give them a bath. In the second case,

104. Article 80G Employment Rights Act.
105. Article 29 Arbeidswet.
106. Article 159 programmawet 22 december 1989, *BS* 30 december 1989, *err. BS* 4 april 1990.
107. Article 20*ter* Arbeidswet.
108. S. De Groof, 'Working Time in Modern Law' in L. Mella Méndez en L. Serrani (eds.), *Work-Life Balance and the Economic Crisis*, Cambridge, Cambridge Scholars Publishing, 2015, (172) 184.
109. A. Supiot, *Beyond Employment. Changes in Work and the Future of Labour Law in Europe*, Oxford, Oxford University Press 2001, 60.

he probably goes back home and asks his companion to take care of the children because he needs some time to recover. The qualitative time dimension I suggest implies that these working activities should not be treated the same in working time law, as they do not have the same impact on the other life sphere.

How this qualitative dimension could be put into practice remains to be seen. However, it does not seem too ambitious to imagine a system where the social partners agree or the legislator decides on the impact of several types of work on the other life sphere. In fact, some examples can already be found that reflect this idea. The stricter rules for night work at a European level exist because it is recognised that working one hour at night is not the same as working one hour during daytime. In a number of national legal systems, such as in Belgium, workers with heavy duties – for instance in the mining industry – are also allowed to retire with fewer years of service than other workers. Finally, it seems that a qualitative dimension is already suggested by the European Commission in the attempts to review the Working Time Directive when it puts forward that on-call time should be counted differently 'i.e. not always on an hour-per-hour basis'.[110]

Working time law's first and primary goal is to limit the worker's availability to his employer in time – which I call working time law's 'demarcation function'.[111] This function, however, is faced with the important challenges of today's society where the distinction between work and private life is fading. A qualitative time approach could in my view be useful to answer this challenge and allow working time law. A qualitative dimension means taking into account the constraints that one's life sphere places on the other, an idea that comes from work-life balance literature. Such a qualitative time approach allows working time law to continue to fulfil its historical and justified functions, which is crucial to pursue the fundamental goals of labour law of human dignity and social justice.

110. Communication from the Commission to the European Parliament, the Council, the European Economic and Social Committee and the Committee of the Regions 21 December 2010, *Reviewing the Working Time Directive (Second-phase consultation of the social partners at European level under Article 154 TFEU)*, COM(2010)801, 10.

111. S. De Groof, 'Working Time in Modern Law' in L. Mella Méndez en L. Serrani (eds.), *Work-Life Balance and the Economic Crisis*, Cambridge, Cambridge Scholars Publishing, 2015, (172) 178.

CHAPTER 5

Making the Business Case for Work-Life Integration in the United States

Katherine S. Drake & Amy K. Brown

§5.01 INTRODUCTION

A leading business problem in the United States (US) is the mismatch between the traditional workplace and the evolving modern workforce. Employee demand for increased work-life integration has grown in the past decade, challenging our accepted work norms. Introducing human resource policies and practices to improve workplace flexibility is one response to the problem, but these policies are not sufficient when implemented in isolation. In order to redesign work to achieve work-life integration, we first need to address and change cultural norms and stigmas that hinder successful outcomes.

In making the business case, we look at examples of success in the private sector as well as at government policies that support work-life integration in the US. Paid family medical leave is offered as one important and needed 'flexibility' policy that also helps recognize and establish a norm of taking time off for life, foundational to work-life integration. The three-phase Accommodate, Accept, and Adapt Model (or 3A Model) is then proposed as a framework for categorizing organizations on a continuum in terms of their work-life integration efforts, from accommodating the needs of individual employees to adapting their cultural norms to support work-life integration. We begin our paper with an overview of key constructs, provide evidence for why it is time to prioritize work-life integration, share what we have learned from policies that support work-life integration, and then conclude with recommendations for moving work-life integration efforts forward.

§5.02 OVERVIEW OF WORK-LIFE INTEGRATION, WORKPLACE FLEXIBILITY, CULTURE, AND REDESIGN

[A] Work-Life Integration

The last decade has witnessed a shift in semantics, away from the term work-life balance, which implies a dichotomy of competing demands on an individual's time, and toward the concept of work-life integration. According to Stewart Friedman, founding director of the Wharton Work/Life Integration project, 'the idea that "work" competes with "life" ignores that "life" is actually the intersection and interaction of four major domains: work, home, community, and the private self.'[1] Instead of focusing on the trade-offs between work and life, the time has come to integrate these different areas of our lives in a more harmonious way.

Jessica DeGroot, founder and executive director of ThirdPath Institute, a non-profit agency focused on the integration of work and personal life, talks about leading an 'integrated life' in this way:

> If you arrange your work and home lives so they fit together to fulfill all your needs, you can create a life that has time for your work as well as time for relationships, family and outside interests. That's what it means to lead an integrated life – to create your 'third path.'[2]

While the concept of work-life integration has been gaining momentum in recent years, Lotte Bailyn made the case for work-life integration as far back as 1993, the year she published *Breaking the Mold: Women, Men, and Time in the New Corporate World*.[3] More than twenty years later, in an interview for Strategy + Business (S + B), Bailyn continues to assert that 'work is completed most effectively ... when people are empowered to come together and figure out how to manage that work collectively, taking into account both the organization's needs and one another's needs outside the office.'[4] As a corollary, when both sets of needs are not reconciled, there is increased risk that employees will encounter stress and conflict between their work and nonwork roles.

To be clear, use of the term 'work-life' integration here is intentional. The case to be made is not limited to those with children living at home or to those who have demanding family roles or obligations. This is not solely a parenting or dependent care issue. More and more employers are acknowledging the many 'life' roles their

---

1. Stewart Friedman, *What Successful Work and Life Integration Looks Like*, Harvard Business Review (7 October 2014), https://hbr.org/2014/10/what-successful-work-and-life-integration-looks-like (accessed 13 January 2017).
2. ThirdPath Institute, *Integrated Life*, http://www.thirdpath.org/integrated-life/ (accessed 13 January 2017).
3. Lotte Bailyn, *Breaking the Mold: Women, Men, and Time in the New Corporate World* (Free Press 1993).
4. Laura W. Geller, *Lotte Bailyn Is Redefining the Rules of Work and Family*, Strategy + Business (10 August 2015) accessed http://www.strategy-business.com/article/00356?gko = 87b29 (13 January 2017).

employees have in addition to and outside of work, involving community, elder care, self-care, and overall well-being.[5]

Kossek and Friede (2006) describe three categories of employer support for work-life integration (which they discuss here in terms of work and family): (1) formal human resource policies and practices; (2) employment conditions; and (3) organizational cultures and norms.[6] They further organize human resource policies and practices into those that allow employees increased workplace flexibility, those that assist employees with their caregiving roles (e.g., employer-provided child or elder-care, financial support for dependent care), and those that provide employees facing challenges with emotional support (e.g., Employee Assistance Programs, hotline, or support groups). As an increasing number of employees in the modern workplace are calling for flexibility as a means to improve work-life integration, we will focus our attention on these specific policies and practices.[7]

[B] Workplace Flexibility

Workplace flexibility can take many different forms. It has been defined in the work and family research community as 'the ability of workers to make choices influencing when, where, and for how long they engage in work--related tasks.'[8] Workplace flexibility options that allow for modification of when an employee works while keeping the total amount of time worked constant include flexible or alternative schedules (where hours worked are not rigidly defined or differ from the office standard) and compressed work weeks (where the same number of hours are worked over a fewer number of days). Flexibility options that also offer adjustments to the total number of hours or how long an employee works include part-time/reduced hours, flex year/part-year work, leaves of absence, compensatory time, job-sharing, and phased retirement. Those that provide employees a choice of where to work for some or all of their time, often by taking advantage of technological advances in mobile applications and virtual networks, are referred to as telework, telecommute, or remote work.

However, flexibility only represents a particular subset of policies and practices that may be offered to help employees achieve better work-life integration. It is important to recognize workplace flexibility as best-suited to address structural challenges within an organization; without a complementary strategy to move the

---

5. Ellen E. Kossek and Alyssa Friede, *The Business Case: Managerial Perspectives on Work and the Family*, in The Work and Family Handbook, Marcie Pitt-Catsouphes, Ellen E. Kossek, and Stephen Sweet (eds.) 612, 611–625 (Erlbaum 2006).
6. Ellen E. Kossek and Alyssa Friede, *The Business Case: Managerial Perspectives on Work and the Family*, in The Work and Family Handbook, Marcie Pitt-Catsouphes, Ellen E. Kossek, and Stephen Sweet (eds.) 612, 611–625 (Erlbaum 2006).
7. WorkplaceTrends.com and Career Arc, *2015 Workplace Flexibility Study*, https://workplacetrends.com/the-2015-workplace-flexibility-study/ (3 February 2015).
8. E. Jeffrey Hill, Joseph G. Grzywacz, Sarah Allen, Victoria L. Blanchard, Christina Matz-Costa, Sandee Shulkin, and Marcie Pitt-Catsouphes *Defining and Conceptualizing Workplace Flexibility*, 11(2) Community, Work & Family, 152, 149–163 (2008).

organization's culture, efforts to affect real and sustainable change in the organization have a reduced likelihood of success.[9]

[C] Workplace Culture

Edgar Schein, a leader in the field of organizational culture, has defined culture as:

> a pattern of shared basic assumptions that was learned by a group as it solved its problems of external adaptation and internal integration, that has worked well enough to be considered valid and, therefore, to be taught to new members as the correct way to perceive, think, and feel in relation to those problems.[10]

In the context of work-life initiatives, culture has been more specifically defined as the 'shared assumptions, beliefs, and values regarding the extent to which an organization supports and values the integration of employees' work and family lives.'[11]

Harrington and James (2006) discuss what they see as a disconnect between an organization's stated work-life policies and the extent to which those policies are actually implemented in practice; they propose that much of this discrepancy can be explained by the presence or absence of a supportive organizational culture.[12] Organizations that exemplify a work-life supportive culture have work-life policies and programmes that are used to a greater degree, resulting in positive outcomes for both the organization and its members.[13] In organizations with formal policies to help employees integrate their work and nonwork roles, a non-supportive work-life culture can weaken the effectiveness of those policies. In other words, the existence of these policies is a necessary but not sufficient condition for employees and organizations to reap the benefits; a positive and supportive workplace culture is a critical determinant of the policies' success.

Thompson et al. (1999) go on to describe three components of work-family culture, which we translate to work-life culture in order to extend beyond the family domain. The first component has to do with the degree to which an organization expects employees to prioritize work time over competing non-work demands, including norms about when, where, and how much an employee works. The second component of work-life culture relates to the 'perceived negative career consequences'

---

9. Ellen E. Kossek and Lewis S. Hammer, *Work-Life Initiatives and Organizational Change: Overcoming Mixed Messages to Move from the Margin to the Mainstream*, 63(1) Human Relations 3 (2010).
10. Edgar H. Schein, *Organizational Culture and Leadership*, 17 (3d ed, Jossey-Bass 2004).
11. Cynthia A. Thompson, Laura L. Beauvais and Karen S. Lyness, *When Work–Family Benefits Are Not Enough: The Influence of Work–Family Culture on Benefit Utilization, Organizational Attachment, and Work–Family Conflict*, 54(3) Journal of Vocational Behavior, 394, 392–415 (1999).
12. Brad Harrington and Jacquelyn B. James, *The Standards of Excellence in Work-Life Integration: From Changing Policies to Changing Organizations*, in The Work and Family Handbook, Marcie Pitt-Catsouphes, Ellen E. Kossek and Stephen Sweet (eds.) 665–682 (Erlbaum 2006).
13. Cynthia A. Thompson, Laura L. Beauvais, and Karen S. Lyness, *When Work–Family Benefits Are Not Enough: The Influence of Work–Family Culture on Benefit Utilization, Organizational Attachment, and Work–Family Conflict*, 54(3) Journal of Vocational Behavior 392–415 (1999).

of using work-life policies or programmes or devoting time to non-work activities or responsibilities, or what we now call 'flexibility stigma',[14] and includes norms about visibility or face time.[15] The third component of work-life culture centres on managerial support for employees' non-work activities or responsibilities.

For workplace policies and practices to have their intended, positive impact for both employees and their employers, it is critical that all components of work-life culture are aligned in their support. Comprehensive workplace redesign efforts have the potential to transform work in this way. As Kossek and Lautsch (2007) so astutely wrote:

> Most working men and women today want to succeed in every dimension of their lives. And when they do, their employers, families, and communities benefit, as do the individuals themselves. Organizations can reap their share of these benefits by transforming their cultures so that people have control over how they manage their priorities. The payoff? A more engaged, energized, and productive workforce, which translates directly into bottom-line performance. To make this change occur, we need to have dialogue to change unhealthy organizational cultures, and we need to remove barriers to redesigning work to support schedule control over where and when one works.[16]

[D] Workplace Redesign

Despite significant changes in the workforce since the 1950s, 'companies and organizations have not adapted to these new realities by changing how work gets done.'[17] Ignoring the many calls for change over the past decades, the forty-hour work week has remained ingrained in American society.[18] Technological advances that vastly improved efficiencies offered a promise of increased leisure time for American workers, but instead, expectations for production and profits increased. Tony Schwartz, founder of the Energy Project, observed that people are working more but never achieving enough.[19] In this work-first culture, those who work the most hours are the most likely

14. Joan C. Williams, Mary Blair-Loy, and Jennifer L. Berdahl, *Cultural Schemas, Social Class, and the Flexibility Stigma*, 69(2) Journal of Social Issues 209–234 (2013).
15. Cynthia A. Thompson, Laura L. Beauvais and Karen S. Lyness, *When Work–Family Benefits Are Not Enough: The Influence of Work–Family Culture on Benefit Utilization, Organizational Attachment, and Work–Family Conflict*, 54(3) Journal of Vocational Behavior 394, 392–415 (1999).
16. Ellen E. Kossek and Brenda A. Lautsch, *CEO of Me: Creating a Life That Works in the Flexible Job Age*, 158 (Wharton School 2007).
17. Redesigning, Redefining Work (RRW) Project and Summit, Stanford University Clayman Institute for Gender Research, http://gender.stanford.edu/redesigning-redefining-work-summit (accessed 15 January 2017).
18. Brigid Schulte, *Overwhelmed: How to Work, Love and Play When No One Has the Time*, 50 (Picador 2014).
19. Tony Schwartz, *The Way We're Working Isn't Working*, 3 (Free Press 2010).

to be deemed successful and committed, and hence rewarded and promoted. Employers continue to place a disproportionate value on face time, and a culture of overwork dominates in the US.[20]

American workers are constantly conflicted by the need to work and the need to care for oneself or others. A meta-analysis of the effects of workplace stressors on health outcomes concluded that work-life conflict is worse for one's health than second-hand smoke and that overwork increases the risk of death by 20%.[21] Loehr and Schwartz (2015) asserted that taking breaks from work to renew one's physical, emotional, mental and spiritual energy leads to higher levels of performance.[22] Thus, caring for oneself leads to increased productivity. These ideas run counter to American work norms that value long hours of work.

ThirdPath Institute frames organizational redesign in terms of creating a twenty-first century workplace. In it, all employees become experts in redesigning work to achieve a 'triple win' – a solution that is good for the employee, good for getting the work done, and good for the colleagues and clients of the employee. All members of the organization, individually and collectively, determine how to work flexibly to meet personal needs alongside the needs of the workplace.[23]

The mismatch between workforce needs and workplace design has left employees feeling unsupported in their work-life integration attempts, and evidence suggests there are business and economic consequences.[24] In response to this identified problem, a national conversation on how to reimagine and redesign work has begun.[25] Work-life integration represents a core value behind this movement.

[E] From Workplace Flexibility to Work-Life Integration: The 3A Model

In thinking through the workplace redesign process, we posit a three phase model of Accommodation, Acceptance, and Adaptation, or 3A Model, that describes how a paradigm shift toward authentic work-life integration occurs within organizations. During the Accommodate phase, employers become willing to accommodate employees with caregiving needs that preclude them from being available at all times or for standard hours of work. Flexibility may be offered to employees on a case-by-case basis, yet the stigma associated with using this flexibility is widespread. In the Accept

20. Heather Boushey and Bridget Ansel, *Washington Center for Equitable Growth*, Overworked America: The Economic Causes and Consequences of Long Work Hours (16 May 2016). http://equitablegrowth.org/report/overworked-america/ (accessed 15 January 2017).
21. Joel Goh, Jeffrey Pfeffer, and Stefanos A. Zenios. *Workplace Stressors & Health Outcomes: Health Policy for the Workplace*, 1(1) Behavioral Science & Policy 43 (2015).
22. Jim Loehr and Tony Schwartz, *The Power of Full Engagement: Managing Energy, Not Time is the Key to High Performance and Personal Renewal*, 4, 40 (Free Press 2003).
23. ThirdPath Institute, *21st Century Workplace*, http://www.thirdpath.org/21st-century-workplace/ (accessed 15 January 2017).
24. Heather Boushey and Bridget Ansel, *Washington Center for Equitable Growth*, Overworked America: The Economic Causes and Consequences of Long Work Hours (16 May 2016). http://equitablegrowth.org/report/overworked-america/ (accessed 15 January 2017).
25. Redesigning, Redefining Work (RRW) Project and Summit, Stanford University Clayman Institute for Gender Research, http://gender.stanford.edu/redesigning-redefining-work-summit (accessed 15 January 2017).

phase, employers begin to recognize the mismatch between the workforce and the workplace and challenge work norms to integrate work and personal lives. Flexible work arrangements are stated as policies and offered more broadly to all employees or to categories of employees (e.g., non-union, US-based). Employers enter the Adapt phase when they intentionally modify the work culture to reflect the changing needs and conditions of the workforce. They strive to create a supportive workplace that lets go of ineffective Industrial era work norms in order to achieve the highest level of performance possible.

§5.03 THE CASE FOR WORK-LIFE INTEGRATION

[A] The Changing Workforce

The work norms of yesterday reflect the workplace of yesterday, but a closer look at the working population of the US today reveals just how much has changed since these norms were established. Add to this picture an understanding of the current labour market, and the business case for work-life integration grows even stronger.

[1] Job Market Changes

According to the US Bureau of Labor Statistics, there are now more job openings than job hires in the US. The number of hires has exceeded the number of job openings for most of the Job Openings and Labor Turnover Survey (JOLTS) history. Since February 2015, this relationship has flipped, with job openings outnumbering hires in most months.[26] Those vacancies are increasingly more challenging to fill, with a growing skills gap and rising attrition rates. Middle-skill jobs, which require more education than high school but less than a four-year degree, comprise the largest segment of the US labour market; as of 2014, middle-skill jobs accounted for 54% of US labour market, but only 44% of the country's workers were trained to the middle-skill level.[27] The average tenure for employees in the US, across age groups, was 4.2 years in January 2016, down from 4.6 years in January 2014; the median tenure of workers ages 55 to 64 (10.1 years) was more than three times that of workers ages 25 to 34 years (2.8 years) in 2016.[28] Considering that younger workers comprise a growing segment of the working population, it appears the competition to attract and retain talent is intensifying.

---

26. Bureau of Labor Statistics, US Department of Labor, *Job Openings and Labor Turnover Survey Highlights November 2016*, p. 2 https://www.bls.gov/web/jolts/jlt_labstatgraphs.pdf (accessed 14 January 2017).
27. National Skills Coalition, *United States' Forgotten Middle*, 27 August 2014 (accessed 17 January 2017).
28. Bureau of Labor Statistics, US Department of Labor, *Employee Tenure in 2016*, p. 1 https://www.bls.gov/news.release/pdf/tenure.pdf 22 September 2016 (accessed 17 January 2017).

[2] Shifting Roles of Men and Women at Home and at Work

Over the past seventy plus years, there have been significant shifts in the roles women and men play in American society, both in the workforce and at home. According to the US Bureau of Labor Statistics, less than 33% of women were in the workforce immediately following World War II;[29] by 1975, this rate had increased to about 47%,[30] and as of December 2016, 58% of women were counted as employed.[31] The increase in labour participation has been even more rapid for mothers, In March 2015, 70% of mothers with children under age 18 were in the labour force, up from 47% in 1975.[32] Meanwhile, the increase in American single-parent families has nearly doubled since 1975.[33]

These statistics demonstrate that the traditional breadwinner-homemaker household is largely a relic of the past, and a considerable proportion of the workforce is left with caregiving responsibilities outside of work. Meanwhile, work policies remain guided by Industrial Era labour laws and policies that were developed under old assumptions, including that workers could focus solely on work because someone else was managing their caregiving responsibilities for them (*see* Table 5.1). The 1950s model of an 'ideal worker' is 'someone who works at least forty hours a week year round. This ideal-worker norm, framed around the traditional life patterns of men, excludes most mothers of childbearing age.'[34] It has become clear that the ideal worker norm is no longer sustainable within the context of modern American society.

Table 5.1 Changing Assumptions of Worker, Work, and the Workplace

Old Assumptions	*Proposed Modern Assumptions*
Ideal worker	Ideal modern worker
Focused on work only	Focused on work as one of several integrated domains of life
Men dominate the workforce	All adults work

29. Bureau of Labor Statistics, US Department of Labor, *BLS Reports December 2015 Report 1059: Women in the Labor Force: A Data Book*, p. 1, https://www.bls.gov/opub/reports/womens-databook/archive/women-in-the-labor-force-a-databook-2015.pdf updated 9 December 2016 (accessed 15 January 2017).
30. Women's Bureau, *U.S Department of Labor, Working Mothers Issue Brief*, p. 1, https://www.dol.gov/wb/resources/WB_WorkingMothers_508_FinalJune13.pdf June 2016 (accessed 15 January 2016).
31. Bureau of Labor Statistics, US Department of Labor, *The Employment Situation – December 2016*, p. 6, https://www.bls.gov/news.release/pdf/empsit.pdf (accessed 15 January 2017).
32. Women's Bureau, *U.S Department of Labor, Working Mothers Issue Brief*, p. 1, https://www.dol.gov/wb/resources/WB_WorkingMothers_508_FinalJune13.pdf June 2016 (accessed 15 January 2016).
33. Women's Bureau, *U.S Department of Labor, Working Mothers Issue Brief*, p. 1, https://www.dol.gov/wb/resources/WB_WorkingMothers_508_FinalJune13.pdf June 2016 (accessed 15 January 2016).
34. Joan Williams, *Unbending Gender: Why Family and Work Conflict and What to do About it*, 2 (Oxford University Press 2000).

Old Assumptions	*Proposed Modern Assumptions*
Worker relies on someone else to handle caregiving responsibilities	Worker also has caregiving responsibilities
Work happens for forty hours in a week and during a prescribed schedule	Workload and schedule may vary based on business and worker needs
Work is completed in the workplace	Work is completed anywhere
More time spent at work leads to greater productivity	Productivity cannot be measured only by time at work
Workers' hours and schedule must be closely monitored to ensure productivity	Adults are trusted to determine when and where to do their work as long as productivity goals are met

Add to this evolving picture the reality that parenting roles have changed, and the situation becomes even more dire. Men are picking up caregiving roles and responsibilities that were traditionally relegated to women in the past, creating an even greater mismatch between current organizational policies and work-life integrated cultures. As a group, modern fathers are more involved with their children than those of previous generations, but they are also experiencing unprecedented levels of work-family conflict.[35] As Levs (2015) writes:

> Why hasn't the corporate world kept up with American family life? Because the people in power are often oblivious to the realities of modern families....It's a vicious cycle. People who don't have a family or make it a priority are rewarded in the workplace. They rise to positions of power. They, then, are responsible for the rules and culture.[36]

Those in the minority who have workplace flexibility policies available to them not only still face a prevalent flexibility stigma associated with taking advantage of these policies but also risk reducing their earnings potential and limiting future career opportunities.[37]

'Today's families report feeling insecure and pressed for time, whether they're high-achieving-dual-career couples, low-income single mothers, or the middle-class families in between. For all kinds of families across the income spectrum, the dual demands of home and out-of-home work cause significant stress.'[38] To help reconcile their work, non-work, and caregiving demands, employees are placing a greater value

35. Gayle Kaufman, *Superdads: How Fathers Balance Work and Family in the 21st Century* (NYU Press 2013).
36. Josh Levs, *All In: How Our Work-First Culture Fails Dads, Families, and Businesses – and How We Can Fix It Together*, 2 (Harper One 2015).
37. Scott Coltrane, Elizabeth C. Miller, Tracy DeHaan, and Lauren Stewart, *Fathers and the Flexibility Stigma*, 69(2) Journal of Social Issues 279 (2013).
38. Heather Boushey, *Finding Time: The Economics of Work-Life Conflict*, 7–8 (Harvard University Press 2016).

on workplace flexibility.[39] In early 2015, WorkplaceTrends.com, a human resource research and advisory membership service, and CareerArc, a global recruiting and outplacement firm, released results from their 2015 Workplace Flexibility Study. They found that 75% of working adults rank workplace flexibility as the most important benefit they desire.[40]

[3] From Baby Boomers to Millennials

According to 2015 data from the US Census Bureau, Millennials, defined by the Pew Research Center as those born between 1981 and 1997, have surpassed the Baby Boomers (born between 1946 and 1964) as the largest living generation numbering 75.4 million.[41] They also recently became the largest generation in the American labour force.[42] Meanwhile, Baby Boomers have been retiring in large numbers every year since 2008, when the oldest members reached eligibility age for Social Security benefits. While some are delaying retirement due to financial pressures, others are considering phased retirement, where they can remain with their current employer and gradually reduce their work hours over time.[43] The combination of these trends is changing the face of the workforce as well as the demand for increased flexibility at work.

Much has been written about the Millennial generation, in particular, as hiring managers compete to attract and retain new talent. Deal and Levenson (2016) reported that Millennials feel entitled to integrate life and work from their first day on the job rather than having to earn a right to it. In fact, they do not want to jeopardize their quality of life for a fulfilling career. Millennials want time for personal activities and interests, not just time with their families. They desire flexibility, a manageable workload, and the ability to control where and when they work, but they have concerns that organizations and managers are not supportive of their values and fear they will risk advancing their careers if they take advantage of work-life policies and

39. The Council of Economic Advisors, Executive Office of the President of the United States, *Work-life Balance and the Economics of Workplace Flexibility*, https://www.whitehouse.gov/sites/default/files/docs/updated_workplace_flex_report_final_0.pdf 2014 (accessed 15 January 2017).
40. WorkplaceTrends.com and Career Arc, *2015 Workplace Flexibility Study*, https://workplacetrends.com/the-2015-workplace-flexibility-study/ (3 February 2015).
41. Richard Fry, Pew Research Center, *Millennials Overtake Baby Boomers as America's Largest Generation*, http://www.pewresearch.org/fact-tank/2016/04/25/millennials-overtake-baby-boomers/ 15 April 2016 (accessed 15 January 2017).
42. Richard Fry, Pew Research Center, *Millennials Surpass Gen Xers as the Largest Generation in the U.S. Labor Force*, http://www.pewresearch.org/fact-tank/2016/04/25/millennials-overtake-baby-boomers/ 11 May 2015 (accessed 15 January 2017).
43. Robert Hutchens, Center for Retirement Research at Boston College, *Phased Retirement: Problems and Prospects*, http://crr.bc.edu/wp-content/uploads/2007/02/wob_8.pdf February 2007 (accessed 15 January 2017).

programmes.[44] The sheer numbers of Millennials in the workforce and their willingness to vocalize what they want may encourage more employers to recognize the value of workplace flexibility for acquiring and retaining a talented workforce.

[4] The Growing Gig Economy

Changes in the demographics of the workforce suggest that organizations will need to adapt in order to compete for talent.[45] Now, not only are employers competing with each other for talent, but they are increasingly competing with the 'gig economy', otherwise known as the 'agile workforce', or those people who are self-employed, working in a temporary, freelance, contract, consultant, or project-based capacity.

While this type of independent working arrangement is not new, the advent of companies that connect workers with jobs through websites or mobile applications is a more recent development that has made finding such work easier. The Workplace 2025 Study by Randstad U.S., a polling of 1,500 executives and 3,160 workers, found that agile workers are expected to comprise as much as 50% of the workforce by 2019.[46] The most common reasons cited for this growth are the belief that agile work can generate more income and better professional growth opportunities than traditional employment,[47] along with an increased desire among workers to have the freedom to manage their own work and lives outside of work.[48] At the same time the demand for agile workers is increasing, employers are realizing the benefits of an on-demand workforce to help them meet business demand in a fast-moving, just-in-time environment.[49]

Organizations that address employees' needs for flexibility will maintain a competitive advantage. Further, once employers genuinely understand the degree to which work lives and personal lives are interdependent, new norms and workplace cultures will develop that are in better alignment with our modern workforce.

---

44. Jennifer J. Deal and Alec Levenson. *What Millennials Want from Work: How to Maximize Engagement in Today's Workforce* (McGraw-Hill 2016).
45. Jeanne C. Meister, and Karie Willyerd, *The 2020 Workplace: How Innovative Companies Attract, Develop, and Keep Tomorrow's Employees Today* (Harper Collins 2010).
46. Randstad, *Workplace 2025: Embracing Disruption in a Post-Digital World*, https://www.randstadusa.com/workforce360/workplace-2025/demystifying-the-future-workforce/ (accessed 8 January 2017).
47. Randstad, *Workplace 2025: Embracing Disruption in a Post-Digital World*, https://www.randstadusa.com/workforce360/workplace-2025/demystifying-the-future-workforce/ (accessed 8 January 2017).
48. Cindy Krischer Goodman, *2017 Looks Like it Will be a Big Year for Workplace Flexibility*, Miami Herald, http://www.miamiherald.com/news/business/biz-columns-blogs/cindy-krischer-goodman/article123839719.html (1 January 2017).
49. Randstad, *Workplace 2025: Embracing Disruption in a Post-Digital World*, https://www.randstadusa.com/workforce360/workplace-2025/demystifying-the-future-workforce/ (accessed 8 January 2017).

[B] Business Benefits of Work-Life Integration

[1] Summary of Research

Visionary business leaders are discovering that changes in workforce demographics are creating a need for workplace cultures to evolve to embrace work-life integration in order to remain productive and profitable. These leaders recognize that people who are engaged in their work and working toward achieving their organization's goals are their most valuable asset.[50] In the US industrial economy, the market value of a company was largely determined by tangible assets such as buildings, land, machinery, and equipment. But in our modern service economy, 75% to 84% of the market value of a company is determined by intangible assets. People, or more precisely the skills people bring to work, are an intangible asset.[51] The value of a company is now largely determined by the value of its people. According to the Conference Board's 2016 CEO Challenge Survey, CEOs' number one concern is people.[52]

Employers need to ensure they have the people they need to meet their business objectives, and offering work-life policies and programmes is a proven way to attract and retain talent and reduce absenteeism and turnover. Research supports other business benefits of work-life programmes, including improved financial performance and shareholder value, increased productivity, and reduced costs.[53]

McNamara et al. (2012) identified a number of additional motivators for employers, including to increase employees' job commitment and engagement, to 'do the right thing' for employees, and to improve morale.[54] Employee engagement has been shown to be strongly connected to business outcomes essential to an organization's financial success, such as productivity, profitability and customer engagement.[55] Conversely, the costs of a disengaged workforce are steep, running into the trillions of dollars.[56] The link between workplace flexibility and employee engagement is supported by a Corporate Voices for Working Families study which concluded that workplace

50. Influenced by the concept of people equity developed by Dr William A. Schiemann author of *Reinventing Talent Management: How to Maximize Performance in the New Marketplace* (John Wiley & Sons 2009) and *The ACE Advantage: How Smart Companies Unleash Talent for Optimal Performance* (Society for Human Resource Management 2012).
51. Jeff Higgins, *Bringing HR and Finance Together with Analytics*, Presentation at the University of Saint Thomas People Analytics Conference, Minneapolis (24 March 2016).
52. Conference Board CEO Challenge 2016 https://www.conference-board.org/ceo-challenge2016/ (accessed 12 January 2017).
53. Fred Van Deusen, Jamie Ladge, Jacquelyn James, and Brad Harrington, *Boston College Center for Work & Family, Building the Business Case for Work-Life Programs*, Boston College Center for Work & Family Executive Briefing Series 2008 https://www.bc.edu/content/dam/files/centers/cwf/research/pdf/BCCWF_Business_Case_EBS.pdf (accessed 15 January 2017).
54. Tay K. McNamara, Melissa Brown and Marcie Pitt-Catsouphes, *Motivators for and Barriers Against Workplace Flexibility; Comparing Nonprofit, for-Profit, and Public Sector Organizations*, 15(4) Community, Work & Family, 491, 487–500 (2012).
55. Gallup 2015 Engagement Survey http://www.gallup.com/poll/188144/employee-engagement-stagnant-2015.aspx (accessed 13 January 2017).
56. Jim Loehr and Tony Schwartz, *The Power of Full Engagement: Managing Energy, Not Time Is the Key to High Performance and Personal Renewal*, 6 (Free Press 2003).

flexibility increases employee retention and engagement, leading to a reduction in turnover costs and greater customer loyalty, ultimately increasing profits for shareholders.[57]

[2] Case Studies

As the demand for talent increases, organizations should consider how flexible work arrangements could increase the pool of qualified applicants for open positions. Arise Virtual Solutions, a leading provider of call centre services, discovered that offering telework increased their access to sources of talent including military spouses, retirees, stay-at-home parents, and people with disabilities. Telework reduced the company's building and real estate expenses, decreased the cost of turnover, and increased their customer service quality and consistency.[58]

Lifetrack, a Minnesota-based non-profit organization working to strengthen families, also found that employees believe having the option to telework is a great benefit. Telework has helped the organization retain employees which reduces costs. It has also helped employees do their best work, which in turn increased productivity.[59]

AFLAC offers a variety of insurance products to over 40 million people worldwide. The company recognized a business need to provide services beyond the traditional 8:00 a.m. to 5:00 p.m. work day. So, the company offered employees the opportunity to work four 10 hour days or three 12 hour days by selecting a shift between 6:30 a.m. and 11:00 p.m. This move not only allowed the company to provide better customer service, it gave employees more schedule control making them happier, more effective and more productive. Giving employees more control over their schedules benefitted the employees, the customers and the company. This in turn had a positive impact on the company's bottom line.[60]

Rossetti is an award-winning design company with expertise and experience in architecture, interior design, and graphics. Employees work flexible hours that may vary according to the season. The company says that having flexible work schedules allows them to attract better employees. And, by having their work and personal lives better in balance, those workers are able to stay better committed to their jobs. This in turn contributed to better overall performance for the company.[61]

The First Bank of Tennessee trained managers at some of its branches on flexibility practices. These managers focused on creating a work environment that was

57. Corporate Voices for Working Families, Business Impacts of Flexibility: An Imperative for Expansion, 12 (2011). https://www.wfd.com/PDFS/BusinessImpactsofFlexibility_March2011.pdf (accessed 13 January 2017).
58. Arise Telework Model, eworkplace Minnesota case study (2016). http://www.eworkplace-mn.com/wp-content/uploads/2015/03/AriseEmployerCaseStudy.pdf (accessed 14 January 2017).
59. Beth Quist, YouTube video posted on www.eworkplace-mn.com (2016). (accessed 13 January 2017).
60. AFLAC Case Study: https://workfamily.sas.upenn.edu/static/casestudy#aflac (accessed 13 January 2017).
61. Rosetti case study (https://workfamily.sas.upenn.edu/static/casestudy#Rosetti) and http://t.rossetti.com/theword/ROSSETTI-RECOGNIZED-FOR-EXEMPLARY-WORKPLACE-PRACTICES (accessed 13 January 2017).

supportive of flexibility and of people's personal lives. The result was that employee retention in the branches with flexibility practices proved to be 50% higher than in other branches. This, in turn, contributed to a greater retention rate of customers at these branches. The bank demonstrated that as employee satisfaction increased, customer retention increased by 7%, which translated into a USD 106 million profit increment in two years' time.[62]

Investing in employees' well-being may also decrease costs for a company. TURCK develops, designs and manufactures technology products. This manufacturing company with a very diverse population of about 500 employees, decided to create a culture of well-being. All employees are eligible for a flexible work arrangement that may include flexible schedules, telework or sabbaticals. Their culture of well-being evolved over many years as the leadership team listened to employees' ideas. Within the manufacturing facility, employees take stretch breaks and there is a walking path. There is an onsite clinic and pharmacy and employees have access to a wellness coach. Recently, the employees were given the opportunity to participate in a Community Supported Agriculture (CSA) programme that provides employees with a share of organic produce weekly through a subsidized payroll deduction.[63] By investing in the well-being of their employees, TURCK has reduced turnover costs and boasts a turnover rate between 1% and 4% when the industry average is between 11% and 15%. In addition to reducing costs by lowering turnover rates, TURCK's well-being initiatives have resulted in creating a healthier population and lower health care costs, as compared to normative data.[64]

Numerous case studies demonstrate how work-life policies, practices and programmes have reduced costs, increased profits and increased productivity. The 2014 National Study of Employers found that retaining and recruiting employees as well as increasing productivity are the most cited reasons for providing employee supportive programmes.[65] Being able to attract, acquire and retain people during a time of increased competition for talented employees is a powerful incentive for companies to develop supports for work and personal life.

§5.04 THE CURRENT STATE OF PAID FAMILY LEAVE IN THE US

In this age of competition for talent, one tangible benefit employers would be wise to offer American employees, in the absence of a federal mandate, is paid family leave (PFL). PFL is a fundamental 'flexibility' policy that supports employees at times when

62. Corporate Voices for Working Families, Business Impacts of Flexibility: An Imperative for Expansion, 18 (2011). https://www.wfd.com/PDFS/BusinessImpactsofFlexibility_March2011.pdf (accessed 13 January 2017).
63. Conversation with Kirk Larson, human resources director, TURCK, March 22, 2016. Presentation by TURCK at the Twin Cities Work Life Think Tank, May, 2015.
64. Lora Geiger, *Culture Development: Evolution of Well-being at TURCK*, 4(2) Worksite Health International (July 2013).
65. Kenneth Matos and Ellen Galinsky, 2014 National Study of Employers, Families and Work Institute http://familiesandwork.org/downloads/2014NationalStudyOfEmployers.pdf (accessed 14 January 2017).

family members need extra care. Companies interviewed by Fast Company cited a range of benefits of PFL, such as attracting and retaining talented workers, increasing staff diversity, and avoiding the expense of hiring and training new employees, all of which can directly affect the bottom line.[66]

A commitment to PFL signals to all employees, not just those planning to have children, the organization's value for their lives outside of work. Once PFL policies are implemented broadly and the taking of this leave (by both men and women) becomes the cultural norm, we foresee that changes in workplace attitudes toward work-life integration and increased flexibility will follow. At this moment in time, members of both the private and public sector are beginning to recognize the significance of paid leave.

[A] Private Sector Policies

The 2016 Bright Horizons Modern Family Index sampled 515 employed women expecting their first child or currently planning to have their first child in the next two years and 665 women and men who had their first child in the past two years and returned to work. The resulting study reported roughly half of new parents changed jobs, sacrificing salary for more 'family friendliness', and 78% considered leaving their employer after the birth of their first child.[67] A 2016 Deloitte Parental Leave Survey of 1,000 part and full-time employed adults across the US found that half of all respondents would rather have more parental leave time than a pay raise.[68] Other studies have suggested that offering paid leave and flexibility at work can increase employee engagement, a factor that is also linked with retention.[69]

Knowing it can cost in the range of 16% to 20% of an employee's salary to hire a replacement, employers have a strong financial incentive to entice new parents to stay.[70] Organizations that have revised and improved their paid leave benefits have recognized the impact on both employee recruitment and retention, including the costs

66. Lydia Dishman, *How Paid Parental Leave Changed in 2016*, Fast Company, https://www.fastcompany.com/3066856/the-future-of-work/how-paid-parental-leave-changed-in-2016 (28 December 2016).
67. Bright Horizons, *When's the Best Time to Start a Family? New Study Says: Ask the Boss!*, http://www.brighthorizons.com/about-us/press-releases/modern-family-index-2016 (17 October 2016); Bright Horizons, *Modern Family Index 2016: Labor Pains: What Employees Expect When They're Expecting*, http://solutionsatwork.brighthorizons.com/~/media/519B7725718044AD943F80F33358E0E1 (accessed 9 January 2017).
68. Deloitte. *Parental Leave Survey*, https://www2.deloitte.com/content/dam/Deloitte/us/Documents/about-deloitte/us-about-deloitte-paternal-leave-survey.pdf (2016).
69. EY, *Global Generations: A Global Study on Work-Life Challenges Across Generations: Detailed Findings*, http://www.ey.com/Publication/vwLUAssets/EY-global-generations-a-global-study-on-work-life-challenges-across-generations/$FILE/EY-global-generations-a-global-study-on-work-life-challenges-across-generations.pdf (2015); Madison Solheid, *Do Parental Leave Policies Affect Employee Engagement at Firms in the United States?* accessed from the University of Minnesota Digital Conservancy, http://hdl.handle.net/11299/181417 (2016).
70. Heather Boushey and Sarah Jane Glynn, Center for American Progress, *There Are Significant Business Costs to Replacing Employees*, https://cdn.americanprogress.org/wp-content/uploads/2012/11/CostofTurnover.pdf (16 November 2012).

associated with turnover.[71] In a January 2016 blogpost, Susan Wojcicki, the CEO of YouTube (a Google company), shared 'the research – and Google's own experience – shows a generous paid maternity leave actually increases retention....When Google increased its paid maternity leave policy from 12-to-18 weeks, we saw the rate at which new mothers quit fall by 50 percent.'[72]

It seems many employers are taking notice. The list of companies offering expanded paid parental leave in the US has taken off in last several years, with the technology sector leading the charge. In 2015, Facebook, Netflix, Adobe, Amazon, and Microsoft joined Yahoo, Apple, and Google in expanding paid leave to birth and adoptive parents regardless of gender. Etsy and Twitter joined their ranks in 2016, as did a number of large companies outside the technology industry, including IKEA, 3M, and Ernst & Young. According to the Society for Human Resource Management (SHRM) annual Employee Benefits Surveys, the percentage of surveyed companies offering paid maternity leave jumped from 21% in 2015 to 26% in 2016, while the percentage of those offering paid paternity leave also increased, from 17% in 2015 to 21% in 2016.[73] It would not be surprising if more companies decide to strengthen their parental leave benefits in 2017.[74]

Although this trend has been moving in a positive direction, according to the US Bureau of Labor Statistics, as of March 2016, only 13% of private industry workers had access to any PFL, up only 2% from March 2012.[75] In other words, at least 100 million Americans had no access to PFL in 2016.[76] A report by the non-profit group Paid Leave for the US (PL+US), an organization advocating for PFL for all American workers, concurs that progress on this issue has not been sufficient; two-thirds of the country's

71. Heather Boushey and Sarah Jane Glynn, Center for American Progress, *The Effects of Paid Family and Medical Leave on Employment Stability and Economic Security*, https://www.americanprogress.org/wp-content/uploads/issues/2012/04/pdf/BousheyEmploymentLeave1.pdf (April 2012).
72. Susan Wojcicki, *Closing the Tech Industry Gender Gap*, Huffington Post, http://www.huffingtonpost.com/susan-wojcicki/tech-industry-gender-gap_b_9089472.html?1453912334 (27 January 2016).
73. Society for Human Resource Management, *2015 Employee Benefits: An Overview of Employee Benefits Offerings in the U.S.*, https://www.shrm.org/hr-today/trends-and-forecasting/research-and-surveys/Documents/2015-Employee-Benefits.pdf (June 2015); Society for Human Resource Management, *2016 SHRM Employee Benefits Full Report*, https://www.shrm.org/hr-today/trends-and-forecasting/research-and-surveys/Documents/2016 SHRM Employee Benefits Full Report.pdf (June 2016).
74. Lydia Dishman, *How Paid Parental Leave Changed in 2016*, Fast Company, https://www.fastcompany.com/3066856/the-future-of-work/how-paid-parental-leave-changed-in-2016 (28 December 2016).
75. Bureau of Labor Statistics, US Department of Labor, *National Compensation Survey: Employee Benefits in the United States, March 2012*, https://www.bls.gov/ncs/ebs/benefits/2012/ebbl0050.pdf (September 2012); Bureau of Labor Statistics, US Department of Labor, *National Compensation Survey: Employee Benefits in the United States, March 2016*, https://www.bls.gov/ncs/ebs/benefits/2016/ebbl0059.pdf (September 2016).
76. Bureau of Labor Statistics, US Department of Labor, *Employee Benefits Survey: Appendix Table 2. Number of Workers Represented, March 2016*, https://www.bls.gov/ncs/ebs/benefits/2016/appendixtable2016_02.htm.

sixty largest companies, as measured by their number of US-based employees, have either no paid leave policy or one that they have not publicly disclosed.[77]

A closer look at the US Bureau of Labor Statistics reports shows the gap in access to PFL is widening between higher income managerial level employees, particularly those in larger companies, and their lower-wage counterparts in other roles. For instance, between 2012 and 2016, 11% more workers in professional and technical services organizations (27% in 2016) gained PFL benefits. In 2016, 24% of the top quartile of wage earners in private industry had access to PFL, while 6% of those in the bottom quartile had such access.[78] In other words, what we are seeing is more highly paid private sector workers getting this benefit while little change is happening for lower wage earners.

This finding in private industry is in contrast to employees in state and local government, where access to PFL has remained stable, at 16% of all workers in 2012 and in 2016. Among these workers, the PFL access gap between higher and lower wage workers is much less, at only a 3 percentage point difference between the top and bottom quartiles.[79]

Keep in mind that these figures exclude self-employed, independent contractor, gig, agile, and other workers who are ineligible for benefits from a permanent employer. The reported level of access is, in actuality, an over-representation of the current state of paid leave in the US. Moreover, it should be noted that the mere offering of a benefit is not enough to ensure the use of that benefit. Many workers, for various reasons, feel pressure to return to work quickly and leave time on the table.

According to results from the 2016 SHRM Employee Benefits Survey, men who receive PFL get on average twenty-two days compared to women's forty-one. On top of that discrepancy, the study reported that only 39% of men offered the paid benefit take all of their eligible time, compared with 63% of women.[80]

We may applaud companies for listening to employees' requests for greater flexibility, including paid leave, but simply including work-life policies in an employee

---

77. Paid Leave for the United States (PL + US), *Forging Ahead or Falling Behind? Paid Family Leave at America's Top Companies*, https://plus.nationbuilder.com/corporate (16 November 2016).
78. Bureau of Labor Statistics, US Department of Labor, *National Compensation Survey: Employee Benefits in the United States, March 2012*, https://www.bls.gov/ncs/ebs/benefits/2012/ebbl0050.pdf (September 2012); Bureau of Labor Statistics, US Department of Labor, *National Compensation Survey: Employee Benefits in the United States, March 2016*, https://www.bls.gov/ncs/ebs/benefits/2016/ebbl0059.pdf (September 2016).
79. Bureau of Labor Statistics, US Department of Labor, *National Compensation Survey: Employee Benefits in the United States, March 2012*, https://www.bls.gov/ncs/ebs/benefits/2012/ebbl0050.pdf (September 2012); Bureau of Labor Statistics, US Department of Labor, *National Compensation Survey: Employee Benefits in the United States, March 2016*, https://www.bls.gov/ncs/ebs/benefits/2016/ebbl0059.pdf (September 2016).
80. Society for Human Resource Management, *2016 SHRM Employee Benefits Full Report*, https://www.shrm.org/hr-today/trends-and-forecasting/research-and-surveys/Documents/2016SHRM Employee Benefits Full Report.pdf (June 2016).

handbook is not enough.[81] Policies will do little to effect change if they are implemented in isolation. Additional cultural supports are necessary for these policies to have their intended impact.

Employees report being hesitant to utilize work-life programmes because of the stigmas attached to them.[82] These stigmas exist because companies have failed to fully integrate work-life policies and practices into their culture. In the words of John Kotter, a preeminent authority on organizational change: 'until new behaviors are rooted in social norms and shared values, they are subject to degradation as soon as the pressure for change is removed.'[83]

At minimum, two critical supportive features must be present in an organization in order for work-life policies to drive organizational success. First, employees should have assurances that using the leave to which they are entitled will not negatively impact their careers; taking advantage of a leave programme must feel safe. Second, the organization's norms around accessing leave, and particularly paternity leave, need to be addressed and, in many cases, a culture shift is warranted.

To address these concerns, some companies are hiring trainers and coaches to help both employees and their managers understand how to manage their teams and their workloads and transition back to work under new paid leave policies.[84] In many instances, more expansive culture change programmes are justified in order to fully realize supports for the modern worker that simultaneously benefits the modern employer.

[B] Government Policies

The progress made by the private sector on paid leave is changing what Americans view as 'standard' and has the potential to spur on changes in policy at the state and even federal level. Government policy is better suited to help level the playing field, as not all employers are in a position to offer a paid leave benefit; larger businesses are more likely to have the resources to provide these kinds of benefits, while smaller companies have a difficult time competing. Government policies help ensure that people in all types of organizations regardless of size, and at all income levels, have equal access to programmes that help them manage their caregiving responsibilities.[85]

81. Joan C. Williams, Mary Blair-Loy and Jennifer L. Berdahl, *Cultural Schemas, Social Class, and the Flexibility Stigma*, 69(2) *Journal of Social Issues* 209–234 (2013).
82. Joan C. Williams, Mary Blair-Loy and Jennifer L. Berdahl, *Cultural Schemas, Social Class, and the Flexibility Stigma*, 69(2) Journal of Social Issues 209–234 (2013).
83. John P. Kotter, *Leading Change*, 14 (Harvard Business School Press 1996).
84. Tara Siegel Bernard, *Why Companies Have Started to Coach New Parents*, New York Times, 22 July 2016, http://www.nytimes.com/2016/07/23/your-money/why-companies-have-started-to-coach-new-parents.html (accessed 15 January 2017).
85. Heather Boushey, *Finding Time: The Economics of Work Life Conflict* (Harvard University Press 2016).

Of 185 countries and territories with information available, the US and Papua New Guinea are the only two that do not guarantee the right to paid maternity leave.[86] A February 2016 report from the Organization for Economic Cooperation and Development ranked the US last out of 41 developed nations due to its lack of a federal mandate for paid maternity leave. The fact that 31 of those 41 countries also mandate paid leave for fathers is further evidence of how far behind the US is on providing support to families.[87]

The effort to redesign work to better accommodate life outside of work is being advanced by proposed and existing policies around paid family medical leave at all levels of government in the US. There is hope that progress at the state level will help spur movement at the federal level, by establishing a solid body of evidence on the benefits of paid leave, thereby further highlighting the need for a federal programme.[88]

Three states are leading the way with their own PFL insurance programmes – California (established in 2004), New Jersey (established in 2009), and Rhode Island (2014); New York state recently passed a programme that will take effect in 2018. (Washington State passed a law in 2007, but the paid leave programme has not been enacted due to lack of a funding mechanism.) In each of these states, all workers make small payroll deductions which go into a state fund. When they need to take time off to care for a new-born, adopted child, or seriously ill relative, they get paid from that fund for up to six weeks, and employers are not responsible for paying their salaries. At least four other states (Massachusetts, New Hampshire, Oregon, and Washington) are making progress on passing PFL programmes; a number of cities are not waiting for state-level change and have enacted their own paid leave programmes, including Pittsburgh, Kansas City, Minneapolis, and Washington, DC.

In California, the state with the longest running PFL programme in the country, workers receive approximately 55% of their earnings up to a maximum weekly benefit of USD 1,173 (as of 1 January 2017) for up to six weeks during a twelve-month period.[89] The California PFL Act has been studied extensively over the last twelve years. Support for PFL in California has been found to cut across age groups, gender, education level, and political affiliation. A 2003 poll of adults in California to gauge public approval of the PFL Act found that 85% of all respondents were in favour of the programme.[90]

A 2016 study of the economic and social impacts of PFL in California found the programme was being widely utilized across gender, age, and income groups for both

86. International Labour Organization, *Maternity and Paternity at Work: Law and Practice Around the World*, http://ilo.org/wcmsp5/groups/public/---dgreports/---dcomm/---publ/documents/publication/wcms_242615.pdf (2014).
87. The Organisation for Economic Co-operation and Development, Social Policy Division, Directorate of Employment, Labour, and Social Affairs, OECD Family Database, *PF2.1: Key Characteristics of Parental Leave Systems*, http://www.oecd.org/els/soc/PF2_1_Parental_leave_systems.pdf (updated 28 February 2016).
88. Josh Levs, *Paid Family Leave Could be a Reality in Trump's America*, Time, http://time.com/4570075/donald-trump-paid-family-leave (14 November 2016).
89. State of California, Economic Development Department, *About Paid Family Leave*, http://www.edd.ca.gov/disability/About_PFL.htm (accessed 9 January 2017).
90. Eileen Appelbaum and Ruth Milkman, Hill Briefing, *Paid Family Leave: Lessons from California*, http://cepr.net/documents/presentations/Milkman_Appelbaum_briefing_Jan2014.pdf (30 January 2014).

bonding with a new-born or adopted child and caring for a seriously ill family member. That said, more women than men have used the benefit, with more claims for bonding than caring submitted. The majority of these women took the full six weeks of the benefit. Researchers have noted a substantial rise in claim rates by men since 2004. However, only about 40% of men took the full six weeks of bonding leave. This finding is consistent with gender differences in paid leave use in private sector companies, outside of California, that offer this benefit.[91]

This study also reported results on the impact of PFL use on job turnover. Bonding and caring claimants who remained employed for one year post-claim were more likely to stay with their pre-claim employer than to move to a different firm. Moreover, a review of all existing data on California employers from 2000 to 2014 found no evidence of increased wage costs or turnover rates associated with increased PFL claim rates. To the contrary, their analysis suggests reduced wage costs and turnover rates since the introduction of PFL in California.[92]

According to a 2011 study, most California employers reported that PFL had either a 'positive effect' or 'no noticeable effect' on productivity, profitability/performance, turnover, and employee morale.[93] In addition, paid leave has been associated with increased employee engagement and loyalty.[94] A January 2017, report by the Center for American Progress compiled findings from existing studies on PFL and concluded that it produces positive outcomes for businesses.[95] There is reason to believe these findings could be replicated at the national level if federal PFL became law.

Building on the successes of California's and other state level PFL programmes, the Family and Medical Insurance Leave Act, or FAMILY Act, was introduced to the 114th US Congress in March 2015. The proposed bill, which was not enacted, would have established a national insurance fund paid for by employee and employer payroll deductions of two-tenths of 1% of a worker's wages, or about USD 2 per week for a typical worker. The benefit would have provided up to twelve weeks of paid leave, during which workers would have received up to 66% of their earnings, to care for a new-born or adopted baby or seriously ill family member.[96]

---

91. Kelly Bedard and Maya Rossin-Slater, *The Economic and Social Impacts of Paid Family Leave in California: Report for the California Employment Development*, http://www.edd.ca.gov/disability/pdf/PFL_Economic_and_Social_Impact_Study.pdf (13 October 2016).
92. Kelly Bedard and Maya Rossin-Slater, *The Economic and Social Impact of Paid Family Leave in California: Report for the California Employment Development*, http://www.edd.ca.gov/disability/pdf/PFL_Economic_and_Social_Impact_Study.pdf (13 October 2016).
93. Eileen Appelbaum and Ruth Milkman, *Leaves that Pay: Employer and Worker Experiences with Paid Family Leave in California*, http://cepr.net/documents/publications/paid-family-leave-1-2011.pdf (2011).
94. National Partnership for Women & Families, *Fact Sheet: The Family and Medical Insurance Leave Act (The FAMILY Act)*, http://www.nationalpartnership.org/research-library/work-family/paid-leave/family-act-fact-sheet.pdf (March 2015).
95. Danielle Corley, Sunny Frothingham and Kate Bahn, Center for American Progress, *Paid Sick Days and Paid Family and Medical Leave Are Not Job Killers*, https://www.americanprogress.org/issues/women/reports/2017/01/05/295908/paid-sick-days-and-paid-family-and-medical-leave-are-not-job-killers/ (January 2017).
96. National Partnership for Women & Families, *Fact Sheet: The Family and Medical Insurance Leave Act (The FAMILY Act)*, http://www.nationalpartnership.org/research-library/work-family/

With the recent election of Donald Trump as president of the US, there is uncertainty about the future of a federal PFL programme. During his campaign, Donald Trump called for six weeks of paid maternity leave for birth mothers whose employers do not already offer coverage. While this could be viewed as progress from a current status of no paid leave for caregivers in the US, there is concern that this proposal does not go far enough and would hinder progress toward gender equity in parenting and in the workplace.[97] The current administration would be wise to heed a post-election poll of Trump voters who largely (68%) support a national PFL programme.[98]

The International Labour Organization, while strongly supporting the need for paid parental and adoption leave as a means 'to assist workers to reconcile work and family responsibilities,' has repeatedly cautioned governments to avoid implementing programmes that, in practice, reinforce traditional gender roles and stereotypes:

> Work–life balance measures, including quality working time schemes, (e.g., part-time work with pro-rata entitlements), should be made available to all women and men, irrespective of their sex and family status, as a way of effectively neutralizing the potential 'penalty' associated with being a worker with family responsibility.[99]

A growing number of private sector employers are realizing the business benefits of PFL. Such leave better equips employees to provide care for themselves and others while simultaneously increasing employee recruitment, engagement, and retention. PFL programmes administered by the government relieve the burden on employers and help level the playing field for businesses large and small. However, the positive impact of these policies is limited by their use. Stigmas and cultural norms that diminish the importance of caregiving and discourage leave-taking in the US must be addressed before the benefits of these programmes will be fully realized. Identifying the barriers to change along with strategies to adapt the workplace to fit the workforce are the next steps to moving work-life integration efforts forward.

---

paid-leave/family-act-fact-sheet.pdf (March 2015); *S. 786 – 114th Congress: Family and Medical Insurance Leave Act*. https://www.govtrack.us/congress/bills/114/s786 2015 (accessed 9 January 2017).

97. Josh Levs, *Paid Family Leave Could be a Reality in Trump's America*, Time, http://time.com/4570075/donald-trump-paid-family-leave (14 November 2016); Lydia Dishman, *How Paid Parental Leave Changed in 2016*, Fast Company, https://www.fastcompany.com/3066856/the-future-of-work/how-paid-parental-leave-changed-in-2016 (28 December 2016).
98. Center for American Progress and GBA Strategies, Memo RE: *American Voters Did Not Endorse Trump's Extremist Policy Agenda in 2016 Election*, https://cdn.americanprogress.org/content/uploads/2016/11/21072333/CAP-2016PostelectionPollingMemo-Final.pdf (accessed 9 January 2017).
99. International Labour Organization, *Maternity and Paternity at Work: Law and Practice Around the World*, http://ilo.org/wcmsp5/groups/public/---dgreports/---dcomm/---publ/documents/publication/wcms_242615.pdf, 69 (2014).

§5.05 MOVING WORK-LIFE INTEGRATION FORWARD

[A] Understanding the Barriers to Change

Work-life integration benefits both workers and employers. As we have shown, there are a number of compelling reasons for companies to adapt to work-life integrated cultures. In helping organizations move forward with work-life integration, it is important to be familiar with the potential barriers that may be preventing them from transforming. The most frequently cited barriers can be categorized into concerns about: equal treatment of all employees, absenteeism, implementation costs (coupled with a lack of payoff), cost-effectiveness, and limited employee interest.[100] Some employers fear the policies will be misused, implementing them will be costly and time-consuming, and clients and customers will not react favourably to the changes. Sharing research findings in support of work-life integration should help alleviate some of these misconceptions, as should providing targeted strategies aimed at transforming work culture.

[B] The 3A Model as a Framework for Paradigm Shift

The 3A Model is a tool to help organizations initiate dialogue about strategies to integrate work and life. This model outlines how organizations may perceive integration initiatives, from accommodation of employee needs to accepting the demand for change to adapting to new cultural norms that support work-life integration (*see* Table 5.2).

Table 5.2 3A Model

Accommodate	*Accept*	*Adapt*
Provide flexible work options	Develop supports for work and personal life Challenge existing work norms	Identify desired outcomes Adjust to new conditions Change culture

Changes in workforce demographics have created a demand for flexible work arrangements, and some companies have responded by accommodating employees' caregiving needs in order to retain them. Other employers recognize and accept the mismatch between the workforce and workplace and attempt to extend supports for work and personal life to all employees. When an organization changes the way they think about work, begins to focus on desired outcomes, adjusts to new conditions by redefining their values, modifies behaviours in support of work-life integration, and is intentional

100. Tay K. McNamara, Melissa Brown and Marcie Pitt-Catsouphes, *Motivators for and Barriers Against Workplace Flexibility; Comparing Nonprofit, for-Profit, and Public Sector Organizations*, 15(4) Community, Work & Family, 491, 487–500 (2012).

about creating a new culture, they have reached the Adapt phase of work-life integration.

[C] Strategies for Adapting the Workplace to Fit the Workforce

The need for strategies to adapt the workplace to fit the workforce, with an emphasis on work-life integration, has been established. These redesign efforts will help organizations adapt to new cultures better suited to support the modern workforce while achieving desired organizational outcomes. Five broad recommendations have emerged from the work-life literature. In addition, OpenWork and the Results Oriented Work Environment (ROWE) are presented as examples of workplace transformation strategies that have proven successful across organizations.

[1] Broad Recommendations

[i] Implement Organizational Culture Assessment

Organizational culture assessment is a useful tool to identify both an organization's current and ideal cultures. Successful transformation to a work-life integrated culture rests on having a clear and objective understanding of the shared norms and expectations in the organization. Implementing a culture assessment encourages honest discussion about the factors that support and promote culture change and growth, as well as those that create resistance and hinder performance.

[ii] Resist Overwork and Face Time

In order to develop successful twenty-first century organizations in the US, it is vitally important to address the current culture of chronic overwork and overemphasis on face time, both physical and virtual 'presence' in the office. This means collectively rejecting a system that reinforces and rewards these norms with pay and promotions. It also means recognizing that 'appearing to work' is not the same thing as productively contributing to an organization's business goals and bottom line. The challenge here is that time spent in the office is easily observed and measurable, while productivity can be complex and more difficult to quantify.

Changing the system starts with openly clarifying and establishing both the work and the non-work priorities that influence achievement of organizational goals. It also involves focusing on results and efficiency rather than on time as the measure of success. Training employees at all levels of the organization on how to manage and flex their time spent on work, to meet both personal and organizational goals, will encourage and bolster this transformation. Essentially, all employees must be supported to set appropriate boundaries around their appropriate levels of work and flexibility, while maintaining positive relationships with their customers, clients, and colleagues.

[iii] Offer Increased Flexibility

Establishing a flexible work environment is foundational to work-life integration, but flexibility can be defined in a plethora of ways, some of which are less advantageous than others. Work can be 'flexed' based on the when work happens, where work happens, how much work is undertaken (workload), how quickly work is produced (pace), and who does the work (delegated or shared), Yet, if flexibility means leaving work early to attend to caregiving responsibilities, and then picking work up again the moment those other responsibilities are attended to, personal wellness will not be achieved and burn-out is inevitable. This may fit the definition of flexibility, but it does not contribute to improved work-life integration.

In contrast, increasing the number of reduced workload or part-time positions available will help minimize burn-out and drive work-life integration. Making reduced work-load positions more available will also expand the pool of available workers, bringing in those who have left the workforce due to an inability to commit to full-time work. In a study of reduced workload professionals over time, findings suggest that reduced workloads enabled talented professional workers to remain in the workforce while maintaining the life outside of work they desired.[101]

Ultimately, successful flexibility is about offering choice--a variety of workload options to people who can manage different levels of workplace demands and have different financial needs--recognizing that everyone's 'balance' needs are unique. One potential solution to managing part-time staff is to shift to project-based rather than time-based work, and likewise billing, and to distribute assignments accordingly. Some employees will take on more projects than others; as long as rewards and promotions are distributed fairly and not reserved for those who assume the most work, this strategy will reinforce a supportive work-life culture.

[iv] Resist the Flexibility Stigma

In conjunction with offering increased flexibility, it is important to transition to new work norms that support rather than stigmatize those individuals who choose to benefit from the available options. Workplaces that facilitate open discussions of everyone's caregiving roles, and the challenges of combining them with work roles, lay the foundation for the use and acceptance of workplace flexibility.

The question remains, how can organizations resist flexibility stigma? The minimum requirement is to put flexibility policies in writing and make them available to everyone in the organization. More importantly, people have to use the flexibility policies in order for the culture to change, and organizations need to demonstrate support for flexibility, starting with the leaders modelling it. Once a norm (e.g., the taking of full paternity leave) is established, pressure to conform to the norm grows and reinforces the norm.

101. Douglas T. Hall, Mary D. Lee, Ellen E. Kossek, and Mireia Las Heras, *Pursuing Career Success While Sustaining Personal and Family Well-Being: A Study of Reduced-Load Professionals over Time*, 68(4) Journal of Social Issues, 741, 759 (2012).

[v] Measure Effectiveness

An important step in any workplace initiative is taking the time to measure and evaluate its effectiveness. Are efforts to increase flexibility contributing to employee recruitment, retention, and engagement? What has the impact been on turnover, absenteeism, productivity and the bottom line? How has the employee and customer experience changed since implementing the policy or programme? These are all questions to ask at all stages of a workplace redesign effort.

As the workforce described on the preceding pages is constantly evolving, the workplace will need to be prepared to change and adapt along with it in order to remain viable and successful. What was effective yesterday may not prove successful today. Meeting the changing needs of the workforce and the business requires ongoing evaluation, always re-evaluating the organizational culture relative to the workforce and assessing what policies and programmes are poised to offer the most benefit. Looking to competitors and other innovative organizations as a benchmark may also help inspire new strategies for workplace redesign to support work-life integration.

What the above recommendations share is an emphasis on providing workers with options for managing their work and their lives. There is not a one-size fits all workplace that will be successful across industries. As Moen et al. (2009) wrote: 'people live, work and raise their families in a dynamic, ever changing environment in which nothing is static – except perhaps the outmoded policies limiting their options.'[102] The twenty-first Century American workplace should instead encourage a values shift away from time invested in work and towards results as the measure of organizational performance and success. Reinforcing existing norms of overwork and face time above all else will only lead to more of the same, as will stigmatizing those who choose a different path of reduced workloads and increased flexibility. Measuring progress on redesign efforts, by assessing culture at the start and formatively evaluating success throughout, will ensure that organizational goals are met and that implemented changes evolve along with the dynamic workforce.

Specific workplace redesign strategies are available to guide organizations through the process. OpenWork and the ROWE are presented as two such examples.

[2] Workplace Transformation Models

[i] OpenWork

According to OpenWork.org: 'OpenWork happens when employees and employers collaborate to reinvent how work is done, for the benefit of all. To OpenWork means to break out of old patterns, establish new cultures of trust and accountability and

102. Phyllis Moen, Erin Kelly and Kelly Chermack, *Learning from a Natural Experiment: Studying a Corporate Work-Time Policy Initiative, Work -Life Policies*, Ann C. Crouter and Alan Booth (eds.) 120 (Urban Institute Press 2009).

create new ways of working to reap huge benefits.'[103] OpenWork provides a platform for encouraging dialogue, innovation and change in the workplace. It is a place for providing research, information and success stories about how flexible work increases job satisfaction, productivity, employee engagement, health and well-being, and employee retention.

OpenWork success stories test work norms, such as the norm of overwork in the US. Tower Paddle Boards disputed the notion that working long hours leads to greater productivity. Frustrated by seeing too many people in the office not working, the CEO of the company challenged employees to complete their day's work in five hours and if they did, they could spend the rest of the day any way they liked. After three months, the experiment was working so well they never returned to the traditional eight-hour work day. Working fewer hours resulted in higher revenues and increased employee loyalty.[104] This success story reveals that long hours of work may no longer be the best strategy for maximizing productivity.

OpenWork is strategic in providing a place to share success stories about integrating work and life that may inspire other organizations to challenge their existing norms. Competing with other organizations who are offering flexible work is a motivating factor for organizations to offer flexible work themselves.[105] These success stories have the potential to inspire more companies to develop supports for integrating work and life.

[ii] Results-Only Work Environment (ROWE)

The Results-Only Work Environment (ROWE) began by challenging the traditional notion of work. In a ROWE, work is something you do, not somewhere you go.[106] Managers manage work through ongoing conversations with individuals about goals, and they coach performance rather than manage people's time. ROWE 'was designed to move employees and supervisors from existing, implicit contracts about the expected amounts of *time at work* toward a more explicit contract based on what is *required by the job* and what are the appropriate measures of employees' *effectiveness in the job*.'[107] The purpose of a ROWE is to create and sustain a high performance work culture for the twenty-first century.[108]

---

103. OpenWork definition from the organization's website, www.openwork.org (accessed 15 January 2017).
104. OpenWork, *Open Work Case Study: Tower Paddle Boards*, http://www.openwork.org/tower-paddle-boards/ (accessed 15 January 2017).
105. Tay K. McNamara, Melissa Brown and Marcie Pitt-Catsouphes, *Motivators for and Barriers Against Workplace Flexibility; Comparing Nonprofit, for-Profit, and Public Sector Organizations*, 15(4) Community, Work & Family, 491, 487–500 (2012).
106. Cali Ressler and Jody Thompson, *Why Managing Sucks and How to Fix It*, 26–27 (John Wiley & Sons 2013).
107. Phyllis Moen, Erin Kelly and Kelly Chermack, *Learning from a Natural Experiment: Studying a Corporate Work-Time Policy Initiative*, in Work-Life Policies, Ann C. Crouter and Alan Booth (eds.) 103 (Urban Institute Press 2009).
108. ROWE mission defined on company website www.gorowe.com (accessed 12 January 2017).

Table 5.3 illustrates key differences between the traditional workplace and a ROWE workplace.

Individuals working in a ROWE focus on being productive and achieving results. They are given complete schedule control to determine how to spend the 168 hours available to them each week. There are not any schedules so no one may be considered late for work or criticized for leaving early. The focus is on how to meet outcomes rather than on time. All meetings are optional and may be conducted in person or virtually. Individuals and work teams figure out how to get the work done in an effective manner. There is no judgment about how you spend your time, and the workplace is laser-focused on the bottom line:[109]

> In a ROWE, people are getting more of what's important done in all aspects of their lives. And managers are setting clear and measurable goals on a continual basis, not as an annual or biannual event. Natural cross-training and an 'I've got your back' team mentality develops, compelling the group to team up on client [customer] needs in a seamless fashion. As a result, client satisfaction goes up.[110]

If an individual in a ROWE does not deliver results, the individual will no longer have a job.

Table 5.3 Traditional Workplace Compared to a ROWE Workplace

From	*To*
A focus on work hours (just being there or 'face time'); supervisor sets hours, schedules	A focus on job requirements (doing work well and on time); individual and team set hours, work times, schedules
Meetings are a regular part of work routine	Meetings held only as needed
Reliance on face-to-face interaction	Varied methods of virtual and transparent communication
A 'reactive' orientation, dealing with crises as they occur	A proactive orientation, early planning to avoid crises where possible
Flexibility arrangements negotiated between individual and supervisor	Flexibility is the norm; team members cross-train to cover for one another and set schedules
If work needs are met, presence is still required	Customized work time and schedules aimed at achieving goals
Essential ingredient: tracking employees' time spent working	Essential ingredient: defining specific nature of job and expectations
Problematic: absenteeism, tardiness, presenteeism	Problematic: not meeting job deadlines, expectations

109. Cali Ressler and Jody Thompson, *Why Managing Sucks and How to Fix It*, 8-13 (John Wiley & Sons 2013).
110. Cali Ressler and Jody Thompson, *Why Managing Sucks and How to Fix It*, 11 (John Wiley & Sons 2013).

Source: Phyllis Moen, Erin Kelly and Kelly Chermack, *Learning from a Natural Experiment: Studying a Corporate Work-Time Policy Initiative*, Work-Life Policies, 107, Eds. Ann C. Crouter and Alan Booth (Urban Institute Press 2009).

ROWE gives people autonomy to do their work and makes them accountable for getting it done.[111] Organizations that have adapted a ROWE culture boost employee performance through motivation – enhancing trust and providing autonomy.[112] Case studies and scholarly research find that ROWE increases productivity, employee well-being, work-life balance, organizational commitment, and job satisfaction while decreasing turnover.[113]

ROWE is an example of work redesigned in a manner that enables individuals to succeed at work and in their personal lives. 'ROWE renounces long hours, visible busyness, and accepting unplanned work as signs of commitment or productivity and validates the daily integration of work and personal life, including the prioritization of personal responsibilities.'[114] ROWE addresses the mismatch between the workforce and the workplace and is an example of a strategy that may be used to adapt to an integrated work-life culture.

Raising awareness of the workplace workforce mismatch and inviting people to rethink work may further propel a paradigm shift necessary for organizations to adapt to integrated work-life cultures. ROWE and OpenWork are two examples of strategies that are being used to shift our mindset from accommodating workers to adapting our organizational cultures to align with the modern workforce.

§5.06 CONCLUSIONS

This chapter presents a discussion about the mismatch between the modern workforce and workplace in the US and proposes that changes in workforce demographics require work redesign that prioritizes work-life integration. These efforts challenge work norms and long held beliefs about work. The evidence provided suggests that a paradigm shift will benefit both workers and their employers.

An overview of constructs was included to clarify their use throughout this paper. There has been a shift from talking about work-life balance and the competing demands on one's time to work-life integration that proposes a need to value the

111. Cali Ressler and Jody Thompson, *Why Managing Sucks and How to Fix It*, 6–7 (John Wiley & Sons 2013).
112. Monique Valcour, *The End of 'Results Only' at Best Buy Is Bad News*, Harvard Business Review March 8, 2013 https://hbr.org/2013/03/goodbye-to-flexible-work-at-be (accessed 14 January 2017).
113. Monique Valcour, *The End of 'Results Only' at Best Buy is Bad News*, Harvard Business Review March 8, 2013 https://hbr.org/2013/03/goodbye-to-flexible-work-at-be (accessed 14 January 2017); Phyllis Moen, Erin Kelly and Kelly Chermack, *Learning from a Natural Experiment: Studying a Corporate Work-Time Policy Initiative*, in Work-Life Policies, Ann C. Crouter and Alan Booth (eds.) 122 (Urban Institute Press 2009).
114. Erin Kelly, S Ammons, Kelly Chermack, and Phyllis Moen, *Gendered Challenge, Gendered Response: Confronting the Ideal Worker Norm in a White-Collar Organization*, 24 Gender & Society, 297–298 (2010).

domains of work and life outside of work and create supports that enable success in both. Work-life integration is not reserved for working parents but is a need and desire of all workers at all stages of the life cycle, regardless of age, gender, or family composition.

The 3A model was introduced to illustrate a continuum of work-life integration efforts in organizations. It is necessary to shift thinking about work-life policies and practices away from accommodating individuals who do not fit the accepted norms and toward adapting to a culture that integrates work and life for the benefit of both individuals and organizations.

The business case for work-life integration demonstrates a need for more flexible work environments driven by changes in the job market along with demographic changes in the workforce. Moreover, flexible work policies and practices produce favourable bottom line results. Success stories were included to illustrate the positive outcomes for workers and employers as well as to share ideas about how organizations are altering their practices and challenging work norms.

The need for the US to offer PFL to all workers is presented as the most critical policy for the government to support and implement. PFL for all lays the foundation that care for oneself and others is valued and important. There is a tremendous demand for supports for life outside of work, the success of which has the potential to benefit both employees and employers.

Considerations for moving work-life integration efforts forward are presented. Recommendations and strategies for adapting the workplace to fit the workforce are offered in pursuit of eliminating the American cultural norm of overwork and corresponding flexibility stigma, and hence creating more productive workplaces with employees who have time for their lives outside of work. OpenWork provides a platform for dialogue and for sharing stories about organizations that are challenging work norms successfully. This effort could lead to new insights for shaping an organizational culture that prioritizes work- life integration. The ROWE takes a different approach by creating a high performance work culture and a process for organizations to adapt to the new culture. This 'results only' culture relinquishes industrial constructs of time by giving people autonomy and trusting them to be accountable. ROWE responds to changing workforce demographics and the need for workplaces designed to support individuals' work-life integration while producing results for organizations.

In conclusion, the mismatch between the modern workforce and traditional workplace in the US is undeniable. Industrial workplace norms are not meeting the current needs of individuals or organizations. Individuals are expressing a growing desire for flexibility and support for work-life integration, and organizations need engaged workers who contribute to their productivity and profitability. Work-life policies and practices challenge work norms and deeply held beliefs about work, but introducing flexibility policies without addressing and adapting work culture will limit the impact of those policies. Following existing wisdom and strategies regarding workplace redesign will move this effort forward. However, considerable opportunity for innovation in this arena remains, and future research is encouraged.

CHAPTER 6

The Third Shift: How Do Professional Women Articulate Working Time and Family Time?

Émilie Genin

§6.01 INTRODUCTION

About thirty years ago, Hochschild and Machung[1] developed the concept of 'second shift' to illustrate the fact that women take care of most of the household and childcare responsibilities despite their massive entrance into the labour market. While the progress since then by women is undeniable, they still spend more time than men in housework and child care, even when they work full time in highly qualified jobs. As a consequence, professional women are particularly affected by work-family conflict.[2]

Work-family conflict is generally defined as the mutual incompatibility between work and family roles.[3] In spite of multiple efforts by researchers to demonstrate the vast array of adverse consequences associated with this conflict for employees – physical and mental health problems, stress, lower levels of job satisfaction, diminished satisfaction with family and personal life in general[4]- and employers as well as absenteeism, increased intention to quit, lower levels of productivity and work

1. A Hochschild & A Machung, *The Second Shift: Working Parents and the Revolution at Home*, New York, Avon books (1990).
2. É Genin, L'empiètement du travail des femmes et des hommes cadres sur leur vie personnelle. *Gestion, revue internationale de gestion*, 34 (3):128–136 (2009); S Parasuraman & C Simmers, Type of Employment, Work-Family Conflict and Well-Being: A Comparative Study. *Journal of Organizational Behavior*; 22(5): 551–568 (2001).
3. J Greenhaus & N Beutell, Sources of Conflict Between Work and Family Roles. *Academy of Management Review*, 10(1): 76–88 (1985).
4. F Amstad, L Meier, U Fasel, A Elfering & N Semmer, A Meta-Analysis of Work-Family Conflict and Various Outcomes with a Special Emphasis on Cross-Domain Versus Matching-Domain Relations, *Journal of Occupational Health Psychology*, 16(2): 151–169 (2011).

commitment[5]- organisational practices and cultures are still slow to change and public policies are not always sufficient to allow working parents to balance work and family life satisfyingly.[6] As a consequence employees, women in particular, are often left to their own devices when managing the different, even contradictory, demands of work and family. They have to adapt and find by themselves ways to balance work and family. In such a context, working from home may appear to be the best – or even the only – option for qualified women (i.e., professionals or managers) to achieve an acceptable balance. Recent research[7] has indeed shown that the latter tend to frequently resume work from home in the evening, at night or during weekends in order to deal with the heavy pressure from work and from home.

We have called this phenomenon the 'Third Shift'. This idea reflects a daily sequence characterised by work – family tasks – back to work. This articulation between work and family is facilitated by the use of mobile technologies.

Based on a literature review as well as on our own research (*see* methodological note), this chapter proposes to explore the third shift: its extent, its causes and consequences. To conclude, we discuss some of the issues raised by the third shift, namely, how it challenges existing public policies and patterns of work regulation, without challenging the traditional gendered division of work in the corporate and in the private spheres.

§6.02 METHODOLOGICAL NOTE

The examples and analyses presented in this chapter emerged from different research projects dealing with the interactions between personal and professional time. Two samples of data are used for the purpose of this chapter (i.e., defining and exploring the causes and consequences of the Third Shift phenomenon, one qualitative and one quantitative.

Sample 1

Sample 1 was collected in Quebec (Canada) between January 2011 and May 2012. It is composed of a set of first hand qualitative data.

The objective of the study for which it was collected was to cover a diversity of situations and not to present a statistically reliable portrait of the population of professionals and managers in Quebec. We thus selected participants using convenience sampling and the snowball method. First of all, organisations of various sectors

5. A Beauregard & L Henry, Making the Link between Work-Life Balance Practices and Organizational Performance. *Human Resource Management Review*, 19: 9–22 (2009).
6. D-G Tremblay & E Genin, Parental Leave: An Important Employee Right, but an Organizational Challenge. *Employee Responsibilities and Rights Journal*, 23(4):249–268 (2011).
7. Genin, *supra* note 2; É Genin, Proposal of a Theoretical Framework for the Analysis of Time Porosity, *International Journal of Comparative Labour Law and Industrial Relations* (2016); É Genin, Technologies mobiles et travail à la maison: mise à disposition ou mode de conciliation? *Interventions Économiques*, 53 (2015); É Genin, Quels facteurs influencent la satisfaction des cadres à l'égard de l'équilibre des temps (personnel et professionnel)? *@GRH*, 10(1), 87–107 (2014).

(public, semi-public, private) were identified. Contact was established with a human resources manager or a senior executive in each organisation to obtain the authorisation to carry out interviews. They also helped us to identify and contact possible participants. The latter were then invited by e-mail to participate in the research.

Twenty-one semi-structured interviews were then carried out with managers and professionals (six men and fifteen women) in the Montreal area (Quebec, Canada). The participants worked in varied fields of activity: health, education, cosmetics and bank/insurance services. They were from 27 to 58 years old, and eleven of them had children (of various ages from babies to adults). All the participants worked fulltime for a unique employer and none of them benefited from a formal telework agreement.

The method used for data collection was semi-structured interviews. The questions were organised following different themes such as: current position and working conditions; working time characteristics; work autonomy; use of the mobile technologies; work performed at the home and work-life balance.

All the interviews were entirely recorded and transcribed. Their duration varied from forty-five to ninety minutes. The data collected were subsequently coded and analysed using the thematic content method and the software QDA Miner (version 4).

Sample 2

Sample 2 is a second hand quantitative data set collected in France by through a Trade Union. The Work and TimeS Survey (*Travail et TempS*) was carried out electronically using the workers' union website for professionals and managers in the Spring of 2012. Participants were contacted directly by the union representative of their specific organisation; or, they accessed the survey directly from the union's website. Access to the survey was unlimited, meaning those participants who accessed the survey online and who freely participated were not required to be union members, although it is unlikely that non-union employees would have taken part. Out of the 3,282 responses obtained, there were 1,842 questionnaires suitable for research purposes; incomplete questionnaires or those filled out by workers who were neither professionals nor managers (their professions were cross-checked) were eliminated.

The sample was made up of 61% men and 39% women. The women in this survey were somewhat over-represented in comparison to the general population of professionals and managers in France, which consists generally of only 34% women.[8] The ages of participants ranged from 22 to 65 years, with an average age of 43. The average time already occupied in a professional position was 7.5 years. The majority of participants (62%) had at least one dependent child under 18: of these professionals and managers 31% had only one child while 48% had two children, 16% had three children and 5% had four or more children. We observe that in the sample there is a significant difference between men and women regarding this category of family life: of the women surveyed 41% did not have children, compared to 36% of the men. The

8. APEC, *Des inégalités professionnelles persistantes entre hommes et femmes cadres*; http://cadres.apec.fr/Emploi/Marche-Emploi/Enquetes-Apec/Enquetes-2011/Femmes-cadres-et-hommes-cadres-des-inegalites-professionnelles-qui-persistent (accessed on 2011).

men also had more children on average than the women (1.3 children per man compared to 1.1 children per woman).

The participants were classified into two subcategories: managers, including those with roles involving employee supervision, and professionals who do not supervise other employees but who possess a specific expertise giving them a similar level of status to that of a manager. Using this classification, the sample includes 47% managers and 53% professionals. Among the managers, 45% supervised between one and five people, 45% from six to fifty people and 10% supervised more than fifty-one people. Employee supervisory responsibilities were positively correlated with age. They were not, however, correlated with gender, which presents a divergence from previous studies[9] where women were less often in supervisory positions than men and usually led smaller teams.

Though the survey was mainly quantitative, containing questions on working time, working conditions, work-life balance, and job satisfaction; it also contained a section for qualitative comments and/or suggestions which was surprisingly well used. More than 300 qualitative comments of managers and professionals on their working conditions, working time, work-life balance and satisfaction in general were available for analysis.

§6.03 GENDER, WORK-FAMILY CONFLICT AND THIRD SHIFT

Many studies have demonstrated that professionals and managers are less satisfied with their work-life balance than workers in other categories of employment.[10] Indeed, the nature of their job induces particular sources of work-family conflict. For example, their work is often stressful, their roles ambiguous and their workload and hours spent at work are generally superior to those of other workers, which in turn generates conflict and dissatisfaction.[11] On the other hand, professionals and managers –men and women- also seem eager to find balance between their work and in other areas of their life.[12]

The analyses conducted on sample 2 confirm these findings. Approximately two thirds of the respondents say they are dissatisfied with work-life balance and lack time for their personal and family activities.

Gender is a very important variable to understand in order to address the variety of mechanisms involved in achieving work-life balance and the way gender makes an impact upon them more specifically. Most authors consider that the determinants of

9. APEC, *supra* note 4.
10. K Allard, L Haas & P Hwang, Exploring the Paradox: Experiences of Flexible Working Arrangements and Work-Family Conflict Among Managerial Fathers in Sweden, *Community, Work & Family*, 10(4): 475–493 (2007); Parasuraman & Simmers, *supra* note 2.
11. Allard et al. *supra* note 10; Amstad et al. *supra* note 4; M DiRenzo, J Greenhaus & C Weer, Job Level, Demands, and Resources as Antecedents of Work–Family Conflict, *Journal of Vocational Behavior*, 78(2): 305–331 (2011); Greenhaus & Beutell *supra* note 3.
12. Allard et al. *supra* note 10.

work-family conflict differ for men and women;[13] given women's traditional caregiving role, they still assume the lion's share of domestic and parenting work. Focusing on this gendered perspective, we can assume that any additional work hours represent a bigger source of work-family conflict for women than for their male counterparts. Considering that professionals and managers generally work longer hours than other categories of workers, work-family conflict is a bigger concern for women than for men in this employment category.

The analyses conducted in sample 2 tend to confirm this statement. There are actually important differences between men and women, in particular, the satisfaction related to domestic and family time is lower for women. For instance, 41% of men declare that they experience a satisfying balance whereas only 33% of women do think so. Additionally, 17% of women declare that balance is almost non-existent against 12% of men. Parents are also less satisfied than non-parents. Not surprisingly, parenting time is still mainly feminine. Important differences have been found between mothers and fathers: whereas 45% of mothers take care of the children every day (before and after work) and, only 31% of fathers do so. Furthermore, 18% of men never take care of the children (because of work) compared to 12% of women.

The results provided by sample 2 thus clearly confirm that (1) work-family conflict remains a huge issue among qualified workforce and; (2) women in this category of employment seem to experience higher levels of conflict that their male counterpart due to their traditional parenting and caregiver role. In sum, achieving work-life balance for professional women is often fraught with difficulties and rife with impediments, even if their positions give them access to more resources.

According to recent French surveys, one in four workers works at home on an occasional or regular basis and; this proportion rises up to 75% among managers and professionals.[14] In sample 2, we find the exact same percentage - 75%- declaring that they work at home. On average respondents work two hours a week from home and no significant differences are observed between men and women. However, the results of previous research[15] and the content analysis carried out with sample 1 tend to show that men and women work at home for different reasons. Women, mothers particularly, tend to work at home to better balance work and family while men do it for other reasons. To deal with the heavy pressure from work and from home, professional women frequently resume work from home in the evening, at night or during weekends in order to finish the work they have no time to do at the office. Given the difficulties they face to balance work and family, working from home may appear to be the best - or even the only - option for them to achieve an acceptable balance.

13. B Gutek, A Searle & L Klepa, Rational versus Gender Role Explanation for Work-Family Conflict, *Journal of Applied Psychology*, 76(4): 560–568 (1991); Parasuraman & Simmers *supra* note 2.
14. JM Bergère & Y Chassard, *A quoi servent les cadres?* Paris: Odile Jacob (2013); A Bozon, A Pailhé, & A Solaz, Le travail empiète pour tous, la famille déborde pour les femmes. Ined Actualités, 11. (accessed on http://www.ined.fr/fr/tout-savoir-population/memos-demo/analyses/travail-famille/2010).
15. Genin, *supra* note 2; Parasuraman & Simmers, *supra* note 2.

In sample 1, nearly half of the mothers declare to systematically resume work in the evening (one hour on average) to be able to leave the office in time to pick up their children:

> '[Working from home] is a good thing to me. If I have to work one hour, I will do it when my baby is asleep or when my daughter is doing her homework ... I can achieve a balance like that, I feel more comfortable. For example, when I leave at 5:00 pm, I do work from home. We receive so many emails; I prefer to respond in the evening rather than at work.'
>
> 'It is important to be available for the employees, to give them time [] But I always leave at 4:00 pm because of my children. I go home and do my things. After that, I resume work [] I work at home every day one or two hours. This gives me independence. I get organized like that. That's the way I can finish all my work and do not get under stress [] At home, my working hours are flexible, that is how I do balance work, family, husband [] I would like to work more at home and less at the office. It is satisfactory; I can do my household at the same time'
>
> 'If I have to leave the office at 3:00 pm because I have family obligations, I will work at home one hour in the evening [] Yes it is regular, I work at home 5 hours a week on average. I find it satisfactory... I think it is important for the employees to know that we are available for them, so I make myself available [] In my generation, we are always torn with the idea that we should be more present for the children and that we spend too much time at work.'

Resuming work from home illustrates a mode of work-family articulation that aims to manage a heavy professional workload and equally heavy domestic and parental workload. This phenomenon is called the 'Third Shift' and reveals a daily sequence of activities characterised by work – family tasks – back to work. Besides reflecting the still widely unequal distribution of parental work between spouses/partners, the Third Shift phenomenon also exemplifies how these working mothers integrate –without really contesting them- the constraints emerging from both the domestic sphere ('I can do my housework at the same time') and the professional sphere ('it is important to be available for the employees'). The third shift also mirrors the fact that these professionals have but little other options to reconcile work and parental demands.

On the contrary, fathers, especially those older respondents- seem to prefer staying later at the office to deal with occasional work overload, precisely because they have the possibility to do so (which women in the same situation do not have); as mentioned by this father of three teenagers:

> I have always been like that, when I am at work, I am at work. I don't mind to put the hours, but when I leave, I leave, I do not work at home [...] My wife is used to it. She knows that my work is very important to me. She accepts that I finish late and arrive later in the evening. I work a lot, but I am fine with that [...] I do not think that working at home would be good for me.

The third shift is then grounded in gendered dynamics. The domestic and parental work being still mainly carried out by women, men can choose to stay later at the office ('my wife is used to it, she accepts'). Yet this possibility does not prevail amongst the mothers interviewed in sample 1. Most of them work a third shift to articulate personal life and professional life, even if it is not still completely satisfactory. The last participant indeed mentions that women 'in my generation, we are always torn with the idea that we should be more present for the children and that we spend too much time at work'.

Let us conclude with an important nuance. The youngest father of sample 1 (34) also acknowledges to use daily mobile technologies to stay connect with his work while spending time with his family. In this respect his behaviour seems closer to the one of mothers than to the ones of the older fathers of the sample. It may be the sign of a generational change. But evidences are scarce and this point needs further development.

§6.04 THE THIRD SHIFT: A SYMPTOM OF THE DEMATERIALISATION OF WORK, DISRUPTIVE TECHNOLOGIES AND GENDER INEQUITY

The Third Shift phenomenon appears to be the result of a conjunction of several factors affecting qualified employment in the twenty-first century. It is a manifestation, or a symptom, of the changing nature of work.

First of all, the Third Shift phenomenon reflects the dematerialisation of work and the widespread use of mobile technologies amongst skilled workers. The nature of their work has shifted from the material to the immaterial and informational. Additionally, mobile technology has made it possible to work almost anywhere at any time: on weekends, on vacation, as well as when commuting. Even before information and communication technologies (ICT) came into widespread use, managers and professionals were taking work home.[16] In itself, work at home is not new and does not require the use of mobile technologies. What *is* new, however, is the extent of the phenomenon (approximately 75% of skilled workers do so). Most of professionals and managers have access to a laptop, and other electronic devices, such as a smartphone, in order to facilitate increased connectivity with colleagues or work-based software systems; they are also frequent early adopters of new technology.[17] Working a third shift from home is thus not just facilitated but also encouraged by the demateralisation of qualified work and the generalisation of ICT. Let us add that in the two samples presented in this chapter, as well as in other research,[18] work at home is rarely formal telework (i.e., framed by a work contract) and it mostly takes place beyond regular office hours. Working a third shift thus often remains informal and unseen work.

16. A Russell Hochschild, *The Time Bind: When Work Becomes Home and Home Becomes Work*, Metropolitan Books (New York, 1997).
17. Bergère & Chassard, *supra* note 14; Bozon et al. *supra* note 14.
18. S Ojala, J Nätti & T Anttila, Informal Overtime at Home Instead of Telework: Increase in Negative Work-Family Interface, *International Journal of Sociology and Social Policy*, 34(1/2): 69–87 (2014).

With the dematerialisation of work came its corollary: the intensification of work. This phenomenon has been largely documented in the literature[19] and is associated to the development of new production models based on just in time[20] and the requirement to do more with less (less resources and less time). Indeed, in our second sample, the respondents clearly perceived this intensification of their work: 65% declare their workload has increased over the past two years (22% consider the increase 'significant'). Furthermore, 43% declare their workload is too heavy and 7% say it is unbearable.

These results indicate that the Third Shift phenomenon is not only a way to articulate work and family but also a response to the increased demands from professional work. It is not simply a change in the place of work; it is the extension of office work into personal time and space. Indeed, most of the studies carried out show that the majority of people who work during their personal time, do so in order to finish tasks that they were not able to complete during normal working hours.[21] Women thus seem particularly affected by work intensification since they already have less time than men to dedicate to professional work.[22] Working from home may well be the only way to finish all their work as expressed by this woman of sample 1:

- Would you say that work at home is an obligation?
- Yes, if I want to reach the objectives, I have to work at home. At the office I do not have time to complete everything then yes, it's an obligation… .

The organisational pressure as well as work intensification can then lead to the development and extension of the Third Shift phenomenon.

Furthermore, the intensification of work along with the accessibility and widespread use of mobile technologies, have resulted in more and more employers expecting employees to be available 24/7 which, may in turn generate an implicit obligation for employees to be available for work.[23] This implicit requirement for permanent availability for work may also pressure women into working a third shift. The constraints are both subtle and fluid. Being available for work when away from the workplace is often presented as optional – one may, after all, choose to keep one's mobile phone turned off or not to check one's email– but the negative consequences of

19. C Kelliher & D Anderson, Doing More with Less? Flexible Working Practices and the Intensification of Work, *Human Relations*, 63(1): 83 (2010).
20. G Vallée, Employees' Obligation to Be Available to Employers: A (New) Pathway to Precariousness or a Source of Flexibility? *International Journal of Comparative Labour Law and Industrial Relations*, 3: 275–279 (2016).
21. A Halford, Hybrid Workspace: Re-spatialisations of Work, Organisation and Management, *New Technology, Work and Employment*, 20(1): 19–33 (2005); S Matusik & A Mickel, Embracing or Embattled by Converged Mobile Devices? Users' Experiences with a Contemporary Connectivity Technology, *Human Relations*, 64(8): 1001–1030 (2011); C Middleton & W Cukier, Is Mobile Email Functional or Dysfunctional? Two Perspectives on Mobile Email Usage, *European Journal of Information Systems*, 15(3): 252–260 (2006).
22. Gutek, et al. *supra* note 13.
23. Vallée *supra* note 20.

not being fully available for work are amply documented in the literature.[24] As a consequence, resuming work from home (by answering emails for example) may be also be the result of an implicit obligation to be available for work after (and before) traditional working hours.[25]

Finally the results of previous research on managers and professionals clearly highlighted how the gendered division of labour affects time allocation of men and women.[26] The fact that women are more likely than men to resume work from home to balance work and family (men tend to do it for different reasons[27]) illustrates the relatively unchanged sexual division of domestic and parental work. While the progress made by women in the professional sphere is undeniable, women still do the lion's share of domestic and parental work, even when they work full time in qualified jobs. To be able to leave the office 'on time,' working mothers tend to resume work systematically in the evening or at night when the children are asleep and the domestic tasks have been accomplished. This behaviour is less often observed among men, who generally prefer to stay later at the office. In brief, women adapt their personal organisation and practices – through work at home – to deal with the conflicting demands of work and the traditional caregiver role. In these situations, working a third shift appears to be the best – or even the only – option hey have while men can choose to stay later at the office or not.

To conclude, the Third Shift phenomenon appears to be embedded in gendered and organisational dynamics such as the dematerialisation of work through technological intermediation and the intensification of work pressures. Such developments challenge existing patterns of work regulation but do not really seem to challenge the gendered organisation of the professional and the personal spheres.

§6.05 DISCUSSION OF THE STAKES FOR THE THIRD SHIFT

In the past twenty years, scholars and policy makers have paid increasing attention to work-life balance.[28] For qualified workers, working at home often constitutes a personal response to incompatibilities between personal and professional demands. ICT tools can offer freedom to those who want to work when and where it suits them, thus providing one means for balancing work and life. In this respect, working a third shift allows a kind of flexible work arrangement, and is thus positively associated with work-life balance. Nevertheless, research exploring the links between work at home and work-life balance has yielded mixed results. Indeed, ICT tools can encourage individuals to extend, without moderation, their occupational activities into their personal time and employers to expect a permanent availability for work.[29] In this

24. J Evans, G Kunda & S Barley, Beach Time, Bridge Time, and Billable Hours: The Temporal Structure of Technical Contracting, *Administrative Science Quarterly* 49(1): (2004); L Perlow, *Sleeping with Your Smartphone*. Boston, Harvard Business Review Press (2012).
25. Genin, *supra* note 7.
26. *Ibid.*
27. Genin, *supra* note 2.
28. Amstad *supra* note 4.
29. Matusik & Mickel, *supra* note 21; Middleton & Cukier, *supra* note 21, Perlow, *supra* note 24.

respect, the Third Shift phenomenon questions the extended of temporal availability that can be decently expected from qualified workers.[30]

Another stake of the Third Shift phenomenon is the definition of work-life balance itself. The individual-centred definition of work-life balance has indeed been criticised because it gives the false impression that work-life balance is an individual problem. This approach does not permit bringing certain underlying social issues to light[31] such as the intensification of work, the implicit obligation to be available for the employer or the persistent gender inequity in the professional and private spheres. If the Third Shift is no longer considered as an individual choice but rather as a social phenomenon reflecting how rigid organisational practices and cultures are and how insufficient public policies are for working parents, it may open the way to a collective reflexion on how to provide them with better work-family policies. An example could be the provision of formal telework agreements instead of informal and unseen work at home.

Finally, the Third Shift questions gender equity. Despite the evolution of the labour force (increased participation of women, dual-earner couples, single parents) and the changing social values regarding work and family, there is still structural inequality for women, inherited from the traditional social roles of men and women.[32] Working from home, to articulate work and family, may as well reinforce the existing sexual division of work or facilitate gender equity. Far from challenging gendered organisation, working a third shift from home could lead to the reproduction and exacerbation of the traditional male model of work.[33] Indeed, as women are willing to organise their work hours differently, they continue to be in charge of the majority of domestic and family tasks, thus creating a vicious circle where they alone bear the burden of work-family balance. On the other hand, the fact that professional women find ways to balance work and family responsibilities while keeping their career on track is encouraging and may well have a positive effect on gender equity. All these questions need further development and are avenues for future research.

§6.06 CONCLUSION

To sum up, the current chapter presented the idea of the Third Shift to qualify the informal work that professional women perform from home in the evening, at night or during weekends in order to deal with the heavy pressure from work and from home. This study, as any other, bears many limits. It is based on two samples from different countries which can make the conclusions weaker due to national differences. Though there certainly are differences between France and Canada, those countries are comparable in terms of economic development and gender equity. Additionally, few

30. Vallée, *supra* note 20.
31. P Moen, From 'Work Family' to the 'Gendered Life Course' and 'Fit': Five Challenges to the Field, *Community, Work and Family*, 14(1): 81 (2011).
32. *Ibid.*
33. P Van Echtelt, A Glebbeek, S Lewis & S Lindenberg, Post-Fordist Work: A Man's World? Gender and Working Overtime in the Netherlands, *Gender & Society*, 23(2): 188–214 (2009).

variations have been observed between the two samples with respect to the individual strategies professionals develop to reach work-life balance even when compared to studies carried out in other countries.[34] This last point is clearly raises an interesting avenue to develop in future research.

34. *Ibid.*

CHAPTER 7

Irregular Work Scheduling and Its Consequences

Lonnie Golden & Jaeseung Kim

§7.01 INTRODUCTION AND OVERVIEW

What are the effects on work-family balance when an employee works on an irregular or on-call type of work shift? How many and which of those employed in the United States (U.S.) work on irregular or on-call work shift times? The integration of work and family is increasingly dependent on employees' ability to receive their preferred work schedule. While some employees have been gaining more autonomy over their hours or schedules, many others actually have less control. Some workers may not mind this, particularly if they lack other responsibilities with which work may conflict. However, for workers with families, having shift times that are variable over the course of a week (or day) complicates their navigation through caregiving, and may indirectly affect employers to the extent it leads to more intense or frequent work-family conflict. This may be true even for those with relatively shorter weekly work hours.

The incidence and effects of unstable work schedules are explored here using General Social Survey (GSS) data and its Quality of Worklife (QWL) modules. Estimates are that from 10% of workers report working these kinds of shifts. Adding in split or rotating shifts, the shares working unstable work schedules climbs to 17% %. A poll in 2016 asking this same question found even higher percentages – 16% and 24%, respectively (*https://ssascholars.uchicago.edu/einet/employment-polls*). It is even higher among part-time employees.[1] Working overtime that is required by the employer is associated with working on an irregular schedule or on rotating/split shifts. By income level, the lowest and also the highest income workers face the most

1. The majority of hourly part-time workers (83%) are found elsewhere to have unstable work schedules (Ruan and Reichman 2014).

irregular work schedules. Having irregular scheduling is, perhaps surprisingly, associated with longer average weekly hours. By occupation type, almost 15% of sales and related occupations have irregular or on-call schedules. By industry, irregular scheduling is most prevalent in personal services, business/ repair services, entertainment /recreation, finance/ insurance/real estate, and retail trade.

Less than 11% of workers on "regular" work schedules report "often" experiencing work-family conflict in contrast with as many as 26% of irregular/on-call shift employees, and 19% of rotating/split shift workers. Similarly, only 20% working on irregular/on-call schedules report "never" experiencing work-family interference, in contrast to 28% of those on "regular" schedules. Multivariate analyzes tests whether or not work-family conflict is worsened not only by longer weekly hours of work, but also by having irregular shift work. Controlling for hours worked per week, employees who work irregular shift times, in contrast with those with more standard, regular shift times, experience greater work-family conflict. The association between work-family conflict and irregular shift work could be similar of different for hourly and salaried workers (when controlling for the latter's relatively longer weekly work hours). Working on split/rotating shift times exacerbates work- family conflict, although slightly less than does working irregular/on-call shifts. There may be lower work-family conflict for those with part-time jobs, however, perhaps entirely attributable to their shorter working hours. The analysis examines whether the adverse effect of irregular and on-call shifts can be moderated or mitigated by having daily schedule flexibility—either an ability to alter their starting and ending times or to take time off during work. If having flexibility moderates some of the adverse negative effect of irregular work schedules on work-family balance, there is a case for law and public policies to enhance such flexibility, even without policies that would attempt to enhance the stability or regularity of shifts.

The results are intended to gauge the possible net improvement of worker well-being with new public policies, such as a legal, protected right to request more flexible stable or predictable work hours' notice of schedules.[2] The results regarding both the sources and reduction of such conflict not only reinforce the existing "business case"[3]—in employers own long term interest—but limiting the extent and prevalence of work hours fluctuation that are at the behest of employers only, underscores the need to adopt preventative public policy measures as well. The results herein provide support for adopting policy measures that would temper fluctuations in the daily and weekly work hours of hourly paid employees. Some already are taking place in states and municipalities across the U.S. It will describe recently passed or proposed reforms of the Fair Labor Standards Act (FLSA).reform measures, to provide a legal, protected "right to request," modeled on the laws in the United Kingdom (U.K.), Australia, New

2. As is argued in Golden (2012a), to further broaden the comprehensive scope considered by Harris (2000).
3. *See* Ben-Ishai (2014); Sweet et al. (2014); Swanberg et al. (2011); Watson and Swanberg (2013); Golden (2012b); Bloom, Kretschmer, and Van Reenen (2011); Boushey and Glynn (2012); Lee and DeVoe (2012); Matos and Galinsky (2011); Lambert and Henly (2010); McGuire, Kenny, and Brashler (2010).

Zealand, the Netherlands, and Germany, and their largely positive experiences for employees, without harm to employers.[4]

§7.02 IRREGULAR SHIFT AND ON-CALL WORKING IN THE U.S. AND ITS POTENTIAL ADVERSE CONSEQUENCES

The plight of employees with unstable or unpredictable work schedules has become increasingly well-documented in the media (Cauthen, 2011; Kantor 2014; Covert 2014, Aarons-Mele 2014) and in the academic literature. Work schedules or shifts that are irregular are consistently found to be associated with assorted adverse outcomes for workers (Costa, Sartori, Akerstedt 2006; Heisz and LaRochelle-Cote 2006; Camerino et al., 2010, Tucker and Folkard 2012; Olsen and Dahl 2010; Haley-Lock and Ewert 2011). There are drawbacks of erratic and uncontrollable work schedules for any employee, particularly those on nonstandard work times (Askenazy 2004; Bohle, et al. 2011; McNamara, Bohle, and Quinlan 2011; Golden et al. 2011; Fagan et al. 2012; Glauber 2013; Wood, Michaelides, and Totterdell 2013; Kelly et al. 2014; Jacobs and Padavic 2015). They can be particularly acute among hourly paid workers, especially with lower incomes (Henly and Lambert 2014; Correll, Trimble-O'Connor, and Williams 2014; Swanberg, Watson, and Eastman 2014; Alexander and Haley-Lock 2013; Watson and Swanberg 2013; Carré and Tilly 2012; McCrate 2012; Lambert, Haley-Lock, and Henly 2012; Martin et al. 2012; Scott et al. 2004). Work times are most irregular for those hourly workers on part-time employment arrangements (Zeytinoglu et al. 2004; Henly, Shaefer, and Waxman 2006; Yildirim and Aycan 2008; Kalleberg 2011). Moreover, it is becoming recognized that when work hours and schedules generally are variable, it undermines elements of well-being, such as sleep time.[5] One such study examined the extent to which work demands, including irregular work schedules, are related to work-family conflict as well as life and job satisfaction among nurses. Irregular work schedules (along with work overload) are the predictors of work-family conflict, and that work-family conflict is in turn associated with lower job and life satisfaction (Yildirim and Aycan 2008). Generally, having to be constantly available for work, not just long hours per se, creates a daily struggle for workers to reconcile competing caregiving and workplace demands (Correll et al. 2014).

Generally, fluctuation in workloads or job demands tends to negatively affect workers' well-being, all else constant, both when it is routine or transient (Wood, Michaelides, and Totterdell 2013). This is mainly because fluctuation creates interference of work with nonwork activity and undermines the effort-recovery process, time needed for rest in between shifts in order to perform effectively. Even when work hours are positively related to indicators of well-being, variability of work diminishes

4. For descriptions by country, *see* Charlesworth and Campbell (2008); Heymann and Earle (2010); Hegewisch (2005).
5. Policy interventions have been recommended to increase sleep time by delaying the morning start time of work or making it more flexible, and offsetting inherent economic disincentives from working fewer hours (Basner, Spaeth, and Dinges 2014). Having an irregular sleep schedule can be just as hazardous for health as insufficient sleep (Locke 2014).

well-being significantly (Wood, Michaelides, and Totterdell 2013; Golden et al. 2013; Golden and Okulicz-Kozaryn 2015). Thus, reducing or minimizing instability in work hours, schedules, and workloads may improve workers' well-being, for a given level of daily or weekly hours and income.[6] Facilitated by new software technology, many employers are adopting a human resource strategy of hiring a cadre of mainly part-time employees whose work schedules are modified, often on short notice, to match the employer's staffing with customer demand at the moment (Lambert, Haley-Lock, and Henly 2012). Such jobs are dis-proportionately found in the service occupations and in the retail and wholesale trade and services industries, such as hospitality and leisure, professional and business services, and health services.[7] Moreover, because precarious employment is concentrated among relatively lower-income earners, it not only exacerbates growing income inequality (Standing 2011), stifling potential economic expansion and underutilizing potential available labor input, but may take a toll on the well-being of workers with families.[8]

§7.03 IRREGULAR SHIFT WORK: FINDINGS USING THE GSS AND ITS SUPPLEMENTS

Which workers are more prone to having variable work schedules? What is the apparent association of having irregular or unpredictable shift times with adverse outcomes for workers with families? This chapter analyzes data from the four most recent GSS QWL modules, for the years 2014, 2010, 2006, and 2002. First, it identifies the proportions of workers who work on regular day shift times and contrasts their characteristics to those on "irregular or on-call" or "split or rotating" shift times. It identifies the work (and personal) characteristics associated with working irregular/on-call shift times. It then analyzes the data, contrasting the reported frequency of work-family interference, by those on irregular versus other types of work shifts, controlling for the duration of their weekly work hours . It also contrasts the

6. *See* Hacker et al. (2014). For example, children's cognitive development, including older children's test scores, have been inversely associated with parents working irregular, nontraditional work shift times (Boots 2004; Boushey and Mitukiewicz 2014; Li et al. 2014). For evidence that mismatches with one's preferred hours (both too long or too short, but the former a bit more than the latter) adversely affects subjective well-being, *see* Wooden, Warren and Drago (2009).
7. *See* Mayer (2014); Luce, Hammad, and Sipe (2014); and Haley-Lock and Ewert (2011).
8. Many state and local laws already have been moving labor laws in the direction away from employee protections (Lafer 2013). Thus, advocates are calling for laws and regulations that could help ease the incidence, frequency, or consequences of having too few or unpredictable work hours. Recent reports and articles include: *Tackling Unstable and Unpredictable Work Schedules: A Policy Brief on Guaranteed Minimum Hours and Reporting Pay Policies* (Center for Law and Social Policy, Retail Action Project, and Women Employed 2014); "State-by-State Reporting Time Pay Laws" (Starosciak 2013); *The Schedules That Work Act: Section-by-Section* (National Partnership for Women & Families and National Women's Law Center 2014); *Short-Shifted* (Luce, Hammad, and Sipe 2014); *Underwriting Bad Jobs: How Our Tax Dollars are Funding Low-Wage Work and Fueling Inequality* (Demos 2013), *Worth Working For* (Peck and Traub 2011); *Families and Flexibility: Reshaping the Workplace for the 21st Century* (Stringer 2014); *Nonstandard Work Schedules and the Well-Being of Low-Income Families* (Enchautegui 2013).

outcomes among the (smaller proportion) of workers who work either a "split /rotating shifts" or afternoon/evening shift times.

In the QWL, a key question asked of the employed is, "Which of the following best describes your usual work schedule?" Respondents may check one of the following: day shift, afternoon shift, night shift, split shift, irregular shift/on-call, or rotating shifts. Figures 7.1 and 7.2 show the descriptive results of the key variables. Figure 7.1 shows that about 10% of the work force reports their work shift to be "irregular or on-call." These are workers that have no regular daily or weekly schedules that are at all predictable. Interestingly, despite the aforementioned technological and industry composition changes since 2002, this proportion does not appear to be escalating over time. Moreover, specifically, those who work irregular or on-call shift times are about 6% of hourly workers, 8% of salaried workers, and 30% of those paid on some other basis (such as contract work). Of course, this 10% figure might well underestimate schedule variation or unpredictability, because those who work a day shift schedule—the great majority, at about 70% to 75% of workers—might have irregular start and end times within the day schedule (or afternoon or night, too). If we add in those who work on split or rotating shift times, about 17% of the employed are on unstable work shifts. In addition, while irregular/on-call shift working has not shown signs of escalating, the proportion on standard day shifts seems to be trending downwards somewhat, coming in at no more than 70% of the employed in 2014, higher in previous survey years. While there is no indication of an upward trend in irregular/on-call working, there is somewhat in split/rotating shift work. Figure 7.2 shows that irregular shift working is in large part, a sectoral phenomenon. It is highest in service sector industries, especially "other," food, hospitality and retail service employment.[9]

Multi-nominal logistic model are conducted to identify the individual work and personal characteristics that are associated, positively or negatively, with the dependent variable "irregular" shift time (also rotating and split shift times) compared to the regular shift, including day and night shifts. *Table 7.1* shows that by income level, there is a clear pattern—being in any income bracket above the lowest (the referent group) diminishes the chances of being on both irregular/on-call and split/rotating shifts(although being in the highest income category, perhaps curiously, does not significantly diminish such chances). The concentration of irregular work hours among lower

9. A recent poll of working adults by the Public Policy Polling (PPP) provides new, and more compelling evidence for the more pervasive extent of irregular shift work and its disproportionate distribution by industry type (n = 1,000). To the question, "Thinking of your main job, which of the following best describes the hours you usually work: a regular day shift, an evening shift, a night shift, a rotating shift, a split shift, an irregular schedule, or something else?" The polls showed that two-thirds work on a regular day shift. Some 5% said their shifts were "rotating" and another 3% were on "split shift." However, fully 16% reported that their shift was "irregular"—higher than in the GSS sample, perhaps indicating a growth in such scheduling. By industry, most pertinently, almost 3 in 10 workers in retail or wholesale trade have work schedules too irregular to specify a time of day. Another 2 in 10 workers in food services or production share that schedule irregularity, while those in professional services have the next highest rate (about the national average), while about one in ten employed in construction and education/health care/nonprofits have irregular schedules. (Not surprisingly, agriculture has the greatest share of workers reporting irregular shifts.)

income workers mirrors the pattern of working nonstandard hours—where the majority of one's hours are outside the 6 a.m. to 6 p.m. range—which consists of 20% of the work force, 15% of those with full-time work (Enchautegui 2013).[10] Those with incomes below the low salary $22,500 have a slightly higher-than-average proportion working irregular shifts (11% versus 10%). In addition, those working irregular shifts or variable hours (rotating or split shifts) work a relatively longer workweek, on average.[11]

Working longer hours has a positive association with working unusual shift times, particularly split/rotating shifts, somewhat also on irregular shift times. This suggests either employers schedule such workers for longer hours than those on regular shifts, and/or that employees don't mind longer hours compared with those on the regular shifts. Because the association is relatively weaker between hours duration and irregular shifts than with hours duration and split/rotating shifts, we may be observing that irregular shift work is more common than split/rotating shifts among part-time workers. However, for workers on irregular schedules, the role of longer hours becomes statistically insignificant when including the effect of having flexibility in work scheduling or not.

10. Such "nonstandard" working hours are associated with receiving not only lower average pay—incidence almost twice as high among the very-low-wage employed—but being employed in the following industries, in sequential order: accommodation and food, arts and entertainment, retail, management and administrative service, transportation and warehousing, nondurable manufacturing, and heath/social assistance. It is also at least twice the overall average for security guards, waiters, laborers, nurses, stock clerks, and building cleaners. In contrast to variable schedules, nontraditional schedules are more common among women, particularly women (though not men) with preschool-aged children, but both variable and nontraditional schedules are more likely among those with less education. However, lower-income men are more likely than lower— income women to work outside standard hours (Enchautegui 2013).
11. Omitted from *Table 7.1* are the co-variates associated with demographic characteristics of workers. Working an irregular/on-call shift or a split/rotating shift are inversely associated with age, but also turns upward at older ages—particularly the split or rotating shift work schedules. Thus, the pattern of distribution of irregular schedules is slightly skewed toward younger workers, but not decidedly so. Being male actually strongly increases being on an irregular shift (gender has no association with working split or rotating shifts). By race, irregular work schedules appear to be greater among whites than non-whites, but this phenomenon is almost entirely attributable to racial differences in income, work hours, and access to flexible work scheduling arrangements. Being married has no relationship to working irregular/on-call shifts, but is associated positively with working more split or rotating shifts. However, this is entirely due to married workers' levels of income and work hours. Perhaps surprisingly, having young children has no influence either way. Education level has little bearing on incidence of working either type of shift, with the exception that having "some college" puts workers more in the split or rotating shift status. Years on the job have no effect either way. There is, however, variation by occupation. In particular, about 15% of workers in sales and related occupations have irregular schedules, while most other occupations are quite near (or in the case of administrative support) far below the national average. By industry sector, irregular scheduling is high relative to the average in the following industries: retail trade (12%), finance/insurance/real estate (12%), business/repair services (15%), personal services (17%), entertainment/recreation (15%) and unsurprisingly, agriculture (19%). Finally, variable work shifts, in particular, irregular and on-call work, appears to be associated with significantly higher reported frequency of having work-family conflict (as shown in the bottom section of *Table 7.1*). Thus, irregular/on-call work is relatively more likely to appear in industries such as Food services; Health services; Retail trade and "other services," in that order.

In our analyses, we introduce two measures of employee-centered types of work schedule "flexibility." These are derived from questions in the QWL module - How often are you allowed to change your starting and quitting times on a daily basis? [Neve;;Rarely; Sometimes; Often r] and, "How hard is it to take time off during your work to take care of personal or family matters?" [Very hard;; Somewhat hard; Not too hard; Not at all hard]. Because of the ordering of responses, these indicate the degree of "flexibility." Both types of flexibility are associated with lesser work-family interference, but in particular, the ability to take time off during the day.

Indeed, the associations of work shift type with flexible work schedules itself appears to be complex. Having an ability to take off time during work, for family or personal needs, is associated with less likelihood of split/rotating and irregular shift working. However, another type of work scheduling flexibility, an ability to vary the starting and ending times of one's work day, is associated with more irregular shift working. Most revealing is that when workers work extra hours beyond their usual workweeks ("mandatory overtime work"), this is associated with a greater likelihood of being on irregular/on-call shift and split or rotating shifts.

The finding that the two indicators of schedule flexibility appear to work in opposite directions for split/rotating and irregular shifts might also reflect a reverse direction of the relationship. When someone's schedule is irregular, taking time off is harder, but changing start and end times becomes easier, thus, an ability to change one's own start and end times may be a proxy for having a more variable schedule. This association between start and stop time flexibility and irregular scheduling is likely to be a reflection of salaried jobs, where such flextime is more common than in hourly jobs or lower-income jobs.[12] In addition, having overtime work that is mandatory (regarded as "required by employer"), as opposed to purely voluntary, is strongly positively associated with being on either irregular or split/rotating shift work. Finally, all prior results remain largely the same (not shown here) when adding controls for the working conditions that would reflect "job demands." [13]

§7.04 IRREGULAR/ON-CALL WORK SHIFTS AND WORK-FAMILY CONFLICT

The measure of work to family conflict is, "How often do the demands of your job interfere with your family life?" *1 Never; 2 Rarely; 3 Sometimes 4 Often [*reversed from the actual survey responses, for clarified interpretation]. Figures 7.3 through 10 show the incidence and degree of work to family interference in the sample, by workers' job, demographic and income characteristics. Figure 7.3 is the issue of focus—Work-Family by Type of Shift. The mean score of "Day Shift" is not much above "rarely," whereas

12. *See* Golden, Wiens-Tuers, Lambert and Henly (2011); Enchautegui (2013).
13. Greater job demands, such as the perception that "there are too few staff to get the work done," may explain at least some of the positive association between having longer work hours and irregular work shift times. Nevertheless, irregular and on-call shift working is arguably a result of an employer strategy of adopting lean staffing of shifts hour-to-hour, while keeping a buffer of employees on the rolls to schedule hours on short notice (*see* Lambert, 2008).

for Irregular Shift workers, it is closer to "sometimes." This suggests that there are about as many workers who say, "often" as there are those who say, "rarely or never." In the descriptive data broken out, only 20% on irregular/on-call shifts report "never" experiencing work-family conflict. This is in contrast to 28% of those on "regular" schedules, and 24% of those on split/rotating shifts. Similarly, the share reporting "often" experiencing such work-family conflict was 26% among irregular/on-call shift employees, and 19% among rotating and split shift workers, whereas less than 11% of those on more regular work schedules report work-family conflict. Figure 7.4, work-family conflict by gender, shows that men experience work-family conflict more frequently than women. This probably owes to their longer average work hours and propensity to work full time jobs as compared to women. Figure 7.5 displays work-family conflict by married status, and shows that married workers clearly have more time conflict, however, perhaps surprisingly, no difference if their spouse works or not. Figure 7.6, work-family conflict by age, shows only slight differences by age, somewhat higher during typical child-rearing years. Figure 7.7, work-family conflict by number of children, shows the biggest jump is between none child and one child, and also somewhat higher than that for those with three or more children. Figure 7.8 work-family conflict by education, shows a somewhat increasing gradation by education level. Figure 7.9, work-family conflict by income, shows a similar, somewhat increased gradation as income levels of households is higher. Figure 7.10, work-family by full-time part-time job status, shows a clearly greater level of conflict for those working full time relative to those in part time jobs. Not surprisingly, given that many workers voluntarily take part time jobs for the very purpose of balancing time at work with nonwork activities and responsibilities.

Table 7.2 shows the multivariate findings of the crux of the research, the seven different models tested. The salient finding comes from when the three types of shift working is included and contrasted—adding in afternoon (evening) and night shift working, and contrasting all three with regular day shift. Irregular/on-call working has the most prominent negative effect on work family balance. Next, when workers report that their shift is either a rotating or split shift schedule, the main effects are almost as strong as those observed for irregular/on-call. While not quite as large, work-family conflict appears to be worsened by working non-day regular shift times, such as late afternoon, evenings or night shift. Thus, there is a clear smooth, gradient in the effects, worsening as shifts move away from the regular daytime shift. By industry, "other services" and somewhat Food Service and wholesale trade has less work-family conflict, relative to the comparison industry of Agriculture/Mining. Split/rotating shifts are greatest in Food Services, Construction and Educational services

Among the control variables in the model, we find no gender difference—Women have no more work to family conflict than men. Having children present in the household adds to work-family conflict, although most of that appears to due to have at least one child. Being Married with a spouse NOT working increases work-family conflict, however, if other spouse is working, there is no significant positive association with time conflict (compared to those not married). Thus, Married workers with spouses have more work-family conflict, but whether there spouse is working or not has no bearing on the level of that positive association.

We find strong evidence that longer weekly work hours are positively associated with work-family conflict, not too surprisingly, given the zero-sum nature of most daily time. When part time versus full time is used in place of number of hours, part time employment appears to reduce the level of work family conflict experienced. The shorter hours of part timers clearly reduces the effects of irregular hours on work family conflict. The association between income and work-family conflict is only slightly more positive at higher income levels. Progressively Higher household income appears to come at the expense of greater degrees of work family conflict. The households that chose not to report their income have no differences in work family conflict to those who did report. Finally, we find that Work to family conflict was higher in 2010 and 2014 than in 2006 and 2002. However, irregular shift working neither increase nor decrease over these twelve years.

In the interaction models, we added interaction terms to see if there are accentuated or diminished effects of irregular/on-call and other nontraditional shift time working for many of these control variables (models in columns 2 through 7). We isolate the findings by industry interactions, in *Table 7.3.* We find that irregularity of schedules is not statistically significantly greater or lesser for women than men. The key interaction term finding is that not only does flexibility moderate or mitigate conflict of work with family, but the combination of irregular shifts and inflexible daily schedules create a double blow to workers' work-life balance." The interaction with part-time jobs also shows that working part time have smaller effects of irregular scheduling than on full timers. When working part time (or not) is substituted for the number of weekly work hours, its interaction term estimates suggest that part time working cushions the negative main effects of the number of work hours. The effect of part time work in relieving work-family conflict is accentuated for those workers on both afternoon and evening shifts and split/rotating shifts, as well as for those on Irregular on-call work. However irregular shift working for part-timers is no less harmful for work-family balancing than it is for full timers.

By workers' paid status, the negative association between irregular scheduling and work-family conflict does not vary between hourly and salaried workers. By industry interactions, three industries reinforce, or create "add-on effects" for irregular shift working—Health and Food services and Retail Trade. Indeed, Retail Trade sector work accentuates the effects on work-family conflict of irregular/on-call and late aft/eve/night shiftwork, but not split/rotating shiftwork.The key findings are that the adverse effects of Irregular work on work-family are robust—it survives adding in a wide range of possible interaction terms. The interactions suggest the effects of irregular and on-call work are intermediated by some conditions that moderate it, some that accentuate it. For example, having more control over daily schedules by employees would reduce work-life conflict or those on the irregular schedules, and part time (shorter shift) hours would help those on split/rotating and irregular shifts better balance work with family responsibilities and time.

§7.05 IMPLICATIONS OF THE FINDINGS FOR PROPOSED LEGAL REFORMS: WHAT CAN BE DONE?

Given the evidence presented here and in other, recent studies of the relationship between irregular or unpredictable work hours and work-family conflict, which policies might prove most effective at mitigating the work-family conflict? Either by reducing the incidence or severity of shift time irregularity over a workweek, or by offsetting the impact by providing workers more choice—to refuse shifts, change shifts or request shifts. Other countries have taken steps to limit this short-term unpredictability of work schedules and promote a legally protected ability of workers to adjust their work schedules?[14] Regarding the latter, an important first step has been proposed in a previous U.S. Congress, and now two states—Vermont and New Hampshire—and a handful of cities have passed—including Seattle San Francisco and a few Bay Area California cities have passed a protected employee "right to request." Many other cities, including New York City, are poised to pass this. A "right to request" changes in work hours, schedules, or location, with protection from retaliation, is modeled on the laws in the U.K., Australia, New Zealand, the Netherlands, and Germany. Such a right to request is intended to protect from retaliation those who choose to limit their work hours or have their schedules adjusted in order to address family duties, to promote continuance of working at one's current job, and to accommodate the choice of parenthood even if labor force withdrawal is affordable (Kulow 2012; Bird and Brown, 2016). The evidence presented suggests that providing that "right" at least on an individual, case-by-case basis would be helpful in part because access to more flexible working arrangements is so disparate by sector. While access is more limited for hourly workers (Sweet et al. 2014; Golden 2009; Lyness et al. 2012; McNamara, Bohle, and Quinlan 2011; Williams and Boushey 2010), salaried workers, perhaps in lower level supervisory positions, might benefit at least as much because they are even more likely to be on irregular work schedules.

The public policies could be built on the private sector's existing voluntary arrangements. They provide a starter model of practices that could become minimum standards that would curb the prevalence of on-call work and increase the regularity of hours by providing minimum advance notice for setting and changing work schedules. Some of the existing voluntary employer initiatives include the store Macy (at its unionized locations), which has agreed to set initially planned work schedules for their employees as far as six months in advance. At Ikea, the aim is at least three weeks. Some companies, such as Whole Foods and Starbucks, let the employees determine their own minimum number of hours per week. Not specifying a minimum for every employee allows some, such as working students, to request only ten to fifteen hours, even though other part-time workers might want a minimum of twenty, or as in Costco,

14. Elsewhere, there are useful compilations and descriptions of other countries' attempts to provide more individual access to control over one's own work hours or schedules and legal protection to requesting it (Andresen, 2015; Berg, Bosch, and Charest 2014; Kassinis and Stavrou 2013; Boushey 2011; Hegewisch and Gornick 2008; Hegewisch 2009; Boulin et al. 2006; Hegewisch 2005;. Labor Project for Working Family, 2014).

a minimum of twenty-four hours per week, posted at least one week in advance (Peck and Traub 2011). Such workers are also empowered to engage in the key practice of shift-swapping. Since much schedule instability found in hourly jobs (outside the more formal, "just-in-time" type of contingent jobs) typically comes in the form of overtime (Williams and Huang 2011), a "right to refuse" unwelcome, short-notice overtime work could be added to the rights to request. Other model practices include the home care staffing agency, Cooperative Home Care Associates, whose Minimum Hours Program features a mix of longer-term, higher-hour cases and shorter-term, lower-hour cases. The company's guaranteed hours program aims to provide workers with sufficient hours to make ends meet, while also allowing the company to cover its caseload with appropriate staffing. CHCA's workers are guaranteed pay for thirty hours of work per week, even if thirty hours of work are not available (*see* Center for Law and Social Policy Retail Action Project, and Women Employed 2014). At Walmart, the Access to Open Hours initiative was a key demand of Making Change at Walmart, a campaign of the United Food and Commercial Workers union. After employee walk-outs and protests over the past two years, spotlighting the company practice of limiting hours and opportunities for part-timers, Walmart agreed to curb such practices, and employees have reported marked improvements in their schedules and well-being generally (Jamieson 2014).[15] Most recently, Dollar General has decided to increase the weekly hours of those employees whose weekly hours were reduced somewhat when their hourly wage rates were raised to compete with other, rival retailers' increases (Ziobro 2015).

The Vermont law establishes a process whereby an employee can request "a flexible work arrangement" for any reason (not just parenting), at least twice per calendar year, and the employer is required to discuss and consider such requests "in good faith." It protects employees who request or use flexible work arrangements from retaliation or discrimination, a key component to prevent such arrangements from becoming a gender segregating practice (*see* Powell 2013). The law is also like the federal legislation in that there are at least eight factors for which the employer may deny the request, either completely or partially, as long as the denial of the request is put in writing. It may be denied as "inconsistent with business operations or its legal or contractual obligations." It includes factors such as the burden of additional costs on business quality, performance, or restructuring, the effect on aggregate employee morale, an inability to meet consumer demand, recruit new staff, reorganize work among existing staff, or an insufficiency of work during periods employee proposes to work instead. There are no studies documenting the experience of employees or employers regarding exercise of the right to request or its processes. In countries that have such a "right to request," the vast majority of requests are granted and the process appears to be without flaws.[16]

In San Francisco, employees with caregiving responsibilities as of January 2014 have a right to request flexible work schedules, under the city's Family Friendly

15. Dave Jamieson, In Wake of Protests, Walmart Workers Find More Hours Within Reach, *Huffington Post*, Posted: April 7, /2014.
16. Over 80% of such requests, after the program was begun, were approved (Hegewisch 2005).

Workplace Ordinance (FFWO). San Francisco employers must inform employees of their new rights and meet tight deadlines for responding formally to requests for flexible or predictable work schedules. Any employee may request a new schedule to help care for a child, a parent age 65 or older, or any family member with a serious health condition. To be eligible, the employee must have worked for the employer for at least six months, must regularly work at least eight hours each week, and must work in San Francisco. An employee may submit a request twice every twelve months, or if there is a "major life event." The employer must meet within twenty-one days of receiving a request and respond in writing within twenty-one days of the meeting. Like both the Vermont law and federal proposal, an employer can deny a request for "bona fide business reasons." San Francisco Board of Supervisors approved new protections for the city's retail workers, which took effect on January 5, 2015. The measures are intended to give hourly-paid retail staffers more predictable schedules and priority access to extra hours of work available. The legislation applies to retail chains with twenty or more locations nationally or worldwide and that have at least twenty employees in San Francisco under one management system (thus affecting about 5% of the city's workforce). The ordinances require businesses to post workers' schedules at least two weeks in advance. Workers will receive compensation for last-minute schedule changes, "on-call" hours, and instances in which they are sent home before completing their assigned shifts. More specifically, workers will receive one hour of pay at their regular rate of pay for schedule changes made with less than a week's notice and two to four hours of pay for schedule changes made with less than twenty-four hours' notice. Moreover, it requires "formula" retail employers (chain businesses subject to the rule) to provide two to four hours of pay to an employee at his regular rate of pay when he is required to be "on-call" for a specified shift but the employer cancels the shift with less than twenty-four hours' notice. Finally, it prohibits formula retail employers from discriminating against employees with respect to their rate of pay, access to employer-provided paid and unpaid time off, or access to promotion opportunities. This will more forcefully protect employees on part-time status, for example, by providing part-timers and full-timers equal access to scheduling and time-off requests.

The *Retail Workers Bill of Rights* which was substantially incorporated into the San Francisco ordinance to protect workers in the city's formula retail chain stores and restaurants. It contained a novel provision (which was not adopted) to promote what it termed, *Full-Time Work and Access to Hours.* If a formula retailer had additional hours of work to offer in job positions held by current part-time workers, it would be required to offer those hours of work first to existing (qualified) part-time employees before hiring additional part-time employees or before hiring through a temporary services agency, staffing agency, or any similar contractor. Access to Hours bills aim to satisfy a preference for adding work hours, among those employees who explicitly request such hours. The "Opportunity to Work" ballot measure passed in 2016 overwhelmingly in San Jose, CA. At SeaTac, Wash., a similar provision was passed as part of "Prop 1." It requires employers covered by the law to offer additional hours or to "promote" part-time workers to full-time work before hiring additional part-timers from outside (Ballotpedia 2013). (It is not yet implemented because a judge blocked enforcement at Seattle-Tacoma International Airport, pending appeal.) The Berkeley Flexible Work Time Initiative was passed overwhelmingly by voters in the November 2014 election. This Berkeley, Calif., City Council must adopt an ordinance that would allow both private- and public-sector workers to request part-time work, and to ask the state and federal governments to draft legislation to give employees a right to shorter or more flexible work hours unless a legitimate business reason for denial of the request was presented in writing.

The passed ordinances contain features that would further incentivize firms to stabilize employees' work schedules, directly or indirectly. This includes required payments for "reporting time" and split-shifting, if not in line with a minimum advance-notice time. It would also help prevent the inadequacy of work hours that often results from calling off workers or sending them home before a shift was scheduled to end, without pay. Eight U.S. states (plus the District of Columbia and Puerto Rico) have legislated various reporting pay laws and policies. These laws and policies, which are sometimes called "show up pay," compensate employees for a minimum number of hours during a work shift for which they have been scheduled, even when the employee is sent home because the employer has no work for him or her to perform. While employees may still be sent home from work, they are guaranteed one or more hours of pay to offset the expenses associated with showing up at work (transportation, childcare, etc.). In California, for non-exempt employees in the mercantile, public housekeeping, and amusement/ recreation industries, if an employee reports to work when required, but is given less than half of the usual/scheduled day's work, the employee must be paid (at her regular rate of pay) for half of the usual/scheduled day's work, but not less than two hours. In Connecticut, a non-exempt employee in the mercantile trade and restaurant industries who reports for duty (by request or permission of the employer) must be paid a minimum of four hours of pay at her regular rate (only two hours for restaurant and hotel workers). Non-exempt employees in the District of Columbia must be paid for at least four hours, payment at the employee's regular rate for the hours worked, plus payment at minimum wage for the hours not worked. In Massachusetts, non-exempt employees (except those in charitable organizations), who are both scheduled to work at least three hours and report on time must be paid for at least three hours at no less than the minimum wage even if no work is available. In New Hampshire, non-exempt employees (except those working for counties or municipalities), must be paid not less than two hours' pay at the regular rate of pay if an employee reports to work at the employer's request (unless the employer makes a good faith effort to notify an employee in advance not to report to work). In New Jersey, if a non-exempt employee reports to work at the employer's request, she must be paid for at least one hour at the applicable wage rate. Non-exempt employees in the restaurant and hotel industries in New York who (by request or permission) report for duty must be paid at least three hours for one shift or the number of hours in the regularly-scheduled shift, whichever is less. Other specific minimum payments are required when workers were scheduled to work two or three shifts. In other "miscellaneous industries and occupations," an employee is entitled to a minimum of four hours of pay, or the number of hours in the regularly-scheduled shift, whichever is less. In Oregon, an employee younger than 18 years old who is required to report for work must be provided sufficient work to earn at least one-half of the amount earned during the minor's regularly scheduled shift. In Rhode Island, an employer who requests or permits a non-exempt employee to report for duty at the beginning of a shift must either provide three hours of work or three hours of pay to that employee. (Alexander, Haley-Lock, and Ruan 2014; Center for Law and Social Policy 2014; Center for Law and Social Policy, Retail Action Project, and Women Employed 2014; Starosciak 2013).

Foreign legislation, upon which further hours stabilization ordinances could be modeled, includes Canada, which has legislated reporting pay requirements in its federal sector and in several of its provinces. The amount of pay owed differs among jurisdictions. In British Columbia (BC) and the Yukon territory, employees must be paid two hours at regular wage, and in BC, four hours must be paid at the regular rate if the shift was scheduled to be over eight hours, and two hours at the regular rate if the shift was not scheduled to be that long or if the reason the employee cannot work is outside of the employer's control. In Ontario, Saskatchewan, New Brunswick, Nova Scotia, Newfoundland and Labrador, and Alberta, compensation is mandated for a minimum of three hours at the minimum wage. In Quebec, Prince Edward Island, and Manitoba, compensation is mandatory at a minimum of three hours at the employee's regular wage. In the Northwest Territories and Nunavut, employees are owed four hours at regular wage if they show up to work to work their shift and less than four hours of work is provided. The federal sector requires three hours at the regular wage. Finally, employees have the right to refuse overtime without repercussions in Saskatchewan, Québec, and Yukon. Wider adoption of such reporting pay requirements might help to compensate employees in ways the labor market is currently not necessarily compensating them for the work-family conflict and stress they experience when regular or overtime work is unpredictable in a given day or week. (Canadian Labour Congress, 2011).

In the U.K., the legal right to request for those with caregiving responsibilities was extended (in July 2014), now allowing all employees (not just caregivers) to request flexible work arrangements, if they have been with a company for at least half a year. An employer can still deny a request if it has a good business reason for doing so. There is now a more formally established appeal process for employees, should they wish to pursue it further. According to a survey, 8% of U.K. workers had submitted a flexible working request to their employer within a week of the law being enacted, while another 11% have said they definitely plan to do so, perhaps in the near future. Roughly 35% of those surveyed said they might consider requesting flexible work hours at some point (Pilon 2014).[17] Thus, the new law may prove to be a popular option for employees, but at the same time, employers will not be overrun with such requests, if only one in three employees are even considering making such a request. In Australia, similarly, the right to request was expanded (in 2009) from parents of preschool-aged children to any employee (with at least twelve months on a full-time or part-time experience with their employer) who has a child up to age 18 (or any

17. The survey was conducted by a conference calling service, *PowWowNow*. Its director was shocked mainly by the finding that 46% of respondents were unaware of the previous law.

caregiving responsibility for a member of his or her immediate family or household), has a disability, is experiencing domestic violence, or is age 55 or older. The age criterion may be regarded as providing a potential bridge or phasing of retirement. No dissatisfaction has been documented by either employees or employers, who must seriously consider a request for flexible working arrangements but may refuse on reasonable business grounds (*see* Skinner and Pocock 2011).

Minimum hours or preventing "zero-hours contracts," which promise no minimum hours of employment) would be designed to keep an employees' hours from fluctuating down to zero hours in any given week (Messenger and Wallott, 2015). The widespread use of "zero-hours" contracts in the U.K. fostered a move on the part of the British government (termed, "BIS 2014-2") in June 2014 to ban the use of exclusivity clauses in such contracts. In France, the regulation of part-time work has been substantially modified by Act No. 2013-504 of June 14, 2013. Not only is the minimum number of working hours of part-time workers set at twenty-four hours per week (or its equivalent calculated over a reference period), except for students, but negotiations regarding the organization of part-time work in companies must be initiated when at least one-third of the workforce in a sector is employed on a part-time basis. This number may be reduced upon request, to deal with personal constraints or to combine several occupations with a view to reaching the equivalent of a full-time job. The first such ordinance in the U.S. was passed in the District of Columbia, but this was narrowly targeted to building services and cleaning workers in large commercial buildings.

Back in the U.S., President Obama directed the federal Office of Personal Management (OPM) to initiate more flexible work and workplace options for the approximately 2 million federal employees. The directive includes a section with a "Right to Request Work Schedule Flexibilities." Agencies must make federal employees aware, on a periodic basis, that they have the right to request work schedule flexibilities available to them under law, pursuant to an applicable collective bargaining agreement, or under agency policy, without fear of retaliation or adverse employment action as a consequence of making such a request. The agencies must facilitate conversations about work schedule flexibilities, including telework, part-time employment, or job sharing arrangements. Supervisors have to confer directly with the requesting employee as appropriate to understand fully the nature and need for the requested flexibility, and carefully respond within twenty business days of the initial request. In addition, other sections provide part-time and job sharing, telework, break times, and private spaces for nursing mothers. The directive goes on to promote "Encouraging Use of Work-Life Programs" generally plus providing help for agencies as to the "Use of Workplace Flexibilities and Work-Life Programs." Finally, it directs the OPM to create, annually update, and publish a Workplace Flexibility Index using data from the Federal Employee Viewpoint Survey, reporting required by the Telework Enhancement Act of 2010, and other appropriate measures of agencies' effective use of workplace flexibilities, reviewable periodically into the future, including issuing reports identifying any "best practices" and the removal of any barriers to or limitations uncovered that may unnecessarily restrict the use of existing workplace flexibilities and work-life programs (The White House 2014).

There have been recent proposals in the U.S. Congress to address this at a national scope. The “Flexibility for Working Families Act” was introduced in the 113th Congress, to give employees a right to request from their employer a change to part-time hours, flextime schedule and most pertinently, a right to request some minimum time of notice for schedule changes.[18] The bill would apply to employers with fifteen or more employees. The legislation would establish a process, which starts with an employee request for a change in any of four different working hour conditions. An employee may apply for a temporary or permanent change in the number of hours the employee is required to work; the times when the employee is required to work or be on-call for work; where the employee is required to work; or the amount of notification the employee receives of work schedule assignments. The employer can deny the request, but if it denies that request, the employer is supposed to propose an alternative arrangement for the employee’s hours, times, place, and/or the employee may pursue a series of meetings to reach a resolution.[19] The Schedules that Work Act of 2014 (H.R. 5159), would have extended this still further in scope. It would provide employees in all companies with fifteen or more employees, not only a right to request more flexible, predictable, or stable hours, but a “Right to Receive” schedule changes for those employees with caregiving or education responsibilities, unless the employer has bona fide business reasons for not doing so. This new right would target four key industries where irregular scheduling (and job growth) has been concentrated. It would require a minimum of fourteen days advance notice for posting schedules. It also would mandate a minimum reporting payment for call-off and one hour’s pay for split-shifting practices. Specifically, the bill would require employers to inform workers in writing of their expected minimum hours and job schedule, on or before their first day of work. If the schedule and minimum hours happen to change, the employer would be required to notify the employee at least two weeks before the new schedule comes into effect. Employers would begin to have to compensate workers when they are sent home from work earlier than planned, paid at their regular rate for four hours or the total length of the workers’ shift if the shift is less than four hours. In addition, they would need to compensate workers at their usual rate for schedules changes, on-call shifts, and split shifts, when the employer changes the schedule less than twenty-four hours prior to a scheduled shift; when the worker is scheduled for an “on-call” or a “call-in” shift, but is not called in; and when the worker is scheduled for a shift interrupted by a non-working period (i.e., not a meal break) (Alexander and Haley-Lock, 2013). This legislation draws on the state legislation described above (Luce, Hammad, and Sipe 2014; Alexander, Haley-Lock, and Ruan 2014).

In sum, there is little movement at the Federal level since the “Schedules that Work Act” was introduced in 2015, but more activity at state and local government

18. Introduced on June 27, 2013, by Rep. Carolyn Maloney (D-N.Y.) and Sen. Bob Casey (D-Pa.). The Secretary of Labor would receive, investigate and attempt to resolve complaints of violations, of sections 6 and 7 of the Fair Labor Standards Act of 1938.
19. If the employee is dissatisfied with the employer’s rejection or alternative, the employee would have the right to receive the decision in writing and then schedule meetings, accompanied by a representative, and if necessary, hearings in a federal court.

levels, to address the underlying sources of the work-family consequences observed in the empirical results, particularly regarding work schedules that are on-call, unstable and cancelled on very short notice. Such schedules -while not necessary escalating over time—afflict a wide variety of employees, although it is concentrated in a few sectors, such as retail trade, food services and other services such as educational and health. Thus, not surprisingly, the initial wave of such legislation has targeted those sectors, yet it would be beneficial for workers with families to gain such protections in any sector. Our key findings -- that the irregular shift-working is harmful to work-family balance, that part-time working does not at all ameliorate that harm, but that flexibility to take off time from work for personal reason shields workers from at least some of that harm - has implications for which type of policies would help reduce the extent and frequency of workers' work-family balance efforts. For example, legally protected rights to request alterations in the daily schedule of hours, and an ability to refuse unwelcome shift times or "extra hours," particularly for part-time employees, would unambiguously facilitate such workers' attempt to better balance work with family responsibilities and time.

Figure 7.1 Work Shift by Survey Year

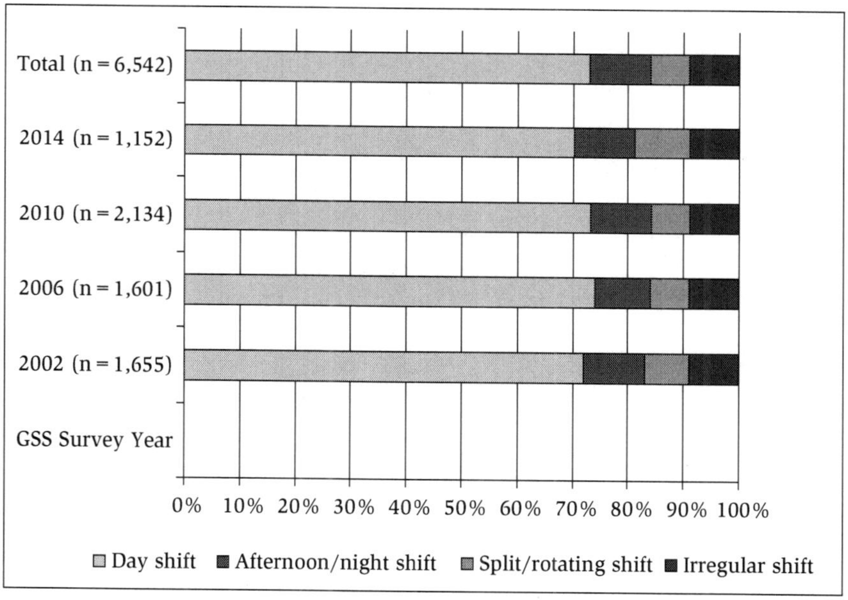

Figure 7.2 Work Shift by Industry Sector

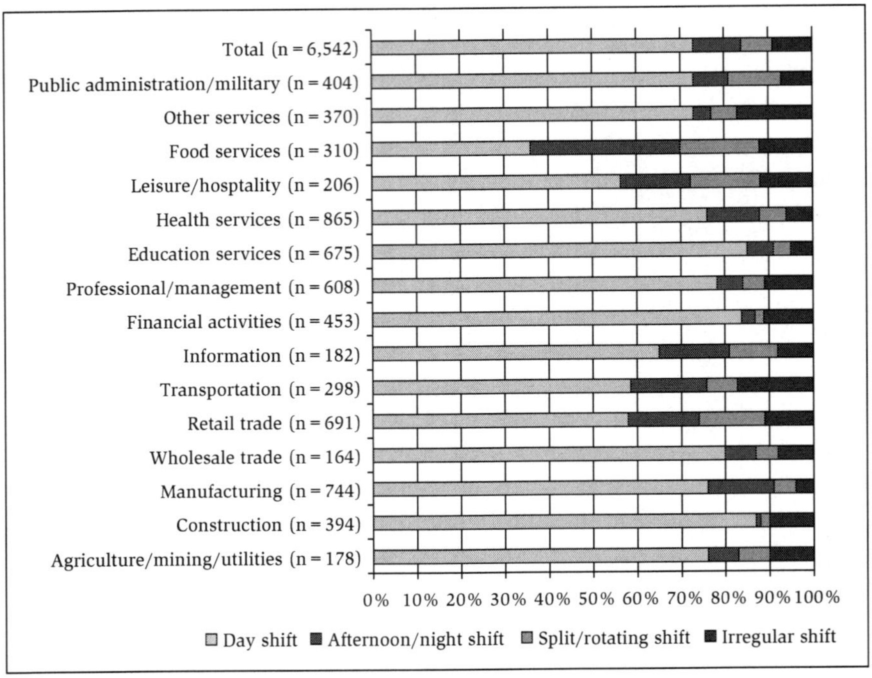

Figure 7.3 Work-Family Conflict by Work Shift

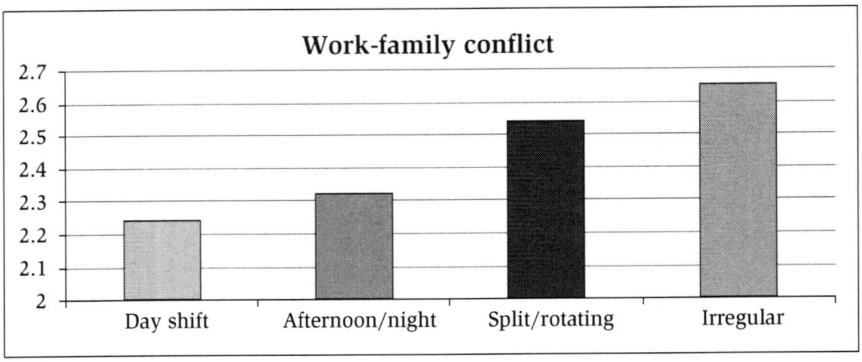

Figure 7.4 Work-Family Conflict by Gender

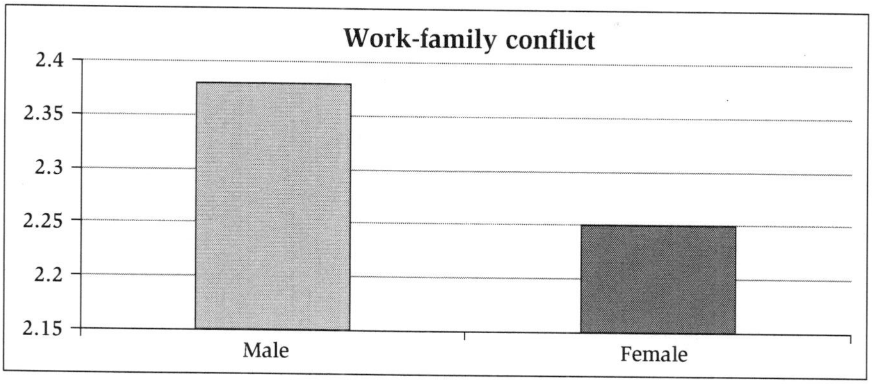

Figure 7.5 Work-Family Conflict by Marital Status and Spouse's Work Status

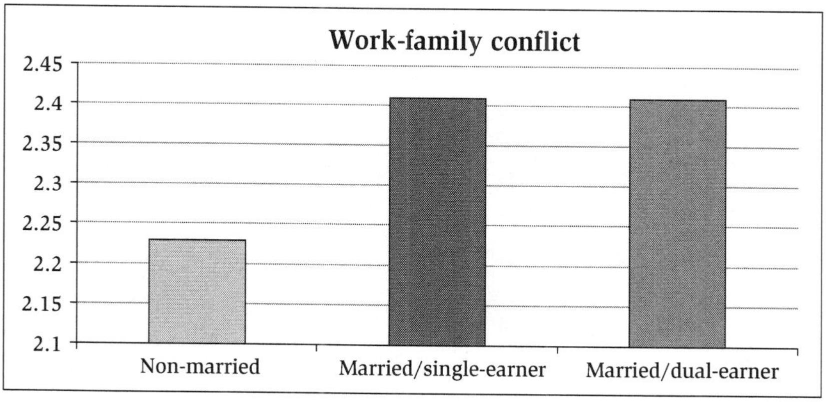

Figure 7.6 Work-Family Conflict by Age

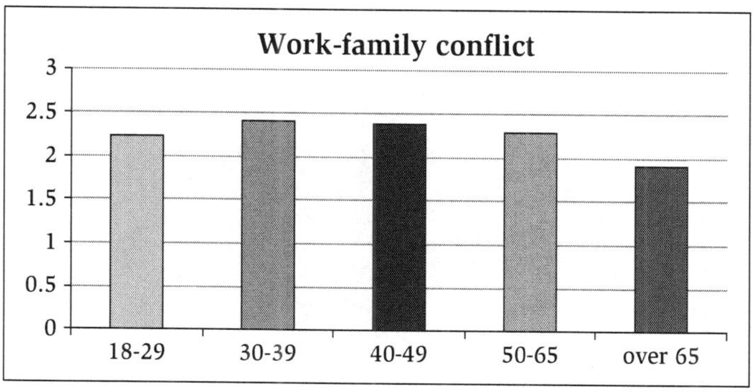

Figure 7.7 Work-Family Conflict by Number of Children in Household (Under Age 12)

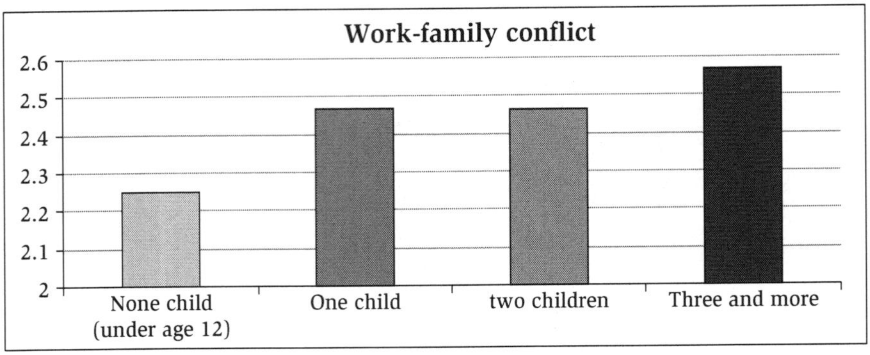

Figure 7.8 Work-Family Conflict by Education

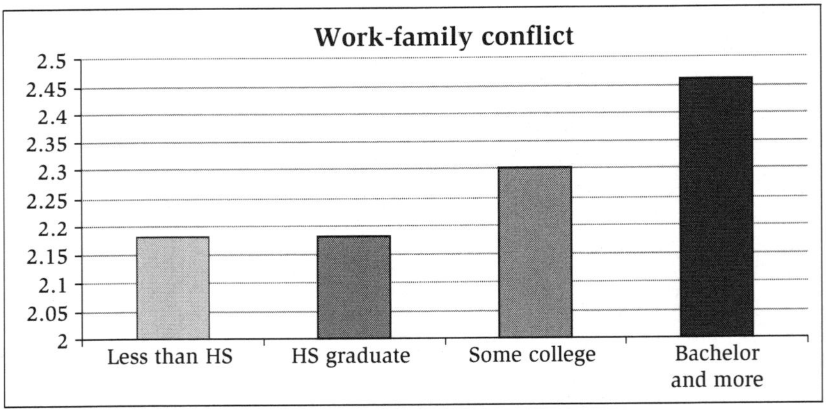

Figure 7.9 Work-Family Conflict by Income

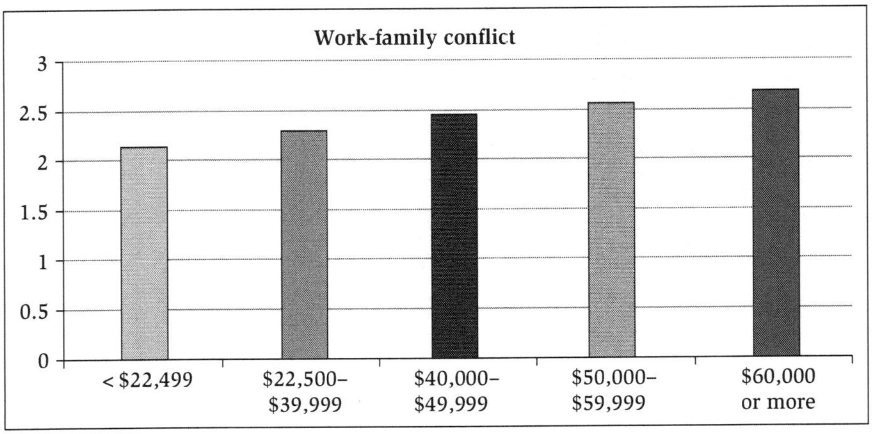

Figure 7.10 Work-Family by Full-time/Part-time Job Status

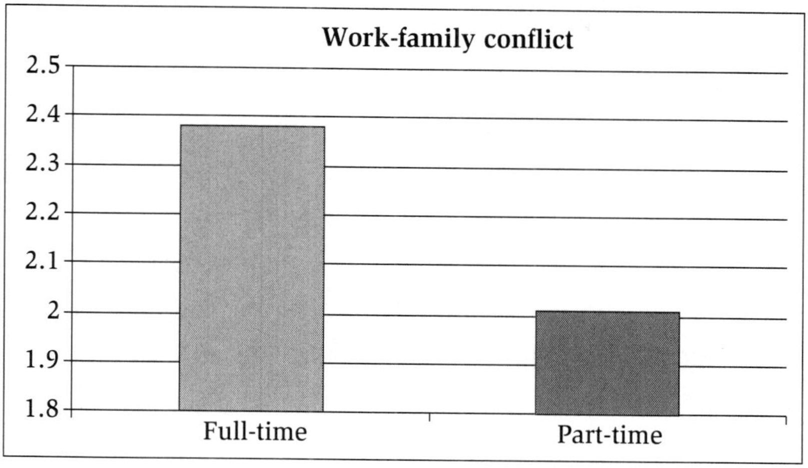

Table 7.1 Multi-nominal Logit Model to Predict Work Shift

	Split/Rotating Shift	*Irregular Shift*	*Split/Rotating Shift*	*Irregular Shift*
	Coef. (S.E.)	*Coef. (S.E.)*	*Coef. (S.E.)*	*Coef. (S.E.)*
How workers paid				
Salaried (ref.)				
Hourly paid	0.885***	-0.188	0.862***	-0.027
	(0.139)	(0.123)	(0.141)	(0.126)
Other paid	1.019***	1.611***	1.074***	1.498***
	(0.182)	(0.123)	(0.184)	(0.125)
Respondent income				
< $22,499 (ref.)				
$22,500–$39,999	-0.385**	-0.448***	-0.385**	-0.442**
	(0.135)	(0.133)	(0.135)	(0.135)
$40,000–$49,999	-0.742**	-0.349*	-0.764***	-0.351
	(0.227)	(0.178)	(0.228)	(0.180)
$50,000–$59,999	-0.340	-0.898***	-0.314	-0.973***
	(0.252)	(0.243)	(0.253)	(0.245)
Over $60,000	-0.149	-0.449**	-0.114	-0.500**
	(0.197)	(0.165)	(0.198)	(0.166)
Working hours	0.0189***	0.008*	0.015***	0.005
	(0.003)	(0.003)	(0.003)	(0.003)
Overtime work is mandatory			0.314**	0.449***

	Split/Rotating Shift	*Irregular Shift*	*Split/Rotating Shift*	*Irregular Shift*
	Coef. (S.E.)	*Coef. (S.E.)*	*Coef. (S.E.)*	*Coef. (S.E.)*
			(0.106)	(0.101)
Ability to take time off during day			-0.146**	-0.189***
			(0.0493)	(0.0482)
Ability to Change start/end time			-0.0668	0.360***
			(0.044)	(0.0452)
N	6,452		6,452	

Note. Reference group is a regular shift (day, afternoon, and night shift); All models are controlled for respondent's education, survey year, age, age squared, race, marital status, having a pre-school child, and years on the job. GSS Quality of Worklife module data, for 2002, 2006, 2010, and 2014. Standard error is in parenthesis. Coef. = coefficient.

***$p < .001$ **$p < .01$ *$p < .05$.

Table 7.2 The Association between Work Shift and Work-Family Conflict and the Interaction Effects

	Model 1	Model 2	Model 3	Model 4	Model 5	Model 6
	Main Model	*Gender Interaction*	*Schedule Flexibility Interaction*	*Schedule Flexibility Interaction*	*Part/ Full Time Interaction*	*Hourly/ Salary Workers Interaction*
	Coef. (S.E.)	*Coef. (S.E.)*	*Coef. (S.E.)*	*Coef. (S.E.)*	*Coef. (S.E.)*	*Coef. (S.E.)*
Education						
High school graduate or less (ref.)						
Some college	0.067*	0.0670*	0.0826**	0.0685*	0.0660*	0.0532
	(0.029)	(0.0290)	(0.0279)	(0.0290)	(0.0295)	(0.0308)
Bachelor and more	0.126***	0.1255***	0.1436***	0.1309***	0.1071**	0.1216***
	(0.032)	(0.0325)	(0.0313)	(0.0326)	(0.0331)	(0.0351)
Survey year						
2002 (ref.)						
2006	0.001	0.0014	-0.0021	0.0012	0.0074	0.0125
	(0.032)	(0.0324)	(0.0312)	(0.0323)	(0.0329)	(0.0343)
2010	0.131***	0.1309***	0.1155***	0.1300***	0.1409***	0.1249***
	(0.030)	(0.0304)	(0.0294)	(0.0304)	(0.0310)	(0.0324)
2014	0.139***	0.1389***	0.1169***	0.1391***	0.1508***	0.1306***
	(0.036)	(0.0358)	(0.0346)	(0.0358)	(0.0365)	(0.0381)
Age	-0.003**	-0.0035**	-0.0030**	-0.0033**	-0.0047***	-0.0036**
	(0.001)	(0.0011)	(0.0011)	(0.0011)	(0.0011)	(0.0012)
Age square	-0.000**	-0.0002**	-0.0002**	-0.0002**	-0.0002***	-0.0002*
	(0.000)	(0.0001)	(0.0001)	(0.0001)	(0.0001)	(0.0001)

	Model 1	*Model 2*	*Model 3*	*Model 4*	*Model 5*	*Model 6*
	Main Model	*Gender Interaction*	*Schedule Flexibility Interaction*	*Schedule Flexibility Interaction*	*Part/ Full Time Interaction*	*Hourly/ Salary Workers Interaction*
	Coef. (S.E.)	*Coef. (S.E.)*	*Coef. (S.E.)*	*Coef. (S.E.)*	*Coef. (S.E.)*	*Coef. (S.E.)*
How workers paid						
Salaried (ref.)						
Hourly paid	-0.161***	-0.1623***	-0.1663***	-0.1642***	-0.2158***	
	(0.030)	(0.0297)	(0.0286)	(0.0300)	(0.0301)	
Other ways paid	0.003	0.0039	-0.0010	0.0114	-0.0009	
	(0.041)	(0.0412)	(0.0397)	(0.0413)	(0.0421)	
Race						
Non-white (ref.)						
White	0.181***	0.1808***	0.1775***	0.1812***	0.1832***	0.1856***
	(0.028)	(0.0278)	(0.0268)	(0.0278)	(0.0283)	(0.0289)
Gender						
Male (ref.)						
Female	0.019	0.0031	0.0008	0.0207	-0.0184	0.0081
	(0.026)	(0.0298)	(0.0250)	(0.0258)	(0.0262)	(0.0274)
Marital status & Spouse's Work Status						
Non-married (ref.)						
Married & single-earner	0.122***	0.1210***	0.1300***	0.1233***	0.1079***	0.1155***
	(0.026)	(0.0264)	(0.0254)	(0.0264)	(0.0268)	(0.0280)
Married & dual-earner	0.117**	0.1174**	0.1094**	0.1184**	0.1081**	0.1157**
	(0.037)	(0.0371)	(0.0357)	(0.0370)	(0.0377)	(0.0397)

	Model 1	*Model 2*	*Model 3*	*Model 4*	*Model 5*	*Model 6*
	Main Model	*Gender Interaction*	*Schedule Flexibility Interaction*	*Schedule Flexibility Interaction*	*Part/ Full Time Interaction*	*Hourly/ Salary Workers Interaction*
	Coef. (S.E.)	*Coef. (S.E.)*	*Coef. (S.E.)*	*Coef. (S.E.)*	*Coef. (S.E.)*	*Coef. (S.E.)*
The number of child (younger than 12 years old)						
None (ref.)						
One	0.198***	0.1973***	0.1970***	0.1993***	0.1887***	0.1957***
	(0.036)	(0.0356)	(0.0344)	(0.0356)	(0.0363)	(0.0374)
Two or more	0.221***	0.2209***	0.2179***	0.2199***	0.1993***	0.1944***
	(0.037)	(0.0370)	(0.0357)	(0.0370)	(0.0377)	(0.0392)
Worker's annual income						
< $22,499 (ref.)						
$22,500–$39,999	0.048	0.0480	0.0579	0.0480	0.0797*	0.0804*
	(0.033)	(0.0326)	(0.0314)	(0.0325)	(0.0337)	(0.0343)
$40,000–$49,999	0.123**	0.1222**	0.1385**	0.1192**	0.1677***	0.1623***
	(0.045)	(0.0455)	(0.0438)	(0.0454)	(0.0466)	(0.0481)
$50,000–$59,999	0.237***	0.2354***	0.2460***	0.2327***	0.2877***	0.2883***
	(0.054)	(0.0540)	(0.0520)	(0.0541)	(0.0552)	(0.0575)
Over $60,000	0.222***	0.2202***	0.2433***	0.2179***	0.3195***	0.3158***
	(0.045)	(0.0455)	(0.0438)	(0.0457)	(0.0461)	(0.0501)
Missing for income cases	-0.029	-0.0290	-0.0164	-0.0240	-0.0135	-0.0118
	(0.038)	(0.0384)	(0.0371)	(0.0384)	(0.0392)	(0.0418)

	Model 1	*Model 2*	*Model 3*	*Model 4*	*Model 5*	*Model 6*
	Main Model	*Gender Interaction*	*Schedule Flexibility Interaction*	*Schedule Flexibility Interaction*	*Part/ Full Time Interaction*	*Hourly/ Salary Workers Interaction*
	Coef. (S.E.)	*Coef. (S.E.)*	*Coef. (S.E.)*	*Coef. (S.E.)*	*Coef. (S.E.)*	*Coef. (S.E.)*
Years working for the job	0.001	0.0012	0.0025	0.0014	0.0014	0.0025
	(0.002)	(0.0015)	(0.0015)	(0.0015)	(0.0016)	(0.0017)
Work hours	0.015***	0.0153***	0.0121***	0.0152***		0.0155***
	(0.001)	(0.0009)	(0.0009)	(0.0009)		(0.0010)
Industry sector						
Agriculture/mining (ref.)						
	0.005	0.0068	-0.0008	0.0073	-0.0452	0.0310
Construction	(0.084)	(0.0836)	(0.0805)	(0.0835)	(0.0850)	(0.0925)
Manufacturing	-0.057	-0.0536	-0.0505	-0.0577	-0.0989	-0.0233
	(0.077)	(0.0772)	(0.0744)	(0.0771)	(0.0786)	(0.0836)
Wholesale trade	-0.162	-0.1578	-0.1882	-0.1628	-0.2127*	-0.0990
	(0.100)	(0.1000)	(0.0963)	(0.0999)	(0.1017)	(0.1098)
Retail trade	-0.008	-0.0051	-0.0172	-0.0133	-0.0660	0.0333
	(0.079)	(0.0787)	(0.0759)	(0.0786)	(0.0801)	(0.0857)
Transportation	0.023	0.0300	-0.0104	0.0197	-0.0017	0.0437
	(0.088)	(0.0877)	(0.0844)	(0.0875)	(0.0892)	(0.0967)
Information	-0.006	-0.0027	-0.0035	-0.0097	-0.0706	0.0445
	(0.098)	(0.0981)	(0.0946)	(0.0981)	(0.0999)	(0.1056)
Financial activities	-0.058	-0.0542	-0.0583	-0.0568	-0.1236	-0.0120
	(0.083)	(0.0830)	(0.0800)	(0.0829)	(0.0844)	(0.0909)

	Model 1	Model 2	Model 3	Model 4	Model 5	Model 6
	Main Model	*Gender Interaction*	*Schedule Flexibility Interaction*	*Schedule Flexibility Interaction*	*Part/ Full Time Interaction*	*Hourly/ Salary Workers Interaction*
	Coef. (S.E.)	*Coef. (S.E.)*	*Coef. (S.E.)*	*Coef. (S.E.)*	*Coef. (S.E.)*	*Coef. (S.E.)*
Professional/ management	-0.068	-0.0644	-0.0564	-0.0655	-0.1395	-0.0306
	(0.080)	(0.0798)	(0.0769)	(0.0797)	(0.0811)	(0.0873)
Education services	-0.004	0.0031	-0.0489	-0.0075	-0.0855	0.0611
	(0.081)	(0.0809)	(0.0779)	(0.0810)	(0.0821)	(0.0869)
Health services	-0.032	-0.0256	-0.0510	-0.0339	-0.0791	0.0217
	(0.078)	(0.0781)	(0.0752)	(0.0779)	(0.0794)	(0.0842)
Leisure/hospitality	-0.082	-0.0786	-0.1003	-0.0801	-0.1634	-0.0525
	(0.096)	(0.0957)	(0.0922)	(0.0955)	(0.0972)	(0.1034)
Food services	-0.035	-0.0297	-0.0594	-0.0463	-0.1062	0.0238
	(0.089)	(0.0891)	(0.0858)	(0.0890)	(0.0907)	(0.0958)
Other services	-0.123	-0.1213	-0.1100	-0.1223	-0.1944*	-0.0955
	(0.085)	(0.0855)	(0.0824)	(0.0854)	(0.0869)	(0.0951)
Public administration	-0.084	-0.0801	-0.0683	-0.0900	-0.1430	-0.0472
	(0.084)	(0.0839)	(0.0809)	(0.0838)	(0.0853)	(0.0896)
Work shift						
Day shift (ref.)						
Afternoon/night shift	0.265***	0.2374***	0.1875***	0.3031***	0.2876***	0.3106**
	(0.039)	(0.0553)	(0.0455)	(0.0659)	(0.0455)	(0.1016)
Split/rotate shift	0.354***	0.3563***	0.2660***	0.3411***	0.4638***	0.2647**
	(0.045)	(0.0644)	(0.0534)	(0.0673)	(0.0516)	(0.0994)

	Model 1	*Model 2*	*Model 3*	*Model 4*	*Model 5*	*Model 6*
	Main Model	*Gender Interaction*	*Schedule Flexibility Interaction*	*Schedule Flexibility Interaction*	*Part/ Full Time Interaction*	*Hourly/ Salary Workers Interaction*
	Coef. (S.E.)	*Coef. (S.E.)*	*Coef. (S.E.)*	*Coef. (S.E.)*	*Coef. (S.E.)*	*Coef. (S.E.)*
Irregular shift	0.401***	0.3506***	0.2874***	0.3106***	0.5036***	0.5183***
	(0.042)	(0.0545)	(0.0481)	(0.0495)	(0.0501)	(0.0743)
Afternoon/night x female		0.0532				
		(0.0749)				
Split/rotate x female		-0.0043				
		(0.0877)				
Irregular x female		0.1156				
		(0.0813)				
Taking time off			-0.2637***			
			(0.0133)			
Afternoon/night x taking time off			-0.1022**			
			(0.0354)			
Split/rotate x taking time off			-0.0615			
			(0.0395)			
Irregular x taking time off			-0.1111**			
			(0.0357)			
Change start/end times				0.0114		
				(0.0119)		
Afternoon/night x change start/end times				0.0132		
				(0.0341)		

	Model 1	Model 2	Model 3	Model 4	Model 5	Model 6
	Main Model	*Gender Interaction*	*Schedule Flexibility Interaction*	*Schedule Flexibility Interaction*	*Part/ Full Time Interaction*	*Hourly/ Salary Workers Interaction*
	Coef. (S.E.)	*Coef. (S.E.)*	*Coef. (S.E.)*	*Coef. (S.E.)*	*Coef. (S.E.)*	*Coef. (S.E.)*
Split/rotate x change start/end times				-0.0227		
				(0.0361)		
Irregular x change start/end times				-0.1354***		
				(0.0338)		
Part-time (ref. full-time)					-0.1703***	
					(0.0426)	
Afternoon/night x part-time					-0.1279	
					(0.0905)	
Split/rotate x part-time					-0.2373*	
					(0.1072)	
Irregular x part-time					-0.2031*	
					(0.0915)	
Hourly paid						-0.1336***
						(0.0330)
Afternoon/night x hourly paid						-0.0390
						(0.1097)
Split/rotate x hourly paid						0.1143
						(0.1127)
Irregular x hourly paid						-0.0107
						(0.1004)

	Model 1	*Model 2*	*Model 3*	*Model 4*	*Model 5*	*Model 6*
	Main Model	*Gender Interaction*	*Schedule Flexibility Interaction*	*Schedule Flexibility Interaction*	*Part/ Full Time Interaction*	*Hourly/ Salary Workers Interaction*
	Coef. (S.E.)	*Coef. (S.E.)*	*Coef. (S.E.)*	*Coef. (S.E.)*	*Coef. (S.E.)*	*Coef. (S.E.)*
N	6,542	6,542	6,542	6,542	6,542	5,753
R-squared	0.151	0.151	0.211	0.152	0.120	0.153

Note. Standard error is in parenthesis. Coef. = coefficient. Ref. = reference category.

*** $p < 0.001$, ** $p < 0.01$, * $p < 0.05$.

Table 7.3 The Interaction Effects of Work Shift with Industry

	Industry Interaction
	Coef. (S.E.)
Afternoon/night shift	0.113
	(0.161)
Afternoon/night x Agriculture/mining	-0.630*
	(0.311)
Afternoon/night x Retail trade	0.407*
	(0.188)
Afternoon/night x Public Admin.	0.468*
	(0.234)
Split/rotate shift	0.171
	(0.176)
Split/rotate x Construction	0.920*
	(0.371)
Split/rotate x Education services	0.513*
	(0.259)
Irregular shift	0.145
	(0.121)
Irregular x Retail trade	0.346*
	(0.167)
Irregular x Health services	0.449*
	(0.178)
Irregular x Food services	0.611**
	(0.211)
N	6,542
R-squared	0.160

Note. Only significant interaction estimates are reported. This model adust for same control variables as the previous models in Table 7.2. Standard error is in parenthesis. Coef. = coefficient. Ref. = reference category.

*** $p < 0.001$, ** $p < 0.01$, * $p < 0.05$.

REFERENCES

Alexander, Charlotte, and Anna Haley-Lock. 2013. "Not Enough Hours in the Day: Work Hour Insecurity and a New Approach to Wage and Hour Regulation." Georgia State University College of Law Legal Studies Research Paper.

Alexander, Charlotte, Anna Haley-Lock, and Nantiya. Ruan, 2014. "Stabilizing Low-Wage Work: Legal Remedies for Unpredictable Work Hours and Income Instability." *Harvard Civil Rights-Civil Liberties Law Review (CR-CL)*, U Denver Legal Studies Research Paper No. 13-43.

Aarons-Mele, Morra. 2014. "Unpredictable Work Hours Are Stressing Too Many People Out." *Harvard Business Review*, August 27.

Andresen, Maike. 2015. "A Look Into the Future: Is Working Time Freedom Apt to Add Value for Different Stakeholders?" *Human Resource Management Practices*, 107–124. Springer International.

Appelbaum, Eileen, Heather Boushey, and John Schmitt. 2014. *The Economic Importance of Women's Rising Hours of Work*. Center for American Progress and the Center for Economic and Policy Research.

Askenazy, Philippe. 2004. "Shorter Work Time, Hours Flexibility and Labor Intensification." *Eastern Economic Journal*, vol. 30, no. 4, 603–14.

Bakst, Dina, Jared Make, and Nancy Rankin. 2011. Beyond The Breadwinner: Professional Dads Speak Out on Work and Family. A Better Balance.

Ballotpedia. 2013. "City of SeaTac 'Good Jobs Initiative' Minimum Wage Increase, Proposition 1." November.

Basner Mathias, AndreaM. Spaeth, and David F. Dinges. 2014. "Sociodemographic Characteristics and Waking Activities and Their Role in the Timing and Duration of Sleep." *Sleep*, vol. 37, no. 12, 1889–1906.

Beninger, Anna, and Nancy M. Carter. 2013. *The Great Debate: Flexibility vs. Face Time—Busting the Myths Behind Flexible Work Arrangements*. Catalyst.

Ben-Ishai, Liz. 2014. *Job Schedules that Work for Businesses*, Center for Law and Social Policy CLASP. http://www.clasp.org/resources-and-publications/publication-1/Job-Schedules-that-Work-for-Businesses.pdf.

Ben-Ishai, Liz, and Hannah Matthews. 2014. *Federal Legislation to Improve Job Schedules and Child Care Access for Low-Wage Workers*, November 19.

Ben-Ishai, Liz, Hannah Matthews, and Jodie Levin-Epstein. 2014. *Scrambling for Stability: The Challenges of Job Schedule Volatility and Child Care*, Center for Law and Social Policy (CLASP).

Berg, Peter, Gerhard Bosch, and Jean Charest. 2014. "Working-Time Configurations A Framework for Analyzing Diversity across Countries." *Industrial and Labor Relations Review*, vol. 67, no. 3, 805–837.

Bernstein, Jared, and Ross Eisenbrey. 2014. *New Inflation-adjusted Salary Test Would Bring Needed Clarity to FLSA Overtime Rules*. Economic Policy Institute report. *http://www.epi.org/publication/inflation-adjusted-salary-testbring-needed/*.

Bird, Robert C., and Elizabeth Brown. 2016. *"The Right to Request as a Model for Flexible Working Time."*

Bloom, Nicholas, ., Tobias Kretschmer, and John. Van Reenen. 2011. "Are Family-Friendly Workplace Practices a Valuable Firm Resource?" *Strategic Management Journal*, vol. 32, 343–367.

Bohle, Philip, Harold Willaby, Michael Quinlan, and Maria McNamara. 2011. "Flexible Work in Call Centres: Working Hours, Work-life Conflict & Health." *Applied Ergonomics*, vol. 42, no. 2, 219–224.

Boots, Shelley Waters. 2004. *The Way We Work: How Children and Their Families Fare in a 21st Century Workplace*, The New America Foundation.

Boushey Heather, and Alexandra Mitukiewicz. 2014. *Job Quality Matters: How Our Future Economic Competitiveness Hinges on the Quality of Parents' Jobs.* Washington Center for Equitable Growth.

Boushey, Heather, and Sarah Jane Glynn. 2012. *There Are Significant Business Costs to Replacing Employees.* Center for American Progress. Washington DC.

Boushey, Heather. 2011. "The Role of the Government in Work-family Conflict." *The Future of Children*, vol. 21, no. 2, 163–190.

Camerino, Donatella, Marco Sandri, Samantha Sartori, Paul Maurice Conway, Paolo Campanini, and Giovanni Costa. 2010. "Shiftwork, Work-Family Conflict Among Italian Nurses, and Prevention Efficacy." *Chronobiology International*, vol. 27, no. 5, 1105–1123.

Canadian Labour Congress. 2011. *Mapping Basic Working Conditions in Employment Standards Laws Across Canada — 2011/2012.* October *www.canadianlabour.ca 14.*

Carré, Françoise, and Chris Tilly. 2012. "Work Hours in Retail: Room for Improvement." Policy Paper No. 2012-012. Kalamazoo, MI: W.E. Upjohn Institute for Employment Research. *http://research.upjohn.org/up_policypapers/12.*

Cauthen, Nancy K. 2011. "Scheduling Hourly Workers: How Last Minute." Just-In-Time Scheduling Practices Are Bad for Workers, Families and Business. *Demos.* New York, March.

Center for Law and Social Policy (CLASP), Retail Action Project (RAP), and Women Employed. 2014. *Tackling Unstable and Unpredictable Work Schedules.*

Center for Law and Social Policy (CLASP). 2014. *Job Schedules that Work for Businesses.* November 26.

Charlesworth, Sara, and Iain Campbell. 2008. Right to Request Regulation: A Panacea for Work/Family Imbalance? Draft, Parliament of Australia.

Chung, Heejung. & Tijdens, Kea. 2013. "Working Time Components and Working Time Regimes in Europe: Using Company-Level Data Across 21 Countries." *International Journal of Human Resource Management*, vol. 24, no. 7, 1418–1434.

Correll, Shelley. J., Kelly, Erin. L., Trimble-O'Connor, Lindsey, & Williams, Joan. 2014. "Redesigning, Redefining Work." *Work & Occupations*, vol. 41, no. 1, 3–17. *doi:10.1177/0730888413515250.*

Costa, Giovanni, Samantha Sartori, and Torbjorn Akerstedt. 2006. "Influence of Flexibility and Variability of Working Hours on Health and Well-Being." *Chronobiology International*, vol. 23, no. 6, 1125–37.

Covert, Bryce. "How Unpredictable Hours Are Screwing Up People's Lives." 2014. *ThinkProgress*, on September 11.

Dahl, Molly, Thomas DeLeire, and Jonathan Schwabish. 2011. "Estimates of Year-to-Year Volatility in Earnings and in Household Incomes from Administrative, Survey and Matched Data." *Journal of Human Resources*, Fall, vol. 46, 750–774.

Delaney, Arthur, and Emily Swanson. 2014. "Less Pay, More Weekend? Some Americans Are Ready To Say Yes." *Huffington Post*, July 26.

Demos, 2013. *Underwriting Bad Jobs: How Our Tax Dollars are Funding Low-Wage Work and Fueling Inequality*, May.

Dynan Karen, Douglas Elmendorf, and Daniel Sichel. 2012. "The Evolution of Household Income Volatility," *The B.E. Journal of Economic Analysis & Policy*, vol. 12, no. 2 (Advances), Article 3.

Enchautegui María E., 2013. *Nonstandard Work Schedules and the Well-Being of Low-Income Families Low-Income Working Families*, Urban Institute, Paper 26, July.

Fagan, Colette, Clare Lyonette, Mark Smith, and Abril Saldaña-Tejeda. 2012. *The Influence of Working Time Arrangements on Work-life Integration or "Balance": a Review of the International Evidence*. International Labour Organization.

Federal Reserve Bank Board of Governors. 2014. *Report on the Economic Well-Being of U.S. Households in 2013*.

Glauber, Rebecca. 2013. *Wanting More but Working Less: Involuntary Part-time Employment and Economic Vulnerability*. The Carsey School of Public Policy at the University of New Hampshire Scholars' Repository.

Golden, Lonnie, Barbara Wiens-Tuers, Susan J. Lambert, and Julia R. Henly. 2011. "Working Time in the Employment Relationship: Working Time, Perceived Control and Work–life Balance." Chapter 10, K. Townsend and A. Wilkinson (eds.) *Research Handbook on the Future of Work and Employment Relations*, Edward Elgar, UK, 188–211.

Golden, Lonnie., Julia. Henly, Susan. Lambert, and Jaeseung. Kim. 2013. "Work Schedule Flexibility for Workers: A Path to Employee Happiness?" *Journal of Social Research and Policy*, vol. 4, no. 2, December, 107–135.

Golden, Lonnie. 2012a. "Becoming Too Small to Bail—Prospects for Workers in the 2011 Economy and 112th Congress," *Indiana Labor Law Journal*, vol. 87, 11.

Golden, Lonnie. 2012b. *The Effects of Working Time on Productivity and Firm Performance: A Research Synthesis Paper*. International Labour Organization.

Golden, Lonnie. 2009. "Flexible Daily Work Schedules in US Jobs: Formal Introductions Needed?" *Industrial Relations*, vol. 48, no. 1, 27–54.

Golden, Lonnie. 2014. *Flexibility and Overtime Among Hourly and Salaried Workers: When You Have Little Flexibility, You Have Little To Lose*. Economic Policy Institute Briefing Paper #385.

Golden, L., and Adam Okulicz-Kozaryn. 2015. *Work Hours and Worker Happiness in the US: Weekly Hours, Hours Preferences and Schedule Flexibility*. Draft.

Gottschalk, Peter, and Robert Moffitt. 2009. "The Rising Instability of U.S. Earnings." *The Journal of Economic Perspectives*, vol. 23, no. 4, Fall, 3–24.

Gottschalk, Peter, Robert Moffitt, Lawrence F. Katz, and William T. Dickens. 1994. "The Growth of Earnings Instability in the U.S. Labor Market." *Brookings Papers on Economic Activity*, 217–272.

Hacker, Jacob S., Gregory A. Huber, Austin Nichols, Philipp Rehm, Mark Schlesinger, Rob Valletta, and Stuart Craig. 2014. "The Economic Security Index: A New Measure for Research and Policy Analysis." *Review of Income and Wealth*, vol. 60, Issue Supplement S1, pages S5–S32.

Haley-Lock Anna, and Stephanie Ewert. 2011. "Waiting for the Minimum: U.S. State Wage Laws, Firm Strategy, and Chain-Restaurant Job Quality," *Journal of Industrial Relations*, vol. 53, no. 1, 31–48.

Harris, Seth D. 2000. "Conceptions of Fairness and The Fair Labor Standards Act," *Hofstra Labor & Employment Law Journal,* vol. 18, 19.

Hegewisch, Ariane. 2005. *Employers and European Flexible Working Rights: When the Floodgates were Opened.* UC Hastings College Center for Worklife Law, Issue Brief, Fall.

Hegewisch Ariane. 2009. *Flexible Working Policies: a Comparative Review,* Institute for Women's Policy Research and the Equality and Human Rights Commission.

Hegewisch, Ariane, and Gornick, Janet. 2008. *Statutory Routes to Workplace Flexibility in Cross-National Perspective.* Institute for Women's Policy Research and the Center For Worklife Law, University Of California Hastings College of the Law.

Heisz, Andrew, and Sébastien LaRochelle-Côté. 2006. "Work Hours Instability." *Perspectives on Labour and Income*, vol. 7, no. 12, 17–20.

Henly, Julia R., and Susan Lambert. 2014. "Unpredictable Work Timing in Retail Jobs: Implications for Employee Work-life Outcomes." *Industrial and Labor Relations Review*, vol. 67, no. 3, 986–1016.

Henly, Julia. R., H.Luke. Shaefer, and Elaine. Waxman. 2006. "Nonstandard Work Schedules: Employer- and Employee-driven Flexibility in Retail Jobs." *Social Service Review*, vol. 80, no. 4, 609–34.

Heymann, Jody, and Alison Earle. 2010. *Raising the Global Floor: Dismantling the Myth that We Can't Afford Good Working Conditions for Everyone.* Stanford, Calif.: Stanford University Press.

International Social Survey Program, Work Orientations III Module, 2005–2006, GESIS, Leibnitz Institute for the Social Sciences

Jacobs, Anna W., and Irene Padavic. 2015. "Hours, Scheduling and Flexibility for Women in the US Low-Wage Labour Force." *Gender, Work & Organization*, vol. 22, no. 1, 1418–1434.

Jamieson, Dave. 2014. "In Wake of Protests, Walmart Workers Find More Hours Within Reach." *Huffington Post*, April 7.

Jensen, Shane T., and Stephen H. Shore. 2008. "Changes in the Distribution of Income Volatility." Johns Hopkins University, mimeo. *arXiv preprint arXiv:0808.1090.*

Jobs With Justice San Francisco. N.d. "Retail Workers Bill of Rights." http://retailworkerrights.com/.

Kalleberg, A.L. 2011. *Good Jobs, Bad Jobs: The Rise of Polarized and Precarious Employment in the United States, 1970s to 2000s.* New York: Russell Sage Foundation.

Kantor, Jodi. 2014. "As Shifts Vary, Family's Only Constant Is Chaos." *New York Times*, August 14.

Kassinis, G. I., and Stavrou, E. T. 2013. "Non-standard Work Arrangements and National Context." *European Management Journal,* vol. 31, no. 5, 464–477.

Kelly, Erin L., Phyllis Moen, J. Michael Oakes, Wen Fan, Cassandra Okechukwu, Kelly D. Davis, and Leslie B. Hammer. 2014. "Changing Work and Work-Family

Conflict Evidence from the Work, Family, and Health Network." *American Sociological Review*, June, vol. 79, no. 3, 485–516.

Kelly, Erin L., and Alexandra Kalev. 2006. "Managing Flexible Work Arrangements in U.S. Organizations: Formalized Discretion or 'a Right to Ask.'" *Socio-Economic Review*, vol. 4, no. 3, 379–416.

Kroll, Steven. 2011. "The Decline in Work Hours During the 2007–09 Recession," *Monthly Labor Review*, April, 53–59. *http://www.bls.gov/opub/mlr/2011/04/art10full.pdf.*

Kulow, Marianne DelPo. 2012. "Legislating a Family-Friendly Workplace: Should It Be Done in the United States?" *Northwestern Journal of Law and Social Policy*, vol. 7.

Labor Project for Working Families. 2014. "Flex Pack: A Toolkit on Organizing, Bargaining and Legislating for Worker-Controlled Flexibility."

Lafer, Gordon. 2013. *The Legislative Attack on American Wages and Labor Standards, 2011–2012*. Economic Policy Institute, Briefing Paper # 364, October 31.

Lambert, Susan J. 2008. "Passing the Buck: Labor Flexibility Practices that Transfer Risk onto Hourly Workers." *Human Relations*, vol. 61, no. 9, 1203–27.

Lambert, Susan J., Peter J. Fugiel, and Julia R. Henly. 2014. *Schedule Unpredictability among Early Career Workers in the U.S. Labor Market: A National Snapshot.* EINet (Employment Instability, Family Well-being, and Social Policy Network) at the University of Chicago.

Lambert, Susan, and Julia Henly. 2010. *Work Scheduling Study: Mangers' Strategies for Balancing Business Requirements with Employee Needs, Manager Survey Results*, University of Chicago School of Social Service Administration.

Lambert, Susan J., Anna Haley-Lock, and Julia R. Henly. 2012. "Schedule Flexibility in Hourly Jobs: Unanticipated Consequences and Promising Directions." *Community, Work & Family*, vol. 15, no. 3, 293–315.

Lambert, Susan, Anna Haley-Lock, and Julia R. Henly. 2012. "Labour Flexibility and Precarious Employment in Hourly Retail Jobs in the U.S: How Frontline Managers Matter," Chris Warhurst et al.(eds.), *Are Bad Jobs Inevitable? Trends, Determinants and Responses to Job Quality in the Twenty-First Century*. London: Palgrave Macmillan.

Lambert, Susan J. 2014. "The Limits of Voluntary Employer Action for Improving Low-Level Jobs."

Marion Crain and Michael Sherraden (eds.), *Working and Living in the Shadow of Economic Fragility.* Oxford University Press, 120.Lewis, Katherine Reynolds. 2014. *How Men Flex: The Working Mother Report*, Working Mother, October 21.

Li, Jianghong, Sarah Johnson, Wen-Jui Han, Sonia Andrews, Garth Kendall, Lyndall Strazdins, and Alfred Dockery. 2014. "Parents' Nonstandard Work Schedules and Child Well-Being: A Critical Review of the Literature." *The Journal of Primary Prevention*, vol. 35, no. 1, 53–73.

Locke, Susannah. 2014. "Why the Workday Should Be 10–6, Not 9–5," *VOX*, December 23.

Luce, Stephanie, Sasha Hammad, and Darrah Sipe. 2014. *Short-Shifted.* Retail Action Project, The Murphy Institute for Worker Education and Labor Studies at the City University of New York, and the Retail, Wholesale and Department Store Union.

Lyness, K. S., J.C. Gornick, P. Stone, and A.R. Grotto. 2012. "It's All About Control: Worker Control over Schedule and Hours in Cross-National Context." *American Sociological Review*, vol. 77, no. 6, 1023–1049.

Martin, James E., Robert R. Sinclair, Ariel M. Lelchook, Jenell L. S. Wittmer, and Kristen E. Charles. 2012. "Nonstandard Work Schedules and Retention in the Entry-Level Hourly Workforce." *Journal of Occupational and Organizational Psychology*, vol. 85, 1–22.

Matos, Kenneth, and Ellen Galinsky. 2011. *Workplace Flexibility in the United States: A Status Report*. Families and Work Institute.

Mayer, Gerald. 2014. "The Increased Supply of Underutilized Labor from 2006 to 2014." *Monthly Labor Review*, November.

McCrate, Elaine. 2005. "Flexible Hours, Workplace Authority, and Compensating Wage Differentials in the U.S." *Feminist Economics*, vol. 11, no. 1, 11–39.

McCrate, E. 2012. "Flexibility for Whom? Control Over Work Schedule Variability in the U.S." *Feminist Economics*, vol. 18, no. 1, 39–72.

McGuire, Jean Flatley, Kaitlyn Kenney, and Phyllis Brashler. 2010. "Flexible Work Arrangements: The Fact Sheet."

McNamara, Maria, Philip Bohle, and Michael Quinlan. 2011. "Precarious Employment, Working Hours, Work-life Conflict and Health in Hotel Work." *Applied Ergonomics*, vol. 42, no. 2, 225-232.

Messenger, Jon, Conditions of Work and Employment Programme of the International Labour Organization). 2015. Information regarding *Loi sur la sécurisation de l'emploi* provided personally to the author.

Murdoch, Jonathan, and Rachel Schneider. 2014. *Spikes and Dips: How Income Uncertainty Affects Households*, US Financial Diaries, December 4.

National Institute for Occupational Safety and Health (NIOSH). 2002, 2006, 2010. General Social Survey Quality of Worklife Supplement. *http://www.cdc.gov/niosh/topics/stress/qwlquest.html.*

National Partnership for Women & Families and National Women's Law Center. 2014. "Fact Sheet: The Schedules That Work Act: Section-by-Section." Washington DC, July.

Olsen, Karen M., and Svenn-Åge Dahl. 2010. "Working Time: Implications for Sickness Absence and the Work–Family Balance." *International Journal of Social Welfare*, vol. 19, no. 1, 45–53.

Public Policy Polling (PPP). 2014, December 9–11.

Peck, Ben, and Traub, Amy. 2011. *Worth Working For: Strategies For Turning Bad Jobs Into Quality Employment* October 11.

Pilon Annie. 2014. "Survey: 11 Percent of UK Workers Want Flexible Hours In Employment," October 27, *http://smallbiztrends.com/2014/10/survey-uk-workers-want-flexible-hours.html.*

Powell, Lane C. 2013. Flexible Scheduling and Gender Equality: The Working Families Flexibility Act under the Fourteenth Amendment. *http://repository.law.umich.edu/mjgl/vol20/iss2/5.*

Prause, JoAnn, David Dooley, and Jimi Huh. 2009. "Income Volatility and Psychological Depression." *American Journal of Community Psychology* vol. 43, no. 1–2, 57–70.

Ruan, Nantiya, and Nancy Reichman. 2014. "Hours Equity Is the New Pay Equity." *Villanova Law Review,* vol. 59, 35.

Shierholz, Heidi. 2013. *Low Wages and Scant Benefits Leave Many In-Home Workers Unable to Make Ends Meet*, EPI Briefing Paper #369, Economic Policy Institute, November 25.

Scott, Ellen K., Kathryn Edin, Andrew S. London, and Rebecca Joyce Kissane. 2004. "Unstable Work, Unstable Income: Implications for Family Well-Being in the Era of Time-Limited Welfare." *Journal of Poverty,* vol. 8, no. 1, 61–88.

Shaefer, H. Luke. 2009. "Part-Time Workers: Some Key Differences Between Primary and Secondary Earners," *Monthly Labor Review*, vol. 3, 3–15.

Shin, Donggyun. 2012. "Recent Trends in Men's Earnings Volatility: Evidence from the National Longitudinal Survey of Youth, 1985-2009," *The B.E. Journal of Economic Analysis & Policy*, vol. 12, no. 2 (Topics), Article 2. *DOI: 10.1515/1935-1682.3339.*

Skinner, N., and Barbara. Pocock. 2011. "Flexibility and Work-life Interference in Australia." *Journal of Industrial Relations*, vol. 53, no. 1, 65–82.

Standing, Guy. 2011. *The Precariat: The New Dangerous Class*. Bloomsbury Publishing UK.

Stringer, Scott M. *Families and Flexibility: Reshaping the Workplace for the 21st Century*. Comptroller's Office. New York City, June 2014.

Starosciak, 2013. Michael. "State-by-State Reporting Time Pay Laws," *Wage and Hour Review*. Posted on February 5.

Swanberg, Jennifer E., Sharon P. McKechnie, Mamta U. Ojha, and Jacquelyn B. James. 2011. "Schedule Control, Supervisor Support and Work Engagement: A Winning Combination for Workers in Hourly Jobs?" *Journal of Vocational Behavior,* vol. 79, no. 3, 613–624.

Swanberg, J. E., Watson, E., and Eastman, M. 2014. "Scheduling Challenges Among Workers in Low-Wage Hourly Jobs: Similarities and Differences Among Workers in Standard-and Nonstandard-Hour Jobs." *Community, Work & Family*, vol. 17, no. 4, 409–435.

Sweet, Stephen, Marcie Pitt-Catsouphes, Elyssa Besen, and Lonnie Golden. 2014. "Explaining Organizational Variation in Flexible Work Arrangements: Why the Pattern and Scale of Availability Matter." *Community, Work & Family,* vol. 17, no. 2, 115–141.

Sweet, S., Besen, E., Pitt-Catsouphes, M., and McNamara, T. K. 2014. "Do Options for Job Flexibility Diminish in Times of Economic Uncertainty?" *Work, Employment & Society*, vol. 28, no. 6, 882–903.

Tucker, Philip, and Simon Folkard. 2012. *Working Time, Health and Safety: A Research Synthesis Paper*. International Labour Organization.

Wang, Wendy. 2013. Fact Tank—Our Lives in Numbers. *Mothers and work: What's "ideal"?* August 19.

Watson, Liz, and Jennifer E. Swanberg. 2013. "Flexible Workplace Solutions for Low-Wage Hourly Workers: A Framework for a National Conversation 1." *American University. Labor & Employment. LF,* vol. 3, 380–522.

The White House. 2014. "Presidential Memorandum—Enhancing Workplace Flexibilities and Work-Life Program." June 23. *https://www.whitehouse.gov/the-press-office/2014/06/23/presidential-memorandum-enhancing-workplace-flexibilities-and-work-life.*

Williams, Joan, and Heather Boushey. 2010. *The Three Faces of Work-Family Conflict.* Center for American Progress.

Williams, Jonathan. 2015. "Groundbreaking Labor Rights Coming Your Way," Jobs with Justice SF, February 3.

Williams, Joan C., and Penelope Huang. 2011. "Improving Work-Life Fit in Hourly Jobs: An Underutilized Cost-Cutting Strategy in a Globalized World." *Available at SSRN 2126291.*

Wood, Stephen, George Michaelides, and Peter Totterdell. 2013. "The Impact of Fluctuating Workloads on Well-Being and the Mediating Role of Work–Nonwork Interference in This Relationship." *Journal of Occupational Health Psychology,* vol. 18, no. 1, 106.

Wooden, M., D. Warren, D., and R. Drago. 2009. "Working Time Mismatch and Well-being." *British Journal of Industrial Relations,* vol. 47, 147–179.

Yildirim, Dilek, and Zeynep Aycan. 2008. "Nurses' Work Demands and Work–Family Conflict: A Questionnaire Survey." *International Journal of Nursing Studies,* vol. 45, no. 9, 1366–1378.

Zeytinoglu, I. W. Lillevik, M. Seaton, J. Moruz. 2004. "Part-Time and Casual Work in Retail Trade: Stress and Other Factors Affecting the Workplace." *Relations Industrielles*, vol. 59, no. 3, 516–542.

Ziliak, James, Bradley Hardy, and Christopher Bollinger. 2011. "Earnings Volatility in America: Evidence from Matched CPS." *Labour Economics*, December, vol. 18, 742–754.

Ziobro, Paul. 2015. "Dollar General Plans to Spend More on Labor This Year." *Wall St. Journal,* March 12.

CHAPTER 8

Through Work-Life-Family Reconciliation to Gender Equality? Slovenia and the United Kingdom's Legal Frameworks Compared

Barbara Kresal & Ania Zbyszewska

§8.01 INTRODUCTION

Work-family reconciliation and work-life balance have been key social policy issues in countries of the European Union (EU) for some time. However, despite the importance assigned to them at the declarative level, practical progress in this realm has not been as significant as might have been expected.[1] On the contrary, recent developments suggest that the discrepancy between policy aspirations and practice, at least in some EU Member States, has only strengthened during the post-2008 economic crisis. There is growing evidence that workers have found it even harder during this period to reconcile their various obligations despite apparent commitment to, and proliferation of, work-family friendly policies.[2]

One reason for this contradiction may be the fact that rather than being ends in themselves, work-family reconciliation and work-life balance are often also instrumental to other policy objectives. Measures introduced under this broad umbrella have been invoked to support a range of goals and aims including employment facilitation

1. *See*, for instance, European Institute for Gender Equality (2015), *Reconciliation of Work, Family and Private Life in the European Union – Policy Review*, Luxembourg: Publications Office of the EU, pp. 39–46; D. Ahrendt, S. Blum, C. Crepaldi, *Families in the Economic Crisis: Changes in Policy Measures in the EU*. Dublin: Eurofound, 2015; and others.
2. *Ibid. See also The Modern Families Index*, Bright Horizons, 2017. Online: https://www.workingfamilies.org.uk/wp-content/uploads/2017/01/Modern-Families-Index_Full-Report.pdf.

and economic growth, gender equality, and job quality, but also those related to demography and the best interest of children and families.[3] Policymakers have suggested that these various objectives are reconcilable, or even complimentary of one another, though researchers have questioned whether this is in fact the case under the current policy regimes.

Perhaps the most paradigmatic pairing of goals that work-family policies are said to co-facilitate, and one that has attracted the most attention, is that of employment growth and gender equality.[4] Various policy bodies, including the EU, have from the early 1990s promoted the notion that helping people achieve better balance between work and family (especially women, given the traditional and persistent gender-based division of roles) can help to boost overall employment rates and contribute to economic growth.[5] In addition to such broader economic benefits, women's participation in the labour markets has also been said to foster gender equality. This is both, because employment can provide the foundation for women's economic independence, and because women's engagement in paid work might also stimulate a more equal sharing between women and men of responsibilities, duties, and burdens associated with unpaid work.[6] Crucially, scholars have stressed, and EU policymakers have also taken note, that for such a redistribution to take place, work-family reconciliation must be promoted for everyone, so as to enable men also to take charge for care and other domestic tasks. Yet while the need for a cultural change in workplaces and homes has been acknowledged and encouraged, and there is a renewed commitment to developing a comprehensive policy approach to work-family/work-life issues at the EU level,[7] some relevant areas of EU law, like regulation

---

3. The perspective of the best interest of the child is often overlooked in discussions of work-life/family balance. However, measures supporting working parents can be regarded also as ones that favour the child.
4. For the theory considering this pairing from the perspective of gender equality, *see*, for instance, J. Lewis, *Work-Family Balance, Gender and Policy*. Cheltenham Edward: Elgar, 2009; A.-M. Mooney Cotter, *Pregnant Pause – An International Legal Analysis of Maternity Discrimination*. London: Ashgate, 2010; J. Fudge, 'Global Care Chains: International Migrant Care Work', *International Journal of Comparative Labour Law and Industrial Relations* 28, No. 1 (2012): 63–69; J. Sipilä, K. Repo, T. Rissanen, *Cash-for-Childcare: The Consequences for Caring Mothers*. Cheltenham: Edward Elgar, 2010; L. Addati, N. Cassirer, K. Gilchrist, *Maternity and Paternity at Work: Law and Practice Across the World*. Geneva: ILO, 2014 and many others.
5. The emphasis on the employment perspective and macroeconomic goals is evident in the EU documents. For instance, the EU 2020 Strategy sets the target of 75% employment rate, which is possible only through raising women's employment. *See also* the new EU initiative on work-life balance (European Commission, *Roadmap for the Initiative 'A New Start to Address the Challenges of Work-Life Balance Faced by Working Families'*, 2015. Online: http://ec.europa.eu/smart-regulation/roadmaps/docs/2015_just_xxx_maternity_leave.en.pdf). The argument that gender gaps contribute to the GDP loss is also made. *See*, e.g., European Parliament, *Report in Creating Labour Market Conditions Favourable for Work-Life Balance* (2016/2017(INI)), 2. 8. 2016 ('GDP per capita losses attributable to gender gaps in the labour market have been estimated at up to 10% in Europe').
6. Overall, a mutually reinforcing relationship between these objectives has been largely assumed, wherein women's equal employment participation would automatically lead to more gender equality. Of course, this relationship could also be understood the other way around, with the cultural change being a precondition for more equality in employment. In reality, there is a continuous hermeneutic interplay between these two.
7. European Commission, *Roadmap, supra*.

of standard working time,[8] for example, have remained unchallenged by this discussion.[9]

To what extent has been the development of EU policy in so far as work-family and work-life-balance policies' egalitarian and economic potential (and symbiosis) translated at the national level? Furthermore, how robust are these commitments in practice when conditions worsen, such as during the crisis? In this chapter, we scrutinize the current legal frameworks for reconciliation of work and family life in two EU members, Slovenia and the United Kingdom (UK). While both countries have long sought to promote women's employment and 'family friendly' workplaces, the two have very different starting points and have taken distinctive approaches to regulating on this issue. From a comparative perspective, beyond the influence of EU norms, we are particularly interested in the extent to which the existing national frameworks enable employees to take advantage of their entitlements, and especially the degree to which they also support redistribution of unpaid work between men and women. Moreover, we consider how robust the two frameworks have remained during the crisis, in so far as de jure rights and de facto ability of workers to uptake them.

The paper is structured as follows. We begin with a brief social and economic overview, to highlight how each of the countries here considered performs on women's employment, and to highlight a number of key institutional differences between the two. Next, we turn to our national case studies. A brief note on the policy development in each country is followed by more detailed examination of the existing legal frameworks for work-family reconciliation. Our analysis of the two frameworks, in section four, focuses on the perspective of their comparative advantage in so far as employee friendliness, equality-promoting potential, and their robustness during the crisis. We conclude with a reflection on the common problems we see in these models, on what at truly egalitarian model of work-family reconciliation might look like, and on just how far from this ideal we still are.

---

8. Researchers have long argued that while flexible working-time arrangements might be indeed crucial to fostering more egalitarian patterns of work, regulation of *standard* work hours is essential. Comparative research on working-time regimes, suggests those regimes where hours of work are less polarized between women and men, and where limitations on long hours work are maintained, are more likely to encourage redistribution of paid and unpaid work: C. Fagan, 'Gendered Time Schedules: Paid Work in Great Britain', *Social Politics* 3, No. 1 (1996): 72; D.M. Figart, E. Mutari, 'Work Time Regimes in Europe: Can Flexibility and Gender Equity Coexist?' *Journal of Employment Research* 34, No. 4 (2000): 847; D. Figart, E. Mutari, 'Europe at a Crossroads: Harmonization, Liberalization, and the Gender of Work Time' *Social Politics* 8, No. 1 (2001): 53; D. Anxo, 'Working Time Patterns Among Industrialized Countries: A Household Perspective' in *Working Time and Workers' Preferences in Industrialized Countries: Finding the Balance*, edited by J. Messenger, Geneva: ILO, New York: Routledge, 2004, pp. 195–211, 60.
9. A. Zbyszewska, 'Reshaping the European Working-Time Regime: Towards a Sustainable Model.' *European Labour Law Journal* 7, No. 3 (2016): 331–347; A. Zbyszewska *Gendering European Working Time Regimes: The Working Time Directive and the Case of Poland*, Cambridge: CUP, 2016.

§8.02 SOCIAL AND ECONOMIC BACKGROUND

Both Slovenia and the UK boast women's employment rates[10] that are at or above the EU average. However, the two countries differ in so far as employment patterns and gender gaps. The gender employment gap (difference in male and female employment rates) is 11.3% in the UK, and 8% in Slovenia, while the EU average is 11.6%.[11] However, if measured in relation to full-time work equivalency, the gender employment gap is 21.2% in the UK and only 10.5% in Slovenia, compared to EU average of 18.2%.[12] Slovenia also has the lowest gender pay gap in the EU (3.2% in 2013), whereas in the UK, the pay gap is 19.7%, which is above the EU average of 16.3%. The overall gender gap in earnings (which measures the combined impact on the average earnings of all working-age women, whether or not employed, as compared with men) is around 13% in Slovenia, 48% in the UK, and 42% in the EU.[13]

The employment patterns also differ in the two countries. In Slovenia, a great majority of women are employed in full-time work, whereas in the UK, a substantial number of women work part-time: in 2014, the share of part-time work for women amounted to 42.5% in the UK (one of the highest in the EU) and to 14.9% in Slovenia, which is less than half of the EU average (32.8%).[14] Women's part-time employment has been steadily growing in Slovenia (it was 7.2% in 1999, 11.1% in 2005, 13.2% in 2009 and 14.9% in 2014), whereas in the UK, it has remained more or less stable over time, with slight downward long-term trend (it was 42.5% in 2009, 42.6% in 2005, 44% in 1999).[15]

Apart from family-friendly legal frameworks, the ability to increase women's employment rate depends, among others, on the organization of child-care services and their accessibility and actual use. Only a small number of EU countries have already reached the Barcelona targets as regards the child-care (33% of children under 3 years of age and 90% of children from 3 years of age to mandatory school age), with Slovenia being one of them. In Slovenia, over 80% of children under 3 years of age and slightly over 90% of children aged 3 to mandatory school age are in formal child-care. In the UK, these figures are much lower, i.e., for the first age group slightly below 30% and for the second age group slightly above 70%; only Greece, Romania and Poland have lower shares.[16]

---

10. If not otherwise specified, the data refer to the age group 20–64.
11. Data for 2014 (European Union, *Equality Between Women and Men 2015*. Luxembourg: Publications Office of the EU, 2016, p. 48). In 2008, women's employment rate was 68.8% in the UK and 68.5% in Slovenia, while the EU average was 62.8%. In 2014: 70.6%, UK, 63.6%, Slovenia, and 63.4%, EU.

    During the crisis, women's employment situation worsened in Slovenia and slightly improved in the UK.
12. *Ibid.*, p. 49. In 2014, women's employment rate measured in full-time equivalent was 56.9% in the UK and 60.3% in Slovenia, with the EU average of 54.5%.
13. *Ibid.*, p. 53. Data for 2010.
14. European Union, *Employment in Europe 2015*. Luxembourg: Publications Office of the EU, 2016, pp. 339, 439, 455.
15. *Ibid.* and European Union, *Employment in Europe 2009*. Luxembourg: Publications Office of the EU, 2009, pp. 179, 183.
16. European Union, *Equality Between Women and Men 2015, supra*, pp. 12–13. Data for 2013.

There are relevant links between the organization of child-care and the effect of parenthood on employment. In all EU Member States, except Slovenia and Denmark, there is a positive link between parenthood and employment rate for men and a negative link for women (the so-called male breadwinner effect – when presence of children causes more women to either leave their paid work entirely or begin working part-time, whereas the opposite is true for men). On the other hand, a shared breadwinner model is an important indicator of gender equality, but dependent to a large extent on adequate provision of child-care. In Slovenia, the link between parenthood and employment is positive for both, men and women: the employment rate of women aged 25–49 with children is – not much, but still – higher than that of women without children (+2%, whereas +13% for men); in the UK the employment rate of women with children is lower (-11%, +8% for men).[17] Unsurprisingly, according to public-opinion surveys, a large number of UK respondents (above EU average) deem improved child-care accessibility the most effective way to increase women's employment, whereas considerably fewer respondents expressed the same view in Slovenia (below EU average).[18]

However, data on care/home work done by women and men show that although in Slovenia a large majority of women participate in paid work on a full-time basis and the gender employment gap is low, they still preform significantly more homework than men do. On average, women spend 4.7 hours per day and men 2.7 hours per day in unpaid work in Slovenia, whereas in the UK, women spend on average 4.3 and men 2.3 hours per days in unpaid work.[19] These figures suggest that the gender equality in professional life in Slovenia has not yet translated into equality in the domestic sphere, where the unequal distribution of responsibilities persists. The public opinion on what should be done to increase time spent by men in care/home says (the results are very similar in Slovenia and in the UK) that better and more flexible – in the meaning of family-friendly – work arrangements and the change of the men and boy's attitudes towards caring activities are those the most needed.[20]

§8.03 LEGISLATIVE FRAMEWORKS

In this section we examine the current legal frameworks that establish work-family and work-life balance entitlements in Slovenia and the UK. Generally speaking, in both countries, there are several interlocking strands of employment law that impinge

17. C. Miani, S. Hoorens, *Parents at Work: Men and Women Participating in the Labour Force*. Brussels: Rand Europe, European Union, 2014, p. 5.
18. European Commission, *Special Eurobarometer: Gender Equality*. European Union, 2015 (Online: http://ec.europa.eu/justice/gender-equality/files/documents/eurobarometer_report_2015_en.pdf), p. 64.
19. OECD, *Time Spent in Unpaid, Paid and Total Work, by Sex* (Online: http://www.oecd.org/gender/data/timespentinunpaidpaidandtotalworkbysex.htm). Other research shows even bigger differences between women and men's domestic activities, with the average data for the EU suggesting women spend twenty-six hours weekly, on average, on caring activities, while men only nine hours (K. Davaki, *Differences in Men's and Women's Work, Care and Leisure Time*. European Parliament, 2016, pp. 31–32).
20. European Commission, *Special Eurobarometer*, *supra*, pp. 69–70.

directly on work and family issues. These include (1) protections of employment status and rights of pregnant workers; (2) rights such as maternity, paternity and parental leaves, and rights to pay during these leaves; (3) protections of contractual position while on leave; and (4) various post leave policies, such as a right to request flexible working, working time regulation in general, emergency leaves. In addition, as already noted, provisions related to child care – its organization and funding – are also integral to reconciling work and family responsibilities. We discuss key elements of each national framework in turn, before moving to our comparative analysis in section four.

[A] Slovenia

[1] Historic Development

Work-family balance has been a long-standing issue on the Slovenian policy agenda, with both the employment promotion perspective and the broader gender equality one playing important roles in its development. Slovenia (at the time a part of the Kingdom of Serbs, Croats and Slovenians, later renamed Yugoslavia) introduced maternity leaves already during the interwar period, following the ratification of the ILO Maternity Protection Convention No. 3 (1919) in 1927. After the World War II, gender equality and full employment for all were strongly supported within a socialist self-management system, and maternity leaves were extended during the 1940s and the 1950s, with full compensation,[21] job protection during pregnancy and maternity leave, and the right to return to their previous job guaranteed. In the 1970s, Slovenian leave policies began to follow the Swedish model of a short maternity leave and a longer paid parental leave that could be shared (transferred) between partners,[22] thereby introducing one of the first policies in Europe that gave also working fathers the possibility to stay at home to take care of a child, with the rights to job protection and pay compensation. Further extensions of leaves in the 1980s were motivated, among others, by discussions on gender equality and promotion of women's full-time employment and economic independence. Since 1970s, high-quality and affordable public child-care services were developed in parallel with leaves.[23]

Slovenia became an independent, capitalist state in 1991, and while labour relations, social security, and social welfare regimes were adapted over the course of transition to the new system, the legislative provisions related to work-family balance

21. M. Korintus, N. Stropnik, 'Hungary and Slovenia: Long Leave or Short?' in *The Politics of Parental Leave Policies: Children, Parenting, Gender and the Labour Market*, edited by S. B. Kamerman and P. Moss. Bristol: Policy Press, 2009, p. 142.
22. Ž. Humer, M. Hrženjak, 'Socialization of Childcare in Slovenia and Its Impact on Informal Care Markets'. *Laboratorium: Russian Review of Social Research*, North America, 8, January 2017 (Online: http://www.soclabo.org/index.php/laboratorium/article/view/648/1717).
23. N. Stropnik, 'Child Care in Slovenia: An Example of a Successful Transition', *Child: Care Health and Development* 27, No. 3 (2001): 263–278 (Online: http://www.academia.edu/18695993/Child_care_in_Slovenia_an_example_of_a_successful_transition).

remained mostly unchanged.[24] In 2001, Slovenia introduced non-transferable statutory right for the fathers – a partially paid paternity leave[25] –, which became 'a great success' in terms of take-up rates, with a great majority of fathers using the compensated part of this leave. The new Parental Protection and Family Benefits Act, which was passed in 2014 to transpose the new EU Parental Leave Directive 2010, will be presented in detail in the following section.

[2] Leaves Associated with Parenthood

The current legislative framework entitles parents in Slovenia to paid maternity, paternity and parental leave if they are employed or self-employed (or have certain status equivalent to it) and are thus subject to compulsory social insurance for parental protection. No qualifying period is required, and the duration of leave is determined in calendar days and is the same for a full-time or part-time absence from work.[26]

Taking up maternity, paternity and parental leave depends solely on the will of the worker/parent who is entitled to it and the employer cannot invoke business or operational needs in order to influence in any way the duration, timing or mode of its use; the employer cannot postpone it, demand adjustments etc. To exercise their leave rights workers are obliged to notify the employer at least, as a general rule, thirty days in advance.

[i] Maternity Leave

Mothers are entitled to a maternity leave in the duration of 105 days, i.e., 15 weeks (28 days prior to the expected date of delivery and 77 days after the delivery). Maternity leave can only be used continuously, without interruptions, and in the form of full-time absence from work. With a few exceptions, it is a non-transferable right.[27]

During the entire period of maternity leave the mother (or another person exercising this right) is entitled to the compensation benefit out of the social insurance scheme, so that an individual employer does not bear any direct financial burden. There is no qualifying period for either the leave or compensation, with the latter calculated on the basis of the employee's average salary (for the last 12 months, or less in case of shorter employment period), and set at 100% of that amount. In 2012, on a 'temporary' basis (due to austerity measures), this rate was lowered to 90%, with some exceptions, and the maximum ceiling was set at double the average salary, about EUR 3,000 per month.

---

24. B. Kresal, K. Kresal Šoltes, G. Strban, *Social Security Law in Slovenia*. Alphen aan den Rijn: Kluwer, 2016, p. 25.
25. *Ibid.*, p. 85. Before that, collective agreements entitled fathers to one to three days' paid leave of absence at the time of the child's birth.
26. Only relevant for paternity and parental leave, which may also be used in the form of partial absence from work, whereas the maternity leave must be used in the form of full work absence.
27. Legislation lists a number of exceptions which, depending on circumstances, can result in the leave (or a part of it) being transferred to the father, the child's grandparents or another person caring for the child.

[ii] Paternity Leave

In 2014, the paid paternity leave was extended from fifteen to thirty days and the unpaid part of it was abolished.[28] The first fifteen days of paternity leave can be used until the child reaches the age of six months (in certain cases 12 months of age), in the form of full-time or part-time absence from work, either in continuity without interruptions or on a day-by-day basis. Additional fifteen days can be used until the child completes the first grade of primary school, after the expiry of parental leave, irrespective of who, mother, father or both in combination used it (*see* below). During the entire period of paternity leave, the father is entitled to a compensation benefit, which follows the same rules as the maternity compensation benefit (in the amount of 100% of previous salary, temporarily reduced to 90% due to the crisis, with the maximum ceiling). The take up rates of these leaves are high. In 2012, for example, 85% of fathers used their paid paternity leave, whereas the take-up rate for an unpaid paternity leave was very low.[29]

[iii] Parental Leave

The new regulation on parental leave introduced in 2014 was a result of a compromise after a heated debate with strong public-opinion opposition against shortening the duration of possible use of parental leave by the mother in order to guarantee a non-transferable part of that leave for the father.[30] As a result, an important conceptual change has been introduced in an attempt to follow the requirements of Directive 2010/18, i.e., parental leave as an individual right of each parent instead of previous shared right of both parents; however, with very broad transferability possibilities. Under the current framework, each parent has a right to parental leave of 130 days whereby, the mother can transfer up to 100 days to the father, while the father can transfer all 130 days to the mother. Therefore, the actual impact of this reform on more equal distribution of parental responsibilities in practice, and its consistency with the spirit of the EU directive is questionable.[31] Adoptive parents are eligible for parental leave under the same conditions and in the same duration as biological parents.

---

28. Due to the crisis and taking into account the financial burdens connected with additional fifteen days of paid paternity leave, the new Act postponed the entry into force of the new regime: twenty days paid paternity leave in 2016, twenty-five days in 2017 and thirty days from 2018 onwards.
29. Committee on the Elimination of Discrimination against Women, *Convention on the Elimination of All Forms of Discrimination against Women: Consideration of reports submitted by State parties under Article 18 of the Convention: Fifth and sixth periodic reports*. United Nations, 2014, p. 37 (Online: http://tbinternet.ohchr.org/_layouts/treatybodyexternal/Download.aspx?symbolno=CEDAW%2fC%2fSVN%2f5-%206&Lang=en).
30. Ž. Humer, S. Panić, *The Policy on Gender Equality in Slovenia*. Brussels: European Parliament, 2015, p. 20 (Online: http://www.europarl.europa.eu/RegData/etudes/STUD/2015/510010/IPOL_STU (2015)510010_EN.pdf).
31. G. Strban, B. Kresal, *Zakon o starševskem varstvu in družinskih prispevkih z uvodnimi pojasnili* [Parental Protection and Family Benefits Act with Introductory Comments]. Ljubljana: Uradni list, 2014, p. 54; B. Kresal, 'Slovénie'. *Revue de droit comparé du travail et de la sécurité sociale*, No. 1 (2014), p. 173.

The parental leave must be used continuously after the expiry of the maternity leave, either in the form of a full or partial absence from work. It cannot be used by both parents at the same time in the form of full absence from work, but they can switch, so that only one parent is on leave at a time, except if they both use it in the form of part-time absence from work. The law also provides for the possibility to postpone a part of it (up to seventy-five days) to be spent at a later point of time, but no later than the child's completion of the first grade of primary school. In certain cases, the parental leave is extended (by ninety days for multiple births or adoptions and a child with special needs; or when there are already two or more children in the family; premature birth etc.). This part of leave can be used by both parents at the same time, even if used in the form of full absence from work.

During the entire period of parental leave, a person is entitled to a compensation benefit which follows pretty the same rules as the maternity compensation benefit (in the amount of 100% of previous salary, temporarily reduced to 90% due to the crisis, with the maximum ceiling of two country's average salaries, approx. EUR 3,000 per month). In case the parental leave is used as part-time absence, the proportional amount of compensation benefit is paid up to full working time.

[iv] The Right to Part-Time Work Due to Parenthood

After the expiry of parental leave, which can be used in the form of part-time absence (with the corresponding pay compensation), there is another possibility for parents to work part-time. It is a statutory right within the parental protection insurance scheme and the employer cannot invoke any business or operation needs against it; the exercise of this right depends solely on the will of an employee, in the same way as the right to maternity, paternity or parental leave.

One of the parents has a right to work part-time until a child is 3 years old. In case of two or more children, the right is prolonged until the younger child completes the first grade of primary school, whereby one year is non-transferable for each of the parents. For a child with severe disabilities, this right is prolonged until the child reaches the age of 18. The employer pays the salary for the part-time work actually done, whereas the parental insurance scheme covers the cost of social security contributions up to full working time. If parents care for four or more children, one of them has a right to cease working due to child-care; the insurance scheme covers the cost of social security contributions until the youngest child completes the first grade of primary school.

Although meant to facilitate work-family balance for working parents, the right to work part-time has been criticized in academic literature in Slovenia when it was first introduced into Slovenian law. From the gender equality perspective, the lower earnings, fewer opportunities in career development, access to training, and the possibility of promotion meant that this right can inadvertently be a source of indirect discrimination of women who are more likely than men to take it up.[32]

[3] Flexible Working Arrangements and Other Rights for Working Parents

Beside rights stemming from the Parental Protection Act described above, working parents are entitled to other rights and protections, as regulated by the Employment Relationships Act 2013. According to a broad general provision the employers are obliged to enable employees to easily reconcile family and employment responsibilities. Direct and indirect discrimination based on family responsibilities is prohibited. The parents enjoy very strong protection against dismissal and they have the right to return to their previous job after leave, including all benefits accumulated during the period of leave.

Out of the health insurance scheme, parents are entitled to paid absence from work with 80% compensation during their caring for a sick child.[33] Parents have the rights to additional annual leave and to use at least one week of it during school holidays. Additional protection (in terms of restrictions) is extended to parents as regards the unfriendly working hours (such as night work, overtime work, work on Sundays and national holidays etc.).

According to the Employment Relationships Act, the worker may request flexible working time and its adjustment, including part-time work, for the purposes of reconciliation of professional and family life. Within this legislative framework, all different family-friendly working-time arrangements are possible, however not as a right, rather as a possibility to request them, whereby the employer can accept or oppose the worker's proposal, but not without any reasonable justification. The employer must justify his decision to refuse or grant such a request in writing, taking into account the operational needs of the business.

[4] The Role of Collective Agreements

In Slovenia, collective agreements – primarily at the sectoral level – play a very important role in regulating employment relations.[34] While a comprehensive approach is still missing in so far as collective negotiations on the issue of work-family balance,

---

32. *See*, for instance, M. Hrženjak, 'Ekonomska neenakost žensk z vidika spolnega pokojninskega razkoraka' [Economic Inequalities of Women from the Perspective of Gender Based Pension Gap], *Delavci in delodajalci* 16, No. 4 (2016): 609–626; B. Kresal, 'Equal Opportunities in Slovenia and EU Anti-discrimination Law' in *Reflections on 20 Years of Social Reform in Central and Eastern Europe*, edited by K. Koldinska and M. Štefko. Prague: Auditorium, 2010, pp. 113–114.
33. For up to seven working days (fifteen days for a child under seven years of age) in each case, which can be extended if necessary up to fourteen (thirty) days and in exceptional circumstances even up to six months.
34. The coverage rate is very high, however falling (around 80%, or 65% according to some research). *See* K. Kresal Šoltes, 'Pravna in vsebinska vprašanja prenove kolektivnih pogodb' [Legal and substantive issues regarding the renovation of collective agreements]. *Delavci in*

there is evidence that social partners are becoming more aware of this issue, and collective agreements do provide for different rights for working parents and include provisions relevant for work-family balance.[35] Among such measures are those that address working time, annual leave, additional paid absence from work for different family-related reasons, additional unpaid leave for family matters and similar, as well as work location. Moreover, many collective agreements provide for the right to request unpaid leave (usually up to thirty days per year). However, employers may invoke operational needs of the business to refuse granting this right. Usually, the possibility to request unpaid leave is not limited to work-family balance reasons.

[5] Child-Care Services

Public child-care services are well-developed and of a high-quality. Consequently, there is a high coverage of childcare (*see* section §8.02). The vast majority of kindergartens are public (93 %) and only 7 % are private. The public child-care services are mainly financed by public resources, and in part also by parents' share which depends on their income. In 2008, the Slovenian Government introduced free institutional care for the second child and all following children, but in 2012, as a part of austerity measures, payment of 30 % of the price for the second child was reintroduced, while care for subsequent children remained free. Public network of childcare is not regarded only as a means to enable both parents to engage in paid work, but also as a means for socialization, education and healthy development, following the principle of ensuring equal opportunities to all children.[36]

[B] United Kingdom

[1] Historic Development

In the UK, the framework of family and work-life balance related rights developed only over the last two decades, as up to the mid-1990s, employees enjoyed few legislated rights in this area. Unlike Slovenia, the UK did not legislate the right to maternity leave until 1975, and even then it applied only to a select number of workers.[37] While the right was extended in the 1980s, the overall deregulatory approach to labour regulation and labour market flexibility championed by the Thatcher and Major governments during the 1980s and early 1990s meant that apart from the broader promotion of

delodajalci 14, No. 2-3 (2014): 287–305; European Union, *Industrial Relations in Europe*. Luxembourg. Publications Office of the EU, 2015, pp. 17–37, Visser, *infra*.

35. K. Kresal Šoltes, B. Kresal, 'Ukrepi za lažje usklajevanje poklicnega in družinskega življenja v kolektivnih pogodbah v Sloveniji' [Measures for Better Reconciliation of Professional and Family Responsibilities in Collective Agreements in Slovenia]. *Delavci in delodajalci* 15, No. 4 (2015): 525–563.
36. Ž. Humer, M. Hrženjak, *supra*, pp. 58–59.
37. The long qualifying periods of employment required under this early scheme meant that not all pregnant workers qualified and could benefit from the leave provisions. Coverage was extended to all employed women in 1993, in order to bring the UK in compliance with Directive 92/85.

non-standard forms of work (i.e., part-time and temporary work) the British state largely refrained from regulating on these issues.[38]

In the mid-1990s, however, the New Labour government headed by Tony Blair ushered in a significant shift in approach to work-family reconciliation, based on the notion that more robust rights for working parents were not necessarily inconsistent with flexibility, and indeed could be good for business and the overall economic efficiency. Beginning with the 1998 *Fairness at Work* paper, which sought to change 'the culture of relationships in and at work and to reflect a new relationship between work and family life',[39] the New Labour administration introduced a range of family-friendly employment rights, primarily derived from EU Directives.[40] Behind its apparent commitment to supporting parents and enhancing equality[41] lay also the more instrumental objective of increasing overall employment figures, as well as that of reducing reliance on social assistance or other forms of public/welfare provision.[42] Thus, the New Labour's 2004 *Choice for Parents,*[43] the 2005 paper *Work and Family: Choice and Flexibility,*[44] and the Work and Families Act 2006, all of which introduced a range of 'family friendly' provisions, also promoted the view that gainful employment for all was the most effective route out of poverty.[45] The Coalition government led by David Cameron, which took over from Labour in 2010, continued its own work-family reconciliation policy largely along that same trajectory, with flagship policies of shared parental leave and broadening of the right to request flexible working.

Today, the various rights that affect reconciliation of work and family and work-life balance can be found in a rather dispersed framework of legal acts and regulations.[46] The next section outlines the key work-family related rights available to British parents.

38. J. Conaghan, 'Women, Work, and Family: A British Revolution?' in *Labour Law in an Era of Globalization*, edited by J. Conaghan, R.M. Fischl and K. Klare, Oxford: Oxford University Press, 2004, pp. 53–74; S. Fredman, *Women and the Law*, Oxford: Clarendon Press, 1997.
39. *Fairness at Work*, Department of Trade and Industry, 1998, p. 2.
40. A. McColgan, 'Family Friendly Frolics? The Maternity and Parental Leave etc. Regulations 1999', *Industrial Law Journal* 29, No. 2 (2000): 125.
41. E. Caracciolo di Torella, 'New Labour, New Dads – The Impact of Family Friendly Legislation on Fathers.' *Industrial Law Journal* 36, No. 3 (2007): 318–328.
42. G. Moffat, 'Work-Life Balance and Employment Law: Cultural Change or Mission Impossible' in *Family Life and the Law: Under One Roof*, edited by R. Probert, London: Ashgate, 2007, p. 135; J. Lewis, M. Campbell, 'UK Work/Family Balance Policies and Gender Equality, 1997–2005.' *Social Politics* 14, No. 4 (2007): 4–30; D. McCann, *Regulating Flexible Work*, Oxford: Oxford University Press, 2008.
43. *Choice for Parents: The Best Start for Children – A Ten Year Strategy for Childcare* (December 2004) HMSO, London.
44. *Work and Family: Choice and Flexibility*, URN05/1298, DTI, October 2005.
45. *Supra* Moffat, p. 142.
46. These include Employment Rights Act 1996, Employment Relations Act 1999, Maternity and Parental Leave Regulations 1999, Employment Act 2002, Work and Families Act 2006, as well as amendments to those main laws enacted by Flexible Working Regulations 2009, Parental Leave Regulations 2013, Childcare and Family Bill 2013, and most recently, Children and Family Act 2014.

[2] Leaves Associated with Parenthood

[i] Maternity Leave

Since 1996, the maternity leave is available to pregnant women hired on the basis of an employment contract (those hired on a contract for services are not eligible),[47] and it is set at a maximum of fifty-two weeks, which is divided into two twenty-six-week portions: the 'ordinary maternity leave' and the 'additional maternity leave'.[48] While pregnant employees do not have to meet a formal qualifying period of service for maternity leave eligibility, the condition that an employer is given at least a fifteen-week notice, creates such a requirement in practice. Eligible employees can choose when to commence leave, so long as it is not before eleven weeks prior to the expected week of childbirth. Apart from the mandatory two-week period (or four weeks for factory workers), employees can also determine how much leave to take.

An employee's job status is protected during maternity leave; dismissals during this period are automatically deemed 'unfair', and potentially regarded as acts of direct discrimination. Similarly, while on leave, employees are entitled to maintain their contractual terms and conditions and accrue benefits. One exception is that while those using the ordinary maternity leave entitlement have the right to return to *the same* job, employers are not required to guarantee the same for women who take the additional leave. The latter are still entitled to return to a position that is suitable and appropriate.[49]

Another important distinction relates to the fact that qualification for the statutory maternity leave does not necessarily guarantee entitlement to the statutory maternity pay, which is payable for up to thirty-nine weeks, so not for the entire period of available leave. Unlike eligibility to the leave itself, entitlement for maternity pay is tied to service and income thresholds. To qualify, in addition to giving the employer an appropriate notice, employees must also provide proof of pregnancy, demonstrate twenty-six weeks of continuous employment before the end of the qualifying week, which is the fifteenth week before expected week of childbirth, and must have earned a minimum weekly salary specified by regulations (currently set at GBP 112, which is equivalent to approximately EUR 130 per week and EUR 530 per month). Eligible employees are then entitled to have 90% of their salary replaced during the first six weeks of leave; thereafter, they receive GBP 140 (approximately EUR 165 per week or EUR 660 per month) or 90% of their usual salary, whichever is lower.

Those mothers who do not qualify for the statutory maternity pay may be able to claim Maternity Allowance from the benefits agency. As in the case of the statutory maternity pay, there are specified (although less onerous) service thresholds that must

47. Access to many employment rights, including family friendly ones is limited by this requirement: G. James, N. Busby, *Families, Care-Giving and Paid Work: Challenging Labour Law in the 21st Century*. Cheltenham: Edward Elgar, 2011.
48. The rights to maternity leave are established by the Employment Rights Act 1996 (ss. 71 and 73), with the details being set out in the Maternity and Parental Leave Regulations 1999, as amended.
49. Refusal of this right to return amounts to an automatic unfair dismissal.

be met to obtain this allowance, but it is also available to self-employed women or women who perform unpaid work in their own or their spouses' business.

[ii] Paternity Leave

Since 2000, fathers wishing to care for a new born child and support the child's mother have been entitled to a paternity leave of one or two weeks. Only fathers who are employees can claim leave entitlements, and in addition, they have to also meet a qualifying service period threshold. Moreover, the amount of leave days a father actually receives depends on the number of days he usually works per week, since it is the latter number that determines the meaning of a week for the purpose of this particular leave entitlement (as opposed to the assumption that a week is five days). The leave has to be taken within the first fifty-six days after the child's birth, and it must be taken in one go.

In order to qualify for the paternity leave pay, in addition to the service requirements, fathers have to also meet an income threshold set at the same level as that which is required for maternity pay entitlement already noted. The statutory paternity pay formula is equivalent to that available to mothers after the initial six weeks of maternity leave.

[iii] Shared Parental Leave

A right to shared parental leave was introduced in 2015, and replaced an earlier scheme of additional paid parental leave for fathers.[50] The maximum duration of this shared leave is essentially equivalent to the number of weeks unused by the mother in relation to her total fifty-two-week maternity leave entitlement. Since mothers are required to take at least two weeks of maternity leave, in practice parents can share up to fifty weeks of parental leave (or forty-eight weeks, where the mother works at a factory). Provided they are eligible, parents are free to split this leave as they choose, and this includes a right for each to split their portion into up to three blocks, and to take the leave at the same time as the other parent or in succession.

As with maternity leave, parents who are eligible to share leave may also be entitled to claim shared parental leave pay. The total number of weeks for which pay can be obtained is still thirty-nine, meaning that in practice sharing parents can, at most, have further thirty-seven (or thirty-five) weeks of paid leave left between them, after the mandatory two (or four) week maternity leave is taken into account.

Eligibility for the shared parental leave is somewhat more complicated than in the case of maternity and paternity leaves. To qualify, parents have to share responsibility for a child, both have to meet specified service periods, and at least one must have been

50. The Work and Families Act 2006 and the Additional Paternity Regulations 2010 established further paternity leave entitlement for qualifying fathers, of up to twenty-six weeks. As in the case of maternity leave, fathers taking this leave had rights to job protection; they were also entitled to statutory paternity pay, set at the same rate as the maternity pay and contingent on meeting the same income requirements.

an employee during the qualifying period. In addition, one of the parents must also meet a specified income threshold. The statutory shared parental leave pay is determined according to the same (90% or a set weekly amount, whichever is lower) formula as that already noted above.

Crucially, the take up of these shared leaves has been very low. According to My Family Care study, only 1% of male employees, in 200 organizations that were surveyed, took the shared parental leave in 2015.[51] Finance was considered to be determinative for 80% of surveyed men and women.

[iv] *Adoption Leave and Other Entitlements for Adoptive Parents*

Parents who adopt a child are also entitled to various leaves, and, with a few distinctions, the entitlements and qualifying conditions for them are very similar to those under the maternity, paternity and shared parental leave schemes and statutory pay.[52]

[v] *Unpaid Parental Leave*

Since 1999, parents are also entitled to additional unpaid parental leave rights, which was introduced to bring UK law in compliance with the EU Council Directive 96/34/EC. The current law provides that employers and employees can reach a customized parental leave arrangement via a collective or workplace agreement, which is then incorporated into the individual employment contracts. Failure to reach such an agreement automatically triggers the default unpaid parental leave provisions contained in regulations.

According to regulations, employees who have been employed continuously for a period of not less than a year and who already have or expect to have responsibility for a child are entitled to take unpaid leave of up to eighteen weeks, for the purpose of caring for the child. The leave can be taken at any time up to the child's fifth birthday (if a child is disabled, up to 18th birthday) or, if the child is adopted, up to the fifth anniversary of its placement with the adoptive family. The leave can be taken in blocks of no less than one week and no more than four weeks can be taken in each individual year.

Importantly, with the view of encouraging fathers to take on a more active caring role, the parental leave entitlement is not transferrable between the parents. To exercise their right to this leave, parents have to provide the employer with a notice (twenty-one days). However, employers may postpone granting the leave for up to six months, when they consider that doing otherwise would unduly disrupt operation of the business. Employees are entitled to reasons in writing when such a decision to

51. *Shared Parental Leave – One Year On – Where are we Now?* My Family Care, 2016 (Online: https://www.myfamilycare.co.uk/news/update/shared-parental-leave-where-are-we-now.html).
52. Also, the 90% income replacement rate is not paid out during the first six weeks of the adoption leave as is the case in relation to maternity leave.

postpone is taken, and with an offer of alternative time period for granting of their request. While there is no statutory requirement to pay employees during their leave period, other terms and conditions of employment remain in place during their absence and there are entitled to return to the same position. However, if a parent takes parental leave to extend earlier maternity or paternity leave, the employer only has the obligation to restore the employee to a suitable and appropriate alternative job. In both cases, seniority and terms and conditions must remain the same.

[3] Emergency Leave

Employment Relations Act 1999 also introduced a right for employee to take a reasonable amount of unpaid time off during work hours in order to provide urgent assistance to dependants. There is no qualifying period of employment for this entitlement, although it is only available to employees. The leave is not intended for caring activities per se, but rather to address unexpected 'emergency' situations. A broad definition of a 'dependant' includes any person living in the same house as the employee or who reasonably relies upon the employee for assistance (this can include not only children, but also parents, tenants, lodgers, etc.). While the legislation does not stipulate periods of notice required or the absolute limits of time that can be taken, employment tribunals have interpreted the latter as 'short' and 'reasonable', with the operational needs of the employer not being relevant to the determination of what is reasonable.[53]

[4] Flexible Working and the Right to Request

The UK governments had long deemed flexibility to be a desirable way to help working people – especially working parents – combine paid work with the care responsibilities involved in family life. In the context of the country's long established long-hours culture for men and short work hours among women,[54] such a right was to also provide an incentive to better redistribute care work and foster active fatherhood.

Originally, the right to flexible working established by the 1996 Employment Rights Act and Flexible Work Regulations 2002 required an employee to have twenty-six weeks of continuous employment to be eligible to make a request. Likewise, a request could only be made on the basis of a need to care for a child, or another person in a dependant relationship with the employee (spouse, civil partner, a relative, a person living at the same address). However, recent legislative changes have extended the right to request to all employees, and beyond reasons of care, reflecting changes in both the conception of who is a carer and the development of a broader focus on work-life balance.

---

53. *Qua v. John Ford Morrison* (2003). In relation to the determination of notice period, the tribunal held that the greater the notice available the more difficult it is for the employee to establish that the need to take leave has to do with an emergency: *Royal Bank of Scotland v. Harrison* 2009 IRLR 28.
54. Fagan, *supra*. Also, *supra* figures cited in section §8.02.

At the same time, however, while the recent changes broadened who is entitled to the right to request they have also relaxed the obligations placed on employers in relation to granting such requests. While in the past employers were required to respond to the employee's request application within a period of twenty-eight days, under current rules this period has been extended to three months. If the employer refuses to accept the request, they must point to one or more of the potential reasons that enumerated by regulation, which relate to operational needs and the running of business. While employees have a right to appeal rejected requests, the 2014 changes have also had procedural implications, in practice making such appeals more difficult and less likely to succeed.

[5] Childcare

In the UK, the state does not take active role in the organization of care for the youngest children, leaving these decisions to parents. Nonetheless, parents are eligible to get financial assistance in paying for childcare, provided that it is delivered by one of the statutorily approved providers. For 3 to 4 year olds, parents can receive subsidies for a set number of weekly hours of care (about fifteen, with plans to extend to thirty as of September 2017); in some circumstances, such subsidies are also available for children under two years old (in disadvantaged families). Apart from subsidies, parents may also qualify for child tax credits, childcare vouchers, or be able to claim back up to 85% of child-care costs. Nonetheless, the net costs of child care are still higher in the UK than in most EU countries.[55]

§8.04 COMPARING THE SLOVENIAN AND UK WORK-FAMILY/LIFE BALANCE REGIMES

Before analysing the more specific points of convergence and divergence between the two national legislative frameworks, a few preliminary observations should be made about the sources and types of regulation that have shaped them.

An obvious point is that as EU Member States Slovenia and the UK are both bound by EU directives and these have provided an impetus for the gradual expansion of rights related to work-family reconciliation, especially in the UK. Slovenia has also ratified the Revised European Social Charter from 1996 (CETS no. 163) and is bound by its provisions on maternity protection (Article 8) as well as on workers with family responsibilities (Article 27), whereas the UK has only ratified the original 1961 Charter (CETS no. 35) and is bound as regards the maternity protection only by Article 8.1. Unlike Slovenia, which has ratified all relevant ILO conventions on maternity protection (Nos 3, 103 and 183) and on workers with family responsibilities (No. 156), the UK has not ratified any of them.

55. According to the OECD's family database and its *Doing Better for Families* report, the net costs of childcare in the UK constituted 26.6% of a family income, compared to the 11.8% OECD average: OECD, *Doing Better for Families*, 2011 (Online: http://www.oecd.org/els/soc/doingbetterforfamilies.htm).

Another preliminary observation relates to the differences in the national sources of regulation that shape the work-family rights available to workers in each country. As outlined above, these frameworks are primarily statutory in both Slovenia and the UK, with collective bargaining playing a secondary one. However, while this is especially true of the UK, where the role of collective agreements in setting standards related to work-family reconciliation is undermined due to the comparatively low rates of unionization and collective bargaining coverage,[56] in Slovenia, the social partners do play a role given the much higher rates of unionization and collective agreement coverage.[57] Thus, as the above discussion detailed, many Slovenian collective agreements include rights for working parents and provisions relevant for work-family reconciliation that go beyond those statutorily prescribed.

Overall, while the influence of the EU – both, through 'hard' law and policy coordination mechanisms – means that there are a number of common elements in the Slovenian and the UK legal frameworks, there are also significant technical and policy, or ideological differences between the two. Rather than enumerate the various points of convergence and divergence, our comparative analysis will focus on three points. We will examine: (1) how the unique features of each framework contribute to its overall employee or family-friendliness; and (2) the degree of egalitarianism (understood as the likelihood that women and men will be equally supported as caregivers in law and practice) that each supports. We will also consider; (3) how the recent crisis has impacted the possibilities available to working parents in Slovenia and the UK.

[A] How Employee Friendly?

Strictness of the legislative framework, in that rights for supporting work-family and work-life articulation cannot be varied or derogated from through the exercise of employer prerogative, is one feature that can be determinative from the perspective of employee friendliness.

In this regard, the Slovenian framework compares favourably: so long as employees seeking to take up their entitlements meet the statutory requirements related to notice periods, timing, and scheduling of leaves, employers cannot, for the most part, refuse or otherwise interfere with the exercise of these rights. This level of strictness or protection is somewhat weaker in the UK framework, where employers can have the last word on employees' ability to draw certain rights (at least in so far as the timing and scheduling of their take up) in a broader range of circumstances, by invocation of business and operational needs. While, as in Slovenia, invocation of this prerogative is not possible in relation to maternity or paternity leaves, employers in the UK do have a say in scheduling of unpaid parental leave and the right to request flexible work. In the first instance, employers have a right to reschedule the requested periods of leave by up to six months, which is potentially a very significant delay given that

56. Trade union density in the UK stands at about 25 %, with collective agreement coverage at about 29.5 %. *See* J. Visser, 'What Happened to Collective Bargaining During the Great Recession', *IZA Journal of Labor Policy* 9, No. 5 (2016).
57. *See supra*, section §8.03[A][4].

only up to four weeks of leave can be requested during a year and the total leave entitlement of eighteen weeks must be taken up by the time the child turns five. Employers in the UK also retain a right to not grant a flexible working request, if specific business reasons justify it. These rights to refuse or reschedule leave request can constitute a barrier to the take up of employee rights,[58] which are not present in the Slovenian model to the same extent. While Slovenian employers also have a say in requests for flexible working, the right to work part-time due to parenthood is shielded from this prerogative.

Is the UK framework more flexible, giving workers more choice over how and when to take up their entitlements as a trade-off for its lower level of protection against employer's right to vary or refuse? This is not necessarily the case either, since similar rights to request flexible work arrangements are available to workers in both countries. While in the UK, the recent extension of the right to request to any employee wishing to work flexibly regardless of their family situation and beyond reasons of care is no doubt a positive development, such a broad right to flexibility is only advantageous in so far as the employer accepts the request in the first place, which the UK law does not guarantee. Moreover, in the UK, a choice to reduce work hours will generally translate into reduced income; a 'penalty' that at least those Slovenian workers who opt for part-time work as a modality of parental leave do not have to bear given the income replacement scheme that tops up their part-time earnings.

Income, or more specifically the level at which income is replaced during periods of child or family-related leaves, is another key distinction between the two frameworks that has important implications for their comparative employee friendliness. Thus, while employees in the UK are entitled to only a slightly lower number of leave weeks than their Slovenian counterparts (or, indeed, to more weeks when the unpaid parental leave is also counted), the latter benefit from a much higher portion of leave weeks that are paid. Income replacement is also much higher in Slovenia, as it is set at 100% (temporarily, due to the crisis reduced to 90%) of usual salary for both women and men for the entire leave period. In the UK, income replacement is guaranteed at 90% of normal salary only during the first six weeks of maternity (and adoption) leave, thereafter being set at a fixed (and very low!) weekly amount of just under GBP 140 or 90% of usual weekly income only if the latter is lower. This means that fathers qualifying to paternity or shared parental leave are only entitled to income replacement calculated based on this latter formula. As will be discussed in the next section, this specific structure of compensation during leaves also has implications for the UK regime's comparative equality disadvantage vis-à-vis the Slovenian model.

Finally, the administration of income replacement in the two systems might also have distinct impact on employee friendliness of each model. In Slovenia, the system of statutory maternity, paternity, and parental leave pay is centralized and employers are not responsible for its administration. In the UK, individual employers remain responsible for covering the partial replacement costs, although they can claim back

58. While evidence collected 2011 suggests a 60% acceptance rate of all requests, there is a disparity between men and women's request, with the latter making more requests and being more likely to be successful: Fourth Work-Life Balance Employee Survey 2011.

the costs of maternity, paternity, and shared leave pay from the state. The extent to which employers perceive management of this process to be a 'burden', however, may have implications for how they will be predisposed to workers who seek to draw on their statutory leave rights. Gender of the employee can be determinative here as well.

[B] How Egalitarian?

Each of the national legislative frameworks examined here establishes more or less equal entitlements for mothers and fathers, or women and men. As such, the frameworks at least formally support equal rights for all parents. Nonetheless, as we suggest below, the structure of the Slovenian framework renders it overall more likely to de facto support combining parental responsibilities with paid work, and more equal sharing of work and family responsibilities between the parents.[59]

A key element intended to support more equal take-up of leaves by mothers and fathers is the 'non-transferability' principle, which prevents the possibility of leave entitlements available to each parents being reallocated between them. In EU law, this principle has been integrated into the Directive on parental leave. However, as the Slovenian and UK examples show, the non-transferability of leaves is insufficient to encourage fathers to take up leave, as the structure of compensation and level of income replacement are crucial, if not determinative, elements affecting take-up of leaves.[60]

In the UK, for example, the non-transferability principle has been incorporated into the *unpaid* parental leave provisions. However, the principle does not apply to the paid shared parental leave, which lets parents choose how to split their entitlement. Parents can certainly choose to share this latter paid leave equally, and both benefit from job protection, maintenance of most conditions of employment, and the right to return to the same or comparable job. Yet, the fact that parents are entitled to income replacement for a only a portion of leave, being thirty-nine weeks *per child* of the possible fifty-two weeks to be split by parents, combined with the relatively low level of income replacement related to this leave, tends to undermine the likelihood of equal sharing. First, the fact that mothers are entitled to somewhat higher compensation during the first six weeks of maternity leave creates an additional incentive for them to use those weeks, leaving even fewer weeks for actual sharing between the parents. Thereafter, parents are likely to make decisions about allocation of the remaining leave on the basis of economic 'loss' (or sufficiency, given the low level of replacement), and the fact that men are more likely to command higher incomes will be determinative in these decisions about how to share leave.

59. The figures (*see* section §8.02) show that while this is true as regards the high share of women in employment (i.e., equal sharing of paid work), the unequal distribution of domestic/parental responsibilities still persists (i.e., unequal sharing of unpaid work). However the figures show a slow positive trend, with men taking on a more active part in parenting and devoting more time to caring activities, especially those of the younger generation.
60. *See*, for instance, J. Cabrita, F. Wohlgemuth, *Promoting Uptake of Parental and Paternity Leave Among Fathers in the EU*, Dublin: Eurofound, 2015; G. B. Eydal, T. Rostgaard, *Fatherhood in the Nordic Welfare States*, Bristol: Policy Press, 2016.

By contrast with the UK, the Slovenian legislative framework provides for more generous paternity leaves, which are not transferable and fully paid, meaning that they are likely to be taken (and indeed are, as the statistics show). In relation to the parental leave, however, the transferability is not entirely gender neutral since women/mothers are *not* entitled to transfer all of their leave to their male partners/fathers of their child, while fathers are able to transfer the entirety of theirs. The principle of non-transferability is also only partially applied in the context of the right to request part-time work for child-related reasons, with only one year being non-transferrable. Thus, if the application of the non-transferability principle in the context of entitlements for parental leave (and part-time work) is considered, the UK regime might appear to be more egalitarian of the two, if only in the formal sense. However, while the Slovenian model appears to retain some assumptions about the priority of maternal care, the fact that both mothers and fathers are entitled to have full income replacement during their leave portions significantly increases the likelihood that men will actually use their allocated leave entitlements.

The egalitarian possibilities of the UK's leave schemes are also limited by the fact that the right to take up and schedule the unpaid parental leave is made contingent on the employer's agreement as to its timing, and the fact that employers have been given the last word on requests of flexible work arrangements. It is not difficult to imagine that cultural and workplace norms and gender stereotypes can interfere with some employers' objectivity in weighing requests for parental leave and flexible working – especially when care obligations are invoked as reasons for these requests –, against organizational needs of firms. Indeed, recent research suggests that men who seek to take advantage of their care-related rights often face obstacles at work.[61] At the same time, assumptions about women being the ones more likely to invoke child-care related rights might also make them more vulnerable to discrimination in hiring.

In addition to various rights that parents may draw on, the Slovenian model also tends to be more egalitarian due to the widespread, and affordable public care services parents can rely on. While public child care delivery is low in the UK, parents do currently benefit from a range of child-care subsidies and some free childcare, and there are plans to extend free child-care for three to four year olds to thirty weekly hours during school terms from September 2017. However, given the levels of funding the government actually commits to early-childhood education, there are already concerns that the quality of care might erode away under this new model, as will its availability to many parents.[62]

[C] Impact of the Crisis

The post 2008 crisis had implications for reforms of the work-family and work-life balance legislative frameworks in both countries. In Slovenia, changes to paternity leave which increased the number of paid leave days for which father are eligible have

61. *The Modern Families Index, supra.*
62. G. Cameron, C. Harding, *No Shortcuts: Quality and the Free Childcare Extension*. Family and Childcare Trust, 2017.

been phased-in gradually, in effect delaying the reform's full effect until in 2018. The austerity measures the Slovenian government adopted reduced different social benefits, including compensation benefits for maternity, paternity and parental leave (as noted above). Since even in Slovenia women are still more likely to take-up these leaves, they were more adversely affected as a result. The reduction in leave compensation may have also provided a disincentive for fathers to take-up these rights, going against the proclaimed policy goal of more equal distribution of parental responsibilities.[63] Other family benefits, such as child-care allowance, have been also reduced and/or became means-tested with negative social consequences.[64]

Similarly, in the UK, the previous Coalition government's flagship reform of expanding the right to request flexible work beyond reasons of care for dependants was introduced during the crisis period. However, in the process, a number of elements of the previous right to request framework were weakened. First, the previous requirement that an employer respond to a workers' request within twenty-eight days of it being made was changed, and currently employers can take up to three months to respond. Moreover, under the current scheme employers have a broader discretion to refuse the employee's request.

Along with its effects at the legislative level, recent evidence suggests that the crisis has also led to overall worsening in employment conditions and the weakening of employees' ability to draw on their existing legal entitlements in order to support the articulation between work and family. In Slovenia, fear of dismissal has placed workers under increased pressure during the crisis, while rationalization processes resulted in intensification of work for some workers, reduction of working hours and thus lower real earnings for others. Precarious work and false self-employment have grown in Slovenia, resulting in more people having difficulties in exercising their rights in practice.[65]

In the UK, many workers still face difficulties with achieving satisfactory balance between the competing demands of work and family life despite the growing number of rights they can draw on.[66] The Modern Families Index 2017 reports that while an increasing numbers of men express the desire to partake in care of their children,[67] evidence shows that during the post-2008 crisis period UK firms have either reduced their commitment to family friendly policies or have used such policies instrumentally,

63. B. Kresal, Nova pravna ureditev materinskega, očetovskega in starševskega dopusta [New Legal Regulation of Maternity, Paternity and Parental Leave]. *Podjetje in delo* 40, No. 3-4 (2014), p. 446.
64. About the impact of the crisis on work-life balance and family policy N. Stropnik, *Investing in Children: Breaking the Cycle of Disadvantage (Slovenia)*. European Union, 2014. Online: http://csdle.lex.unict.it/Archive/LW/Data%20reports%20and%20studies/Reports%20%20from%20Committee%20and%20Groups%20of%20Experts/20140505-015801_NetworkIESI2013-2_SLOVENIA_report_April14pdf.pdf; European Institute for Gender Equality, *supra*, p. 41.
65. D. Senčur Peček, 'Samozaposleni, ekonomsko odvisne osebe in obstoj delovnega razmerja' [Self-employed, economically dependent persons and existence of an employment relationship]. *Delavci in delodajalci* 14, No. 2-3 (2014): 201-220.
66. *The Modern Families Index*, *supra*.
67. *Ibid*.

to achieve costs savings and other business and operational needs.[68] As in Slovenia, this period also led to intensification and extensification of work, as firms turned to 'lean' management styles and redundancies.[69] Thus, while official figures report a reduction in overall hours of work in the UK, suggesting a lessening of reliance on long-hours culture, evidence suggests that most workers in fact spend an increasing number of hours catching up on work at home, in evenings and during weekends.[70] The blurring of boundaries between home and work is partly due to the prevalent use of information technologies to communicate and deliver work, but there is evidence that poor job design contributes to this as well. Importantly, research suggests that despite changing social norms around men's involvement in care provisions, fathers face various constraints when they seek to work less or more flexibly in order to spend more time with their children. In the context of 'lean' organizational culture of cuts and redundancies, some fathers are reporting reluctance (or fear) to request the sorts of arrangements that would suit them better.[71] Thus, there appears to be an increasing gap between employer attitudes and employee desires for more balanced work-life articulation, and this is especially prevalent when younger workers are considered.[72]

§8.05 CONCLUSIONS

This chapter considered two examples of legal frameworks for work-family and work-life balance to assess whether the progressive development of EU policy in this area has translated into national regimes that are in fact employee friendly and egalitarian. We were also interested in how the commitment to helping parents reconcile and redistribute their responsibilities for paid work and unpaid care has fared under the general retrenchment experienced across most social policy fields during the post-2008 crisis period, especially in relation to existing legal rights or development of new ones.

While Slovenia and the UK have distinctive starting points and approaches to work-family policy, our analysis revealed that there are some significant points of convergence in the two countries' policies, especially with regards to their egalitarian potential and its shortcomings. And while this is not itself surprising, given that both countries have operated under the influence of EU norms, the flaws of these common policy points suggest broader limitations of the current approach adopted at the EU level; they also suggest how this approach could be reformed to be more effective in practice.

---

68. A. Smith, '"The Magnificent 7[am]?" Work-Life Articulation Beyond the 9[am] to 5pm] "Norm"' New *Technology, Work and Employment* 31, No. 3 (2016) : 209–222; S. Lewis, D. Anderson, C. Lyonette, N. Payne, S. Wood, 'Public Sector Austerity Cuts in Britain and the Changing Discourse of Work-Life Balance,' *Work, Employment, Society* (published online: 4 May 2016) doi.org/10.1177/0950017016638994.
69. *Ibid.*
70. *The Modern Families Index*, *supra*, cites that 72% of polled workers reported taking work home on evenings and weekends with 41% of workers doing so 'often or all the time'.
71. *Ibid.*
72. *Ibid.*

To begin, we note that while creating opportunities for parents to more equally distribute care responsibilities is essential to fostering work-family reconciliation culture that is also egalitarian; simply making it possible transfer of leave rights – or other child-care related rights – to the father is not an effective way of facilitating equal sharing. Such a right to transfer has existed in the Slovenian legal framework since 1975, thus long before the country's EU accession. In practice, the right did not see much take up until fairly recently, when it was combined with other measures such as a non-transferable, dedicated, and fully paid paternity leave. The UK experience, although very different in so far as a relatively recent development of father's entitlements, nonetheless also supports the view that enabling transfer of leaves between parents is unlikely to facilitate their uptake by fathers, as the relative unpopularity of the recently enacted shared leave scheme illustrates. The fact that the income replacement guaranteed during that latter leave is set at such a low rate – especially in light of the gap between men and women's work hours and incomes in the UK – creates a further financial disincentive. Thus, while gendered assumptions about how women and men should share care work are present in both countries, the UK's legislative framework continues to maintain structural incentives for mothers to stay at home even as policymakers claim the need to challenge cultural stereotypes and legislate rights that formally appear to treat women and men equally.

While prescribing leave entitlements as individual, non-transferrable rights for each parent is one alternative to the problems associated with transferable leave rights that is already present in EU policy and has been integrated in both national frameworks we considered, our analysis suggests non-transferability is also insufficient. Again, the key problem is the model of income replacement or compensation during leave. As we have suggested, formally equal entitlements are meaningless, apart from their symbolic value, when financial differentials between women and men's real incomes are not actively accounted for by pay compensation schemes. Parental leave can be regarded as an effective work-family balance measure that also promotes gender equality only in so far as it is paid at an adequate rate; otherwise it remains a tool for reinforcing gender-based division of labour wherein both men and women are deprived of a chance to more equally partake in and benefit from opportunities created by paid work on the one hand and participation in family life on the other.

Therefore, for work-family reconciliation policies to be egalitarian, leave policies must be designed as non-transferable equal rights for all parents, which attract high level, if not full, income replacement, and which are of adequate length but flexible as regards the mode of its use. Access to high-quality, affordable, accessible child-care services – designed depending on the length of the leave and needs of the working parents – is of course also an essential component of a worker friendly and egalitarian work-family reconciliation framework, as it enables parents to return to work upon completion of leave. Likewise, provisions that enable flexible work are also crucial, but our analysis confirms that such flexibility must be embedded in a strong rights-based framework. Such a framework is a necessary precondition of an employee-friendly and egalitarian work-family reconciliation model, as working parents must have guaranteed rights, not merely possibilities and rights to request that are dependent on employers' prerogatives.

Unfortunately, the gap between what a progressive and integrated model of work-family reconciliation ought to be and what it is in practice has only widened in the recent, post-2008 crisis period; a paradoxical development given the growing number of 'family friendly' rights in both Slovenia and the UK, and the policy mantra that work-family reconciliation is essential to co-facilitating a range of social and economic objectives.

REFERENCES

Addati, L., Cassirer, N., Gilchrist, K., *Maternity and Paternity at Work: Law and Practice Across the World*. Geneva: ILO, 2014.

Ahrendt, D., Blum, S., Crepaldi, C., *Families in the Economic Crisis: Changes in Policy Measures in the EU*. Dublin: Eurofound, 2015.

Anxo, D., 'Working Time Patterns Among Industrialized Countries: A Household Perspective' in *Working Time and Workers' Preferences in Industrialized Countries: Finding the Balance*, edited by J. Messenger, Geneva: ILO, New York: Routledge, 2004, pp. 195–211.

Cabrita, J., Wohlgemuth, F., *Promoting Uptake of Parental and Paternity Leave Among Fathers in the EU*. Dublin: Eurofound, 2015.

G. Cameron, C. Harding, *No Shortcuts: Quality and the Free Childcare Extension*. Family and Childcare Trust, 2017.

Caracciolo di Torella, E., 'New Labour, New Dads – The Impact of Family Friendly Legislation on Fathers.' *Industrial Law Journal* 36, No. 3 (2007): 318–328.

Choice for Parents: The Best Start for Children – A Ten Year Strategy for Childcare (December 2004) HMSO, London.

Committee on the Elimination of Discrimination against Women, *Convention on the Elimination of All Forms of Discrimination Against Women: Consideration of Reports Submitted by State Parties Under Article 18 of the Convention: Fifth and Sixth Periodic Reports*. United Nations, 2014.

Conaghan, J., 'Women, Work, and Family: A British Revolution?' in *Labour Law in an Era of Globalization*, edited by J. Conaghan, R.M. Fischl and K. Klare, Oxford: Oxford University Press, 2004, pp. 53–74.

Davaki, K., *Differences in Men's and Women's Work, Care and Leisure Time*. European Parliament, 2016.

Eydal, G.B., Rostgaard, T., *Fatherhood in the Nordic Welfare States*, Bristol: Policy Press, 2016.

European Commission, *Roadmap for the Initiative 'A New Start to Address the Challenges of Work-Life Balance Faced by Working Families'*, 2015.

European Commission, *Special Eurobarometer: Gender Equality*. European Union, 2015.

European Institute for Gender Equality, *Reconciliation of Work, Family and Private Life in the European Union*. Vilnius, 2015.

European Parliament, *Report in Creating Labour Market Conditions Favourable for Work-Life Balance* (2016/2017(INI)), 2. 8. 2016.

European Union, *Equality Between Women and Men 2015*. Luxembourg: Publications Office of the EU, 2016.

European Union, *Employment in Europe 2015*. Luxembourg: Publications Office of the EU, 2016.

European Union, *Industrial Relations in Europe*. Luxembourg. Publications Office of the EU, 2015.

European Union, *Employment in Europe 2009*. Luxembourg: Publications Office of the EU, 2009.

Fagan, C., 'Gendered Time Schedules: Paid Work in Great Britain' *Social Politics* 3, No. 1 (1996): 72–106.

Fairness at Work, Department of Trade and Industry, 1998.

Figart, D.M., Mutari, E., 'Work Time Regimes in Europe: Can Flexibility and Gender Equity Coexist?' *Journal of Economic Issues* 34, No. 4 (2000): 847–871.

Figart, D.M., Mutari, E., 'Europe at a Crossroads: Harmonization, Liberalization, and the Gender of Work Time' *Social Politics* 8, No. 1 (2001): 36–64.

Fredman, S., *Women and the Law*, Oxford: Clarendon Press, 1997.

Fudge, J., 'Global Care Chains: International Migrant Care Work', *International Journal of Comparative Labour Law and Industrial Relations* 28, No. 1 (2012): 63–69.

Hrženjak, M., 'Ekonomska neenakost žensk z vidika spolnega pokojninskega razkoraka' [Economic Inequalities of Women from the Perspective of Gender Based Pension Gap], *Delavci in delodajalci* 16, No. 4 (2016): 609–626.

Humer, Ž., Hrženjak, M., 'Socialization of Childcare in Slovenia and Its Impact on Informal Care Markets'. *Laboratorium: Russian Review of Social Research*, North America, 8, January 2017.

Humer, Ž., Panić, S., *The Policy on Gender Equality in Slovenia*. Brussels: European Parliament, 2015.

James, G. Busby, N., *Families, Care-Giving and Paid Work: Challenging Labour Law in the 21st Century*. Cheltenham: Edward Elgar, 2011.

Korintus, M., Stropnik, N., 'Hungary and Slovenia: Long Leave or Short?' in *The Politics of Parental Leave Policies: Children, Parenting, Gender and the Labour Market*, edited by S.B. Kamerman and P. Moss, Bristol: Policy Press, 2009, 135–157.

Kresal, B., 'Slovénie'. *Revue de droit comparé du travail et de la sécurité sociale*, No. 1 (2014): 172–173.

Kresal, B., Nova pravna ureditev materinskega, očetovskega in starševskega dopusta [New Legal Regulation of Maternity, Paternity and Parental Leave]. *Podjetje in delo* 40, Nos 3–4 (2014): 433–446.

Kresal, B., 'Equal Opportunities in Slovenia and EU Anti-discrimination Law' in *Reflections on 20 Years of Social Reform in Central and Eastern Europe*, edited by K. Koldinska and M. Štefko, Prague: Auditorium, 2010, 109–120.

Kresal, B., Kresal Šoltes, K., Strban, G., *Social Security Law in Slovenia*. Alphen aan den Rijn: Kluwer, 2016.

Kresal Šoltes, K., 'Pravna in vsebinska vprašanja prenove kolektivnih pogodb' [Legal and substantive issues regarding the renovation of collective agreements]. *Delavci in delodajalci* 14, Nos 2–3 (2014): 287–305.

Kresal Šoltes, K., Kresal, B., 'Ukrepi za lažje usklajevanje poklicnega in družinskega življenja v kolektivnih pogodbah v Sloveniji' [Measures for Better Reconciliation of Professional and Family Responsibilities in Collective Agreements in Slovenia]. *Delavci in delodajalci* 15, No. 4 (2015): 525–563.

Lewis, J., *Work-Family Balance, Gender and Policy*. Cheltenham Edward: Elgar, 2009.

Lewis, S., Anderson, D., Lyonette, C., Payne, N., Wood, S., 'Public Sector Austerity Cuts in Britain and the Changing Discourse of Work-Life Balance,' *Work, Employment, Society* (published online: 4 May 2016).

Lewis, J., Campbell, M., 'UK Work/Family Balance Policies and Gender Equality, 1997–2005.' *Social Politics* 14, No. 1 (2007): 4–30.

McCann, D., *Regulating Flexible Work*, Oxford: Oxford University Press, 2008.

McColgan, A. 'Family Friendly Frolics? The Maternity and Parental Leave etc. Regulations 1999'. *Industrial Law Journal* 29, No. 2 (2000), pp. 125–143.

Miani, C., Hoorens, S., *Parents at Work: Men and Women Participating in the Labour Force*. Brussels: Rand Europe, European Union, 2014.

Moffat, G., 'Work-Life Balance and Employment Law: Cultural Change or Mission Impossible.' in *Family Life and the Law: Under One Roof*, edited by R. Probert, London: Ashgate, 2007, 135–158.

Mooney Cotter, A.-M., *Pregnant Pause – An International Legal Analysis of Maternity Discrimination*. London: Ashgate, 2010.

My Family Care, *Shared Parental Leave – One Year On – Where Are We Now?* Online: https://www.myfamilycare.co.uk/news/update/shared-parental-leave-where-are-we-now.html.

OECD, *Time Spent in Unpaid, Paid and Total Work, by Sex*. Online: http://www.oecd.org/gender/data/timespentinunpaidpaidandtotalworkbysex.htm.

OECD, *Doing Better for Families*, 2011. Online: http://www.oecd.org/els/soc/doingbetterforfamilies.htm.

Senčur Peček, D., 'Samozaposleni, ekonomsko odvisne osebe in obstoj delovnega razmerja' [Self-employed, economically dependent persons and existence of an employment relationship]. *Delavci in delodajalci* 14, No. 2–3 (2014): 201–220.

Sipilä, J., Repo, K., Rissanen, T., *Cash-for-Childcare: The Consequences for Caring Mothers*. Cheltenham: Edward Elgar, 2010.

Smith, A., '"The Magnificent 7[am]?" Work-Life Articulation Beyond the 9[am] to 5pm] "Norm"' New *Technology, Work and Employment* 31, No. 3 (2016): 209–222.

Strban, G., 'Vpliv nadzornih institucij na uresničevanje pravice do socialne varnosti' [The Influence of the Supervisory Institutions on the Implementation of the Right to Social Security – Are Benefits in Slovenia (In)adequate?]. *Delavci in delodajalci* 15, No. 4 (2015): 477–499.

Strban, G., Kresal, B., *Zakon o starševskem varstvu in družinskih prispevkih z uvodnimi pojasnili* [Parental Protection and Family Benefits Act with Introductory Comments]. Ljubljana: Uradni list, 2014.

Stropnik, N., *Investing in Children: Breaking the Cycle of Disadvantage (Slovenia)*. European Union, 2014.

Stropnik, N., 'Child Care in Slovenia: An Example of a Successful Transition'. *Child: Care Health and Development* 27, No. 3 (2001): 263–278.

The Modern Families Index, Bright Horizons, 2017.

Visser, J., 'What Happened to Collective Bargaining During the Great Recession', *IZA Journal of Labor Policy* 9, No. 5 (2016) (published online 13 May 2016).

Work and Family: Choice and Flexibility, URN05/1298, DTI, October 2005.

Zbyszewska, A., 'Reshaping the European Working-time Regime: Towards a Sustainable Model.' *European Labour Law Journal* 7, No. 3 (2016): 331–347.

Zbyszewska, A., *Gendering European Working Time Regimes: The Working Time Directive and the Case of Poland*, Cambridge: CUP, 2016.

CHAPTER 9

"This Is Not an Ideal, Man": Restructuring the Ideal Worker Norm

Ifat Matzner-Heruti

§9.01 INTRODUCTION

Working caregivers in Israel and in the United States (U.S.) find integrating their work and family responsibilities extremely challenging. Many of them realize that being a successful worker and also an involved caregiver is virtually a "mission impossible." Whereas several provisions aiming at aiding working parents have been enacted in the last decades, they were mainly focused on enabling workers to take leave—whether paid or unpaid—at times of birth or sickness.[1] Undoubtedly, enabling workers to take such leave is of utmost importance, yet it is insufficient given the prevalence of the ideal worker norm in numerous workplaces. According to this norm, the ideal worker is someone who has to fulfill inflexible workplace demands, such as working full-time and overtime without taking time-off for family responsibilities.[2] The assumption is, however, that this norm privileges fathers but discriminates against working mothers who cannot be ideal workers due to their domestic responsibilities.[3] Such assumption, I argue, is a major reason for the pervasiveness of the total and strict practices in many workplaces that are responsible for the seemingly unyielding work-family conflict. This chapter, therefore, attempts at expanding the work-family debate and research by focusing on fathers, examining how the ideal worker norm is manifested in the lives of many Israeli and American fathers today. In order to do so, the chapter uses masculinities[4] scholarship and analyzes the complex interconnection of masculinities

1. *See infra* section §9.02.
2. *See infra* section §9.02.
3. *See infra* section §9.03.
4. The term "masculinities" is used in the plural form to emphasize that masculinity has numerous impressions and multiple meanings. Masculinities identities are neither fixed nor natural, but are

norms, fatherhood, and work practices in both countries. Such interconnection exposes the messages that fathers receive, according to which their familial contribution, as well as their manhood, is measured by the amount of money they earn, not by the nurture they provide.[5] And because workers in Israel and in the U.S. are evaluated in terms of time, namely the number of hours they work,[6] fathers have to invest most of their time and energy to working, at the expense of their familial responsibilities. The requirement to perform as an always-available ideal worker does not affect fathers uniformly but rather depends on each father's multiple identities and social strata. Essentially, being socially expected to serve as an ideal worker comes with a price fathers have to pay—both those who are able to adhere to the strict norms of the workplace and certainly those who are not. Only when we deconstruct the ideal worker norm with regard to men and fathers can we evaluate the sacrifices they make. Such a deconstruction might be the way to finally dismantle the entrenchment of workplace norms and ameliorate working caregivers' hurdles.

This chapter proceeds in four parts. Part I starts with a cross-national examination of Israeli and American fathers and fatherhood via the lens of masculinities theory's core principles. It shows that masculinity imperatives are in tension with caregiving by fathers, resulting in fathers' difficulties to conceptualize their own identity as fathers. These imperatives include rejecting anything regarded as feminine; constantly proving their masculinity to other men (and to women); and providing economically for their families. The Part demonstrates that these imperatives operate both in Israel and in the U.S., yet they are influenced by each country's specific characteristics. In addition, this Part analyzes the changes in the construction of mothers' dual role as caregivers and employees in Israel and in the U.S., and the impact of these changes on the construction of fathers' dual role. Part II examines, by means of comparison, the role of the Israeli and American states, employers and courts in the creation and stagnation of the father "as a breadwinner" imperative. It shows that while the two countries differ in the level of public support they provide to working parents, they both place fathers as secondary caregivers. It also demonstrates that similar working norms are operating in both countries, according to which the ideal

---

rather socially constructed and manifested through performances. *See* Nancy E. Dowd, *Masculinities and Feminist Legal Theory*, 23 Wis. J.L. Gender & Soc'y 201, 241 (2008) [hereinafter Dowd, *Masculinities and Feminist Legal Theory*]; *see also* Nancy E. Dowd, The Man Question: Male Subordination and Privilege, 26–27 (2010) [hereinafter Dowd, The Man Question]; Masculinities and the Law: A Multidimensional Approach 28 (Frank Rudy Cooper and Ann C. McGinley eds., 2012) [hereinafter Masculinities and the Law]; Frank Rudy Cooper, *"Who's the Man?": Masculinities Studies, Terry Stops, and Police Training*, 18 Colum. J. Gender & L. 671, 684 (2009) (quoting Paul Smith, *Introduction* to Boys: Masculinities in Contemporary Culture 1, 3 (Paul Smith ed., 1996); Richard Collier, *Masculinities, Law, and Personal Life: Towards a New Framework for Understanding Men, Law, and Gender*, 33 Harv. J.L. & Gender 431, 471–472 (2010); Ann C. McGinley, *Work, Caregiving, and Masculinities*, 34 Seattle U. L. Rev. 703, 706–707 (2011).

5. *See infra* section §9.01[C].
6. *See* Daphna Hacker, Michal Frenkel and Yael Braudo-Bahat, *Working Families in Israeli Law: Between Neo-Liberalism and Human Rights*, in Gender in Israel 682, 704–705 (Margalit Shilo and Gideon Katz eds., 2011) (contending that Israel and the U.S. share the same neo-liberal organizational culture according to which good workers are measured by the number of hours they work).

worker is considered to be the one who dedicates most of his time and energy to work, without taking time-off for familial responsibilities. What is more, when working caregivers litigate their cases, trying to challenge workplace time demands, courts have been reluctant for the most part to undermine these demands. Such reluctance strengthens the ideal worker norm, making the integration of home and work almost impossible.

After analyzing the multiple ways that the ideal worker norm is reinforced by the Israeli and the American laws, workplaces and courts, Part III aims at deconstructing this norm with regard to working fathers. It uses masculinities theory to exemplify that whereas feminist legal theories argue that men have been privileged by the ideal worker norm, such norm negatively affects fathers. Furthermore, as long as this norm continues to be regarded as a privilege for fathers we can expect little success in achieving gender equality in the home and in the workplace. Hence, investigating how fathers have been impacted by the demands to function as breadwinners and ideal workers sheds light on the complex and multidimensional aspects of these demands in a way that will ultimately lead to their revision and modification. The last part of this chapter develops a twofold strategy to ameliorate fathers' work-family conflict. It uses both core principles of masculinities and neo-institutionalism theories to examine workers' and organizations' motives with regard to work-family policies. The examination demonstrates that employees and organizations are susceptible to similar influences when deciding whether to use work-family policies (employees) or adopting them (organizations). Fathers, for instance, might use these policies if other fathers at their workplace were openly involved in nurturing. Likewise, organizations might decide to adopt certain policies if other organizations in their field did so. Realizing that there is a "domino effect" among employees themselves and among organizations means that work-family advocates should invest their efforts not only in creating legal reforms, but also in collaborating with human resources professionals at leading organizations in order to modify structural norms.

§9.02 MASCULINITIES IMPERATIVES AS MANIFESTED IN THE LIVES OF ISRAELI AND AMERICAN FATHERS

Masculinities scholarship, a cross-disciplinary field of research that emerged in the 1970s and 1980s,[7] investigates the ways men are affected by patriarchy.[8] According to masculinities research, there are universal and common masculine characteristics in societies. Nevertheless, in every particular society the sense of "manhood" has its own

7. *See* MASCULINITIES AND THE LAW, *supra* note 4, at 1. For an overview of the research of major sociologists, *see* DOWD, THE MAN QUESTION, *supra* note 4, at 28. Nevertheless, the research has developed in other disciplines as well, such as psychology, criminology, feminist theory, queer theory, anthropology, and geography. *See* McGinley, *supra* note 4, at 706.

8. The theory focuses on men and their experiences, and its purpose is to shed light on the ways masculinity produces power but at the same time disadvantages men in patriarchal societies. *See* MASCULINITIES AND THE LAW, *supra* note 4, at 4. Moreover, it exposes the assumptions pertaining to manhood and the various ways in which such assumptions justify ideas and institutions. *See* Cooper, *supra* note 4, at 684–685.

nuances depending on the traditions and cultural context of the specific society.[9] Men's identities, therefore, "are constituted through diverse and socially-contingent practices that, within certain contexts, may be experienced in different ways."[10] Examining masculinities within context is important methodologically as it focuses the attention on the specific aspects of the situation and the system men operate within.[11] Israeli and American masculinities identities are thus influenced by the characteristics of their society and culture, and are shaped by and within those features.[12] And clearly, the way masculinities norms are constructed and understood within each of the societies shapes men's role as fathers.

Many of the core principles of masculinities theory come into force when we deal with fathers, hence via looking through the lens of the theory we will be able to detect the obstacles and difficulties Israeli and American men face as fathers.[13] Researches in Israel and in the U.S. have demonstrated that the gendered division of caregiving and household work is still persistent in both countries: Israeli and American fathers spend less time than mothers caring for children and even less time doing housework.[14] While fathers in both countries do more childcare and household work than their own fathers used to do, mothers still do disproportionately more.[15] A lot has been written about the reasons for this pervasive gendered division, focusing mainly on women's socialization to perform the domestic duties as well as the incompatibility between workplace norms and mothers' needs.[16] As accurate as these explanations might be, they provide merely

9. *See* Cooper, *supra* note 4, at 684; *see also* David Morgan, *Epilogue*, in MAKING MEN INTO FATHERS: MEN, MASCULINITIES AND SOCIAL POLITICS OF FATHERHOOD 281 (Barbara Hobson ed., 2002) [hereinafter MAKING MEN INTO FATHERS].
10. *See* Collier, *supra* note 4, at 472.
11. *See* MASCULINITIES AND THE LAW, *supra* note 4, at 85.
12. *See* Einat Hollander, *"The New Israeli Man?" Changes in Constructions of Masculinity in an Inter-Generational Perspective* 65 (2007) (unpublished Ph.D. Thesis, Department of Sociology and Anthropology, Bar-Ilan University, 2007) [Hebrew].
13. *See* Dowd, *Masculinities and Feminist Legal Theory, supra* note 4, at 243.
14. In the U.S., *see* Nancy E. Dowd, *Fatherhood and Equality: Reconfiguring Masculinities*, 45 SUFFOLK U. L. REV, 1047, 1053 (2012); *see also* Joan C. Williams and Stephanie Bornstein, *Caregivers in the Courtroom: The Growing Trend in Family Responsibilities Discrimination*, 41 U.S.F. L. REV. 171, 174 (2006); Keith Cunningham-Parmeter, *Men at Work, Fathers at Home: Uncovering the Masculine Face of Caregiver Discrimination*, 24 COLUM. J. GENDER & L. 253, 255 (2013). In Israeli, *see* Nadav Peretz, *The Abandonment of Fathers as Families' Surveillance: Fathers in the Legal Discourse in Israel, in* ABANDONING STATE – SURVEILLANCING STATE: SOCIAL POLICY IN ISRAEL, 1985–2008, 273 (2010) [Hebrew]; Arianne Renan-Barzilay, *Working Parents: Multidimensionalism and Working-Class Social Feminism—A New Theoretical Framework for Reconciling Work and Family in Israel*, 35 TEL AVIV UNIV. L. REV. 310–312 (2012) [Hebrew]; Daphna Hacker and Michal Frenkel, *Active Parenthood and Employment Equal Opportunities: The Need to Change the Characteristics of the Labor Force, AVODA, HEVRA AND MISHPAT 275, 279 (2005) [Hebrew].*
15. For American data, *see* Dowd, *supra* note 14, at 1053; For Israeli data, *see* Daphna Hacker, *Motherhood, Fatherhood and Law: Child Custody and Visitation in Israel*, 14(3) SOCIAL AND LEGAL STUDIES 411 (2005).
16. *See*, e.g., Nicole B. Porter, Caregiver Conundrum Redux: *The Entrenchment of Structural Norms*, 91(4) Denv. UL Rev. 963, 966 (2013); Joan C. Williams and Allison Tait, *Mancession or "Momcession"?: Good Providers, a Bad Economy, and Gender Discrimination*, 86 CHI.-KENT. L. REV. 857, 875 (2011) (contending that "the workplace culture is male-dominated and defined by norms of extreme masculinity"); CATHARINE A. MACKINNON, TOWARD A FEMINIST THEORY OF THE STATE 224 (1989); Joan Acker, *Hierarchies, Jobs, Bodies: A Theory of Gendered Organizations*, 4

partial answers. Masculinities theory complements the vast feminist and work-life research by shifting the focus to men, investigating the reasons for men's lack of involvement in caregiving and housework. It shows that throughout their lives men are subject to masculinity imperatives pertaining to their "proper" role as men and fathers. The three main imperatives include rejecting anything regarded as feminine; constantly proving their masculinity to other men (and to women); and providing economically for their families. While these three imperatives operate both in Israel and in the U.S., they are influenced by each country's specific norms, as will be analyzed below.

[A] Avoid Acting in a Feminine Way

One of the strongest imperatives of manhood requires men to reject all things defined as feminine which clearly include caregiving.[17] Providing care is associated with women as it requires being soft and empathetic and men receive the message that it is not their "natural" role.[18] As astutely described by Professor Nancy Dowd:

> [A]t the core of fatherhood, however, is a tension that resonates in the contemporary practice of fatherhood. Fatherhood is one of the critical life roles for men, but care of children is significantly at odds with the concept of masculinity.[19]

Not surprisingly, several studies have shown that fathers feel more comfortable performing some kinds of caregiving tasks rather than others,[20] and they also tend to "masculinize" care.[21] Indeed, as professors Marsilio and Roy have demonstrated, "practical and cultural forces often complicate men's vision of themselves as fathers and their ability to nurture their children."[22] Israeli culture and norms thus provide an even greater challenge for Israeli fathers to function as caregivers. In Israel, there is a strong connection between masculinity and militarism due to historical reasons, and on-going security problems.[23] Thus, in order to attain hegemonic masculinity,[24] one

---

GENDER & SOC'Y 139 (1990); Kathryn Abrams, *Gender Discrimination and the Transformation of Workplace Norms*, 42 VAND. L. REV. 1183 (1989); JOAN C. WILLIAMS, RESHAPING THE WORK-FAMILY DEBATE: WHY MEN AND CLASS MATTER 88 (2010) [hereinafter WILLIAMS, RESHAPING]; Dowd, *supra* note 14, at 1061–1063.

17. *See* Dowd, *supra* note 14, at 1063.
18. *Id.* at 1063 (contending that "care is perceived as soft, vulnerable, weak—all characteristics associated with women, and again, to be rejected, at whatever cost by men").
19. *See* DOWD, THE MAN QUESTION, *supra* note 4, at 105.
20. *See* Kathryn Abrams, *Cross-Dressing in the Master's Clothes*, 109 YALE L.J. 745, 760–762 (2000) (book review).
21. *See* Dowd, *supra* note 14, at 1063–1064; *see also* Kathleen Sylvester and Kathleen Reich, *Making Fathers Count, Assessing the Progress of Responsible Fatherhood Efforts*, SOCIAL POLICY ACTION NETWORK, *available at* http://www.aecf.org/upload/publicationfiles/making%20fathers%20count.pdf 22 (2011).
22. *See* WILLIAM MARSIGLIO AND KEVIN ROY, NURTURING DADS: FATHERHOOD INITIATIVES BEYOND THE WALLET 4 (2012).
23. The connection between masculinity and militarism in Israel is especially salient due to the historical process which identified the Zionist Jew as masculine and as a fighter. The Zionist movement, which emerged in Europe during the nineteenth century, was aimed at creating the new Jew as masculine and a fighter. The movement wanted to change the image of the old

should also be a fighter.[25] That is, there is a direct link between serving in the army in combat units, willing to sacrifice your life for the country, and being regarded as a good citizen.[26] This social imperative does not go along with nurturing and softness so required in caring for children. There is a similar link in the U.S., as serving in the military "confers privilege, most notably, the notion of full citizenship because of the literal sacrifice of [men's] bodies."[27] However, whereas serving in the military is optional in the U.S. and regarded as only one route to being considered a good American citizen, it is mandatory in Israel[28] and provides *the* measurement for being regarded as a "real" Israeli. Thus, Israeli fathers might find nurturing as even more at odds with masculinity norms than their American counterparts, given the militaristic society they live in.

[B] Located Within a Hierarchy

Another masculine trait that has a direct impact on the way Israeli and American men are involved in caregiving is hierarchy: both the hierarchies among men themselves and those of men on women.[29] The hegemonic masculine man in Israel manifests the prevalent hierarchies in the Israeli society: This man should be Jewish and white; he

European Jew, who was perceived as weak and vulnerable, which made him an easy target for hatred and hostility. In contrast, the body of the new Jew was supposed to be tall and masculine, and he was expected to be assertive and self-confident. For more on the historical process of creating the masculine Jew, *see* Orna Sasson-Levi, *Masculinity as a Protest: Identity Construction Among Blue-Collar Soldiers,* 5(1) ISRAELI SOCIOLOGY, A JOURNAL OF THE STUDY OF SOCIETY IN ISRAEL 17 (2003) [Hebrew]; Hollander, *supra* note 12, at 66; Danny Kaplan, *The Construction of Combat Emotions as a Central Site of "Sexonality,"* 5(1) ISRAELI SOCIOLOGY, A JOURNAL OF THE STUDY OF SOCIETY IN ISRAEL 50 (2003) [Hebrew]; Yohai Hakak, *Who Is a Hero? Changes in the Construction of the Haredi Masculine Body due to the Interaction with the Secular Masculine Body,* 11(1) ISRAELI SOCIOLOGY, A JOURNAL OF THE STUDY OF SOCIETY IN ISRAEL 163 (2009); Yair Seltenreich, *Masculinity, Respect and Body in the PJCA Settlements of the Galilee During the Settlement Period,* 11(1) ISRAELI SOCIOLOGY, A JOURNAL OF THE STUDY OF SOCIETY IN ISRAEL 137–157 (2009).

24. The concept of "hegemonic masculinity" was coined by R.W. Connell, a leading theorist of masculinities. This form of masculinity is the socially preferred one in a given culture, however only a minority of men might actually enact it. *See* R.W. Connell and James W. Messerschmidt, *Hegemonic Masculinity: Rethinking the Concept,* 19 GENDER & SOC'Y 829, 832–833 (2005).
25. Not surprisingly, most of the studies that deal with Israeli masculinities have been focused on the military and its effects on Israeli men. *See* Danny Kaplan, *Introduction,* in R.W. CONNELL, MASCULINITIES 16 (2009) [Hebrew]; *see also* Hollander, *supra* note 12, at 72.
26. *See* Hollander, *supra* note 12, at 54–55.
27. DOWD, THE MAN QUESTION, *supra* note 4, at 58.
28. Serving in the army is mandatory in Israel for both men and women. A lot have been written and said about Israeli women's service in the military, and a full discussion of this complex issue is beyond the scope of this study. However, at the risk of diminishing the seriousness and depth of the issue, it is worth mentioning that the military is perceived as a masculine organization, and has a significant role in reinforcing gender roles in the Israeli society. *See,* e.g., Noya Rimalt, *Women in the Sphere of Masculinity: The Double-Edged Sword of Women's Integration in the Military,* 14 DUKE J. GENDER L. & POL'Y 1097 (2007); Orna Sasson-Levy, *Constructing Gender Identities Within the Israeli Army* (2000) (unpublished Ph.D dissertation, Hebrew University) (on file with the Hebrew University Library) [Hebrew]; Sasson-Levi, *supra* note 23, at 54; Hollander, *supra* note 12, at 70–72.
29. *See* Dowd, *supra* note 14, at 1065–1066.

needs to belong to the upper-middle class; should be heterosexual; and not feminine.[30] Given that the hegemonic masculine man in the U.S. currently "is an elite Anglo white heterosexual male,"[31] there are many similarities between hegemonic masculinity in Israel and the U.S. However, "white supremacy" is defined differently in the two countries. In the U.S., race is the primary system of oppression in a way that often overshadows the patriarchal dividend.[32] American black men's subordinated status in the hierarchy of masculinities is reinforced due to a combination of gender, race, and class.[33] In Israel, however, the "black" man is distinguished not necessarily by his race but rather by his nationality or ethnicity.[34] In other words, men in Israel might inhabit a privileged gender category (i.e., men) and a subordinated ethnical category (i.e., Arab).[35] The military service establishes and reinforces hierarchies among men and its central role goes beyond the service itself and affects social, national, and educational aspects as well.[36] It is valued as a qualification for occupying political leadership in Israel as can be seen by the large number of generals in all Israeli cabinets throughout the years.[37] Similarly, serving in the U.S. military is also prized as a qualification for obtaining political positions as well as for receiving entitlements such as educational and health benefits.[38]

In order to maintain their place in the hierarchical order, men feel a constant pressure to prove their masculinity,[39] which strongly affects their level of involvement in caregiving. Indeed, research has shown that peer behavior has a major impact on fathers in both countries: When asked what might affect their level of engagement in caregiving, Israeli and American fathers said that in order for them to be more openly engaged as parents, other working fathers need to publicly exhibit their participation in parenting as well.[40] Along these lines, fathers find it difficult to co-parent in an equal

---

30. *See* Hollander, *supra* note 12, at 78.
31. *See* Masculinities and the Law, *supra* note 4, at 87.
32. *Id.* at 30.
33. *Id.* at 92, and also at 85, and at 29; *see also* Dowd, The Man Question, *supra* note 4, at 150.
34. Israel is a multi-ethnic society in a very complex manner, which can be divided into two main levels: the first division is between Jews and Arabs; the second division is between Jews from different origins - Ashkenazi v. Sephardi. "Mizrahim" or "Sephardim" are Jews of Middle Eastern, Central Asian, or North African descent. These divisions have an impact on class stratification as well, and Ashkenazi-Jews occupy the upper strata in society, whereas Sephardi-Jews occupy less desirable social positions, and Israeli-Arabs occupy the bottom strata. *See* Meir Yaish, *Class Structure in a Deeply Divided Society: Class and Ethnic Inequality in Israel, 1974–1991*, 52 The British J. Sociology 414 (2001).
35. Whereas in the American context, "men could be seen as inhabiting a privileged gender category (i.e., men) and a subordinated racial category (i.e., black)." *See* Masculinities and the Law, *supra* note 4, at 85.
36. *See* Hollander, *supra* note 12, at 71.
37. *Id.* at 39.
38. *See* Dowd, The Man Question, *supra* note 4, at 58.
39. *See* Masculinities and the Law, *supra* note 4, at 3.
40. *See* Darren Rosenblum, *Unsex Mothering, Toward a New Culture of Parenting*, 35 Harv. J.L. & Gender 110 (2012); *see also* Dror Gershoni, *New Fatherhood in Israel—A Gender Perspective on Masculinity and Fatherhood in the Institutional and Marital Context* 63 (2004) (unpublished M.A. Thesis, Dep't of Soc. & Anthro., Bar-Ilan University) (on file with the Bar-Ilan University Library) [Hebrew] (In his study of Israeli fathers, Gershoni's interviewees have said that in order for them to be more openly engaged in care, employers need to change their perceptions, and other working fathers need to publicly exhibit their participation in parenting). Peer behavior

and collaborative way with other men when there are multiple parents.[41] Multiple parents have become a common phenomenon due to the increase in divorce rates in both countries and the likelihood that one—or both—of the biological parents will re-marry or cohabit with other partners.[42] Since co-parenting requires collaboration and connection, the hierarchy norm of masculinities might undermine the possibility of a successful cooperation between the parents—the biological and non-biological ones—to the detriment of children.[43]

[C] Being the Family Provider

Israeli and American fathers countries are expected to provide for their families economically and their ability—or inability thereof—to be breadwinners comes to define their identity as men.[44] The strong correlation between achieving success in the workplace and being regarded as masculine means that fathers' familial contribution is measured by money, not caregiving.[45]

While contemporaneously fathers in both countries are expected to be the primary breadwinners, American fathers were historically supposed to be the sole breadwinners, having homemaker-wives.[46] This is in contrast to their Israeli counterparts, whose wives have always been expected to be *both* caregivers and employees, albeit to put nurture before paid work.[47] The role of Israeli women as both workers and caregivers was developed with the creation of the new state.[48] Women were expected

has a greater effect on men than the behavior of their own fathers or their partners. *See* DOWD, THE MAN QUESTION, *supra* note 4, at 112.

41. *See* Dowd, *supra* note 14, at 1065–1066.
42. *Id.* at 1066; In Israel, *see* Ayelet Blacher-Prigat and Daphne Hacker, *Parents or Strangers: Common and Desired Legal Status of Parent's Partners*, 40 MISHPATIM 6–7 (2010) [Hebrew]; Hacker, *supra* note 15, at 411.
43. *See* Dowd, *supra* note 14, at 1066; *see also* DOWD, THE MAN QUESTION, *supra* note 4, at 108 (arguing that "[m]ultiple fatherhood is not uncommon, but what appears to be uncommon is multiple nurturing fathers").
44. *See* Ifat Matzner-Heruti, *"Dare to Care": The Complicated Case of Working Fathers Alleging Sex and Parental Discrimination – A Comparative Analysis*, 23 J. L. & POLICY 101 (2014).
45. *See* Abrams, *supra* note 20, at 759–760 (arguing that the social expectation of men to perform as "ideal workers" without family responsibilities arises from "more pervasive gender norms that link masculinity with the ability to perform as the family provider"); *see also* MAKING MEN INTO FATHERS, *supra* note 9, at 62 (arguing that "indeed, part of the very definition of proper masculinity, and good fatherhood, in the United States has been economic self-support"); DOWD, THE MAN QUESTION, *supra* note 4, at 110; Ann C. McGinley, *Masculine Law Firms*, 8 FIU L. REV. 423, 440 (2013); Shelley J. Correll, Erin L. Kelly, Lindsey Trimble O'Connor and Joan C. Williams, *Redesigning, Redefining Work*, 41(1) WORK AND OCCUPATIONS 3, 4 (2014). With regard to the Israeli context, *see* Gershoni, *supra* note 40, at 60.
46. This is a generalization and does not reflect the lives of women of color and working-class women who have always worked outside their homes. *See* Martha Chamallas, INTRODUCTION TO FEMINIST LEGAL THEORY 25 (2003).
47. Michal Frenkel, *Has the Motherhood Wall Collapsed? Work Family Strategies of Hi- Tech Women in Israel*, The Israeli Women's Network Publication Series 11–12 (2003).
48. *See* Dafna N. Izraeli, *The Women Workers' Movement: First Wave Feminism in Pre-State Israel*, in PIONEERS AND HOMEMAKERS: JEWISH WOMEN IN PRE-STATE ISRAEL 183–209 (Deborah Bernstein ed., 1992); *see also* Mordehai (Moti) Mironi, *Work, Family, and the Law in Israel*, 27 COMP. LAB. L. & POL'Y J. 487, 489 (2006).

to give birth[49] and care for children, but also to take part in the labor market. However, their financial contribution was supposed to provide only the second income.[50] Thus, Israeli families comprised of a father as a sole breadwinner and a mother as a sole homemaker were always an exception,[51] and there was a low legitimacy for mothers whose "only" job was to raise their children.[52] Consequently, employment laws were enacted to provide working mothers with entitlements in order for them to combine work and family, such as the Employment of Women Law.[53] This law, enacted as early as 1954, established certain rights to be given to working mothers, such as paid maternity leave.[54] Aside from paid maternity leave, Israeli working mothers are entitled to certain arrangements aiming at allowing them to combine their work and family duties.[55]

By comparison, American mothers were historically expected to solely take care of the children and the home, while their husbands were supposed to be the economic providers, earning wages capable of singularly supporting the family.[56] As Professor Catherine Albiston explains, this family wage ideology came as a response "to the changing economic system brought about by industrialization and the upheavals that threatened male exclusive competence and authority in the economic realm."[57] During this process, separate spheres of responsibility were established: Women were identified with the private sphere of the home and with task-oriented labor, whereas men were identified with the public sphere outside the home and with time-disciplined labor.[58] This gender division of labor led to far-reaching consequences, changing the value and importance of work. Working full time for wages in the industrial economy meant independence and citizenship whereas working part time or working at home meant dependency.[59] The changing norms, therefore, were to define what work actually is.[60] Yet, the American workforce has undergone dramatic changes in the last

49. *See* Mironi, *supra* note 48, at 487–488 (arguing that "demography and birth rate have become an issue of national security" in Israel); *see also* Frenkel, *supra* note 47, at 11.
50. *See* Hollander, *supra* note 12, at 77–78.
51. *See* Hacker, *supra* note 15, at 411.
52. *See* Frenkel, *supra* note 47, at 11–12; *see also* Peretz, *supra* note 14, at 272.
53. Employment of Women Law, 1954 S.H. 154.
54. *Id.* § 6. The law mandates that a woman must be employed in order to be eligible for paid maternity leave which demonstrates Israel's encouragement of women to work outside their homes. Women who work in their own homes are not considered workers hence they are not entitled to a maternity allowance (or unemployment pay). *See* RUTH HALPERIN-KADDARI, WOMEN IN ISRAEL: A STATE OF THEIR OWN 124 (2004).
55. For example, they might be entitled to a shortened workday; they have the right to use the services of an on-site employer-provided day care center (in case there is one); they have the right to take up to eight days of paid leave per year to take care of a sick child. *See* Employment Equal Opportunities Law, 5748-1988, §4.
56. *See* Catherine Albiston, *Institutional Inequality*, WIS. L. REV. 1093, 1118–1119 (2009). Yet, as Martha Chamallas expressed, women of color and working-class women have always worked outside their homes. *See supra* fn. 46.
57. *See* Albiston, *supra* note 56, at 1118.
58. *Id.*
59. *Id.* at 1111.
60. *Id.* at 1111–1112.

half of the twentieth century when many women entered it,[61] and the majority of families nowadays include dual-earner couples.[62] Moreover, the American family's construction has also changed, and there are more and more single-parent families due to increases in both the divorce rate and the number of never-married parents.[63] Nevertheless, despite these changes, the family wage ideal is still a powerful norm[64] requiring fathers to be the main breadwinners.[65] By the same token, women still suffer the "motherhood penalty,"[66] which is reflected in the difficulties they face when trying to combine work and familial responsibilities.[67]

To sum up, the value of understanding masculinities' core insights is to bring a much richer picture of male privilege,[68] and expose the gender "policing" of men and fathers. Such "policing" includes the demand of men to avoid acting in a "feminine" and soft way; the importance of hierarchy to manhood, which pressures men to constantly prove their manliness; and the breadwinner norm. Fathers' role in Israel and in the U.S. was historically constructed around economic responsibility, and they were expected to function as the primary breadwinners (in Israel) or sole breadwinners (in the U.S.). Changes in the American workforce have led to an erosion of the breadwinner/homemaker household model. Yet, American fathers are still required to be the primary providers, and they consequently perceive breadwinning as their main role as husbands and parents.[69] Their Israeli counterparts are also expected to function as the main providers, and, at most, "help" their wives with childrearing and household chores.[70] Thus, in both countries, fathers' role as nurturers is regarded as voluntary and optional, not as part of their identity as men,[71] and consequently they are often seen as secondary and even incompetent parents.[72]

In the next part, I would like to demonstrate how the elements of masculinities analyzed above are reinforced by Israeli and American governments, workplaces and

61. *See* Catherine Albiston, *Institutional Perspectives on Law, Work, and Family*, 3 ANNU. REV. LAW SOC. SCI. 397, 399 (2007); *see also* JANET C. GORNICK AND MARCIA K. MEYERS, FAMILIES THAT WORK: POLICIES FOR RECONCILING PARENTHOOD AND EMPLOYMENT 7 (2003); Haya Stier and Avital Sella-Dotan, *Work-Family Balance in the Era of Intensive Work*, in HEAVY WORK INVESTMENT: ITS NATURE, SOURCES, OUTCOMES, AND FUTURE DIRECTIONS 225 (Harpaz and Snir ed., 2014).
62. *See* http://taxfoundation.org/blog/america-has-become-nation-dual-income-working-couples.
63. *See* Albiston, *supra* note 61, at 400; *see also* Stier and Sella-Dotan, *supra* note 61, at 225.
64. *See* Laura T. Kessler, *Transgressive Caregiving*, 33 FLA. ST. U. L. REV. 45 (2005).
65. *See* Albiston, *supra* note 56, at 1152; *see also* Abrams, *supra* note 20, at 759–760.
66. Shelley J. Correll et al., *Getting a Job: Is There a Motherhood Penalty?* 112 AM. J. SOC. 1297, 1298, 1334 (2007).
67. *Id.* (arguing that "employed mothers are the group of women that now accounts for most of the 'gender gap' in wages"); *see also* Joan C. Williams and Nancy Segal, *Beyond The Maternal Wall: Relief For Family Caregivers Who Are Discriminated Against On The Job*, 26 HARV. WOMEN'S L. J. 77 (2003).
68. *See* MASCULINITIES AND THE LAW, *supra* note 4, at 30; *see also* Douglas P. Schrock and Michael Schwalbe, *Men, Masculinity, and Manhood Acts*, ANNUAL REVIEW OF SOCIOLOGY, 277, 288–289 (2009).
69. *See supra* section §9.01[C].
70. *See* Hollander, *supra* note 12, at 77–78.
71. *See* Matzner-Heruti, *supra* note 44, at 161; *see also* Dowd, *supra* note 14, at 1061–1062; DAPHNA HACKER, PARENTHOOD AND THE LAW, CUSTODY AND VISITATION CONSTRUCTION UPON DIVORCE 77–150 (2008) [Hebrew].
72. *See* DOWD, THE MAN QUESTION, *supra* note 4, at 120.

courts. Specifically, I will examine how the ideal worker model infuses the breadwinner norm in a way which generates significant difficulties for working fathers to be involved caregivers.

§9.03 THE ROLE OF THE ISRAELI AND AMERICAN GOVERNMENTS, EMPLOYERS, AND COURTS IN THE REINFORCEMENT OF THE MASCULINE BREADWINNER NORM

The previous part has shown that masculinities imperatives shape Israeli and American men's understanding with regard to their paternal role and obligations as fathers: The cornerstone of these obligations is to care for their families financially which essentially means that fathers should be primarily committed to market work.

Work-family policies in both countries intensify fathers' primary commitment to the workplace, albeit differently, depending upon each country's culture, tradition and history, to name but a few.

To begin with, while both counties can be classified as liberal welfare states[73] with common law systems, they differ in the level of their governments' interference. The Israeli state was founded on social-democratic values, including a strong emphasis on governmental intervention in the social and economic spheres.[74] By comparison, the American state's emphasis has been focused on ideals of self-sufficiency with minimal governmental interference,[75] and there is a strong reliance on employer-based benefits.[76] Americans must secure their wages from the market, and provide care for their families—rather than the state.[77] Such assumption has a significant impact on men, as astutely asserted by Orloff and Monson:

> The emphasis ideologically and materially on private sources of welfare—both cash and care—has been consequential for gender relations, and men's positions. The strong emphasis on private responsibility for all but the aged means that

73. *See* Hila Shamir, *The State of Care: Rethinking the Distributive Effects of Familial Care Policies in Liberal Welfare States*, AM. J. COMP. L. 953, 960 (2010) (characterizing Israel and the U.S. as liberal welfare states based on the typology of Gosta Esping-Andresen: GÖSTA ESPING-ANDERSEN, *THE THREE WORLDS OF WELFARE CAPITALISM* (1990)).
74. *See* Avraham Doron, *Is a Balanced Attitude towards the Welfare State Possible?* 12 LABOR, SOCIETY AND STATE 516 (2010) [Hebrew] (contending that from the 1930s to the end of the 1970s, the hegemony of the labor movement, as well as its belief in a social-democratic regime, including strong interferences in social and economic life, was dominant in Israel. However, since the 1980s, the Israeli society has been in the process of leaning towards the radical-right in many spheres, including the socio-economic). Interestingly, Israeli society is influenced by the U.S. and is turning away from ideals of social solidarity to ideals of individualism and worshipping personal economic success. *Id.* at 528 (arguing that Israel, as a post-industrial society, is undergoing a profound cultural change). The salient change could be seen in its departure from historical ideals of social solidarity and equality to ideals of individualism and personal economic success); *see also* Peretz, *supra* note 14, at 272 (arguing that the Israeli welfare state is going through major changes in terms of moving away from a social-democratic welfare policy to a neo-liberal policy); Hacker et al., *supra* note 6, at 686-687.
75. *See* Lisa Bornstein, *Inclusions and Exclusions in Work-Family Policy: The Public Values and Moral Code Embedded in the Family and Medical Leave Act*, COLUM. J. GENDER & L. 10, 77 (2000).
76. *See* Albiston, *supra* note 56, at 1105.
77. *See* MAKING MEN INTO FATHERS, *supra* note 9, at 62-64.

men's identities—as fathers, citizens, workers—are not forged within the welfare state, but outside it, or even in opposition to it.[78]

Israel and the U.S. thus differ as to the level of legal and public support provided for families. For instance, the Israeli antidiscrimination provision defines parents as a protected group in the workplace,[79] whereas its American antidiscrimination counterpart lacks such protection.[80] In addition, the U.S. government provides almost no direct support for families,[81] including paid family leave.[82] The Israeli law, in comparison, provides paid family leave on the occasions of birth or adoption of a baby.[83] Moreover, Israeli parents might be allowed to work shortened days, depending upon their workplace's policy.[84] To be clear, not all of the Israeli mandates are framed in a

78. *See* Making Men into Fathers, *supra* note 9, at 89.
79. Employment (Equal Opportunities) Law, 5748-1988, SH No. 38, § 2(a) [hereinafter EEO Law].
80. Civil Rights Act of 1964, 42 U.S.C. § 2000e-2 (1964). Title VII of the Civil Rights Act of 1964 was enacted to prohibit discrimination against employees in the workplace. Title VII provides: "[i]t shall be an unlawful employment practice for an employer . . . to discriminate against any individual with respect to his compensation, terms, conditions, or privileges of employment, because of such individual's race, color, religion, sex, [and] national origin." *Id.* § 2000e-2(a)(1). A few states have specific prohibitions in their employment discrimination protections based on family responsibilities. In Alaska, for example, the statute prohibits discrimination based on "parenthood," *inter alia. See* Alaska Stat. § 18.80.200 (2006). In the District of Columbia, an employer cannot discriminate against an employee based on "family responsibilities". *See* D.C. Code Ann. § 2-1402.11 (2001). There are sixty-three local jurisdictions in twenty-two states in addition to Alaska and the District of Columbia that prohibit this type of discrimination. *See* Stephanie Bornstein and Robert J. Rathmell, *Caregivers as a Protected Class?: The Growth of State and Local Laws Prohibiting Family Responsibilities Discrimination*, Ctr. for WorkLife Law, U.C. Hastings Coll. of L. 1, 1 (2009), http://www.worklifelaw.org/pubs/LocalFRDLawsReport.pdf.
81. *See* Gornick and Meyers, *supra* note 61, at 107; *see also* Martha A. Fineman, The Autonomy Myth: A Theory of Dependency 14 (2004); Making Men into Fathers, *supra* note 9, at 30; Bornstein, *supra* note 75, at 77 (contending that "[t]he United States has done little to help working families. We lack any comprehensive national policy."); Lori Jablczynski, Note, *Striking a Balance Between the "Parental" Wall and Workplace Equality: The Male Caregiver Perspective*, 31 Women's Rts. L. Rep. 309, 313 (2010) (arguing that "America still lacks adequate social backing for caregivers and their familial obligations."); Nancy E. Dowd, *Work and Family: Restructuring the Workplace*, 32 Ariz. L. Rev. 431, 469 (1990) (asserting that "[t]he primary role of the law in the work-family relationship has been non-intervention...") On the importance of supportive policies, and the lack of such ones in the U.S., *see* Jane Waldfogel, *What Children Need* (2006).
82. Family and Medical Leave Act of 1993, 29 U.S.C. §§ 2601–2654 (1994) In order to be eligible for the leave, the worker must have worked for at least twelve months prior to taking the leave, and for at least 1,250 hours during these months. Further, the worker must be part of a workplace where there are more than fifty employees within seventy-five miles. *Id.* at §101(2)(A)(ii). The U.S. is the only country in the developed world that does not provide paid parental leave. *See* Rosenblum, *supra* note 40, at 104; *see also* Gornick and Marcia, *supra* note 61, at 123 (2003). Four states, however, provide paid family leave. *See* http://www.nolo.com/legal-encyclopedia /paid-family-leave-states-29854.html (last visited 03.09.2016). Other states are considering leave legislation as well. *See* Caldwell G. Collins, *Note: Home Alone: Is This the Best We Can Do? A Proposal to Amend Pending Parental Leave Legislation*, 29 Wash. U. J.L. & Pol'y 301, 310–312 (2009).
83. Employment of Women Law, 1954 S.H. 154, § 6. Israeli laws also include paid leave to care for a sick child, sick parent or sick spouse: *see*, respectively, Sick Pay (Absence from Work Due to Child's Illness) 1993, Sick Leave Law (Leave Due to a Parent's Illness) 1993, Sick Leave Law (Leave Due to a Spouse's Illness) 1998. Moreover, employees are entitled to a paid leave in cases of their own health problems. *See* Sick Leave Law 1976.
84. EEO Law § 4(a) states that "[w]here, in accordance with the terms of employment customary at her place of work, a woman employee has any entitlement by virtue of her being a parent, such

gender-neutral stance; some of them state that only if the mother cannot use the benefit can the father, under some conditions, assume the role of a caregiver.[85] This unequal distribution manifests Israel's view of fathers as secondary caregivers who have a residual role as nurturers.

Not only are legal mandates—or lack of them thereof—convey to fathers the message that they are secondary caregivers, but also workplaces. The ideal worker norm is prevalent in both countries—good and devoted workers are considered to be those who dedicate most of their time and energy to their employers, without taking time-off for family (or other) responsibilities.[86] In fact, employees in both countries are measured according to the time they spend at work, and not surprisingly, they work more hours than their counterparts in other industrialized countries.[87] While the increase in working hours mainly affects professionals and managers,[88] more and more professions have also begun to require longer working days.[89] The requirement to stay long hours at work forces workers to devote most of their time and energy to work, perpetuating the breadwinner model and maintaining a workforce committed to putting work first in a way that also serves the whole capitalist system.[90] Even when Israeli and American fathers expressed equal views regarding caregiving, the daily stress at work along with fear of being unemployed, especially at times of recession, reinforce gendered order and hegemonic masculinity.[91] Therefore, fathers feel a major responsibility to succeed at work, in a workforce which is becoming more and more demanding and competitive. In this way, gender norms of masculinities nourish the breadwinner norm, signaling to fathers that by being the family providers they are

---

entitlement shall also be accorded to a male employee at the workplace where the aforesaid term of employment is customary ... ."

85. *See* Matzner-Heruti, *supra* note 44, at 116–118 (analyzing section 4 of the EEO Law and its gendered eligibility requirements); *see also* Ifat Matzner-Heruti, *All You Need Is Leave? Rethinking the Concept of Paternity Leave*, 21 CARDOZO J.L. & GENDER 475 (2014).
86. *See* Joan Williams and H.C. Cooper, *The Public Policy of Motherhood*, 60 J. SOC. ISSUES 849 (2004); *see also* Williams and Segal, *supra* note 67, at 114. In Israel, *see* Hacker and Frenkel, *supra* note 14, at 278; *see also* Hacker et al., *supra* note 6, at 682–684.
87. *See* GORNICK AND MEYERS, *supra* note 61, at 59; *see also* Jerry A. Jacobs and Kathleen Gerson, *Toward a Family-Friendly, Gender-Equitable Work Week*, 1 U. PA. J. LAB. & EMP. L. 457, 458 (1997–1998); Williams and Cooper, *supra* note 86, at 852; WILLIAMS, RESHAPING, *supra* note 16, at 90; Belinda M. Smith, *Time Norms in the Workplace: Their Exclusionary Effect and Potential for Change*, 11 COLUM. J. GENDER & L. 271 (2002); Rosenblum, *supra* note 40, at 107; Williams and Segal, *supra* note 67, at 114. In comparison, the law in Israel defines the work-week in Israel as forty-three hours a week, however, in practice many workplaces demand their workers to work more hours. *See* Renan-Barzilay, *supra* note 14, at 327; *see also* Hacker and Frenkel, *supra* note 14, at 278; Hacker et al. *supra* note 6, at 704–705; and also http://www.haaretz.com/print-edition/news/experts-israelis-among-most-overworked-people-in world1.270790;http://www.ynet.co.il/articles/0,7340,L3760210,00.html [Hebrew] (asserting that many Israelis work sixty hours a week or more).
88. *See* Smith, *supra* note 87, at 277; *see also* WILLIAMS, RESHAPING, *supra* note 16, at 90. In Israel, *see* Renan-Barzilay, *supra* note 14, at 327.
89. *See* Erin L. Kelly, *Discrimination Against Caregivers? Gendered Family Responsibilities, Employer Practices, and Work Rewards*, in HANDBOOK OF EMPLOYMENT DISCRIMINATION RESEARCH: RIGHTS AND REALITIES 341, 350 (Laura Beth Nielsen and Robert Nelson eds., 2005); *see also* Smith, *supra* note 87, at 277. In Israel, *see* Renan-Barzilay, *supra* note 14, at 327.
90. *See* Abrams, *supra* note 20, at 760; *see also* Dowd, *supra* note 14, at 1061.
91. In Israel, *See* Gershoni, *supra* note 40, at 72–73. In the U.S., *see* Williams and Tait, *supra* note 16.

regarded as masculine men.[92] As manifested in the words of an Israeli father who equally shares caregiving and household duties with his wife:

> From my experience, and from the experience of my friends, the desire to put the family first – and not just pay lip service – clashes with things that are perceived as very masculine. What will you tell yourself, or your neighbors? That you were an amazing father?[93]

His American counterpart similarly connects working and being masculine by asserting: "As a man you have no status at all if you do not work."[94] Indeed, voluminous studies have shown that workplaces—both in Israel and in the U.S.—often penalize working fathers who "dare" to be more engaged and active as parents.[95] What is more, the studies demonstrate the Gordian knot between masculinity and breadwinning, showing that Israeli and American fathers who deviate from their traditional roles not only jeopardize their work status but also their manly façade.[96] Therefore, many Israeli fathers have come to accept and even justify workplace requirements to dedicate many hours to work, worrying that if they do not, they might lose their jobs.[97] Yet, the research has documented another phenomenon: in order to avoid the penalties of noncompliance but still be able to fulfill familial responsibilities, American fathers have found several strategies to cope with their conflicting demands. For instance, some use informal, under-the-radar flexibility, which means being secretive about their engagement in work-family related activities.[98] While this kind of strategy enables fathers to maintain their ideal worker façade, it does not help transform the organizational culture into a supportive one for fathers (and other caregivers).[99] It is worth mentioning the experience of divorced fathers who need to recalibrate their working schedules to meet their children's needs in the absence of a mother. According to a recent study conducted in Israel, divorced fathers adopt various work-family strategies, including flexible work arrangements, setting new expectations with supervisors, and

---

92. *See* Chuck Halverson, *Notes, From Here to Paternity: Why Men Are Not Taking Leave Under the Family and Medical Leave Act*, 18 Wis. Women's L.J. 257, 263 (2003); *see also* Dowd, *supra* note 14, at 1061–1062; Williams and Tait, *supra* note 16, at 864.
93. *See* Naomi Darom, *Israeli Fathers Who Want it All: But Can They Get a Job After Being Stay-at-Home Dads?*, Haaretz (May 18, 2013, 1:50 PM), http://www.haaretz.com/weekend/magazine/israeli-fathers-who-want-it-all-but-can-they-get-a-job-after-being-stay-at-home-dads.premium-1.524313.
94. *See* Andrea Doucet, *"It's Almost Like I Have a Job, But I Don't Get Paid": Fathers at Home Reconfiguring Work, Care, and Masculinity*, 2 FATHERING 277, 278 (2004).
95. *See* Matzner-Heruti, *supra* note 85, at 482–484.
96. *Id.*
97. *See* Gershoni, *supra* note 40, at 60, 72–74.
98. *See* Jamie J. Ladge, Beth K. Humberd, Brad Harringtin and Marla Baskerville Watkins, *Updating the Organization Man: An Examination of Involved Fathering in the Workplace*, The Academy of Management Perspectives 29 (2014); *see also* Joan C. Williams, Mary Blair-Loy, and Jennifer L. Berdahl, *Cultural Schemas, Social Class, and the Flexibility Stigma*, 69(2) J. Soc. Issues 209, 221 (2013); Erin Reid, *Why Some Men Pretend to Work 80-Hour Weeks*, Harvard Business Review (April 28, 2015), https://hbr.org/2015/04/why-some-men-pretend-to-work-80-hour-weeks&cm_sp=Article-_-Links-_-End%20of%20Page%20Recirculation (showing that by using creative ways to balance work and life, men were able to "pass" as ideal workers and at the same time work less than other men who did not use such ways).
99. *See* Ladge et al., *supra* note 98, at 29.

working shorter days.[100] The study also showed that divorced fathers are able to combine work and family better than married fathers due to employers' and colleagues' supportiveness.[101] While married fathers are expected to have a wife who is responsible for childrearing, divorced fathers lack such an "in-house caregiver" and thus their familial duties receive support at work.

The above analysis shows that workplaces affect the kinds of strategies workers pursue to combine work and family, emphasizing workplaces' compelling power to encourage or discourage men from fulfilling caregiving duties. Clearly, a supportive atmosphere toward male caregivers within the organization is critical for their real ability to combine work and family, as will be further elaborated below.[102]

Having encountered an unsupportive environment and workplace discrimination has led several Israeli and American fathers to sue their employers. Yet these fathers, as well as other plaintiffs who try to challenge workplace norms, often find little solace in courts. For the most part, courts in Israel as well as in the U.S. have been reluctant to challenge or criticize well-engrained structural norms and practices. An example of the Israeli courts' attitude can be found in the Supreme Court's refusal to hear a case in which the plaintiff, an investigator in the Israeli police, was required to attend a fourteen-week course far from her home.[103] Because this course was to begin a few months after she had had a baby, she refused to participate in it, arguing that the course's conditions constitute discrimination against parents, mainly mothers. She further claimed that this course could be operated under other conditions that would not require her to leave her home.[104] This case had the potential of questioning and challenging work practices that were not compatible with parents' obligations. However, rather than investigating whether those practices can be done in other, more accommodating ways, the Supreme Court chose not to decide it.[105] By failing to provide legal protection for caregivers, the court gave the employer unfettered discretion to its seemingly gender-neutral policy that essentially places a burden on caregivers.

Whereas the Supreme Court's reinforcement of total working norms is expressed in its reluctance to decide the case, a similar view of accepting—indeed strengthening—the ideal worker model is manifested in several cases decided by the Israeli regional and national labor courts.[106] Interestingly, these cases were brought to courts by fathers who asked to get benefits similar to their female colleagues. Specifically, the plaintiffs asked to work shortened days, arguing that it is a benefit

100. Laliv Cohen-Israeli and Larissa Remennick, *"As a Divorcee, I Am a Better Father": Work and Parenting among Divorced Men in Israel*, 56.7 *Journal of Divorce & Remarriage* 535 (2015).
101. Laliv Cohen-Israeli, *Care and Career*, 13(3) Fathering 215 (2015).
102. *See infra* section §9.04.
103. *See* Hacker and Frenkel, *supra* note 14, at 275–278; *see also* Hacker et al. *supra* note 6, at 706.
104. *See* Hacker and Frenkel, *supra* note 14, at 275–278.
105. The judges suggested that the plaintiff withdraw the plea. *Id.*
106. For an in-depth analysis of cases brought to labor courts by Israeli fathers who argued they were discriminated against at work due to their sex and parental status, *see* Ifat Matzner-Heruti, *"Daddy's gone to work, he'll return when the moon comes out": An Examination of Policies for Reconciling Fatherhood and Employment*, 6 Ma'Asei Mishpat 67 (2014) [Hebrew]; *see also* Matzner-Heruti, *supra* note 44.

conferred to working mothers and thus should apply to them as well.[107] The regional labor courts ruled in favor of the plaintiff fathers, and the National Labor court reaffirmed.[108] Ironically, while these decisions might seem as undermining the ideal worker norm, they are actually reinforcing it: The rational of the courts was that enabling fathers to work an hour less would enable mothers to work more hours.[109] The courts encourage mothers to work like ideal workers in order for them to be equal to men in the workplace.

The courts reiterated this rational in other decisions as well. For example, in deciding whether working fathers are entitled to monetary benefits the same as their female colleagues, the judges ruled against the fathers.[110] Working fathers, decided the courts, do not need incentives to stay long hours at work whereas mothers do:

> [T]he essence of the monetary benefit as "mother's prerogative" is to encourage working mothers to stay at work for long hours in order to fulfill job demands. In this way of promoting mother-teachers' status and salary, the goal of establishing substantive equality between mother-teachers and father-teachers is achieved.[111]

The courts' focus on hours is unclear and disturbing because these cases dealt with teachers—a profession in which the number of hours worked is not and should not be the measure for evaluation.

The Israeli Courts' tendency to reinforce the long working hour days is also manifested in cases interpreting the Hours of Work and Rest Law.[112] This law, legislated in 1951, regulates working times and states that a working week will be comprised of forty-five hours (later reduced to forty-three hours).[113] Whenever workers are asked to work beyond these hours, they will be compensated with overtime pay.[114] However, the law includes a list of employees who are excluded from it, such as policemen, sailors and members of an air-crew.[115] Aside from these specific occupations, there are other two groups of workers excluded: employees who fulfill duties that require "a special degree of personal confidence,"[116] and employees whose work conditions and circumstances make it "impossible for the employer to control their working hours and hours of rest."[117] Those who are excluded are entitled to a global payment, regardless of the hours they work. Throughout the years, more and more positions have been excluded from the law by employers who employed their workers for many hours without paying them overtime.[118] Indeed, most of the cases brought to courts involved the question of whether the law should have been applied

107. *See* Matzner-Heruti, *supra* note 44, at 118–119.
108. *Id.* at 119–120.
109. *Id.* at 119–126.
110. *Id.* at 126–129.
111. National Labor Court [NLC] 547/08 Medinat Israel v. Levi Shlomo [*State of Israel v. Levi*] (February 27, 2013), Nevo Legal Database (by subscription) § 57.
112. Hours of Work and Rest Law, 5711–1951.
113. *Id.* § 3.
114. *Id.* § 16.
115. *Id.* § 30(a)(1)-(4).
116. *Id.* § 30(a)(5).
117. *Id.* § 30(a)(6).
118. *See* Hacker et al., *supra* note 6, at 704.

and the employee had to receive the overtime pay or alternatively, the employee's position rightly fell within the exceptions.[119] When deciding these cases, however, the courts never inquired whether or not the employers' demand to work overtime is at all justified or whether such a practice is even economically rational.[120] Instead, according to the courts' neo-liberal approach, it is totally fine to require someone to work overtime as long as they get paid for it.[121]

American courts have also been reluctant to challenge existing practices of full-time work, inflexible schedules and no-leave policies.[122] Since work practices have become so well entrenched, courts regard them as natural and normal, taking them for granted as necessary for businesses without either seeing them as a form of gendered social organization, or challenging their necessity.[123] In her article, Nicole Porter uses jurisprudence under the Americans with Disabilities Act (ADA), showing that courts reaffirm employers' refusal to modify workplace structural time norms for employees with disabilities.[124] Claiming that such time norms are essential functions of the job and thus cannot be modified has been employers' main argument, and courts usually accepted it.[125] Analyzing ADA cases and demonstrating that courts have been reluctant to challenge or criticize workplace norms as unfitting to workers with disabilities has led Porter to the conclusion that litigation might not be the most effective strategy to solve work-family conflicts.[126] Indeed, scholars and advocates have been debating whether or not litigation involving Title VII has the ability to change workplace norms.[127] The most persuasive critique doubts Title VII's ability to re-examine and change the structure and norms of the workplace in such a way as to enable caregivers to take family leave and have flexible work arrangements.[128] As data show, plaintiffs who usually succeed in persuading the courts that they have been discriminated against due to their sex were those who worked like ideal workers and wanted to continue to work as ones without challenging time norms.[129] This is probably what led Ariel Ayanna's lawyers to use the illogical claim that he was able to be both an ideal

119. *See* Sharon Aharoni-Goldenberg, *Unpaid Overtime – Implications and Proposals for Change*, 13 LABOR, SOCIETY AND LAW 236–237 (2013).
120. *See* Hacker et al., *supra* note 6, at 705–706.
121. *Id.* at 706.
122. *See* Albiston, *supra* note 61, at 414; *see also* Nicole B. Porter, Caregiver Conundrum Redux: *The Entrenchment of Structural Norms,* 91(4) Denv. UL. Rev. 963, 972 (2013).
123. *See* Albiston, *supra* note 61, at 413–414; *see also* Porter, *supra* note 122, at 986–987.
124. *See* Porter, *supra* note 122, at 981–986.
125. *Id.* at 982.
126. *Id.* at 986–989.
127. *Id. See also* Michelle A. Travis, *Recapturing the Transformative Potential of Employment Discrimination Law,* 62 WASH. & LEE 1. REV 7 (2005).
128. This is due to the current problems facing lawyers when using the claim of disparate treatment theory and also because of the way courts have examined disparate impact theory with regard to work practices. *See* Porter, *supra* note 122, at 986–987; *see also* Albiston, *supra* note 56, at 1136–1151.
129. *See* Albiston, *supra* note 61, at 413–414; *see also* Albiston, *supra* note 56, at 1153-1154; Kelly, *supra* note 89, at 356; Porter, *supra* note 122, at 972–973.

worker and an involved caregiver.[130] Ayanna, a male lawyer, had worked for a private law firm that adhered to the billable hour system,[131] according to which employees are measured by the hours they put in: the more hours the better. Knowing that challenging the billable hour system would probably be futile, he claimed that he was in fact able to meet the job requirements but nevertheless was discriminated against and eventually unlawfully fired due to his sex and his fulfillment of caregiving duties:

> Ayanna's caregiving responsibilities never detracted from his fulfilling the requirements of his position at Dechert. Ayanna regularly was at the office until 7:00, 8:00, 9:00 p.m. or even later, and he often worked late into the night from home. He never missed a deadline and was never unavailable even if he was not physically in the office.[132]

What is more, Ayanna claimed that the firm had a "macho" culture and its message to the male associates and partners was clear: familial responsibilities are not a man's role.[133] Arguing against the firm's "machismo" culture and at the same time claiming that he adhered to it essentially strengthens such culture of working very long hours without being involved as a parent. Ultimately, the court issued an order in the firm's motion for summary judgment,[134] dismissing Ayanna's claim of disparate treatment sex discrimination.[135]

To sum up this part, current policies and norms both in Israel and in the U.S. strengthen the ideal worker requirement and expect men and fathers to fulfill it, making care an economic responsibility at the expense of an emotional one.[136] Israeli laws provide some support for parents, yet differentiate between mothers' and fathers' eligibility, locating fathers as secondary caregivers. The American state, in comparison, lacks even the minimal accommodation of paid sick leave and parental leave, as well as a federal antidiscrimination law protecting caregivers. Lack of public support creates a heavy burden on fathers to financially provide for the family.[137] In other words, the role of a breadwinner in the current U.S. economy "fails to incorporate nurture, sacrificing nurture for gender-defined economic responsibility."[138]

With regard to working hours, many workplaces both in Israel and in the U.S. expect their employees to fulfill face-time full-time and even overtime requirements which leave almost no time for other activities besides work. Yet, when plaintiffs try to challenge these requirements, courts in both countries are reluctant to restrain

130. Complaint and Jury Demand, Ayanna v. Dechert, LLP, 914 F. Supp. 2d 51 (D. Mass. 2012) No. 110-CV-12155, 2010 WL 5344371. For a detailed analysis of this case, *see* Matzner-Heruti, *supra* note 44, at 145–157.
131. *See* Complaint and Jury Demand, *supra* note 130, at para. 52.
132. *Id.* para. 66.
133. *Id.* para. 11.
134. *Ayanna*, 914 F. Supp. 2d at 53.
135. *Id.* at 57.
136. *See* Dowd, *supra* note 14, at 1057–1058.
137. *See* Making Men into Fathers, *supra* note 9, at 61; also at 62; *see also* Marsiglio and Roy, *supra* note 22.
138. *See* Nancy E. Dowd, *Fathers and the Supreme Court: Founding Fathers and Nurturing Fathers*, 54 Emory L.J. 1271, 1321 (2005).

employers' time demands, thus help to reinforce work and caregiving as mutually exclusive.

After analyzing the strengthening of the ideal worker norm by state laws (or lack of laws), workplaces and courts, in the next part I would like to deconstruct this norm by using masculinities theory. I contend that the assumption that the always-available ideal worker norm privileges men and fathers and discriminates "only" against women and mothers is a major reason for its pervasiveness. This is also why work-family policies have had little success thus far in achieving gender equality in the home and in the workplace.

§9.04 DECONSTRUCTING THE IDEAL WORKER NORM

Masculinities theory's main purpose is to interrogate how men, as gendered subjects, are situated in relation to a certain policy since such interrogation enriches discussions of equality and subordination.[139] Evidently, in much of the scholarship about gender equality in the workplace, men have been depicted as privileged and as those who are not affected by the conflict between home and work.[140] According to the prevalent theme in this scholarship, the workplace has been historically constructed by and for men, because they could work long hours outside their homes since their wives took care of the domestic duties, namely the household and care for the family members.[141] Consequently, the theme goes, the contemporary ideal worker norm that requires employees to take no time-off for caregiving fits men's lives, and therefore, constitutes gender discrimination against women and mothers.[142]

While this theme demonstrates an important aspect of the difficulties and discrimination women and mothers have endured at work, it lacks a crucial aspect: being required to be an ideal worker is not necessarily a privilege for all men, as men are not a one-dimensional group. Analyzing the ideal worker model with the usage of masculinities theory helps to shed light on the complex and multidimensional aspects of this model in a way that will ultimately lead to its revision and modification.

First, the assumption that men benefit from the workplace structure is essentializing as it assumes that all men benefit from the prevalent rigid and inflexible workplace norms of working many hours. Yet, such an assumption ignores hierarchies

139. *See* Dowd, *supra* note 4, at 204; *see also* Masculinities and the Law, *supra* note 4, at 4.

140. *See*, e.g., Laura T. Kessler, *Transgressive Caregiving*, 33 Fla. St. U. L. Rev. 10 (2005); *see also* Brad Harrington et al., The New Dad: Caring, Committed and Conflicted 36 (2011), *available at* http://www.bc.edu/content/dam/files/centers/cwf/pdf/FH-Study-Web-2.pdf; Making Men into Fathers, *supra* note 9, at 26; Kelli K. Garcia, *The Gender Bind: Men as Inauthentic Caregivers*, 20 Duke J. Gender L. & Pol'y 1, 1–2 (2012). In Israel, *see* Haya Stier, *The Inter-Relations Between Work for Pay and Family Work*, 7 Sotsilogia Yisraelit [Israeli Sociology] 143, 146 (2005) [Hebrew] (arguing that while there is a vast amount of literature dealing with the implications of family responsibilities on women's work patterns, a comparable discussion with regard to men is almost non-existent).

141. *See*, e.g., Catharine A. MacKinnon, Toward a Feminist Theory of the State 224 (1989); Joan Acker, *Hierarchies, Jobs, Bodies: A Theory of Gendered Organizations*, 4 Gender & Soc'y 139, 146–147 (1990).

142. *See* Williams and Segal, *supra* note 67, at 80.

among men, and as masculinities theory has exposed,[143] there are power differences among men and not all of them are advantaged by the traditional masculine work culture. For instance, the situation of working-class, poor, and minority men, uncovers the notion that the ability to perform as a breadwinner is tied to class privilege as well as to race and ethnicity, *inter alia.*[144] Therefore, stating that work is a privilege refers to a specific group of men—those who work in high-status, highly paid jobs. Second, and related to the previous point, even those who are considered as privileged at work and "pass" as ideal workers, suffer at the personal level as fathers and partners. As Professor Joan Williams argues:

> Breadwinners, even affluent ones, also feel the pressure of being a family's sole support...the straightjacket of conventional masculinity hurts not only men unable to live up to socially accepted male roles but also the many men who play those roles well but ultimately feel imprisoned by them.[145]

Indeed, a growing body of literature has demonstrated the damages caused by heavy work load, showing that overwork entails negative health outcomes.[146] The increased demands of the workforce takes a heavy toll on men who are expected to provide for their families and therefore are forced to fulfill total time norms. Furthermore, adhering to the ideal worker norm entails personal and familial sacrifices as it requires men and fathers to subordinate their relationship with partners and children for wage work.[147] Third, many fathers cannot adhere to the total work demands and function as ideal workers due to their marital status or sexual orientation: As divorce rates are on the rise both in Israel and in the U.S.,[148] more and more fathers face a new reality in which they need to integrate work and home differently than the way they used to. Interestingly, this new reality enables some fathers to "re-discover" their fatherhood and they report an increased paternal involvement in comparison to the past, when they were still married.[149] Yet, they are required to calibrate their priorities, including the adjustment of their work schedule in order to meet their children's needs, and hence for many such fathers, this new era of enhanced fatherhood means also the diminishment of their status as ideal workers.[150] Likewise, fathers in same-sex families need to set a division between work outside and inside the home which, in the absence of a woman, is not based on gendered assumptions, and thus at least one of the men cannot adhere to strict working time norms.[151]

---

143. *See supra* section §9.01[B].
144. *See* Making Men into Fathers, *supra* note 9, at 18, 63; *see also* Williams, Reshaping, *supra* note 16, at 81.
145. *See* Williams, Reshaping, *supra* note 16, at 83.
146. *See* Dowd, *supra* note 4, at 230; *see also* Aharoni-Goldenberg, *supra* note 119, at 222–224; Stier and Sella-Dotan, *supra* note 61, at 226.
147. *See* Williams, Reshaping, *supra* note 16, at 81; *see also* Dowd, The Man Question, *supra* note 4, at 110.
148. *See* Belcher-Prigat and Hacker, *supra* note 42, at 6–7; *see also* Renan-Barzilay, *supra* note 14, at 313–314; Cohen-Israeli, *supra* note 101, at 213. In the U.S., *see* Dowd, *supra* note 14, at 1055.
149. *See* Cohen-Israeli and Remennick, *supra* note 100, at 547.
150. *See* Cohen-Israeli, *supra* note 101, at 213.
151. Dara Purvis, *The Sexual Orientation of Fatherhood,* MICH. ST. L. Rev. 983, 997–1005 (2013).

Yet, besides life circumstances which force fathers to take a greater role in child rearing, a growing number of Israeli and American fathers today realize that they want to be more involved in their children's lives.[152] Many state that they do not want to be like their own fathers, who barely spent time with them as children.[153] Indeed, an increased number of fathers regard parenting as a central part in their lives:[154] they are spending more time with their children today than did their counterparts three decades ago,[155] and are also more involved in housework duties, such as cooking and housecleaning.[156] However, with growing responsibilities comes an enlarged work-family conflict. Israeli and American fathers, especially in dual-earner families, are experiencing more work-family conflicts than their counterparts thirty years ago—and more than present-day mothers.[157] Professor Daphna Hacker demonstrates the predicament of Israeli fathers today:

> Fathers today are exposed to contradicting images of maleness and fatherhood, ranging from the ideal rational, competitive worker who is expected to invest all his time and energy in the job market to the "new father," who is expected to spend time at home and create meaningful emotional relations with his children. In fact, there are no binding social scripts that guide and shape fathers' behavior, neither during marriage nor after divorce.[158]

The complexity in many fathers' lives today could explain the persistent gap between fathers' expressed desire to be more involved at home—and their actual involvement.[159]

---

152. *See* Kari Palazzari, *The Daddy Double-Bind: How the Family and Medical Leave Act Perpetuates Sex Inequality Across All Class Levels*, 16 COLUM. J. GENDER & L. 429, at 444; *see also* Ellen Galinsky, Kerstin Aumann, James T. Bond, *Times Are Changing: Gender and Generation at Work and at Home* 14 (2011), *available at* http://familiesandwork.org/site/research/reports/Times_Are_Changing.pdf [hereinafter *Times Are Changing*]; Dowd, *Masculinities and Feminist Legal Theory, supra* note 4, at 239; Anne-Marie Slaughter, *Why Women Still Can't Have it All, available at* http://www.theatlantic.com/magazine/archive/2012/07/why-women-still-cant-have-it-all/309020/; WILLIAMS, RESHAPING, *supra* note 16, at 89. In Israel, *see* Hacker and Frenkel, *supra* note 14, at 284.
153. *See* Marianne Cooper, *Being the "Go-To Guy": Fatherhood, Masculinity, and the Organization of Work in Silicon Valley*, 23(4) QUALITATIVE SOCIOLOGY 379, 391 (2000). In Israel, *see* Hacker and Frenkel, *supra* note 14, at 284.
154. *See* Palazzari, *supra* note 152, at 444.
155. *See Times Are Changing, supra* note 152; *see also* Dowd, *Masculinities and Feminist Legal Theory, supra* note 4, at 239.
156. *See* Cohen-Israeli and Remennick, *supra* note 100, at 537.
157. *See Times Are Changing, supra* note 152, at 18–19; *see also* HARRINGTON ET AL, *supra* note 140, at 4; Michelle A. Travis, *The Future of Work-Family Policy: Is "Choice" the Right Choice?: Review of Women & Employment: Changing Lives and New Challenges*, 13 EMP. RTS. & EMP. POL'Y J. 385, 417 (2009). In Israel, *see* Gershoni, *supra* note 40, at 73–74.
158. *See* Hacker, *supra* note 15, at 419.
159. *See* Abrams, *supra* note 20, at 760–762; *see also* Michael Selmi, *Family Leave and the Gender Wage Gap*, 78 N.C.L. REV. 707, 755 (2000); Lars Plantin, *Different Classes, Different Fathers? On Fatherhood, Economic Conditions and Class in Sweden*, 10(1) COMMUNITY, WORK AND FAMILY 93–110 (2007); HARRINGTON ET AL., *supra* note 140, at 15; and also at 31; Laura T. Kessler, *The Attachment Gap: Employment Discrimination Law, Women's Cultural Caregiving, and the Limits of Economic and Liberal Legal Theory*, 34 U. MICH. J.L. REFORM 371, 420 (2001). In Israel, *see* Gershoni, *supra* note 40, at 73–74.

Lastly, arguing that the ideal worker norm constitutes discrimination solely or mainly against women virtually strengthens the norm that women are—and should continue to be—the primary caregivers. Thus, when scholars and advocates demand that the workplace be restructured, or "accommodated," to adjust to women's needs, they are not only stagnating women's status but also men's, albeit in a distinctive way: Such a view assumes that men, as ideal workers, are privileged, while women, who cannot function as ideal workers due to their caregiving duties, are discriminated against. This notion implicitly—though unintentionally—sees market work as superior to care work. Yet, when looking at work and care differently we can argue that many Israeli and American mothers today might even be in a better position than fathers in terms of combining work and family. To begin with, working mothers have more legal arrangements and benefits as parents than fathers, especially in Israel.[160] Moreover, mothers' usage of work-family entitlements is viewed more favorably than that of fathers' usage.[161] Therefore, even when statutes—in Israel or in the U.S.—are framed in a gender-neutral language, it is mothers who, for the most part, will use these entitlements.[162] To be clear, many mothers in both countries still pay a price at work for this integration,[163] yet fathers pay a price for their lack of integration in their personal and family life. Seeing care work as more important than market work—or, at least, as equally important—highlights working fathers' sacrifices and compelled disadvantages.

To conclude, it is about time we started exploring the impacts of workplace norms on men and fathers. As this Part has demonstrated, being required to be the ideal worker entails significant hardship for fathers—both for those who cannot achieve this ideal in the first place, and those who do. Hence, in order for work-family policy to be effective and not merely formal, the connection between masculinities imperatives and the provider status must be identified, analyzed and challenged.[164] The last part of this chapter will suggest new insights for how to effectuate social change for male working caregivers, and ultimately for all working caregivers. Drawing on new-institutionalism theory and revealing its linkage to masculinities theory might be key to mitigating fathers' work-family conflicts.

---

160. *See supra* section §9.02.

161. *See* Dowd, *supra* note 14, at 1059 (arguing that it is possible for women to balance work and family). As was discussed before, Israeli and American fathers who use work-family arrangements are often regarded as men who deviate from their proper gendered role. *See supra* section §9.02.

162. With respect to family leave, for example, only a miniscule number of Israeli fathers have taken leave following the birth of a baby. *See* Matzner-Heruti, *supra* note 85, at 476. Likewise, American fathers have taken less family leave in comparison to mothers. *See*, e.g., A. Armenia and N. Gerstel, *Family Leaves, the FMLA and Gender Neutrality: The Intersection of Race and Gender*, 35 SOC. SCI. RES. 871, 886–887 (2006); *see also* http://www.forbes.com/sites/learnvest/2013/06/14/why-men-dont-take-paternity-leave/; Halverson, *supra* note 92, 259–61; Gillian Lester, *A Defense of Paid Family Leave*, 28 HARV. J.L. & GENDER 1, 69 (2005); Michael Selmi, *Is Something Better than Nothing? Critical Reflections on Ten Years of the FMLA*, 15 WASH. U. J.L. & POL'Y 65, 75 (2004).

163. An impressive amount of research has been done about workplace discrimination against women and mothers.

164. *See* Abrams, *supra* note 20, at 761.

§9.05 MASCULINITIES THEORY MEETS NEO-INSTITUTIONALISM THEORY

Masculinities theory suggests a complicated linkage between being a man and being a provider which places a heavy burden on fathers. This linkage also explains why most Israeli and American fathers are reluctant to use legal entitlements, such as family leave and flexible work arrangements. If most fathers do not use legal mandates, it seems pointless to advocate for more mandates. Rather, our efforts should be invested in other directions that have more potential to really help caregivers.

In this last part I would like to develop a twofold strategy to ameliorate fathers' work-family conflict. I use core principles from masculinities theory to shed light on the reasons why working fathers are deterred or encouraged to use work-family entitlements. In addition, I use core principles from neo-institutionalism theory to analyze organizations' motives to adopt certain work-family policies. Integrating these theories will allow for a novel and nuanced insight that could enrich the work-family debate.

[A] What Influences Fathers to Use Work-Family Policy? The Effect of the Organizational Environment

The answer to the question of what causes fathers to use work-family entitlements is rather simple: their workplace environment. Supervisors play a key role in helping or discouraging male employees to integrate work and family demands, and fathers will use work-family entitlements if their employers are supportive of such a behavior.[165] Initially, supervisors have to communicate the available entitlements properly to their employees and convey the message that the latter are encouraged to use them.[166] Hence, organizations that have merely formal work-family policies can be misleading in a way that does not expose the real unsupportive organizational atmosphere towards male caregivers.[167] These policies may remain practically decoupled from the organization's norms and practices and consequently have little effect on changing the behavior of managers and their attitudes towards working caregivers.

However, not only supervisors impact fathers' level of work-family integration but also their peers.[168] Fathers will use the organization's policies if other male employees do the same.[169] Put another way, fathers emulate their male colleagues' behavior and chances become higher that the former be more involved as caregivers if the latter are. Several studies affirm that, demonstrating that team members' behavior

165. *See* Stier and Sella-Dotan, *supra* note 61, at 236–237; *see also* Albiston, *supra* note 61, at 411.
166. *See* Stier and Sella-Dotan, *supra* note 61, at 233; *see also* Jacobs and Gerson, *supra* note 87, at 472; Julie Holliday Wayne and Bryanne L. Cordeiro *Who Is a Good Organizational Citizen? Social Perception of Male and Female Employees Who Use Family Leave*, 49 SEX ROLES 233, 244–245 (2003).
167. *See* Albiston, *supra* note 61, at 409–411; *see also* Catherine R. Albiston, *Bargaining in the Shadow of Social Institutions: Competing Discourses and Social Change in Workplace Mobilization of Civil Rights*, 39 LAW & SOC'Y REV. 11 (2005); Stier and Sella-Dotan, *supra* note 61, at 233.
168. *See* Stier and Sella-Dotan, *supra* note 61, at 237.
169. *See supra* note 40, and accompanying text.

has a major impact on employees' use of work-family entitlements.[170] These data corroborate one of masculinities theory's core principles that men feel the constant need to prove their masculinity to other men: "[w]e are under the constant careful scrutiny of other men. Other men watch us, rank us, grant our acceptance into the realm of manhood. Manhood is demonstrated for other men's approval."[171] Hence, men will not display their involvement in caregiving lest other men scrutinize them and regard this behavior as unmanly. Therefore, fathers will be more involved in caregiving if their male colleagues are, and their supervisors encourage such behavior, which proves that a supportive atmosphere toward male caregivers within the organization is critical.

Organizations can foster a supportive environment for caregivers by informing the workers that integrating their multiple life responsibilities is acceptable and allowed.[172] Moreover, they can convey the message that the ideal worker is virtually an unrealistic ideal and no one should invest all of his time and energy in work. They can also give employees more control over their own time, knowing that not only will it help the worker, but it will be good for the business as well.[173]

[B] What Influences Organizations to Adopt Work-Family Policy? The Effect of the Organizational Field

When exploring what influences organizations to adopt certain work-family policies, an interesting finding comes up: they are emulating other organizations in their field.[174] While it was common to contend that organizations adopt work-family policies only for economic reasons or because they fear legal sanctions, neo-institutionalism theory has shown that organizations, similar to social actors, actually copy the behavior of other organizations.[175] Indeed, organizations might adopt more generous work-family policies than they are required by law, if their organizational counterparts had them. A fascinating example for the mimetic element can be tracked in the decisions of many tech companies, one following the other, to expand their paid parental leave policies.

---

170. *Id.*
171. *See* Michael S. Kimmel, *Masculinity as Homophobia: Fear, Shame, and Silence in the Construction of Gender Identity, in* THE GENDER OF DESIRE: ESSAYS ON MALE SEXUALITY 25, 33 (2005); *see also* MICHAEL S. KIMMEL, MANHOOD IN AMERICA: A CULTURAL HISTORY (1996) (providing a history of U.S. masculinity).
172. *See* Stier and Sella-Dotan, *supra* note 61, at 236–237.
173. A significant amount of studies has examined the effect of work-family arrangements on the organization's bottom line. *See, e.g.,* Byron Y. Lee and Sanford E. DeVoe, *Flextime and Profitability*, 51 INDUS. RELATIONS 298 (2012) (this study, conducted in Canada, examined the effect of flextime on profitability. The findings indicate "that flextime increases profitability when implemented within a strategy centered on employees but decreases profitability when implemented within a strategy focused on cost reduction"); *see also* Phyllis Moen, Erin L. Kelly and Rachelle Hill, *Does Enhancing Work-Time Control and Flexibility Reduce Turnover? A Naturally Occurring Experiment*, 58 SOC. PROBS. 69 (2011); Williams and Segal, *supra* note 67, at 78–79 (providing references for the human resource literature on the "business case"); Ladge et al., *supra* note 98, at 2 (reporting that organizations that encourage work-family integration generate positive work-related outcomes).
174. *See* Albiston, *supra* note 61, at 406–407.
175. *Id.* at 407.

Companies like Amazon, Apple, Microsoft, Yahoo and Facebook now offer generous paid maternity and paternity leave.[176] For instance, Facebook provides the company's workers around the world with four months of paid parental leave (regardless of their gender).[177] Not long after Facebook's announcement, e-bay also declared its new policy of parental leave.[178] Evidently, creating work-family policies is related to the specific industry, and tech companies extend their benefits in order to retain and attract workers. To be sure, neither of the companies is obliged by law to provide paid family leave which shows that other forces alongside legal sanctions drive organizations to adopt work-family policies. This is not to say that state's enactment of legal mandates is not important as a means of enabling workers to integrate their work and family. It does say, however, that organizations might adopt policies regardless of state laws. Nevertheless, it is important to remember that while there is no doubt that the enactment of paid family leave policies by tech companies is a blessed step, companies might also change their policies just as easily. This is in contrast to state laws that involve a complicated legislative process on the one hand, and which are more difficult to change once enacted, on the other hand.

To conclude, masculinities theory and neo-institutionalism theory complement each other in a way that helps to explain critical processes both within the organization and among a cohort of organizations of the same industry. At the organization level, it has been shown that formal work-family policies will not suffice inasmuch as they are supported and encouraged by supervisors and coworkers. While the organizational environment affects employees' usage of work-family benefits in general, a supportive environment is especially important with regard to male caregivers. This is because male workers who display their involvement in caregiving in an unsupportive workplace risk both their work status and their manly front which are tightly connected.[179] Alternatively, fathers will display their role as caregivers only if other male employees will. At the organizational field level, a similar dynamics occurs, as neo-institutionalism theory has shown that not only are workers imitating others but also organizations are. Organizations' desire to receive legitimacy within the field is not less strong than their wish to produce compliance with legal mandates. As the processes occurring in many tech companies show, when certain organizations decide to provide their workers with work-family policies beyond the law's requirements, other organizations might follow. Therefore, real change on the ground for male caregivers is significantly hinged upon their organization. Realizing the "domino effect" both among

176. Alicia Adamczyk, *These Are the Companies with the Best Parental Leave Policies,* MONEY (11.4.15), http://time.com/money/4098469/paid-parental-leave-google-amazon-apple-facebook/.

177. Chloe Angyal, *Facebook Announces Four Months of Paid Parental Leave for All Employees,* THE HUFFINGTON POST (11.27.2015 11:45 pm ET), http://www.huffingtonpost.com/entry/facebook-announces-four-months-of-paid-parental-leave-for-all-employees_us_56592f7ee4b079b2818a75b4.

178. Valentina Zarya, *This is the Latest Tech Company to Update Its Parental Leave Policy,* FORTUNE (12.4.15 3:15 pm EDT), http://fortune.com/2015/12/04/tech-company-leave/.

179. *See supra* section §9.01[C].

organizations and employees themselves leads to the conclusion that crafting work-family policies must be done in conjunction with human resources professionals at leading organizations.[180]

§9.06 CONCLUSION

Looking at the work-family imbalance of working fathers through different cultural contexts reveals how fathers' ability to combine work and caregiving is determined by the confluence of legal rules with background rules and social norms. As the comparative analysis of masculinities norms between Israel and the U.S. showed, both societies reinforce the notion that breadwinning is connected to masculinity and therefore fathers should adhere to the strict norms of the workplace in order to be able to provide for their families. However, the requirement to function as an ideal worker comes at a personal and familial price fathers in both countries often pay. This chapter furthered the argument that exposing this price is crucial not only for ameliorating fathers' work-family conflicts but also for dismantling the entrenchment of workplace norms. In order to dismantle these norms, attention should be given to the role of organizations in promoting or hindering fathers' work-family integration. Thus, this chapter suggested using insights from neo-institutionalism theory in connection with masculinities theory to shed light on the motives that drive organizations to adopt work-family policies and fathers to use them.

180. *See* Albiston, *supra* note 61, at 408; *see also* Williams and Segal, *supra* note 67, at 117.

CHAPTER 10

Teleworking in Iberian Labour Law as a Measure of Reconciling Work and Family Life and Working Time Control as the Key to Avoid the Blurring of the Boundaries Between Work and Family Life*

Lourdes Mella Méndez

§10.01 TELEWORKING IN IBERIAN LABOUR LAW (PORTUGAL AND SPAIN) AS A MEASURE OF RECONCILING WORK AND PERSONAL AND FAMILY LIFE

The two countries on the Iberian Peninsula (Portugal and Spain), despite sharing the same geographical, social and political space in the European Union, display significant differences in the regulation of their labour markets. An area in which these differences are displayed is in teleworking or, more broadly, distance work.

In Portugal, the implementation of the European Framework Agreement on Teleworking (EFAT), of July 2002, was made directly through the Labour Code (hereinafter LC) of 2003. In this way, an immediate implementation of teleworking at the state legislative level was chosen and detailed regulation was set out in several Articles (233–243), which address – following the European Agreement model – many of the basic and problematic aspects of this legal figure. For example, it covers the concept and formalities of teleworking, the contractual freedom of the parties, the need for equal treatment of teleworkers and the rest of the workforce, the protection of

* This paper is a result of the National Research Project carried out by MINECO (Spain), entitled 'Legal analysis of Telework in Spanish and Comparative Law' (DER2013-43615-R), leading by Prof. Lourdes Mella.

privacy, health and safety at work, the working time and freedom of work schedule, the secondary duties of the company (such as training) and the worker, and, finally, the participation and collective representation of the interests of these workers by the bodies of ordinary representation. According to Article 233 LC, teleworking is 'a labour service performed with legal subordination, usually outside the employer's business and by means of the use of information and communication technologies'. Although the Portuguese legislature acted quickly and regulated teleworking thoroughly, at first, the reconciliation of the work/life balance was not considered directly. This had to be rectified later, and even twice, to cater for the different situations of teleworkers.

The first of these reforms was in 2009, profoundly modifying the Portuguese Code of Labour,[1] also with regard to telework, whose regulation was altered both from a formally (now located in the new Articles 165–171) materially, as several Articles were merged into one and others were modified. The definition of teleworking is now in the current Article 165 LC, which maintains the previous wording, except the expression 'out of the *employer's* business', as the word 'employer' has been removed. Aside from that little variation, one of the most significant changes was introduced by the influence of Law 112/2009, of 16 September, which established the legal regime for the prevention of domestic violence, protection for, and assistance of, its victims; and repealed the Law 107/99, of 3 August, and Decree Law 323/2000, of 19 December. Following the provisions of the Act, the new Article 166.2 LC provides for the right of the worker, who is a *victim of domestic violence,* to carry out their work remotely, when this is consistent with the activity performed.

The second of the aforementioned reforms was made in 2015 and focused on regulating teleworking as an option for the worker who *has a child less than three years of age.* This reform is the result of Law 120/2015, of 1 September, which aims to strengthen the rights of working parents to reconcile work and family life with this option for working and living. This amendment modifies Article 166 LC, adding some new sections (discussed *below* in more detail), while redrafting sections 5, 6, 7 and 8.

With these two modifications, the field of teleworking is developing in Portugal, legally and progressively, with the reconciliation of private family and working lives of the working person. Certainly, compared with ordinary cases, in which the employer enters into 'a contract for the subordinated provision of teleworking' with an internal or external worker (Article 166.1 LC), with the two recent reforms the approach is very different, because teleworking is set in legislation as a *unilateral right of the worker.* More specifically, if the employee meets the requirements set out in the legislation, the employer cannot deny their right to work outside the company, if requested. The right to teleworking does not depend on the consent of the employer, but the concurrence of legal requirements for the specific case. In a similar vein, there are authors who understand that the specific rules that apply to the ordinary case that the teleworker is

1. Approved by Law n° 7/2009 of 12 February, with the alterations introduced by Laws n° 105/2009 of 14 September; 53/2011 of 14 October; 23/2012 of 25 June; 47/2012 of 29 August; 69/2013 of 30 August and 27/2014 of 8 May.

already part of the company[2] do not apply to the cases set out in the reforms, which enjoy a special privileged status.[3]

If the specified legal conditions are met, the employer may not decline the request for teleworking from a worker who is the victim of domestic violence or who wants to reconcile their working and family lives, and especially if the care of a child under three years of age is involved, as pointed out in Article 166.4 LC. Therefore, if the employer refuses a request unjustifiably, the worker can take one of the following steps: to temporarily suspend the contract,[4] and that by analogy with the provisions for the inability to transfer from one place to another; to judicially demand the fulfilment of the request for teleworking; to terminate the contract at will and with fair cause;[5] or even to pursue civil or administrative liability, as the behaviour of the employer is classified as a serious offence.[6]

In Spain, the situation as regards telework is very different, at least at the legal level. Certainly, the state legislature did not address this issue until 2012, as the implementation of EFAT was made through the National Agreement for collective bargaining on 30 January 2003, which, in its seventh chapter, reflected the commitment of business and trade unions to promote the adaptation of its content in the Spanish context. So, the development of telework was left in the hands of ordinary collective agreements, which generally did not make references to teleworking or, if they did, included references in a clause style with general ideas but without a clear commitment to implementing teleworking by the social partners. Arguably, this situation began to change with the Labour reform of 2012, which amended the former Article 13 Workers' Statute (hereinafter WS) entitled 'home working contract' to include a new reference to 'distance work'. Under section 1 of the amended Article of WS, distance work is defined as 'that in which the provision of labour activity takes place predominantly in the worker's home or another place freely chosen by them, alternatively to the workplace of the company'. The following sections of the Article include a general reference to the form of the contract and to the equal rights of these workers with the rest of the workforce. An example of this is the reference to the right of these workers to remuneration as a professional group, to training for employment, mobility and promotion, protection, health and safety, and finally, to the enjoyment of rights of collective representation.

However, nothing is expressly stated in Article 13 WS on the use of distance work and, specifically, teleworking, as a means of reconciling work and family life. This omission is particularly significant as Paragraph III of the Preamble of the Law 3/2012 of 6 July, responsible for the current wording of that provision, refers to telework as a particular form of work that fits perfectly with the productive and economic model pursued by favouring the flexibility of enterprises in the organization of work and to

2. Article 167 LC.
3. de Oliveira Carvalho, C.: 'Social protection of victims of domestic violence in Portugal', *Revista Internacional y Comparada de Relaciones Laborales y Derecho del Empleo*, 2013, V. I, n°. 4, p. 18.
4. Article 296.2 LC.
5. Article 394.2 LC.
6. Article 166.8 LC. Take in account the lapse of the legislator, because that provision refers to the business breach of the provisions of section 3 Art. 166 LC, but it should say section 4.

'optimise the relationship between work and personal and family life', which should be understood as a clear reference to the reconciliation of both. Against this silence on the part of the state, the specific legislation on telework in the different autonomous communities and collective agreements set teleworking as a measure of conciliation, as will be seen *below*.

Even schematically, once highlighted the evolution of the regulation of telework in Spain and Portugal, it is clear that increasing focus of the legislature on this new way of working is needed in both countries. Undoubtedly, the fact that since the adoption of the AFET in 2002 the Portuguese legislature has considered it appropriate to include its regulation in the Labour Code (in 2003), in a detailed and thoughtful way to adapt to new social changes, it reflects the seriousness and interest with which teleworking has been, and is, treated in Portugal, which contrasts sharply with the late and poor legal regulation of the same area in Spain.

[A] Teleworking as a Way of Helping Victims of Domestic Violence

One of the most difficult and important situations in which teleworking can be used as a special employment measure to help workers is in situations of domestic violence.

In Portugal, Article 166.2 LC relates to this, albeit indirectly, as the particular circumstance of the worker being a victim of domestic violence is not mentioned expressly. According to that provision, once these conditions are met, as laid down in Article 195.1 LC, 'that worker has the right to exercise their work in the teleworking regime, when this one is consistent with the activity carried out'. The reference of the first provision to the second one implies to have to take in account the regime of the 'transfer' or geographical mobility (in Spanish terms and in a broad sense), temporary or permanent, configured as a unilateral right of the victim of domestic violence worker (and regulated in the second Article). More clearly, the Portuguese legislature links the two rights of victims of domestic violence (transfer from one establishment to another within the same company and the change from on-site working to teleworking) to the same requirements, as, after all, in both cases it is about relocating or moving the worker from one place to another, and for the same reasons. So, the first requirement that the worker-victim has to meet to be entitled to these labour transfers is fulfilling the two conditions relating to the domestic violence situation that he or she is experiencing, which are cumulative. These are: (1) the filing of a criminal complaint ('*queixa-crime*') against the aggressor; and (2) the leaving of the family home at the time that the transfer takes effect.[7]

Before discussing these requirements, it is already clear that in Portugal, a victim of the domestic violence is a person who, regardless of gender and age, suffers acts of physical, psychological or sexual violence, in accordance with the provisions of Article 152 of the Penal Code.[8] In addition, this Article extends further the concept of victim for

7. Cf. Pimenta Fernandes, T.: *O regime jurídico da mobilidade geográfica do trabalhador em Portugal. Uma análise crítica à luz do direito espanhol.* Doctoral thesis defended in April 2016 at the University of Santiago de Compostela. Manuscript copy, pp. 307 et seq.
8. Cf. Art. 2 Law 112/2009, cited above.

the purposes of the commission of a criminal offence, to include the spouse or former spouse; a person of the same or different sex with whom the aggressor has, or has had, a relationship, even without having cohabited with them; a member of immediate family, and particularly a defenceless person living in the family home, especially on the grounds of age, disability, serious illness or economic dependence.

This broad concept of a victim of domestic violence is positively valued, as it extends legal protection to a large number of people affected by such violence. In a different way, the Spanish law starts with a very strict concept of a victim of gender violence. Indeed, the Organic Law 1/2004 of 28 December, on comprehensive protection measures against gender violence (hereinafter, OLCPMGV), 'aims to act against violence that, as a manifestation of discrimination, the inequality and power relations between men and women, are exerted on the latter by those who are, or have been, their spouses, or those who are, or have been, linked to them by similar relationships of affection, even without cohabitation.'[9] Intentionally, the Spanish legislator reserves the status of victim of gender violence – as well as labour rights associated with it – for the women who, as a social risk group traditionally discriminated against by men, require special protection. Of course, this does not prevent the man who suffers gender violence from enjoying the general protection of the law, and those who commit gender violence against men are equally reprehensible. However, it is clear that the legislature did not intend to equate men and women as victims of gender violence, which is subject to the effects of labour market measures.

In Portuguese law, the first condition required for granting a transfer[10] – and therefore the move to teleworking – is the filing of a *criminal complaint* against the aggressor, which is important as it reflects the will of the victim to end with the situation of domestic violence. However, as domestic violence is a crime of a public nature in Portugal, it is also possible that the criminal proceedings are opened by complaint filed by any other person, or when the prosecutor or judge are aware of the crime by other means (even without submission of the complaint). Somehow, with that initial stimulus (complaint or direct involvement of the authorities), a criminal investigation and system protection for the victim is triggered, and the victim is granted – by the judicial authority or the competent police service – the so-called 'status of victim of domestic violence', and a document guaranteeing the victim will have this status.[11] However, in exceptional and duly justified circumstances, victim status may also be granted without prior criminal complaint being made by the body responsible for citizenship and gender equality in public administration.[12]

In the case of teleworking, the literal interpretation of Article 195.1 LC should be accepted, which only requires the 'filing of the criminal complaint' and not the later granting of 'victim status', so the employer cannot require it in the first instance when deciding on a request for teleworking. This interpretation is more favourable to the employee, although, of course, if necessary, the aforementioned statute must also be

9. Article 1 Law, cited above.
10. Article 195.1 LC.
11. Article 14.1 and 2 Act 112/2009, cited above.
12. Article 14.4 Law 112/2009, already cited.

accepted as a valid way of proving compliance with the legal requirements to access the form of distance work.[13] Although not required by the legislature, it seems logical to understand that if the mentioned statute is cited by the worker, the employer must accept it in order to demonstrate the situation of domestic violence, which, after all, it is what it is about (teleworking is a unilateral right of the victim).

In Spain, access of victims of gender violence to special labour rights also requires the proof of that violence. Such evidence shall be provided in 'the protection order for the victim, although, exceptionally, evidence of such a situation can be provided in the report of the Public Prosecutor indicating that the applicant is a victim of gender violence until the protection order' is issued.[14] The protective order is granted, upon request[15] or ex officio, by the Judge of Violence against Women and, where appropriate, the judge on call, who must act in accordance with Article 544 of the Criminal Procedure Act.[16] Through a unique and immediate judgment (a judicial writ), the protection order permits the taking of all protection measures – both criminal and civil in nature – for the victim and, at the same time, activates the mechanisms for assistance and social protection that the State, the autonomous communities and local governments provide in these situations. In other words, the protection order acts as a means of access to any of the protective measures provided by law for victims of domestic violence, providing victims with a comprehensive protection status and unifying the various means available for this purpose.

Returning to the Portuguese case, the second condition required for Portuguese victims of domestic violence deserves some criticism, because it shows the lightness with which the legislator reverts from the teleworking regime to the transfer or mobility one provided in Article 195 LC, and related to this, it should be recognized that *'the leaving of the family home* at the time it (the measure) becomes effective' is not always logical or desirable. Indeed, although at first, it may seem reasonable to require that the worker-victim leave the family home at the time of the transfer as a means of protecting himself, and even if it is justified by the change in workplace, it is not always so straightforward. As the Portuguese doctrine has highlighted, it may be the case that leaving the family home is not necessary, for example, because the new workplace is near the family home (thus does not require change of address)[17] and the judge has issues a restraining order to keep the aggressor away from the family home. It can also happen that the victim has already left the family home by the time the transfer takes effect, for example, when the person is receiving medical treatment away from home

13. In a similar vein, Vaz Marecos, D.: *Código do Trabalho anotado*, 2nd edition (Coimbra, 2012), p. 408.
14. Article 23 OLCPMGV. Cf. Article 544*ter* Criminal Procedure Act, introduced by Law 27/2003 of 31 July, regulating the order of protection of victims of domestic violence.
15. Of the victim, family, prosecutor or other entities or agencies of welfare, public or private, which were aware of the existence of any of the crimes or offences of gender violence.
16. Article 62 of Law 1/2004, which extends the protection order to the victims of gender violence.
17. Although the term 'transfer' may relate to the Spanish expression 'geographical mobility' of Art. 40 WS, both legal terms do not equate to the same thing, as in the Portuguese system there can be transfer without a change of the worker's address, but in the Spanish law there cannot (as long as that expression is understood in the strict sense). Therefore, when used in the Spanish context, 'transfer' must be understood broadly.

and the place of work and only a change of address facilitates the compatibility between the treatment and work schedules.[18] Therefore, the dependence of the right to the previously discussed labour measures (transfer and teleworking) on the forced abandonment of the family home, imperative in any case, and without any margin of personal appreciation by the parties to the contract, and, where appropriate, by the competent authorities (the trial judge), seems an excessive requirement and, perhaps, unnecessary and harmful to the worker concerned.[19]

Indeed, this same negative assessment also applies to the requirement in the case of teleworking. Of course, if you take into account that the usual place of work in this type of work (outside the company) is the family home itself, there is no sense in making access to it conditional upon the abandonment of the home by the worker. Although it can be argued that the worker can still provide services from elsewhere according to their availability (from a rented place) or a community telecentre, such options are not always feasible in specific cases, therefore, a reinterpretation of this requirement is the best solution here. More precisely, what should be required, in general, is the leaving the family home of the aggressor (in cases of cohabitation, as it is not always necessary) and staying away from it; otherwise, it would be hurting and 'punishing' the victim, who would be forced to leave his home and prevented from working from it.

In any case, if this radical approach does not succeed, which would place the obligation of leaving the home onto the other party involved in the family conflict, a restrictive interpretation of the requirement above is supported, which would permit exceptions to it. One of them could be when, for example, in view of the circumstances of the case, the leaving of the victim is neither necessary to safeguard their personal safety and security nor timely, as he or she wants to provide services for the company from home. In the latter case, if the risk persists to the life and personal safety of the person, it is argued that the departure should be imposed on the offender. However, there are authors who, even using a restrictive interpretation of the aforementioned requirement, never consider the transfer of the obligation of leaving to the aggressor, even in cases of teleworking. So, in these cases, if there is a risk to the personal safety or the physical or mental health of the victim or a change in circumstances is considered appropriate, working from the family home is prevented by the legal requirement compelling the victim to leave their home.[20]

Along with this double condition, which determines the transfer of the worker-victim of violence (Article 195.1 LC), the other requirement that necessarily has to concur in Portuguese law so that the victim can undertake teleworking is that the activity carried out *is compatible* with the new way of working remotely.[21] Thus, it can be asserted that the first two conditions are subjective in character, as they concern

---

18. Ravara, D.: *Violência doméstica. Implicações – sociológicas, psicológicas e jurídicas do fenómeno. Manual pluridisciplinar,* coordinado por Paulo Guerra y Leuília Gago (abril 2016), pp. 352 et seq.
19. Likewise, de Carvalho Oliveira, C., *supra.*, p. 14. Also, Vasconcelos, J.: 'Sobre a proteção da vítima de violencia doméstica no Direito do Trabalho Português', *Revista de Direito e Estudos sociais,* 2010, 1-4, pp. 118 et seq.
20. In this regard, Ravara, D., *supra.*, p. 352.
21. Article 166.2 LC.

requirements that depend on the worker, and the third condition is more objective, as it affects the work of the company, which is also related to the management and organizational skills of the employer. This condition is also required for the transfer, as Article 195.2 LC provides that the employer may postpone – but never reject – the taking effect of it until 'there is a compatible job available' in the new workplace. Therefore, it seems that in both cases the transfer is conditional upon the prior work activity (in development within the company) being provided in that location normally. The idea is that the changing of workplaces should affect neither the labour activity nor its productivity, which is related to defending the legitimate interests of the employer. Certainly, the personal and private interests of the victim of domestic violence must be addressed, but only as far as possible, which requires that they are compatible with their duties as part of the employment relationship. However, it does not seem that the application of teleworking can be postponed on basis of 'overriding requirements related to the operation of the company or service' (Article 195.2 LC). A broad interpretation of this argument is not possible, which only expressly provides for the transfer, but not for teleworking; the Article 166.2 LC does not even mention such a situation.[22]

In the case of teleworking, on-site activity will be compatible with the new way of working when the worker is able to continue working outside the company naturally, that is, with the same level of performance and productivity reached on-site. Obviously, the necessary contact with managers and colleagues can be maintained using the current sophisticated technological tools, so prior inclusion of workers in a team cannot be an automatic ground for rejection of the application for teleworking. In any case, the peculiarities of the particular case must be examined and determined accordingly and, if doubt remains, granting the request of the worker is advisable, even it is just to test it or for a certain period of time. As holder of managerial and organizational power, the employer has the competence to assess the compatibility of the labour activity of the worker with its development outside the company.[23] However, the collective agreement on teleworking can provide for, for example, consultation on the compatibility with the workers' representatives or other bodies, especially in case of doubt. In addition, the agreement can facilitate the task of determining the compatibility issue by including a list of posts and work activities that are viable to be undertaken outside the company.

Moreover, if the activity that the worker undertakes in the company is difficult to carry out outside the company, it is always possible that, by agreement of the parties, a different task is assigned to him for completion in the new workplace (worker's home or other available place). Now, it goes without saying that in such a case the worker must meet legal requirements and professional qualifications required to carry out this new task.

22. Likewise, Abrunhosa e. Sousa, D., 'O enquadramento legal teletrabalho em Portugal', in *Revista de Derecho Social y Empresa*, 2016, n° 6 (in press).
23. Thus, Palma Ramalho, R.: *Direito do Trabalho. Part II. Situaçaos Laborais individuais*, 4th edition (Lisbon, 2012), p. 296.

Under Spanish law, Article 21.1 OLCPMGV sets out the labour rights of worker-victims of gender violence, which are mainly geographical mobility and changing workplaces (as in Portuguese law), but also the reduction or reorganization of their working hours, the suspension of employment but keeping the job, and the termination of the employment contract. These rights are applied under the terms provided in the Workers' Statute.[24] The aforementioned provision of the OLCPMGV does not expressly recognize the transfer to telework or distance work as a right of the worker-victim of gender violence. However, such a possibility should be defended, given the broad terms of the Article 37.8 WS. Indeed, according to this provision, a worker who is a victim of gender violence is entitled to 'changes in working time, through the adaptation of the work schedule, the application of flexi-time or *other forms of organisation of working time which are used in the company*'. Undoubtedly, the significance of the latter part of the quotation (in italics) is that it opens the door to new ways of working in order to protect the affected worker, such as teleworking, whether total or partial, and in the latter case, combining periods of employment on-site and off-site.

However, even accepting that the aforementioned Article 37.8 WS covers the teleworking for worker-victims of violence, the Spanish model on this point provides less protection than the Portuguese one, and this is because:

(1) There is not a provision which clearly and directly recognizes this new way of working as a right of the worker (unlike in Portugal), but there is an ambiguous expression, which is understood as including, among others, the possibility of teleworking.

(2) The possibility of using teleworking is not automatic and is not always guaranteed, as it must be a form of working 'that is already used in the company'. If it is not so, the employer has no obligation to introduce a teleworking plan for the specific case, or grant the individual request of the worker.[25] In other words, the economic interests of the company must be respected, too, and the company must only work with labour measures that have already been implemented and are familiar to it, without having to take on new ones. Moreover, even if teleworking as a form of work already exists in the company, the application of the worker must meet the requirement of compatibility with the organization of business in the company, and, in particular, the continuity or normal progression of work outside of that. More clearly, if teleworking is requested, the position of the worker must be compatible with distance work to ensure proper performance of duties and to avoid damage to the business.

However, it is clear that, when it comes to assessing the compatibility between the organization of work or characteristics of the position occupied by worker and teleworking, the employer has to take a generous approach, in

24. Articles 37.8, 40.3*bis* and *ter*, 48.6, 52.d), 53 and 55.5.b) WS.
25. Gala Durán, C.: 'Gender violence and Labour Law: an approach to the various measures envisaged', *Labour Relations*, n°. 10, 2005, p. 38.

order to grant the application when possible. In other words, the denial of a request to change to teleworking must be based on absolute incompatibility, in the sense of a total impossibility to allow the request of the worker, for example, because the position is not objectively suitable for undertaking distance working. It is not enough that the request causes disruption for the company, damages slightly its economic interests or requires a special organizational task; the relevance of the legally protected good and the vulnerability of the worker – a victim of a difficult situation of gender violence – demand a clear effort to adapt to the new situation on the part of the company.[26]

(3) For the daily exercise of these rights, it is necessary to focus, first, on the provisions of the collective or individual agreement.[27] The collective agreement refers to the agreement in the ordinary collective agreement or a specific agreement between the company and workers' representatives. The individual agreement is the direct agreement with the affected workers, which is relevant when no collective agreement exists or the collective agreement has been improved by the individual. Secondly, if there is no agreement, the responsibility for the realization of these rights falls on the applicant worker. So, the worker themselves – a victim of gender violence – will be the one who will decide what type of changes need to be made to reconcile work and private life at that particular time.

However, the legal attribution of this decision-making power to the worker should not be regarded as a *carte blanche* for him or her, in the sense that the employer is obliged to accept any measure requested. In fact, the employer may decline a request based on his managerial and organizational power, in which case the worker will have to go to the social jurisdiction to defend their right.[28] From a critical point of view, it would have been appropriate that the legislature had included minimum terms of exercise of the right, in order to unify the regime applicable to it and increase legal certainty. Indeed, perhaps it would have been more appropriate that the placing of the burden of responsibility on the worker for the realization of the right through the measure requested was accompanied by its immediate enforceability, in the case of business discrepancies. In such a case, the worker-victim would be immediately protected through the granting of the requested measure of teleworking and, if necessary, the burden for challenging the introduction of the measure would be placed on the employer.

Moreover, a review of existing collective agreements highlights the poor regulation of teleworking in general, and, more so, of its links with the specific purpose of

26. Menéndez Sebastián, P., and Velasco Portero, T.: *The incidence of gender violence in the employment contract,* Madrid (Cinca), 2006, p. 75.
27. Villalba Sánchez, A., 'Gender violence *versus* domestic violence. Spanish-Portuguese perspective', in AAVV volume: *Gender violence and Labour Law. Current studies on critical points*, led by Lourdes Mella (Madrid, 2012), p. 759.
28. Procedure established in Art. 139 Law 36/2011 of 10 October, regulating the Social Jurisdiction. Art. 37.8, second paragraph, WS.

protecting victims of gender violence. This is also the case with the regulation that the various Spanish autonomous communities are undertaking to promote the implementation of telework in the public sector. According to some of these regulations, when there are several requests for teleworking from the same administrative unit, and is not feasible to grant all requests, criteria are established under which the beneficiaries will be selected, and in these cases, being a victim of gender violence is regarded as being significant.[29] However, a criticism can be made of the fact that the mere mention of being a victim of gender violence is regarded as significant without any request for further details being supplied.

[B] Teleworking as a Way of Helping Working Parents with Young Children

Another case – perhaps the most common – where telework is used as an individual right to facilitate the reconciliation of work and personal life of the worker it is when this one has the responsibility to care for minor children. In Portugal, as already noted, the most recent reforms relating to telework (Law 120/2015 of 1 September) aim to strengthen the rights of working parents to reconcile work and family life, offering teleworking for this particular way of working and living. That Law gives new wording to Article 166.3 LC, which now states that, 'apart from the situations referred to in the previous Article (domestic violence), the worker with a child aged up to 3 years is entitled to exercise their labour activity through teleworking, when this is compatible with the activity performed and when the employer entity has the resources and means to that end.' So, a unilateral right of the worker, male or female, to provide services outside the company, in order to facilitate the care of a child of less than three years of age, is set out by the legislator. This right is valued positively as it is a true measure of reconciliation with significant potential to adjust the work/life balance, and thus support parenthood, and, eventually, an increase in the birth rate.[30]

There are two conditions for the exercise of this right by workers who are in this type of family situation – both objective in nature. First, compatibility of the labour activity with the new way of working remotely is required. As this is a feature in common with the other case previously analysed, we can apply here what was said there, and the second condition is that the company has the resources and means for the introduction of telework. On this last requirement, a focus should be placed on avoiding fraud on the part of the company, for example, if it fraudulently claims an inability to provide such resources as a means of denying the right of the worker. Perhaps it would be appropriate for the individual or collective agreement to establish

29. Cfr. Art. 6 of the Decree of the Governing Council of Castile and Leon 9/2011 of 17 March, regulating the off-site working day by teleworking in the Administration of the Community of Castile and Leon. Also Art. 6.3.a) Decree 57/2013 of 12 August, approving the provision of services from public employees in teleworking regime in the Administration of the Regional Government of Castile-La Mancha.
30. ABRUNHOSA e SOUSA *(supra)*, telework for workers with children of less than three years of age acts as an extension of maternity or paternity leave, but it neither costs for the social security system nor implies a loss of income for those concerned.

the possibility that third parties (i.e., workers' representatives) can also verify the truth of such claims and, even if they are true, to allow the worker to provide the technical means required to do their job off-site. Of course, the employer must make every effort to ensure the realization of these individual rights of the worker, who has delicate circumstances in his personal life and also has to reconcile them with his working life. In this regard, collective agreements may also improve legal regulation, for example, by increasing the age of the children who are cared for by a working parent for that parent to be entitled to access to telework.

Under Spanish law, the situation is quite different to the Portuguese one, as the most important rule at the state level (contained in Article 13 WS) does not relate, in any way, teleworking with the reconciling work and family life, and, in particular, with the care of young children. The legal rules approved by the Autonomous Communities in recent years to promote the implementation of teleworking in the regional public sector are clearer, however. These rules cite giving public employees the flexibility to work from home as one of the main purposes of teleworking, thus contributing to the reconciliation of personal, family and work life, and increasing job satisfaction among public employees.[31] Thus, the legislator wants these rules 'to have a trickle-down effect to the private sector, so that the benefits of this type of work can be extended to society as a whole.'[32]

In this regard, collective agreements in the private sector also tend to focus on teleworking as a means of reconciliation. In any case, it is expressly stated that 'the goal of teleworking policy is to provide employees an alternative way of working outside the office and to facilitate working from home when, for any reason, the worker cannot go to the office, but it is fit for work.' As one of these reasons is the care of relatives, it is clear that it 'supports the reconciling of work and family life.'[33] In some cases, it has been expressly recognized that company management and employee representation 'positively value the advantages that the provision of this type of working method provides to the company and its workers', because it has facilitated 'a marked improvement in reconciling work and family life, contributing to more flexible working conditions.'[34] Similarly, the 'improvement in the working environment of the company and the motivation of the workforce' has been noted, all without a reduction in productivity levels among staff.[35]

31. For example, Art. 2.2 Decree 9/2011, already cited. In a similar sense, Art. 13 Order of 20 December 2013, together with the Vice-President and Ministry of Presidency, Public Administration and Justice and the Ministry of Finance, through which accreditation, working time, flexi-time and teleworking is regulated for public sector employees in the Community of Galicia; and Art. 1.2 Decree 127/2012 of 6 July, whereby off-site working in the form of teleworking is regulated in the Autonomous Community of Extremadura.
32. Explanatory Memorandum of Decree 36/2013 of 28 June, through which the teleworking is regulated in the Autonomous Community of the Balearic Islands.
33. IX Annex of the III Collective Agreement 'Nokia Solutions and Networks Spain, SL' (EGD Resolution of 14 April 2015; State Official Bulletin -hereinafter SOB- of 25 April).
34. Article 89 Collective Agreement 'Companies linked to Telefónica Spain, SAU, Telefónica Móviles Spain, SAU and Telefónica Solutions Information Technology and Communications, SAU' (EGD Resolution of 28 December 2015; SOB of 21 January).
35. Article 15.7 IV Collective Agreement 'Repsol YPF, SA' (EGD Resolution of 21 March 2012; SOB of 4 April).

Consistent with this initial approach, both regional regulations and collective agreements often set the reconciliation of work and family life as one of the criteria to be taken into account in order to select workers applying to provide services off-site. Regarding family life, caring for a disabled person over a certain age (usually 65) or caring for a minor, are two generally favourable circumstances.[36] In such cases, other circumstances are also taken into account. These include the degree of disability of the person or the official recognition of the social security benefits received;[37] the extent to which the person cared for is included in the labour market, and any salary that is earned; whether or not a single-parent family exists; the degree of the relationship between the worker and the person cared for; and the simultaneous presence of several protected situations (e.g., a minor or older person with disabilities).

Focusing on the case of *minors*, the granting of telework is usually conditional upon the minors not exceeding a maximum age, which can be any age up to the age of 18 until (e.g., 12[38] or 14),[39] although sometimes the standard includes a scale by age (0 to 18) and the score goes from more to less, as the age increases.[40] Sometimes the concept of 'children' is understood in a broad sense, including not only the natural and adopted children, but also other minors under guardianship or fostering (permanent, adoptive or simple), both those of the worker requesting teleworking and those of his or her spouse or partner.[41] As the aim of these legal provisions is to increase the birth rate, it is possible to find some cases in which the pregnancy of the worker alone is considered a ground for access to telework,[42] which is very positive.

In terms of comparison between the two countries studied, the general conclusion is that the legal regulation of telework in the Portuguese system has an approach clearly aimed at protecting the personal and family lives of workers and facilitates their professional development. Thus, the Portuguese legal regulations clearly deserve a *positive* assessment unlike the Spanish law, where such an approach is lacking in the most important state legislation in this area (Article 13 WS). The configuration of teleworking as an individual right of the worker based on personal circumstances, such as those discussed in the Portuguese context, is absent from Spanish system.

Although some regional standards (which regulate teleworking for the public sector) and some agreements do cite teleworking as a measure of reconciliation, this

36. Article 61 of the II Collective Agreement 'ONO Group (Cableuropa and Tenaria, SA)' (EGD Resolution of 11 June 2013; SOB of 1 July): 'there will be preference for those candidates who have dependents (minor children, disabled or elderly persons to care for)'; Art. 43 III Collective Agreement 'Nokia Solutions and Networks Spain, SL', cited.
37. Article 7 Decree 45/2013 of 5 December, through which off-site working civil servants and employees, in the form of teleworking, is regulated in the Autonomous Community of La Rioja and its Autonomous Bodies (LROB of 13 December, 2013), requires permanent disability.
38. Article 6.1 Government Council Decree 9/2011 of Castile and Leon, *supra* cited; Art. 6.1 Decree 92/2012 of 29 May, approving the agreement on off-site working in the form of teleworking for public employees of the Basque Country and its autonomous bodies.
39. Article 8.1 of Extremadura Decree 127/2012 of 6 July, above. In some, the norm is valued differently depending on the age of the child and whether they have disabilities. For example, Art. 7.2 of Decree 36/2013 of 28 June, cited.
40. Article 7.2 Decree 36/2013 of 28 June, said.
41. Article 6.1 Decree of the Governing Council of Castile and Leon 9/2011, quoted.
42. First additional provision of Decree of the Governing Council of Extremadura 127/2012 of 6 July.

legal loophole is not clearly covered, the ideal would have been that the Workers' Statute enshrined teleworking into national law and set it out as a clear method of reconciliation for workers and not just as a business cost-saving measure. Accordingly, it is necessary to recommend that the Spanish legislature follows the example of its Portuguese counterpart, in order to improve the current regulation of telework in Spain and to reconfigure it, legally, as a true measure of reconciliation. Note the importance of the introduction of such type of measures and their positive impact on, for example, the birth rate and the care of the dependents and older persons – two interests in a society that is increasingly ageing. Clearly, this new way of working may be a good option to meet this goal.

§10.02 WORKING TIME CONTROL AS THE KEY TO AVOID THE BLURRING OF THE BOUNDARIES BETWEEN WORK AND FAMILY LIFE

[A] Risks of Working Outside the Workplace

As discussed *above,* working off-site has the great advantage of facilitating the reconciliation of work and family, and this is because the place where the private life is fostered becomes the host for the other aspect of life (working life). In other words, the family home becomes, in most cases, a common space for work and family development, removing spatial barriers between the two aspects of life. Without doubt, the merging of these two aspects of life into one place will lead to new challenges for the worker to ensure that they function successfully on both fronts. One of the main challenges is organizing working time and family time adequately. Failure to so, can easily result in problems arising from a *poor interaction* between these two aspects and can lead to poor performance on the part of the worker, if, for example, they experience continuous interruptions (by others in the family home) and, therefore, lack focus on the task at hand. In this sense, although the work life and private life are lived in the same physical space, it should be noted that they neither can – nor should – be lived in the same temporal space, because the person either works or rests, and one cannot do both things 'at the same time' well. More clearly, the respective times for work and rest should be clearly demarcated, with the time for each being used exclusively for the purpose originally planned. Logically, flexibility and alternation to those times is a different matter and can be arranged in order to suit to the particular personal and family circumstances of each worker.

On the other hand, it is possible that some imbalances may arise in relation to the limits of work and rest times, either in favour of the former or the latter. In the former, health problems can be caused by overworking, such as physical and mental exhaustion, 'workaholism' or techno-stress may appear.[43] In the latter, in which the swing is in favour of rest time, the problems are related to a breach of the previously set working

43. Mella Méndez, L., 'Safety and health in telework', in AAVV volume: *Distance work and teleworking. Studies on their legal status in Spanish and Comparative Law,* editor L. Mella (Madrid, 2015), pp. 190 et seq.

hours and thus the performance of the worker, which may be a reason for a disciplinary action being taken. Therefore, it is clear that, regardless of the where the workplace is located, work and rest time must be strictly observed to respond to the legitimate interests of both the employer and the worker.

In order to achieve the desired goal of the teleworking experience and to ensure success for both parties to the contract, it may be appropriate to require a professional and personal profile of the worker concerned. In this vein, for example, the 'White Paper of Teleworking' of the Spanish company *Repsol* states that 'not all employees can join the programme' of teleworking, as 'a particular professional profile, capabilities and enough skills are required of them in order to keep their commitments at a distance, managing their own time, space and resources' adequately and efficiently. The person in question must demonstrate abundantly 'responsibility for self-management, discipline and motivation' and also an 'adequate performance over the time.'[44] Certainly, the greater the freedom and flexibility that teleworking involves, the greater the responsibility to organize working time and rest time adequately, and, certainly, not all personal profiles meet such requirements. Without doubt, this must be taken into account both in the selection of the worker and in the determination, from the outset, of the kind regime of teleworking to implement and its specific circumstances.

Regarding the teleworking regime, one of the most recommended models is partial in character, thus involving the combination of on-site and off-site work, and in which it is easier to maintain employee-employer contact. This approach avoids some labour risks, especially those of a psychosocial nature, resulting from the poor interaction or distinction between work and rest times; and, where appropriate, can detect and solve them as soon as possible. In this sense, the AMET protects – even without mentioning it – part-time teleworking in two of its clauses. One is the first, defining telework as a form of work organization in which the labour activity is carried out off the premises of the company on a 'regular' basis. The latter expression quoted, although setting out distance work as a routine or something normal, does not seem to demand exclusivity in it. In other words, what is normal is not necessarily exclusive or absolute and, therefore, the regular teleworking protects periods (even short periods) in which the work is performed on-site. The other clause of interest is the ninth, which, in its third paragraph, provides that the employer shall ensure 'that some measures are taken to prevent the isolation of teleworkers in relation to other employees of the company, such as providing them with opportunities to meet regularly with their peers and access to information' of the company. This clause also highlights the need for the worker to maintain some personal contact with the company and co-workers.

Following the European Agreement, Spanish law states clearly that work activity will be carried out at a location chosen by the worker and 'in an alternative way to its on-site development in the workplace' (Article 13.1 WS). This provision thus enshrines a part-time teleworking model, in which periods of distance work and on-site work will occur at intervals and durations agreed by the parties, as long as the former type of

44. Http://www.repsol.com/imagenes/es_es/libro_blanco_tcm7-627218.pdf.

work is prevalent. Similarly, the Portuguese LC states that 'the employer must avoid the isolation of the worker, especially through the maintenance of regular contact with the company and other workers.'[45] In short, these periods in the company are beneficial to the employee, as they allow him or her to maintain contact with managers and peers, strengthening personal and professional relationships and avoiding the effects of physical isolation.

On the other hand, in relation to the specific circumstances in which teleworking can be developed, the computer link between the worker and the company is of particular importance, whether unilateral (company-worker or *vice versa*), bilateral (bidirectional) or non-existent. In the first two cases, the technological contact between the parties facilitates more easily the corporate control of the work activity, including compliance with working hours; in the latter case, we must think of more traditional methods.

[B] Working Time in Distance Work and Its Control by the Employer

To the extent that teleworking is included in the field of Labour Law, the principle of equal treatment between the teleworker and the rest of the workforce applies, so the working time of that worker is subject to the maximum daily and weekly limits set out under law. Thus, this equality implies that, in the case of the distance worker, annual maximum normal working hours, overtime (until a maximum annual number) and the corresponding minimum daily, weekly and yearly periods of rest, will apply, as required by the Working Time Directive 2003/88/EC. This Directive sets out minimum health and safety requirements for the organization of working time, in particular minimum rest periods and maximum weekly working time, among other aspects.

In Spain, these limits of maximum working time and minimum rest are a reflection of the duty set out in Article 40.2 Constitution, which compels public authorities to limit working time to protect the health of workers. Certainly, health is linked to rest time, and this in turn depends on the length of the working day being limited. Therefore, although Article 13 WS does not expressly say so, the general rules laid down in terms of working time in Articles 34–38 WS have to be applied to teleworking. Among such rules is the eight hours per day and four hours per week (average annual total) of ordinary working time and the eighty hours per year maximum of possible overtime. Thus, despite the silence of the legislature, the principle of equal treatment for all workers of the company justifies the supplementary application of these rules. Similarly, in Portugal, the right of the teleworker to be subject to 'the limits of the normal working period' is specified, as with the rest of the workforce (Article 169.1 LC), which is, generally, also eight working hours per day and forty hours per week, a maximum overtime[46] and the enjoyment of breaks provided by law.[47]

---

45. Article 169.3.
46. Article 228 LC provides the maximum number of overtime hours, which are 175 and 150, depending on the size of the company is small, medium and large, respectively.
47. Articles 203.1 and 211 LC.

As teleworking is performed under a contract subject to Labour Law, it is clear that the employer – the holder of managerial and organizational power – has the right to give orders and instructions and to control the labour activity of workers in its different aspects,[48] including the maximum and minimum legal limits on working time, already mentioned. Indeed, it is about controlling whether workers respect, on the one hand, the working time they have committed to (which is important for productivity); and, on the other hand, the necessary rest, essential for good health. Only the respect of the boundaries between the two elements facilitates a healthy balance, as when those boundaries become blurred, broken or removed, the employment relationship is unbalanced and, can potentially (if rest time is affected) becomes harmful to the worker.

In order to ensure the control of the working day of teleworker, the employer first has to establish *clear guidelines on working time* (duration of the regular workday and, if appropriate, extraordinary workdays) and breaks (minimum or maximum), being respectful of legal and conventional regulations; and then, for the worker, he has to provide some *tools for measuring the working time* completed. These tools vary depending on the system of communication that exists between the contracting parties, which also determines the extent of collaboration by the worker.

Regarding the first aspect (the working time of teleworkers), it must be noted that, in Spain, despite the silence of Article 13 WS, the collective bargaining and the regulations of the autonomous communities reflect a preference for maintaining the same working hours and timetable for all employees of the company, regardless of the place from which they provide services. The primacy of the interests of the company and the possibility that the worker has to be present to cover certain on-site services requires that, even facilitating their relocation, the teleworker has to complete the same working time with the same schedule as their colleagues in the workplace, in order to be in a position to collaborate with them at any time. Thus, some collective agreements expressly state that the working time of the teleworker will be the general working time set out in the agreement and the timetable will be determined 'by the general schedule of the department to which the teleworker belongs';[49] or that the working time and timetable of teleworker will be the detailed in the collective agreement with a general character.[50] Similarly, some regional regulations, although acknowledging that teleworking may involve flexi-time, provide for the establishment of 'minimum periods of interaction' between the worker and the employer to work in a coordinated manner, especially in view of the service needs.[51]

48. Article 20.3 WS.
49. Article 74 XII Collective Agreement 'HIBU Connect' (EGD Resolution of 28 May 2013; SOB of 12 June). Also Annex V (working conditions of teleworkers, n°. 1) Collective Agreement 'Companies linked to Telefónica Spain, Telefónica Móviles and Telefónica Spain Information and Communications Solutions', cited.
50. Article 38.2.3 Collective Agreement 'Orange Espagne' (EGD Resolution of 5 August 2014; SOB of 21 August).
51. Article 8.5 Decree 92/2012 of 29 May, the Basque Country and its Autonomous Bodies, already cited.

It should be noted that this requirement limits one of the great advantages of teleworking, which is the flexibility in terms of time and personal freedom to perform the work activity when it suits the worker, even at night, weekends or holidays. Of course, the worker can always perform the tasks during these periods, but if the normal working day of the company has been completed, the teleworker would be overworking and eliminating rest periods.

In order to regulate this, in some Spanish agreements certain time flexibility is permitted in teleworking, with respect to the general schedule observed in the company, although it is subject to the requirements (together or separately) set forth below. So, teleworking outside normal hours: (1) must be requested by the worker and previously be agreed with the company (the employee's supervisor);[52] (2) must be objectively justified in terms of activity and professional commitments of the job, and, in any case, it must not negatively impact on other colleagues and work organization in the company;[53] (3) must respect the maximum duration of ordinary and extraordinary working time and the days and weeks rest in between; and (4) must maintain the same levels of productivity that teleworking would produce in normal time.[54] The specific changes must be documented in writing in an addendum to the original contract (if they do not appear in it from the outset). As shown, there is a limited or 'exceptional' flexibility, and it also must be agreed with the company.

As regards the Portuguese case, it should be noted that the previous version of the Labour Code (the 2003) contained a fairly detailed regulation concerning working time of the teleworker. It indicated, on the one hand, that this worker was subject to 'the maximum daily and weekly working time limits', applicable to workers who did not perform distance work,[55] and, on the other hand, that the teleworker could 'be exempted from the timetable',[56] which gave the worker maximum flexibility. However, the current regulation of LC (2009) scarcely regulates the working time of the teleworker, as it merely establishes that the normal work period must appear in the contractual document and that this period is subject, under the principle of equal treatment, to the general 'limits'.[57] However, nothing mentioned in relation to the work schedule expected to be followed by the teleworker, which seems to be a matter to be specified by the parties of the contract. In any case, although the aforementioned possibility of time exemption no longer appears in the provision related to teleworking, its application to the case can still be defended, which is also confirmed in the general regulation of the 'exemption from work schedule', regulated in Articles 218 and 219 LC. According to the former, by written agreement, the worker who provides services under a teleworking regime may be exempt from the work schedule (subsection c).

52. Article 36 Collective Agreement 'Thales Spain GRP, SAU' (EGD Resolution of 23 November 2015; SOB of 9 December).
53. *Ibid.* Also Art. 61.3 Collective Agreement 'ONO Group' (EGD Resolution of 11 June 2013; SOB of 1 July).
54. *Ibid.*
55. Article 240 LC 2003.
56. Article 241 LC 2003.
57. Articles 166.5 and 169.1 LC.

Moving on to other issues, with regard to the control of working time, it should be noted that in Spain, the Workers' Statute contains some references to working time control, as provided for under Article 12.5.h) for part-time workers,[58] or, the more generally under Article 35.5. According to this latter Article, 'the control of working time is the responsibility of the company', who has to 'register the working time of the worker day by day and total it in the period set for the payment of remuneration, delivering a copy of that registration to the worker in the corresponding receipt.' It is clear, then, that the obligation of the company to register the working hours of every worker, and the subsequent delivery of the daily summaries of hours worked to them, is already necessary in relation to ordinary working hours, and not only when overtime is completed. In this sense, it is important to mention here the recent ruling of the Spanish National Court of 4 December 2015,[59] which states the importance of that registration, since such control of the working day is 'necessary' to know the actual working hours of the workforce and, consequently, to assess if the work schedule is adhered to in its strict terms, or, on the contrary, if there is a deficit or excess in working hours completed, calculated annually. In other words, it said that daily control is the only means by which to verify compliance with the normal working hours, and the specific terms of such compliance. Thus, it is clear whether overtime is completed and, where applicable, documentary evidence exists, so register provides legal certainty in relation to the working hours truly completed by workers.

Without that daily and documented control neither the employer nor the Labour Inspectorate (indeed nobody, except the worker) can easily ascertain the hours worked. Therefore, in cases of alleged breaches of the previously agreed terms (fewer hours of work completed than agreed), the employer will have the responsibility of proving the breach. On the contrary, if the allegation is the performance of overtime, the worker will bear the burden of proof of its completion.[60]

In Portugal, the current Labour Code provides expressly that the employer must keep a register of working time – both ordinary and extraordinary[61] – of all workers, even those who are exempt from a work schedule and/or provide services outside the company. Such a register must indicate the start and end of working time and the interruptions that occur and do not count towards hours completed. In the event that the subject is exempt from the work schedule, it seems to be sufficient an indication of the days and hours worked is provided. When the worker provides services *outside* the

58. 'The working time of part-time workers will be registered every day and totalled on a monthly basis, delivering a copy to the employee, together with the receipt of wages, of the summary of all hours worked in each month, both ordinary and complementary, referred in Paragraph 5. The employer shall keep the monthly summaries of time records for a minimum period of four years. In case of breach of those registration obligations, the contract is presumed to be full-time, unless evidence of the partial nature of the services' is provided.

59. N° resource 301/2015.

60. For Judgement from Superior Tribunal of Justice of Castile-Leon (Valladolid) of 3 February 2016 (application number 2229/2015), even if it has not established a control system of working time, the employer must pay worker for overtime if the employee can prove it was completed. Otherwise, this would be equivalent 'to creating a space for impunity and lawlessness in distance work and home work'.

61. Articles 202 and 231 LC, for ordinary and extraordinary work, respectively.

company, the employer must ensure that the employee endorses the record as soon as they return to the company or, if necessary, he must sign and send the employer the record, within fifteen days from the completion of the work.[62] This verification seeks the agreement of the worker with the information contained in the record, through them checking the data and giving their approval by signing it, since, after all, is the worker who works off-site himself who best knows the details of this work schedule.

Portuguese doctrine understands that this legal mention (referring to the worker providing services outside) is perfectly applicable to teleworker,[63] so, if the teleworker provides services through a mixed model of teleworking, upon returning to the company, he revises the document within the cited period of fifteen days. If the period of work outside the company is longer in duration that fifteen days, the company must send the registration of working hours to the worker, who then prints the corresponding document and signs (or signs directly, if the thing documented is posted) and then returns it to the company duly endorsed, regularly, and within a fortnight of receipt. The employer must keep these records for five years, and ensure that they are available for immediate consultation. A breach of this obligation involves a serious infringement.[64]

Of course, this corporate obligation of controlling the working hours completed by the worker also applies in the event that the worker provides services at a distance and, in particular, from the family home. Indeed, it is not possible to allege that a violation of the privacy of the home has been committed; neither by the employer to refuse to comply with his duty to control working time, nor by the worker to prevent that the same being carried out. In fact, if the connection between the company and the worker is *interactive* or *online*, controlling remote labour activity can be done through new information and communication technologies, 'by checking the connection of the worker to the corporate intranet and their activity on the network.'[65] In any case, it is anticipated that control of the working time is asserted through the periods of agreed interconnection, that is, by 'sending control emails' when the agreed work starts and ends, or through another similar system.[66] A collective agreement provides that the signing of 'presence control' by the worker will be completed on the computer installed at home, 'through the employee portal on the intranet'.[67] In other words, the teleworker may be required to communicate the beginning and end of their working hours, powering the so-called 'presence device', which helps the employer to monitor the compliance with working time (ordinary and extraordinary).

This interactive and technological control of working time deserves two additional comments. On the one hand, from the point of view of privacy, such control is easy and 'does not imply, in principle and in normal conditions, an invasion of space

62. N° 3 of the Arts. 202 and 231 LC.
63. Cfr. Abrunhosa e Sousa, D., *supra*.
64. Article 202.1 and 2 LC.
65. Judgement of Superior Tribunal of Castile-Leon (Valladolid) of 3 February 2016, cited.
66. Article 9.3 Decree 36/2013 of 28 June, the mode of service is regulated by telework in Autonomous Community of the Balearic Islands.
67. Article 75 XII Collective Agreement 'HIBU Connect', cited.

protected under the concept of family home'.[68] In any case, these telematic control systems support different modes depending on the task performed by the worker, who must be promptly informed of these systems. The employer must also report them to the representative bodies and others previously agreed. Logically, it is always necessary that these systems respect the dignity of the individual concerned and are proportionate to the objective pursued, as required by clause 6 of the AFET.

On the other hand, this interactive control of the working time of teleworker is particularly suitable when the latter follows the same schedule of work of the company. Thus, workers who are subject to the regular schedule of the company tend to be interconnected with it, and *vice versa*, so that corporate control of their working days and schedules is technologically possible. This correlation between the common company schedule and interactive control is reflected in some agreements, by stating that 'the worker must be working and available *online* during the hours of mandatory presence that the working calendar establishes'.[69]

In the event that the teleworker provides services *offline* – as in the traditional sense of home working[70] – the company can meet its obligation of controlling working time by setting: (1) clear rules on maximum working hours and rest; and (2) reporting and controlling instruments to be used by the worker himself, so the worker bears the main responsibility for his management.[71] In any case, it must be noted that, even taking responsibility for meeting those standards, it is more difficult for the employer to verify whether the employee meets them or not; in fact, in many cases, employee performance and, consequently, remuneration, is usually fixed on the basis of units or pieces of work completed, without taking into account the hours worked completing the tasks. In some cases, a combination of both methods is provided, and although performance is evaluated based on the meeting of objectives or the delivering of outcomes, the use of 'technological means as an additional control instrument to verify the work carried out'[72] is established.

If the results of the company control show that the teleworker exceeds their working hours with a clear blurring of boundaries between working time and rest time, and this poses a clear danger to their physical or mental health (e.g., psychosocial risks), the employer can, and should, take measures to protect the worker, in order to prevent the situation from worsening. Initially, these measures may include, for example, tightening the interactive control over the teleworker, making him subject to the common work schedule of the company, promoting more contact and presence in the corporate headquarters (attendance at courses, meetings and other activities in

68. Judgement of Superior Tribunal of Castile-Leon (Valladolid) of 3 February 2016, cited.
69. Article 38.2.3 Collective Agreement 'Orange Espagne', cited.
70. Article 13.4 WS in its pre-reform 2012 version: 'every employer employing homeworkers shall make available a document for controlling the performed labour activity, which must include the name of the worker, the type and amount of work, the amount of delivered raw materials, the agreed rates for wage determination, the delivery and receipt of elaborate objects *and a few other aspects of the employment relationship* of interest to the parties'. The registration of working time could be included in the 'other aspects of the employment relationship'.
71. In this regard, clause 9 EFAT, in the framework of legislation, collective agreements and company rules applicable, 'the teleworker manages the organisation of their working time'.
72. Article 8.1 Decree 57/2013 of 12 August, cited.

common), and providing the employee with specific information and training on the dangers of overworking for the health of the worker, and other similar preventive activities. Although it is not strictly necessary, the best thing is that these measures are taken in collaboration with workers' representatives, particularly specialists in the prevention of occupational labour risks, and the Labour Inspectorate.

Finally, if the behaviour of the worker does not change and the management of his working and rest time continues to breach regulations, the employer can, and should, take further and definitive measures to end this way of working. These measures may include the termination of teleworking and the return of the teleworker to the company, or even the taking of disciplinary action against the employee for not obeying company orders. All these actions should reflect the legitimate exercise of corporate powers and be designed to ensure safe working for the workforce.

CHAPTER 11

Work-Life Balance in the Modern Workplace: A Comparative Analysis of the Turkish and European Multinational Companies Operating in Turkey

Gürol Özcüre, Nimet Eryiğit & Harun Demirkaya

§11.01 INTRODUCTION

This chapter's main objective is to explore and evaluate Turkey's current work-life balance policy from the perspective of the adoption of international norms – in particular, International Labour Organization (ILO) Conventions and the EU Labour Law Directives. Another aim of this study is to analyse the application and adoption of the international norms in Turkish modern workplace. We discuss the implications of employment and care regimes for the work-family reconciliation of working mothers in Turkey. In Turkey, as in other South East European and Mediterranean welfare states, a largely informal care market has developed in which migrant women can find work. Italy's care regime is characterized by 'explicit familialism', as options other than informal family care are not readily available.

We used The European Foundation for the Improvement of Living and Working Conditions (Eurofound) survey results, particularly 6th European Working Conditions survey results, to compare the EU Member States with Turkey. In addition, to analyse company situations in national and multinational companies operating in Turkey, we developed a survey that included the Turkish and European multinational companies located in İstanbul and the Kocaeli province, which are the most industrialized areas of Turkey.

As OECD figures show, Turkey is one of the world's open market economies. According to EWCDB of ETUI, the number of Multinational Companies (MNCs) operating and investing in Turkey has reached to over 500. The analysis is based face-to-face interviews with workers. A questionnaire was sent to 44 employees and we researched work-life balance company applications in Turkey and compared it with the EU companies and policy perspectives (the EU Directives and Europe 2020 targets). Similar surveys are rarely found in academic literature in Turkey. For instance, a survey was conducted among 201 persons (106 female, 95 male) who worked in a Turkish hospital in Ankara by Tekingündüz, Kurtuldu and Öksüz, which found that job satisfaction affects family-work conflict positively, but affects job stress negatively. On the other hand, job stress affects work-family conflict and family-work conflict positively, but affects job satisfaction negatively.[1]

As Turkey is a candidate for membership of the EU, in this chapter we discuss the implications of employment and care regimes for the work-family reconciliation of working mothers in Turkey. In Turkey, as in other South East European and Mediterranean welfare states, a largely informal care market has developed in which women can find work. Turkey's care regime is characterized by 'explicit familialism', as options other than informal family care are not easily available. We will also analyse the Commission's annual progress reports on Turkey regarding work-life balance, which aim to monitor the progress of EU candidate countries towards the fulfilment of the EU *acquis* for EU membership.

§11.02 GENERAL SCOPE: WORK-LIFE BALANCE IN TURKEY

Historically in Turkey, women were emancipated but remained unliberated, as highlighted in scientific literature written by Toprak (1990) and Kandiyoti (1987), who pointed to the implicit difference between formal equality and liberty in Turkey. Women sought autonomy from tradition and the right to speak up as individuals.[2] The conservative Justice and Development Party (*Adalet ve Kalkınma Partisi-Ak Parti*), in power since 2003, has prioritized measures aimed at protecting the family. The policies of the Ministry of Family and Social Policy made social aid accessible to more than 6 million families in 2012, and 70% of aid is paid to women at home for taking care of the elderly, sick or disabled, or for sending their children to school. It should be noted, however, that some social policy experts have criticized these policies for encouraging women to stay at home.[3]

The participation of women in the labour market in Turkey is very low and Turkey's care regime is characterized by 'explicit familialism', as options other than informal family care are not readily available. According to the EU main policy areas

1. Selahattin Tekingündüz, Aysu Kurtuldu & Sibel Öksüz, *İş-Aile Yaşam Çatışması, İş Tatmini ve İş* Stresi Arasındaki İlişkiler, Siyaset, Ekonomi ve Yönetim Araştırmaları Dergisi, 27–42.Yıl: 3, Cilt: 3, Sayı: 4 (2015).
2. Yeşim Arat, 'On the Emancipation of Women in Contemporary Turkey', *Emancipation in Exile Perspectives on the Empowerment of Migrant Women,* 47–52 (Ed. Nermin Abadan-Unat, Gretty Mirdal, İstanbul: İstanbul Bilgi Üniversity Press, 2015).
3. Sema Erder, 'Changing Forms of "Vicibility versus Invisibility" Concerning Women in Conservative Societies in the Urban Context', *Emancipation in Exile Perspectives on the Empowerment of Migrant Women,* 55–64 (Ed. Nermin Abadan-Unat, Gretty Mirdal, İstanbul: İstanbul Bilgi Üniversity Press, 2015).

relating to the work-life balance, the main issues are parental, maternity and paternity leave; childcare facilities; care for relatives; entry into the labour market; and the regulation of flexible, fixed-term and part-time jobs. There is much talk today of the 'work-life balance' issue between government policymakers, academics and social partners in Turkey. Although policies are less successful than expected, recently there have been some positive legal developments in this area, however, the working hours in Turkey remain among the highest in Europe. The main question is how far can the law intervene to ensure that workers are able to allocate sufficient time to family life. Another question is how does paid and unpaid leave allow parents more time to care for their children and other dependent family members, and how can it encourage people with caring responsibilities, mainly women, to continue working or re-enter the labour market.

Childcare institutions have been seen as a means of providing women with greater opportunities in the labour market, so that they can adopt male behaviour in the labour market while outsourcing their caring activities. Work-life balance describes the desire of all individuals – not just those with family responsibilities – to attain a balance between their paid work and their life outside work, from childcare and housework to leisure and self-development. Work-life balance has traditionally had a relatively narrow focus on health, stress-related burnout, working hours, maternity leave, and formal employment. The history of contemporary economies in the European Continent shows us that full employment policies in labour market families with two adults, dependent children and elderly relatives, requires women to work. The EU Directives concerning work-life balance aimed to support reconciling work and family life, and state support for childcare and care for the elderly.[4]

Paid and unpaid maternity leave was introduced by the EU Directives in 1990s in most of the EU countries including the United Kingdom (UK). Access to care services and benefits are conditional upon nationality, residence, and migratory status. Several women reported having been excluded, for instance, from public crèches due to their children's undocumented status; in this respect, informal work can also complicate access to services whose waiting lists give precedence to women in (regular) paid employment. Access to services is especially critical for women with children under the age of three, while care-work reconciliation is, instead, facilitated by the longer opening hours of schools which are also free of charge and open to children of undocumented mothers. Informal resources are, however, crucial to successful reconciliation processes.[5]

There are three ways to close the female pay gap: (i) increase the hours worked by women; (ii) increase the participation of women in the labour market; and (iii) increase the representation of women in high-productivity sectors. These three ways implicitly question the current situation that drives women to work part-time and provide the lion's share of unpaid services, such as care-giving and housework.

---

4. Jane Jenson, 'The European Social Model: Gender and Generational Equity', *Global Europe Social Europe*, 150–151 (Eds. Anthony Giddens, Patrick Diamond and Roger Liddle (Polity Press, Cambridge, 2006).
5. Gwyneth Pitt, *Employment Law*, 140–154 (5th Ed., London: Sweet & Maxwell 2004).

Reducing the part-time employment rate of women, and their share of unpaid hours, will be key to capturing women's economic potential in Western Europe. After the introduction of the Open Method of Coordination (OMC) and the 'Lisbon Strategy (2000)' goals for more and better employment, the female employment rate increased 51% to 60% and general employment rate increased to 70% until 2010, after which there was a notable lack of progress. The Europe 2020 Strategy renewed the target generally as 75% for men and women aged between 20 and 64 until 2020.[6]

Prof. Blanpain insisted that the European Union (EU) must have its own specific social policy and full-fledged labour law, because the expression 'labour law' is used in Article 156 of the Treaty on the Functioning of the European (TFEU), where the promotion of labour law needs close cooperation between the Member States. The national labour law usually limits itself to regulating employment in the private sector, while European Labour Law also covers employment in the public sector and the regulation of the equal treatment of men and women. The Europe 2020 Strategy aims to increase the labour market participation of women as a precondition for boosting economic growth and for tackling the demographic challenges from a gender equality perspective. Conditions should also be created to support the supply of adequate, affordable, high quality childcare services for pre-school age children.[7]

The European Institute for Gender Equality required information on gender equality and gender mainstreaming from the accession and candidate countries including Turkey. he Charter of Fundamental Rights of the European Union dated 12 December 2007 (replacing the Charter of 2000) which was given legal effect through the Lisbon Treaty, as set out in Article 6.1, is important for Turkey's future policy framework. The Charter's list of rights includes equality between men and women and the 'reconciliation of family and professional life'. The reconciliation of work and private life was identified as an important aspect of gender equality and concrete targets to be achieved by 2010 were to provide childcare to at least 90% of children between three years of age and the mandatory school age, and to at least 33% of children under three years of age in the EU. Flexicurity policies also address the reconciliation of work and private life. To promote reconciliation between work and family life, policies regarding childcare provisions are necessary. Securing coverage of targeted children by 2010 is a useful benchmark at Member State level. The Pact for Gender Equality and the European Alliance for Families should also contribute to a lifecycle approach to work, in particular by facilitating the transition from education to the labour market. Guideline 8 promotes a lifecycle approach to work through better reconciliation of work and private life and the provision of accessible and affordable childcare facilities and care for other dependants of family.[8]

6. Jean-Claude Barbier, *Changes in Political Discourse from the Lisbon Strategy to Europe 2020: Tracing the Fate of 'Social Policy'* Working Paper 2011.01 (Brussels: European Trade Union Institute 2011).
7. Roger Blanpain, *European Labour Law*, 74–75 (14th Ed., The Netherland: Wolters Kluwer Law & Business 2014).
8. *Ibid.*, at pp. 264–286.

[A] The ILO and the Council of Europe Work-Life Balance Conventions Affecting Turkish Labour Law

Turkey, as a member of the United Nations (UN) and ILO since 1932, endorsed the principles and rights set out in the Constitution (1982) and in the Declaration of Philadelphia, and has undertaken to work towards attaining the overall objectives. Also, Turkey as a member of the Council of Europe since 1949 and a candidate country to the EU, has to respect the ILO norms and to promote and realize them in good faith in accordance with the ILO Constitution. The principle of 'Equality and Prohibition of Discrimination' is promoted by the 1948 Declaration of Human Rights of the UN, which provides in Article 2 that:

> Everyone is entitled to all the rights and freedoms set for in the Declaration without distinction of any kind, such as race, colour, sex, language, religion, political or other opinion, national or social origin, property, birth or other status. Furthermore, no distinction shall be made on the basis of the political, jurisdictional or international status of the country or territory to which a person belongs, whether it be independent, trust, non-self-governing or under any other limitation of sovereignty.[9]

The placement of all parental responsibilities solely on women and the traditional distribution of roles are among the most important obstacles to equality in the working life of women in Turkey. According to International Convention on the Elimination of All Forms of Discrimination Against Women (CEDAW) Article 12/2(c), Turkey is under an obligation to encourage the provision of supportive social care services to enable parents to combine family obligations with work responsibilities. According to the official data, there are not enough nursing rooms or child, elderly, and disabled care centres in Turkey.[10]

Turkey needs to take measures to regulate work-life balance in accordance with ILO Conventions (No. 156 (workers with family responsibilities), No. 175 (part-time work), No. 177 (home work), and No. 183 (protection of motherhood)). Turkey also committed to equality between men and women in the negotiation process with the EU as a candidate country for full membership. ILO Convention No. 156, dated 1981, sets out the right to parental leave after the maternity leave, and for working women and men with family responsibilities to be allowed leave in cases of sickness of their children. The Convention also aims to eliminate the discrimination of workers with family responsibilities and to introduce a prescribed international labour standard in this respect, in as much as, he/she who wants to become and remain integrated in the labour force, and to re-enter the labour force after an absence due to family responsibilities, should be facilitated to do so. According to ILO Convention No. 183, dated 2000, breastfeeding should be permitted once or twice a day, or working hours should be reduced accordingly. These hours will be paid as the time worked. Under ILO

9. The UN, *The Universal Declaration of Human Rights (UDHR)*, http://www.un.org/en/universal-declaration-human-rights/ (accessed on 10 December 2016).
10. Kadriye, Bakırcı, *Gender Equality in Employment in Turkish Legislation with Comparisons to EU and International Law*, J. Workplace Rights, Vol. 15(1), 3–25 (2011).

Convention No. 123, dated 1965, the women's employment regulation requires men to participate in family child care responsibilities. Under the Revised Social Charter, Turkey is under an obligation to enable workers with family responsibilities to enter and remain in employment, as well as to re-enter employment after an absence due to those responsibilities. This includes the provision of facilities for vocational guidance and training (Article 27.a).[11]

According to Article 10 of the Constitution of 1982, all individuals are equal without any discrimination before the law, irrespective of language, race, colour, sex, political opinion, philosophical belief, religion and sect, or any such considerations. In 2004, parliament adopted constitutional amendments that introduced the following provision: 'Men and women shall have equal rights. The State has the duty to ensure that this equality is put into practice.' In September 2010, a referendum on constitutional amendments resulted in the incorporation of the following words: 'Measures ensuring equality between men and women would not be considered a violation of the principle of equality.' As a result, the state is now obliged to take positive measures to achieve de facto equality between men and women. On the other hand, Article 50 of the Constitution remains untouched. According to Article 50, paragraph 2 of the Constitution, no one shall be required to perform work unsuited to his/her age, sex, and capacity. Minors, women, and persons with physical or mental disabilities shall enjoy special protection with regard to working conditions. The inclusion of minors and persons with mental disabilities in the same paragraph as the reference to women gives the impression that women are not equal citizens but legally restricted persons, who do not have full legal capacity. They are weak, helpless, and in need.[12] The provisions in the Regulation on the Employment Conditions of Pregnant and Breastfeeding Women and Nursing Rooms and Childcare Centres that stipulate only the number of women employees required before nursing rooms and childcare centres need to be provided (Article 15/1 and 2) and the provisions on the use of these facilities by the children of women employees (Article 16) should be amended in a way that observes equality.[13]

In the Charter on Fundamental Social Rights of Workers of 1989, reconciliation is framed as a means of reconciling 'family life and occupation' and the Commission programme that followed shows that family life means having children. The introduction of reconciliation policies is also associated with the acceptance that policies may interfere with giving birth and providing education, whereas the Court rejected the EU going that far until the mid-1980s. During the 1990s, the areas concerned were extended. The 1998 employment guidelines regard caring for the elderly as belonging to the work-family reconciliation dilemma, as well as working time and the duration of the contracts.

11. *Ibid.*, at pp. 11–12.
12. *Ibid.*, at pp. 7–8.
13. *Ibid.*, at p. 20.

[B] The EU Work-Life Balance Policy Affecting Turkish Labour Law

The issue of reconciliation first appeared at the EU level in the 1974 social action programme referring to the articulation between 'family responsibilities' and 'job aspirations'. In the Charter on Fundamental Social Rights of Workers of 1989, reconciliation is framed as a means of reconciling 'family life and occupation' and the Commission programme that followed shows that family life means having children. The introduction of reconciliation policies is also associated with the acceptance that policies may interfere with giving birth and providing education. The EU policy action began to facilitate the reconciliation of work and family life. Firstly, the EU parental leave Directive concerned the reconciliation of working and family life (Directive No. 96/34 of 3 June 1996 on the framework agreement on parental leave (1996) OJL145/4 and Directive 2010/18[14] of 8 March 2010 implementing the revised Framework Agreement on parental leave and repealing Directive 96/34/EC). This Framework Agreement sets out the minimum requirements. On 26 March 2010, at an informal meeting of EU equality ministers, it was decided that the same target rate for the employment of both men and women (75%) should be set. In line with the Europe 2020 Strategy[15] 75% of people aged 20–64 should be in work by 2020. Europe's current average employment rate is at 69% for those aged 20–64. Only 63% of women are in work compared to 76% of men.[16]

The Amsterdam Treaty (1997) created a roadmap for integrating work-life balance policy into the European Employment Strategy (EES). The Employment Guideline 18 of the EES, entitled Equal Opportunities, which relates to equality between men and women and the reconciliation of work and family life (work-life balance), is important for this study. Care of the elderly and child care services in the EU have also gained importance. Guideline 7 also relates to work-life balance policies such as those on maternity leave, child care, and flexible working regulations. Work-life balance policies involving the provision of affordable care and innovation in the manner in which work is organized should be geared towards increasing employment rates, particularly among women. The European 2020 Strategy target is to raise the employment rate for women and men aged 20–64 to 75% by 2020.[17] These trends seem to match closely the aspiration of employees to combine work-life balance successfully. Increased flexibility in working time arrangements also helps to integrate more people into the labour market and enhance employment opportunities.[18]

Article 33 of the Charter of Fundamental Rights states: '*To reconcile family and professional life, everyone shall have the right to protection from dismissal for a reason connected with maternity and the right to paid maternity leave and to parental leave*

14. (2010) OJ L68/13.
15. Communication from the Commission, Europe 2020, A strategy for smart, sustainable and inclusive growth, COM(2010) 2020 final, Brussels.
16. Nurhan Süral, *An Assessment of the Pregnancy and Maternity Related Provisions of the Labor Legislation* (İÜHFM C. LXXII, S. 2, 442, 2014).
17. Roger Blanpain, *European Labour Law*, 294–296 (14th ed., Wolter Kluwer Law & Business, The Netherlands, 2014).
18. Frank, Hendrickx, *European Labour Law Handbook*, 138 (Tilburg: Tilburg University).

following the birth or adoption of a child.' Article 24 of the Charter of Fundamental Rights, moreover, states: *'Equality between women and men must be ensured in all areas, including employment, work and pay. The principle of equality shall not prevent the maintenance or adoption of measures providing for specific advantages in favour of the underrepresented sex.'* Article 3 TEU states that the Union shall combat social exclusion and discrimination. Moreover, Article 8 TEU asserts that the Union shall aim to eliminate inequalities and to promote equality between women and men.

Directive 2010/18/EU of 8 March 2010 implementing the revised Framework Agreement on parental leave concluded by BUSINESSEUROPE, UEAPME, CEEP and ETUC and repealing Directive 96/34/EC39 (the Parental Leave Directive) had to be transposed into national law by 8 March 2012. Male and female workers are entitled to an individual right to parental leave on the grounds of the birth or adoption of a child to take care of that child until a given age up to eight years to be defined by Member States and/or social partners. The main improvement is that the individual right to parental leave has to be granted for a period of four months – one more month than according to the former Parental Leave Directive. In order to encourage a more equal take-up of leave by both parents, the new Parental Leave Directive emphasizes the non-transferability of at least one of the four months. There is still no obligation to provide totally or partially paid parental leave. At the end of parental leave, workers shall have the right to return to the same job or, if that is not possible, to an equivalent or similar job. Parents returning from parental leave may request changes to their working hours or patterns for a set period of time. Employers have to consider and respond to such requests, taking into account both employers' and workers' needs.

The patriarchal family structure is characteristic of traditional Turkish society, and household affairs and care duties are generally undertaken by women. Turkey's legal rules on pregnancy and maternity leave for working women are found mainly in The Constitution of the Turkish Republic (1982) and Labor Law No. 4857 (2003). The Civil Servants Law No. 657 and the Social Insurances and General Health Insurance Law No. 5018 (2008) also contains some regulations for civil servants and workers. Article 10 of the Constitution of Turkish Republic states that women and men have equal rights and that the State is responsible to ensure that every Turkish citizen is treated equally, according to Article 41 of the Constitution of the Turkish Republic. In terms of labour, household and care duties are traditionally carried out by women, and the concept of sharing household duties with a spouse is an unfamiliar one. The Turkish Labour Law No. 4857 is not woman friendly as much as family friendly. Today, 39% of women are unpaid family workers.[19]

The Sack Law introduced new types of leave and made substantial (generous) increases in the duration of the current forms of leave for civil servants and workers with a permanent employment contract in the public sector. On 22 May 2012 the European Parliament adopted a resolution from an EU 2020 Perspective for women in Turkey. Amongst other things, the European Parliament underlined the very low female participation rate in the Turkish labour force, which is well below the targets

19. ILO, http://www.ilo.org/wcmsp5/groups/public/---europe/---ro-geneva/documents/meetingdocument/wcms_359818.pdf (accessed 21 April 2017).

envisioned by the EU's 2020 Strategy, and called on the Turkish government to establish a national plan of action in order to ensure greater participation of women in the labour market. Turkey accepted the Turkish National Employment Strategy (2014–2013) and the EU Employment Strategy. As stated in '*Female Labor Force Participation in Turkey: Trends, Determinants, and Policy Framework,*' a report prepared jointly by Turkey's State Planning Organization and the World Bank, pregnancy and childcare are important constraints to women's employment. Women interviewed in Istanbul stated that they would have to pay between 500 and 600 TL (between approx. EUR 210 and EUR 250) per month for childcare only if they decided to work, and other additional costs for household help. These costs would use up most of their additional earnings.[20] The rate of female employment and participation in the labour in Turkey is low.[21]

The poverty rate in Turkey is higher than the EU average. Although, as a middle-income country, Turkey does not suffer extreme poverty, the food and non-food poverty rate accounts for 18.08% of the population. This means that close to 13 million people in Turkey are poor. Furthermore, the poverty rate seriously differs between urban and rural areas; the rural poverty rate (38.69%) is four times higher than that of urban areas (8.86%). Regional differences also exist in terms of the poverty rate. In South Eastern and Eastern Anatolia, poverty prevails more than in other parts of Turkey.[22] The current persistent at-risk-of-poverty rate shows the percentage of the population living in households where the equivalised disposable income was below the at-risk-of-poverty threshold set at 60% of median equivalised household income for the current year and for at least two out of the preceding three years. In 2015 percentage of poor was 1.58%, while it was 1.62% in the previous year.[23]

As regards Turkey's relationship with the EU and negotiations in the area of social policy, two opening benchmarks for Turkey were determined and had to be fulfilled in order to be able to open negotiations for Chapter 19 with the European Union Council in 2007. These opening criteria related to union freedom and undeclared work. The first benchmark concerned ensuring full trade union rights in line with EU standards and relevant ILO Conventions (No. 87 Freedom of Association and No. 98 Right to Organize and Collective Bargaining), in particular, the right to strike and the right to collective bargaining both in public and private sectors. The second benchmark was the submission of an action plan for the transition, implementation and enforcement of the relevant the EU *acquis* with a view to including the whole labour force. Regarding the first benchmark, two new laws were enacted to ensure full trade union rights in line with EU standards. The Law on Trade Unions and Collective Labour

20. Nurhan Süral, *An Assessment of the Pregnancy and Maternity Related Provisions of the Labor Legislation* (İÜHFM C. LXXII, S. 2, 444, 2014).
21. European Parliament resolution of 22 May 2012 on a 2020 Perspective for Women in Turkey (2011/2066 (INI)http://www.europarl.europa.eu/sides/getDoc.do?pubRef=-//EP//TEXT+TA+P7-TA-2012-0212+0+DOC+XML+V0//EN&language=EN (accessed on 10 October 2016).
22. TurkStat, Poverty Rate Investigation (February 2013), http://www.tuik.gov.tr/PreHaberBultenleri.do?id=21867 (accessed on 25 December 2016).
23. TurkStat, Poverty-Rate Investigation (December 2016), http://www.turkstat.gov.tr/PreHaberBultenleri.do?id=21867 (accessed on 25 December 2016).

Agreements entered into force in 2012 but still remains far from the EU standards. As regards the second opening benchmark, the action plan was drafted and sent to the Commission on 30 April 2010.

Chapter 19 of the EU-Turkey accession negotiations on social policy and employment contains a total of 164 actions for the adoption of EU Social end employment policy, which consist of: Labour Law (15 actions), undeclared work (15 actions), health and safety at work (5 actions), social dialogue (7 actions), employment (30 actions), European Social Funds/Instrument for Pre-Accession Assistance (IPA) (2 actions), social inclusion (17 actions), social protection (20 actions), anti-discrimination (8 actions), equal opportunities (13 actions), and capacity building of institutions (32 actions).

[C] Work-Life Balance Regulations in the 2003 Turkish Labour Act

By combining work and life balance, the 2003 Turkish Labour Act has become a key element in safeguarding workers' employment rights under flexible arrangements and improving equality in the modern workplace. The new Labour Act No. 4857 brought increases for the worker in annual leave with pay and maternity leave. Article 5 of Act No. 4857 provides that '*no discrimination based on sex can be made in the business relations. The employer can not treat a worker differently in concluding the labour contract, establishing the conditions thereof, implementation and thereof due sex or pregnancy unless biological reasons or those pertaining the work qualifications oblige.*' The reconciliation of work and family responsibilities requires policies on the recognized rights of child-bearing parents to care for their children, and pre-school education. Birth related permissions can be divided into three groups which consist of maternity leave, paternity leave and breastfeeding leave. It is also possible to reconcile work and family responsibilities through sick, elderly and disabled care leave. Amendments regarding unpaid leave rights and part-time working rights for female employees was published in Official Gazette number 29882 on 8 November 2016, and entered into force on the same day. According to the new law, a working woman who gives birth while earning a minimum wage earns the full salary while working half day. The Amending Law has introduced some changes to Labour Law No. 4857. Below is a brief summary of changes introduced by the Amending Law, specifically as regards the Labour Law.

Paid maternity leave period before and after childbirth, the right to unpaid leave for female employees after a period of paid maternity leave of up to 6 months, and the right to breastfeeding leave amounting to 1.5 hours until the child reaches 18 months of age regulated under Article 74 of the Turkish Labour Act No. 4857. The maternity leave period regulated in the Turkish Labour Act as 16 weeks is over to 14 weeks which ahead of the EU and ILO regulations. According to Articles 17 and 18, during the maternity leave period, women workers are protected against termination of the labour contract.[24] In addition to the above rights, a female employee may, following the end of paid maternity leave, take unpaid leave for up to half of her weekly working hours on the following terms upon request:

(a) 60 days for the first birth;
(b) 120 days for the second birth;
(c) 180 days for the third or more births.

30 days will be added to the above-mentioned periods in the case of multiple births and the period will be 360 days in case the child is disabled. Provisions as to breastfeeding leave cannot be applied within such periods. At this point, the question arises as to whether the female employee may still use her right to unpaid leave for up to 6 months following the end of part-time working rights or not. It is still not clear how such leave rights will be used. One of the amendments introduced by the Amending Law is that if a female employee wants to use her right to unpaid leave within the above-mentioned periods, a part-time working monthly allowance will be granted to such a female employee by the Unemployment Fund provided that the following conditions are fulfilled:

(1) The female employee shall apply to the Turkish Employment Organization within 30 days of the end of her maternity leave.[25]
(2) 600 days' unemployment insurance premiums shall have been paid before childbirth in the name of the female employee.
(3) The female employee shall be working for at least half of the weekly working hours.[26]

The part-time working allowance term will be half of the weekly working hours (22.5 hours) regulated by law, and the daily wage will be gross daily minimum wage. The Amending Law is not clear yet on how the 22.5 weekly part-time working hours will be split among the days of the week. From the letter of the Amending Law on the right to unpaid leave for up to half of the weekly working hours, we understand that such a period is deemed to be half of the daily working hours or to correspond to the half of the weekly working hours. Another point which requires clarification is how the payment from the unemployment fund which is set as the gross daily minimum wage

24. Kadriye Bakırcı, 'Türk Hukukunda İş ve Aile Sorumluluklarının Uzlaştırılması': Uluslar arası Hukuk ve AB Hukuku Çerçevesinde Bir Değerlendirme', *Emek Piyasasında Toplumsal Cinsiyet Eşitliğine Doğru İş ve Aile Yaşamını Uzlaştırma Politikaları*, Derleyen: İpek İlkkaracan, 63-67 (İstanbul: İTÜ Bilim, Mühendislik ve Teknolojide Kadın Araştırmaları ve Uygulamaları Merkezi ve Kadının İnsan: Hakları Yeni Çözümler Derneği 2010).

25. Save, for compelling reasons, in the case that the female employee does not apply within thirty days of the date when the paid maternity leave ends, the payment will be made by deducting the amount of the time elapsed during the application period from the total time for which part-time working allowance is deserved.

26. The part-time working stated herein should not be confused with the part-time employment known in practice as part-time employment model. The part-time working stated herein was introduced by the Amendment Law and only female employees have the right to benefit from it.

amount will apply to employees who receive higher wages than the minimum wage. This will certainly not cause any loss of rights for employees who receive minimum wages, but employees with salaries higher than such minimum wage will be facing a loss of rights. In addition to the foregoing amendments, another amendment introduced by the Amending Law is that should the female employee dies during or after the childbirth, the unused maternity leave will be granted to the father. Whether 'unused leave' refers solely to the maternity leave or the female employee's unpaid leave up of to six months remains unclear.[27]

There are some other actions to be taken in addition to the legal liabilities such as protecting pregnant and breastfeeding women, the provision of breastfeeding rooms and nurseries by legally liable firms, and the guarantee that women returning from maternity leave come back to an equal and equivalent position. Some important steps to be taken are increasing the access of women to flexible working hours, especially in light of childcare responsibilities; training for parents on achieving the work-life balance; providing experience and information sharing platforms; and enabling the children to visit working places.

[D] Part-Time Working Rights for Parents in Turkey[28]

According to the amendment to Article 74 of the Turkish Labour Act No. 4857 and the Regulation on Parental Leave or Part-Time Work after Unpaid Leave supports women's employment in Turkey, requires an improvement in the level of education of women and aims to reduce low-paid work for women. It also aims to eliminate the lack of knowledge and skills of women. Another aim is removing the unregistered economy from childcare services. Social and gender approaches and traditional views of women's work are still a huge obstacle in rural areas in Turkey. In contrast, it seems that employers have used the system of home work provided by sub-contracting to dismantle the production process in order to avoid the risks created by demand fluctuations in the textile sector. Work such as seasonal work, temporary work, home work, and part-time work results in unstable and precarious work that is often associated with and common in female employment in Turkey. As already mentioned, women continue to be overrepresented in part-time work in Turkey. The contracting of female workers is increasing in lower-paid sectors. After the end of above-mentioned periods of paternal leave, one of the parents may request from his or her employer to work part-time until the beginning of the month after the child's compulsory education begins. Such requests are must be granted by legally by employers in Turkey. Employers cannot refuse or use such a request as a justifiable reason for termination of an employment contract.[29]

27. Cem Kılıç, Çalışan annelerin hakkını yemeyelim, *Milliyet Gazetesi*, 9 Ekim 2016, p. 13.
28. Procedures and principles as to which sectors and jobs are suitable for part-time working and practice will be specified by regulations to be announced by Ministry of Labour and Social Security.
29. Posta Gazetesi, Anneye yarım iş tam maaş ödeme, 11 Eylül 2016, p. 10.

The employee who is working part-time as stated above, may return to his or her job full-time provided that she or he informs the employer in writing with at least one month's notice on the condition that the employee will not be entitled to benefit from the same right to part-time work for the same child. In such a case, if there has been a replacement in the position, the contract of the employee who has replaced the part-time employee will be terminated automatically. With this change, it becomes evident that the employer should be agreeing a fixed-term employment contract with the replacement employee up to the time when the replaced employee will be returning to his or her job, and such an employment contract should emphasize that the replacement employee is in fact recruited for the position of the replaced employee. Another important point is that should one of the parents be unemployed, the other working parent cannot request part-time work.

The sub-contract system that is commonly used in the confectionary sector around Istanbul in particular, has adversely affected female participation in the labour market in Turkey. Comparing Turkey with the EU countries it is clear that the work-life balance policies in the EU countries result in 32.6% of women working in part-time jobs and 9.5% of men working in part-time jobs. These policies, which were implemented successively in most of the European countries during the 1990s, have recently been on the agenda of the policymakers in Turkey. Recent research shows that the reconciliation policies have positive results such as increasing the female activity rate and balancing work and private life. However, they also have adverse effects like exacerbating the problem of the unequal distribution of unpaid work between men and women and hindering women's access to full-time jobs.[30]

[E] Employees Adopting a Child under Three Years of Age

One of the parents or adoptive parents adopting a child under three years of age may use the paid maternity leave for eight months from the date on which the child is adopted. The person adopting a child who is under three years of age, individually or together with their spouse, may request to work part-time from the date on which the child is adopted. Female or male employees adopting a child under three years of age may use the right to unpaid leave which amounts to half of the weekly working hours upon their request. They may also take part-time working allowance within this period if the above stated relevant conditions are met. Lastly, a person adopting a child under three years of age, individually or together with their spouse, may benefit from unpaid leave of up to six months from the date on which the child is adopted. Although the amendments appear positive at first glance, criticisms have been voiced on the grounds that it will cause several difficulties and confusions for employers. It will be possible to further interpret the procedures and principles of implementation of recent amendments in detail once the regulations are issued by the Ministry of Labor and Social

30. Çağla Ünlütürk Ulutaş, *İş ve Aile Yaşamını Uzlaştırma Politikaları: Türkiye'de Yeni Politika Arayışları*, Ankara Üniversitesi SBF Dergisi, 723–750, Cilt 70, No. 3 (2015).

Security, the Ministry of Finance, the Department of Social Security, and the Treasury.[31]

In Turkey, in Labour Law No. 4857 and the Civil Servants Law No. 657, there is no leave entitlement under the title of 'Parental leave.' A worker may request leave for a valid reason and this may be a family-related reason. In the Civil Servants Law, there are forms of leave such as 'excuse leave' and 'compassionate leave' that may be used for family-related reasons. An 'excuse leave' is a ten-day period of paid leave to which a second ten-day period of paid leave may be added within one year. 'Compassionate leave' is three months' paid leave, plus three months' paid leave, plus eighteen months' unpaid leave. Unpaid sabbatical leave of one year to be used altogether or in two parts is granted to civil servants who have completed five (previously ten) years of service. Sabbatical leave can only be taken once throughout the entire period of service. It cannot be used when the civil servant is serving in a region which is subject to martial law, a state of emergency or a disaster. Permanent workers employed in the public sector are entitled to an unpaid compassionate leave of six months plus six months. Workers permanently employed in the public sector are also entitled to unpaid sabbatical leave of six months upon the completion of ten years of employment. This sabbatical leave can only be taken once in the entire period of employment.[32]

The standard of labour legislation in Turkey, as a candidate country for EU membership, has a step closer to the legal norms of employees' rights in the European Union countries, by the enactment of Law No. 6645 adopted in Parliament and published in the Official Journal, on 23 April 2015 in Turkey. One notable change brought about by this Law was the introduction of new types of paid leave, leave of absence with pay or paid time off work into Labor Law No. 4857. New concepts of leave concerning working parents are as follows:

(i) **Adoption leave:** in the case of the adoption of a child the employee is entitled to three days of paid leave.
(ii) **Paternity leave:** an employee whose spouse has given birth is entitled to five days' paid leave.
(iii) **Shared parental leave for disabled child:** employed parents whose child has at least 70% disability or chronic disease based on a medical report, shall be allowed to take up to ten days' of paid leave a year for attending the treatment of the child; on condition that leave may be taken only one of the parents and without interruption or in segments.

In labour law terminology the terms 'parental leave or family leave' include **maternity leave**, **paternity leave** and a**doption leave,** and are designed to give parents time to care for a newborn or an adopted child or a child with a disability or chronic disease. Employees in Turkey were previously entitled only to the maternity leave

31. Özbek Attorney *Partnership, Novalties introduced to Turkish Labour Law* (http://www.ozbek.av.tr/publications/novalties-introduced-to-turkish-labor-law-by-the-law-no-6663/) (accessed on 25 December 2016).
32. Nurhan Süral, *An Assessment of the Pregnancy and Maternity Related Provisions of the Labor Legislation* (İÜHFM C. LXXII, S. 2, 450, 441–456, 2014).

which also contains the nursing leave which is granted to women in case of pregnancy and childbirth, three days' paid leave for marriage, and three days' bereavement leave in the event of the death of the employee's mother, father, spouse, brother or sister, or child. By the above-mentioned legislative arrangement another three types of parental leave are now available for Turkish employees – three days' paid leave for **adoptive parents,** five days' paid leave for **fathers with a newborn child**, and ten days' paid leave for the **parents of disabled or chronically ill children**.

[F] National Action Plans, Employment Strategies and Development Plans for Gender Equality in Turkey

In the National Action Plan for Gender Equality of Turkey 2008–2013, objectives and strategies for action are developed for the areas of education, economy, poverty, power and decision-making, health, media and the environment. In the economic area, strategies to increase women's employment in line with the Ninth Development Plan of Turkey (2007–2013) include: (1) revising the existing Labour Law in order to incorporate definitions based on gender equality; (2) taking the necessary measures against all kinds of discrimination faced by women with regard to entry into and performance in employment and working life; (3) expanding care services for children and for sick, disabled and elderly people, and enhancing their accessibility; (4) making legal arrangements on parental leave in order to share the childcare responsibilities between mothers and fathers; and (5) providing information to home-based working women about the opportunities to benefit from the social security system.

In the Tenth Development Plan of Turkey (2014–2018),[33] the chapter on the status of family and women states that:

> The family structure in Turkey has been transforming from the extended family to the nuclear family and the relationships among the family members have also been changing. For reconciliation of family and working life, alternative models such as flexicurity, parental leave, extending and increasing the accessibility of nurseries and child care services will be implemented. Component-3: Conserving Dynamic Population Structure; 1. Strengthening harmony of family and working life; 2. Extending high quality, affordable and accessible nursery and preschool facilities. Program Targets a-) Protecting family welfare and strengthening family institution b-) Strengthening intergenerational solidarity • Harmonizing work and family life.[34]

The assessment of the work-life balance and related measures indicates that the following documents have a strategic importance in forming the policymaking target groups and individuals at risk: (i) Tenth Development Plan; and (ii) Strategic Plan of The ministry of Family and Social Policy.[35]

33. Republic of Turkey, Ministry of Development, *Tenth Development Plan* (2014–2018) was approved at the 127th plenary session of The Grand National Assembly of Turkey, on 1 July 2013.
34. *Ibid.*, at pp. 40–41.
35. Utku Balaban, *Social Inclusion Practices in Turkey: An Employment-Oriented Strategy for 2014–2018* (Ankara: Ankara University).

The National Employment Strategy of Turkey (2014–2023) aims to create more and better jobs by 2023 when the Republic of Turkey will celebrate its centennial. The Strategy was published in the Official Gazette on May 30, 2014. There are 40 concrete targets, 57 policy measures and 201 actions grouped under four main pillars. The Strategy sets ambitious employment targets. Turkey has also prepared its first employment and social reform programme. The current high unemployment rate (10.7% in 2014 and 10.3% in 2015) is far from the 5% target in 2023. The female rate of participation in the labour market is as low as 32.2%, and the female employment rate is very low as 29.6%, while the male (15–64 years) participation rate (75.6%) and employment rate (69.5%) are at levels comparable to the EU. The general employment rate target is 55% in 2023. The youth unemployment rate is high (16.9% in 2014), as is the level of undeclared work (undeclared employment rate was 33.6% in 2014). The target level is under 15% in 2023. Turkey's current main problems are insecure flexibility, precarious employment and unskilled labour for female employment in this area.

A recent project started which aims to support the registered employment of women through widening home based childcare in Turkey. The project is co-funded by the Turkish Republic and European Union in order to ensure the return of working mothers to their employment after having children. According to the project, working mothers who have children between 0–2 years of age are granted financial support of EUR 300–EUR 390 monthly in case they employ a child caregiver. From the beginning of the project, approximately EUR 15 million was given to about 7,000 mothers, and 8,000 caregivers benefited from the project. The project was introduced in March 2015 in the pilot provinces of İzmir, Bursa and Antalya, and as of 1 December 2016, **Istanbul and Ankara** will be included in the scope of the project, and the level of support will be increased from EUR 320 to EUR 416 for single mothers, and mothers with disabled children. Applications are starting on 28 November 2016 and can be made through Turkish Social Security Organization.[36]

The number of beneficiary mothers is limited to 3,500 in İstanbul and 1,500 in Ankara. Mothers will be chosen from the applicants, and this is a big obstacle for the project. According to the rule of project, beneficiaries must be Turkish citizens and will be chosen among mothers with a child aged between 0–24 months who work full-time, reside in the same house as the child, earn less than the monthly minimum wage (monthly TRY 3,249 in 2016) and employ a full-time child caregiver. According to the project, to be eligible, the caregiver must be a Turkish citizen, must reside in the same province as the mother and child, must have notified at least thirty days full-time social security premium, must not to be a first degree relative of the mother or father of the child, or a third degree relative if she or he is cohabiting with the parent (grandparents are not deemed as caregiver), must be educated to at least primary level, and must be 18 years of age.

36. Social Security Organization, *Evde çocuk bakımı*, www.sgk.gov.tr and www.evdecocukbakimi .net (accessed on 18 November 2016).

[G] 2016 Progress Report of the EU for Turkey; Latest Data of Women Employment in Turkey

The 2016 Progress Report of the EU for Turkey states:

> Employment rates were 75.3% for men aged 20 to 64 and 32.5% for women aged 20–64 in 2015. The employment rate of Turkey has increased slightly from 75% for men and 31.6% for women respectively, but the female rate remains far below the national target. The general employment rate of Turkey has reached 53.9% as an EU candidate country, but the rate is found to be very low when comparing it to the EU Member States. The unemployment rate also increased further to 10.3% for those aged 15 and over and remains significantly higher for women in 2015. The youth unemployment rate rose to 18.3% in 2015, and almost a third of all young people are not in employment, education or training. Strong regional disparities also persist in employment. State subsidies of reduction in social security contributions and tax exemptions to employers for hiring additional young men or women were extended to December 2020. In the field of equality between women and men in employment and social policy, women continue to be predominantly employed in low-skilled jobs and their representation at management levels is extremely low. The gender pay gap remains problematic. Legislation on part-time work for working parents has been adopted. The lack of institutions and services to care for children, the elderly and sick people, including for long-term care, continue to hinder women's employment due to the gender bias for caring responsibilities.[37]

According to the Commission's Turkey 2016 Progress Report the Turkish economy is well advanced and can be considered a functioning market economy. Economic growth strengthened in 2015, but is slowing again in 2016 while unemployment remains relatively high. The Turkish economy has grown at an average annual rate of 3.7% over the past three years, and this was solely driven by domestic demand, particularly based on growing household consumption and public spending. Private investments remained relatively weak, while the contribution of net exports was negative. The government's Economic Reform Programme for 2016–2018 projects an overly optimistic macroeconomic scenario in which GDP growth strengthens, while unemployment, inflation and the current account deficit decrease. The effects of the failed coup on the overall economic situation are still difficult to assess. Restoring and maintaining investor confidence will in any case require the rule of law and independence of the judiciary to be respected.[38] According to the Commission's Turkey 2016 Progress Report, the number of jobs increased but is still below the growth rate of the labour force. In 2015, employment increased by 2.7%, which was less than the 3% growth rate of the labour force. Despite the low proportion of women actively looking

---

37. Republic of Turkey, Ministry of Development, *The Tenth Development Plan* 59–60 (Ankara, Republic of Turkey, Ministry of Development, 2014–2018).
38. The European Commission, *Turkey 2016 Report*, SWD(2016) 366 final Commission Staff Working Document Turkey 2016 Report Accompanying the document Communication from the Commission to the European Parliament, the Council, the European Economic and Social Committee and the Committee of the Regions 2016 Communication on EU Enlargement Policy {COM(2016) 715 final}, pp. 32–35.

for work, their unemployment rate remains significantly higher than the unemployment rate for men. In addition, about one third of women who are considered to be employed are in fact unpaid family workers in the agricultural sector. Almost a third of young people are not in employment, education or training. The efficient functioning of the labour market continued to be impeded by a lack of flexibility, for example in labour contracts, while undeclared work remained widespread. This calls for a deepening and widening of labour market reforms, which also need to be more inclusive.[39]

§11.03 COMPARISON OF THE SIXTH EUROPEAN WORKING CONDITIONS SURVEY IN 2015 AND OUR SURVEY IN 2016 RESULTS IN TURKEY

The European Working Conditions Survey (EWCS) was completed in twenty-eight European Union (EU) Member States, five candidate countries – one of which was Turkey – and two European Free Trade Association (EFTA) countries – Norway and Switzerland – in 2015. EWCS is an authoritative source of cross-national data about working conditions in these areas. A sixth survey was undertaken in 2015 covering thirty-five countries. Candidate countries including Turkey are being supported by the EU IPA. Survey sample size ranges between 1,000 and 3,300 people in each country (2,000 in Turkey) excluding some EU countries with a greater sample size. The questionnaire includes several questions about working life. EWCS's were completed in Turkey during the time period September-December 2015.[40] This chapter analyses several aspects of flexibility, and their associations with employees' work-life balance. The analyses were based on the sixth wave of the European Working Conditions Survey completed in 2015. We used data of the sixth survey, in 2015, covering the twenty-eight EU Member States, the five EU candidate countries (Albania, the former Yugoslav Republic of Macedonia, Montenegro, Serbia, and Turkey), as well as Switzerland and Norway, based on the hierarchical cluster analysis. As autonomy enables the adjustment of working time to meet obligations, needs, and activities in private life, it is expected to advance a better work–life balance.[41] The target sample size was 1,000. To reflect the larger workforce in larger countries, the target was increased to 1,200 in Poland, 1,300 in Spain, 1,400 in Italy, 1,500 in France, 1,600 in the UK and 2,000 in Germany and Turkey. The total sample size for the sixth EWCS in all 35 countries is 43,850 interviews. Finally, the **interview** format was face-to-face, at the respondents' homes.[42]

---

39. *Ibid.*, at p. 33.
40. Eurofound, *Sixth European Working Conditions Survey – Overview Report*, Publications Office of the European Union, Luxembourg (2016), pp. 12–13.
41. Timo Anttila, Tomi Oinas, Mia Tammelin & Jouko Natti, *Working-Time Regimes and Work-Life Balance in Europe*. European Sociological Review, Oxford University Press, Vol. 31(6), 713–724 (2015).
42. Eurofound, http://www.eurofound.europa.eu/print/surveys/european-working-conditions-surveys/sixth-european-working-conditions-survey-2015/ewcs-2015-methodology (accessed on 13 January 2017).

In our study, in order to make a comparable study we have chosen some questions (fourteen) from the EWCS and added five demographic questions. We wanted the respondents to spare their valuable time for us, so we selected the most important part of the questions. Our questionnaire had forty-three responses composing of 30.2% women and 69.8% men between the dates 5 December to 15 December 2016. Respondents were aged between 30–49 mostly. They all live and work in Kocaeli and Istanbul Province of Turkey.

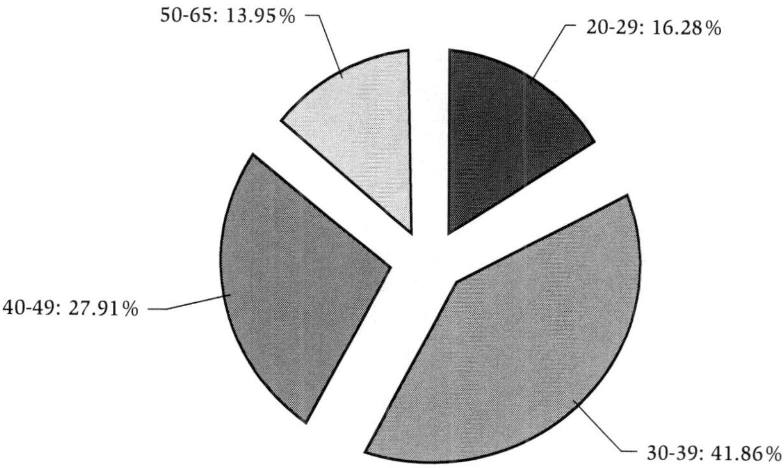

51.2% were managers, 41.9% were employees and 7.0% were senior managers. Mostly managers and employees took in part in our survey. Companies' capital structures were as following: 75.6% national and 12.2% is European MNCs. Three per cent were more than *50%* European MNCs, and lastly 4.9% were more than *50% national.*

Question 44 = 'How well do your working hours fit in with family or social commitments outside work?' For the 'Not at all well' answer, Turkey's score (7%) is higher than the European Union score (4%). For the 'Not very well' answer, Turkey's score(19%) is higher than the European Union score (15%).For the 'Very well' answer, Turkey's score (16%) is lower than the European Union score (28%).For the 'Well' answer, Turkey's score (59%) is higher than the European Union score (53%). Data is based on *Question 44* from the sixth *European Working Conditions Survey (2015).*[43] Answers to this question in our survey do not present much difference in terms of the percentages of the sample. In the EWCS we can compare Turkey and the European

43. Eurofound, http://www.eurofound.europa.eu/surveys/data-visualisation/sixth-european-working-conditions-survey2015?locale = EN&dataSource = EWCS2016&media = png&width = 740&question = y15_Q88&plot = euBars&countryGroup = linear&subset = agecat_3&subsetValue = All (accessed on 5 January 2017).

Union according to the answers of the question 'How often in the last 12 months have you worried about work when you were not working?'

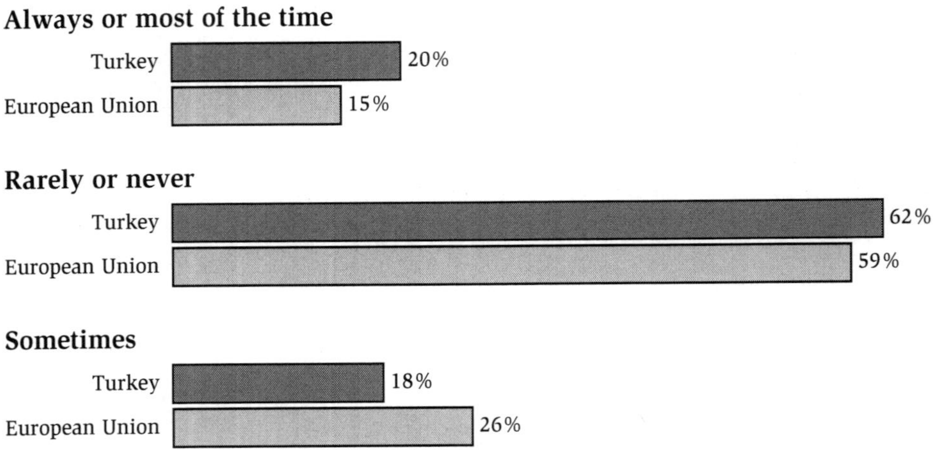

The EWCS results for the 'Always or most of the time' answer, Turkey's score (20%) is higher than the European Union score (15%). For the 'Rarely or never' answer, Turkey's score (62%) is higher than the European Union score (59%). For the 'Sometimes' answer, Turkey's score (18%) is lower than the European Union score (26%),[44] However, according to the our survey the answers are: 4.9%: always; 29.3%: mostly; 29.3%: sometimes; 26.8%: rarely; and 9.8%: never. We can interpret this result as increasing anxiety about work during non-working hours. In the EWCS we can compare Turkey and European Union according to the answers of the question 'How often in the last 12 months have you felt too tired after work to do some of the household jobs which need to be done?'

44. Data is based on question 45a from the sixth 'European Working Conditions Survey' (2015). http://www.eurofound.europa.eu/surveys/data-visualisation/sixth-european-working-conditionssurvey2015? locale=EN&dataSource=EWCS2016&media=png&width=740&question=y15_Q88&plot=euBars& countryGroup =linear&subset=agecat_3&subsetValue=All (accessed 15 September 2016).

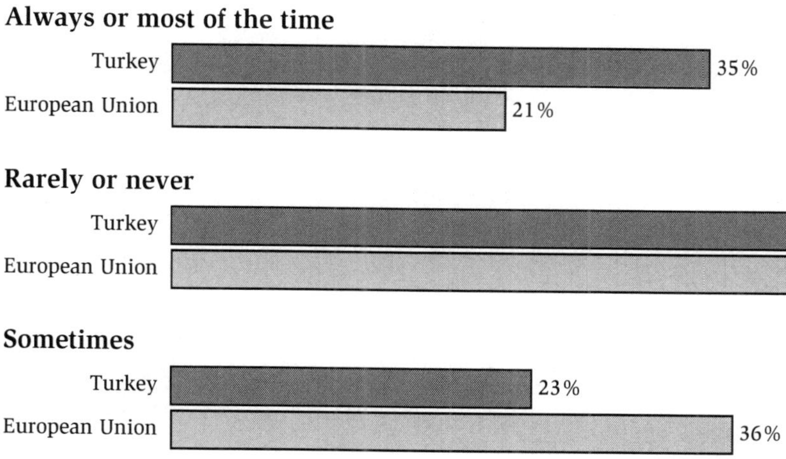

For the 'Always or most of the time' answer, Turkey's score (35%) is higher than the European Union score (21%).For the 'Rarely or never' answer, Turkey's score (42%) is equal to the European Union score (42%). For the 'Sometimes' answer, Turkey's score (23%) is lower than the European Union score (36%). Data is based on *Q* from the sixth *European Working Conditions Survey (2015)*. However according to our survey the answers are: 7.3%: always; 48.8%: mostly; 36.6%: sometimes; 4.9%: rarely; and 2.4%: never. We can interpret this result as increasing tiredness after working hours during household jobs. In the EWCS we can compare Turkey and European Union according to the answers of the question 'How often in the last 12 months have you found that your job prevented you from giving the time you wanted to your family?'

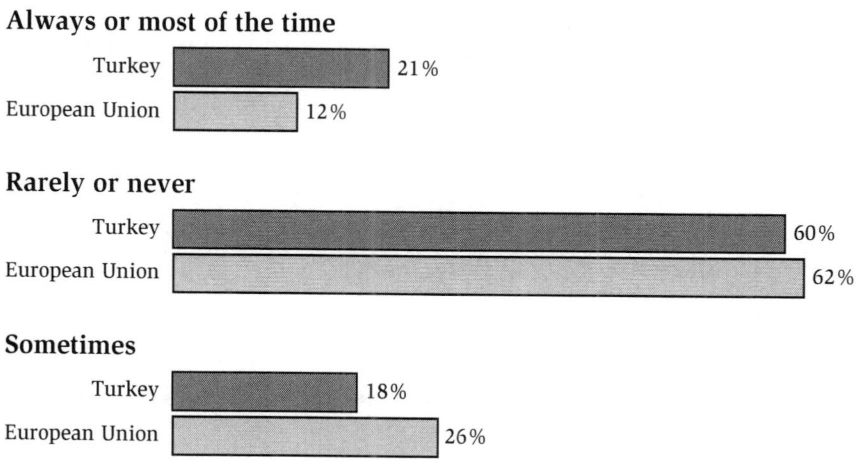

For the ‘Always or most of the time’ answer, Turkey’s score (21%) is higher than the European Union score (12%). For the ‘Rarely or never’ answer, Turkey’s score (60%) is lower than the European Union score (62%).For the ‘Sometimes’ answer, Turkey’s score (18%) is lower than the European Union score (26%). Data is based on *Question 45c* from the sixth *European Working Conditions Survey (2015)*. However, according to our survey the answers are: 4.9%: always; 36.6%: mostly; 41.5%: sometimes; 14.6%: rarely; and 2.4%: never. We can interprete this result as decreasing time spared for family because of working hours. In the EWCS we can compare Turkey and European Union according to the answers of the question ‘How often in the last 12 months have you found it difficult to concentrate on your job because of your family responsibilities?’

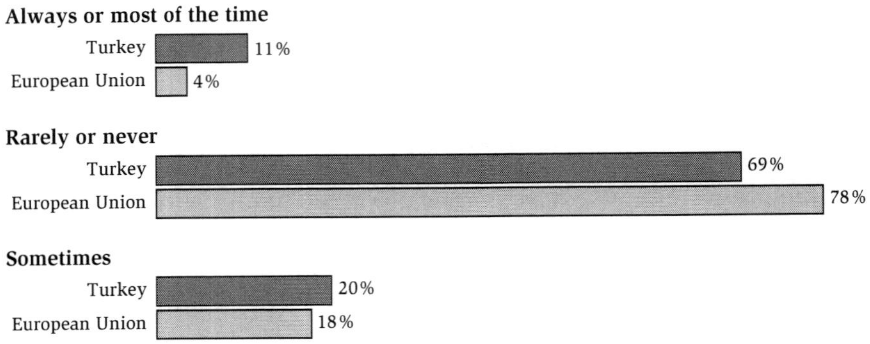

For the ‘Always or most of the time’ answer, Turkey’s score (11%) is higher than the European Union score (4%).For the ‘Rarely or never’ answer, Turkey’s score (69%) is lower than the European Union score (78%). For the ‘Sometimes’ answer, Turkey’s score (20%) is higher than the European Union score (18%). Data is based on *Question 45d* from the sixth *European Working Conditions Survey (2015)*.[45] However, according to our survey the answers are: 0.0%: always; 7.3%: mostly; 41.5%: sometimes; 34.1%: rarely; and 17.1%: never. We can interpret this result as increasing rate of disconcentration on work because of being unable to respond to the family responsibilities. In the EWCS we can compare Turkey and European Union according to the answers of the question ‘How often have you worked in your free time to meet work demands?’

45. http://www.eurofound.europa.eu/surveys/data-visualisation/sixth-european-working-conditions-survey-2015?locale=EN&dataSource=EWCS2016&media=png&width=740&question=y15_Q88&plot=euBars&countryGroup=linear&subset=agecat_3&subsetValue=All (accessed on 5 January 2017).

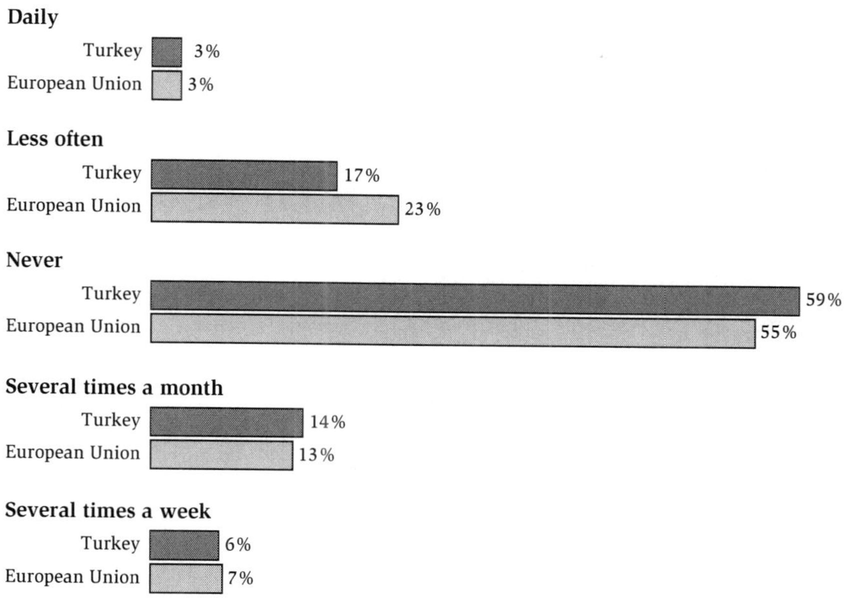

For the 'Daily' answer, Turkey's score (3%) is equal to the European Union score (3%). For the 'Less often' answer, Turkey's score (17%) is lower than the European Union score (23%). For the 'Never' answer, Turkey's score (59%) is higher than the European Union score (55%).For the 'Several times a month' answer, Turkey's score (14%) is higher than the European Union score (13%).For the 'Several times a week' answer, Turkey's score (6%) is lower than the European Union score (7%).Data is based on *Question 46* from the sixth *European Working Conditions Survey (2015)*.[46] However, according to the our survey the answers are: 2.6%: daily; 33.3%: less often; 10.3%: never; 43.6%: several times a month; and 10.3%: several times a week. We can interpret this result as increasing time spent during free times at work in the last twelve months. Q47 = 'Is it difficult to take an hour or two off to take care of personal or family matters during working hours?' For the 'Difficult' answer, Turkey's score is (26%) lower than the European Union score (34%). For the 'Easy' answer, Turkey's score (74%) is higher than the European Union score (66%). Data is based on *Question 47* from the sixth *European Working Conditions Survey (2015)*.[47] Answers to this question in our survey do not present much difference in terms of the percentages of the sample. To sum up the results of our survey in the context of EWCS 2015, we see negative signs in terms of work-life balance in Turkey. Two surveys were completed with a one-year

46. Eurofound, http://www.eurofound.europa.eu/surveys/data-visualisation/sixth-european-working-conditions-survey (accessed on 5 January 2017).
47. http://www.eurofound.europa.eu/surveys/data-visualisation/sixth-european-workingconditions-survey-2015?locale = EN&dataSource = EWCS2016&media = png&width = 740&question = y15_Q88&plot = euBars&countryGroup = linear&subset = agecat_3&subsetValue = All (accessed on 28 December 2016).

difference. We assert that in a year there had been negative facts influencing work-life balance in Turkey. In fact it is hard to make a comparison when the sample sizes and characteristics are different in two surveys, but we have tried to lessen the effect of this difficulty by choosing a sample from the most industrialized regions of Turkey. Even though our sample size is rather smaller than the EWCS sample, it represents the most industrialized part of Turkey. On the other hand, face-to-face interviews were used as the method in EWCS; we completed our survey through an online questionnaire. The EWCS could not reach some regions in Turkey both because of security reasons and highly secured upper class sites in the urban area. In the table below the characteristics of the sample of the EWCS in Turkey is discussed.

In the EU28, some 81% of workers feel there is a good fit between their work and family or social commitments. Men are more likely to say that their working hours do not fit with their private commitments, with 20% of men indicating this compared to 16% of women. Workers with care responsibilities more often report a poor fit. Employees in permanent contracts, self-employed persons and part-time workers report a good fit more often than the EU average. A small majority of workers (56%) would like to work the same hours as they do currently and 30% would like to work fewer hours. When paid and unpaid work are looked at together, women continue to work more hours than men – fifty-five hours per week, as against forty-nine for men. Men work more hours in their paying job, but women do the most unpaid working hours. Some 21% of workers state that they are too tired after work to do necessary household tasks. Some 33% of managers worry about work outside working hours – compared to just 9% of plant and machine operators. Working asocial hours or in a supervisory position makes it more likely that work–family conflict will arise. Single parents and workers in households with children experience greater difficulty. Workers in the job quality profiles differ in terms of their work–life balance and the work–family fit they experience. Workers in 'smooth running' jobs have the strongest positive association with work–life balance. In addition, these workers are shown to be the least affected by work–family conflict and have a preference for working more hours. These favourable associations could be explained by the prevalence of part-time work within this job profile and some difficulties in making ends meet. Workers with 'high flying' jobs are more likely to have a preference for working fewer hours, and work–family conflict is less prevalent than in the other profiles except for the 'smooth running' cluster. The other three job profiles show a negative association with work–family conflict -particularly the 'under pressure' cluster. Related to the poor working time quality and poor quality social environment for this profile, work–family conflicts in both directions are common. Unsurprisingly, workers in this profile are most likely to want a reduction in their working hours. People who work long hours (over forty-eight hours per week) are twice as likely as the average to want to work less. Conversely, nearly three times as many people working short hours (twenty hours per week or fewer) want to work more hours than the average.

Table 11.1 EWCS 2015 Sample Characteristics in Turkey

TURKEY

Category	*Label*	*Class Size in LFS ('000)*	*Proportion in LFS*	*Number of Respondents in EWCS*	*Unweighted Proportion in EWCS*	*Weighted Proportion in EWCS*
Gender x Age						
1	Male, 15-24	2637.4	0.102	201	0.101	0.104
2	Male, 25-39	7966.1	0.307	611	0.321	0.308
3	Male, 40-59	6599.3	0.254	511	0.256	0.256
4	Male, 60 +	1038.2	0.040	86	0.043	0.042
5	Female, 15-24	1291.8	0.050	85	0.043	0.051
6	Female, 25-39	3389.8	0.131	306	0.153	0.132
7	Female, 40-59	2613.5	0.101	151	0.076	0.098
8	Female, 60 +	394.6	0.015	14	0.007	0.010
Total		*25930.7*	*1.000*	*1995*	*1.000*	*1.000*
Occupational Groups (ICSO-08)						
isco1	Managers	1340.8	0.052	49	0.046	0.052
isco2	Professionals	2384.8	0.092	157	0.148	0.093
isco3	Technicians and associate professionals	1391.2	0.054	92	0.087	0.056
isco4	Clerical support workers	1731.3	0.067	73	0.069	0.066
isco5 + isco0	Service and sale workers + Armed forces	4753.5	0.183	263	0.248	0.186

Category	*Label*	*Class Size in LFS ('000)*	*Proportion in LFS*	*Number of Respondents in EWCS*	*Unweighted Proportion in EWCS*	*Weighted Proportion in EWCS*
isco6 + isco8	Skilled agricultural, forestry and fishery workers + Plant and machine operators and assembles	6731.7	0.260	135	0.127	0.252
isco7	Craft and related trades workers	3690.2	0.142	167	0.158	0.145
isco9	Elementary occupations	3901.9	0.151	124	0.117	0.151
Total		*25930.9*	*1.000*	*1060*	*1.000*	*1.000*
Activity of employer (NACE REV 2.0)						
a-e	Agriculture & Industry	10780.6	0.416	663	0.341	0.411
f,h,j	Construction, Transport, ICT	3257.4	0.126	230	0.118	0.127
g,i	Trade, accommodation and food services	4936.5	0.190	408	0.210	0.191
k-n,r-u	Non-public services	3276.1	0.126	333	0.171	0.127
o-q	Public services	3680.2	0.142	311	0.160	0.144
Total		*25930.8*	*1.000*	*1945*	*1.000*	*1.000*
Region						
1	Istanbul	5096	0.197	380	0.190	0.197
2	West Marmara	1262	0.049	96	0.048	0.049
3	Aegean	3766	0.145	298	0.149	0.143

Category	Label	Class Size in LFS ('000)	Proportion in LFS	Number of Respondents in EWCS	Unweighted Proportion in EWCS	Weighted Proportion in EWCS
4	East Marmara	2634	0.102	232	0.116	0.107
5	West Anatolia	2550	0.098	188	0.094	0.098
6	Mediterranean	3149	0.121	239	0.120	0.120
7	Central Anatolia	1246	0.048	134	0.067	0.053
8	West Black Sea	1646	0.063	158	0.079	0.061
9	East Black Sea	979	0.038	74	0.037	0.037
10	Northeast Anatolia	734	0.028	40	0.020	0.027
11	Middle East Anatolia	1091	0.042	28	0.014	0.039
12	Southeast Anatolia	1779	0.069	133	0.067	0.069
Total		*25932*	*1.000*	*2000*	*1.000*	*1.000*

Source: http://www.eurofound.europa.eu/sites/default/files/ef_survey/field_ef_documents/6th_ewcs_-_technical_report.pdf (accessed on 10 January 2017).

§11.04 CONCLUDING REMARKS

MNCs implement work-life balance policies to benefit their workers to reduce stress, lower the worker's tendency to leave firms, boost productivity, and increase the worker's engagement and commitment to the firm, thus reducing absenteeism and improving productivity. Also, these policies could improve the financial performance of the companies, although, empirical evidence regarding the outcomes of work-life balance policies is still scarce.[48]

The number of MNCs is increasing operating and investing in Turkey. The reason why MNCs in general investing in their Turkish operations? Labour costs are the main driver and inhibitor of MNC investment, and when we asked to same question we got the answer that labour costs are only a part of the fact. When we asked the managers what factors led companies to invest in Turkey, the main reason was the availability of a skilled workforce in the Kocaeli and İstanbul province. Although the study did not focus on SME (small- and medium-sized enterprises), this is a significant survey on work-life balance practices in MNCs in Turkey based on a representative sample. It covers both Turkish-owned and European-owned firms.

Employment life in Turkey is still far from flexible. There are still excessively rigid rules and applications far from the EU and ILO standards. There has been some progress in the area of social policy and employment, where the rate of unregistered employment has been decreasing (currently 33.6% in 2014), but important gaps remain with the EU average. Social dialogue mechanisms do not function effectively. Labour law needs to be amended and enforced for the benefit of the entire workforce. Working conditions, including health and safety at work have yet to be addressed. Anti-discrimination, social inclusion and social protection policies and practices need to be improved. Full membership to the EU remains in question due to mutual distrust and objections which have brought the membership negotiations almost to a halt.

Nowadays, the majority of Turkish people are reluctant as regards Turkey's membership to the EU, but this depends on conjuncture. The percentage of supporters of the EU-Turkey integration process was higher before the 2008 economic crisis in Turkey, also in the EU. According to the European Commission:

> Turkey is a candidate country and a strategic partner for the European Union. Its dynamic economy provides a valuable contribution to the prosperity of the European continent. Turkey's strategic location also underlines the importance of further cooperation. Active and credible accession negotiations provide the most suitable framework for exploiting the full potential of EU-Turkey relations. The accession process, which no alternative can replace, promotes EU-related reforms and provides an important basis for strengthening economic competitiveness and trade opportunities. Accession negotiations need to regain momentum. The EU should remain an important anchor for Turkey's economic and political reforms. In this regard, it is in the interest of both Turkey and the EU.

48. Consolacion Adame-Sancez, Tomas F. Gonzalez-Cruz & Clara Martinez-Fuentes, *Do Firms Implement Work-Life Balance Policies to Benefit Their Workers or Themselves?*, Journal of Business Research Vol. 69, 5519–5523 (2016).

As women become more involved in the Turkish labour market the demand for childcare and care of the elderly and disabled will also increase. When, today, more work-life balance policy in Turkey has focused on how to increase employment rates of women, families from the lower income group which cannot afford commercial care services and existing widespread home care option have become increasingly ineffective and have decreased. For that reason, women's traditional care roles are weakening in Turkey.

Due to the traditional family model that today does not exist, and the care services that have solved the problem, intergenerational solidarity is more difficult. Turkey must also ratify the ILO Conventions related to work-life balance, and it amended some labour law regulations in 2016 in accordance with the ILO and the EU norms. Further steps and amendments are needed to meet international norms and the EU Directives. Flexible working arrangements must be renewed according to the EU flexicurity approach. Childcare services insurance, old-age care insurance and family benefits insurance must be created which currently do not exist in Turkish social security system. Undeclared work must also be eliminated, so that those with family responsibilities can benefit.

The housework contribution of men is much further away from solving the current caregiver deficit. The only way to improve caregiver shortage is to extend the role of the state in this area. The current situation in working conditions also makes it difficult to establish work-life balance. Indefinite work regulations, lower wages, and increased working hours increase work-life conflict. In this case, women are forced to choose between having a child or participating in employment. The result is high employment-low birth or low income-low employment in Turkey.[49]

49. Ç. Ünlütürk-Ulutaş, 'İş ve Aile Yaşamını Uzlaştırma Politikaları: Türkiye'de Yeni Politika Arayışları', Ankara Üniversitesi SBF Dergisi, Cilt 70, No. 3, 2015, 723–750.

CHAPTER 12

Exploring the 'Boundary Control Paradox' and How to Cope with It: A Social Theoretical Perspective on Managing Work-Life Boundaries and Work-Life Balance in the Late Modern Workplace

Pascale Peters, Robert J. Blomme, Anne van Heertum & Daantje Derks

§12.01 INTRODUCTION

[A] The Scholarly Debate on the Blurring of Boundaries Between Work and Non-work

In view of enhanced global competition (and the associated work intensification felt in organisations) and the growing numbers of single parent and dual earner families combining work and informal care, both characterising life in late modernity (Giddens, 1990), an increasing number of workers have to simultaneously cope with multiple and intensified role obligations, expectations and responsibilities. A large number of these workers may struggle to achieve both work and life satisfaction (Peters, 2000). In search of work-life balance, they have to enact role taking that fits their (multiple) role identities, with a minimum of negative work-life interactions (work-life conflict) and a maximum of positive work-life interactions (work-life enhancement) (Clark, 2000; Friedman & Greenhaus, 2000; Geurts, Taris, Kompier, Dikkers, Van Hooff, & Kinnunen, 2005; Greenhaus & Beutell, 1985; Greenhaus & Powell, 2006; Grzywacz, Almeida, & McDonald, 2002). In order to achieve this, personal control over boundary crossings is important. Individuals' boundary control perceptions do not relate to personal traits, but can be viewed as workers' psychological interpretations of perceived control over one's boundary environment (Kossek, Ruderman, Braddy, & Hannum, 2012).

In response to workers' growing need to have more personal control over their work-life boundaries, the management concept of 'New Ways of Working' (NWW) has become popular in the late modern workplace (Peters, 2011). According to the Dutch National NWW Barometer 2013, for example, more and more organisations in the Netherlands have introduced HR policies and practices associated with NWW (2011: 43%, 2012: 53%, 2013: 64%) (Van der Meulen, 2014). NWW can be viewed as a workforce philosophy in which the needs of the individual worker are central and combined with an associated bundle of HRM practices (Peters, Poutsma, Van der Heijden, Bakker, & De Bruijn, 2014) that allow individual workers, enabled by new information and communication technologies (ICT), to determine how, where, when and with whom they work (Bijl, 2009; Gates, 2005). Having access to NWW practices, workers are believed to use their time more efficiently and to plan their own work hours and work locations according to their personal preferences, meanwhile taking responsibility for their own work tasks and those of their teams (Peters, Den Dulk, & Van der Lippe, 2009; Peters et al. 2014).

Although NWW generally has a positive connotation (cf., Ten Brummelhuis, Bakker, Hetland, & Keulemans, 2012), and in the Netherlands is even actively advocated and supported by the national and local governments as well as social partners (Peters, 2011), the literature presents telework, an important feature of NWW, to have some striking paradoxical outcomes (Boell, Cecez-Kecmanovic, & Campbell, 2016). On the one hand, due to the greater autonomy and flexibility associated with NWW, workers in NWW contexts have the ability to better coordinate work and non-work responsibilities, something which is shown to enhance workers' work-life balance, job satisfaction, and productivity. On the other hand, however, NWW is also shown to increase workers' work-life conflict, something which reduces their work-life balance, job satisfaction and productivity. Boell and colleagues (2016) show these inconsistent telework outcomes to result from the diversity of the nature of work undertaken by knowledge workers and the perceived differences in the suitability of different tasks for telework. That said, they argue that a deeper investigation of aspects of work (e.g., its complexity, individual experiences and the diversity of work activities and ICT enactment in work practices) is necessary for gaining a better understanding of telework and its seemingly inconsistent outcomes and implications (p. 126).

In response to this, in this contribution, we will argue that the seemingly inconsistent outcomes and implications of NWW may be attributed to how individuals' enhanced autonomy and flexibility and the permeability of the boundaries between workers' work and non-work domains (associated with NWW or telework), possibly intended as a Human Resource Management (HRM) strategy to provide workers with more 'boundary control' to better combine work and non-work obligations, may rather negate workers' perceptions of boundary control among those who are vulnerable to pressure from both supervisors and teammates to be always available for work (cf. Derks, Duin, Tims, & Bakker, 2015), also during hours that were traditionally regarded as off-work hours (such as the weekend), a development that is enabled by NWW. We suggest that this explanation reflects what we will refer to as the *'boundary control paradox'* according to which NWW practices such as enhanced autonomy and flexibility of individual workers foster the emergence of new 'availability norms and behaviours' that may rather reduce individuals' perceived boundary control. This may especially be the case when autonomy and flexibility run parallel with other NWW practices such as output management and teamwork that shift the responsibilities for the management of work activities to individual workers and their teams (Peters et al. 2009; Peters et al. 2014). As a consequence of the loss of perceived boundary control, workers may allow work to enter the non-work domain more frequently, possibly leading to more work demands and associated strain spilling over from the work domain into the non-work domain, a phenomenon which will be experienced by workers as 'work-life conflict' coming at the expense of workers' work-life balance, job satisfaction and productivity (Rothbard, Philips, & Dumus, 2005; Ter Hoeven, Van Zoonen, & Fonner, 2016).

[B] The Societal Debate on Blurring of Boundaries Between Work and Non-work

Over the past decade, the above-described workplace and household trends and their potential to disrupt the work-life balance, job satisfaction and productivity of workers and their families have (re)kindled the societal debate on both the need and the effectiveness of nations' and organisations' regulations regarding workers' availability for paid work outside traditional office hours. Well-known examples are the policies introduced by the German companies Volkswagen, BMW and Daimler, who have implemented explicit regulations regarding workers' e-mail communication during off-work hours to prevent (unwanted) interruptions from work activities in the non-work domain. Recently, a Dutch newspaper article (NRC-Handelsblad, Friday 6 January 2017, p. E3) also debated the new French labour regulation, introduced on 1 January 2017, to give workers in organisations employing more than fifty workers the right to disconnect from the paid work domain ('le droit à la déconnexion') and to even ignore work-related e-mails sent outside formal working hours in order to combat negative work outcomes such as work-life imbalances. According to the newspaper article, organisations in France will not be sanctioned directly if they fail to comply with this new regulation, but workers in these organisations who suffer from work-related stress and burn-out are believed to have a stronger position in court, where their employers may be held responsible for the workers' lack of work-life balance and well-being.

Some scholarly experts interviewed in the newspaper article stated that this type of regulation can be viewed as a positive development, since it can pressure organisations to introduce sustainable HRM policies and practices geared at restoring individual workers' boundary control and allowing them to segment the work and non-work domains in order to prevent work-life conflict. Other experts in the newspaper article, however, considered the regulation too paternalistic and argued that this type of policy intervention is out-dated in view of the contemporary societal transition from an industrial or modern model (Giddens, 1990) (characterised by standardised working hours, for most people relating to the nine-to-five office hours and weekends-off pattern) to a post-industrial or late modern model (*ibid.*) in which both individuals and organisations are in need of more flexibility regarding when and where to work in a global 24/7 economy.

In line with our argumentation presented in this contribution, the newspaper article (NRC-Handelsblad, Friday 6 January 2017, p. E3) suggested that organisational culture rather than formal labour market or organisational policies can, in the final analysis, actually reverse the trend towards work activities interrupting time slots that were traditionally, and maybe also according to the preferences of many workers and their families, preserved for non-work activities.

[C] Our Contribution to the Debates on the Blurring of Boundaries Between Work and Non-work

In this chapter, we hope to contribute in several ways to the contemporary scholarly and societal debates on work-life balance in post-industrial or late modern workplaces in general, and on the blurring of boundaries between work and non-work in particular.

First, we will present a brief historical backdrop of the modernisation process (globalisation and individualisation) (Giddens, 1990) that has led to what we refer to as the boundary control paradox, as introduced above. We shall do this by showing how reflexive modes of (boundary) control in the labour market and household domains have developed in the course of the de-traditionalisation of work-family positions as they apply to many Western countries (cf. Giddens, 1990). This account, a shortened and slightly adapted version of Chapter 3 in Peters (2000), will be sketchy in many parts; this was done on purpose as its main goal was to gain a better understanding of the emergence of NWW and the boundary control paradox.

Second, in order to familiarise the reader with how the blurring of boundaries between work and non-work has been dealt with in the scholarly work-life literature, we will present an overview of the key concepts used in the increasingly popular Boundary Theory (Ashfort, Kreiner, & Fugate, 2000; Kossek et al. 2012; Kreiner, 2006; Kreiner, Hollensbe, & Sheep, 2009; Nippert-Eng, 2008). This overview will be concluded by presenting preliminary results of an empirical survey study building on Boundary Theory that the authors of this chapter conducted among 162 knowledge workers in two subsidiaries of a large multinational company in the Netherlands and Belgium that have implemented NWW in order to enhance their workers' work-life balance.

Finally, we will conclude our chapter with a discussion on how sustainable HRM (De Prins, De Vos, Van Beirendonck, & Segers, 2015; Ehnert, 2014) can try to actively cope with the boundary control paradox felt by individual workers at the shop floor level, which also implies the use of a 'paradox lens' that is based on a number of seminal writings in organisation studies (cf. Jarzabkoswki, Lê, & Van de Ven, 2013; Lewis, 2000; Smith & Lewis, 2011) and that is increasingly used in HRM studies as well

(Peters & Lam, 2000; Putnam, Myers, & Gailliard, 2014). We feel that this paradox lens allows us to better grasp the complexities surrounding the boundary control debates and to formulate important implications – not only for future research, but also for labour market and organisational policies – in order to further these debates on whether control over work-life boundaries, particularly in the context of NWW, needs to be and in fact can be regulated in such a way that workers, organisations and society at large are able to truly reap the benefits of NWW, both in the shorter and in the longer term.

§12.02 HISTORICAL BACKGROUND OF THE BOUNDARY CONTROL PARADOX

[A] Control in the Modern Workplace

What is certain from history is that 'the process of "social control"– the process of the capitalist system seeking to ensure that there is a well-disciplined workforce available' (Veal, 1987, p. 66) has been at the basis of a constant struggle between the employing classes and the workers, the former attempting to impose order and discipline and the latter attempting to maintain freedoms (*ibid.*, p. 67). In order to be kept in check, productive workers were subjected to close managerial control. With the introduction of the labour contract and on-going industrialisation, time had become money. Time-oriented manufacture was introduced to enhance productivity, and for production to be mechanized it was necessary to enlarge its scale and to extend markets (Wallerstein, 1983). The worker now became a 'small cog in a large machine'. The new production methods were based on routinisation of tasks, a minute division of labour and operative duties involving only the most rudimentary levels of discretion, judgments and skills (Brown & Scase, 1991).

In the early post-war period, the model that we now call the traditional 'breadwinner model' had found its way into the statutes and regulations of the expanding welfare state (Tijdens, 1998), with the individual couple forming the basis of labour market and social security policy and, consequently, the gender bias part and parcel of labour market regulations, social law, tax systems, school system and time-spatial planning, to name but a few domains. Throughout industrial modernity, it was common for women and men to live in highly segregated role relationships, with women's time being seen as the economy's buffer or time reservoir (Beck, 1992; Elchardus, 1996).

The success of the breadwinner model was helped by the top-ranking productivity gains witnessed during the twenty-five years or so following the war. Over that period, union power had grown as well, and working time regulation had become based on a collectively bargained social democratic Keynesian compromise (Hunnicutt, 1988). The overall picture was that of employees gaining more rights through nationwide and industry-wide bargaining, working rigid schedules and operating under close supervision in a tightly structured and hierarchical workplace with persistent male dominance; in spite of incipient changes, men were largely the sole breadwinners and women were relegated to hearth and home.

The oil crisis of the 1970s (1973 and 1979) deeply affected post-war economic and socio-political life in the Western world, as did the later collapse of the Socialist empire (Beck, 1994; Hobsbawm, 1995). Automation and robotisation had already pushed up industrial redundancies. Cheap labour in the Third World, and the absence of effective trade unions there, pulled more mass production away from Western markets. This was aggravated by the high labour costs associated with the social benefits that European workers had gained not long before (Brown & Scase, 1991). In short, the 1970s saw the advent of a new global division of labour, a characteristic of industrialism (Giddens, 1990).

[B] Control in the Late Modern Workplace

After the 1980s, the labour scene went through a period of deep transformation. The enhanced flexibilisation of labour included a general reduction of the working week, whilst flexible labour contracts and part-time work gradually gained ground. The latter development especially allowed women to enter the labour market in larger numbers, which in turn led to an increase of dual earner households. Besides enriching their lives, women's paid work also improved their household budget. Representing a major change, the period and its aftermath saw bargaining for collective agreements go back to a decentralised level whilst provisions in law and regulations extended the scope for more individualised schedules and regimens. The needs of employers and employees alike called for greater differentiation in terms and conditions for labour participation. Employers and unions unanimously began to underscore the importance of responsible and self-reliant employees being given a greater say in the timing of their work, particularly in the face of global competition.

The post-war supply economy was succeeded by a consumer economy in which market niches for low-volume quality goods offered high profit margins to both manufacturers and distributors (Brown & Scase, 1991). World markets became more uncertain, competitive pressures more accurate and profit margins less predictable. In addition, shorter product cycles made constant innovation and trade with new products and services necessary in order to survive (*ibid.*). The key requisite for these developments was, of course, wholesale computerisation. Without advanced ICT, there could never have been any such thing as fast market responses on a global scale involving innovation and flexible designing, customised or small-batch production and swift logistics, all the while maintaining product reliability, quality control and sustainable cost.

To enhance their agility and spread the risk of failure from the vicissitudes of the market and business cycles, large organisations began to concentrate on their core business, farming out the functions that might not pull their weight all the way or encumber the corporation in times of hardship. They also split up their operations into smaller accountable units or units with corporate status. This tended to make hierarchies a lot flatter, and it made empowerment and commitment throughout their structure more obvious propositions (Maxwell, 1997). It also made it more difficult for employees to find a match between personal capabilities and long-term career prospects within the same firm (Elchardus, 1991). As a matter of fact, employers became less inclined to offer permanent contracts, and also employees became less prepared to defer gratification in exchange for promises of advancement or life-time employment.

The requirements of faster reactions to a globalising market set the trend for a new type of employee to become task oriented rather than time oriented, with a greater span of control and accountability (Reich, 1992). Teamwork is critical for this type of worker, who is typically highly skilled and more committed to corporate goals, with gratitude deriving not only from income, but also from personal fulfilment in a sociable setting into which home-life and leisure elements spill over. This makes for a type of control by positive reinforcement and for any coercive intervention to be diffuse and mediated.

In late modern times, social control over time in households changed, too. Women developed a new market attitude, based on a new identity. Higher educational levels made it natural for women to use their qualifications and pursue a career. Outside jobs became more attractive, with women's wages not merely thought of as supplementing male income. Wage freezes and new consumerism, reflected in an urge for more modern personal lifestyles, made it increasingly desirable, if not necessary, for households to gain a dual income. Employers became more adaptive to the desire for convenient schedules towards multiple roles. At the level of legislation, the individual rather than the married couple became the basic unit for taxation, the labour market and social security systems. More women no longer wanted a full and life-long dependence on spousal income, and many younger career women insisted on their spouses taking their share in unpaid work. More males placed a higher value on an affective relationship with their children and were prepared to sacrifice part of their leisure time for it. Despite this, however, the unequal division of work (paid and unpaid) lasted long.

The workplace and household developments sketched above underline the inadequacy of the traditional work/leisure dichotomy. De-traditionalisation of rules and relations of control made the temporal and spatial location of time use (and the division of work across genders) a matter of negotiation, with all parties involved reflexively contributing to the continuity and change in work-family positions. On the whole, the boundaries between work and home became more flexible and permeable, both temporally and spatially, with the development of information and telecommunication technology, teleworking and flexible working systems such as NWW as well as through less personal workplace relations and greater personal commitment. The account presented above shows that in late modern life, multiple bargaining tables are important now that the temporal and spatial locations of work and non-work may overlap, which implies that employees, employers, line managers, colleagues, clients and of course spouses and other parties may all have an influence on the rules and relations of control, also over work-life boundaries.

§12.03 BOUNDARY THEORY AND ITS KEY CONCEPTS

[A] Constructing Boundaries Between the Work and Non-Work Domains

In the post-modern scholarly work-life debate, Boundary Theory has functioned as the foundational theory in understanding how individuals actively manage (the boundaries between) their work and private domains (Ashfort et al. 2000; Chesley, 2005; Kossek, Noe, & DeMar, 1999; Kreiner, 2006; Nippert-Eng, 2008). Boundary Theory investigates how individuals construct their own psychological, physical and temporal boundaries around their work and non-work domains and roles to classify and simplify their daily lives (Ashfort et al. 2000; Nippert-Eng, 1996). As individuals are increasingly exposed to significant role responsibilities from both the work and non-work domains, both the management and the classification of someone's environment becomes more complicated (Clark, 2000). Especially with the emergence of NWW, the physical and temporal locations of work and non-work activities have become less fixed than what used to be the case in the industrial or modern era in which working from nine to five during five days per week and having weekends off had become the norm and standard work pattern for most workers. At present, however, enhanced work autonomy and flexible work practices, both of which characterise NWW (Peters et al. 2014), have enabled boundaries between the work and non-work domains to become blurred.

[B] Flexibility and Permeability of Work and Non-Work Boundaries

Individuals can be taken to maintain, construct and negotiate their work and private roles in different ways (Ashfort et al. 2000; Duxbury, Higgings, Smart, & Stevenson, 2014; Kossek et al. 1999; Kossek et al. 2012). Through taking active steps, they may manage their role transitions, i.e., the way in which they switch, psychologically and/or physically, between their different role responsibilities (Duxbury et al. 2014). Ashfort et al. (2000) describe two concepts that affect the process of role transitions: (1) the flexibility; and (2) the permeability of a role boundary. Flexibility refers to roles which can be enacted on various physical and temporal locations. This refers to the 'when and where' of workers' role enactment (Sundaramurthy & Kreiner, 2008). Permeability refers to roles which are enacted during the execution of another role; hence, it refers to how roles are psychologically and/or behaviourally located *in other roles*. This refers to the 'what' of a role boundary, i.e., the extent to which a role can spill over into another role (*ibid.*).

[C] Managing Work-Life Interruptions

In daily life, employees are increasingly exposed to simultaneous work and private role responsibilities and expectations. Consequently, they have to engage in boundary cross-role interruption behaviours. This type of behaviour refers to the degree to which individuals allow interruptions from one role into another (Kossek et al. 2012). Boundary cross-role interruptions can occur in two directions. On the one hand, we can distinguish *work-private interruptions*, which indicate how often an employee works on his or her work-related tasks outside of the 'planned' work hours. Some of these interruptions may be planned; others may be unpredicted. On the other hand, we can distinguish *'private-work interruptions'*, which indicate how often a worker spends time on private demands during 'planned' work hours. Also the predictability of these interruptions may vary (Ter Hoeven et al. 2016).

[D] Work-Life Role Identities

The direction in which interruptions are allowed, i.e., how an individual worker manages and determines a boundary management strategy either to avoid or to stimulate role interruptions, may depend on someone's role identity (Kossek et al. 2012). Here, role identity refers to the social construction of someone's identity in a role, consisting of core (important) and non-core (less important) aspects of the self (Ashfort et al. 2000; Kossek & Lautsch, 2012). Individuals with a stronger work identity (meaning that when this is more dominant, one is more work-centric) will give higher priority to their work role-related responsibilities than individuals with a private identity (meaning that when this is more dominant, one is more private-centric) (Kossek et al. 2012). Someone's role identity may determine the direction(s) into which an individual allows interruptions of work role-related activities in a non-work related activity, or *vice versa* (Kossek et al. 2012). In this contribution, the primary focus is on the frequency of work interruptions in private activities, since this type of interruption is also central in the societal debate on the blurring of boundaries between the work and non-work domains.

[E] Preferred and Enacted Boundary Management Strategies

Boundary Theory acknowledges that individuals differ in terms of their *preferred* boundary management strategies on a continuum from preferring weak boundaries, i.e., highly integrated roles, to preferring stronger boundaries between roles, i.e., highly segmented roles (Kossek et al. 2012; Kreiner et al. 2009). When individuals prefer more permeable boundaries, they prefer a world in which their work and private roles are more *integrated*. For example, workers can prefer to be available for telephone calls with colleagues during weekends. Conversely, a preference for impermeable boundaries implies that workers prefer a world in which the work and private domains are more separated or segregated. For example, workers can prefer not to answer work-related e-mails during time off from work.

In daily practice, however, individuals' preferred boundary management styles can deviate from their actual boundary management styles. The actual demarcations that workers create or experience between their core life domains can be referred to as their 'enacted boundary management strategy' (Ammons, 2013, p. 50). Workers' enacted boundary strategies can also vary on a continuum from managing to keep weak boundaries, characterised by highly integrated roles, to managing to keep stronger boundaries, characterised by highly segmented roles (Clark, 2000; Kossek et al. 2012; Kreiner et al. 2009). For example, enacted integration occurs when workers telephone with colleagues about work-related matters during their private time. Segmentation occurs, for example, when workers do not answer e-mails after their daily work hours. As enacted boundary strategies vary on this continuum, high segmentation indicates low integration, and *vice versa*.

Since people vary in their preferences for integration or segmentation, both boundary management styles can be seen as 'rational' ways to handle different role responsibilities. Generally speaking, the primary goal of individuals is choosing that particular boundary management strategy that minimises problems in achieving different role obligations (Rothbard et al. 2005). As individuals can be seen as active builders in determining their own role boundaries (Clark, 2000; Nippert-Eng, 1996), it is generally assumed that they will enact their preferred boundary management style.

[F] Boundary Management Incongruence

In more traditional workplaces, workplace flexibility and permeability between work and non-work was generally low, which simply limited most workers' integration of work and non-work activities. However, the introduction of new ICT such as the 'work mobile phone' weakened the traditional boundaries between the work and private domains and allowed greater degrees of integration for those who would prefer this. According to the Person-Environmental (P-E) Fit Theory (Kristof, 1996), it is important that employees' preferences can be aligned within their environmental conditions, as a higher degree of fit fosters more positive work and private outcomes such as job satisfaction and well-being (Dawis & Lofquist, 1984; Kreiner, 2006). Fit occurs when the workplace provides conditions (such as flexibility and permeability) in which individuals are able to enact their preferred levels of integration or segmentation. Nevertheless, when the conditions of the workplace do not 'supply' the resources that enable workers to enact their preferred boundary management strategy, a mismatch or discrepancy occurs (Kreiner, 2006). Kreiner and colleagues (2009) refer to this (mis)fit as 'boundary management (in)congruence'. The larger the difference between enacted and preferred boundary management strategies becomes, the more incongruence will develop.

[G] Boundary Control

Besides boundary management preferences, also the conditions of the workers' environment (Chen, Powell, & Greenhaus, 2009; Kristof, 1996) can influence the extent to which workers enact a certain degree of integration or segmentation (Chen et al. 2009). NWW work environments can enhance the flexibility and permeability of workers' boundaries, which determine whether or not workers' work and non-work roles can actually be integrated. However, even though NWW in principle enables both the integration and segmentation of work and non-work activities, in practice, workers might not be able to realise their preferred boundary management style as this may depend on their perceptions of the degree of 'boundary control'. That is, the enacted boundary management style is determined by the degree to which individual workers perceive that they have control over managing their own boundaries between work and non-work (Kossek et al. 2012), i.e., the extent to which they believe that they can influence the 'timing, frequency, and direction of boundary crossings to fit their identities and multiple role demands' (*ibid.*, 115). When true boundary control is lacking, it is not possible for individuals to (fully) live up to their preferred boundary management styles (Ammons, 2013; Ashfort et al. 2000; Kreiner et al. 2009).

[H] Availability Culture: Relevant Others' Norms and Behaviours

Misfit or incongruence may occur when the workplace is characterised by conditions that represent (perhaps team-related) work demands that pressure workers to enact an integration strategy, possibly to a degree that they do not prefer. Hence, the mere possibility of (virtual) connectivity can force workers into enacting integration (Leonardi et al. 2010), regardless of their own boundary management preferences. One of the factors underlying misfit may be organisational culture (Ashfort et al. 2000), which has become increasingly important in NWW contexts where traditional office hours have lost their meaning and norms and values guide workers' time allocation and work behaviours. In fact, an 'always available' culture can be viewed as one of the key characteristic of work in today's society.

The term 'perceived availability pressures' refers to the degree to which workers experience their supervisors and colleagues to expect them to be available for work during off-work hours. In addition to these norms, availability pressures may also arise from relevant others' availability behaviours, for example when the workers' supervisors or colleagues send or respond to work-related messages outside formal working hours (Derks et al. 2015). Of course, besides availability pressures from within the organisation, also customers or household members can impose certain availability pressures on employees. Some customers, for example, may expect and assume that workers are constantly available (Kreiner et al. 2009).

[I] The Boundary Control Paradox

In this contribution, we argue that an availability culture (perceived availability norms and behaviours) can negate workers' boundary control, in turn impacting their enacted boundary management behaviours and possibly enhancing work-life conflict. The development of ICT allows people to contact others at any time and any place, which pressures workers to be permanently available for work activities. This may particularly be the case in the context of NWW, where workers are expected to take more responsibility for the management of their own and their team's work (Peters et al. 2009; Peters et al. 2014). In other words, due to the new technologies, individuals may not only be enabled to behave more autonomously and flexibly and to send messages to others, but they may also expect others – or be expected by others – to reciprocate immediately (Derks et al. 2015). This creates new 'availability' norms which are rather informally shared by actors inside and outside organisations and which may influence the degree to which workers feel pressured to be available after work hours (Derks et al. 2015; Piszczek & Berg, 2014). Generally speaking, individuals are believed to comply with group norms. They may have internalised and/or adapted to the norms and behaviours of important others in the social environment that they want to be part of (supervisors and colleagues who share work-related tasks, the same workforce and/or profession) (Bandura, 1977; Derks et al. 2015). Particularly supervisors may have an important authority role, and workers tend to live up to expectations (norms) of these higher-placed persons. In addition, workers may tend to imitate the behaviours of important others (Derks et al. 2015; Manz & Sims, 1981), perhaps specifically in the case of teamwork.

In view of the growing importance of teamwork in the late modern workplace, teammates may pressure individuals to work over the weekend. Their work behaviours may in turn be copied by other teammates, and so forth, ultimately leading to what we called the boundary control paradox that workers have to cope with. Although NWW presents individual workers with more individual control over how to manage their work-life boundaries, the perception of having actual boundary control may be negated by the perceived norms and behaviours of relevant others. Since all individual workers, and not just one particular worker, in the organisation or team may be given a greater say over when, where and with whom to work, paradoxical tensions stemming from the need to simultaneously comply to team needs and workers' personal needs can limit the individual workers' perception of boundary control.

Workers' responses to boundary control-related tensions determine their enacted boundary management strategies and possibly their experience of work-life conflict. For example, when one colleague starts e-mailing on a Sunday morning, it is logical in view of constant connectivity and workers' team responsibilities that others will follow this example, as they want to confirm social group norms and behaviours. Generally, availability expectations held by both supervisors and colleagues have a major impact on workers' work-related behaviours. Workers may feel that they need to respond to these availability expectations, for example by answering the requests of others immediately. Consequently, they may perceive to have little boundary control and allow interruptions of work in the non-work domain (Ashfort et al. 2000, 484; Derks et al. 2015; Morris & Venkatesh, 2000), even when this may not be in line with their boundary management preferences. Kreiner et al. (2009) expect that employees working in organisations which demand them to be available for work-related questions outside formal working hours will ultimately also experience more work-home conflict (cf. Derks et al. 2015).

[J] Preliminary Insights from an Empirical Case Study

As work-life scholars, the authors of this contribution are also particularly interested in the impact of (workers' perceptions of) organisations' availability culture on workers' perceived boundary control, their enacted boundary management strategies and the degree of work-life conflict. Therefore, we conducted a cross-sectional study in a case organisation in the building sector, with roughly 44,900 employees at 2,300 locations in more than 40 countries in Western and Northern Europe, Eastern Europe-Central Asia, North America, Asia-Pacific and the Africa-Mediterranean Basin. The case organisation's ambition was to provide customers with superior-quality and innovative products at competitive prices, to open up prospects for its shareholders and to offer all its workers attractive jobs. The initial analyses presented in this chapter were based on data collected among workers in subsidiaries in the Netherlands (employing 584 workers) and Belgium (employing 1,413 workers). The organisation's HR philosophy is reflected in sustainable business practices by respecting the environment and simultaneously trying to make their employees feel satisfied and appreciated. Consequently, the company was certified as a 'Top Employer'.

In May 2015, we gathered data by distributing a digital questionnaire among 224 knowledge workers in the organisation; a large majority of these had formal access to NWW practices designed to meet workers' changing work-life needs, which enhanced their work-life balance. These NWW practices included flexible working, homeworking and flexible network systems. Workers appreciated the NWW conditions, and resistance among the organisation's knowledge workers was low. The survey was carried out anonymously, took approximately 15–20 minutes, and all respondents participated on a voluntary basis. After a reminder had been sent, the final response rate was 72.77%. In total, 163 respondents participated in the study, all with permanent and mostly full-time contracts with the organisation. Of these respondents, 95 worked in the Netherlands and 67 in Belgium. The sample consisted of 53 women and 109 men. Average tenure was 14.67 (SD = 10.43) years, ranging from a few months to 39 years.

In our empirical study, a particular focus lay on the role of the case organisation's availability culture [both normative availability expectations, the degree to which employees perceive normative pressures from their supervisor and colleagues to be available after working hours, and the perceived behavioural availability aspects of important others within the organisation, the degree to which employees perceive that their supervisor and colleagues are available for work-related issues after working hours (Derks et al. 2015)] in workers' perceived 'boundary control' [whether they are able to control the boundaries between the work and non-work domains (Kossek et al. 2012)] and how this impacts their 'enacted boundary management strategy' [i.e., their actual integration behaviour implying more frequent interruptions from work in the non-work domain (Kossek et al. 2012)] and, ultimately, their work-life conflict [the experience of negative interactions between the work and non-work domains resulting from time pressures and strain spilling over from the work domain into the home domain (Geurts et al. 2005)]. Our preliminary results revealed that both supervisors' and colleagues' availability norms and behaviours can exercise pressures on workers' work-life conflict. However, the underlying explanatory paths proved to be different.

Strikingly, *supervisors' availability behaviours* did not impact any of the key variables in our model, but their *availability norms as perceived by workers* did have an impact. Although the normative pressures resulting from workers' perceptions of their supervisors' availability norms did not directly affect workers' perceived boundary control, these affected workers' actual integration behaviours to be more frequent. This implies that workers vulnerable to their supervisors' norms allowed work activities to interrupt the non-work domain more frequently when they thought that their managers expected this from them. Since workers' actual integration behaviours also related to higher levels of work-life conflict, supervisors' availability norms indirectly affected workers' perceived work-life conflict, i.e., time pressures due to work demands and work-related strain more frequently spilled over from the work domain into the home domain. In addition to that, even when workers did not enact greater integration of work and non-work activities, they experienced more work-life conflict when they expected their supervisor to have higher availability norms.

A different influence was found regarding workers' perceptions of the norms and behaviours of their colleagues. In this case, workers' *perceptions of their colleagues' norms* did not play a significant role. However, it was rather the *availability behaviours of their colleagues* that impacted workers' experience of boundary control, their enacted integration style and also, albeit indirectly, namely through their perceived boundary control and enacted integration, their experience of work-life conflict. When workers perceived that their colleagues were available after working hours (e.g., online in the evenings or during weekends), they experienced lower control over their own work-life boundaries and enacted more integration themselves, which in turn indirectly enhanced work-life conflict. However, colleagues' work behaviours after office hours did not directly affect the individual workers' work-life conflict.

These preliminary outcomes, revealing different effects of availability norms and behaviours of supervisors and colleagues, may be explained by the higher position in the organisational hierarchy that supervisors, possibly also in NWW context, have. Obviously, workers were not directly influenced by the availability norms they thought their colleagues had. Conversely, supervisors' availability behaviours were not found to have an impact on workers' perceptions of their own boundary control, enacted work-life integration and work-life balance; rather, a lower level of perceived boundary control, enacted integration and, indirectly, work-life balance could be explained by the flexible work behaviours of colleagues. Possibly, in the context of NWW, workers identify less with the availability behaviours of their supervisors, as the distance between individual workers and their leaders may be larger than between them and their colleagues (teammates). Moreover, supervisors may be viewed to have different tasks which may need to be done over the weekend without directly impacting individual workers' work behaviour. However, when colleagues are perceived to be working over the weekend and communicate with individual workers, the latter may identify with the needs of their colleagues, or they may have requested the information sent by their colleagues themselves. In line with our boundary control paradox, particularly in contexts where teamwork and shared leadership have been introduced, thus increasing the responsibilities of individual workers and their teammates, individual workers' perceptions of personal control over their work-life boundaries may be negated.

§12.04 CONCLUSION AND DISCUSSION

[A] Exploring the Boundary Control Paradox and How to Cope with It

In comparison with the traditional, industrial or modern workplace, the post-industrial or late modern workplace can be characterised by a loss of traditional 'checks and balances' regarding the number and the temporal and physical locations of working hours (Peters, 2000). In theory, in a 24/7 economy, all hours of the day and week can be allocated to work (or to non-work). With regard to work efforts, the sky has become the limit. Especially in view of today's fiercer labour market competition in global markets, workers' long hours, permanent availability and their swifter responses to (market and work) demands can be viewed as a competitive advantage for organisations, teams and individual workers (Peters & Van der Lippe, 2007). In fact, in the final analysis, the anticipated productivity gains associated with flexible working and permeable boundaries characterising NWW have been shown to play a major role in the decisions of many organisations that have introduced this new work style (Peters & Batenburg, 2015). For these organisations, NWW is expected to bring several organisational benefits, such as enhanced profitability, organisational commitment, enhanced collaboration, knowledge sharing, innovative employee behaviour and increased employee and customer satisfaction (cf. Baane, Houtkamp, & Knotter, 2010), probably underlying the boundary control paradox experienced at the shop floor level.

In this contribution, we introduced the boundary control paradox in late modern workplaces and argued that workers who are vulnerable to the availability pressures (norms and behaviours exercised by supervisors and colleagues) may find themselves experiencing lower degrees of boundary control (perhaps rather than higher degrees of boundary control), fostering the enactment of work-life integration (i.e., frequent interruptions of work in private life domains), a process which, in turn, has the potential to enhance workers' experience of work-life conflict. And even when workers experience control over their work-life boundaries, we found that they more often enact integration as a boundary management strategy when they experience that they need to be available for work after formal working hours. Moreover, our preliminary analyses also showed that the availability culture can also directly impact workers' experience of work-life conflict. That is, besides the time that is taken up by integrating work into the non-work domain and that comes at the expense of time available for non-work activities (such as family, leisure and recreation), the pressures from relevant others in the workers' work domains (particular the supervisors in our case) can also cause strain which spills over into the non-work domain, a development which may be reflected in higher levels of work-life conflict.

[B] Sustainability Policies and Practices

In this concluding section, we will discuss how organisations (and other labour market stakeholders) may need to respond to this boundary management paradox in ever more flexible labour markets through the development of what is termed sustainable

HRM policies and practices (De Prins et al. 2015; Ehnert, 2014). The scholarly and societal debates briefly presented in the Introduction stress the importance for nations and organisations to develop policies that can address the boundary control paradox in late modern workplaces. In the emerging field of Sustainable HRM, in line with the triple bottom line of Corporate Social Responsibility ("Planet, People Profit") applied to SHRM in the ROC (respect, openness and continuity) model (De Lange & Koppens, 2007), sustainability HRM policies are viewed as 'a specific form of personnel management that is explicitly linked with the environment of the organisation, which is focused on respect for the human workforce and in which the interests of the employer, the workers and societal interests are *balanced* with each other' (De Prins et al. 2015, p. 319). De Prins and colleagues' notion of sustainable HRM underlines the need for organisational policies to pay greater attention to three factors: *respect* for internal and external stakeholders (e.g., by paying attention to workers' work-life balance and their well-being); *openness* or environmental awareness, including an outside-in and inside-out perspective on HRM (e.g., by paying attention not only to competition in the labour market but also to workers' obligations outside work and by acting upon the societal plea to take work-life balance and health issues into account); and finally *continuity* or a long-term approach to organisations' and individual workers' economic and societal sustainability (e.g., with respect to the economic and social performance of the organisation and individual workers by paying attention to performance, job satisfaction, work-life balance and well-being).

[C] Active Responses to Paradoxical Pressures

Sustainable HRM scholars (cf. Ehnert, 2014) argue that too little has so far been done to improve the sustainability and the quality of working life in the late modern workplace. In line with Ehnert, however, we argue that an active response to the reported boundary control paradox may prevent the paradoxical outcomes regarding workers' work-life balance, job satisfaction and productivity that were researched by Boell and colleagues (2016). In Ehnert's list of criteria for sustainable HRM, organisations' and workers' awareness and ability to actively cope with the paradoxical tensions experienced by organisations and individual workers, possibly explaining the reported paradoxical outcomes, can be viewed as one of the core issues of sustainable HRM (Ehnert, 2014).

In the paradox literature, paradoxical *tensions* underlying paradoxes (experienced by actors at multiple organisational levels) are defined as 'contradictory yet interrelated elements of organisation that seem logical in isolation but inconsistent and oppositional in conjunction and yet persistent over time' (Jarzabkoswki et al. 2013, p. 245; Lewis, 2000). Jarzabkowski and colleagues (2013) and Peters and Lam (2015) showed that paradoxes in organisations' structures can spill over to the individual level (in our case, workers and their teammates and maybe supervisors) and how newly created paradoxes at different analytical levels co-evolve. Their findings indicate the inter-linkages between the organisational and shop floor levels which help to understand stakeholders' paradox responses. In line with this, we argue that the boundary control paradox experienced in late modern workplaces can be viewed to signal *role-performance paradoxical tensions* caused by organising paradoxical tensions spilling-over into contradictions within micro-level actors' roles, as these may demand performing contradictory, opposing roles and activities. The role performing paradoxical tensions (Jarzabkowski et al. 2013) stem from the complex organisational goals and differentiated structural units, in this case the work and home domains that increasingly overlap. Performance paradoxical tensions may especially arise when actors have no clear structure or template on how to behave in particular situations, such as the emerging NWW work environments in which traditional office hours and clear job descriptions have lost meaning (Peters, 2000).

In the light of the account above, the boundary control paradox experienced at the shop floor level can be linked to three key paradoxes experienced at the organisational level (Ehnert, 2014) that have their origins perhaps situated mainly outside organisational borders [i.e., globalisation (work intensification) and individualisation (the need for task combination)] and, hence, outside the direct circle of influence of intra-organisational stakeholders. The associated organisational paradoxical tensions may have trickled down to the shop floor level resulting in the boundary control paradox. Despite that stakeholders in organisations can't influence its sources, they have to deal with the paradoxical situation by adopting sustainable (HRM) policies, practices and practices.

Ehnert distinguishes the following key paradoxes HRM has to cope with: The '*efficiency-substance paradox*: this paradox relates to the tensions that organisations (and HRM professionals) experience when they try to deploy resources more *efficiently* (which is increasingly important in view of fiercer global competition and individualisation) while trying to *sustain its future resources* (e.g., by paying attention to workers' work-life balance, job satisfaction, and productivity); The *efficiency-responsibility paradox*: this paradox relates to the tensions that organisations (and HRM professionals) experience between trying to achieve both *enhancing efficiency* and *gaining social legitimacy*. The latter has become increasingly important in the light of the societal discourse on corporate social responsibility as reflected, for instance, in the German and French national debates and the new boundary control regulations in these nations.

In both paradoxes presented above, efficiency can relate to organisations' as well as teams' and workers' (households') needs for flexibility to manage work as well as non-work more efficiently which may be achieved through the use of NWW. Efficiency, however, needs to be balanced with maintaining a satisfied, productive and healthy workforce (substance) and societal legitimation, respectively. The third paradox Ehnert labels the *present-future paradox* which relates to the tensions that organisations (and HRM professionals) experience between short and long-term effects resulting from their HRM policies and practices. In the light of this chapter, it is relevant to note that organisations often focus on the short-term effects of NWW without paying attention to its unintended long-term consequences of work intensification characterising the late modern workplace. However, the boundary paradox mechanism described in this contribution, resulting from the initial provision of enhanced boundary control to both individual workers and their colleagues (teammates), under the condition of more responsibility for achieving own and their teams' deadlines in view of work intensification may foster an available culture that rather negates workers' perceptions of boundary control and (too much) work-life integration, all of which may ultimately result in higher levels of work-life conflict. This eventually may also affect workers' work-life balance, job satisfaction and productivity.

According to Ehnert (2014), the three key organisational paradoxes discussed above are present in organisations because of the often contradictory rationalities and the plurality that have come to characterise organisations and households in late modernity. Therefore, organisations and individual workers need to recognise these paradoxes (and how their tensions spill over into lower organisational levels) in order to create innovative and sustainable solutions. Since underlying paradoxical tensions stem from polarised cognitive and social constructions due to stakeholders differentiating the one pole (efficiency, for instance) of a phenomenon (NWW, for instance) from the other (substance or legitimation, for instance), these tensions and how they lead to paradoxical tensions (such as boundary control paradoxical tensions at the shop floor level) are not always easy to recognise. Polarisation can mask the simultaneousness and the interrelated character of conflicting truths, rather than viewing the poles as two sides of the same coin ('NWW').

Paradoxical tensions are often not recognised and therefore perceived in organisations as dilemmas involving 'either-or-responses', with a sole focus put on one pole (e.g., efficiency and applauding the long hours and availability of workers, also over the weekend, as is allowed in NWW) whilst the other is ignored (e.g., substance, resulting in work-life conflict, a loss of work satisfaction and performance). The policies adopted by the German companies and the French national government restricting workers' e-mail communication during off-work hours to prevent (unwanted) interruptions from work activities in the non-work domain may be an example of such a passive response, intended to cope with the 'substance pole' only (hoping that regulation restores boundary control and combats work-life conflict). Of course, the right to disconnect from the paid work domain and to even ignore work-related e-mails sent outside formal working hours in order to combat work-life conflict may come across as appealing. However, in view of the needs of organisations, teams and individual workers for both more efficiency and flexibility, this solution ignores this important pole of NWW (the need for flexibility) which in view of labour and household trends calls for customised and individualised boundary management styles (either integration or segmentation), something which may imply that individual workers need to work and communicate outside hours which in early modernity used to be viewed as office hours.

In fact, paradoxical tensions associated with 'NWW' and 'boundary control' experienced by organisations and individual workers and relevant others may be enhanced by *defensive and reinforcing responses,* for example those that are given attention to in the media. It should be questioned, however, whether there are other ways to *explore and actively manage* the paradoxical tensions surrounding NWW (such as the boundary control paradox), namely by consciously taking *both poles of the paradox simultaneously into account* and accepting that paradox demands a 'both-and-response' (Jarzabkowski et al. 2013; Lewis, 2000; Smith & Lewis, 2011).

[D] Implications for Scholarly Research and for Policies and Practices

Although the recent boundary control policies suggested in the European labour market debate can be viewed as important signals to organisations, HRM professionals, supervisors, individual workers, teammates and clients, boundaries between work and non-work should not be rigid, but may need to be negotiated on a daily basis, taking into account the needs of all parties. Therefore, the German and French examples may not provide real solutions to fully understand or to re-conceptualise workers' experiences of paradoxical tensions. In fact, it is worth mentioning here that a growing number of workers rather hold a preference for work-life integration and experience less work-life conflict when they use their smartphones after working hours more frequently (Derks, Bakker, Peters, & Van Wingerden, 2016). Moreover, longitudinal research has shown that combinations or bundles of (perceived) NWW practices (telework, job autonomy, output management) can, on average, improve work engagement and reduce burn-out, also in the longer run (Peters, Kraan, & Van Echtelt, 2013).

This does not imply, of course, that NWW and boundary control issues should not be carefully looked at, since implementing output management as a single practice can negatively affect well-being (Peters et al. 2013). In addition, merely implementing NWW practices does not predict more work-related flow, since employees only experience more work-related flow when they themselves feel empowered, use telework opportunities and experience trust in their relationships with supervisors and colleagues (Peters et al. 2014). In order to implement NWW, trust is an important factor, as trust is needed for workers and other stakeholders to negotiate their work-life boundaries.

Therefore, we advocate to manage the boundary control paradox with active responses, for example by debating how to combat work intensification, to change an 'always available' culture in organisations and to see how HRM policies can truly support a diverse workforce with various preferences regarding how to manage work-life boundaries in order to achieve balance. This implies exploring, coping and trying to deal with paradox on a longer-term basis while accepting paradoxes associated with NWW and boundary control as inherent work conditions in order to go beyond 'reinforcing cycles' that result from stakeholders' defensive paradox responses (cf., Smith & Lewis, 2011). This means that stakeholders in the scholarly and societal debates on work-life balance and the blurring of boundaries need to openly and critically examine their polarised perceptions in order to either learn to live with the paradox or to be willing to balance the elements underlying tension (*acceptance*), to directly address, discuss and work through the sources of the tensions (*confrontation*) by reducing social strain, for example by using humour to ease tensions, or to move to a higher plane of understanding in which paradoxical elements are understood as complex interdependencies rather than stakeholders' competing interests (*transcendence*) (cf., Lewis, 2000).

We feel that the paradox lens enables us to better grasp the complexities surrounding NWW and the boundary control issue. It may also aid current scholarly and societal debates on whether control over work-life boundaries, particularly in the context of NWW, needs to be and in fact can be regulated for workers, organisations and society at large, so that they may be able to truly reap the benefits of NWW, both in the shorter and in the longer term. Future research employing a paradox lens could examine how organisations and their stakeholders perceive and engage in the process of balancing and managing so-called 'ambidextrous', or 'paradoxical strategic challenges' in the light of dynamic market and institutional developments to simultaneously encourage 'paradoxical poles' (Lewis, 2000), for example those associated with legitimation, fairness, flexibility, commitment, autonomy, control, sustainability, effectiveness and efficiency (Peters & Lam, 2015).

Our contribution has indicated that more research is needed in this regard. For example, future research could focus on the conditions under which workers perceive access to NWW practices to improve work-life balance and under which they perceive to actually have the potential to reduce work-life conflict. Of course, both the positive and the negative effects of NWW should be monitored permanently, not only regarding work-life conflict and well-being in the short run, but also, for example, to combat stereotyping based on workers' work-life integration or segmentation behaviours which may affect workers' career opportunities in the longer run. Since employers often stick to their views of the 'ideal worker' (an ambitious employee who is permanently available, visible or stand-by all the time, 'willing to go the extra mile,' with no other obligations outside the work domain), candidates who choose to segment work, or rather to integrate work without their work efforts being noticed, might not be selected for promotions. Consequently, these workers' capabilities and ambitions may be overlooked (Bleijenbergh, Gremmen, & Peters, 2016).

REFERENCES

Ammons, S. K. (2013). Work-family boundary strategies: Stability and alignment between preferred and enacted boundaries. *Journal of Vocational Behavior*, 82(1), 49–58.

Ashforth, B. E., Kreiner, G. E., & Fugate, M. (2000). All in a day's work: Boundaries and micro role transitions. *Academy of Management Review*, 25(3), 472–491.

Baane, R., Houtkamp, P., & Knotter, M. (2010). *Het nieuwe werken ontrafeld. Over bricks, bytes & behaviour*. Assen: Van Gorcum.

Bandura, A. (1977). *Social learning theory*. Oxford, UK: Prentice-Hall.

Beck, U. (1992). *Risk society. Towards a new modernity*. London: Sage Publications.

Beck, U. (1994). The reinvention of politics: Towards a theory of reflexive modernisation. In U. Beck, A. Giddens, & S. Lash (1994). *Reflexive modernisation. Politics, tradition and aesthetics in the modern social order*. Cambridge: Polity Press.

Bijl, D. (2009). '*Aan de slag met het nieuwe werken*, http://www.aandeslagmethnw.nl/Libraries/ Boek_concepten/Aan_de_slag_met_Het_Nieuwe_Werken_pdf.sflb.ashx.

Bleijenbergh, I., Gremmen, I., & Peters, P. (2016). Timing ambition: How temporal structures regarding working hours and ambition affect career advancement among women part-time workers. *Scandinavian Journal of Management*, 32(4), 179–188.

Boell, S. K., Cecez-Kecmanovic, D., & Campbell, J. (2016). Telework paradoxes and practices: The importance of the nature of work. *New Technology, Work and Employment*, 31(2), 114–131.

Boswell, W., & Olson-Buchanan, J. (2007). The use of communication technologies after hours: The role of work attitudes and work-life conflict. *Journal of Management*, 33, 592–610.

Brown, P. & Scase, R. (eds). (1991). *Poor work. Disadvantage and the division of labour*. Milton Keynes/Philadelphia: Open University Press.

Chen, Z., Powell, G. N., & Greenhaus, J. H. (2009). Work-to-family conflict, positive spillover, and boundary management: a person-environmental fit approach. *Journal of Vocational Behavior*, 74, 82–93.

Chesley, N. (2005). Blurring boundaries? Linking technology use, spillover, individual distress and family satisfaction. *Journal of Marriage and the Family*, 26, 1237–1248.

Clark, S. C. (2000). Work/family border theory: A new theory of work/family balance. *Human Relations*, 53(6), 747–770.

Dawis, R. V., & Lofquist, L. H. (1984). *A psychological theory of work adjustment: An individual-differences model and its applications*. Minneapolis: University of Minnesota Press.

De Prins, P., De Vos, A., Van Beirendonck, L., & Segers, J. (2015). Sustainable HRM for sustainable careers: Introducing the 'Respect Openness Continuity (ROC) model'. In A. De Vos & B. I. J. M. Van der Heijden (eds). *Handbook of research on Sustainable Careers* (pp. 319–334). Cheltenham, UK/ Northampton, MA, USA: Edgar Elgar.

Derks, D., Bakker, A. B., Peters. P. & Van Wingerden, P. (2016). Work-related smartphone use, work–family conflict and family role performance: The role of segmentation preference. *Human Relations*, 69(5) 1045–1068.

Derks, D., Van Duin, D, Tims, M., & Bakker, A.B. (2015). Smartphone use and work-home interference: The moderating role of social norms and employee work engagement. *Journal of Occupational and Organizational Psychology*, 88(1), 155–177.

Duxbury, L., Higgins, C., Smart, R., & Stevenson, M. (2014). Mobile technology and boundary permeability. *British Journal of Management*, 25(3), 570–588.

Ehnert, I. (2014). Paradox as a lens for theorizing sustainable HRM. Mapping and coping with paradoxes and tensions. In I. Ehnert, W. Harry, & K. J. Zink (eds), *Sustainability and human resource management: Developing sustainable business organizations* (pp. 247–272). Heidelberg: Springer.

Elchardus (1991). Rationality and the specialization of meaning. A sociological approach to the allocation of time. In G. Antonides, W. Arts, & W. F. Van Raaij (eds) (1991). *The consumption of time and the timing of consumption. Toward a new behavioural and socio-economics. Contribution in honour of Amitai Etzioni*. Amsterdam: North Holland.

Elchardus, M. (1996). *De gemobiliseerde samenleving. Tussen de oude en een nieuwe ordening van de tijd*. Brussel: Koning Boudewijnstichting.

Friedman, S. D., & Greenhaus, J. H. (2000). *Work and family – allies or enemies? What happens when business professionals confront life choices.* New York: Oxford University Press.

Gates, B. (2005). *The new world of work.* Retrieved from: https://www.microsoft.com/mscorp/execmail/2005/05-19newworldofwork.mspx.

Geurts, S. A. E., Taris, T. W., Kompier, M. A. J., Dikkers, J. S. E., Van Hooff, M. L. M., & Kinnunen, U. (2005). Work-home interaction from a work psychological perspective: Development and validation of a new questionnaire, the SWING. *Work and Stress*, 19, 319–339.

Giddens, A. (1990). *The consequences of modernity*. Cambridge: Polity Press.

Greenhaus, J. H., & Beutell, N. J. (1985). Sources of conflict between work and family roles. *The Academy of Management Review,* 10, 76–88.

Greenhaus, J. H., & Powell, G. N. (2006). When work and family are Allies: A theory of work-family enrichment. *Academy of Management Review,* 31, 72–92.

Grzywacz, J.G., Almeida, D.M., & McDonald, D.A. (2002). Work-family spillover and daily reports of work and family stress in the adult labor force. *Family Relations*, 51, 28–36.

Hobsbawm, E. (1995). *Een eeuw van uitersten. De twintigste eeuw 1914–1991*. Utrecht: Het Spectrum B.V.

Hunnicutt, B.K. (1988). *Work without end. Abandoning shorter hours for the right to work*. Philadephia: Temple University Press.

Jarzabkoswki, P., Lê J.K., & Van de Ven, A.H. (2013). Responding to competing strategic demands: How organizing, belonging, and performing paradoxes coevolve. *Strategic Organization*, 11(3), 245–280.

De Lange, W. & Koppens, J. (2007). *De duurzame arbeidsorganisatie: Een geloofwaardig vervolg op maatschappelijk verantwoord ondernemen.* Amsterdam: WEKA Uitgeverij.

Kossek, E. E., & Lautsch, B. A. (2007). *CEO of me: Creating a life that works in the flexible job age*. Upper Saddle River, N.J.: Prentice Hall.

Kossek, E. E., Noe, R. A., & DeMarr, B. J. (1999). Work-family role synthesis: Individual and organizational determinants. *International Journal of Conflict Management*, 10(2), 102–129.

Kossek, E. E., Ruderman, M. N., Braddy, P. W., & Hannum, K. M. (2012). Work–nonwork boundary management profiles: A person-centered approach. *Journal of Vocational Behavior,* 81(1), 112–128.

Kreiner, G. E. (2006). Consequences of work-home segmentation or integration: A person-environment fit perspective. *Journal of Organizational Behavior*, 27(4), 485–507.

Kreiner, G. E., Hollensbe, E. C., & Sheep, M. L. (2009). Balancing borders and bridges: Negotiating the work-home interface via boundary work tactics. *Academy of Management Journal,* 52(4), 704–730.

Kristof, A. L. (1996). Person-organization fit: An integrative review of its conceptualizations, measurement, and implications. *Personnel Psychology*, 49(1), 1–49.

Lewis, M. W. (2000). Exploring paradox: Towards a more comprehensive guide. *The Academy of Management Review*, 25(4), 760–776.

Manz, C. C., & Sims, H. P. (1981). Vicarious learning: The influence of modeling on organizational behavior. *Academy of Management Review*, 6(1), 105–113.

Maxwell, G. A. (1997). Empowerment in the UK hospitality industry. In M. Foley, J. Lennon, & G. Maxwell (1997). *Hospitality, tourism and leisure management. Issues in strategies and culture*. London: Cassell.

Morris, M. G., & Venkatesh, V. (2000). Age differences in technology adoption decisions: Implications for a changing work force. *Personnel Psychology*, 53, 375–403.

Nippert-Eng, C. E. (2008). *Home and work: negotiating boundaries through everyday life*. Chicago, I. L.: University of Chicago Press.

Peters, P. (2000). *The vulnerable hours of leisure. New patterns of work and free time in the Netherlands, 1975-95*. Amsterdam: Thela Thesis.

Peters, P. (2011). *Flexible working time arrangements: Exchange of good practice. Discussion Paper, the Netherlands*. http://ec.europa.eu/justice/gender-equality/files/exchange_of_good_practice_nl/nl_discussion_paper_nl_2011_en.pdf

Peters, P. & Batenburg, R. (2015). Telework adoption and formalization in organizations from a knowledge transfer perspective. *International Journal of Work Innovation*, 1(2/3), 251–270.

Peters, P., Den Dulk, L., & Van der Lippe, T. (2009). The effects of time-spatial flexibility and new working conditions on employees' work–life balance: The Dutch case. *Community, Work & Family*, 12(3), 279–297.

Peters, P., Kraan, K., & Van Echtelt, P. (2013). Floreren onder condities van Het Nieuwe Werken: minder burn-out, meer toewijding? *Tijdschrift voor Arbeidsvraagstukken*, 3(29), 304–321.

Peters, P. & Lam, W. (2015). Can employability do the trick? Revealing paradoxical tensions and responses in the process of adopting innovative employability enhancing policies and practices in organizations. *Zeitschrift für Personalforschung*, 29(3–4), 235–258.

Peters, P., Poutsma, E., Van der Heijden, B., Bakker, A.B., & De Bruijn, T. (2014). Enjoying new ways to work: An HRM process approach to study flow. *Human Resource Management*, 53(2), 271–290.

Peters, P. & Van der Lippe, T. (2007). The time-pressure reducing potential of telehomeworking: The Dutch case. *Internal Journal of Human Resource Management*, 18(3), 430–447.

Piszczek, M. M., & Berg, P. (2014). Expanding the boundaries of boundary theory: Regulative institutions and work–family role management. *Human Relations*, 67(12), 1491–1512.

Putnam, L. L., Myers, K. K., & Gailliard, B. M. (2014). Examining the tensions in workplace flexibility and exploring options for new directions. *Human Relations*, 67(4), 413–440.

Rothbard, N. P., Philips, K. W., & Dumus, T. L. (2005). Managing multiple roles: Work-family policies and individuals' desire for segmentation. *Organizational Science*, 16, 243–258.

Smith, W., & Lewis, M. (2011). Toward a theory of paradox: A dynamic equilibrium model of organizing. *Academy of Management Review,* 36(2), 381–403.

Sundaramurthy, C., & Kreiner, G. E. (2008). Governing by managing identity boundaries: The case of family businesses. *Entrepreneurship Theory and Practice*, 32(3), 415–436.

Ten Brummelhuis, L. L., Bakker, A. B., Hetland, J., & Keulemans, L. (2012). Do new ways of working foster work engagement? *Psicothema*, 24(1), 113–120.

Ter Hoeven, C. L., Van Zoonen, W., & Fonner, K. L. (2016). The practical paradox of technology: The influence of communication technology use on employee burnout and engagement. *Communication Monographs*, *83*(2), 239–263.

Tijdens, K. (1998). *Zeggenschap over arbeidstijden. De samenhang tussen bedrijfstijden en flexibilisering van personeelsbezetting*. Den Haag: Wellboom/Delwel.

Van Der Meulen, N. (2014). *De staat van het nieuwe werken: resultaten van de nationale HNW barometer 2012.* Rotterdam School of Management. Rotterdam: Erasmus Universiteit. file:///C:/Users/HP/AppData/Local/Temp/Erasmus_Work_Research_2014_-Resultaten_van_de_Nationale_HNW_Barometer_2013.pdf

Veal A.J. (1987). *Leisure and the future. Leisure and recreation studies 4.* London: George Allen & Unwin.

Wallerstein, I. (1983). *Historical capitalism.* Norfolk: Thetford Press Limited.

CHAPTER 13

Precarious Work and Work-Family Reconciliation: A Critical Evaluation of New Zealand's Regulatory Framework

Amanda Reilly & Annick Masselot

A new class of workers, referred to as the 'precariat',[1] is emerging both internationally[2] and within New Zealand.[3] Precarious work is often understood as work that 'departs from the normative model of the standard employment relationship ... [which] is poorly paid and incapable of sustaining a household'[4] but it is also more broadly identified by its characteristics. The New Zealand Council of Trade Unions, has identified uncertainty of job duration, irregular hours, fluctuating pay, limited access to paid leave, poor representation and input at work on wages and conditions, limited access to training and inferior rights and conditions at work as characteristics of precarious work.[5]

1. Standing, Guy. *The Precariat: The New Dangerous Class* (London and New York: Bloomsbury Publishing, 2011).
2. Kalleberg, Arne, *Good Jobs, bad jobs: The rise of polarized and precarious employment systems in the United States, 1970s-2000s* (Russell Sage Foundation, 2011); Keune, Maarten, *Trade union responses to precarious work in seven European countries*, 5(1) International Journal of Labour Research 59–78 (2013); Fudge, Judy, *Precarious Migrant Status and Precarious Employment: The Paradox of International Rights for Migrant Workers*, 34(1) Comparative Labor Law and Policy Journal 95–132 (2012).
3. Wilson, Margaret, *Precarious Work – New Zealand Experience*, 39(2) New Zealand Journal of Employment Relations 22–33 (2014).
4. Fudge, Judy & Owens Rosemary (eds.), *Precarious Work, Women, and the New Economy: the Challenge to Legal Norms* (Hart Publishing, 2006), p. 3.
5. New Zealand Council of Trade Unions, *Under Pressure: A Detailed Report into Insecure Work in New Zealand* (NZCTU, 2013) http://www.union.org.nz/wp-content/uploads/2016/12/CTU-Under-Pressure-Detailed-Report-2.pdf (accessed 19 December 2016), p. 6. *See also* Tucker, Deborah, *Precarious' Non-Standard Employment – A Review of the Literature* (Labour Market Policy Group, Department of Labour, 2003).

Neoliberal reform, focused on Gross Domestic Product, de-unionisation and de-regulation of labour standards have contributed to growth in this phenomenon.[6] Legal protections, rooted in industrial modes of production and based on an out-dated male bread winner/female caregiver social norm,[7] are inadequate in this new environment.[8] Employment law protections are often tied to the legal status of employee while increasing numbers of workers do not fit into this category. Even when relevant, such protections are under-enforced.[9] Unions and collective bargaining as a cornerstone of workers' protection have also been undermined by the decline of the Union movement.

Productivity improvements and the need to reduce costs for business dominate the discourse around work regulation[10] and work-family regulation largely targets elite women's needs rather than those at the margins of the workforce.[11] Yet, precarious workers, whose work is characterised by poor pay, low levels of legal protection, job insecurity and limited ability to support a household,[12] are those most in need of work

6. Quinlan, Michael, *The 'pre-invention' of precarious employment: the changing world of work in context*, 23(4) *The Economic and Labour Relations Review* 3–24 (2012).
7. Fudge & Owens, *Precarious Work, Women, and the New Economy: the Challenge to Legal Norms*; Bornstein, Stephanie, *Work, Family, and Discrimination at the Bottom of the Ladder* 19(1) Georgetown Journal on Poverty Law & Policy, 1–42 (2012); Crompton, Rosemary, *Employment and the Family: The reconfiguration of Work and family Life in Contemporary Societies* (Cambridge University Press, 2006).
8. Vosko, Lea, *Managing the Margins Gender, Citizenship, and the International Regulation of Precarious Employment* (Oxford University Press, 2010); Forstater, Mathew, *Working for a better world Cataloging arguments for the right to employment* 41(1) *Philosophy & Social Criticism*, 61–67 (2015); Ministry of Business Innovation and Employment, Playing by the Rules: Strengthening Enforcement of Employment Standards Discussion Document (May 2014) [CAB Min (14) 19/7 refers]; Caracciolo di Torella, Eugenia & Annick Masselot, *Work and Family Life Balance in the EU law and policy 40 years on: still balancing, still struggling*, 2 European Gender Equality Law Review, 6–14 (2013); Masselot, Annick, *The Right and Reality of Flexible Working Arrangements in New Zealand*, in Families, Care-Giving and Paid Work, Grace James & Nicole Busby (eds.) (Edward Elgard Publishing, 2011) 69–85; Handy, Jocelyn, *Maintaining Family Life Under Shiftwork Schedules: A Case Study of a New Zealand Petrochemical Plant*, 39(1) *New Zealand Journal of Psychology*, 7–14 (2010).
9. Vosko, Lea, Martha MacDonald & Ian Campbell (eds), *Gender and the Contours of Precarious Employment* (Routledge, 2009); Kalleberg, Arne L., *Nonstandard Employment Relations: Part-Time, Temporary and Contract Work*, 26 Annual Review of Sociology, 341–365 (2000); Kalleberg, Arne L., *Precarious Work, Insecure Workers: Employment Relations in Transition*, 74(1) American Sociological Review, 1–22 (2009).
10. Houseman, Susan, *Why Employers Use Flexible Staffing Arrangements: From and Establishment Survey*, 55(1) Industrial and Labor Relations Review 155–162 (2001); Pennycook, Matthew, Giselle Cory & Vidhya Alakeson, *A Matter of Time: The Rise of Zero-Hour Contracts* (Resolution Foundation, 2013), http://www.resolutionfoundation.org/wp-content/uploads/2014/08/A_Matter_of_Time_-_The_rise_of_zero-hours_contracts_final_1.pdf (accessed 7 December 2016).
11. Williams, Joan C. & Heather Boushey, *The Three Faces of Work-Family Conflict: The Poor, the Professionals, and the Missing Middle* (Center for American Progress and Work Life Law, 2010), https://cdn.americanprogress.org/wp-content/uploads/issues/2010/01/pdf/threefaces.pdf (accessed 7 December 2016); Caracciolo di Torella, Eugenia & Annick Masselot, *Reconciling Work and Family Life in EU Law and Policy* (Palgrave Macmillan, 2010).
12. Fudge & Owens, *Precarious Work, Women, and the New Economy: the Challenge to Legal Norms*; New Zealand Council of Trade Unions, *Under Pressure: A Detailed Report into Insecure Work in New Zealand*,; National Women's Law Center, *The Schedules That Work Act: Giving Workers the Tools They Need to Succeed* (2014) http://www.nwlc.org/sites/default/files/pdfs/schedules_that_work_act_fact_sheet_7.22.14.pdf (accessed 7 December 2016); PEPSO, *It's More Than*

family reconciliation support. Such workers frequently have greater family responsibilities than others, and are forced to take jobs that permit them to fulfil these responsibilities.[13] These workers are thus in need of work family reconciliation measures. Work family reconciliation is concerned with the *need* workers may have to manage their time in order to take care of their families.[14] The concept of work family reconciliation is distinguishable from the concept of work-life balance which is to do with the *desire* to limit the involvement in paid activities in order to pursue other interests (e.g., further education) with the overall aim of contributing to individuals' wellbeing.[15]

This paper considers the problem of precarious workers and work family reconciliation within the context of New Zealand. New Zealand has many of the same features as other Western post industrial countries but it also has some of its own peculiarities linked to colonisation and its relationship with the indigenous people as well as a heavy reliance of agriculture and tourism for its wealth. Although New Zealand has followed the same trends towards deregulation as other countries, New Zealand legislators and unions have made some attempts at addressing work family reconciliation needs which are here discussed. The central research question this contribution explores is whether New Zealand's legal framework is fit for the purpose of supporting precarious workers in work-family reconciliation. Three areas are considered: the right to request flexibility, regulation of working time and the role and efficacy of unions in facilitating work family reconciliation. This analysis is located within a consideration of work family reconciliation needs and the demographics of the precarious workforce.

§13.01 WORK FAMILY RECONCILIATION AND PRECARIOUS WORK IN NEW ZEALAND

Precarious work is characterised by job insecurity and irregular and unpredictable hours. Overwork is also a potential characteristic of precarious work as precarious workers are susceptible to work overload due to economic pressure. The lack of voice inherent in the precarious workers' position contributes to reinforcing worker's lack of control over their working time.[16] Non-standard hours, long hours, intensified work and shift work reduce opportunities for workers to socialise and enjoy personal and

Poverty: Employment Precarity and Household Well-being (February 2013) http://pepsouwt.files.wordpress.com/2013/02/its-more-than-poverty-feb-2013.pdf (accessed 7 December 2016).

13. Hofäcker, Dirk & Stefanie König, *Flexibility and Work-life conflict in time of crisis: a gender Perspective*, 33(9) International Journal of Sociology and Social Policy, 613–635 (2013); Fursman, Lindy & Nita Zodgekar, *Making It Work: The Impacts of Flexible Working Arrangements on New Zealand Families*, 35 Social Policy Journal of New Zealand 43–54 (2009).
14. Caracciolo di Torella & Masselot, *Reconciling Work and Family Life in EU Law and Policy*.
15. *Ibid*.
16. Underhill, Elsa, and Michael Quinlan, *How Precarious Employment Affects Health and Safety at Work: The Case of Temporary Agency Workers*, 66(3) Relations Industrielles/Industrial Relations, 397–421 (2011), p. 405.

family leisure time.[17] They also have a depressing effect on workers' physical and mental health which can affect the quality of time away from work.

Irregular and unpredictable hours also raise challenges in terms of work-family reconciliation. Inadequate notice of work schedules makes arranging childcare and transportation difficult.[18] Irregular hours result in irregular pay making it difficult to meet basic expenses and workers experience stress from not knowing the amount of income they will receive each week. For many precarious workers, working hours are at the discretion of their employer and, whilst many experience a shortfall of hours, a sizeable proportion of temporary workers work forty hours or more.[19] The volume of working hours impacts directly on employees' ability to resolve work family conflict.[20] This is relevant because New Zealanders work typically long hours,[21] and this workplace culture impacts negatively on work family reconciliation.[22] Too many hours of work leave little time for family life and working overtime impacts negatively on individuals' perception of their work family balance.[23] Over time work is particularly negative on work family reconciliation when it is imposed by employers as opposed to being the results of a personal choice by the employee.[24]

Identifying precarious workers is challenging as such workers are not identified as a discrete category in national statistical surveys. In New Zealand, as elsewhere, a range of contractual forms of work arrangement have evolved with many workers not fitting into a standard employer employee contractual relationship (with the associated rights which attach to standard contract of employment.) These include part-time work, fixed-term contracts, temporary agency work, work with flexible hours, tele-working and home working, and 'zero-hour work'. Although not all forms of non-standard work are precarious with all associated problems, many are.

---

17. International Labour Organisation, *From Precarious Work to Decent Work: Outcome Document to the Workers' Symposium on Policies and Regulations to combat Precarious Employment* (ILO, 2012) p. 38, http://www.ilo.org/wcmsp5/groups/public/---ed_dialogue/---actrav/documents/meetingdocument/wcms_179787.pdf (accessed 11 December 2016).
18. National Women's Law Center, *The Schedules That Work Act: Giving Workers the Tools They Need to Succeed.*
19. Statistics New Zealand, *Flexibility and security in employment: Findings from the 2012 Survey of Working Life* (2013), http://www.stats.govt.nz/browse_for_stats/income-and work/employment_and_unemployment/flexibility-security-employment.aspx (accessed 7 December 2016).
20. Jacobs, Jerry and Kathleen Gerson, *The Time Divide: Work, Family and Gender Inequalities* (Harvard University Press, Cambridge, 2004).
21. Fursman, Lindy, *Working Long Hours in New Zealand: A Profile of Long Hours Workers Using Data from the 2006 Census* (Department of Labour, March 2008), http://thehub.superu.govt.nz/sites/default/files/Working%20Long%20Hours%20in%20New%20Zealand%2C%20A%20Profile%20of%20Long%20Hours%20Workers%20Using%20Data%20From%20The%202006%20Census.pdf (accessed 22 December 2016).
22. Fursman, Lindy & Nita Zodgekar, *Making It Work: The Impacts of Flexible Working Arrangements on New Zealand Families.*
23. Eurofound, *Fifth European Working Conditions Survey* (Publications Office of the European Union, 2012) http://www.eurofound.europa.eu/sites/default/files/ef_publication/field_ef_document/ef1182en.pdf (accessed 22 December 2016); Van der Hulst, Monique and Sabine Geurts, *Associations between overtime and psychological health in high and low reward jobs* 15(3) Work & Stress 227–240 (2001).
24. Porter, Gayle, *Work, work ethic and work excess*, 17(5) Journal of Organizational Change and Management, 424–439 (2004).

The diagram below indicates the approximate distribution across different forms of non-standard work in New Zealand.[25]

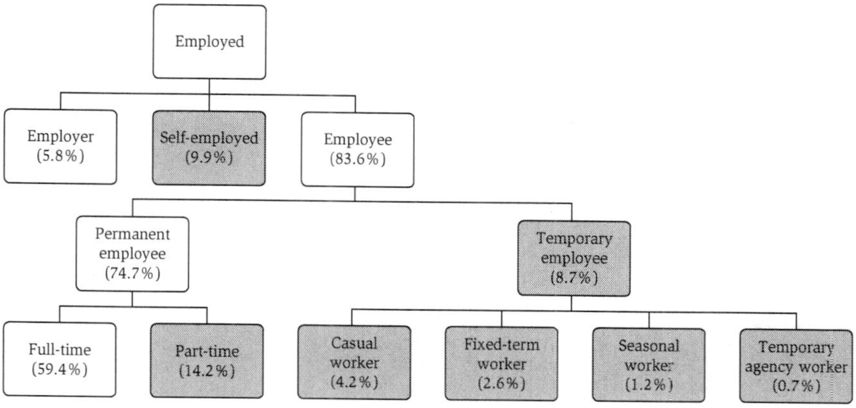

Temporary worker is an umbrella terms encompassing a number of different legal arrangements which may raise different work-family issues as well as making one size fits all regulation inappropriate.

Casual workers, i.e., 'employees hired on a periodic basis as need arises'[26] are typically in a short-term employment relationship with no expectation of on-going work or mutuality of obligations between the parties. By contrast, zero hour contract workers are in an on-going employment relationship characterised by a contract which contains no guaranteed hours for the employee.[27] The use of zero-hour contracts in New Zealand was growing until recently,[28] however, as will be discussed in the section on regulation of working hours, such arrangements are now illegal. Seasonal workers, i.e., workers whose jobs are only available at certain times of the year are also temporary workers. Such workers are most likely to work in agriculture, fisheries and forestry.[29]

25. Distribution of non-standard work in New Zealand New Zealand Workforce Structure. Source: Statistics New Zealand, *Survey of Working Life* (December 2012), http://www.stats.govt.nz/browse_for_stats/income-and-work/employment_and_unemployment/SurveyofWorkingLife_HOTPDec12qtr.aspx (accessed 20 December 2016); Note: Shaded cells are categories of non-standard work. Percentages do not add to totals due to the exclusion of residual categories from the diagram.
26. Brosnan, Peter & Pat Walsh, *Employment Security in Australia and New Zealand*, 8(3) Labour & Industry: a journal of the social and economic relations of work, 23–41 (1998).
27. Pennycook et al., 2013), *A Matter of Time: The Rise of Zero-Hour Contracts*.
28. O'Meara, Patrick, *Flexibility and Employment Laws: Labour law not working for those in insecure work*. Radio New Zealand Insight Programme (16 November 2014), http://www.radionz.co.nz/national/programmes/insight/audio/20157262/insight-for-16-november-2014-flexibility-and-employment-laws (accessed 7 December 2016).
29. Statistics New Zealand, *Flexibility and security in employment: Findings from the 2012 Survey of Working Life*.

Most seasonal workers are male[30] and Māori and Pacific ethnicities have a higher likelihood of being in seasonal employment.[31]

Not all temporary workers are precarious workers, and some choose this form of work for personal reasons. However, Dixon's 2009 study[32] indicated that temporary workers are exposed to higher levels of insecurity and workers experience greater variability in hours and an increased likelihood of working nonstandard hours.[33] She also found that more than half of all workers' hours of work changed from week to week to suit the employer's needs. This was especially the case for casual workers (62%), but less common among fixed-term workers (32%). Nearly a fifth of both casual and temporary agency workers had limited advanced notice of work schedules, with 18% and 19% respectively being told their work schedule only one day or less in advance. Work outside of standard working hours was also common; 43% of casuals and 45% of seasonal workers did at least some of their work in non-standard hours. Seasonal work appears to be more stable than other forms of temporary work; nearly half of all seasonal workers always knew their work schedules.[34] However, Dixon's study[35] indicated that seasonal workers had the highest incidence of all temporary workers for non-standard working hours. They also have a high (23%) incidence of working long hours (forty-five hours or longer per week) and high incidence of experiencing physical symptoms as a result of their work, with 15% saying that they often or always experienced physical problems or pain.

There is no available data on workers who are ostensibly self-employed but who are essentially dependent contractors (which does not exist as a separate legal category in New Zealand). Nonetheless, it seems likely that such workers may also be adversely affected by unreliable work and irregular schedules.

While the above discussion has focused on non-standard work, non-standard work does not necessarily equate to precarious work although it is generally viewed as one indicator of precariousness. It is possible to be ostensibly employed in a permanent position but in real terms to feel that employment is insecure or to lack security or control over working hours. The New Zealand Council of Trade Unions estimates that at least 30% of New Zealand's workforce is in insecure work (including the ostensibly permanently employed) using the criteria identified above. Conversely not every person in non-standard employment is a precarious worker. Many highly paid IT workers are not and some workers express a preference for remaining in non-standard work.

In conclusion, while it is difficult to be precise about the exact number of precarious workers who may be experiencing work family reconciliation issues in New

30. Dixon, *A profile of temporary workers and their employment outcomes*, p. 6.
31. Statistics New Zealand, *Flexibility and security in employment: Findings from the 2012 Survey of Working Life*, p. 13.
32. Dixon, Sylvia, *A profile of temporary workers and their employment outcomes* (New Zealand Department of Labour, 2009), http://www.mbie.govt.nz/publications-research/research/labour-market-and-skills/temporary-workers.pdf (accessed 19 December 2016).
33. Standard working hours are 7am to 7pm, Monday to Friday.
34. Statistics New Zealand, *Flexibility and security in employment: Findings from the 2012 Survey of Working Life*, p. 21.
35. Dixon, *A profile of temporary workers and their employment outcomes*.

Zealand, it is clear that precarious work exists as a phenomenon. It is also apparent that regulating work-family reconciliation is challenging in that precarious work is not concentrated under a single legal form of legal form. Precarious work is also found across different sectors with different scheduling needs. Industries with the highest usage of temporary workers are education and training, and retail, accommodation and food services, where nearly 1 in 5 (both 17%) of their workforce are temporary.[36] Employers in these sectors have different needs than those employing seasonal workers. A casual retail assistant may only be required for a few hours every now and again but long intense hours may be required to harvest fruit.

So far the discussion has focused on precarious workers in general, however, New Zealand precarious workers are not a homogenous group and their work-family reconciliation needs vary. The Council of Trade Union (CTU) has, amongst others identified Māori and Pacific workers as well as migrants as particularly at risk. The challenges faced by men and women may vary too and vary across the life cycle.

Precarious employment has a disproportionate ethnic divide with Māori and Pacific workers being disproportionately over-represented in insecure work.[37] In absolute terms, the majority of the temporary workforce is New Zealand-born European but when viewed proportionately, Māori workers have the highest incidence of working in temporary jobs at 13%, followed by Pacific workers at 10.7%.[38] In addition, Māori and Pacific ethnic groups combine high fertility rates with much lower female employment rates and may have different cultural pressures[39] with regard to gender and family and community responsibility norms.[40]

Immigrants are susceptible to exploitation and often find themselves in precarious work.[41] Anderson and Tipples argue that migrant workers commonly end up in insecure work as they try to find an entry point into the labour market. Immigrant workers are susceptible to accepting precarious employment due to language and cultural barriers or unfamiliarity with their employment rights.[42] This also exposes them to exploitation by employers. There is evidence that migrant workers are being

36. Statistics New Zealand, *Flexibility and security in employment: Findings from the 2012 Survey of Working Life* (2014), http://www.stats.govt.nz/browse_for_stats/income-and-work/employment_and_unemployment/flexibility-security-employment.aspx (accessed 11 December 2016).
37. New Zealand Council of Trade Unions, *Under Pressure: A Detailed Report into Insecure Work in New Zealand*, p. 26.
38. Statistics New Zealand, *Flexibility and security in employment: Findings from the 2012 Survey of Working Life*, p. 6.
39. Mikaere, Ani, *Colonising myths-Maori realities: He rukuruku whakaaro* (Huia Publishers, 2011).
40. The Māori and Pacific culture are not grounded in the betterment of the individual. These cultures place greater emphasis on family and community obligations. Therefore, cultural traditions might add expectations on Māori and Pacific individuals which can cause conflict with working time obligations.
41. McLaren, Eva, Patrick Firkin, Paul Spoonley, Ann Dupuis, Anne de Bruin, and Kerr Inkson, *At the margins: contingency, precariousness and non-standard work*, 1 Labour Market Dynamics Research Programme, Research Report Series (2004), as cited by New Zealand Council of Trade Unions, *Under Pressure: A Detailed Report into Insecure Work in New Zealand*, p. 26.
42. Anderson, Danaë, *Are vulnerable workers really protected in New Zealand?* 39(1) *New Zealand Journal of Employment Relations*, 52–67 (2014), p. 52.

overworked, underpaid and have no written employment agreements.[43] Anderson and Tipples argue that the exploitation of migrant workers is made worse by the weak monitoring and enforcement of labour law.[44] Migrant workers may also have unique work family reconciliation challenges relating to responsibilities to extended family members in other countries amongst other things.

The challenges of precarious work transcend gender boundaries, but there are gendered implications. Nearly six in ten temporary workers in New Zealand are women[45] at least in part due to work family conflict.[46] Women are still largely responsible for unpaid household work and frequently assume the role of primary caregiver. Thus women with childcare responsibilities may choose to participate in temporary work for the flexibility it purports to offer as a method of resolving the conflict.[47] Unfortunately, temporary work, especially temporary work with uncertain continuity and/or irregular work schedules, is no panacea for work-family conflict. A worker may accept work which conflicts with their care responsibilities because they fear not being offered future work opportunities if they refuse. Precarious work also impacts on working fathers. An EEO Trust survey[48] found that 80% of fathers wanted to spend more time with their families. Eighty-two per cent of working fathers said their paid work negatively affected the amount of time they spent with their children. Fifty-two per cent said that their paid work affected the quality of time spent with their children. Fathers in the survey cited several workplace situations which negatively impact on their ability to balance work and family commitments, including lack of flexibility of hours and unpredictable hours, unsupportive work cultures, travel to and location of work, and low uptake of work-life provisions.

Childcare is not the sole care responsibility workers can experience. Eldercare is the unpaid care of an elderly relative by providing 'personal care, household assistance, administrative support, social and emotional support.'[49] As the population ages, many workers, particularly older workers, find themselves balancing paid work with care for elderly relatives. Caring for the elderly is less predictable than childcare responsibilities and the strategies for meeting these needs often rely on traditional methods of using leave entitlements.[50] This is problematic for precarious workers who

43. *Ibid.* p. 54.
44. *Ibid.* p. 56.
45. Statistics New Zealand, *Flexibility and security in employment: Findings from the 2012 Survey of Working Life*.
46. Owens, Rosemary, *Engendering Flexibility in a World of Precarious Work*, in Fudge, Judy & Owens Rosemary (eds.), *Precarious Work, Women, and the New Economy: the Challenge to Legal Norms* (Hart Publishing, 2006) 329-352, p. 329.
47. Connelly, Catherine & Daniel Gallagher, *Emerging Trends in Contingent Work Research*, 30(6) Journal of Management, 959-983 (2004), p. 968.
48. EEO Trust, *Fathers in Paid Work Toolkit* (2003), http://eeotrust.org/content/docs/toolkits/Father%20and%20paid%20work%20toolkit.pdf (accessed 11 December 2016).
49. Davey, Judith & Sally Keeling, *Combining work and Eldercare: a study of employees in two City Councils who provide informal care for older people* (2004), http://thehub.superu.govt.nz/sites/default/files/Combining%20Work%20and%20Eldercare%2C%20a%20study%20of%20employees%20in%20two%20City%20Councils.pdf (accessed 11 December 2016), p. 14.
50. Herring, Jonathan, *Caring and the Law* (Hart Publishing, 2013).

cannot plan with certainty because of uncertain hours and work schedules and limited access to leave entitlements.[51]

In conclusion, given the varied work-family reconciliations needs of both precarious workers, and the varied needs of employers in different sectors, designing any 'one size fits all' legislative solution is challenging and possibly counterproductive. A more individualised tailored approach seems called for.

§13.02 RIGHT TO REQUEST FLEXIBILITY

The concept of flexible work came to the forefront of New Zealand employment law not primarily to solve work-family conflict but as a tool for employers to adapt quickly and more adequately to globalised market competition.[52] Employer-defined flexibility can lead to less predictability and discretion for employees, as wells as an increase in irregularity of work hours, which in turn leads to lower income and higher insecurity for workers.[53] Thus, the flip side of flexibility for employers is precariousness and increased work-life conflict for employees.

However, flexibility does not have to the benefit employers exclusively. It was discussed above how the work family reconciliation needs of precarious workers may vary across a life time and depend upon a range of factors including gender and ethnicity. It was also mentioned that different sectors legitimately have different requirements. The ability to tailor individualised solutions which are flexible to the individual and to the employer has advantages over statutorily dictated standard working conditions.

New Zealand has taken some positive steps towards achieving this ideal. Employees (including temporary and other non-standard workers) have a statutory right to request flexibility. This is covered by Part 6AA of the Employment Relations Act 2000 (as amended successively by the Employment Relations Amendment (Flexible Working Agreements) Act 2007 and by the Employment Relations Amendment 2014), which provides the right to request flexible working arrangements.

Originally modelled on a similar UK provision,[54] which exclusively addressed the need of parents of young and disabled children, the 2007 New Zealand law was designed to facilitate more broadly the needs of employees with their more general care obligations. It represented a significant development for the right to care[55] and

51. James, Grace and Emma Spruce, *Workers with Elderly Dependants: Employment Law's Response to the Latest Care-Giving Conundrum*, 35(3) *Legal Studies* 463–479 (2015).
52. Masselot, Annick, *Gender Implications of the Right to Request Flexible Working Arrangements: Raising Pigs and Children in New Zealand*, 39(9) New Zealand Journal of Employment Relations, 59–71 (2015).
53. Hofäcker & König, *Flexibility and Work-life conflict in time of crisis: a gender Perspective*.
54. Employment Relations Amendment (Flexible Working Agreements) Act 2007, which added part 6AA to the Employment Relations Act 2000. *See also* Levin-Epstein, Jodie, *How to Exercise Flexible Work: Take Steps with a 'Soft Touch' Law*, Work Life Balance Brief No 3. (Centre for Law and Social Policy, 2005); Hegewisch, Ariane, *Flexible working policies: a comparative review* (Equality and Human Rights Commission, 2009).
55. *See* Busby, Nicole, *A Right to Care? Unpaid Care Work in European Employment Law* (Oxford University Press, 2011).

constituted a world premiere in relation to valuing unpaid care work. In 2014, however, an amendment (which entered into force on 6 March 2015) removed the criteria of care and thus, moved away significantly from the original intention to facilitate a better reconciliation between family and work commitments. Section 69AA(a)[56] of the 2007 Act was replaced by a new section which extended the statutory right to all employees, not just those with care responsibilities. Moreover, originally the right to request was limited to employees who had been employed by the same employer for a period of six month, but this limitation was also removed in 2014. Technically, this right is now available to all employees including those in non-standard work from the beginning of employment, whether they have care obligations, or they simply want to enjoy a better work-life balance.

Prima facie this development is positive. However, in the context of work family reconciliation there are some problematic aspects. The legislation now lacks clear underpinning principles which value the reconciliation of work and family or recognise the reality of unpaid care. The removal of the care criteria from the right to request flexible working arrangements arguably makes the care-giving provided by men and women invisible. Care is no longer valued (not even symbolically) and this entrenches the idea that production and reproduction are disconnected in New Zealand society.

An employer, faced with multiple requests by employees for flexibility is not provided with any justification for prioritising work-family reconciliation motivated requests. The desire of one employee to take time off to train for a marathon is exactly on a par with the need of another employee to take an aging parent to the doctor. Moreover, highly valued employees with bargaining power are much more likely to benefit from this right than precarious workers.

The right to request flexible working arrangement can arguably be classified as symbolic. Indeed, while it pays lip service to the idea of work family reconciliation, the dominant focus remains on work productivity. Another point to note is that the statutory right only confers a right to request; employees have always had the right to negotiate and renegotiate the terms of their contract of employment. Although, under the legislation, the employer has the obligation to consider seriously the request for flexible working arrangement, such a request could easily be refused as this obligation is weak. All the law provides for is a right to a process for a fair and timely consideration of a request, rather than a right to flexibility. An employer may refuse the request by providing explanations as to the (business related) reasons for the refusal.[57] The fact that employers are able to decline on business grounds demonstrates the continuing paramountcy of the employer's needs as opposed to employees' need for work family reconciliation. This theme continues in the next section where it is shown that although symbolic steps have been taken towards regulation to mitigate the worst of employer scheduling practices, the employer's needs are still treated as superior to that of employees.

---

56. Under the 2007 Act, Section 69AA(a) states that the object of this Part is to provide '...certain employees with a statutory right to request a variation of their working arrangements if they have the care of any person'.
57. S69AAF of the employment relations Act 2000.

It is also difficult for employees to challenge the refusal of an employer based on business related grounds. Employees, especially those in precarious work often lack the business organisation knowledge (and/or financial and/or emotional ability) to be able to challenge the employer's decision. In addition, the law does not empower employees to challenge the reasons put forward by the employer, as it only allows employees to challenge employers who do not deal with the request in accordance with the specified process. In this case, the matter can be referred to a Labour Inspector, then to mediation, and then only to the court system (the Employment Relations Authority). Even if an employee finds the courage and the energy to contest their employer's refusal, the penalty is paltry. According to S 69AAJ, an employer who does not comply with the process of considering seriously a request for flexible working arrangement is liable to a penalty not exceeding NZD2,000. Such an amount is so insignificant and token, that it cannot be considered as a viable deterrent to employers. In addition, the remedy is ill-adapted to the aim of the provision, as the need for flexibility cannot me met with monetary penalty.

As a result, this statutory right is seldom exercised. Although many employees have requested flexible work arrangements, few have used the formal procedure. The 2011 review of the 2007 amendment shows that among current employees, 43% reported that they have made a request for flexible working arrangement to their employer and a large majority of these requests were approved.[58] However, the request for flexible working arrangement was often not based on the statutory rights.[59] There is, to date, no reported case law around this provision.

Highly qualified, skilled workers, which New Zealand is short of, inherently have the bargaining power to request changes in their terms and conditions of employment. Precarious workers lack bargaining power altogether. The law, as it currently stands is insufficient to change this.

§13.03 REGULATION OF TIME IN NEW ZEALAND

Some key scheduling issues were identified above as problematic for precarious workers leading to work family reconciliation issues, including the problem of over-work due to income insecurity, irregular working hours, changes to rosters at short notice, and insufficient or no guaranteed hours. Following a successful campaign by the unions and in particular UNITE,[60] the New Zealand legislature has recently turned its mind to improving worker's control of their working hours. Consequently, New Zealand law was changed on 1 April 2016 as six new sections (67C–67H) were inserted

58. Department of Labour, *Review of Flexible Working Arrangements in New Zealand Workplaces* (Department of Labour, 2011).
59. *Ibid.*
60. Treen, Mike, *How UNITE took on the Fast Food Companies over Zero Hour contracts and won* (UNITE, 2015) http://www.unite.org.nz/how_unite_took_on_the_fast_food_companies_over_zero_hour_contracts_and_won?recruiter_id=26272 (accessed 19 December 2016); *see* further next section.

into the Employment Relations Act 2000.[61] These reforms represent a step in the right direction to improve work family reconciliation. Nevertheless, it remains questionable whether such reforms go far enough.

New Zealand workers, in real terms, have little protection against overwork. The legal system lacks the comprehensive working time regulations that exist in the European Union countries. Although, there is a maximum working hours provision which establishes a forty-hour, five-day working days per week, the protection it provides is weak. Section 11B of the Minimum Wage Act 1983 prevents an employer from fixing working hours above forty hours per week, *unless this is agreed to* by both parties.[62] These hours can be varied from week to week with agreement between the parties. Subsection (3) of that section also requires that where working hours are fixed at under forty hours per week, both parties must endeavour to fix daily hours so that work hours are not worked on more than five days per week.[63] There is no entitlement to an overtime premium for working above the forty hour maximum, but this can be achieved by agreement between the parties.[64]

The fact that maximum hours may be varied by agreement between the parties makes it doubtful that precarious workers would be able to access any protection against overwork through this provision. Given the weak bargaining power of precarious workers, it would be difficult to refuse an employer's request to alter working hours above the maximum. This is especially true where the employee has no guarantee of on-going work (casuals and temporary agency workers), or the worker is not directly employed within the organisation who has day-to-day control over them (temp agency workers).

In any case, many workers might worry that, refusing to agree to the employer's request to work above the forty hours week, might lead to their hours being drastically reduced in retaliation. It should be noted, however, that a recent amendment to the

61. The focus here is on regulation of working hours however it is worth noting that New Zealand law also provides workers with other leave entitlements which may address work-life balance issues. *I.e.*, Parental leave is provided by the Parental Leave and Employment Protection Act 1987. Paid parental leave is conditional to continuous period of employment and eligibility of the mother. Paid annual as well as sick and bereavement leaves are protected by the Holidays Act 2003. These rights are conditional to continuous employment criteria. Employees are entitled to four weeks' paid annual holiday after twelve months of continuous employment under section 16 of the Holidays Act 2003. The Holidays Act also sets out entitlements to time-and-a-half pay for workers working on public holidays and alternative holiday if the public holiday falls on an ordinary working day for the employee. However, these provisions are available are largely only for those in standard employment and are frequently tied to continuity of service which it may be difficult for precarious workers to establish.
62. Section 11B(2) Minimum Wage Act 1983: 'The maximum number of hours (exclusive of overtime) fixed by an employment agreement to be worked by any worker in any week may be fixed at a number greater than 40 if the parties to the agreement agree.'
63. Section 11B(3) Minimum Wage Act 1983: 'Where the maximum number of hours (exclusive of overtime) fixed by an employment agreement to be worked by any worker in any week is not more than 40, the parties to the agreement must endeavour to fix the daily working hours so that those hours are worked on not more than 5 days of the week.'
64. This section is an obscure requirement of New Zealand law which has had a limited effect in workplaces.

Employment Relations Act 2000 S67F[65] provides protection against such victimisation, provided that the agreement does not contain an availability provision that provides for the payment of reasonable compensation to the employee for making himself or herself available to perform work under the availability provision. Therefore, New Zealand employers may not adversely treat employees who refuse additional hours where there is no availability agreement, which is positive but questions remain as to whether in real terms precarious workers will be able to access this protection given the unbalanced bargaining power between the parties. Also the law contains no prohibition against treating employees who *have agreed* to an availability provision adversely.

In addition to the issue of long working hours, precarious workers are exposed to a lack of certainty with regards to working hours as well as to irregular schedules. Irregular hours, uncertain and unpredictable work schedules deprive precarious workers of the ability to plan and balance their work commitments with their family commitments.[66] Irregular hours result in uncertain and variable pay, contributing to financial pressures which in turn makes it harder for precarious workers to decline work when it is offered.

Providing advance notice of work schedules allows workers to plan work and personal commitments as well as to determine their income in advance, allowing for financial planning and certainty. For this reason, laws providing for the advance notice of work schedules are in effect in several jurisdictions[67] as well as compensation for cancelled shifts.[68] In a recent change to New Zealand law S67C of the Employment Relations Act requires hours of work to be agreed upon between employee and employer as well as to be written into an employees' individual or collective agreement.[69] Hours of work includes the 'number of guaranteed hours' of work, 'the days of the week on which work is to be performed' and 'the start and finish times of work' as well as any flexibility around days and hours of work. This requirement for specificity must be seen as a minor positive development in that it does give employees some indication of the employer's expectation at the outset but employers retain the ability to require flexibility.

---

65. Section 67F was inserted into the Employment Relations Amendment Act 2000, on 1 April 2016, by section 9 of the Employment Relations Amendment Act 2016 (2016 No 9).
66. Shagvaliyeva, Sussanna, and Rashad Yazdanifard, *Impact of flexible working hours on work-life balance*, 4 *American Journal of Industrial and Business Management* 20–23 (2014); Hofäcker & König, *Flexibility and Work-life conflict in time of crisis: a gender Perspective*; Masselot, *Gender Implications of the Right to Request Flexible Working Arrangements: Raising Pigs and Children in New Zealand*.
67. *See* for instance the new regulation adoption in San Francisco, US. Jamieson, Dave, *A Landmark Workers 'Bill of Rights' Passes Unanimously in San Francisco*, Huffington Post (25 November 2014), http://www.huffingtonpost.com/2014/11/25/retail-worker-bill-of-rights-san-francisco_n_6221642.html (accessed 22 December 2016).
68. *See* for example the US Congress proposal for regulation of part-time Schedules, also known as the 'Schedules that Work Act': Kasperkevic, Jana, *Elizabeth Warren to help propose Senate bill to tackle part-time schedules*, The Guardian (23 July 2014), http://www.theguardian.com/money/us-money-blog/2014/jul/23/elizabeth-warren-senate-bill-part-time-schedules (accessed 22 December 2016).
69. Section 67C was inserted into the Employment Relations Amendment Act 2000, on 1 April 2016, by section 9 of the Employment Relations Amendment Act 2016 (2016 No 9).

More significantly the newly introduced section 67G of the Employment Relations Act[70] relates to cancellation of shifts. Under this section the employer cannot cancel a shift unless a reasonable period of notice is given beforehand and reasonable compensation is paid to the employee, if the employer cancels a shift without giving reasonable notice (section 67G(2)). The notice period must be specified in the employee's employment agreement. If it is not specified, then the employer must pay the employee reasonable compensation for the notice specified in the employment agreement (section 67G(3)(b)). If neither reasonable notice nor reasonable compensation is specified in the employee's employment agreement, then the employee is entitled to receive the full amount they would have normally earned working the cancelled shift.

This provision must be welcomed in that it forces employers to plan ahead and compensate employees for shift cancellation. However, the repeated use of the word 'reasonable' in the provision introduces a problematic and subjective element, which might need to be clarified though litigation. Indeed, what is 'reasonable' for the business might not be 'reasonable' for the worker's family life.

In addition to long working hours and irregular and uncertain hours, insufficient hours are also an issue for precarious workers. There has been another recent positive development in New Zealand law around the regulation of 'zero hour' contracts.[71] 'Zero hour' contracts are distinct from casual contracts. Under casual contracts, while the employer has no obligation to offer work, the employee has no obligation to accept work when it is offered. With 'zero hour' contracts, workers not only have no guarantee of work, they are obliged to accept work if and when it is offered. Most pernicious of all is that sometimes employers will make 'zero hour' workers sign exclusivity clauses which mean that employees cannot seek work from other employers. 'Zero hour' contracts thus add to the complexity of managing work family reconciliation for precarious workers. Not only is work not on a regular schedule, when it is offered it cannot be refused, potentially leading to both underemployment as well as intense overwork in times of high employer demand.

Since 2016, New Zealand law effectively prohibits the use of 'zero hour' contracts. S67D of the Employment Relations Act[72] introduces the concept of 'availability'. This provision allows employers to require availability from employees but only if agreed hours of work are specified, and those agreed hours include guaranteed hours of work among those agreed hours. Furthermore, the availability provision has to be based on reasonable grounds and the employee has to be provided with reasonable compensation for making him/herself available for work (s67D3(a) and (b)). This means that employers cannot demand availability from employees without

70. Section 67G was inserted into the Employment Relations Amendment Act 2000, on 1 April 2016, by section 9 of the Employment Relations Amendment Act 2016 (2016 No 9).
71. Brinkley, Ian, *Flexibility or insecurity? Exploring the rise in zero hours contracts* (The Work Foundation, 2013) http://mbsportal.bl.uk/taster/subjareas/hrmemplyrelat/twf/164297flexibilityinsecurity13.pdf (accessed 22 December 2016).
72. Section 67D was inserted into the Employment Relations Amendment Act 2000, on 1 April 2016, by section 9 of the Employment Relations Amendment Act 2016 (2016 No 9).

reason and employees required to be available must have at least two guaranteed hours. Thus, effectively 'zero hour' contracts are now prohibited.

While the intention of this provision is to prevent egregious abuse of 'zero hour' contracts, much discretion is given to the employer to determine what is 'reasonable'. S67(d)(5) provides that in considering whether there are genuine reasons based on reasonable grounds for including an availability provision, an employer must have regard to all relevant matters, including the following:

> whether it is practicable for the employer to meet business demands for the work to be performed by the employee without including an availability provision; as well (b) the number of hours for which the employee would be required to be available; and (c) the proportion of the hours referred to in paragraph (b) to the agreed hours of work. It is thus clear that, as with the right to request flexibility, primacy is to be given to the employer's business needs.

Furthermore employees who have agreed to an availability provision cannot refuse to be available during the agreed hours unless reasonable compensation for availability is not written into the contract. 'Reasonable' is not explicitly defined, however, S67(d)(6) provides that compensation payable under an availability provision must be determined having regard to all relevant matters.[73]

Finally, S67H prohibits unreasonable restrictions on 'secondary employment'. Employers cannot restrict secondary employment for employees, unless the employer has reasonable grounds and the reasons behind these grounds are stated in the employee's employment agreement. Here again the employer is only required to act 'reasonably' but reasonableness is not defined and presumably once again the employer's business requirements are likely to take precedence over the employees' work family reconciliation needs.

In conclusion, while the 2016 amendments ostensibly address some of the worst of the scheduling issues, there is a high degree of flexibility to agree on arrangements which may be very un-family friendly in real terms. While workers with real bargaining power may now have additional leverage in bargaining terms and employers have been given some direction as to how specific they must be in reaching agreements, the fact remains that precarious workers may have little choice but to agree to less than optimal work arrangements. Having agreed, the law offers little in the way of redress. Indeed, a worker who has agreed to an availability provision may explicitly be subjected to detriment, if they refuse hours. Furthermore, the requirements that employers should be reasonable are vague although implicitly it does give primacy to the employer's business needs. Further clarification may be needed through a process of litigation. It

73. Section 67(d)(6) Compensation payable under an availability provision must be determined having regard to all relevant matters, including the following:
    (a) the number of hours for which the employee is required to be available:
    (b) the proportion of the hours referred to in paragraph (a) to the agreed hours of work:
    (c) the nature of any restrictions resulting from the availability provision:
    (d) the rate of payment under the employment agreement for the work for which the employee is available:
    (e) if the employee is remunerated by way of salary, the amount of the salary.

remains to be seen whether precarious workers will have the time or the means to bring litigation forward.

§13.04 UNION INITIATIVES WITH REGARD TO SCHEDULING AND REGULARITY OF HOURS

Statutory regulation of working hours can be beneficial, however, as noted above the requirements of individual sectors vary as do the work family reconciliation needs of individuals and families. In this context, unions can potentially play an important role in negotiating specific solutions tailored to the needs of industry as well as those of the family.

The weak bargaining power of precarious workers has been identified as a key limitation on the efficacy of rights to request flexibility and enforcement of legislative protections.[74] The purpose of labour law classically has been seen as redressing the inherent imbalance of power between workers and employers by empowering unions to act for workers.[75] This principle is explicitly acknowledged in New Zealand's Employment Relations Act which states at section 3 that the object of this Act is – (a) to build productive employment relationships through the promotion of good faith in all aspects of the employment environment and of the employment relationship…(ii) by acknowledging and addressing the inherent inequality of power in employment relationships [and by] (iii) promoting collective bargaining.

Unfortunately however, since the 1990s the power and coverage of New Zealand unions was significantly and intentionally undermined by the Employment Contracts Act.[76] This was replaced in 2000 by the more union friendly Employment Relations Act but the damage had been done and union membership is not high, particularly in the private sector, and it seems to be in a process of gradual decline. As of 2016 it sat at roughly under 20% of the employed workforce.[77]

74. Conaghan, Joanne, *Time to dream? Flexibility, families and the regulation of working time*, in Fudge, Judy & Owens Rosemary (eds.), *Precarious Work, Women, and the New Economy: the Challenge to Legal Norms* (Hart Publishing, 2006), 101–130.
75. Kahn-Freund, Otto, *Labour and the Law* (2nd ed., Stevens, 1977) (1977), p. 6; Anderson, Gordon and John Hughes, *Employment Law in New Zealand*, 6–11 (LexisNexis NZ, 2014); Collins, Hugh, *Labour Law as a vocation*, 105(3) Law Quarterly Review, 468–484 (1989).
76. Anderson, Gordon, *Labour Law in New Zealand* (2nd ed., Wolters Kluwer, Alphen aan den Rijn, 2015).
77. 'In the June 2016 quarter, around 1 in 5 employees belonged to a union, with most union members in full-time employment (86.9 percent) and in a permanent job (92.1 percent). Although the sex split for employees was similar (50.9 percent male, 49.1 percent female), women were more likely to be union members than men (6 in 10 or 58.7 percent).' Statistic New Zealand, *Union membership and employment agreements – June 2016 quarter* (2016), http://www.stats.govt.nz/browse_for_stats/income-and-work/employment_and_unemployment/improving-labour-market-statistics/union-memship-emplymt-agmt.aspx (accessed 19 December 2016).

Despite the stated commitment to unions, in real terms, legislative support is limited and consequently there is insufficient support for bargaining for the improvement of work family reconciliation. Unlike many other European countries,[78] New Zealand does not have extension bargaining. Collective contracts do not extend beyond the members of the union. In addition, although there is a guiding principle that all parties are required to act in good faith, unlike in other countries (such as France and Spain),[79] there is no legislative requirement for employers to bargain on particular terms and conditions. Consequently, New Zealand employers are increasingly trying to exclude from collective bargaining fundamental terms such as pay rates.[80]

Furthermore, while New Zealand unions certainly aim to better the working conditions of precarious workers, precarious workers are often not union members. Unions therefore do not have a mandate to act on behalf of such workers. While it is difficult to be precise with regards to numbers of precarious workers due to aforementioned categorisation issues, it is clear that temporary/non-standard workers have lower trade union participation, with only 22.4% of temporary workers being union members; casual workers had the lowest membership at 14.8%.[81]

New Zealand unions also do not have extensive resources to command and have to tread a difficult line in terms allocating those resources *vis-à-vis* their responsibilities to dues paying members. The weakening of the union movement has moreover indirect flow on effects; the NZCTU argues that the increase in insecure work and lower union participation has eroded workers' knowledge of their employment entitlements.[82] This in turns weakens the ability of the regulatory system to assist precarious workers. Even where laws exist, workers may not have the knowledge to access and/or the financial ability enforce them; casual workers have been found to have the lowest level of knowledge of their legal entitlements.[83]

Despite these limitations, New Zealand unions have had some success in improving workers' control over working hours, including workers in sectors where precarious work is prevalent. In order to do so, unions have been using a variety of means, which we discuss below.

---

78. Traxler, Franz, *Collective bargaining in the OECD: developments, preconditions and effects*, 4(2) European Journal of Industrial Relations, 207–226 (1998); Traxler, Franz, and Martin Behrens, *Collective bargaining coverage and extension procedures* (2002) http://www.eurofound.europa.eu/observatories/eurwork/comparative-information/collective-bargaining-coverage-and-extension-procedures (accessed on 19 December 2016).
79. Artiles, Antonio Martín, *Work-life balance in collective bargaining examined* (2005), http://www.eurofound.europa.eu/observatories/eurwork/articles/work-life-balance-in-collective-bargaining-examined (accessed 19 December 2016); Gregory, Abigail, and Susan Milner, *Trade Unions and Work-life Balance: Changing Times in France and the UK?* 47(1) British Journal of Industrial Relations, 122–146 (2009).
80. *First Union Inc v Jacks Hardware and Timber Limited* [2015] NZ EmpC 230.
81. Statistics New Zealand, *Flexibility and security in employment: Findings from the 2012 Survey of Working Life*, p. 6.
82. Statistics New Zealand, *Flexibility and security in employment: Findings from the 2012 Survey of Working Life*, p. 45.
83. Dixon, *A profile of temporary workers and their employment outcomes*, p. 34; Whatman, Richard, Craig Armitage & Richard Dunbar, *Labour Market Adjustment under the Employment Contracts Act*, 19(1) *New Zealand Journal of Industrial Relations* (1994).

Unions have, to an extent, been able to influence public policy through their campaigns and participation in policy forums. New Zealand unions have, in particular, been at the forefront of advocating for better control over working time. In 2013, the New Zealand Council of Trade Unions published a comprehensive report entitled: *Under Pressure: Insecure Work in New Zealand*[84] to investigate the prevalence and spread of insecure work in New Zealand, and the impact it has had on New Zealand workers. This report also encouraged unions to lead campaigns against insecure work and a number of unions have run campaigns to focus on specific issues faced by precarious workers.[85]

Most encouragingly, UNITE, a small union, has been unexpectedly successful in challenging and ending zero hour contracts in the fast food sector through a savvy combination of a media campaigning and collective bargaining.[86] Not only did UNITE convince all of the fast food chains to agree to terms in collective agreements banning zero hour contracts, but the media campaign was picked up by mainstream media leading ultimately to law change around zero hour contracts discussed above.

Unions have also had some success in achieving favourable judgments for workers through the process of strategic litigation. For example, *Idea Services Limited v. Dickson*[87] dealt with workers required to sleep over in residential care settings. The Supreme Court ultimately held that a person required to be on-site or available for work is entitled to compensation, even if that person is not performing work duties. As a result, John Ryall, Secretary of the Service and Foodworkers Union (now e Tu) expressed the view that litigation to secure workers' rights was now preferable to collective bargaining.[88] 'We decided there's got to be a better way than (collective bargaining)[...]I think these cases will continue, until such time as there is a collective bargaining system in place.'

However, collective bargaining, litigation and campaigning through public forums are not necessarily discrete strategies as the long running Ports of Auckland industrial dispute demonstrates. In late 2011, Ports of Auckland became engaged in a dispute with workers represented by the Maritime Union of New Zealand. This began as a rostering dispute; the Maritime Union opposed the Port's proposals to change the rostering system.[89] The Port argued that more flexible rostering was necessary to match workers with port traffic, but the union opposed this arguing that the current rostering

84. New Zealand Council of Trade Unions, *Under Pressure: A Detailed Report into Insecure Work in New Zealand*.
85. For example the FIRST union which represents workers in Finance, Industrial (Textile and Wood) Retail, Stores & Transport successfully campaigned against a New Zealand bank who wanted to increase flexibility in its employment contracts and reduce advance notice of schedules: McNicol, Hamish, John Anthony and Narelle Henson, ANZ workers walk off the job (10 October 2014), http://www.stuff.co.nz/business/industries/10601614/ANZ-workers-walk-off-the-job (accessed 17 January 2017).
86. Treen, *How UNITE took on the Fast Food Companies over Zero Hour contracts and won*.
87. *Idea Services Limited v Dickson* [2011] NZSC 55 SC 25/2011.
88. https://unitenews.wordpress.com/2015/03/11/nz-labour-letter-march-2015/ (accessed 19 December 2016).
89. NZCTU & MUNZ, *Port of Auckland Dispute Fact Sheet* (2012), http://www.munz.org.nz/wp-content/uploads/2012/01/Port-of-Auckland-Dispute-Fact-Sheet-3-Feb-2012.pdf (accessed 17 January 2017).

system provided a balance between the flexibility required by the Port and the certainty of stable and reliable hours for the workers. The union argued that the proposal removed protections for workers against long hours, reduced their entitlements to breaks and sick leave and provided no guarantees of work and hours. Furthermore, the compensatory pay increase offered no real compensation because the hours become unstable. At its heart this was a work family reconciliation issue. Workers were concerned about the impact the proposed roster changes would have on their family lives by reducing their ability to plan and make commitments.

This dispute ran for four years, until a new collective settlement was finally reached in February 2015. Over the years of the dispute, the union utilised a number of techniques to achieve its ultimate bargaining aim including strikes, the involvement of the International Transport Workers Federation and International Longshore and Warehouse Union, street protests, and litigation over breaches of good faith by the employer in bargaining.

It is clear that unions can play an integral role in addressing the challenges experienced by precarious workers. Successful union campaigns can increase awareness of work family challenges and can encourage either legal change or change in standard human resources practice as well as raise awareness of existing legal rights where such exist.

Unions also contribute to clarifying the law. Overall, while New Zealand has adopted new legislation provisions around zero hour contracts and regulating shift work, there is considerable vagueness and scope for interpretation around the concept of 'reasonableness'.[90] Thus, it is likely that there will be a need for further union funded litigation.

However, amidst a context of declining union participation, unions are presented with a quandary of whether to focus on achieving solutions for their members or campaigning to improve the working lives for all. While New Zealand unions have taken up the challenge of campaigning for all workers as noted by the late Helen Kelly:

> One of the challenges we haven't cracked is the resourcing model for all this new work. While we rely on those that can access the rights to bargaining and union membership to fund these campaigns we will always be running them on a shoe string.[91]

§13.05 CONCLUSION

The central research question this contribution explored is whether New Zealand's legal framework is fit for the purpose of supporting precarious workers in work-family reconciliation.

Precarious workers encounter a number of work family reconciliation challenges including lack of control of scheduling, overwork or insufficient work all of which flow

90. *See* our previous discussions on flexible working arrangement.
91. Kelly, Helen, *Speech to the CTU conference* (14 October 2015), https://thestandard.org.nz/helen-kellys-speech-to-the-ctu-conference/ (accessed 17 January 2017).

from employer requirements for flexibility. The precarity of their working arrangements makes it difficult for precarious workers to gain control of their working hours since there is an inherent inequality of bargaining power in their position giving them limited ability either to negotiate better terms for themselves or to exercise rights they may technically be entitled to in law. Limited knowledge of existing rights compounds these problems.

Regulation to improve the ability of precarious workers to reconcile their work family needs is complex as precarious workers are not concentrated in any one sector or contractual arrangement. Precarious workers are also not a homogenous group and have their own individual needs.

There have been some positive developments in New Zealand law including the extension of the right to request flexibility to all workers and the outlawing of zero hour contracts. However enforcement mechanisms are weak and the penalties for non-compliance by employers are token. The law changes are also underpinned by an emphasis on the employer's needs and what is reasonable from the employer's perspective.

Unions remain the best hope for precarious workers and it would seem that as commented by the late Helen Kelly:

> New Zealand working people more than ever need the institutional strength they build through unions to organise themselves, to give them a say in this society and to win justice and fairness for them and their families.[92]

Unions are well placed contribute to equalising the bargaining power of precarious workers while at the same time working with employers to craft sector specific work family reconciliation terms and conditions in collective contracts. Union can also enforce existing rights and raise awareness of these rights. Given resource constraints, New Zealand unions have achieved some notable wins including successfully lobbying for law change. However, New Zealand unions have limited coverage and resources and the legal framework does not do enough to support unions in this important work. Extension bargaining and explicitly requiring employers to bargain on work-family reconciliation and scheduling issues could considerably strengthen unions' ability to benefit precarious workers. If this were coupled with stronger penalties for employer non-compliance, gains would be possible. However, the fundamental emphasis on the employer's needs as opposed to worker's rights to care for their families would likely remain an obstacle to significant improvements.

REFERENCES

Case Law

Idea Services Limited v. Dickson [2011] NZSC 55 SC 25/2011.
First Union Inc v. Jacks Hardware and Timber Limited [2015] NZ EmpC 230.

92. Kelly's *final speech to the CTU Conference.*

Literature

Anderson, Danaë, *Are Vulnerable Workers Really Protected in New Zealand?* 39(1) New Zealand Journal of Employment Relations 52–67 (2014).

Anderson, Gordon, *Labour Law in New Zealand* (2nd ed., Wolters Kluwer, Alphen aan den Rijn, 2015).

Anderson, Gordon and John Hughes, *Employment Law in New Zealand* (LexisNexis NZ, 2014).

Artiles, Antonio Martín, *Work-life Balance in Collective Bargaining Examined* (2005), http://www.eurofound.europa.eu/observatories/eurwork/articles/work-life-balance-in-collective-bargaining-examined (accessed 19 December 2016).

Bornstein, Stephanie, *Work, Family, and Discrimination at the Bottom of the Ladder*, 19(1) Georgetown Journal on Poverty Law & Policy, 1–42 (2012).

Brosnan, Peter & Pat Walsh, *Employment Security in Australia and New Zealand*, 8(3) Labour & Industry: A Journal of the Social and Economic Relations of Work, 23–41 (1998).

Brinkley, Ian, *Flexibility or Insecurity? Exploring the Rise in Zero Hours Contracts* (The Work Foundation, 2013), http://mbsportal.bl.uk/taster/subjareas/hrmemplyrelat/twf/164297flexibilityinsecurity13.pdf (accessed 22 December 2016).

Busby, Nicole, *A Right to Care? Unpaid Care Work in European Employment Law* (Oxford University Press, 2011).

Caracciolo di Torella, Eugenia & Annick Masselot, *Work and Family Life Balance in the EU Law and Policy 40 Years On: Still Balancing, Still Struggling*, 2 European Gender Equality Law Review, 6–14 (2013).

Caracciolo di Torella, Eugenia & Annick Masselot, *Reconciling Work and Family Life in EU Law and Policy* (Palgrave Macmillan, 2010).

Collins, Hugh, *Labour Law as a Vocation*, 105(3) Law Quarterly Review, 468–484 (1989).

Conaghan, Joanne, *Time to Dream? Flexibility, Families and the Regulation of Working Time*, in Fudge, Judy & Owens Rosemary (eds), *Precarious Work, Women, and the New Economy: the Challenge to Legal Norms* (Hart Publishing, 2006), 101–130.

Connelly, Catherine & Daniel Gallagher, *Emerging Trends in Contingent Work Research*, 30(6) Journal of Management, 959–983 (2004).

Crompton, Rosemary, *Employment and the Family: The Reconfiguration of Work and Family Life in Contemporary Societies* (Cambridge University Press, 2006).

Davey, Judith & Sally Keeling, *Combining Work and Eldercare: A Study of Employees in Two City Councils Who Provide Informal Care for Older People* (2004) http://thehub.superu.govt.nz/sites/default/files/Combining%20Work%20and%20Eldercare%2C%20a%20study%20of%20employees%20in%20two%20City%20Councils.pdf (accessed 11 December 2016).

Department of Labour, *Review of Flexible Working Arrangements in New Zealand Workplaces* (Department of Labour, 2011).

Department of Labour, *Survey of Labour Market Adjustment under the Employment Contracts Act*, prepared by Colmar Brunton Research (August 1997).

Dixon, Sylvia, *A Profile of Temporary Workers and Their Employment Outcomes* (New Zealand Department of Labour, 2009), http://www.mbie.govt.nz/publications-research/research/labour-market-and-skills/temporary-workers.pdf (accessed 19 December 2016).

EEO Trust, *Fathers in Paid Work Toolkit* (2003), http://eeotrust.org/content/docs/toolkits/Father%20and%20paid%20work%20toolkit.pdf (accessed 11 December 2016).

Eurofound, *Fifth European Working Conditions Survey* (Publications Office of the European Union, 2012), http://www.eurofound.europa.eu/sites/default/files/ef_publication/field_ef_document/ef1182en.pdf (accessed 22 December 2016).

Forstater, Mathew, *Working for a Better world Cataloguing Arguments for the Right to Employment* 41(1) Philosophy & Social Criticism, 61–67 (2015).

Fudge, Judy, *Precarious Migrant Status and Precarious Employment: The Paradox of International Rights for Migrant Workers*, 34(1) Comparative Labor Law and Policy Journal, 95–132 (2012).

Fudge, Judy & Owens Rosemary (eds), *Precarious Work, Women, and the New Economy: The Challenge to Legal Norms* (Hart Publishing, 2006).

Fursman, Lindy, *Working Long Hours in New Zealand: A Profile of Long Hours Workers Using Data from the 2006 Census* (Department of Labour, March 2008), http://thehub.superu.govt.nz/sites/default/files/Working%20Long%20Hours%20in%20New%20Zealand%2C%20A%20Profile%20of%20Long%20Hours%20Workers%20Using%20Data%20From%20The%202006%20Census.pdf (accessed 22 December 2016).

Fursman, Lindy & Nita Zodgekar, *Making It Work: The Impacts of Flexible Working Arrangements on New Zealand Families*, 35 Social Policy Journal of New Zealand 43–54 (2009).

Gregory, Abigai, & Susan Milner, *Trade Unions and Work-Life Balance: Changing Times in France and the UK?* 47(1) British Journal of Industrial Relations, 122–146 (2009).

Handy, Jocelyn, *Maintaining Family Life Under Shiftwork Schedules: A Case Study of a New Zealand Petrochemical Plant*, 39(1) *New Zealand Journal of Psychology*, 7–14 (2010).

Hegewisch, Ariane, *Flexible Working Policies: A Comparative Review* (Equality and Human Rights Commission, 2009).

Herring, Jonathan, *Caring and the Law* (Hart Publishing, 2013).

Hofäcker, Dirk & Stefanie König, *Flexibility and Work-Life Conflict in Time of Crisis: A Gender Perspective*, 33(9) International Journal of Sociology and Social Policy, 613–635 (2013).

Houseman, Susan, *Why Employers Use Flexible Staffing Arrangements: From and Establishment Survey*, 55(1) Industrial and Labor Relations Review 155–162 (2001).

International Labour Organisation, *From Precarious Work to Decent Work: Outcome Document to the Workers' Symposium on Policies and Regulations to Combat Precarious Employment* (ILO, 2012), http://www.ilo.org/wcmsp5/groups/

public/---ed_dialogue/---actrav/documents/meetingdocument/wcms_179787.pdf (accessed 11 December 2016).

Jacobs, Jerry & Kathleen Gerson, *The Time Divide: Work, Family and Gender Inequalities* (Harvard University Press, 2004).

James, Grace & Emma Spruce, *Workers with Elderly Dependants: Employment Law's Response to the Latest Care-Giving Conundrum*, 35(3) Legal Studies, 463–479 (2015).

Jamieson, Dave, *A Landmark Workers 'Bill of Rights' Passes Unanimously in San Francisco*, Huffington Post (25 November 2014), http://www.huffingtonpost.com/2014/11/25/retail-worker-bill-of-rights-san-francisco_n_6221642.html (accessed 22 December 2016).

Kahn-Freund, Otto, *Labour and the Law* (2nd ed. Stevens 1977).

Kalleberg, Arne L., *Good Jobs, Bad Jobs: The Rise of Polarized and Precarious Employment Systems in the United States, 1970s–2000s* (Russell Sage Foundation, 2011).

Kalleberg, Arne L., *Precarious Work, Insecure Workers: Employment Relations in Transition*, 74(1) American Sociological Review, 1–22 (2009).

Kalleberg, Arne L., *Nonstandard Employment Relations: Part-Time, Temporary and Contract Work*, 26 Annual Review of Sociology, 341–365 (2000).

Kasperkevic, Jana, *Elizabeth Warren to Help Propose Senate Bill to Tackle Part-Time Schedules*, The Guardian (23 July 2014), http://www.theguardian.com/money/us-money-blog/2014/jul/23/elizabeth-warren-senate-bill-part-time-schedules (accessed 22 December 2016).

Kelly, Helen, *Speech to the CTU Conference* (14 October 2015), https://thestandard.org.nz/helen-kellys-speech-to-the-ctu-conference/ (accessed 17 January 2017).

Keune, Maarten, *Trade Union Responses to Precarious Work in Seven European Countries*, 5(1) International Journal of Labour Research, 59–78 (2013).

Levin-Epstein, Jodie, *How to Exercise Flexible Work: Take Steps with a 'Soft Touch' Law*, Work Life Balance Brief No 3 (Centre for Law and Social Policy 2005).

Masselot, Annick, *Gender Implications of the Right to Request Flexible Working Arrangements: Raising Pigs and Children in New Zealand*, 39(9) New Zealand Journal of Employment Relations, 59–71 (2015).

Masselot, Annick, *The Right and Reality of Flexible Working Arrangements in New Zealand*, in Grace James & Nicole Busby (eds), *Families, Care-Giving and Paid Work* (Edward Elgard Publishing, 2011) 69–85.

McLaren, Eva, Patrick Firkin, Paul Spoonley, Ann Dupuis, Anne de Bruin & Kerr Inkson, *At the Margins: Contingency, Precariousness and Non-standard Work*, 1 Labour Market Dynamics Research Programme, Research Report Series (2004).

McNicol, Hamish, John Anthony & Narelle Henson, *ANZ Workers Walk Off the Job* (10 October 2014), http://www.stuff.co.nz/business/industries/10601614/ANZ-workers-walk-off-the-job (accessed 17 January 2017).

Mikaere, Ani, *Colonising Myths-Maori Realities: He Rukuruku Whakaaro* (Huia Publishers, 2011).

Ministry of Business Innovation and Employment, *Playing by the Rules: Strengthening Enforcement of Employment Standards Discussion Document* (May 2014) [CAB Min (14) 19/7 refers].

National Women's Law Center, *The Schedules That Work Act: Giving Workers the Tools They Need to Succeed* (2014), http://www.nwlc.org/sites/default/files/pdfs/schedules_that_work_act_fact_sheet_7.22.14.pdf (accessed 7 December 2016).

New Zealand Council of Trade Unions (NZCTU), *Under Pressure: A Detailed Report into Insecure Work in New Zealand* (NZCTU, 2013) http://www.union.org.nz/wp-content/uploads/2016/12/CTU-Under-Pressure-Detailed-Report-2.pdf (accessed 19 December 2016).

New Zealand Council of Trade Unions (NZCTU) & Maritime Union of New Zealand (MUNZ), *Port of Auckland Dispute Fact Sheet* (2012), http://www.munz.org.nz/wp-content/uploads/2012/01/Port-of-Auckland-Dispute-Fact-Sheet-3-Feb-2012.pdf (accessed 17 January 2017).

New Zealand Government, *Employment Relations Amendment Bill 2013, Explanatory Note* (New Zealand Government, 2013), http://www.legislation.govt.nz/bill/government/2013/0105/6.0/DLM5160202.html (accessed 11 December 2016).

O'Meara, Patrick, *Flexibility and Employment Laws: Labour Law Bot Working for Those in Insecure Work*. Radio New Zealand Insight Programme (2014), http://www.radionz.co.nz/national/programmes/insight/audio/20157262/insight-for-16-november-2014-flexibility-and-employment-laws (accessed 7 December 2016).

Owens, Rosemary, *Engendering Flexibility in a World of Precarious Work*, in Fudge, Judy & Owens Rosemary (eds), *Precarious Work, Women, and the New Economy: The Challenge to Legal Norms* (Hart Publishing, 2006) 329–352.

Pennycook, Matthew, Giselle Cory & Vidhya Alakeson, *A Matter of Time: The Rise of Zero-Hour Contracts* (Resolution Foundation, 2013), http://www.resolutionfoundation.org/wp-content/uploads/2014/08/A_Matter_of_Time_-_The_rise_of_zero-hours_contracts_final_1.pdf (accessed 7 December 2016).

PEPSO, *It's More Than Poverty: Employment Precarity and Household Well-Being* (February 2013), http://pepsouwt.files.wordpress.com/2013/02/its-more-than-poverty-feb-2013.pdf (accessed 7 December 2016).

Porter, Gayle, *Work, Work Ethic and Work Excess*, 17(5) Journal of Organizational Change and Management, 424–439 (2004).

Quinlan, Michael, *The 'Pre-invention' of Precarious Employment: The Changing World of Work in Context*, 23(4) The Economic and Labour Relations Review 3–24 (2012).

Shagvaliyeva, Sussanna & Rashad Yazdanifard, *Impact of Flexible Working Hours on Work-Life Balance*, 4 American Journal of Industrial and Business Management 20–23 (2014).

Statistic New Zealand, *Union Membership and Employment Agreements – June 2016 Quarter* (2016), http://www.stats.govt.nz/browse_for_stats/income-and-work/employment_and_unemployment/improving-labour-market-statistics/union-memship-emplymt-agmt.aspx (accessed 19 December 2016).

Statistics New Zealand, *Flexibility and Security in Employment: Findings from the 2012 Survey of Working Life* (2014), http://www.stats.govt.nz/browse_for_stats/income-and-work/employment_and_unemployment/flexibility-security-employment.aspx (accessed 11 December 2016).

Statistics New Zealand, *Flexibility and Security in Employment: Findings from the 2012 Survey of Working Life* (2013), http://www.stats.govt.nz/browse_for_stats/income-and-work/employment_and_unemployment/flexibility-security-employment.aspx (accessed 7 December 2016).

Statistics New Zealand, *Survey of Working Life* (December 2012), http://www.stats.govt.nz/browse_for_stats/income-and-work/employment_and_unemployment/SurveyofWorkingLife_HOTPDec12qtr.aspx (accessed 20 December 2016).

Standing, Guy, *The Precariat: The New Dangerous Class* (A&C Black, 2011).

Traxler, Franz & Martin Behrens, *Collective Bargaining Coverage and Extension Procedures* (2002), http://www.eurofound.europa.eu/observatories/eurwork/comparative-information/collective-bargaining-coverage-and-extension-procedures (accessed on 19 December 2016).

Traxler, Franz, *Collective Bargaining in the OECD: Developments, Preconditions and Effects*, 4(2) European Journal of Industrial Relations, 207–226 (1998)

Treen, Mike, *How UNITE Took on the Fast Food Companies over Zero Hour Contracts and Won* (UNITE, 2015), http://www.unite.org.nz/how_unite_took_on_the_fast_food_companies_over_zero_hour_contracts_and_won?recruiter_id=26272 (accessed 19 December 2016).

Tucker, Philip & Celia Rutherford, *Moderators of the Relationship between Long Work Hours and Health*, 10(4) Journal of Occupational and Health Psychology 465–476 (2005).

Underhill, Elsa & Michael Quinlan, *How Precarious Employment Affects Health and Safety at Work: The Case of Temporary Agency Workers*, 66(3) Relations Industrielles / Industrial Relations, 397–421 (2011).

Van der Hulst, Monique & Sabine Geurts, *Associations Between Overtime and Psychological Health in High and Low Reward Jobs*, 15(3) Work & Stress 227–240 (2001).

Vosko, Lea, *Managing the Margins Gender, Citizenship, and the International Regulation of Precarious Employment* (Oxford University Press, 2010).

Vosko, Lea, Martha MacDonald & Ian Campbell (eds), *Gender and the Contours of Precarious Employment* (Routledge, 2009).

Wakeling, Adrian, *Give and Take? Unravelling the True Nature of Zero-Hours Contracts* (2014), http://www.acas.org.uk/media/pdf/6/n/Acas-Policy-Discussion-Paper-Zero-Hours-May-2014.pdf (accessed 9 December 2016).

Whatman, Richard, Craig Armitage & Richard Dunbar, *Labour Market Adjustment under the Employment Contracts Act*, 19(1) *New Zealand Journal of Industrial Relations* (1994).

Williams, Joan C. & Heather Boushey, *The Three Faces of Work-Family Conflict: The Poor, the Professionals, and the Missing Middle* (Center for American Progress and Work Life Law, 2010), https://cdn.americanprogress.org/wp-content/uploads/issues/2010/01/pdf/threefaces.pdf (accessed 7 December 2016).

Wilson, Margaret, *Precarious Work – New Zealand Experience*, 39(2) New Zealand Journal of Employment Relations 22–33 (2014).

CHAPTER 14

Regulating Work-Life Balance: The Contemporary Swedish Experience

Niklas Selberg

§14.01 WORK-LIFE BALANCE: REVITALISING A CLASSICAL CONCERN FOR LABOUR LAW

'Control over the time of the worker lies at the heart of the contract of employment', Hugh Collins reminds us, and places the issue of time at the centre of social, political and legal conflicts around regulations of labour.[1] At the core of the contract of employment lies a bargaining act about time in which the employer will purchase a worker's time rather than the products of her labour. Increasingly, conceptualisations such as work/life balance have been used as a framework to analyse and debate questions of the organisation and regulation of the labour market. While a stronger general emphasis on the need for a balance between 'work' and 'life' can be noted, there has yet to be a concrete development in terms of regulations directly applicable between the parties to the employment contract – although the notion of work/life balance is to some extent acknowledged in international legal instruments, such as the Charter of Fundamental Rights of the European Union,[2] the Revised European Social Charter of 1996 of the Council of Europe[3] and the 1981 Convention concerning Workers with Family Responsibilities of the International Labour Organisation.[4] The European Commission is determined to accompany the European Pillar of Social Rights with 'initiatives to address the challenges of work-life balance faced by working families',

1. Hugh Collins, The Right to Flexibility, pp. 99–124, In: Joanne Conaghan & Kerry Rittich (eds.) Labour Law, Work, and Family. Critical and Comparative Perspectives, Oxford University Press, 2005.
2. Article 33, OJ 2012/C 326/02.
3. Article 27.
4. *See* §14.05 below.

linking this to its commitment 'to promoting social upwards convergence and strengthening the social dimension of European integration'.[5] Furthermore, voices in legal academia – Zbyszewska[6], Busby[7] and Collins[8] – have presented convincing arguments for reforms of the social and legal organisation of work in the direction of social sustainability.

The regulation of (working) time is central to labour and employment law, and has historically been at least partially dominated by the bilateral imagery that comes about in the shadows of the conflict of interests between the two sides of industry. Debates on working time are often about competing visions of flexibility – as either a resource for workers or for the employer.[9] Legal scholars have attempted to unpack the power dimensions of working time by conceptualising the function of time in labour law as limiting the subordination of workers.[10] The classical theme of labour law is present in discourses on work/life balance and debates on working time legislation, but it is also broadly acknowledged that working time regulation is more complex than balancing the interests of the parties to the employment contract. While advising against leaving working time regulation to either the employer solely or to collective bargaining, Supiot claims that:

> it is no longer possible to claim to consider working time regulation from the sole viewpoint of the employer, or exclusively as the organisation of time spent working for wages. Any regulation or deregulation of working time organisation involves the fabric of human life, both individual and social. More than ever, working time deregulation is harmful to the public interest.[11]

Working time is thus perceived as a matter that should not be left entirely to the parties to the work relationship or to the agents of collective autonomy, and something that cannot be defined solely in terms of the outcome of the conflict of the immediate

5. COM(2016) 710, Commission Work Programme 2017. Delivering a Europe that protects, empowers and defends, p. 10 (cf. COM(2008) 635 A better work-life balance: stronger support for reconciling professional, private and family life).
6. Ania Zbyszewska, Reshaping EU Working-Time Regulation: Towards a More Sustainable Regime, European Labour Law Journal, Vol. 7, No. 3 (2016), pp. 331–347, Ania Zbyszewska, Gendering European Working Time Regimes. The Working Time Directive and the Case of Poland, Cambridge University Press, 2016.
7. Nicole Busby, A Right to Care? Unpaid Care Work in European Employment Law, Oxford University Press, 2011.
8. Hugh Collins, The Right to Flexibility, pp. 99–124, In: Joanne Conaghan & Kerry Rittich (eds.) Labour Law, Work, and Family. Critical and Comparative Perspectives, Oxford University Press, 2005.
9. Jeff Kenner, Re-evaluating the concept of working-time: an analysis of recent case law, Industrial Relations Journal, Vol. 35 (2004) pp. 588–602.
10. Cf. Alain Supiot, On-the-Job Time: Time for Agreement, The International Journal of Comparative Labour Law and Industrial Relations, 1996, pp. 195–211, Alain Supiot, Beyond Employment. Changes in Work and the Future of Labour Law in Europe, Oxford University Press, 2001, Jeff Kenner, Regulating Working Time–Beyond Subordination?, In: Stephen Weatherill (ed.), Better Regulation, Hart Publishing, 2007, pp. 195–217.
11. Alain Supiot, On-the-Job Time: Time for Agreement, The International Journal of Comparative Labour Law and Industrial Relations, 1996, pp. 195–211, p. 210f.

interests of each side of industry. The theme of balance further leads labour law beyond its well-known set of direct contractual relations.[12]

Against this backdrop, the present chapter will provide an overview of the work/life balance discourse[13] in Swedish labour law, together with an overview of Swedish regulation - legislation and collective agreements - pertinent to work/life balance, as conceptualised in terms[14] of the distribution of regulatory power between worker and trade union and employer over (a) the total amount of work to be performed, (b) when in time this work is to be performed and (c) the possibilities on part of workers to suspend work without at the same time be in breach of the employment contract.[15]

§14.02 WORK/LIFE BALANCE IN SWEDEN: A HISTORICAL OVERVIEW

In the early stages of industrialisation, working time differed strongly between sectors and enterprises. Industrial conflicts occurred over salaries and working time. The issue of working time was brought up in parliament by Social democrats but was repeatedly struck down. Collective agreements in the form of tariffs on wages and working time were however concluded from as early as the 1890s. The lack of firm regulations about this matter implied that the length of the workweek simply followed the market forces of supply and demand of work.[16]

Following a period in which the general working time decreased somewhat for many workers through collective bargaining, the issue of working time became a political matter in the shadow of the riots and revolutionary tendencies of the 1910s. Not until 1919, under mounting pressure brought about not least because of the Russian revolution and the strong mobilisation of organised labour across Sweden, did the parties in parliament agree to a regulated workday of eight hours; the law was temporary, and not fully established until ten years later. Up until 1920 the working time had been regulated through collective agreements; for many occupations, this meant a workday of about ten hours. However, several exceptions to the law remained; domestic workers were exempt, as were farm workers, care workers and many

12. Cf. Kenner's discussion: 'in the context of the debate about the compatibility of working and family life, there needs to be less dependency on the outmoded idea of the worker being in a relationship of subordination in which he or she has to be protected by the employer.' Jeff Kenner, Re-evaluating the concept of working-time: an analysis of recent case law, Industrial Relations Journal, Vol. 35 (2004) pp. 588-602, p. 601.
13. Jenny Julén Votinius, Föräldrar i arbete. En könskritisk undersökning av småbarnsföräldrars arbetsrättsliga ställning, Makadam förlag, 2007 is a comprehensive text in Swedish on this topic.
14. This is the labour law perspective on the matter, reflected e.g., in Folke Schmidt, Löntagarrätt, Reviderad upplaga 1994 ombesörjd av Tore Sigeman under medverkan av Ronnie Eklund, Håkan Göransson och Kent Källström, Juristförlaget, 1994, pp. 239–245, Kent Källström & Jonas Malmberg, Anställningsförhållandet, Iustus förlag, 2016, pp. 222–228, Erik Danhard, Tid för arbete - en betraktelse över en kontraktuell fråga, In: Kerstin Ahlberg (ed.) Vänbok till Ronnie Eklund, Iustus förlag, 2010, pp. 111–133.
15. Annual vacation is thus not covered in this chapter.
16. Lotti Ryberg-Welander, Arbetstidsregleringens utveckling. En studie av arbetstidsreglering i fyra länder, Lund Studies in Sociology of law, 2000, p. 158.

others.[17] The temporary law on working time for industrial workers limiting the workweek to forty-eight hours, eight hours per day for six days, was partially motivated with the need to cater to 'the needs of workers for family life, for taking parts in civil affairs and need for opportunities to educate themselves'.[18]

Sociologist Eva Schmitz highlights the gender politics of the labour movement's working time regulation policies. A few years prior to the successful legislation of the eight-hour working day, trade unions and the Social democrats had banned employers from hiring women for (usually relatively well-paid) night shifts. The reason given was the protection of women's health and wellbeing. These same organisations nonetheless readily agreed to exempt mostly women-dominated occupations from reduced working time.[19]

Employers and right wing political parties fiercely opposed working time legislation. The temporary legislation was in place until 1930, when a permanent law was enacted. Working time legislation did not cover most workers; by the mid-1950s, only about a third of the workforce was covered by this kind of legislation. The law applicable to industrial workers was complemented by other pieces of legislation, also through amendments to health and safety legislation.[20]

In 1957 the workweek stipulated by law was shortened to forty-five hours. At this point in time the reform of a shortened workweek was perceived as a deliberate choice between leisure time, social reforms and increases in salaries; or in other words between consumption today, or consumption tomorrow. The reform of 1957 explicitly perceived of leisure time as something that could be assigned a price and bargained with between the labour market parties.[21]

Following a period in which the labour market parties entered into collective agreements shortening the workweek legislation was enacted in 1970 shortening the workweek to forty hours (in effect 1973).[22] This is still the legislated amount of hours on a normal workweek (*see* §14.03 below). A few years later, in 1976, the retirement age was lowered by two years while vacation time was extended to five weeks for all employees. According to Isidorsson, these reforms all worked to de facto shorten the working time.[23]

17. Tommy Isidorsson, Striden om tiden. Arbetstidens utveckling i Sverige under 100 år i ett internationellt perspektiv, Göteborgs universitet, Historiska institutionen, 2001, p. 58.
18. Government Bill 1919:247, p. 17f. Lotti Ryberg-Welander, Arbetstidsregleringens utveckling. En studie av arbetstidsreglering i fyra länder, Lund Studies in Sociology of law, 2000, p. 159.
19. Eva Schmitz, Kvinnor, kamrater... Kvinnans roll i arbetarrörelsens uppbygge till slutet av 1930-talet, 1982, p. 16f.
20. Lotti Ryberg-Welander, Arbetstidsregleringens utveckling. En studie av arbetstidsreglering i fyra länder, Lund Studies in Sociology of law, 2000, p. 161.
21. Lotti Ryberg-Welander, Arbetstidsregleringens utveckling. En studie av arbetstidsreglering i fyra länder, Lund Studies in Sociology of law, 2000, p. 164f.
22. Lotti Ryberg-Welander, Arbetstidsregleringens utveckling. En studie av arbetstidsreglering i fyra länder, Lund Studies in Sociology of law, 2000, p. 166f.
23. Tommy Isidorsson, Striden om tiden. Arbetstidens utveckling i Sverige under 100 år i ett internationellt perspektiv, Göteborgs universitet, Historiska institutionen, 2001, p. 70ff.

In her analysis of the relationship between work and family life in modern Swedish history, economic-historian Maria Stanfors points to what can be conceptualised as progressive waves of economic expansion and increasing gender equality.[24] During certain periods, characterised by increased demand of labour, especially in sectors dominated by women, women's salaries have risen and their economic independence has stabilised. Stanfors identifies the first progressive wave as taking place in the 1920s, when sectors such as administration, commerce, care and education opened up to women. Two decades later, another progressive wave brought reforms in the area of education, alongside legislation that abolished discriminatory obstacles for women. The most significant period, however, came during the 1960s and 1970s, according to Stanfors, who concludes that those processes that 'led to change during earlier dynamic and emancipatory periods returned with greater force during these decades'.[25] Thus, a strong expansion in the field of education took place alongside a significant increase in women's labour force participation. Changes in family policy made it easier for women to work whilst raising a family. Measured quantitatively, these changes were substantial, according to Stanfors, both in terms of employment rates and in terms of wages. In qualitative terms, however, there was a strong continuity in terms of a gendered division of labour. The labour market continued to be segregated both horizontally and vertically, with women relegated mainly to labour within the reproductive sphere. Furthermore, their entry into the labour market was not matched by men's entry into unpaid, domestic work.[26]

§14.03 WORK/FAMILY BALANCE IN SWEDEN: AN EMPIRICAL OVERVIEW

Ever since the 1960s, Sweden has been in the forefront of women's labour market participation. However, the gendered division of labour persists in paid as well as unpaid work, and women still use about 75% of the parental leave benefit days. The reconciliation of private and professional life is framed as an issue of gender equality[27] and has been since the end of the 1960s.[28] While the differences between women's and men's work-life balance increased during the 1970s and 1980s[29], there is a tendency towards more equal time-use. Statistics Sweden measure time-use among citizens ages 20–64 years, and their data indicates gendered patterns that tend to vary with age and social situation. Below is an excerpt from the annual report on gender and equality in Sweden, illustrating (figure 14.1) the average time use for women and men from 1991

24. Maria Stanfors, Mellan arbete och familj. Ett dilemma för kvinnor i 1900-talets Sverige, SNS Förlag, 2007.
25. Maria Stanfors, Mellan arbete och familj. Ett dilemma för kvinnor i 1900-talets Sverige, SNS Förlag, 2007, p. 132.
26. Maria Stanfors, Mellan arbete och familj. Ett dilemma för kvinnor i 1900-talets Sverige, SNS Förlag, 2007.
27. Cf. Ann Numhauser-Henning, The Policy on Gender Equality in Sweden, European Parliament, Study for the FEMM Committee, 2015.
28. Roger Klinth, Göra pappa med barn: den svenska pappapolitiken, Boréa förlag, 2002.
29. Maria Stanfors, Mellan arbete och familj. Ett dilemma för kvinnor i 1900-talets Sverige, SNS Förlag, 2007, p. 90.

to 2011 and (figure 14.2) the extent of part time work among women and men.[30] It shows that women in general spend less time in paid work and more time in unpaid work than men, and that women - especially in the ages where they have small children - more often work part time.

Figure 14.1 Employed Who Work Part-Time by Age, 1987, 2000 and 2015

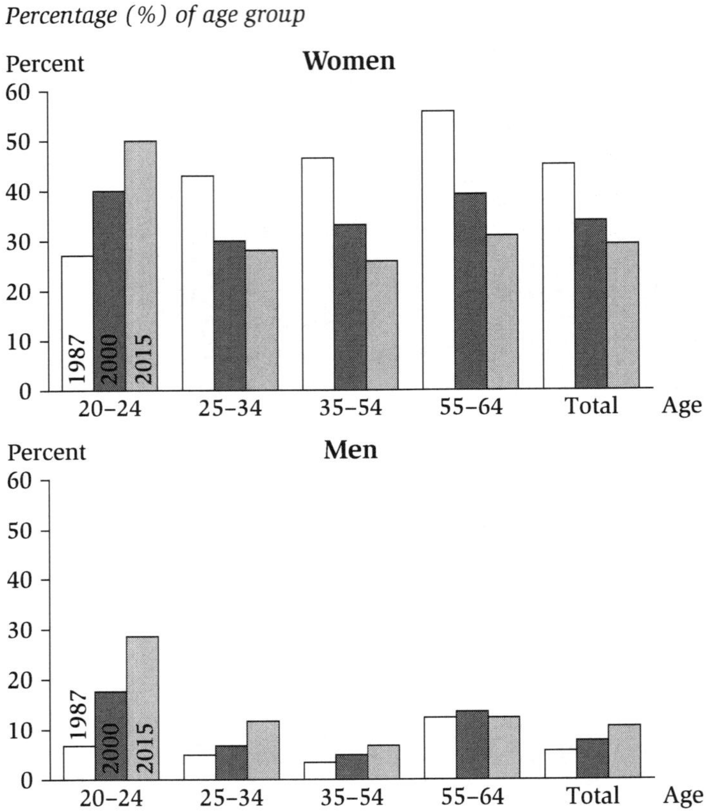

Source: Labour Force Survey (LFS), Statistics Sweden.

30. Statistics Sweden, Women and men in Sweden: Facts and figures, 2016.

Figure 14.2 Average Time Use for Persons Aged 20–64, 1990/1991, 2000/2001 and 2010/2011

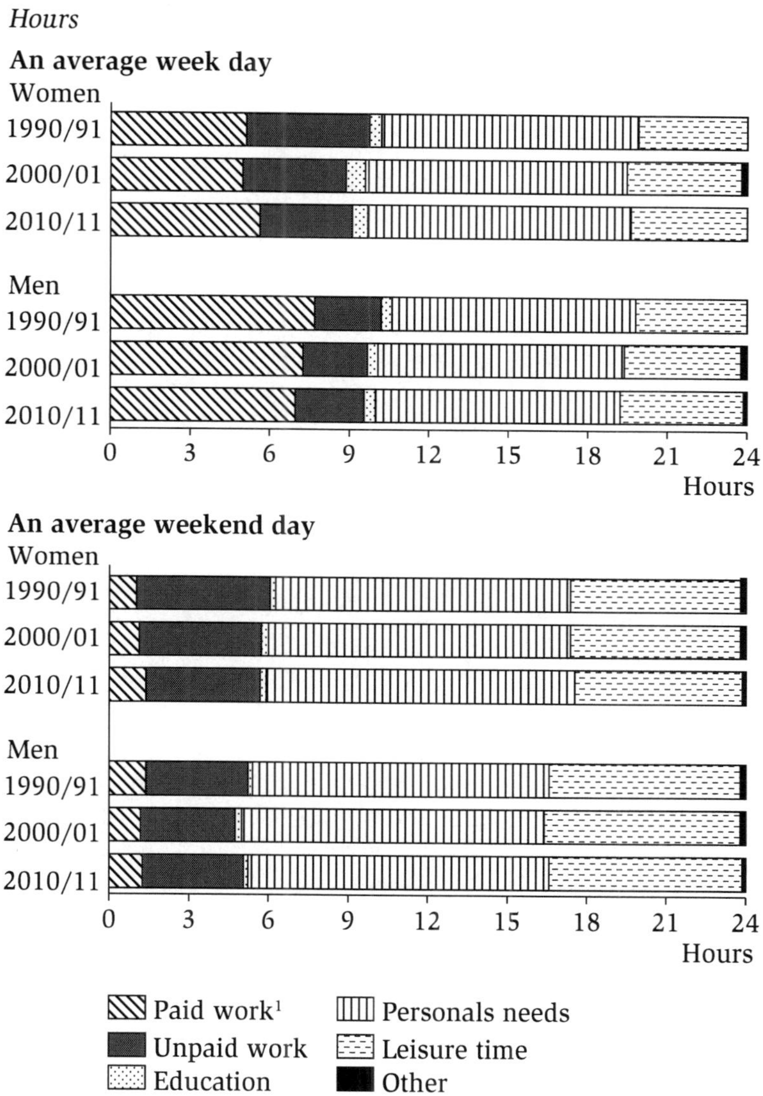

1 Including lunch and travel to and from work.

Source: Time Use Study, Statistics Sweden.

Statistics Sweden confirms that seen over an entire week (i.e., seven days), women and men (ages 20–64) spend an average of eight hours per day at work (paid work, gainful employment, unpaid work and housework). Men spend about ninety minutes more on paid work than women. Women have increased their paid working time by about half an hour since the early 1990s, while men have decreased their paid working time by about forty-five minutes, marking a shift towards increased gender equality in terms of work/life balance. Time use differs not just but between men and women, but significantly over the different stages of the life cycle. Single parents with small children (often women) spend most time on unpaid work, whereas single men aged 20–44 without children spend the least time on unpaid work. Cohabiting parents with small children spend more time on unpaid work than parents with older children, and the women spend around six hours more per week than the men. Most of this time is spent on housework. Women still take care of children and relatives in need more than men do.

Sweden has one of the lowest rates in the OECD of employees working very long hours (50 hours or more per week) (about 1%, the average is 13%). According to OECD, full-time workers in Sweden devote an average of 63% or 15.2 hours of their day to personal care (eating, sleeping, etc.) and leisure. This is on par with the OECD average of 15 hours.[31]

While Sweden is ranked high on the OECD Better Life Index, the gender segregated labour market has gendered effects on well-being. Austerity measures in the public sector since the crisis of the 1990s have impacted women specifically, who have a higher degree of sick leave and burnout; one study indicates that women in the age group of 35–44 years old are most affected.[32]

§14.04 SWEDISH LABOUR LAW AND INDUSTRIAL RELATIONS: AN OVERVIEW

Swedish labour relations are characterised by high levels of unionisation; 70% in the ages 16–64 years in all sectors 2014, and also by a high degree of collective agreement coverage; 91% in the ages 16–64 years in all sectors 2014.[33]

The legislator has, as a matter of explicit policy, systematically promoted the unionisation rates and the coverage of collective agreements. Swedish labour law is comprehensible and covers since the 1970s employment protection, vacation, health and safety at work, employee involvement etc. To a large extent these laws are semi-mandatory, leaving a vast space for derogation (both more and less favourable for employees) from the legislated rights in the form of collective agreements. Collective autonomy is a prominent feature of Swedish labour regulation. In Sweden no legislation exists on minimum wages, leaving the matter almost entirely for collective agreements to set wages.[34]

31. OECD Better Life Index, 2016.
32. Sofia Norlund et al., Burnout, working conditions and gender – results from the northern Sweden MONICA Study, *BMC Public Health* 2010, 10:326.
33. Swedish National Mediation Office, Avtalsrörelsen och lönebildningen, Medlingsinstitutets årsrapport, 2015, p. 42ff.
34. Petra Herzfeld Olsson & Erik Sjödin, The Fissured Workplace: Some Responses to Contemporary Challenges in Sweden, Comparative Labour Law and Policy Journal, Vol. 37 (2015), pp. 143–162.

It is often said that trust, co-operation and mutual understanding characterise Swedish industrial relations and the relationship between employers and trade unions, and also that this entails on part of employers an acceptance of trade unionism. Furthermore, employers are said to appreciate trade union contribution to the day-to-day running of the company, while trade unions are said to pragmatically accept both the employer's freedom to manage the business and technological change. By means of statutory rules on information and co-operation local trade unions partake in almost every aspect of workplace operations.[35]

Trade unions participate in the company operations primarily by representation on the board, in health and safety committees and co-determination negotiations. The channel for employee representation is the trade union; employees do not directly elect their representatives. The trade union's right to negotiate before the employer makes managerial decisions is the most important aspect of trade union participation. The duty on part of management to negotiate cover matters located at the core of entrepreneurial control, e.g., appointment of managers, investment decisions/policies, marketing policies, adoption of budgets, closure of plants, introduction of new technology.[36]

§14.05 REGULATING WORK-LIFE BALANCE: EU-LAW, INTERNATIONAL LABOUR STANDARDS AND NATIONAL LEGISLATION – AND COLLECTIVE AGREEMENTS

Since 1919 Swedish law has contained rules on working time. Ever-present in the Swedish legal regulation of working time has been the prominent role of collective autonomy; accordingly, the main dilemma in the legislative processes has been how the law most adequately can relate to collective agreements (*see* §14.06 below) and how the most benevolent interplay between different types of norms (law and autonomous regulation) can be maintained.[37]

In 1970 a general law on working time replaced a system of sectorial legislation in which different laws applied to different parts of the labour market (e.g., bakeries, farms, restaurants), while at the same time expanding the applicability of the legislation on working time.[38]

The present Working Time Act (1982:673) was enacted in 1982 and changed in 1996 and 2004 in order to transpose EU-directives on working time.[39] In the *travaux préparatoires* to the 1982 Act it is explicitly stated that the adequate distribution of working hours is a 'shared responsibility' of the labour market parties.[40] Similarly, in

35. Reinhold Fahlbeck, Nothing Succeeds as Success. Trade Unionism in Sweden, Juristförlaget i Lund, 1999.
36. Reinhold Fahlbeck, Employee Participation in Sweden. Union Paradise and Employer Hell or...?, Juristförlaget i Lund, 2008.
37. Legislative Inquiry 2001:91.
38. Government Bill 1970:5, pp. 10–19.
39. Today Directive 2003/88/EC of the European Parliament and of the Council of 4 November 2003 concerning certain aspects of the organisation of working time, OJ, L 299, 18.11.2003, pp. 9–19.
40. Government Bill 1981/82:154, p. 17.

2004 the *travaux préparatoires* rejects a suggestion to create a more detailed sectorial legislation (in the case of daily rest) since such a move could be considered as a sign of declining faith in the labour market parties' abilities to handle regulating the particularities of their respective sectors.[41]

The notion that the collective autonomy of the labour market parties is particularly important in Swedish law was present in the transposition process regarding EU-law on working time. EU-law[42] on working time was in 1996 transposed into Swedish law solely through the introduction of a provision stating that collective agreements providing less protection than stipulated in the directive was null and void and that the employer in such an instance would be liable to pay damages for the breach.[43] The idea was to construct a kind of transposition of the directive through changes to already existing collective agreements.[44] Detailed national legal rules transposing EU-law on working time – e.g., daily and weekly rest and maximum amount of working time – followed after the Commission had sued Sweden in 2004 (the claim was conceded[45]).[46] The possibility of invoking the contentious and much-debated opt-out clause[47] in the directive regarding the maximum forty-eight-hour workweek is dismissed by the Swedish government in the *travaux préparatoires*.[48]

The Framework Agreement on Inclusive Labour Markets of 2010 does not play any important role in Swedish labour market regulation.[49]

The European Social Charter of the Council of Europe of 1961 contains a rule on working time in relation to the Article about just conditions of work: the parties undertake 'to provide for reasonable daily and weekly working hours, the working week to be progressively reduced to the extent that the increase of productivity and other relevant factors permit'.[50] Sweden has not ratified this Article of the Charter, neither in 1962, nor in 1996 when the Revised European Social Charter of the Council of Europe was adopted. The Swedish government's explanation for abstaining from ratification is concern for the collective autonomy of the labour market parties: the labour market parties – not the state – are primarily responsible for maintaining reasonable working hours, it is explicitly stated in the *travaux préparatoires*.[51] While the Swedish government identified overwhelming difficulties in ratifying the Article on

41. Government Bill 2003/04:180, p. 38.
42. Then Council Directive 93/104/EC of 23 November 1993 concerning certain aspects of the organization of working time, OJ L 307, 13.12.1993, pp. 18–24.
43. Government Bill 1995/96:162, Legislative Inquiry 1995:92.
44. Government Bill 2003/04:180, p. 16. Cf. Ds 1994:74 and Legislative Inquiry 1995:92 on the discrepancies between the directive and Swedish collective agreements.
45. Case C-287/04, Commission v Sweden, Judgment 26/05/2005, nyp, ECLI:EU:C:2005:330.
46. Government Bill 2003/04:180.
47. Cf. the joined cases C-397/01 to 403/01, judgment 5/10/2004, ECR 2004 I-8835, ECLI:EU:C:2004:584 and Catherine Barnard, Simon Deakin and Richard Hobbs, Opting Out of the 48-Hour Week: Employer Necessity or Individual Choice? An Empirical Study of the Operation of Article 18(1)(b) of the Working Time Directive in the UK, Industrial Law Journal, Vol. 32, No. 4, 2003, pp. 223–252.
48. Government Bill 2003/04:180, p. 33.
49. Between BUSINESSEUROPE/UEAPME, CEEP AND ETUC of the 25th of March 2010.
50. The European Social Charter, Art. 2.1.
51. Government Bill 1997/98:82, p. 17, Ds 1997:65, p. 17, Government Bill 1962:175, p. 10.

reasonable working hours, it saw in 1997 no problems in ratifying Article 27 on rights of workers with family responsibilities, i.e., 'to take into account their needs in terms of conditions of employment'. In ratifying this Article the government cites not only all of labour law presently on the books in Sweden, but also all of the welfare state programmes on childcare, financial support for children, etc.[52]

The Swedish stance towards international labour standards regarding working time is characterised by a certain amount of disinterest. Sweden has *not ratified* a number of ILO conventions on working time, e.g., the Convention Limiting the Hours of Work in Industrial Undertakings to Eight in the Day and Forty-eight in the Week (No. 1, 1919),[53] the Convention concerning the Regulation of Hours of Work in Commerce and Offices (No. 30, 1930),[54] the Convention concerning Weekly Rest in Commerce and Offices (No. 106, 1957),[55] the Convention concerning Hours of Work and Rest Periods in Road Transport (No. 153, 1979)[56] and the Convention concerning Night Work (No. 171, 1990).[57]

The ILO Convention concerning the Reduction of Hours of Work to Forty a Week (No. 47, 1935) was however ratified by Sweden – in 1982, when it was noted that 'no formal obstacles' to Sweden ratifying the convention existed.[58] Furthermore Sweden has ratified i.a. the Convention concerning the Application of the Weekly Rest in Industrial Undertakings (No. 14, 1921)[59] and the Convention concerning Seafarers' Hours of Work and the Manning of Ships (No. 180, 1996).[60]

No actions were taken in Sweden following the adoption of the 1965 ILO Recommendation, No. 123, Employment (Women with Family Responsibilities), addressing particularly women's family responsibilities. The Swedish government argued that this instrument 'risked giving the impression that women ought to uphold a unique position on the labour market – and this would counteract rather than promote a rapid development towards true equality between men and women on the labour market'.[61] The 1981 ILO Convention, No. 156, concerning Equal Opportunities and Equal Treatment for Men and Women Workers: Workers with Family Responsibilities, replacing the 1965 instrument, was the result of a Nordic initiative in the ILO and was ratified by Sweden.[62]

In a sense Sweden has taken a quite ambivalent stance towards ILO conventions regarding working time; the regulation of working time must, according to repeated statements by the government in the *travaux préparatoires*, be designed with consideration taken only to national circumstances, and conventions on the matter can be

52. Government Bill 1997/98:82, p. 33f. Ds 1997:65, p. 32.
53. Government Bill 1921:361.
54. Government Bill 1931:32.
55. Government Bill 1958:46.
56. Government Bill 1980/81:79.
57. Government Bill 1991/92:98.
58. Government Bill 1936:15, Government Bill 1981/82:166, p. 12.
59. Government Bill 1923:198.
60. Government Bill 1999/2000:119.
61. Government Bill 1966:19, p. 32.
62. Government Bill 1981/82:166, p. 10f.

ratified only to the extent that they reflect what is already settled Swedish legislation.[63] Swedish labour law in general and working time regulation in particular is as such not often in breach[64] of international labour standards, so the reluctance on part of Sweden towards ratifying the ILO-conventions in question is not based in any hostility towards the level of protection (the substantive content of) afforded by the norms, but instead in the degree of detail in these norms. Legislating to this degree of detail is perceived as a threat to the collective autonomy of the labour market parties.[65] Since international labour standards are detailed and ratification implies an equally detailed legislation a disharmony comes about in relation to the Swedish model for industrial relations in which legislation provides quite open ended norms that come with vast possibilities of derogation (both to the better and to the worse) in collective agreements.[66]

§14.06 THE INTERPLAY BETWEEN LEGISLATION AND COLLECTIVE AGREEMENTS AND THE SANCTIONS FOR BREACH OF WORKING TIME NORMS

Working time is in Sweden regarded as one dimension of the working environment.[67] The Work Environment Act (1977:1160) thus not only mentions (Chapter 2, Section 1) 'the organisation of working time' (together with forms of remuneration) as an aspect of the organisation of work, that possibly can lead to physical strain or mental stress, illness and accidents but also refers (Chapter 2, Section 10) to the Working Time Act (1982:673) as *lex specialis*. The Working Time Act (1982:673) on its part refers (Section 1) to the working environment legislation as containing 'general protective provisions of relevance to the organisation of working time'.

The Working Time Act (1982:673) represents a particular type of regulation, located at the same time within both public and private law. First of all, the law has a public law character: the rules on the maximum amounts of working hours (*see* §14.03 below) together with the rules on scheduling (*see* §14.04 below) are sanctioned either by public law means, i.e., orders and prohibitions decided by the Work Environment Agency combined with the threat of a conditioned financial penalty (Section 22), or criminal law sanctions (a fine or imprisonment) (Section 23), or financial penalties calculated as 448 SEK[68] for each hour of unpermitted working time for each employee (Section 26).

Secondly, the Act can – in its entirety or partly – be replaced by a collective agreement. In a collective agreement concluded or approved by the national level of a

63. Legislative Inquiry 1968:66, p. 121, Government Bill 1970:5, p. 105.
64. Stina Lagergren, The Influence of ILO Standards on Swedish Law and Practice, International Labour Review, Vol. 125, No. 3, 1986, pp. 305–328, Petra Herzfeld Olsson, Folkrätten i arbetsrätten, In: Rebecca Stern & Inger Österdahl (eds.) Folkrätten i svensk rätt, Liber förlag, 2011, pp. 204–229.
65. Government Bill 1970:5, p. 105.
66. Reinhold Fahlbeck, Derogation from Labour Law Statutes under Swedish law, Juridisk tidskrift 2006/07 pp. 42–56.
67. Government Bill 1990/91:140, p. 35f.
68. SFS 2016:863.

trade union the legislated rules on the maximum amount of work allowed can be opted out from (Section 3). EU-law limits the collective autonomy as regards working time: it is not possible to stipulate less favourable conditions for the employees than what is given by the directive 2003/88/EC (Section 3). A collective agreement in breach of directive 2003/88/EC would be invalid insofar of the breach (Section 3) and an employer applying a collective agreement containing provisions in breach of directive 2003/88/EC shall pay damages for the loss that arises and for the violation that has occurred (Section 24a). Furthermore, contracting out of the Act implies changes as regards the system for sanctioning working time regulation: if an employer is in breach of a collective agreement that has replaced the Act entirely or partly, s/he shall pay damages according to the Co-determination Act (1976:580) (Section 25).[69] An employer in breach of a collective agreement on working time shall thus pay damages covering the actual losses following the breach, and these losses shall be calculated with consideration given to also the afflicted persons' 'interest in compliance with statutory provisions or provisions in the collective bargaining agreement and to factors other than those of purely economic significance', i.e., punitive damages (Sections 54–55 of the Co-determination in the Workplace Act [1976:580]). Finally, the presence of the collective agreement precludes financial penalties: that type of sanction can follow only in case the 'employer has infringed the provisions [...] without the support of a collective agreement' (Section 26).

§14.07 THE ROLE OF TRADE UNIONS

Before making managerial decisions to change the general organisation of working time, the employer must on her own accord negotiate with a trade union party to a collective agreement with the employer. This negotiation is required by the Co-Determination Act (1976:580) (Section 11), and does not do away with the employer's right to unilaterally decide upon this matter.[70] In case the employer is changing the organisation of working time regarding one employee, the trade union that particular person is a member of have a right to this type of negotiation, regardless of the presence of collective agreement in the employer's operations (Section 13).

To the extent working time legislation is semi-discretionary (*see* §14.06 above) trade union and employer can, in the form of a collective agreement, contract around it, thus creating an autonomous working time organisation. The employer is to apply the generally applicable terms in the collective agreement also on workers that are not members of the trade union party to the collective agreement.[71]

The peculiar rule on a priority right of interpretation regarding the duty to perform work applies in the context of collective agreements on the organisation of working time. According to Section 34 of the Co-Determination Act (1976:580); where a dispute arises between an employer and a trade union that are bound by the same collective agreement in respect of a member's duty to perform work pursuant to the

69. Cf. AD 2017:6, AD 2003:17.

70. Government Bill 1975/76:105, app. 1, p. 354. Cf. AD 2008:8, AD 1979:19.

71. Section 3 Working Time Act (1982:673), Sections 23-31a Co-Determination Act (1976:580).

agreement, the trade union's position shall apply until such time as the dispute has been finally adjudicated.[72] For example, in the case of a dispute about whether there is stipulated in the collective agreement an obligation to work overtime, the trade union's interpretation (not that of the employee) of the agreement (i.e., disputes of rights only) shall prevail, until the court have decided the matter.

§14.08 THE QUANTITY OF WORK TO BE PERFORMED

[A] Full Time or Part Time Work? The Role of the Contract of Employment

The quantity of work to be performed is defined by the agreement by the parties to the contract, i.e., the employer and employee decides the total amount of work in the employment contract. In other words the quantity of work the employee is to perform does not form part of the employer's right to direct work.[73]

The maximum amount of work the parties to the employment contract can agree to is however stipulated by the Working Time Act (1982:673) (*see* §14.03 below).

If an employer wants to permanently change the quantity of working hours s/he must come to an agreement with the employee, or terminate the contract of employment in accordance with the Employment Protection Act (1982:80).[74]

These premises pave the way for a particular employer practice that recently became controversial in Sweden regarding the cutting back on the amount of working hours the employer obtains from his or her employees. In case an enterprise – according to the employer's opinion – needs to lower its production costs a shortage of work comes into existence, legally speaking (i.e., the cost saving decision is to employ fewer workers on full-time and instead more workers on part-time). In this situation the employer can offer the employees new contracts that refer to fewer working hours, and if the employees refuse this proposal they are in legal terms understood to have declined a reasonable offer of alternative work (i.e., their old positions but with fewer hours), and from this follows that the employer is free to terminate their contracts of employment. In many instances the employees will be likely to sign this new agreement. In effect this practice implies that the employer has not unilaterally terminated the employees and the seniority principle is thus not applicable to this particular way of handling redundancy or shortage of work.[75] What's at stake here seems generally speaking to be that instead of the seniority principle deciding that the last person(s) hired will be left entirely without employment, employees with more years on the job will be partly affected by the shortage of work. Trade unionists are

72. Cf. AD 2016:32, AD 1998:33.
73. Erik Danhard, Tid för arbete – en betraktelse över en kontraktuell fråga, In: Kerstin Ahlberg (ed.) Vänbok till Ronnie Eklund, Iustus förlag, 2010, pp. 111–133, Kent Källström & Jonas Malmberg, Anställningsförhållandet, Iustus förlag, 2016, p. 222, AD 1984:76.
74. AD 1984:28, AD 1984:76, AD 1985:72, Kent Källström & Jonas Malmberg, Anställningsförhållandet, Iustus förlag, 2016, p. 222.
75. AD 2016:69; cf. AD 2012:16, AD 2012:47, AD 1987:42, AD 2016:53.

voicing discontent in relation to the Labour Court case (of November 2016) on this matter and are calling for the legislator to intervene and put an end to this practice.[76]

As a matter of course EU-law on protection against discrimination on the grounds of part-time work is transposed into Swedish legislation.[77]

[B] A Preferential Right to Increased Working Hours

The Employment Protection Act (1982:80) (Section 25a) provides part-time employees with a preferential right to increased working hours. Under certain circumstances the employer is obliged to satisfy an increased demand for labour by increasing the working hours of a part-time employee. The employee must have notified the employer of his or her desire to work more hours. The preferential right to increased working hours only applies to tasks that the employee is qualified to fulfil. Furthermore, on the one hand this right is confined to the organisational unit (establishment) in which the employee already is employed, but on the other hand the right to increased working hours is not restricted to the same area of employment. Most importantly the preferential right to increased working hours for part-timers is conditioned on the fact that an increase of a particular employee's working hours must actually satisfy the increase in demand for work on part of the employer. If an increase in working hours does not solve the problem at hand for the employer – no preferential right to an increase in working hours exist. This implies e.g., that no such right is at hand on part of a certain employee in case an employer needs additional work performed only at a time when this employee already is scheduled to work.[78] However, this right in the hands of part-timers takes precedence over the right to re-employment on part of former employees once made redundant. If many part-timers invoke their particular right, the seniority principle will decide who is to be given more work-hours. Section 25a of the Employment Protection Act (1982:80) does not hinder employers from conducting re-organisations of their operations that might significantly lessen the actual importance of the preferential right to increased working hours.[79]

[C] Working Hours: Normal and Overtime – and the Obligation to Work Overtime

Regular working time is limited to forty hours per week, but it is possible under particular circumstances (i.e., where necessary with regard to the nature of the work or the working conditions in general) to allow calculating regular working time as a

76. http://www.lag-avtal.se/nyhetsarkiv/handels-arbetsgivaren-rundar-las-med-hyvling-6587328.
77. Council Directive 1997/81/EC of 15 Dec. 1997 concerning the Framework Agreement on part-time work concluded by UNICE, CEEP and the ETUC, [1998] OJ L 14/9. Cf. Hanna Pettersson, Discrimination against Part-Time and Fixed-Term Workers: A Critical Legal Positivist Analysis, The International Journal of Comparative Labour Law and Industrial Relations, Vol. 31, No. 1 (2015), pp. 47–66.
78. Government Bill 1996/97:16, p. 49.
79. AD 2009:9, AD 2012:41.

maximum of an average of forty hours per week for a period of at most four weeks (Section 5 of the Working Time Act [1982:673]).

The definition of *overtime* relates to what is contractually agreed as the standard working amount for a particular employee (*see* §14.01 above). Overtime, for full-time workers, in the absence of a collective agreement, is defined as working time in excess of either regular working time and on-call time as defined in Sections 5 and 6 of the Act (Section 7 of the Working Time Act [1982:673]). And in the presence of a collective agreement on working time (and this is indeed most common) overtime is, for full-time workers, defined as working time in excess of regular working time and on-call time as stipulated in the collective agreement (Section 7 of the Working Time Act [1982:673]). For part-time workers 'additional [or extra] working time' is working time in excess to the employees working time and on-call time under the employment contract (Section 10 of the Working Time Act [1982:673]). The employer is - if a special need is present - allowed to exact a maximum of 200 hours of additional working time per employee over a calendar year (Section 10 of the Working Time Act [1982:673]).

Is the employee obliged to work overtime when this is asked of her? This question is not regulated in legislation, but usually in collective agreements. It is not entirely clear whether - in the absence of regulation in collective agreement - the employee must work overtime if so ordered. Danhard claims that an employee 'normally is obliged to work overtime to a certain extent', as long as the overtime as such is allowed, but also that personal circumstances on part of the employee is relevant in defining this obligation.[80] Källström and Malmberg emphasise that this issue is to be solved with reference to the practice of the workplace, and/or sector, and individual circumstances.[81] This is thus a point in which arguments in court proceedings based in the standard of work/life balance would be allowed and could possible come to play a substantive and original role in regulating working time. No case law exists in which the worker has used this kind of argument in opposing an order to work overtime.

The employer must keep records concerning overtime, additional working time and on-call time, and the employee and the trade union is allowed to inspect those records (Section 11 of the Working Time Act [1982:673] and AFS 1982:17, AFS 2000:9).

On-call time - i.e., time when the employee is at the disposal of the employer at the place of work to carry out work activities as needed - may be claimed up to a maximum of forty-eight hours per employee over a period of four weeks, or fifty hours per calendar month (Section 6 of the Working Time Act [1982:673]).

A particular rule applies to overtime in *emergency situations* (Section 9 of the Working Time Act [1982:673]).

The limit to the amount of working hours that can be exacted is set by EU-law. The Working Time Act (1982:673) reflects the EU-directive 2003/88/EC Article 16(b) and states that the total amount of working time - i.e., including all types of working

80. Erik Danhard, Tid för arbete - en betraktelse över en kontraktuell fråga, In: Kerstin Ahlberg (ed.) Vänbok till Ronnie Eklund, Iustus förlag, 2010, pp. 111-133, p. 121, Cf. Kent Källström & Jonas Malmberg, Anställningsförhållandet, Iustus förlag, 2016, p. 225.
81. Kent Källström & Jonas Malmberg, Anställningsförhållandet, Iustus förlag, 2016, p. 225.

time – per every seven day period may amount to an average of at most forty-eight hours during a reference period of at most four months (Section 10b).

§14.09 REGULATING WORK INTENSITY: A HEALTHY WORKLOAD?

Swedish health and safety legislation has since 1980 operated on the assumption that there is a clear general link between the actual social organisation of the work place and the psychological and social well-being of workers, which also affects workers as human beings, i.e., after the end of the working day.[82] This assumption was in 2015 transferred into a binding norm in the form of a provision enacted by the Swedish Work Environment Agency on 'Organisational and social work environment' stipulating that 'The employer shall see to it that the work tasks and authority assigned to the employees do not give rise to unhealthy workloads' and 'that the resources shall be adapted to the demands in the work.'[83] The non-binding recommendation accompanying this rule suggests that this objective can be achieved through 'Reducing the amount of workload, changing the order of priority, varying work tasks, providing opportunities for rest and recovery, applying other work methods, increasing staffing or supplying knowledge' and also by 'leadership that makes regular dialogue with employees possible' coupled with the constant investigation of risks related to the work load.[84] Furthermore, in relation to workloads it is also stipulated that the employer shall see to it that the employee not only knows what tasks s/he is to perform, the sought after results of work and the methods to be deployed, but also 'which work tasks are to be prioritized when available time is not enough for all work tasks to be performed'.[85]

The non-binding explications accompanying the provision conceptualise the employer's process of allotting work in terms of counterbalancing 'a certain amount of work' with 'resources'. The situation to be avoided – an 'unhealthy workload' – is defined as the state of affairs in which the demands in work 'more than temporarily exceeds the resources' thus creating an imbalance that 'becomes unhealthy if it is prolonged and the opportunities of rest and recovery are insufficient'. Demands in work is explained in terms of that which demands 'repeated efforts', such as 'workload, degree of difficulty, time limits, and physical and social conditions', while 'resources' are that which contributes to achieving the objectives of work, e.g., 'working methods and work equipment, competence and staffing, reasonable and clear objectives, feedback on effort, opportunities for control in the work, social support from managers and colleagues, and opportunities for rest and recovery'.[86]

---

82. This was evidenced in a non-binding norm (a 'general advice', i.e., a recommendation) from the Swedish Work Environment Agency; AFS 1980:14.
83. AFS 2015:4 Organisational and Social Work Environment, Section 9.
84. AFS 2015:4, Section 9.
85. AFS 2015:4, Section 10.
86. AFS 2015:4, Section 4.

These rules must be understood as reflecting a norm regarding the proper work intensity. This implies that the government agency responsible for enforcing health and safety regulation is tasked with supervising the ratio between amounts of work to be performed and the number of workers allotted to that endeavour. Since these rules are in the form of a government agency issued provision they are not semi-mandatory; the labour market parties cannot contract out of them. A set of rules stipulating the degree of intensity in work comes close to the core of the exchange that is the employment relationship. If the agency decides that an employer must allot more workers to a certain task, this will render the operation more costly for the employer. Indirectly this makes work more expensive; the employer must pay a higher price for the same output. Regulating work intensity is thus closely connected to regulating the price of work and has bearing on what work is worth to the employer. Health and safety legislation in its entirety of course always influences the bottom line for the employer, but this connection becomes more salient in the context of the regulation of work intensity. These rules also provides for a shifting role of the state on the labour market. The cornerstone of the Swedish/Nordic system for industrial relations is collective autonomy for the labour market parties, and this is especially so regarding wage formation (e.g., no minimum wage legislation exists). Setting the price for labour is left to collective bargaining (*see* §14.04 above).

The enactment of government agency provisions on work intensity is somewhat surprising, given the fact that for reasons related to collective autonomy of the labour market parties Sweden chose not to ratify the European Social Charter Article on reasonable working hours (*see* §14.05 above).

The regulation of work intensity adds a dimension to the debate on work-life balance. The standard of 'balance' becomes relevant not only in relation to the matters of the total amount of work to be performed and the scheduling of this work, but also for the actual content of work.

§14.10 A REDUCTION IN WORKING TIME? A FAILED LEGISLATIVE PROPOSAL

Parallel to aspirations to *prohibit* (*see* §14.07 below) part-time employment apparently runs the idea of creating a *right* to part-time employment. A committee inquiry was some years ago tasked with empowering employees as regards decisions on the total amount of work to be performed (i.e., a matter regulated by the contract of employment; *see* §14.01 above). The committee's proposal was however later tabled by the government referencing the possibility on part of the labour market parties to regulate this matter in collective agreements. Legislating would infringe upon the hailed collective autonomy of the Swedish industrial relations model.

The proposal was to create a right on part of employees to have up to a quarter of full-time off from work, distributed as a part of all workdays, or in its entirety on one day. In contrast to other legislation on leave from work, the employee must not provide a reason for wanting to be off from work. Only in the case that the decrease in working hours on part of an employee would amount to a 'considerable inconvenience' on part of the employer it was to be possible to decline a request to work fewer hours. This inconvenience must be larger than only having to get a substitute, e.g., large increases in costs, and the operation becoming seriously backed up. Naturally the employee must not use the time off from work to compete with the employer. To qualify for the right to less working-hours the employee must have been employed two years in the enterprise. The period for being off from work on the basis of the proposed legislation was limited to a maximum of two years. The employee was to give the employer a three months' notice that he or she was exercising this right. It was to be possible to terminate the decrease in working hours with a month notice to the employer. An employee exercising his or her right according to the proposed legislation was not to be terminated or punished in any way because of this.[87]

Since the total amount of work an employee is to perform is regulated in the employment contract with the employer, any possibility to unilaterally change, as in the proposed legislation, would amount to a breach of the principle *pacta sunt servanda*. In invoking this legislation the employee could unilaterally change the content of the contract, as regards the total amount of working hours.

§14.11 A REDUCTION OF WORKING TIME? STATE POLICIES AND COLLECTIVE AGREEMENTS

The prospect of introducing a shortened normal working time has been the subject of analysis in government inquires on a number of occasions in recent years. The official assumption seems to be that shortening the normal workweek leads to a lack of revenues, as compared to not implementing this reform, and that the issue of the possibility of working less ought to be conceptualised in terms of deciding on how to handle this trade-off.[88] From the perspective of workers this analysis implies a choice between working less and higher wages. Of course; the forty hour workweek is still the law of the land.

Many collective agreements stipulate a system for decreasing the normal amount of work. These systems usually resemble the regulation of compensation for having performed overtime work. When fulfilling a certain defined amount of work hours (e.g., a full week) the employee will be afforded a certain amount of hours on a time bank. The employee can withdraw time from this bank in the form of either paid time off from work, pension or cash. The system is flexible in the sense that the employee can choose between more spare time and earning extra money while working the

87. Legislative Inquiry 2005:106.
88. Legislative Inquiry 2002:58, Legislative Inquiry 2002: 6, cf. Legislative Inquiry 1988:54, Legislative Inquiry 1989:53, Legislative Inquiry 1992:27.

normal amount of hours. Often sectoral collective agreements delegate to the labour market parties on plant level to decide to implement this kind of scheme.[89]

§14.12 A RIGHT TO FULL-TIME EMPLOYMENT? A FAILED LEGISLATIVE PROPOSAL

Is it possible to conceive of a legislated right to full-time employment? How would such a law be designed? Some years ago a committee investigated this matter and presented a proposal for introducing into Swedish labour law a legislated right to full-time employment.

The proposed legislation contained a rule – applicable to employers with more than ten employees – stating that an employment contract must refer to full time work. To this general rule exceptions were allowed under the following circumstances. The employer was to be allowed to contract for part-time work up to the amount of one-seventh of the total number of employees. When this amount was reached, the employer was to be allowed a further part-time employment contract if the employee gave his or her consent, and the law permitted it. Thus, in three situations part-time employment was to be allowed for more than one seventh of an employer's workforce: if the employee was to work in parallel also for another employer, if the part-time job was a substitute position, or if the employer proved that s/he does not need the amount of full-time work for tasks that the employee is qualified to carry out. Furthermore, exception from the general rule prohibiting part-time employment was to be allowed in case the employee expressed a desire to be employed part-time. This was perceived as a critical point, and it was suggested that this route was to be closed if someone had before been offered a part-time position conditioned on him or her requesting part-time employment and if the person offered a position had not requested part-time employment, and been rejected by the employer. The rule on employee opt-out of the protection afforded by the right to full-time work is complex in attempting to secure a true and relevant consent on part of the employee in relation to an employer offering part-time work. If the employer had employed on part-time in breach of the suggested legislation, the employee was to petition the court that would declare the employment contract to one of full-time.[90]

This proposal was critiqued heavily in the legislative process and tabled by the government while remitting the matter to the labour market parties and their autonomous regulation.[91]

Part-time workers have a preferential right to increased working hours (*see* §14.02 above).

89. Jonas Malmberg, Maria Byrgren & Mikael Hansson, Kartläggning av arbetstidsförkortningar 2000-2003, Arbetslivsrapport 2003:15.
90. Legislative Inquiry 2005:105.
91. Report from parliamentary committee on the labour market; bet. 2011/12:AU13, p. 19f.

§14.13 SCHEDULING AND THE ALLOTTING OF WORKING HOURS

[A] Scheduling: The Right to Direct Work, Trade Union Negotiations and Notification to the Employee

Swedish law considers the scheduling of the agreed quantity (*see* §14.01 above) of work as being part of the employer's right to direct work. Forming part of the managerial prerogative it is possible for the employer to decide on scheduling within the boundaries set by the Working Time Act (1982:673), which does not contain much rules on the matter. As long as the employer remains within the confines of this Act, s/he can decide freely about when work is to be carried out.[92]

The employer can enter into collective agreements about scheduling (*see* §14.04 and §14.06 above and §14.05 below).

In absence of collective regulation on the matter: to what extent is the employer allowed to unilaterally decide to implement changes to scheduling? A clear and distinct answer cannot be given. Källström and Malmberg argue that the employer's unilateral right to change scheduling is not all-encompassing: essential and far-reaching changes to scheduling cannot be allowed, since this would be in breach of basic pre-requisites of the individual contracts of employment, and furthermore; when deciding this matter a court is to take into consideration the type of work, and both sectorial and employer practice.[93] This reference to the individual employment contract and the conditions upon which this was concluded, opens up for possibilities for the work/life balance norm to play a separate and productive role in regulating working time. The employee would have to argue that the contract of employment was concluded on the assumption that a certain type of work/life balance was afforded the employee, and that the employer's decision is to be understood as contrary to this. However, no such case law exists today.

Changes in scheduling might trigger an obligation on part of the employer to negotiate with the trade union of the affected employee (*see* §14.07 above).

According to Section 12 of the Working Time Act (1982:673) the employer must notify employees about changes to the scheduling of normal working hours and on-call time at least two weeks in advance. In case the character of the employer's business demands it, or if events could not have been anticipated this notification can be delivered with shorter notice.

[B] Scheduling as an Aspect of the Working Environment

Some aspects of scheduling are regulated outside of the Working Time Act (1982:673). Since working hours is considered part of the general working environment (*see* §14.06 above), the Swedish Work Environment Agency is mandated with regulating scheduling using public law's means. The public law setting implies that employees do not

---

92. AD 1960:20, AD 1968:9, AD 1984:108, AD 2016:35, 2008:28, 1983:14, 1981:174, 1979:66, Kent Källström & Jonas Malmberg, Anställningsförhållandet, Iustus förlag, 2016, p. 227.
93. Kent Källström & Jonas Malmberg, Anställningsförhållandet, Iustus förlag, 2016, s. 228.

have any rights based on the Agency's provisions and that different kinds of fines are the most important sanctions for breaches. The Working Environment Agency is also responsible for enforcing this type of labour regulation. After an extensive period of deliberations and controversy between the labour market parties, the Agency decided in 2015 a provision on 'Organisational and social work environment' stating 'The employer shall take any steps necessary in order to counteract scheduling of working hours leading to ill health among the employees.'[94] The general non-binding recommendations accompanying this provision mentions shift work, night work, split shifts, a large amount of overtime work, long work shifts and 'far-reaching possibilities of having to work at different times and places, with expectations of being constantly reachable' as possible sources of ill-health among employees. How the employer makes use of his or her scope of action in relation to scheduling within the framework of the Working Time Act (1982:673) is thus regarded as a working environmental matter that the Working Environment Agency is to watch over.[95]

[C] Scheduling and Pro-active Actions Favouring Non-discrimination and Equal Opportunities

Outside of labour law, scheduling is regulated in the Discrimination Act (2008:567). The Act's section on 'active measures' for achieving non-discrimination and equal opportunities is relevant in relation to many aspects of the employment relationship, but also for scheduling. This aspect of the anti-discrimination legislation forms part of public law and is sanctioned with a type of fine – employees are thus not given rights in these provisions. The Equality Ombudsman is tasked with enforcing the rules on active measures in the form of orders to implement changes to the business combined with the threat of a fine in case the employer remains passive in relation to the order (Discrimination Act [2008:567] [Chapter 4]). The employer has a general obligation (i.e., s/he will otherwise be fined) to proactively prevent discrimination and to positively further equal opportunities in relation to all grounds of discrimination; sex, transgender identity or expression, ethnicity, religion, disability, sexual orientation, age. Furthermore, the employer must also present active measures in relation to working conditions, terms and conditions of employment and 'possibilities to combine gainful employment and parenthood' (Discrimination Act [2008:567] [Chapter 1, Section 5, Chapter 3, Sections 1–5]). This responsibility on part of employers to support employees in their role of parent was introduced in 1990 and was at that point only related to sex: the provision explicitly mentioned that the objective was to 'aid both women and men in combining gainful employment and parenthood'. The *travaux préparatoires* highlighted the importance of men taking on more parental responsibilities (i.e., parental leave).[96] Up until 2017 the provision on employer responsibilities in relation to combining employment and parenthood was confined to the discrimination

94. AFS 2015:4, Section 12. These rules replaced an older and non-binding norm; AFS 1980:14 with similar content.
95. Government Bill 1990/91:140, p. 35f. (*See* §14.06 above.)
96. Government Bill 1990/1991:113, p. 70f, p. 100.

ground sex.[97] In 2008 it was realised that the provision targeted men and women to the extent that it was deemed necessary to state in the *travaux préparatoires* that measures to 'collectively stimulate' men in the form of support and encouragement must not be carried out in such a way so that direct discrimination of women came about in the form of less appreciation for the same effort; taking parental leave.[98] From 2017 onwards a change in the law renders the provision formally relevant for all grounds of discrimination and not only sex, and today the provision is conceptually explicitly geared towards employees that are parents, not women nor men.[99]

What does the responsibility to aid employees in their role as parents imply? This matter is referenced in the *travaux préparatoires*, with the overarching comment that the demands differ following the local conditions of the employer's operations as regards obstacles and possibilities for positive change. Suggestions for measures that are aligned with the objective of aiding employees in combining parenthood and gainful employment are defining taking time off from work in order to care for children as a merit, limiting overtime and work on unsocial hours, allowing part time work on all positions (also on higher levels), introducing flexible scheduling arrangements, enabling to work from home (via Internet and technical means provided by the employer), review long-term plans for staffing and scheduling to secure possibilities for parental leave, maintaining contacts between the workplace and the parent at home with children (providing information about developments at work, meetings and opportunities for skills development, etc.).[100]

[D] Legislated Periods of Rest

The Working Time Act (1982:673) defines the overall space within which the employer is allowed to exact work from the employee on the basis of the employer prerogative.

The Working Time Act (1982:673) provides all employees with the right to a minimum daily rest period of eleven consecutive hours in any twenty-four hour period. Derogations are temporarily allowed if they are rendered necessary by special circumstances that the employer could not have foreseen, provided that the employee is given a corresponding compensatory rest period. The daily rest period shall include the hours between midnight and 05.00. Derogations may be made if the work – in view of its nature, the needs of the general public or other special circumstances – must be carried out between midnight and 05.00 (Section 13).

Furthermore, the Working Time Act (1982:673) provides all employees with a minimum uninterrupted weekly rest period of thirty-six hours per every seven-day period. Weekly rest does not include periods spent on stand-by (i.e., when the employee is permitted to leave the workplace but must remain at the employer's disposal in order to carry out work when the need arises). As far as possible, weekly

97. Government Bill 2007/08:95, s. 330f, p. 536.
98. Government Bill 2007/08:95, p. 331.
99. Government Bill 2015/16:135, p. 40, p. 44f.
100. Government Bill 1990/91:113, p. 70f, 100, Government Bill 2007/08:95, p. 330f, 536, Government Bill 2015/16:135, p. 40, 45f.

rest shall be scheduled to weekends. Derogations from the rule on weekly rest periods may be made on a temporary basis if this is caused by a special circumstance that the employer could not have foreseen. A derogation of this kind is only allowed if the employee is given a corresponding compensatory rest period (Section 14).

[E] Collective Agreements on the Allocating of Working Hours

Collective agreements regulating scheduling of work contain a variety of designs and regulatory solutions.[101]

It is commonplace that sectoral collective agreements *delegate* to the trade union and employer on plant level to agree on scheduling. The employer is thus obliged to negotiate with the local level trade union. In case an agreement cannot be achieved the employer's will prevails.

Collective agreements on scheduling of working time are sometimes construed with provisions on a *fallback mechanism*. This defines a solution for when the parties are unable to reach an agreement, in effect usually strengthening the trade union's bargaining position.

Framework agreements define a space within which the employer is free to schedule work. Going outside of the frames set by the agreement presupposes consent from the plant level trade union.

Unilateral employer regulation is allowed by some collective agreements. This type of regulation is merely a reminder of the employer prerogative, i.e., what would be the starting point in absence of a collective agreement (or if the collective agreement does not regulate working time).

Regulation in *individual agreement* between employer and employee is stipulated by some collective agreements. What is demanded from the employer is substantial negotiations with the employee, and in case an agreement is not reached the employer decides. Collective agreement provisions of this kind are sometimes supplemented with *guidelines* stating that the interest of employees is to be catered to.

Collective self-scheduling enables the workforce to staff the organisation taking into account criteria set by the employer regarding the amount of workers needed per shift. The employees distribute night and day shifts and weekends among themselves, and the employer exercises his or her right to decide on scheduling only in case the employees fail to reach an agreement. The liability in relation to the legality of this type of schedule remains however solely on the employer. The system might be conceptualised as the employer voluntarily abstaining from exercising his or her right to schedule work.

Collective agreements can provide a rule on framework within which scheduling is to be done, and on occasion this provision particularly mentions work/life balance:

> Scheduling of working hours shall take into consideration the needs of the enterprise as well as the needs and requests of the employee regarding the quantity

101. David Johnsson & Jonas Malmberg, Avtalsutveckling på arbetstidsområdet, Arbetslivsrapport 1998:2 is the source for this entire section.

and allotting of working hours. Scheduling shall – to the largest extent possible – be oriented towards considering the possibilities of the employee of combining work with family and social life.

The case law of the Labour Court however indicates that such broad language on the allotting of work is of a limited normative effect. In interpreting this provision the Labour Court has decided that it does not by itself prevent the employer from implementing split shifts for a worker covered by the agreement. Barring split shifts would demand an explicitly agreed rule on the matter.[102]

§14.14 LEGISLATED RIGHTS TO ABSENCE FROM WORK

[A] The Protection Against Termination of Employment and Absence from Work

The Swedish Employment Protection Act (1982:80) stipulates that employment contracts of unspecified duration can be terminated only if the employer can prove just cause for dismissal is at hand in a certain case (Section 7). This broadly applicable legal standard is the cornerstone of employment protection (it is a mandatory rule), and defines indirectly i.a. the situations in which employees are allowed to be absent from work without the employment contract being terminated. The case law of the Labour Court is immense on this point and has covered e.g., unauthorised absence, illnesses and incarceration following criminal conviction.[103] The court carefully assesses and balances the opposing interests of the parties to the dispute and considers a large amount of circumstances when deciding cases about just cause for dismissal relating to individual employees. Since this rule is a generally applicable norm in the form of a quite open-ended balancing operation the employee party to a case would be able to deploy arguments relating to the work/life balance standard.[104] As of yet this has however not explicitly been done.

[B] Parental Leave and Care for Ill Relatives

The Parental Leave Act (1995:584) provides six types of parental leave for care of children (Sections 4–9): *Maternity leave*, i.e., full-time leave for a female employee following the birth of her child and while breastfeeding, *full-time leave* for a parent until the child has reached the age of eighteen months or, provided the parent is then receiving full parental benefit, during a period after that point, *part-time leave with parental benefits*, i.e., leave for a parent in the form of a reduction of normal working hours by three quarters, half, one quarter or one eighth while the parent is receiving parental benefit at three quarters, half, one quarter or one eighth of the full rate,

102. AD 2010:2.
103. *For example* AD 1981:120, AD 1992:77, AD 2011:71, AD 2003:50, AD 2006:83, AD 1999:26, AD 1981:51, AD 2004:30, AD 1978:86, AD 2011:26, AD 1979:87.
104. Kent Källström & Jonas Malmberg, Anställningsförhållandet, Iustus förlag, 2016, p. 140ff, passim.

part-time leave without parental benefits, i.e., leave for a parent in the form of a reduction of normal working hours by up to one quarter, until, in most cases, the child has reached the age of eight, *leave with temporary parental benefit*, i.e., leave for an employee's temporary care of a child, and *leave with child-raising allowance*, i.e., full-time leave or leave in the form of a reduction of normal working hours by half for a parent of a child for whom full child-raising allowance is paid.

The total amount of parental benefits is 480 days to be divided (it is possible to use parental benefits for fractions of a workday) between the parents during a time up until the child is twelve years old (Social Insurance Code [2010:110] [Chapter 12, Section 12]).

Essentially the Parental Leave Act (1995:584) supplements the Social Insurance Code (2010:110) (Chapters 12–13): an employee with a right to state administered parental benefits according to public law, has a right in relation to his or her employer to exercise this right by being off from work. The corresponding basic function of being a labour law counterpart to a social/public law scheme has the Act on Allowances and Time Off for Carers (1988:1465). The Parental Leave Act (1995:584) together with the Entitlement to Time Off for Urgent Family Reasons Act (1988:209)[105] transpose EU-directives on pregnancy and maternity/paternity issues into Swedish law.[106]

[C] Studies

The Study Leave Act (1974:981) provides employees with 'an in principle unrestricted right to leave of absence for studies'.[107] The extent of the right to leave is related to the studies, and no legal limits apply regarding length (Section 1). The leave can be for full-time or part-time. The right to leave concerns all types of studies, as long as they are 'structured', and they do not have to be related to the employee's profession or the like. The employer is allowed to postpone the leave of absence for up to six months, but if s/he wants to postpone it's starting point more than six months after the date of the application, the trade union must provide its consent (Section 5). The law applies to all types of employment relationships (part-time, full-time, temporary employment *etc.*). The only qualifications regard length of employment: the employee must have been employed six months before the leave, or for at least twelve months during the last two

105. Cf. AD 2016:24, AD 2003:70.
106. Council directive 92/85/EEC of 19 October 1992 on the introduction of measures to encourage improvements in the safety and health at work of pregnant workers and workers who have recently given birth or are breastfeeding (tenth individual Directive within the meaning of Art. 16(1) of Directive 89/391/EEC), Directive 2006/54/EC of the European Parliament and of the Council of 5 July 2006 on the implementation of the principle of equal opportunities and equal treatment of men and women in matters of employment and occupation (recast) (Art. 2.2.c), Council directive 2010/18/EU of 8 March 2010 implementing the revised Framework Agreement on parental leave concluded by BUSINESSEUROPE, UEAPME, CEEP and ETUC and repealing Directive 96/34/EC. *See* Jenny Julén Votinius, Troublesome Transformation – EU Law on Pregnancy and Maternity Turned into Swedish Law on Parental Leave, In: Mia Rönnmar (ed.) Labour Law. Fundamental Rights and Social Europe, Swedish Studies in European Law Volume 4, 2011, pp. 137–152.
107. Government Bill 1974:148, p. 89.

years (Section 3). An employee invoking this law is protected from employer retaliation and termination of employment because of the leave and has a right to return to work in case s/he quits the studies (Sections 8–10). The trade union has the priority right to interpretation of the act (Section 11).

The motivation of the Act was in the beginning of the legislative process explicitly understood to be related to the interest of work/life balance. A departmental working group preparing a draft version of the law pointed to the 'great difficulties most workers have in combining education with gainful employment and obligations towards the family etc.',[108] but these considerations were not elaborated upon in the final proposal to parliament. At this stage of the legislative process more overarching issues concerning the difficulties of workers to study on their spare time together with a general societal interest in a well-educated citizenry was invoked.[109]

[D] Job Hunts

The Employment Protection Act (1982:80) provides an employee who has received notice of termination, during the period of notice, with a right to reasonable leave of absence from the employment with full employment benefits in order to visit an employment agency or otherwise seek work (Section 14).

A particular piece of legislation provides an employee that has been off from work because of illness with a right to be off from this job in order to try out another employment. The Act on a right to try out other work because of reasons of illness (2008:565) is essentially motivated by a desire to facilitate the return to waged work of persons who have been away from the labour market because of sickness.[110]

[E] Starting a Business

The Right to Leave to Conduct a Business Operation Act (1997:1293) entitles employees to have leave from her or his employment to conduct a business operation (Section 1). This particular right to time off from work refers to one period, for six months and on a full time basis. The employee is not allowed to compete with the employer's operation. Furthermore, the leave from work must not involve 'significant inconvenience' for the employer's operation (Section 3). The employee must give notice to the employer at least three months prior to the commencement of this leave (Section 5). The employee has the right to discontinue his or her leave and resume work, but the employer may postpone the return to work for at most one month (Section 7).

108. Ds A 1974: 2.
109. Prop. 1974:148, p. 53ff.
110. Prop. 2007/08:151.

[F] Commissions of Trust in Trade Unions and Political Office

The Local Government Act (1991:900) provides workers with a right to time off from work – 'to the extent necessary' in order for them to hold political office, e.g., as a representative to the municipal assembly and/or members of different committees, in the municipality (Chapter 4 Section 11). Furthermore, workers have, according to the Instruction of Government, a right to time off from work to function as a member of parliament (Chapter 4 Section 10).

The Workplace Union Representative Act (1974:358) secures time off from work in order for workers to be elected as trade union representatives for the trade union party to the collective agreement at the enterprise/workplace. The right to time off from work represents what is reasonable in relation to the circumstances prevailing at the workplace (Section 6). The employer and the trade union are to deliberate on the scheduling of this kind of time off, and it must not interfere severely with the employer's operations (Section 6).

[G] Retirement

The Employment Protection Act (1982:80) contains a right on part of employees to remain in employment up to the end of the month when he or she attains the age of 67 – unless the employer can show just cause for dismissal (Section 32a). The time of retirement is an instance in which the just cause rule (Section 7) does not apply: If an employer wants an employee to retire when he or she reaches the age of 67 the employer shall give the employee at least one month's written notice (Section 33). Furthermore, an employee who has reached the age of 67 is not entitled to more than one month's notice of termination and do not have a preferential right to re-employment after having been made redundant (Section 33). This implies not only that an employee who has reached the age of 67 is first in line to termination of contract in case of redundancy, but more importantly that the employer in effect is allowed to hire another person to do the tasks hitherto performed by the 67 year old thus making him or her redundant.

§14.15 CONCLUDING DISCUSSION: WORK/LIFE BALANCE FROM THE PERSPECTIVE OF LABOUR LAW

The organisation of working time is – as indicated in this chapter – subject to a vast amount of regulation in Swedish labour law; legislation, agency provisions, case law, collective agreements and individual employment contracts. The standard of work/life balance is however conspicuously absent from the forefront of Swedish labour market discourse, even in relation to regulations pertinent to the organisation of working time. Instead, other values and considerations – i.a. collective autonomy, the role of trade unions, health and safety of workers, employment protection, gender equality – are present as prime motivators for labour law regulation of the organisation of working time and issues regarding work/life balance. The standard of balance in relation to work/life seems still partly external to Swedish industrial relations and labour law. In Sweden a substantial part of all work performed is covered by collective agreements, and these agreements regulate, in close proximity, both wages and working hours. The fact that the setting of wages and working hours are delegated to the autonomous processes of the labour market parties seems to at least historically to have created difficulties for the impact of a norm such as work/life balance in the design of terms and conditions of work. The notion of work/life balance – e.g., shorter hours and/or employee influence over scheduling – is apparently not easily forged into the regulatory output of collective bargaining and industrial conflict. The trade-off inherent in collective bargaining is commonly perceived to be relating to a choice between more spare time or a higher salary. This resonates with a dialogue between Weeks and Marx pointing to the need for continued reflection on the organisation of working time in our time.

In her seminal analysis of the 'problem' with work, Kathi Weeks argues that we seem to have difficulties with grasping the power relations of both work and the family systematically. Like the marriage relation, she says, the employment relation is often experienced and imagined not as a social institution but as a unique relationship. Work, according to Weeks, is continually reified, in that it is viewed as part of the natural order rather than as a social convention.[111] The same may be said of the time aspect of work, as it is generally understood in the labour movement. Karl Marx unpacked the central facets of working time by explaining its role in the labour process in terms of absolute and relative surplus value, placing the question of working time and work intensity firmly at the centre of the capitalist mode of production.[112] However, feminist scholars have pointed out that Marx's analysis leaves out the work that takes place outside of production, the labour historically undertaken by women in the reproductive sphere. This work, traditionally underemphasised in analyses of accumulation, in fact plays a central role to production as well as to reproduction and care. Since unwaged 'reproductive' work is what makes waged 'productive' work possible on a daily and generational basis, it should be considered socially necessary labour, and as such 'part and parcel of the capitalist mode of production', according to Weeks.[113] Thus, the issue of tensions between work time and non-work time is more complex than one may find at the outset, as it involves gendered power dynamics.[114]

Naturally, a worker is not 'free', just because she is 'free from work' in the sense temporarily off from her job. The legal right to be off *from* work seems nevertheless to

111. Kathi Weeks, The Problem with Work. Feminism, Marxism, Antiwork Politics, and Postwork Imaginaries, Duke University Press, 2011, p. 3.
112. Karl Marx, Capital, Volume I, Ch. 16.
113. Kathi Weeks, The Problem with Work. Feminism, Marxism, Antiwork Politics, and Postwork Imaginaries, Duke University Press, 2011, p. 24.
114. Ania Zbyszewska, Reshaping EU Working-Time Regulation: Towards a More Sustainable Regime, European Labour Law Journal, Vol. 7, No. 3 (2016), pp. 331–347, Ania Zbyszewska, Gendering European Working Time Regimes. The Working Time Directive and the Case of Poland, Cambridge University Press, 2016.

be related to possibilities of exercising rights *at* work – while correspondingly a subordinated position at work renders difficult to exercise the right to be off from work. Thus the interplay between regulation applicable between the parties to the employment contract and systems for actually sustaining the worker while she is not working is crucial.

CHAPTER 15

Family Responsibilities Accommodation in Canada: Individual Solutions to a Collective Dilemma

Mathilde Valentini & Stephanie Bernstein

§15.01 INTRODUCTION

Various legal norms have been adopted over time to promote reconciliation between work and family responsibilities. For instance, although the International Labour Organization's (ILO) almost universally ratified Discrimination (Employment and Occupation) Convention[1] (no. 111) does not explicitly prohibit discrimination based on family status, the ILO's Committee of Experts considers that it is included in the protected ground of sex[2] and that it can constitute a 'distinction, exclusion or preference which has the effect of nullifying or impairing equality of opportunity or treatment in employment'.[3] In an attempt to specifically address the issue of work-family balance, in 1981 the ILO adopted the Workers with Family Responsibilities Convention (no. 156), ratified to date by forty-four countries; Canada is not among them.[4] The aim of this convention is to enable workers with family responsibilities to

1. Discrimination (Employment and Occupation) Convention (25 June 1958), 362 U.N.T.S. 31.
2. *Ibid.*, Art. 1(1)a). *See* International Labour Office, *Equality in Employment and Occupation* § 37, 15 (International Labour Conference, 1996), http://www.ilo.org/public/libdoc/ilo/P/09661/09661(1996-83-4B).pdf (accessed 25 November 2016).
3. Discrimination Convention (1958), 362 U.N.T.S. 31, *supra* n. 1, Art. 1(1)b). *See* International Labour Office, *supra* n. 2, § 53–54, 20–21.
4. Workers with Family Responsibilities Convention, 1981 (23 June 1981), 1331 U.N.T.S. 295. *See also* ILO, Workers with Family Responsibilities Recommendation, 1981 (No. 165), 67th ILC Sess (23 June 1981).

engage in employment without being subject to discrimination.[5] It recognizes that the problems of workers with family responsibilities are part of a larger public concern and that national policies should take work-family conflict into account.[6] Some authors see this Convention as imposing a duty for employers to accommodate employees based on their family status.[7] As for the United Nations, the Convention on the Elimination of All Forms of Discrimination Against Women (CEDAW), also almost universally ratified, underlines the necessity of promoting social policy to enable parents to combine work with family responsibilities in order to avoid 'discrimination against women on the grounds of marriage or maternity and to ensure their effective right to work.'[8]

At a national level, measures such as the limitation of working time, childcare leave, other leave for family caregiving, and, more recently, the 'right to request' flexible work arrangements[9] have been integrated into different countries' legislation, including in Canadian jurisdictions. Although other jurisdictions around the world prohibit discrimination based on family status,[10] the treatment of discrimination –

5. International Labour Office, *supra* n. 2, § 54, 21; International Labour Office, *Women at Work: Trends 2016*, 78 (International Labour Organization, 2016), http://www.ilo.org/wcmsp5/groups/public/---dgreports/---dcomm/---publ/documents/publication/wcms_457317.pdf (accessed 25 November 2016).
6. Workers with Family Responsibilities Convention, 1981, 1331 U.N.T.S. 295 *supra* n. 4, preamble.
7. Pierre Verge & Dominic Roux, *Un milieu de travail diversifié: l'apport de l'obligation d'accommodement raisonnable selon le droit international et le droit canadien*, 12 PISTES, § 24, 6 (2010), https://pistes.revues.org/1696 (accessed on 25 November 2016). This duty would arise from Art. 4 of the Convention, which states that 'all measures compatible with national conditions and possibilities shall be taken … (b) to take account of [the needs of workers with family responsibilities] in terms and conditions of employment and in social security'.
8. Convention on the Elimination of all Forms of Discrimination Against Women, Art. 11(2)(c) (18 December 1979), 1249 U.N.T.S. 13. Regional instruments also prohibit this form of discrimination: *see* for example the *European Parliament's Directive on Equality of Men and Women in Employment*, which addresses the need to reconcile family responsibilities with work, for example through the establishment of flexible working-time arrangements, as a way to address 'the problem of the continuing gender-based wage differentials and marked gender segregation on the labour market'. Directive 2006/54/EC of the European Parliament and of the Council of 5 July 2006 on the implementation of the principle of equal opportunities and equal treatment of men and women in matters of employment and occupation (recast) preamble, OJ L 204/23 (2006).
9. The right to request is the right of an employee to ask his or her employer for a flexible work arrangement on a permanent or temporary basis, generally for care responsibilities, without binding obligations on the employer. To date, no Canadian jurisdiction has adopted the 'right to request', although it is being discussed for inclusion in federal labour standards legislation. *See* Stéphanie Bernstein & Mathilde Valentini, *Redefining the 'Normal' Worker: Law and Policy Choices for Work-Family Balance in Canada*, 27 New Solutions (2017) (forthcoming).
10. For example, in Australia, *see* e.g., Belinda Smith, *It's About Time – For a New Regulatory Approach to Equality*, 36 Fed. L. Rev. 117 (2008); *Id.*, *What Kind of Equality Can We Expect from the Fair Work Act?* 35 Melb. U. L. Rev. 545 (2011); in Ireland, *see* e.g., Olivia Smith, *Litigating Discrimination on Grounds of Family Status*, 2 Fem. Leg. Stud. 175 (2014); in the United States, *see* e.g., Joan C Williams & Stephanie Bornstein, *Evolution of 'FReD': Family Responsibilities Discrimination and Developments in the Law of Stereotyping and Implicit Bias*, 59 Hastings L.J. 1311 (2007).

particularly on the basis of family responsibilities – by Canadian courts is, in some respects, unique to Canada.[11]

In this chapter, we focus on recent developments in Canadian employment discrimination law, which establish a duty to accommodate workers on the basis of their family responsibilities. This contribution aims to critically assess the potential and the limits of this approach. To do so, we first briefly trace the evolution of Canadian employment discrimination law, before turning to the rise of family status as a protected ground and the legal test that has emerged from the case law in recent years. Courts have established that when such discrimination occurs, employers have an obligation to accommodate employees whose working arrangements present a considerable obstacle to fulfilling their family responsibilities and who have demonstrated that they have failed in their attempts to fulfil these obligations without accommodation. Based on examples from the case law, we illustrate how the duty to accommodate can help workers reconcile their work and their family responsibilities.[12] This solution can in effect be particularly beneficial for some workers, but it also presents shortcomings that we will discuss in the last part of the chapter.

§15.02 THE DUTY TO ACCOMMODATE IN CANADIAN EMPLOYMENT DISCRIMINATION LAW

The concept of a duty to accommodate first appeared in the United States during the 1960s and was subsequently imported into Canadian anti-discrimination case law, in instances where a prima facie case of discrimination had been established.[13] Despite its

11. British Columbia Law Institute, *Human Rights and Family Responsibilities: Family Status Discrimination under Human Rights Law in British Columbia and Canada*, 93, www.bcli.org/sites/default/files/Family_Status_Study_Paper.pdf (accessed 25 November 2016). *See also* Belinda Smith, *Rethinking the Sex Discrimination Act: Does Canada's Experience Suggest We Should Give Our Judges a Greater Role?, in Sex Discrimination in Uncertain Times* 235, 255 (Margaret Thornton ed., ANU Press 2010).
12. We studied the case law on family responsibilities discrimination in all the Canadian jurisdictions, as of 2 May 2014, the date of the seminal case, *Canada (Attorney General) v. Johnstone*, 2014 FCA 110, until 1 January 2017. Canadian cases referred to in this text can generally be found online at www.canlii.org.
13. The *Civil Rights Act of 1964*, Pub. L. No. 88-352, 78 Stat. 241 was enacted, and in 1966, the Equal Employment Opportunity Commission issued a guideline for employers to treat employees without discrimination based on religious grounds and to accommodate their needs. This guideline was revised in 1967 to specify the obligation to accommodate employees, but due to the restrictive interpretation by the Courts, in 1972, the Congress modified the *Civil Rights Act* to define the term 'religion' and to specifically add the requirement of reasonable accommodation unless the employer can show that this would constitute undue hardship. *See* Ravi Malhotra, *The Legal Genealogy of the Duty to Accommodate American and Canadian Workers with Disabilities: A Comparative Perspective*, 23 Wash. U. J.L. & Pol'y 1, 18–19 (2007); Mark L. Berlin, *Reasonable Accommodation: A Positive Duty to Ensure Equal Opportunity*, Can. Hum. Rts Y.B., 137, 143–144 (1984–1985); Steven L. Willborn, *Reasonable Accommodation in the United States, in Reasonable Accommodation in the Modern Workplace: Potential and Limits of the Integrative Logics of Labour Law* 9, 9–11 (Roger Blanpain & Frank Hendrickx eds., Kluwer Law International 2016); Christian Brunelle, *Discrimination et obligation d'accommodement en milieu de travail syndiqué* 104–105 (Yvon Blais 2001).

origins in US law, the concept has actually been more broadly and deeply integrated into Canadian law.[14]

As in many other countries, Canadian courts first recognized direct discrimination, then acknowledged the existence of indirect discrimination and systemic discrimination. Direct discrimination occurs when an employer distinguishes, by a rule or a practice, an employee on a clearly prohibited ground.[15] The essence of this type of discrimination lies on the generalization, 'about a person's ability to perform a job based on membership in a group sharing a common personal attribute such as age, sex, religion, etc.'[16] During the 1960s and 1970s, the intent to discriminate generally had to be proven, but this is no longer the case.[17]

Human rights tribunals then began to recognize indirect discrimination. In the 1985 judgment *Ontario Human Rights Commission v. Simpson-Sears*[18] which concerned work schedules that impeded the practice of a particular religion, the Supreme Court of Canada endorsed this concept. This decision was inspired by the disparate impact theory[19] discussed in 1971 by the United States Supreme Court in *Griggs v. Duke Power Co.*[20] For the Supreme Court of Canada, indirect discrimination occurs in the workplace when:

> an employer for genuine business reasons adopts a rule or standard which is on its face neutral, and which will apply equally to all employees, but which has a discriminatory effect upon a prohibited ground on one employee or group of employees in that it imposes, because of some special characteristic of the employee or group, obligations, penalties, or restrictive conditions not imposed on other members of the work force.[21]

---

14. Malhotra, *supra* n. 13. *See also* Sandra Fredman, *Comparative Study of Anti-discrimination and Equality Laws of the US, Canada, South Africa and India* 55–59 (European Commission, Directorate-General for Justice 2012), http://dx.publications.europa.eu/10.2838/82208 (accessed 22 December 2016). For a general overview of the duty to accommodate in Canada, *see* Kevin Banks, *Reasonable Accommodation as Equal Opportunity, in Canadian Employment Law, in Reasonable Accommodation in the Modern Workplace: Potential and Limits of the Integrative Logics of Labour Law* 27 (Roger Blanpain & Frank Hendrickx eds., Kluwer Law International 2016).
15. Direct discrimination in the United States is known as disparate treatment theory. *See* Risa Lieberwitz, *Employment Discrimination Law in the United States: On the Road to Equality?, in New Developments in Employment Discrimination Law* 1, 5 (Roger Blanpain, Hiroya Nakakubo & Takashi Araki eds., Kluwer Law International 2008).
16. *Central Alberta Dairy Pool v. Alberta (Human Rights Commission)* [1990] 2 S.C.R. 489.
17. William Black, *From Intent to Effect: New Standards in Human Rights*, 1 C.H.R.R. C/1 (1980); Rosalie Silberman Abella, *Equality in Employment: A Royal Commission Report* 8 (Ministry of Supply and Services Canada 1984).
18. [1985] 2 S.R.C. 536 (The requirement to work on Saturdays had an adverse effect on an employee who belonged to the Seventh-Day Adventist Church).
19. For more information on disparate impact theory (as opposed to disparate treatment theory, or direct discrimination), *see* Lieberwitz, *supra* n. 15, at 20–25.
20. 401 U.S. 424 (The requirement of a high school diploma as a condition for employment had the effect of excluding a higher proportion of black applicants).
21. *Simpsons-Sears* [1985] 2 S.R.C. at 551.

Two years later, in 1987, the Supreme Court of Canada referred for the first time specifically to systemic discrimination.[22] This notion is complex and subtle, being linked to structural inequities: 'Rather than approaching discrimination from the perspective of the single perpetrator and the single victim, the systemic approach acknowledges that by and large the systems and practices we customarily and often unwittingly adopt may have an unjustifiably negative effect on certain groups in society.'[23]

In 1999, the Supreme Court of Canada abolished the need for a claimant to identify the type of discrimination of which she or he alleges to be a victim.[24] Direct, indirect and systemic discrimination are now all subject to a unified legal test and employers have therefore a duty to accommodate employees who are victims of all forms of discrimination.[25] Thus, in Canada today, when a person alleges employment discrimination, she must first make a prima facie case[26] of discrimination and once this is established, the burden of proof shifts to the employer to justify the discriminatory policy or practice by demonstrating that it constitutes a bona fide occupational requirement, from which then flows the duty to accommodate.

First, to establish a prima facie case of discrimination, employees are required to prove (1) that they possess a characteristic protected by the applicable human rights legislation;[27] (2) that they experienced adverse treatment on the part of their employer; and (3) that the protected characteristic was a factor in the adverse impact.[28]

When this is established, the employer can demonstrate that the policy or the practice is a bona fide occupational requirement. This second step involves three requirements. The employer must show (1) a rational connection between the adopted

---

22. *Canadian National Railway Company v. Canada (Human Rights Commission)* [1987] 1 S.C.R. 1114.
23. Abella, *supra* n. 17, at 9.
24. *British Columbia (Public Service Employee Relations Commission) v. BCGSEU* [1999] 3 S.C.R. 3 (also known as the *Meiorin* judgment).
25. The aim of this chapter is not to analyse the subtleties in the interpretation by the courts of the different types of discrimination since the *Meiorin* decision. While we have stated for simplicity's sake that in this Supreme Court of Canada judgment the question of the different types became moot, in fact, courts and tribunals apply this unified test rather unevenly. *See* e.g., *Moore v. British Columbia (Education)*, 2012 SCC 61, ¶¶ 58–60.
26. The Supreme Court of Canada defines a prima facie case as 'one which covers the allegations made and which, if they are believed, is complete and sufficient to justify a verdict in the complainant's favour in the absence of an answer from the respondent-employer': *Simpsons-Sears* [1985] 2 S.R.C. at 558.
27. Labour, employment and human rights legislation varies from jurisdiction to jurisdiction in Canada. The Constitution recognizes the exclusive legislative powers of the provinces regarding property and civil rights and matters of a merely local or private nature, while the powers of the federal Parliament are limited to certain enterprises and undertakings (e.g., interprovincial and international transportation, banking, telecommunications) and to the field of unemployment insurance. Fewer than 10% of Canadian employees work in federally regulated workplaces (*Constitution Act, 1867* (UK), 30 & 31 Vict., c. 3, ss 91–92). There are thus fourteen legislative jurisdictions in Canada: ten provinces (British Columbia, Alberta, Saskatchewan, Manitoba, Ontario, Quebec, New Brunswick, Nova Scotia, Prince Edward Island and Newfoundland), three territories (Yukon, Northwest Territories and Nunavut) and the federal jurisdiction.
28. *Moore*, 2012 SCC 61, ¶ 33. In this judgment, the Supreme Court uses the terms 'adverse treatment' and 'adverse impact' which are not be confused with the use of the terms 'disparate treatment' and 'disparate impact' in US law. *See* Lieberwitz, *supra* n. 15.

standard and the performance of work; (2) a sincere belief in the need for the standard; and (3) the reasonable necessity of the standard to achieve the legitimate work-related purpose.[29]

The third requirement involves the demonstration that 'it is impossible to accommodate individual employees sharing the characteristics of the claimant without imposing undue hardship upon the employer.'[30] Such hardship must be substantial, and an accommodation request that would involve some inconvenience or operational upset would be insufficient to constitute undue hardship.[31] This last criterion represents an important difference with the US standard, according to which accommodation requiring more than a minimal cost to the employer constitutes 'undue hardship.'[32] The duty to accommodate employees in Canada has thus emerged out of this third requirement. It creates a positive obligation for employers as it requires them to act proactively in response to discrimination in the workplace.[33]

The duty to accommodate now forms an integral part of Canadian labour and employment law. Michael Mac Neil indicates four specific trends or reasons that could explain the importance of the human rights tradition in this area.[34] First, legislation on human rights directly addresses discrimination in the workplace. For example, section 7 of the federal *Canadian Human Rights Act* targets discrimination at work: 'It is a discriminatory practice, directly or indirectly, (a) to refuse to employ or continue to employ any individual, or (b) in the course of employment, to differentiate adversely in relation to an employee, on a prohibited ground of discrimination.'[35] Second, human rights are implicitly incorporated into all collective bargaining agreements in Canada.[36] Employees can thus make claims of discrimination through the grievance procedure

29. *Meiorin* [1999] 3 S.C.R. 3 ¶ 54.
30. *Ibid.*
31. *Central Okanagan School District No. 23 v. Renaud* [1992] 2 S.C.R. 970.
32. *Trans World Airlines, Inc. v. Hardison*, 432 U.S. 63 (1977). *See also* Willborn, *supra* n. 13, at 17.
33. The duty to accommodate can also be applied in other sectors such as housing or education, but most of the cases arise in the employment context, particularly with respect to religious freedom and disability. Pierre Bosset, *Les fondements juridiques et l'évolution de l'obligation d'accommodement raisonnable, in Les accommodements raisonnables: quoi, comment, jusqu'où ?*: Des outils pour tous 3, 13–17 (Myriam Jézéquel ed., Yvon Blais 2007).
34. Michael Mac Neil, *Labour Law and Discrimination on the Basis of Marital and Family Status* 9–11 (Labour Law Conference – The Charter and Human Rights at Work: 25 Years Later, University of Western Ontario, 27 October 2007), http://http-server.carleton.ca/~mmacneil/Family_Status_MacNeilPaperRevisedAugust08.pdf (accessed 21 December 2016).
35. *Canadian Human Rights Act*, R.S.C. 1985, c. H-6, s. 7.
36. *Parry Sound (District) Social Services Administration Board v. O.P.S.E.U., Local 324*, 2003 SCC 42. Canada has a strong culture of collective bargaining. In 2014, unionization rate in Canada was 26.4%, while the average in OECD countries was 16.7% and 10.7% in the United States: OECD.Stat, *Trade Union Density*, http://stats.oecd.org/Index.aspx?lang=en&SubSessionId=35f71dd2-d504-4e31-aaa3-73fd5a2960dc&themetreeid=13# (accessed on 25 November 2016). In Canada, the certified union in a workplace has an exclusive right of representation of all workers who can thus no longer negotiate individually with the employer: *see Isidore Garon ltée v. Tremblay; Fillion et Frères (1976) inc. v. Syndicat national des employés de garage du Québec Inc.* [2006] 1 S.C.R. 27. For more information on collective labour relations in Canada, *see* D.D. Carter, G. England, B. Etherington & G. Trudeau, *Part II. Collective Labour Relations, in International Encyclopaedia for Labour Law and Industrial Relations* 203 (Roger Blanpain & Frank Hendrickx eds., Kluwer Law International 2000); Michael Mac Neil, Michael Lynk & Peter Engelmann, *Trade Unions in Canada* (Aurora, Canada Law Book, 2007 Update).

provided for in their agreement, even if it does not explicitly proscribe such discrimination. Third, the arbitrators[37] who hear discrimination cases have jurisdiction to interpret and apply human rights standards that are not expressly integrated into the collective agreement.[38] Fourth, if a claim arises regarding a discriminatory practice in a workplace, the union can be held jointly responsible for discrimination, so unions must actively participate in the process of accommodating an employee.[39]

Protected grounds of discrimination in Canada vary according to the human rights legislation of each jurisdiction, but most laws protect against discrimination based on the grounds of race, national or ethnic origin, colour, religion, sex, sexual orientation, age, mental or physical disability, marital status and family status.[40] This last ground is one of the most recent to have been added to Canadian human rights legislation[41] and has lately received an increasing amount of attention by Canadian scholars and jurists.[42] This recent recognition by the courts of family responsibilities discrimination has the potential to help workers to better balance their work and family life.

§15.03 ACCOMMODATING WORKERS BASED ON THEIR FAMILY RESPONSIBILITIES: THE EVOLVING LEGAL TEST

Family status constitutes a prohibited ground of discrimination in employment – and in other contexts such as housing or the provision of services normally offered to the public – in almost all Canadian jurisdictions, except two.[43] The term 'family status' was

37. Notwithstanding some limited exceptions, in Canadian labour law, grievances arising in unionized workplaces are heard by arbitrators who are named and paid for by the parties to the collective agreement.
38. *Parry Sound*, 2003 SCC 42. Workplace human rights claims can be adjudicated by arbitrators when the business is unionized or by specialized human rights tribunals. *See* generally Elizabeth Shilton, *Choice, but No Choice: Adjudicating Human Rights Claims in Unionized Workplaces in Canada*, 38 Queen's LJ 461 (2013); **Halsbury's Laws of Canada, *Labour* HLA-419 (LexisNexis 2016)**.
39. *Renaud* [1992] 2 S.C.R. *See also* Mac Neil, Lynk & Engelmann, *supra* n. 36, Ch. 11.
40. For more information on enumerated grounds of discrimination in Canada according to jurisdiction, *see* Halsbury's Laws of Canada, *Discrimination and Human Rights* HDH-53 - 223 (LexisNexis 2013).
41. British Columbia Law Institute, *supra* n. 11, at 23.
42. *See* e.g., Elizabeth Shilton, *'Family Status' Discrimination: New Tool for Transforming Workplaces, or Trojan Horse for Subverting Gender Equality?* (LLRN Inaugural Conference, Universitat Pompeu Fabra, 13–15 June 2013) http://papers.ssrn.com/sol3/papers.cfm?abstract_id=2330294 (accessed 21 December 2016); Mac Neil, *supra* n. 34; Melody Jahanzadeh, *Family Status Accommodation: The Road to an Amalgamated Approach* 2 W. J. Legal Stud. (2012).
43. *Canadian Human Rights Act*, R.S.C. 1985, c. H-6, ss. 3(1), 7 (Federal jurisdiction); *Human Rights Code*, R.S.B.C. 1996, c. 210, s. 13 (British Columbia); *Alberta Human Rights Act*, R.S.A. 2000, c. A-25.5, s. 7(1) (Alberta); *Saskatchewan Human Rights Code*, S.S. 1979, c. S-24.1, ss. 2(1)(m.01)(iv), 16 (Saskatchewan); *Human Rights Code*, S.M. 1987–88, c. 45, s. 9(2)i) (Manitoba); *Human Rights Code*, R.S.O. 1990, c. H-19, s. 5 (Ontario); *Human Rights Act*, R.S.N.S. 1989, c. 214, s. 5(1)(d), (r) (Nova Scotia); *Human Rights Act*, R.S.P.E.I. 1988, c. H-12, ss. 1(1)(d), 6(1)a) (Prince Edward Island); *Human Rights Act*, S.N.L. 2010, c. H-13.1, ss. 9(1), 14 (Newfoundland and Labrador); *Human Rights Act*, R.S.Y. 2002, c 116, ss. 7(k), 9(b) (Yukon); *Human Rights Act*, S.N.W.T. 2002, c. 18, ss. 5(1), 7(1) (Northwest Territories); *Human Rights*

included in human rights legislation mostly during the 1980s and 1990s, but jurisdictions do not all interpret the notion in the same way. Five provinces and territories have defined 'family status' as consisting only in a parent-child relationship,[44] two jurisdictions have adopted a broader definition – being related to a person by blood, marriage or adoption[45] –, and five jurisdictions have left the term undefined.[46]

Family status encompasses both the status itself and the corresponding responsibilities related to this state. The first aspect is quite clear in the case law. It includes complaints based on absolute status and relative status.[47] For example, an employer cannot require the hiring of only single workers or workers without children (absolute), nor can an employer discriminate against an employee because of the identity or the actions of a member of his or her family (relative). The second dimension of family status – family responsibilities – has been recognized by courts and specialized tribunals in Canada, which, however, remain divided as to the applicable test to determine what constitutes discrimination.

One of the first decisions to acknowledge that family status encompassed family responsibilities was rendered by the Canadian Human Rights Tribunal in 1993.[48] In *Brown v. Canada (Department of National Revenue)* [*Brown*],[49] a neutral rule that required customs inspectors at the Toronto Airport to work rotating shifts had an adverse impact on a mother who was unable to find a person to care for her child at night.[50] The tribunal concluded that the complainant established a prima facie case of discrimination. The term 'family status' extended to the condition of being a parent and to the duties and obligations associated with this state,[51] and the complainant possessed these characteristics.

This decision is important because it places family responsibilities discrimination in the context of work-family balance: the tribunal states 'We can therefore understand the obvious dilemma facing the modern family wherein the present socio-economic trends find both parents in the work environment, often with different rules and

Act, S.Nu. 2003, c. 12, ss. 7(1), 9(1) (Nunavut). Family status is not a prohibited ground in the human rights legislation of the provinces of Québec and New Brunswick.

44. These provinces are Ontario, Nova Scotia, Saskatchewan, Prince Edward Island, and Newfoundland and Labrador (the Newfoundland and Labrador's definition includes stepchild and adoptive child, as well as step-parent and adoptive parent): R.S.O. 1990, c. H-19, s. 10; R.S.N.S. 1989, c. 214, s. 3(h); S.S. 1979, c. S-24.1, s. 2(1)(h.1); R.S.P.E.I. 1988, c. H-12, s. 2(h.11); S.N.L. 2010, c. H-13.1, s. 2(i).
45. These jurisdictions are Alberta and Nunavut: R.S.A. 2000, c. A-25.5, s. 44(1)(f); S.Nu. 2003, c. 12, s. 1.
46. These jurisdictions are the federal jurisdiction, Manitoba, Yukon, British Columbia, and Northwest Territories: R.S.C. 1985, c. H-6; S.M. 1987-88, c. 45; R.S.Y. 2002, c. 116; R.S.B.C. 1996, c. 210; S.N.W.T. 2002, c. 18.
47. *B v. Ontario (Human Rights Commission)*, 2002 SCC 66. Family status encompasses 'complaints based on the particular identity of a family member' (¶ 40). The Supreme Court did not mention obligations or duties arising from the family status.
48. The Canadian Human Rights Tribunal is a specialized tribunal that rules at the first level in the federal jurisdiction.
49. 1993 CanLII 683 (C.H.R.T.). The complaint alleged discrimination on two grounds, namely sex (pregnancy) and family status (for her first child).
50. Since her husband was a police officer and also subject to rotating shifts.
51. *Brown*, 1993 CanLII 683 (C.H.R.T.), at 15.

requirements.'[52] For the tribunal, the human rights legislation[53] regarding family status discrimination 'is a clear recognition ... of a parent's right and duty to strike [the balance between family needs and employment requirements] coupled with a clear duty on the part of an employer to facilitate and accommodate that balance.'[54] It was thus determined that human rights legislation had a role to play in reducing work-family conflict.

Since this decision, two trends have emerged in the case law with regard to the appropriate test to establish a prima facie case of discrimination in matters of family responsibilities. One originated in the province of British Columbia and is a more restrictive test, and the other comes from the federal jurisdiction and is more liberal. The first group of cases followed the British Columbia Court of Appeal's[55] decision *Health Sciences Association of British Columbia v. Campbell River and North Island Transition Society* [*Campbell River*].[56] This case concerned a mother of four children, one of whom was diagnosed with a major psychiatric disorder.[57] Her work schedule had permitted her to care for her son after school until her employer modified it to finish at 6:00 pm.[58] As her son required substantial parental attention, she claimed that her employer had a duty to accommodate her by reinstating her previous schedule. The court did acknowledge that the change in work hours was discriminatory, but to arrive at this finding, it elaborated a particular test: 'a prima facie case of discrimination is made out when a <u>change</u> in a term or condition of employment imposed by an employer results in a <u>serious interference</u> with a <u>substantial parental</u> or other family duty or obligation of the employee (emphasis added).'[59] The court explained the need to make the prima facie test more difficult to meet in the case of the prohibited ground of family status by the 'great mischief'[60] these kinds of claims might create in the employment context. Indeed, many workers struggle with work-family conflict. Therefore, in order to avoid disruption in the workplace, the court created a different test from the one applicable to other prohibited grounds of discrimination.[61] According to the court, in the vast majority of cases where there is a conflict between family and work, it would be difficult to meet the requirements of a prima facie case of discrimination.[62] In other words, human rights legislation was not designed to help workers balance their work and family life.

The second group of cases followed a decision rendered two years later by the Canadian Human Rights Tribunal in *Hoyt v. Canadian National Railway*.[63] Ms. Hoyt

---

52. *Ibid.*, at 20.
53. In this case, the *Canadian Human Rights Act*, R.S.C. 1985, c. H-6.
54. *Ibid.*
55. The Court of Appeal is the highest court in the province of British Columbia.
56. 2004 BCCA 260.
57. *Ibid.*, ¶ 7.
58. *Ibid.*, ¶ ¶ 9–10.
59. *Ibid.*, ¶ 39.
60. *Ibid.*, ¶ 38.
61. *See* Section §15.02.
62. *Campbell River*, 2004 BCCA 260 ¶ 39.
63. 2006 CHRT 33. In this case, the tribunal had to rule on a double complaint for sex and family status discrimination. The sex complaint was related to the failure of the employer to accommodate the plaintiff due to the pain she was experiencing in her pregnancy (¶¶ 25–36).

was assigned to work on Saturdays, as was her husband who worked for the same employer. She was able to make child care arrangements for all but three Saturdays, so she asked her employer to modify her schedule for these three days. Instead, he proposed that she take unpaid leave.[64] The tribunal upheld the complaint and stated that the test developed in *Campbell River* created a double standard depending on which ground of discrimination was being invoked: 'It would, in my view, be inappropriate to select out one prohibited ground of discrimination for a more restrictive definition.'[65] So the tribunal came back with the *Brown* test – which applies the usual test in matters of discrimination – to establish a prima facie case of discrimination based on family status: 'Ms. Hoyt demonstrated on the evidence that she was a parent and that she was incurring the duties and obligations of parenthood... CN's direction that she could stay home those Saturdays, but that she would not be paid, meant that she was unable to participate equally and fully in employment with her employer.'[66] In regard to the general human rights discrimination test, the 'great mischief'[67] apprehended in the workplace by accommodation requests to balance work and family responsibilities should therefore be examined at the second step, when the employer has the opportunity to demonstrate that the impugned policy or practice is a bona fide occupational requirement and that the required accommodation would cause undue hardship.[68]

In a judgment rendered in 2014, *Canada (Attorney General) v. Johnstone* [*Johnstone*],[69] the Federal Court of Appeal[70] tried to resolve the divergent approaches in the case law. Ms. Johnstone and her husband worked for the Canada Border Services Agency at the Toronto airport, and both had unpredictable work schedules with day, evening and night shifts.[71] It was impossible for Ms. Johnstone to find daycare for her two children outside of normal daycare hours. She was able to rely on family members three days a week, so she asked to have a fixed schedule three days a week, with thirteen-hour shifts to keep her full-time status.[72] Her employer then offered her a fixed schedule, but she would lose her full-time status and lose benefits,[73] so she filed a complaint for discrimination based on her family status.[74] The court granted her claim and rejected the *Campbell River* test.

The main difference between the *Campbell River* test discussed above and the Johnstone test is that in the latter case the court clearly rejects the requirement that the employee demonstrate that there has been a change in his or her working arrangement. In essence, however, the *Johnstone* decision still imposes a different burden of proof then the one applied for other prohibited grounds. To make a pr*ima facie* case of

64. *Ibid.*, ¶¶ 37–43.
65. *Ibid.*, ¶ 120.
66. *Ibid.*, ¶ 129.
67. *Campbell River*, 2004 BCCA 260 ¶ 38.
68. *Hoyt*, 2006 CHRT 33, ¶ 121. *See Meiorin* [1999] 3 S.C.R. 3 ¶ 54.
69. 2014 FCA 110.
70. The Federal Court of Appeal is the highest court in the federal jurisdiction.
71. *Johnstone*, 2014 FCA 110 ¶¶ 5, 7.
72. *Ibid.*, ¶ 11.
73. *Ibid.*, ¶ 8, 10.
74. *Ibid.*, ¶¶ 108–109.

discrimination based on family status, in the case of childcare obligations, the worker would have to prove:

> (1) that a child is under his or her care and supervision; (2) that the childcare obligation at issue engages the individual's legal responsibility for that child, as opposed to a personal choice; (3) that he or she has made reasonable efforts to meet those childcare obligations through reasonable alternative solutions, and that no such alternative solution is reasonably accessible and (4) that the impugned workplace rule interferes in a manner that is more than trivial or insubstantial with the fulfilment of the childcare obligation.[75]

The Federal Court of Appeal finally found that Ms. Johnstone's situation met these criteria and that her employer should have accommodated her by granting her a fixed schedule and maintaining her full-time status. It should be noted that the Federal Court of Appeal stated that the burden of proof should be the same for all the enumerated grounds.[76] It nevertheless defined quite a different test to establish a prima facie case of discrimination on the ground of family status. Since this judgment, courts and specialized tribunals in Canada have mostly applied this test to prove a prima facie case of discrimination related to family responsibilities.[77]

Despite the issue of the applicable burden of proof, it is clear that human rights law in Canada protects workers with family responsibilities, and that their employers have a positive duty towards them. The duty to accommodate is often invoked in situations involving childcare, but it also applies to other situations, such as eldercare. According to the Ontario Human Rights Commission, 'The ground of family status may therefore embrace a range of circumstances where there are no blood or adoptive ties, but relationships of care, responsibility and commitment that resemble a parent-child relationship'.[78] Indeed, in 2015, the Federal Court, in *Canada (Attorney General) v. Hicks,*[79] acknowledged that family status includes taking care of a dependent adult, in this case a mother-in-law who had been placed in a long-term care facility.[80]

---

75. *Ibid.*, 110 ¶ 93.
76. *Ibid.*, ¶ 81.
77. *See* e.g., *Fleming v. Treasury Board (Canada Border Services Agency)* 2016 PSLREB 96 ¶¶ 120–122; *Miraka v. A.C.D. Wholesale Meats Ltd.*, 2016 HRTO 41 ¶ 41; *Canadian National Railway Co. v. Unifor Council 4000* [2015] C.L.A.D. No. 213 ¶¶ 23–27; *Partridge v. Botony Dental Corporation*, 2015 ONCA 836 ¶¶ 87–89. In the province of British Columbia, the *Campbell River* test continues to apply (*See* e.g., *Kenworthy v. Brewers's Distributor Ltd.* 2016 BCHRT 54 ¶ 85; *Ma v. Cleator* 2014 BCHRT 180, ¶ 235). Some courts and tribunals have proposed a test that is more comparable to the general test applicable to the other protected grounds (*See* e.g., *SMS Equipment Inc. v. Communications Energy and Paperworkers Union, Local 707 (c.o.b. Unifor, Local 707-A)*, 2015 ABQB 162 ¶ 77; *Misetich v. Value Village Stores Inc.*, 2016 HRTO 1229 ¶¶ 42–48).
78. Ontario Human Rights Commission, *Policy and Guidelines on Discrimination Because of Family Status*, 10 (Toronto, Ontario, 2007) http://www.ohrc.on.ca/sites/default/files/attachments/Policy_and_guidelines_on_discrimination_because_of_family_status.pdf (accessed 21 December 2016). The Ontario definition of family status is limited to the parent-child relationship. *Human Rights Code*, R.S.O. 1990, c. H-19, s. 10.
79. 2015 FC 599.
80. The federal jurisdiction does not define the term 'family status'. *Canadian Human Rights Act*, R.S.C. 1985, c. H-6.

The evolution of the test to establish family status discrimination shows that there was initially a liberal approach to the question in *Brown* where it was recognized that family responsibilities must be taken into account in the workplace to guarantee full and equal participation in employment. A more restrictive test was developed and essentially maintained, although the notion of 'family' was expanded. As we will see from other examples in the case law, the duty to accommodate offers benefits to some workers, particularly with respect to the greater control over their working time, a key element in the reduction of work-family conflict.

§15.04 IS THE DUTY TO ACCOMMODATE AN EFFECTIVE MEANS TO FACILIATE BALANCING WORK AND FAMILY RESPONSIBILITIES?

Accommodation based on family responsibilities can take many forms and can be on a temporary or on a permanent basis. It can be invoked in different contexts and has the potential to provide a personalized solution for workers, depending on the conflicts they experience with family responsibilities. For example, the duty to accommodate has been invoked successfully by an employee to avoid an assignment in another city.[81] It has, however, been also invoked unsuccessfully by an employee who tried to be transferred to another city to live closer to his children who were with their mother after the parents separated.[82] Another case involved an employee who requested to telework from home to be able to nurse her child: her claim was unsuccessful.[83] In the context of wrongful dismissals, some employees have succeeded in proving that they were discriminated against on the basis of their family responsibilities and that their employer should have accommodated them. For example, an employee managed to successfully challenge his termination due to missed work days to care for his two young children and his sick wife.[84] Another worker who asked her employer to extend her parental leave for a month because she was not able to find childcare for her son during this period also saw her dismissal as a result of her employer's refusal

81. *Canadian National Railway v. Seeley*, 2014 FCA 111 (The employee had been laid off, but remained on a seniority list. While living in Brûlé, Alberta with her husband and their two children, her employer called her back to cover a shortage of employees in Vancouver (a distance of about 1000 km). The employee sought accommodation on account of her parental obligations and asked not to be transferred, but to remain on the seniority list. The Federal Court of Appeal confirmed that she had been discriminated against because of her family status and that her employer should have accommodated her).
82. *Fleming*, 2016 PSLREB 96 (The employee and his ex-wife had joint custody of their two children with him having unrestricted access. As he was living at a distance of about 500 km from them, it was hard to exercise his right of access to his children).
83. *Flatt v. Canada (Attorney General)*, 2015 FCA 250, leave to appeal refused 2016 SCR 8 (The employee requested to telework from home full-time for a year following the end of her maternity leave because she wished to continue nursing. The claim based on discrimination on the grounds of sex and family status was rejected).
84. *Miraka*, 2016 HRTO 41 (The employee alleged that his employer discriminated against him because of his family status and his disability. He stayed at home for two days to care for his one-year-old and four-year-old children, because his wife, who normally took care of them, was ill herself. The third day, the employee went to work but had to leave early because he suffered great pain, which was diagnosed as a hernia.).

overturned.[85] As we can see, the duty to accommodate can potentially apply to multiple situations, on a temporary or on a permanent basis.

Much of the case law regarding family responsibilities discrimination and the duty to accommodate is related to hours of work and scheduling. Indeed, all the seminal cases summarized above involve work schedules.[86] Since the *Johnstone* judgment, an employer's duty to accommodate by modifying work schedules has often been invoked. For example, a professor confronted significant difficulties when her classes were scheduled before 9 a.m. or after 5 p.m. and she could not find reliable childcare for her two children, one of whom had severe health issues, due to her unpredictable schedule which changed each term.[87] She established a prima facie case of discrimination and the arbitral panel determined that her employer should have accommodated her, unless this would have resulted in undue hardship.[88] In another case, an employee successfully invoked her employer's duty to accommodate her to avoid having to perform overtime since she had to pick up her daughter on time otherwise she would have lost her place at the daycare.[89]

Also, some workers, especially single mothers, have successfully asked to only be scheduled days in order to be able to fulfil their family responsibilities. For example, in *SMS Equipment Inc. v. Communications Energy and Paperworkers Union, Local 707 (c.o.b. Unifor, Local 707-A),*[90] the Alberta Court of Queen's Bench confirmed the decision of an arbitrator who decided that the requirement to work rotating day and night shifts discriminated against an employee who was a single mother and who had requested to only work day shifts:

> the Grievor's parenting responsibilities are extraordinary. She is a single mother of two children under the age of six, with no childcare support from the children's

---

85. *Clark v. Bow Valley College*, 2014 AHRC 4 (During her parental leave, the worker realized that there was an error in the duration of her leave. She then asked her employer to extend her leave by one month, which he refused to do. Since she did not return to work during that month, the employer considered that she had abandoned her position and terminated her employment).
86. *Brown*, 1993 CanLII 683 (C.H.R.T.) at 2 (The employee asked to have a day schedule); *Campbell River*, 2004 BCCA 260 ¶ 10 (The employee asked to reinstate her old schedule); *Hoyt*, 2006 CHRT 33 ¶ 42 (The employee asked to modify her schedule so that she would not have to work for three Saturdays); *Johnstone*, 2014 FCA 110 ¶ 11 (The employee asked to have a fixed schedule with a compressed work week).
87. *Fanshwe College of Applied Arts and Technology v. Ontario Public Service employees Union (Zavitz-Govan Grievance)* [2015] O.L.A.A. No. 265.
88. *Ibid.*, ¶ 83. *See also Partridge*, 2015 ONCA 836 (The employer's requirement that the employee be available to work until 6:00 pm discriminated against her because she was not able to pick up her children at day-care on time and there was no proof that the employer could not have accommodated her without undue hardship).
89. *Canada Post Corporation v. Canadian Union of Postal Workers (Weber Grievance, CUPW 560-10-00070, Arb Swan)* [2016] C.L.A.D. No. 64 (The employee, a full-time letter carrier, was the mother of a pre-school aged daughter. She used to drop her off shortly after 6:00 a.m. and pick her up at 4:00 p.m. The employer restructured her delivery route and required her to perform overtime when the delivery was incomplete. The employee claimed that she was not able to do overtime because she had to pick up her child on time and she had no alternative childcare arrangement. The arbitrator concluded that she was victim of discrimination because of her family responsibilities and that her employer should have accommodated her).
90. 2015 ABQB 162.

> fathers or any other family members. She is working a non-traditional job (female welder) on a non-traditional shift (nights) in a non-traditional pattern (rotating).[91]

The court concluded that the employer had to accommodate the worker because 'the Employer called no evidence to justify the requirement that all employees work rotating night and day shifts, and no evidence that accommodating the Grievor would cause it undue hardship.'[92] In another case, the worker was the sole support of her two young children and had no family members who could assist her.[93] Before having her children, she worked on two-week rotating shifts, with day and evening shifts. When she returned to work after her first maternity leave, she exchanged evening shifts for day shifts with a co-worker.[94] When returning after her second maternity leave, she asked her employer to schedule her only on day shifts, because her daycare closed at 6:15 p.m. The accommodation request was granted, but only for a period of two months.[95] The tribunal decided that the worker had made a case that she had experienced family status discrimination and ordered the employer to continue to schedule her on day shifts.[96] In these last cases, the employers' duty to accommodate was particularly beneficial to workers with irregular or unpredictable schedules.

The duty for employers to individually accommodate workers because of their family responsibilities can thus be useful for workers to gain some control over their working time. In a legislative context such as Canada's, where standards regarding employees' control over their working time are objectively weak,[97] the duty to accommodate can sometimes be the only way for a worker to find the means to better balance family and work obligations. As we have seen however, the legal test to prove family status discrimination is relatively hard to meet.

§15.05 MAINTAINING THE BURDEN ON THE INDIVIDUAL WORKER: SOME OF THE LIMITS OF THE DUTY TO ACCOMMODATE

The duty to accommodate workers based on their family status sends a strong message to Canadian employers, who can no longer pretend to claim that there is an impermeable divide between employees' work and family life. Even though many employers in Canada[98] and elsewhere are encouraged to, and in fact do, voluntarily try to accommodate workers, voluntary standards are not sufficient. Different measures can also be

91. *Communications, Energy, and Paperworkers Union, Local 707 v. SMS Equipment Inc. (Cahill-Saunders Grievance)* [2013] A.G.A.A. 41, ¶ 62.
92. *SMS Equipment Inc.*, 2015 ABQB 162 ¶ 90.
93. *Tomlinson v. Runnymede Healthcare Centre*, 2015 HRTO 4, ¶¶ 2, 6.
94. *Ibid.*, ¶ 4.
95. *Ibid.*, ¶ 5.
96. *Ibid.*, ¶¶ 19, 27.
97. *See* Judy Fudge, *Control Over Working Time and Work-Life Balance: A Detailed Analysis of the Canada Labour Code, Part III*, 24–42 (Report prepared for the Federal Labour Standards Review, 2006) https://dspace.library.uvic.ca:8443/bitstream/handle/1828/1014/Fudge%20COntrol%20over%20working%20time%20.pdf?sequence=1&isAllowed=y (accessed 22 December 2016).
98. *See* e.g., Government of Canada, Canadian Centre for Occupational Health and Safety, Work/Life Balance, http://www.ccohs.ca/oshanswers/psychosocial/worklife_balance.html

negotiated through collective bargaining and hence become legally binding on the parties to the collective bargaining agreement. It should, however, be borne in mind that the possibility of collective bargaining is necessarily contingent on the presence of unions in the workplace, which varies considerably from jurisdiction to jurisdiction in Canada and according to sector of activity and firm size.[99] While these initiatives have no doubt had an impact in many Canadian workplaces, the duty to accommodate is distinct in that it is binding on the employer and applies to all workers, be they unionized or not, part-time or full-time, temporary or permanent, etc.

The duty to accommodate based on a worker's family responsibilities is, however, still limited in comparison to the extent of an employer's duty in the case of other types of discrimination. As we have seen, the courts express a great reluctance to treat 'family status', defined as including the responsibilities that flow from this status, as they would treat other protected grounds of discrimination. As Elizabeth Shilton points out: 'It is the pervasiveness of the family status problem that poses the threat.'[100] Family responsibilities and work can interfere with each other on a regular basis and the vast majority of workers have some form of family responsibility. The courts are thus loath to treat all work arrangements that have a negative impact on family responsibilities as discriminatory. In response to this reluctance, the test established to prove a prima facie case of discrimination is more onerous. Indeed, the majority of the decisions to date deal only with whether or not the employee has met the test at the first step, without even analysing the employer's defence of a bona fide occupational requirement and the subsequent duty to accommodate.[101] It is more difficult to make a prima facie case of discrimination on the basis of family responsibilities because the employee has to prove that he or she first tried to self-accommodate by finding another solution outside of the workplace.[102] In our view, this requirement is incorrect.

The general test to establish a prima facie case of discrimination on other grounds does not require that the claimant demonstrate that she or he first tried to independently find another solution. It is only at the second step that the employer can attempt to justify the impugned standard by insisting that the employee has the obligation to co-operate in the accommodation process and seek reasonable solutions. In this sense, '[the] search for accommodation is a multi-party inquiry'[103] which includes the

(accessed 21 December 2016). The CCOHS clearly states that a lack of work-family balance is a source of occupational psychosocial risks and provides employers with suggestions to reduce work-family conflict.

99. Institut de la statistique du Québec (ISQ), *Regard statistique sur la couverture syndicale au Québec, ailleurs au Canada et dans les pays de l'OCDE* (Québec, Canada, 2014) http://www.stat.gouv.qc.ca/statistiques/travail-remuneration/presence-syndicale/couverture_syndicale_qc-canada-ocde.pdf (accessed 14 January 2017).

100. Shilton, *supra* n. 42, at 24.

101. *See* e.g., *Johnstone*, 2014 FCA 110 ¶¶ 12, 109 (The employer did not even argue that accommodating Ms. Johnstone by offering her a fixed schedule would cause him undue hardship); *Fanshwe College* [2015] O.L.A.A. No. 265 ¶ 82 (The employer did not present evidence of a bona fide occupational requirement); *SMS Equipment Inc.*, 2015 ABQB 162 ¶ 90.

102. The third factor in *Johnstone*, 2014 FCA 110 ¶ 93 is: 'that he or she has made reasonable efforts to meet those childcare obligations through reasonable alternative solutions, and that no such alternative solution is reasonably accessible'.

103. *Renaud* [1992] 2 S.C.R. 970 at 994.

participation of the claimant. Since the *Johnstone* judgment, some courts and specialized tribunals have begun to criticize this confusion in the test and reaffirm the importance of protecting against discrimination based on family responsibilities in the same manner as for other protected grounds:

> a self-accommodation element ... is not required with respect to other prohibited grounds of discrimination. This is unnecessary and contrary to the objects of human rights law. It is unnecessary because a finding of discrimination does not automatically follow once a prima facie case is established. It is only when the complainant establishes a prima facie case and the respondent fails to justify the rule or conduct that discrimination will be found.[104]

It remains to be seen if more recent decisions will eventually dominate the case law and will have the effect of simplifying the test for employees who claim discrimination related to their family responsibilities. The duty to accommodate workers with family responsibilities would then be applied in the workplace in the same way as it is for other protected grounds such as disability and religion.[105] The duty to accommodate on these last grounds is firmly established in all Canadian workplaces.

In unionized workplaces, the duty to individually accommodate workers because of their family responsibilities can present some advantages when it has not been possible for different reasons to collectively bargain such measures to enhance work-family balance. For employees whose work schedules interfere in a substantial manner with their family responsibilities, the existence of an employer's duty to accommodate allows them to ask for a schedule change, independently of other considerations, such as their employment status (*part-time v. full-time*) or their seniority in the workplace. Indeed, the principle of seniority is the cornerstone of collective bargaining in Canada.[106] This well-entrenched principle ensures formal equality at work by eliminating – or at least greatly reducing – favouritism on the part of the employer, but, at the same time, may negatively affect women or minority groups because they often do not have access to the same conditions of employment.[107] As regards family responsibilities, young parents may sometimes be among the last to choose their work schedules given their low seniority in the workplace. The duty to accommodate allows the employee, the union and the employer to put aside the general seniority rule in a particular case and jointly seek a solution for a more inclusive work environment that takes into account the worker's family responsibilities.

However, this solution is not as easy as it seems. The duty to accommodate on an individual basis raises the question of the potential for tension between collectively bargained rights and individual human rights in the workplace.[108] In the Canadian labour culture of firm-based collective bargaining, accommodation may be perceived as a case of individual interests overriding collectively bargained rights. Formal

104. *SMS Equipment Inc.*, 2015 ABQB 162 ¶ 77; *See also Misetich*, 2016 HRTO 1229 ¶ ¶ 42–48.
105. *See* Banks, *supra* n. 14, at 37–40.
106. Brunelle, *supra* n. 13, at 318–326.
107. Adelle Blackett & Colleen Sheppard, *Collective bargaining and equality: Making connections*, 142 Int'l Lab. Rev. 419, 433–434 (2003).
108. *Ibid.*

equality is still well entrenched in the workplace: the just employer is often seen to be the one who treats all employees in the same way.[109] Differential treatment of employees can be perceived as favouritism. Remedies adapted to the specific situation of an individual worker may therefore foster resentment among co-workers[110] and have the effect of marginalizing the accommodated worker.[111] No doubt with time, organizational cultures will change and be more willing to accept accommodations for family responsibilities as being the norm, and not the exception. In the meantime, however, it can be said that family responsibilities are still seen as an individual problem that does not require the participation of workplace actors to find a solution.

§15.06 CONCLUSION: THE NEED FOR A PARADIGM SHIFT

This chapter has explored family status discrimination in Canadian employment law and the duty of employers to reasonably accommodate workers on this ground. Family status is a relatively recent protected ground of discrimination in Canada and courts and specialized tribunals have acknowledged that it includes responsibilities associated with this status. In the last years, workers in different contexts have invoked this form of discrimination, most often in an attempt to gain some control over their working time and to lessen work-family conflict. The duty to accommodate can thus be an effective means for workers, particularly women, to balance their work and family life. Despite the promise of using anti-discrimination legislation to this end, this chapter has also underlined some of the limits of the individual accommodation approach to reconciling work and family.

One of these limits is that the duty for employers to accommodate individuals on the basis of their family situation does not promote a rethinking of work organization at a broader level, nor necessarily promote institutional change.[112] Several decisions deal with unsocial working hours and the need for employees to gain more control over their working time. Instead of responding to this problem on a case-by-case basis, through anti-discrimination laws, it may be more effective to modify minimum standards legislation, which applies to all workplaces within a given jurisdiction, so that it contains provisions that enable all workers to have such control. There should more generally be a paradigm shift, from a working time model based on the

109. Christian Brunelle, *L'accommodement raisonnable dans les entreprises syndiquées: Une valse à mille temps?* 33 Gestion 59, 60 (2008).

110. Studying the right to request flexible work arrangements in England, Hegewich came to the same conclusion regarding the potential resentment of the workers who had asked for such measures. Ariane Hegewisch, *Flexible working policies: a comparative review* 43 (Report no. 16, Institute for Women's Policy Research, UK, 2009) https://www.equalityhumanrights.com/sites/default/files/research_report_16_flexible_working_policies_comparative_review.pdf (accessed 22 December 2016).

111. *See* Shelagh Day & Gwen Brodsky, *The Duty to Accommodate: Who Will Benefit?* 75 Can. B. Rev. 433 (1996).

112. *See* Shilton, *supra* n. 42; Colleen Sheppard, *Individual Accommodation Versus Institutional Transformation: Two Paradigms for Reconciling Paid Pork and Family Responsibilities, in Les 15 ans du Tribunal des droits de la personne et les 30 ans de la Charte des droits et libertés de la personne*, 379 (Yvon Blais, 2005) papers.ssrn.com/sol3/papers.cfm?abstract_id=2298101 (accessed 22 December 2016).

'unencumbered worker', without family obligations, to one which takes into account the needs – and the equality rights – of workers with care responsibilities.[113] As William and Bornstein point out in response to a call for accommodation based on family responsibilities in the United States: '... rather than requiring individualized accommodations, what is necessary is one key shift to the norm of a balanced worker – a norm based on the not-so-heroic assumption that most adults have ongoing caregiving responsibilities.'[114]

Moreover, the duty to accommodate does not take into account the gendered nature of the distribution of family responsibilities. The great majority of the decisions mentioned in this chapter involve women who are making a claim to be accommodated in order to fulfil their family responsibilities. This is not surprising given the consistent data on the inequitable sharing of family responsibilities between women and men in Canada,[115] as well as elsewhere.[116] The duty to accommodate workers because of their family responsibilities applies, in theory, indifferently to women and men but the more frequent claims brought by women underline the fact that gender roles are still well entrenched in our society, as well as the need for more transformative legislation. While legal mechanisms such as the duty to accommodate individuals remain necessary to enable women to stay in employment, other, more collective, measures are needed to further encourage men to assume their share of care work. Indeed, an essential component of work-life balance is a more equitable redistribution of care work between women and men. As stated in the ILO *Convention on Workers With Family Responsibilities* (no. 156), adopted more than 35 years ago, it is essential to '[recognize] that the problems of workers with family responsibilities are aspects of wider issues regarding the family and society which should be taken into account in national policies, and [to recognize] the need to create effective equality of opportunity and treatment as between men and women workers with family responsibilities and between such workers and other workers.'[117]

113. Bernstein & Valentini, *supra,* n. 9.
114. Williams & Bornstein, *supra* n. 10, at 1325.
115. Anne Milan, Leslie-Anne Keown & Covadonga Robles Urquijo, *Families, Living Arrangements and Unpaid Work* 20–25 (Component of Statistics Canada Catalogue no. 89-503-X, Women in Canada: A Gender-based Statistical Report, 2011) http://www.statcan.gc.ca/pub/89-503-x/2010001/article/11546-eng.pdf (accessed 13 January 2017).
116. International Labour Office, *supra* n. 5, at 19–21.
117. Workers with Family Responsibilities Convention, 1981, 1331 U.N.T.S. 295 *supra* n. 4, preamble.

CHAPTER 16

Reconciliation of Work and Private Life as Key Element for Sustainable Work Throughout the Life Course

*Greet Vermeylen, Agnès Parent-Thirion, Mathijn Wilkens & Jorge Cabrita**

§16.01 INTRODUCTION

Gender equality and work-life balance are inherently part of the European policy agenda, including the Employment strategy as part of EU2020. It is also a part of the reflection on the European pillar of social rights. Indeed, whether and how men and women in Europe can engage in paid work depends very much on how well they can reconcile work with private life. Throughout the life course, private life needs, particularly care responsibilities, need to be taken care. This issue is one of the key elements in the conceptual framework of sustainability of work throughout the life course for men and women (Eurofound 2015). Another way of considering it is to consider it along the ideas behind Amartya Sen's capabilities theory, whereby capabilities for work-life balance stand for creating the opportunities and facilities for men and women to engage in work and combine it with their private life (Hobson and Fehlen, 2009). These facilities could for instance be working time options (adaptation of working hours, such as part time work), family leaves, working time arrangements (organisation of working hours, being able to take time off at short notice to take care of private needs), as well as social infrastructure, such as care facilities for dependent relatives, crèches, school and afterschool care. For all, it is the combination of measures which determines how good one can reconcile one's work and one's private time needs.

* The authors state that the opinions stated in this chapter are theirs and do not engage Eurofound.

Eurofound's working definition of sustainable work over the life course (Eurofound 2015) means that working and living conditions are such that they support people in engaging and remaining in work throughout an extended working life. For work to be sustainable, two elements need to be considered: work on the one hand, referring to the quality of the job and the work environment (and the impact on health, well-being and skills development over the life course), and the individual on the other hand, referring to the interaction between work and private life, considering how the characteristics and circumstances of are catered for, such as time needs for private life, particularly care or health needs. These private time needs can vary very much depending on the intensity of care or health needs, such as for children, other dependents in needs of care or one's own health. Hence, there is not a one fits all solution to make 'work sustainable over the life course'. In particular circumstances and situations, a different solution – combination of measures and facilities- can help men and women to reconcile their work demands with private time demands. Furthermore these time needs can change over the life course, whereby certain solutions can be more appropriate for particular phases or issues in life, for instance the children of different age, disabled relatives, elderly parents or a partner with health issues might require different solutions.

From a gender equality point of view, both employment participation for men and women can be encouraged and facilitated through reconciliation policies and workplace practices. However, it is equally important to reflect on the division of work in the private sphere, the so-called unpaid work among the partners.

§16.02 RESULTS FROM THE 6TH EWCS: WORKING TIME AND RECONCILIATION BETWEEN WORK AND PRIVATE LIFE

The 6th European Working Conditions Survey, a survey of workers in thirty-five countries, sheds some light on working conditions and their impact on reconciliation in the European Union. Indeed, a crucial element to understand working conditions of people is to understand how they organise their time over the different activities in their life, both working life and private life. We only have twenty-four hours in a day in which we need to juggle our time, together with our family members.

When we look at working time, we need to consider both paid working time and unpaid working time, time spent on activities in the private sphere, such as care and household tasks. Throughout working life, different times needs arise in the private sphere. Care responsibilities for children, grandchildren, disabled and elderly dependents are more intensive at particular times of our life

The division of time over the different aspects of our life depends very much on the compromises and choices which are made at household level as well as the social infrastructure and organisation of society (Muckenberger and Boulin, 2002) (cfr *infra*). Indeed, opening hours of shops and services determine private time needs for workers, in the sense that one needs to be able to organise one's private life in the constraints of both one's job and the 'times of the cities'.

There are big differences between men and women in the division of working time. While men work on average more working hours in the main paid job, women do take the biggest bulk of the unpaid working time. This is true for full time and part time workers. The number of hours spent on average is the second job is very low for men and women. There are hardly any differences in average commuting time of men and women (three hours per week).

§16.03 WORKING TIME DURATION

Over the years, working time has been decreasing for men and women. This goes in two ways: less people work very long working hours and more people work part time. There is however still a gendered pattern with regard to working hours. Less people work very long working hours: whereas 18% of workers in 2005 worked forty-eight hours or more per week, this has gone down to 15% in 2015. Men (21%) work more often very long working hours than women (9%). The opposite pattern can be found with part time work: part time work, working less than thirty-four hours per week has gone up from 21% in 2005 to 29% in 2015. Women (42%) work more often part time than men (16%). One striking thing is that short part time work (less than twenty hours per week) has gone up more dramatically for men (from 5% in 2005 to 10% in 2015) than for women (from 17% in 2005 to 22% in 2015). Some of these short part time working hours might be involuntary part time work. Also, there are quality differences among different forms of part time, with voluntary and longer part times usually associated with better quality (Fagan et al., 2014, Messenger 2004).

Among the countries, however, different working time patterns can be noted: in some countries, both men and women work full time, working around the 37.5 - 40 hours per week, and those with more variety, both in terms of more workers working longer hours (usually men) and those with more part time workers (and in these cases more women than men working shorter hours on average).

Figure 16.1 Average Usual Weekly Working Hours per Country (All Workers, Women and Me)

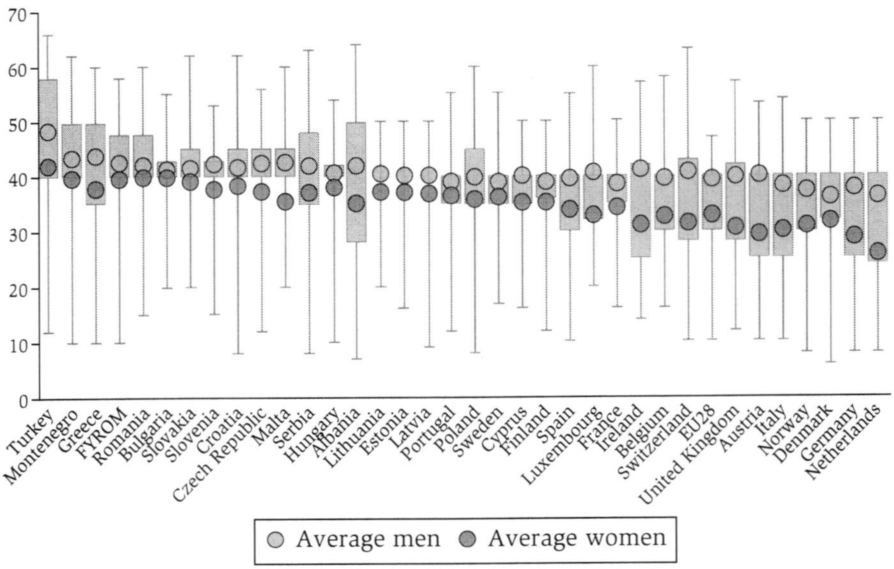

Taken from Eurofound (2016), Sixth European Working Conditions Survey: overview report, p. 55

Legend: The grey both represents the interquartile range (50% of workers) and the whiskers represent the 5th and 95th percentile.

§16.04 PAID AND UNPAID WORKING TIME

When reflecting upon reconciliation issues, one needs to consider overall working time, that is both paid and unpaid working time. This paints a very different picture. Indeed, the bulk of the 'unpaid' work, done in the private sphere, such as care and household activities, remains done by women. The amount of unpaid working hours increases when there are children in the household, both for men and women, but for women much more than for men. The 6th EWCS shows that while women decrease their working hours on average with the arrival of children in the household but increase their unpaid working hours dramatically. For men, they slightly increase their working hours in paid and unpaid work, but not to the same extent in the latter case: In households without children, men work on average forty hours in paid work and five hours in unpaid work compared to thirty-six hours in paid work and twelve hour in unpaid work for women. In households with the youngest child under the age of seven, men work forty-one hours in paid and fifteen hours in unpaid work, compared to thirty-two hours in paid and thirty-nine hours in unpaid work for women. The amount of unpaid work decreases when children get bigger, but the difference between men and women remains. Interestingly, Eurofound 2013 shows that when men engage more in care activities in the rush hour of life, it is often when they are in particular working time settings (organisation and duration).

Next to paid working time in the main job and unpaid working time, working time in the second job, if there is one and commuting time needs to be considered. However, on average for workers in the EU there are hardly any differences and are very low on average.

Figure 16.2 Paid and Unpaid Work over Life Stages for Women and Men (Hours per Week, EU 28)

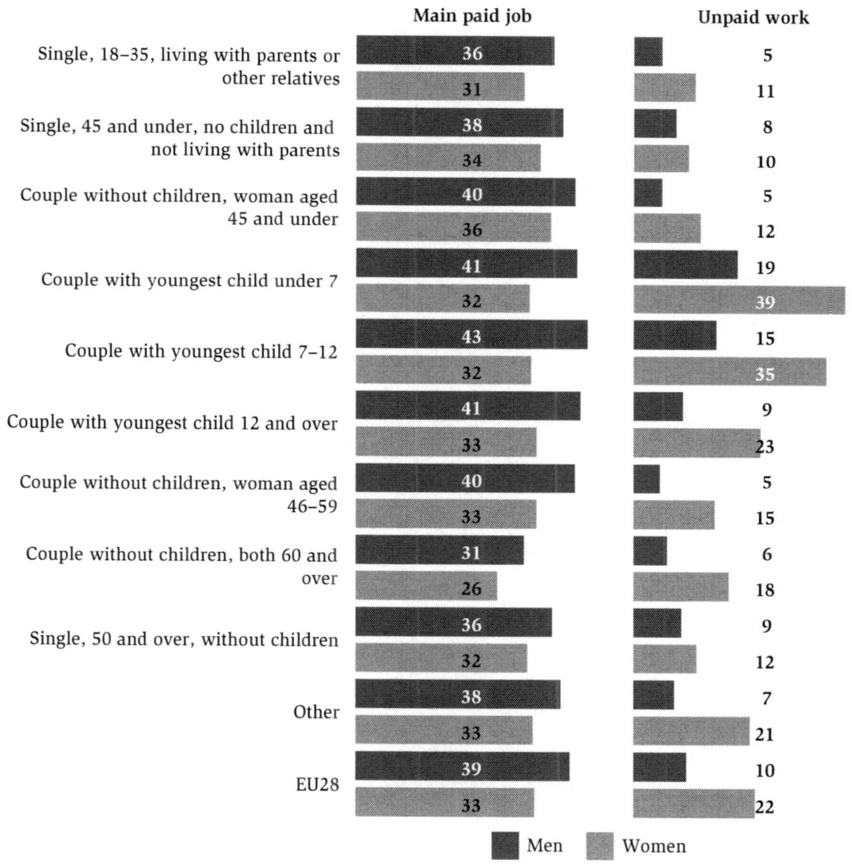

Taken from Eurofound (2016), Sixth European Working Conditions Survey: overview report, p. 117

§16.05 WORKING TIME ORGANISATION

The way working time is organised also crucial for work-life balance. First of all, atypical working times might have an impact on organisation of private life: more than half of the workers work at least one Saturday a month and around one third one Sunday a month, one in five does night work and/or shift work (of the shift workers nearly have rotating shifts). Atypical working times are more done by men than by women.

Secondly, when we look at regularity, also important for work-life balance, 29% workers report that they have low regularity in their working hours, more men (33%) than women (25%). In terms of changes in the work schedule: 69% of workers (67% of men and 70% of women) have not changes in their work schedule, and when they occur, for 18% they know several days or weeks in advance, for 8% they know the day before and 5% they know the same day only. Particularly, little predictability has a strong negative impact on work-life balance. 12% of workers have been requested to come into the office at short notice, slightly more men (13%) than women (11%).

Thirdly, for more than half (55%) working time arrangements are set by the company with no possibility for change, one in ten (9%) can choose between fixed schedules and one in five(19%) has flexitime, meaning that they can vary between certain schedules. The last group (around 17%) report that they can determine freely their working hours. There is hardly any difference between women and men, but women slightly report more than their working time arrangements are set by the company with no possibilities for change (57%).

Fourthly, 65% of workers (68% of men and 63% of women) report that it is easy (25%) or fairly easy (40%) to take an hour or two off during working hours to take care of personal or family matters.

§16.06 BLURRING FRONTIERS BETWEEN WORKING AND NOT WORKING (FOR PAY)

Nearly one worker in four (23%) reports that they have worked in their free time to meet work demands several times a month, 10% does so several times a week and 3% daily. Men (24%) do so slightly more than women (22%) several times a month, but there are no gender differences for those who do this more frequently. Differences are often related to the job and employment status: managers (48%), professionals (39%) and skilled agricultural workers (33%) do it most often, and the same is true for self-employed workers with (51%) as well as without employees (37%) in comparison with employees (20%).

§16.07 ICT AND WORKING TIME

Technologies have changed where we can work. Recent findings (Eurofound and ILO, 2017) show that work-life balance is in many cases one of the drivers for introducing telework by companies. Workers are usually in favour of being able to decide where they can work, not only to reconcile work with private life but also to be able to work without being constantly interrupted by colleagues. While regular telework is overall still quite low (3% of workers), another 10% does it occasionally and 5% is does high mobile telework/ICT mobile work. Said this, within the EU, big differences can be found: where there are less than 10% T/ICTM workers (all three groups together) in Italy in Greece, this goes up to more than 30% of the workers in Denmark, Sweden and the Netherlands. The effect on work-life balance however is very mixed: not all T/ICTM workers report better results with regard to a good fit between work and private life, they work more often very long hours and work more often in their private time, the so-called blurring frontiers between work and private life. The effect is strongest for those who do supplemental telework (on top of the work done in the office) instead of substitutional telework (for instance one or two days at home instead of in the office). The effect however is still most positive for those who have working time autonomy, that is who have some say over when they work. T/ICTM workers also report more often that they can take some time off at short notice for private reasons. While most countries have some legislation and/ or national/sectorial agreements following the lines of the European Framework Agreement on Telework (outlining some rules for regular telework), referring to some clauses that can be implemented in company agreements and/or practices if they want to introduce telework, currently a new movement starts to reflect on the boundaries to working time, through 'a right to disconnect'. Companies have started to introduce limits to when emails can be sent or computers being switched off after too long working. Sectorial agreements and legislation have been developed or are being developed to reflect on measures to reduce the constant availability and working, for instance in France and Germany, often in the context of mental health policies.

§16.08 WORK-FAMILY CONFLICTS

Work and private life are not separate parts of our life. Negative spill-overs from work to private life or from private life to work, work-family conflicts, can lead to work-related outcomes, such as impacting on job satisfaction, organisational commitment and engagement; to non-work related outcomes, such as life, family and marital satisfaction and strain, as well as health-related outcomes, particularly psychological strain, mental health problems and absenteeism (Allen et al., 2000, Amsted et al., 2011 and Annink et al., 2016). Negative spill-overs from private life to work are a lot less reported by workers: 4% of worker report that they found it always or most of the time difficult to concentrate on the job because of their family responsibilities, and 3% report that their family responsibilities prevented them from giving the time to their family. There are very little gender or occupational differences among workers. It seems to hint that those with most problems have either found a way of reconciling work with their private responsibilities or that they have left the labour market.

Negative spill-overs from work to private life are more commonplace. 14% of workers report that they always or most of the time kept on worrying about their job when not working. The differences are mostly related to the kind of job the workers do:

managers (31%) and professionals (21%) report more problems, compared to workers in elementary occupations (9%) and plant and machine operators (9%). One worker in five (20%) report that they always or most of the time felt too tired after work to do some of the household jobs that need to be done. This is slightly more the case for women (22%) than men (20%). It is reported most by managers (26%), skilled agricultural workers (25%), plant and machine operators (25%) and service and sales workers (24%) on the one hand and least by workers in elementary occupations (13%) on the other hand. 11% of workers report that they always or most of the time found that their job prevented them from giving the time they wanted to their family. Managers (16%) and service and sales workers (14%) report most problems and clerical support workers, workers in elementary occupations and technician (each 9%) report least problems. Self-employed with employees and, to a lesser degree, self-employed without employees report more negative spill-overs from work to private life than employees.

§16.09 RECONCILIATION ISSUES

Both working time duration and organisation are important for work-life balance (Fagan, 2012). Around one worker in five (18%) in the 6th EWCS report that they have a bad fit between working life and private life, slightly more the case so for men (20%) than women (16%), which might be related to adaptive choices, whereby women take jobs which can be reconciled better with their private life and/or have shorter working hours. More problems with work-life balance arise when there are children in the household. Working time arrangements and options can play a useful role. Work-life balance is associated negatively with long working hours, irregular and asocial working hours (nights, weekends) as well as for those working in their free time to meet work demands (often facilitated through ICTs). Shorter working hours, having some say over your working time, but particularly being able to take time off at short notice are associated with a more positive fit between work and private life. It needs to be noted that while allowing workers to take time off at short notice to take care of private issues, such as taking an hour to bring your child to the dentist, is not necessarily costly for employers, but comes up as one of the strongest factors in the analysis. It might not be possible in all work situations, but where it is possible, it is really worthwhile to do the organisational effort.

§16.10 WORKING TIME OPTIONS AND WORKING TIME PREFERENCES

When considering working time preferences, that is whether people would like to increase, decrease or keep the same working hours if they had a choice and provided that they have to earn a living, more than half of the workers (58%) report that they are happy with to work the same hours than they currently work, same result for women and men. However, nearly one in three (28%) would like to work less than currently (31% of men and 25% of women) and 14% would like to work more than currently (11% of men and 16% of women).

While (temporary) reduction of working time might be positive for work-life balance, it is not always associated with positive other outcomes from a gender equality point of view (Fagan 2014), nor the preferred option for many workers in part time: 37% of the part timers would like to increase their working hours if they could, compared to 7% of the full timers. Therefore, it is important to reflect on transitions between working time options (back to full time), the way part time is organised (e.g., longer part time, like working four days out of five), which might have less negative consequences for the career prospects of the workers. For some workers it might be useful to interrupt work for a certain time to take care of care responsibilities, through leave arrangements, such as maternity and paternity leave, parental leave as well as carers' leave.

§16.11 FAMILY LEAVES

National legislation provides for family leaves. Not in all countries, the same leaves are available and they definitely are not shaped in the same way. There are huge differences across countries with regard to existence of the leave (and entitlement), the length of leave (in weeks, months, years), and whether and how much it is remunerated/paid (generosity of leave entitlements). While in all countries, leaves are associated with pregnancy and maternity leave, paternity leave exists is most countries but parental leave and carers' leave is not always available. We also bump here into an issue of inequality between women and men, with women everywhere taking the main bulk of all leaves. In an increasing number of countries, initiatives are taken to try and encourage uptake for fathers of parental leave.

§16.12 MATERNITY LEAVE AND PATERNITY LEAVE

Maternity leave is available and mandatory in all countries, even though duration, both of all leave and of the mandatory period (if there is one), as well as the remuneration is not equal for all workers in all countries and across countries. The duration varies between eight weeks and fifty-eight weeks overall, the maternity allowance varies between flat rate in Ireland, 70% in Czech republic, Slovakia and Hungary on the one hand and 100% in Austria, Croatia, Denmark, Estonia, France, Germany, Greece, Lithuania, Luxembourg, Malta, the Netherlands, Norway, Poland, Portugal, Slovenia, Spain, on the other hand. In Lithuania and Latvia there is no minimum mandatory period to take, while it varies between two weeks in Slovenia, Denmark, Hungary and UK on the one hand and thirty-four weeks in Slovakia. Either the public authorities or employer (or both) is responsible for paying the maternity allowance. A specific issue is the access and uptake of maternity leave for self-employed which is usually shorter than for (permanent) employees. In some countries part of the maternity leave can be shared with the father, usually only a period (e.g., after the first six weeks). In Sweden and Portugal no difference is made between maternity, paternity and parental leave.

Paternity leave now exist in nearly all countries, except Cyprus, Germany and Ireland, the duration varies between one day and ninety days. There are statutory provisions in the other countries, but in terms of length, paternity leave varies considerably in terms of working days, from one compulsory day in Malta (two in the public sector), two days in Greece, Luxembourg, the Netherlands, Spain and Italy (four days in 2018), five days in Hungary and Romania, seven days in Croatia, ten days in Belgium, Estonia, Latvia and Sweden, eleven days in France, thirteen days in Spain, fourteen days in Denmark, Norway, Poland and the UK, fifteen days in Bulgaria Portugal to the more 'generous' Member States where it extends to thirty days in Lithuania and Slovenia and fifty-four days in Finland.

§16.13 PARENTAL LEAVE

In parental leave there is equally a considerable variety among countries, not only in entitlement (whether it exists), duration (from a couple of months up to three years) and whether and how much it is remunerated (not remunerated, flat rate/ a percentage of average earnings in the country, a percentage of one's salary, and the amount often depends also on the amount of leave that is being taken). In many countries, there are also rules about the division of the leave among partners, with in some countries dedicated periods for each parent. Indeed, attempts are made to encourage uptake of parental leave by fathers through specifically dedicated periods for each of the parents.

Parental leave can be allocated in different ways, as a family entitlement, that can be divided between the parents, an individual entitlement or a mixed entitlements, that is part family and part individual entitlement. In fourteen Member States, parental leave can be shared by the parents. This is the case for Austria, Bulgaria, Croatia, Cyprus, Denmark, Estonia, Finland, Germany, Hungary, Lithuania, Poland, Romania, Slovakia and Slovenia. In twelve EU Member States, it is an individual entitlement that cannot be shared. This is the case for Belgium, France, the Czech Republic, Greece, Ireland, Italy, Latvia, Luxembourg, Malta, the Netherlands, Spain and the United Kingdom. In the remaining Member States (Portugal and Sweden) and in Norway, parental leave comprises two parts, one that can be shared and one that cannot be shared.

Remuneration is an important element: often decision are taken at household level whereby financial calculations are important determinants whether one and/or two and whom can take up the leave according to remuneration and replacement rates.

For eight Member States, there is no cash benefit associated with parental leave: in Croatia, Cyprus, Greece, Ireland, Malta, the Netherlands, Spain and the UK, parental leave, if taken, is unpaid. The cash benefits associated with the take-up of parental leave are paid either flat rate or a percentage of the salary which varies between 30% and 100%, sometimes depending on the length of uptake. It is flat rate in Belgium, the Czech Republic, France, Hungary (for the last stage of leave entitlements), Luxembourg, Poland (for the last stage of leave entitlements), Slovakia and Sweden (for part of leave entitlements). In Austria, the recipient can choose between a flat rate or an income dependent benefit. In the other Member States with such benefits, the amount concerned is a proportion of the individual's most recent salary – 30% in Italy, 60% in

Poland, 67% in Germany, 70% in Finland, 80% in Austria (in one leave option), and up to 100% in Denmark and in Portugal (for the shortest length).

A last issue is take-up of parental leave by fathers and mothers. In all countries, fathers are more reluctant to take up leave, which might have to do with a series of elements, including information about the leave available, the leave compensation (and pay disparities), availability and flexibility of child care facilities, prevailing family organisation models and how it is perceived and embedded in the workplace (culture) and whether the leave can be taken up in a flexible way. Often this could be a way of overcoming the fear of being away for too long from the workplace having a negative impact on career prospects for both men and women.

There are a number of examples of measure to encourage fathers to take up parental leave through quota or financial bonuses. Examples of father quotas are Finland, Norway and Sweden. The 'daddy month' in Finland is an earnings-based paternity allowance (70%) which increased the paternity allowance to twenty-five days and can be taken when the other parent is also on leave. While uptake is still quite low (32%), it is a fivefold increase with before. In Norway, there is a father quota of 10 weeks. In Sweden, 90 days are reserved for each parent, and 300 days can be split. Another example is the 'family time bonus' which was introduced in Austria in March 2017, paternity leave reserved for fathers within 2 months after the birth. Also the amount of parental leave is higher when both take leave: in the case of a flat rate paid parental leave option, the time is between 12–28 months if only one of the two parents take leave but increases to 15–35 months if both take leave (20% is not transferable) and in case of the income dependent option, paid 80% of the salary for 12 months if one partners takes it and 14 months if both take it plus a partner bonus of EUR 500.

§16.14 CARERS' LEAVE

A special issue to carers leave: 80% of the care is done by informal carers in the European Union: many workers have to give up work in order to take care of dependant relatives, other than small children, in need of care. This is least organised in most of the countries, while there are some exceptions. Short term leave, usually linked with sickness of a relative, is relatively well organised (between six to seven days and thirty year) and paid more generously, but longer term leave, more relevant for on-going elderly and disabled care is a lot scarcer and often unpaid.

Short term care leave, between six to seven days and thirty days, is usually more generously remunerated than short term leave. Examples are for instance the Netherlands, where it is paid at 70% of the remuneration. In Germany, workers can also apply for interest free loans for short term leaves. Usually, no consent from the employer is needed. One exception is Finland where the employer and employee need to agree upon this.

Example of long term care leave are for instance carers leave in Spain, for up to two years but unpaid, in Sweden it is sixty days per year but paid as replacement similarly as sick leave (120 days in case of sick child). In other countries, a relatively flexibly organised reduction of working hours can be another way of engaging in these care responsibilities, e.g., Germany, UK, the Netherlands. In the latter case, the employer needs to justify in case of refusal. In the context of potentially longer working lives, it might be useful to reflect on how this could be embedded more systematically, to be able to take care for elderly parents or a partner. There has been a call from nongovernmental organisations (NGOs) and the European Parliament for a 'Carers' Directive' including giving care credits to workers.

Next to leaves, in some countries the worker has the right to reduce their working hours if they want, such as in Lithuania for workers who are nursing sick family members, and in Spain both sick family members and disabled family members. In the Netherlands, long term care leave and reduction of working hours can be asked for a wider circles of acquaintances, and include the care for a sick neighbour or friend (provided they are not hospitalised).

§16.15 SOCIAL INFRASTRUCTURE

Last but not least, care infrastructure such as crèches, school and afterschool care as well as (semi) residential care or home care infrastructure (with services at home) for other dependents are constructive for those with care responsibilities. Availability, quality, price, traditions, opening hours and 'flexibility' (adapted to needs of workforce) are again very important determinants whether this is a real possibility for those who could benefit from it to combine work with care responsibilities.

Particularly, equal access to quality services for all groups is important, including children living in low-income families (Eurofound 2015c and 2016a): some differences across countries can be found in the availability of places, the cost as well as the quality.

Furthermore, the schooling system plays an important role: indeed, while, if available, infrastructure for small children is usually available all day, in several countries, school times are only half day or shorter than usual working days, and afterschool care is not always available, good quality or affordable. Afterschool clubs do exits privately or organised via voluntary organisations but accessibility has not been organised. Initiatives to organise afterschool care via schools starts to develop in several countries, such as Belgium, Ireland, UK. Next to this informal child care can be provided by the wider relatives circle (e.g., grandparents). In Belgium, certain social insurance providers can provide a child minder for a sick child from the second day of sickness onwards. It also needs to be considered in conjunction with other family arrangements such as parental leave (Eurofound 2015c).

With regard to long term care facilities for disabled or other relatives in needs, the situation is less organised and not systematically captured across Member States as many different options are available. The following possibilities exist: home care, residential care, semi-residential care (e.g., day care and respite care). Again the differences are related to availability, quality and cost of these services. In some countries, the social insurance fund organises a series of services, such as home services and respite care for carers, such as in Belgium. In other countries, only private services are available and/or public services are means tested.

§16.16 DIFFERENT NEEDS AT DIFFERENT TIMES THROUGHOUT THE LIFE COURSE

Last but not least: reconciliation measures consist of a mix of different possible solutions consisting in care infrastructure, family leaves, working time options and working time arrangements, being able to adapt your working hours to your private needs including flexitime, predictable hours, being able to take time off at short notice. It is the combination of the different facilities which enhance the capabilities for work-life balance. It depends also on the (cultural) preferences and the needs of the workers throughout their working life. Gender equality is an important element and the issue remains how to try and facilitate/ encourage as much as possible both partners to engage in private life activities throughout the life course.

Some of the arrangements might have unintended negative side effects. Telework a couple of days a week could be useful for work-life balance, but this might depend very much on the kind of care one needs to give (e.g., might be more complicated with small children) and might lead to trying to juggle to do different things at the same time or working very long hours. Therefore, it needs to be structured carefully.

Different needs at different times: the care needs for small children might be different than those of bigger children who need some minding but maybe less intensively. A frail relative who might need intensive care has different care needs than an elderly parent for whom one needs to go to the doctor or do administration/cooking a few times a week. Therefore, there is 'not a one fits all solution', but a wide range of working time arrangements, options and leaves could enhance the worker's capabilities for reconciling work and private life and sustainable work. Ensuring that both men and women can work if they want and can continue to participate in work relies on actions from all policymakers and companies.

BIBLIOGRAPHY

Allen T., Herst D., Bruck C. and Sutton M., *Consequences associated with work-to-family conflict: a review and agenda for future research*, Journal of Occupational Health Psychology, Vol. 5 no. 2, (2000), pp. 278-308

Amsted F., Meier L., Fasel U., Elfering A., Semmer N., *A meta-analysis of work-family conflict and various outcomes with special emphasis on cross-domain versus matching domain relations*, Journal of Occupational Health Psychology, Vol. 16 no. 2 (2011), pp. 151-169

Annink A., Den Dulk L., Steijn B., *Work-family conflict among employees and self-employed across Europe*, Social Indicators Research, Vol. 126 no. 2 (2016), pp. 571-593.

Eurofound, *working life profiles*, https://www.eurofound.europa.eu/observatories/eurwork/comparative-information/working-life-country-profiles.

Eurofound, *Foundation Focus: Work-life balance: creating solutions for everyone*, Dublin, (2016a).

Eurofound, *Sixth working conditions survey - overview report*, Publications Office of the European Union, Luxembourg (2016b).

Eurofound, *Sustainable work throughout the life course: national policies and strategies*, Publications Office of the European Union, Luxembourg (2016c).

Eurofound, *Maternity leave provisions in the EU Member States: duration and allowances*, Dublin (2015a).

Eurofound, *Promoting uptake of parental and paternity leave among fathers in the European Union*, Dublin (2015b).

Eurofound, *Early childhood care: Accessibility and quality of services*, Publications Office of the European Union, Luxembourg (2015c).

Eurofound, *Sustainable work over the life course: concept paper*, Dublin (2015d).

Eurofound, Working and caring: reconciliation measures in times of demographic change, Dublin (2015e).

Eurofound, *Foundation Focus: Sustainable work: towards better and longer working lives*, Dublin (2014).

Eurofound, *Working time and work-life balance in a life course perspective*, Dublin (2013).

Eurofound, Parenting support in Europe, Dublin (2012).

Eurofound, *Parental leave in European companies*, Dublin (2007).

Eurofound and International Labour Organisation, *Working anytime, anywhere: the effects on the world of work*, Publications Office of the European Union, Luxembourg, and the International Labour Office, Geneva (2017).

Fagan C., Lyonette C., Smith M., Saldana-Tejeda A., The influence of working time arrangements on work-life integration or 'balance': a review of the international evidence, ILO, Geneva (2012).

Fagan, C. & Norman, H., *Work-Life Balance Revisited: a reconciliation policy mix to ease the constraints faced by parents: External report commissioned by and prepared for the use of the European Commission*, Directorate-*General Justice, Brussels* (2015).

Fagan, C., Norman, H., Smith, M. & González Menéndez, M. C., *In search of good quality part-time employment*, ILO, Geneva (2014).

Barbara Hobson (ed.), *The agency gap in work–life balance: Applying Sen's capabilities framework within European contexts*, Social Politics, Vol. 18 no 2, Barbara Hobsonbarbara.hobson@sociology.su.se (2011) pp. 147–167.

Hobson B. and S. Fahlén, *Applying Sen's Capabilities framework to work family balance within a European context: Theoretical and empirical challenges, REC-WP 03/2009, Working Papers on the Reconciliation of Work and Welfare in Europe*, RECWOWE Publication, Dissemination and Dialogue Centre, Edinburgh (2009).

Messenger J. (ed.), *Working time and workers' preferences in industrialised countries: finding the balance*, Oxon, Routledge (2004).

Muckenbergen U. and J.Y. Boulin, *Times of the city, new ways of involving citizens*, Concepts and Transformation, Vol. 7 no. 1 (2002), pp. 73–91.

CHAPTER 17

Work-Life Balance, Time and Money: Identifying the Work-Life Balance Priorities of Working Class Workers

Tracey Warren

§17.01 INTRODUCTION

How do we spend our time? How might we organize our time better so that our lives are improved? These questions have inspired thinkers for centuries. This chapter outlines and offers a critique of a significant modern formulation of those longstanding philosophies: the dominance of 'time poverty' in how we understand 'work-life balancing'.

Time is a fundamental element of peoples' everyday lives. Discussions around the importance of time are rooted in sociology, social policy, economics, history, philosophy and multiple other disciplines. Fundamental to this academic debate is how the time spent in paid work connects with the time dedicated to other aspects of life. Social theorists, from Marx[1] in 1859 to Durkheim[2] in 1912 up to Wajcman[3] in 2015, and with Becker,[4] Elias,[5] Adam[6,7] Gershuny[8] and many others in between, have highlighted

1. Karl Marx, *Preface to a Contribution to the Critique of Political Economy*. Various prints (first published in 1859).
2. Emile Durkheim, *The Elementary Forms of Religious Life*. New York: Free Press (1965), first published (1912).
3. Judy Wajcman, *Pressed for Time: The Acceleration of Life in Digital Capitalism*. Chicago: University of Chicago Press (2015).
4. Gary Becker, 'A Theory of the Allocation of Time', *Economic Journal*, 75, 493–517 (1985).
5. Norbert Elias, *Time. An Essay*. Oxford: Blackwell (1992).
6. Barbara Adam, *Time and Social Theory*. Cambridge: Polity Press (1990).
7. Barbara Adam, *Timewatch. The Social Analysis of Time*. Cambridge: Polity (1995).
8. Jonathan Gershuny, *Changing Times – Work and Leisure in Postindustrial Society*. Oxford: Oxford University Press (2000).

the central role that time plays in organizing lives. The importance of having enough time for personal fulfilment and the challenges involved in coordinating life's multiple times are main undercurrents in academic thinking. Time has critical ramifications beyond academia too. Time is pivotal in movements throughout history that sought to improve working lives, and in policy formulation to support workers, job seekers and their families.

The specific temporal position that underpins these discussions is one in which the time spent in and on work should not overwhelm the rest of a person's life. A chief argument is that workers should not spend too many hours in their jobs. A dedicated literature has grown up around the concern with working 'too much'. In 1899 Veblen[9] asked about the relationship between time spent on work and leisure, querying whether a society would prevail in which leisure time would be extolled over work time. This work versus leisure time theme re-emerged strongly towards the end of the twentieth century, with a pessimistic backdrop. Fears began to be expressed about an expansion of very long hours in the workplace. Harried lives, time-squeeze and time-poverty were placed firmly on academic agendas, particularly in societies in which the social organization of work time was being destabilized following the economic crises of the 1970s. In the USA, sociologist Schor[10] was to memorably problematize the idea of a 'long hours' culture'. In her 1991 *The Overworked American* she critiqued so-called greedy organizational environments that were demanding too many hours from workers (and see Schor 2010[11]). From USA sociology too, Hochschild's (1997) influential *The Time Bind*[12] identified the detrimental impact that longer hours in the workplace can have on family time (*see also* Robinson and Godbey, 1997[13]). There were also time debates in Europe, with writers such as Garhammer (1998),[14] Gershuny (2000)[15] and Nowotny (2005)[16] all exploring whether time poverty was a major (re)-emerging social problem. One paradox in these debates is that long hours working may well have actually decreased over time, still workers report feeling

9. Thorstein Veblen, *The Theory of the Leisure Class*. London: New English Library Limited (1963, published originally in 1899).
10. Juliet Schor, *The Overworked American: The Unexpected Decline of Leisure*. New York: Basic Books (1991).
11. Juliet Schor, *Plenitude: The New Economics of True Wealth*, New York: Penguin (2010).
12. Arlie Russell Hochschild, *The Time Bind. When Work Becomes Home and Home Becomes Work*. New York: Henry Holt and Company (1997).
13. John P. Robinson and Geoffrey Godbey, *Time for Life. The Surprising Ways Americans Use Their Time*, Pennsylvania University Park: Pennsylvania State University Press (1997).
14. Manfred Garhammer, '*Time Poverty in Modern Germany*', Society and Leisure, 21, 327, 352 (1998).
15. Gershuny, *Changing Times*.
16. Helga Nowotny, *Time: The Modern and Postmodern Experience*; Cambridge: Polity Press (2005).

more time rushed (Bianchi et al. 2006[17]; Golden 2009[18]; Jacobs and Gerson 1998[19]; Roberts 2002[20]; Wajcman 2015[21]). We return to the 'experience' of time later.

Worker movements have long campaigned against too many work hours. The famous union slogan '8 hours for work, 8 hours for sleep, 8 hours for what we will' dates back to the nineteenth century when a battle was being fought for an eight-hour work-day. The 1800s in Britain also saw a struggle to protect the 'St Monday' tradition, so-called because workers typically did not work on Mondays, as industrialization demanded (and ultimately won) Monday as a usual day of work. Employers, trying to impose a structured working week, began to remove the Monday holiday, replacing it with a Saturday half-holiday, but were met with widespread resistance (*see* Thompson 1967[22]). Much later in Europe, workers' aims to curtail very long hours had success in the EC's 1993 Working Time Directive, which set minimum rest periods (daily, weekly, annually), limits to night-time work, as well as maximum weekly work hours, including overtime, of forty-eight. Ensuring that sufficient time is free from paid work was also fundamental to other EC directives, including around parental leave: that established rights to three months' unpaid leaves from paid work for women and men having or adopting a child. The 1997 Part-time Work Directive had 'too many' hours as its backdrop too since it supports the employment rights of those whose hours are reduced because, historically, any deviation from full-time employment meant exclusion from employment protection.

This concern with 'too much' work and policy responses aimed at addressing the problem is well-known in the long-established study of time and of employment. 'Too much' work was to become a staple in the new dedicated study of work-life balance that emerged in the 1990s (Lewis et al. 2016[23]), as we show next.

§17.02 THE CENTRALITY OF TIME: LONG HOURS, WORK-LIFE BALANCE AND MIDDLE CLASS WORKERS

Do the number of hours that people spend in the labour market integrate smoothly with the rest of their lives or overwhelm them? Replicating the above earlier debates, 'too many' hours became central both to theoretical understandings of work-life balance

17. Suzanne M. Bianchi., John P. Robinson and Melissa Milki, *The Changing Rhythms of American Family Life*. New York: Russell Sage (2006).
18. Lonnie Golden, 'Brief History of Long Work Time and the Contemporary Sources of Overwork', *Journal of Business Ethics*, 84, 2, 217–227 (2009).
19. Jerry A. Jacobs and Kathleen Gerson, 'Overworked Individuals or Overworked Families? Exploring Trends in Work, Leisure and Family Time', *Work and Occupations*, 28, 1, 40–63 (2001).
20. Ken Roberts, *Are Long or Unsocial Hours of Work Bad for Leisure?* in G. Crow and S. Heath (eds) *Social Conceptions of Time: Structure and Process in Work and Everyday Life*. London: Palgrave (2002).
21. Wajcman *Pressed for Time*.
22. Edward Palmer Thompson, 'Time, Work-Discipline and Industrial Capitalism', *Past and Present: A Journal of Scientific History*, 38, 56–176 (1967).
23. Suzan Lewis, Deirdre Anderson, Clare Lyonette, Nicola Payne and Stephen Wood, 'Public Sector Austerity Cuts in Britain and the Changing Discourse of Work-Life Balance', Work, Employment and Society, OI: 10.1177/0950017016638994 (2016).

and to dedicated campaigns to promote a better work-life balance for workers. On the latter, in the UK for example, the charity 'Working Families' celebrates an annual '*National Work Life Week*' when it publicises the 'Go Home on Time Day'. The Trades Union Congress' '*Work your Proper Hours Day*' also places work-life balance up front in its campaign against long working weeks.

This focus on 'too many' hours arose because spending very long hours in work can be highly problematic for work-lives. 'Too many' hours have been identified, rightly, as a route to work-life imbalance because workers can be left with far too few hours to dedicate to other areas of their lives. Time for sleep and time for 'what we will' is sacrificed when the working week grows unchecked. Negative outcomes of long hours include poor physical and mental health for workers themselves (Eurofound 2016[24]), whilst their families, friends and communities suffer from the workers' long absences and reduced well-being.

Whilst a long hours' culture can have negative effects on individuals, families and societies, the overly dominant focus on very long hours in the study of work-life balance is nevertheless problematic. It is driven by the experiences of a specific group of workers: those working in higher not lower level occupations. Some of the longest weeks are worked by otherwise privileged individuals employed at the top of the occupational hierarchy. Workers in the very highest level jobs can face some of the most extreme time pressures, with total time commitment often expected from the most senior staff. These are the long hours' workers who are most likely to say that they would prefer to work shorter weeks (Fagan 2003[25]). Extrapolating individual level work-time up to the level of a household means that the longest hours arise in couples when both partners are in long hour jobs in higher level posts. Accordingly, the lives of many middle-class mixed-sex couple families are known to be time-poor, time-squeezed or time-rushed. Hence such dual earner middle-class couples dominate studies of household work-life balance: where they report, rightly, on their lack of joint quality family time.

This is not to deny that long hours working is prevalent too for many workers in low waged occupations, but the reasons for their long weeks and the conditions of their working lives are rather different. Put simply, working class workers are more likely to be compelled to work over-time and/or multi-job for financial reasons (Crompton and Lyonette 2008[26]; Fagan et al. 2008[27]; Lautsch and Scully 2007[28]). Accordingly, these

24. Eurofound *Sixth European Working Conditions Survey – Overview Report*, Luxembourg: Publications Office of the EU (2016).
25. Colette Fagan, *Working-Time Preferences and Work-Life Balance in the EU: Some Policy Considerations for Enhancing the Quality of Life*, Luxembourg: Office of Official Publications of the European Communities (2003).
26. Rosemary Crompton and Clare Lyonette, *Mothers' Employment, Work-life Conflict, Careers and Class* in J. Scott, S. Dex, H. Joshi (eds). *Women and Employment. Changing Lives and New Challenges*, Cheltenham: Edward Elgar (2008).
27. Colette Fagan, Linda McDowell, Diane Perrons, Kathryn Ray and Kevin Ward *Class Differences in Mothers' Work Schedules and Assessments of their 'Work-life Balance' in Dual-earner Couples in Britain* in J. Scott, S. Dex, H. Joshi (eds). Women and Employment. Changing Lives and New Challenges, Cheltenham: Edward Elgar (2008).
28. Brenda A. Lautsch and Maureen A. Scully, 'Restructuring Time: Implications of Work-Hours Reductions for the Working Class', *Human Relations*, 60, 5, 719–743 (2007).

long hours' workers are less likely to say that they would prefer a shorter working week than are their long-hours peers in higher level jobs (Warren 2015[29]). Because they are also less likely to 'kvetch' about their long hours (Hammermesh and Lee 2007[30]), they feature less in work-life balance studies.

Such class differences in work-time intersect with the gendering of time (Bryson 2007[31]; Sirianni and Negrey 2000[32]). In the UK, for example, a one and a half earner model persists for mixed-sex couples, but this is especially the case amongst working class families. So, though many working class men do work long hours, their female partners are more likely to work part-time or not at all than are middle class women, especially if they have dependent children. As a result, the work-life balancing of working-class couples is less likely to be impacted by their having joint very long paid working weeks (Warren and Lyonette, 2015[33]).

In contrast, working class workers are more likely than the middle classes to experience work-time underemployment: wanting to work extra, not fewer hours. Work-time underemployed workers comprise those involuntary part-timers who want to work full-time; part-timers preferring longer hour (though still part-time) jobs; and full-timers who would like to up their working weeks (Bell and Blanchflower 2013[34]). Work-time underemployment is classed. Levels of all types of work-time underemployment are higher among the working than middle class, and their levels of underemployment rose after the great recession of 2008-9 (Alexander and Haley-Lock 2015[35]; Warren 2015[36]). *Labour Force Survey* figures for 2015 show that almost three million employed people in Britain wanted more hours[37] (9% of the employed population).

Yet, extraordinarily, wanting to work *more* (not fewer) hours figures rarely in work-life balance debates. Conceptualising work-life imbalance as largely about time and, more narrowly still, about its squeeze is a specific, classed partial understanding of what work-life and its balance or imbalance might mean. The heavy concentration on long hours of work in academic debates mirrors how researchers 'measure' work-lives. If we explore the leading social surveys (because the wording used to explore topics is both unambiguous and readily available), it is revealing to see how

29. Tracey Warren, 'Work-Life Balance/Imbalance: The Dominance of the Middle Class and the Neglect of the Working Class', *British Journal of Sociology*, 66, 4, 691–717 (2015).
30. Daniel S. Hammermesh and Jungmin Lee, 'Stressed Out on Four Continents: Time Crunch or Yuppie Kvetch?', *Review of Economics and Statistics*, 89, 2, 374–383 (2007).
31. Valerie Bryson, *Gender and the Politics of Time: Feminist Theory and Contemporary Debates*, Bristol: The Policy Press (2007).
32. Carmen Sirianni and Cynthia Negrey, 'Working Time as Gendered Time', *Feminist Economics*, 6, 1, 59–76 (2000).
33. Tracey Warren and Clare Lyonette, *The Quality of Part-Time Work in Britain* in F. Green, A. Felstead and D. Gallie (eds). *Unequal Britain at Work: The Evolution and Distribution of Intrinsic Job Quality in Britain*, Oxford: Oxford University Press (2015).
34. David Bell and David Blanchflower, 'Underemployment in the UK Revisited', *National Institute Economic Review*, 224: F8-F22 (2013).
35. Charlotte Alexander and Clare Haley-Lock, 'Underwork, Work-Hour Insecurity, and a New Approach to Wage and Hour Regulation', *Industrial Relations*, 54, 4, 695–716 (2015).
36. Tracey Warren, 'Work-Time Underemployment and Financial Hardship: Class Inequalities and Recession in the UK', *Work, Employment and Society*, 29, 2:191–212 (2015).
37. Just over three million wanted fewer hours and were willing to take less pay to achieve that. LFS, Q4, 2015, ONS 2016.

they inquire about work-lives. Take the *European Social Survey*: respondents were asked 'how satisfied are you with the balance between the *time* you spend on your paid work and the *time* you spend on other aspects of your life?' (italics added). Asked about the pressures on their paid work, respondents score the extent to which they: 'never seem to have enough *time* to get everything done in my job'. Asked about pressures from paid work, they rate how far they 'find that your job prevents you from giving the *time* you want to your partner or family'. They are not asked whether a *lack* of paid work undermines their work-life balancing.

The narrow conceptualization and incomplete measurement of work-life im/balance means that the type of work challenges facing many working-class workers, and their families, have gone unseen in the study of work-life balance or only been partially recognized.

§17.03 OTHER TEMPORAL DIMENSIONS OF WORK-LIFE IM/BALANCE

If we return again to the dedicated study of time we can see that academics in that multi-disciplinary tradition have long recognized that focusing only on working 'too many' hours will produce a fractional understanding of inequalities in time (Bittman and Wajcman 2000[38]; Epstein and Kalleberg 2001[39]; Presser 2006[40]; Southerton 2006[41]; Wajcman 2015[42]). Indeed, it was not just the absolute number of working hours that fuelled growing fears over time poverty, rather anxieties about other temporal dimensions to our lives flourished too. So-called 'quality time' became understood as not just about having the right amount of non-work time, but also (1) having some control over time; (2) having free time at the right point of the day and week; and (3) having work and free time that fit with the temporal rhythms of family, friends and the community (Reisch 2001[43]). These are influential and established arguments in the dedicated study of time. They stress the importance of moving beyond only quantifying the number of hours worked to consider also how time is experienced. All three additional dimensions of quality time can be applied to the temporality of work-life balancing, and class is central to each one.

First, consider work-time autonomy. Workers in higher level jobs are typically far more able to control when, where and how they work than are other employees. Their working days are less likely to be rigidly controlled by others, and they have more

38. Michael Bittman and Judy Wajcman, 'The Rush Hour: The Character of Leisure Time and Gender Equity'. *Social Forces*, 79, 1, 165–89 (2000).
39. Cynthia F. Epstein and Arne L. Kalleberg, 'Time and the Sociology of Work. Issues and Implications', *Work and Occupations*, 28, 1, 5–16 (2001).
40. Harriet B. Presser, *Employment in a 24/7 Economy: Challenges for the Family*. in D. Perrons., C. Fagan., L. McDowell., K. Ray., and K. Ward. (eds) *Gender Divisions and Working Time in the New Economy. Changing Patterns of Work, Care and Public Policy in Europe and North America*. Cheltenham: Edward Elgar (2006).
41. Dale Southerton, 'Analysing the Temporal Organization of Daily Life: Social Constraints, Practices and Their Allocation', *Sociology*, 40, 3, 435–454 (2006).
42. Wajcman Pressed for Time.
43. Lucia A. Reisch, 'Time and Wealth. The Role of Time and Temporalities for Sustainable Patterns of Consumption', *Time and Society*, 10, 367–385 (2001).

flexibility available over when their work starts and ends, and over length and type of breaks. The lower down the occupational hierarchy, the less of this 'time elasticity' is available to workers. Working class employees are over-concentrated in jobs where the work-time is tightly monitored. Workers in retail and restaurants, for example, or in warehouses, fast food outlets such as MacDonald's, and in call centres, all stand out for being subject to intense levels of surveillance of their work-time. The monitoring of their time can verge on the extreme. Academic studies have highlighted tight controls of 'clocking in' and out of work at call centres (via thumb-print or eye scanning, for example), and highly regulated toilet breaks (Bain et al. 2002[44]). Union campaigns and media investigations have exposed scandals involving severe temporal control of workers employed at large warehouse distribution centres. At the 'Sports Direct' warehouse in the Midlands of England, notorious examples include workers penalized harshly for any time infringements (including taking a short break for a drink of water), and such a culture of fear that workers avoided taking sick leave when they were ill (a sick leave resulted in a 'strike', six strikes led to dismissal). Ambulances were called regularly to the warehouse for medical emergencies, one woman gave birth in the workplace toilet; and local schools reported children coming into school ill because their parents could not risk taking a care day (the Guardian 2016[45]). The intrusive monitoring of the working day and the compulsory high speed of work experienced by thousands of Amazon warehouse staff has seen similar media investigations (BBC 2013[46]).

The greater levels of autonomy over their work-time that are enjoyed by middle class workers are increased further because they tend to be in a better position to create extra time by outsourcing their domestic work. The vast majority of employers of domestic cleaners, child-carers and nannies, 'handymen' and gardeners are middle class families, whilst, of course, cleaning, child-caring and nannying, handy-work and gardening are important sources of employment for the working classes, including migrant workers (Kilkey et al. 2013[47]; Lutz 2016[48]) who simultaneously have to organize their own caring, cleaning and home maintenance.

Working class workers also face more problems with the second and third additional temporal dimensions to work-life balance: having their work/non-work time at the right time; and coordinating with family members' time. Working class employees are over-concentrated in jobs that are marked by unsocial work-time, including shift work. Both are known to impact negatively on workers' sleep patterns

44. Peter Bain, Aileen Watson, Gareth Mulvey, Phil Taylor and Gregor Gall, 'Taylorism, Targets and the Pursuit of Quantity and Quality by Call Centre Management', *New Technology, Work and Employment*, 17, 3, 170–185 (2002).
45. Guardian, the, *Mike Ashley Running Sports Direct Like 'Victorian Workhouse'*, 22 July (2016).
46. BBC, *Amazon, the Truth Behind the Click*, BBC Panorama, 29 November (2013).
47. Majella Kilkey, Diane Perrons and Ania Plomien, *Gender, Migration and Domestic Work: Masculinities, Male Labour and Fathering in the UK and USA*, London: Palgrave Macmillan (2013).
48. Helma Lutz, (ed) *Migration and Domestic Work: A European Perspective on a Global Theme*, New York: Routledge (2016).

and health, with evidence of heightened problems ranging from fatigue and anxiety to cancer (Eurofound 2016[49]).

Third, shift and unsocial working also desynchronizes the time schedules of workers from those of their family and friends (Lesnard 2008[50]). Shared sleeping time with partners is affected as are joint family meal times, and there are difficulties in planning social commitments, particularly when shifts rotate (Presser 1995[51]; Golden 2015[52]). This desynchronization of family time is acute when members work different times of the day or night in so-called split or opposite schedules. In a previous paper, the author collated the intense family-time challenges created by a partner working away from home. In classic studies of men's working class jobs, railway workers who lodged away from home, long-distance lorry drivers, and deep sea fishermen were all experienced, in varying ways, as 'strangers' to their families (Warren 2003[53]).

§17.04 WORK-LIFE BALANCE AND MONEY

The heavy focus on time in discussions around work-life balance, and on long hours within that, has meant that the types of imbalance that are more likely to impact the working class are neglected. One glaring area of neglect is the role played by money in balancing a work-life.

Experiencing and fearing financial hardship are rarely analysed as 'work-life' matters. Yet we know that having enough money is fundamental to achieving the basics of a quality life. Everyday accounts of working-class lives are saturated with reports of acute financial difficulties and/or fears that problems might develop. Moreover, the contemporary background to our work-lives has been one of deepening economic inequalities. In the UK, financial problems are so intense for some people that they have been forced to resort to charitable food banks for essentials: figures for food bank use rocketed after 2008 (Garthwaite 2016[54]). Loan sharks, who lend money at extortionate interest rates to those on low incomes, have proliferated, whilst pawn shops offering high-interest loans in exchange for personal items (commonly but not only jewellery) now dot UK shopping streets, particularly in working class neighbourhoods (O'Hara 2015[55]). Multiple research studies with low income workers after the recession document working class lives marked by financial strain, with people scraping by, reporting relentless and demoralizing everyday worries about spending and accumulating debts. Parents recount caring for children whilst being unable to

49. Eurofound, *Sixth European Working Conditions Survey.*
50. Laurent Lesnard, 'Off-scheduling Within Dual-Earner Couples: An Unequal and Negative Externality for Family Time', American Journal of Science, 114, 2, 466 (2008).
51. Harriet B. Presser, 'Job, Family and Gender: Determinants of Non-standard Work Schedules Among Employed Americans in 1991', *Demography*, 32, 4, 577–598 (1995).
52. Lonnie Golden, *Irregular Work Scheduling and Its Consequences*, Economic Policy Institute, Briefing Paper #394, April 9, (2015).
53. Tracey Warren, 'Class- and Gender-Based Working Time? Time Poverty and the Division of Domestic Labour', *Sociology*, 37, 4: 733–754 (2003).
54. Kayleigh Garthwaite, *Hunger Pains. Life Inside Foodbank Britain.* Bristol: Policy Press (2016).
55. Mary O'Hara, *Austerity Bites: A Journey to the Sharp End of Cuts in the UK.* Bristol: Policy Press (2015).

heat their homes or afford hot water, and the daily 'heat or eat' dilemma is a reality for far too many (Shildrick and MacDonald 2013[56]). Those 'just about managing' financially attracted a neat government acronym in late 2016 ('JAMS') but no serious policy commitment to ease their deepening problems. Rather, at the time of writing, further cuts in public spending will impact hardest on those who are already struggling (the Resolution Foundation 2016[57]). Such outright material hardship and financial anxiety surely undermine anyone's quest for a balanced work-life.

§17.05 WORK-LIFE BALANCE, TIME AND MONEY

If we return yet again to the study of time, it is well-known there that strong links exist between time and money. We can go back to Veblen's influential consideration of leisure and work time where he identified the rich as potentially becoming the future 'leisure class', being financially able to dedicate their time to leisure not paid work. Schor argued that the long hours' culture arose first amongst high income workers, on Wall Street for example, stimulated by and supporting their heightened levels of consumption. The contrast is extreme between lives characterized by such income wealth/time poverty and the income-poverty/time-wealth associated with being unemployed (Sullivan 2008[58]). Furthermore, this chapter is underlining the point that individuals can be both time- and income-poor.

These vital debates have begun to be mirrored in the dedicated study of work-life balance. Studies by prominent work-life researchers identify how time pressures for many middle class workers go hand-in-hand with higher incomes. So, though middle class dual full-time households, for example, face some of the most acute time pressures on their work-lives, their material resources help ease their balancing (Fagan et al. 2012[59]; Chatzitheochari and Arber 2012[60]; Crompton and Lyonette 2008[61]). Working class households typically face less time squeeze, but have fewer material resources to balance their lives. They are more at risk of severe instability in work-life balancing, in the short and longer terms, rooted in their current and prolonged financial insecurity. Financial shocks due to employment change (e.g., job loss or forced

56. Tracy Shildrick and Robert MacDonald 'Poverty Talk: How People Experiencing Poverty Deny Their Poverty and Why They Blame 'the Poor', *The Sociological Review*, 61, 2, 285–303 (2013).
57. Resolution Foundation *Under New Management: Options for Supporting 'Just Managing' Families at the Autumn Statement*, London: RF, http://www.resolutionfoundation.org/wp-content/uploads/2016/11/Under-new-management.pdf (2016).
58. Oriel Sullivan, 'Busyness, Status Distinction and Consumption Strategies of the Income Rich, Time Poor', *Time and Society*, 17, 1, 5–26 (2008).
59. Colette Fagan, Clare Lyonette, Mark Smith and Abril Saldaña-Tejeda, *The Influence of Working Time Arrangements on Work-life Integration or 'Balance': A Review of the International Evidence*, Geneva: ILO (2012).
60. Stella Chatzitheochari and Sara Arber, 'Class, Gender and Time Poverty: A Time-Use Analysis of British Workers' Free Time Resources', *The British Journal of Sociology*, 63, 3, 451–471 (2012).
61. Rosemary Crompton and Clare Lyonette, *Mothers' Employment, Work-life Conflict, Careers and Class*, in J. Scott, S. Dex, H. Joshi (eds) *Women and Employment. Changing Lives and New Challenges*, Cheltenham: Edward Elgar (2008).

reduction in hours, Hacker et al. 2013[62]) are more common for the working classes, whose financial safety nets (in the form of assets and savings held, and being able to borrow) are likely to be meagre or non-existent (Hills et al. 2013[63]). Similarly, these workers are also less able to cope with the monetary ramifications of such family-related financial shocks as divorce and bereavement. These elements, and more, of what it is to feel financially secure or at risk of or in hardship provide the economic foundations for balancing work-lives.

Clearly then, lack of time and lack of money both impact negatively on work-life balance. The types of imbalance that workers experience differ, and the magnitude of the impact of each form of imbalance on overall wellbeing varies too. In previous research, the author identified the forms of work-life imbalance that arise from various work-time problems (working very long hours, being work-time dissatisfied, lacking time autonomy, having unsocial hours); imbalance caused by financial insecurity; and work-life imbalance where both time and financial problems coexist (Warren 2015[64]). Exploring the distribution of the assortment of forms of work-life imbalance throughout the work-force, that study led to a rather different conclusion about class and work-life balance in the UK. It was one in which working class workers were far more likely to experience both temporal and financially based work-life imbalance than were the middle classes. This was, in part, because so few of the middle classes were financially insecure but also because they worked social hours with more work-time autonomy than the working classes. That study concluded too that being financially work-life balanced, not time-balanced, was more important for achieving a satisfactory life overall. Yet despite money trumping time, still time not money dominates work-life balance policies.

§17.06 WORK-LIFE BALANCE POLICIES: TIME AND MONEY

Work-life balance is important. Where policies do exist to support work-life balance, they are provided by one or a combination of: cross-national agreements (e.g., EU directives), state-level legislation, and voluntary employer initiatives, depending upon the national setting (Den Dulk et al. 2013[65]). Work-life balance has increasingly become part of everyday discourse at all these multiple levels of the formulation of programmes, certainly in the most developed economies (Kossek and Friede, 2006). Take the level of the firm: work-life balance has been related to such key workplace matters as employee recruitment, turnover and progression; worker stress and ill

62. Jacob S. Hacker, Philipp Rehm and Mark Schlesinger, 'The Insecure American: Economic Experiences, Financial Worries, and Policy Attitudes', *Politics*, 11, 1, 23–49 (2013).
63. John Hills, Jack Cunliffe, Ludovica Gambaro and Polina Obolenskaya, *Winners and Losers in the Crisis: The Changing Anatomy of Economic Inequality in the UK 2007-2010*, Social policy in a cold climate research report, SPCCRR02. London: LSE (2013).
64. Warren *Work-life balance/imbalance.*
65. Laura Den Dulk, Sandra Groeneveld, Ariane Ollier-Malaterre and Monique Valcour, 'National Context in Work-Life Research: A Multi-Level Cross National Analysis of the Adoption of Work-Life Arrangements in Europe', *European Management Journal* 31, 5, 478–94 (2013).

health; job commitment and satisfaction; and productivity (McCarthy et al. 2010).[66] Thus a strong business case has been made for work-life balance enhancements in the workplace. Firms can increase their own competiveness by appealing to a wider diversity of employees who, attracted by and rewarded with better work conditions, are stimulated to remain committed to the organization, thus reducing costs to the firm of replacing workers and re-training new staff. Better supported workers have been found to engage more fully in their work, and this can improve their own performance and that of the firm too (Kossek et al. 2010[67]). Undoubtedly the business case is valuable as a way to persuade firms to take up work-life balance in their company ethos, but questions of equality and social justice in the workplace should not fall secondary to the case for economic growth (Collier 2015[68]; Lewis et al. 2016[69]). Outside the workplace too, better work-life balance has been attributed with improving quality of life for workers themselves and, moving beyond a focus on the individual, enhancing the everyday lives of any partners, children, extended family and friends (Lewis et al. 2007[70]).

Yet, though work-life balancing has spread into everyday policy discourse, the language used to talk about it has been oversimplified, limiting in turn the policy responses that are seen to be possible. The language we use: 'can set up a linguistic/conceptual trap... which limits wider comprehension of the phenomenon and particularly the origins of the issues, obscuring the potential to open up new visions or alternative futures' (Lewis et al. 2007: 362). Policies targeted at fostering work-life balance, whether by states or firms, are limited because they invariably cluster around the too narrow notion of work-life balance as 'having enough time'. Such 'family-friendly' temporal-based provision as flexible working, carers leave schemes, and career breaks tend to dominate policy formation.

Not only are such policies limited in vision, they also appeal to a limited section of the overall workforce. Despite the growth in work-life balance policies, and notwithstanding decades of innovative work by researchers and campaigners, as well as some HR departments and policy makers, to broaden its appeal, work-life balance is still seen largely as a problem for working mothers, imbalance solvable by initiatives that are taken up mainly by these women. The most established work-life balance

66. Alma McCarthy, Colette Darcy and Geraldine Grady, 'Work-Life Balance Policy and Practice: Understanding Line Manager Attitudes and Behaviors', *Human Resource Management Review*, 20, 2, 158–167 (2010).
67. Ellen E. Kossek, Suzan Lewis, and Leslie B. Hammer, 'Work–Life Initiatives and Organizational Change: Overcoming Mixed Messages to Move from the Margin to the Mainstream', *Human Relations*, 63, 1, 3–19 (2010).
68. Richard Collier, 'Naming Men as Men in Corporate Legal Practice: Gender and the Idea of "Virtually 24/7 Commitment" in Law', *Fordham Law Review*, 83, 5 (2015).
69. Lewis, Anderson, Lyonette, Payne, and Wood *Public Sector Austerity Cuts in Britain and the Changing Discourse of Work-Life Balance.*
70. Suzan Lewis, Richenda Gambles, and Rhona Rapoport, 'The Constraints of a 'Work-life Balance' Approach: An International Perspective', *International Journal of Human Resource Management*, 18, 3, 360–373 (2007).

language is avowedly gender neutral and inclusive (Kossek et al. 2006[71]), yet a 'generic female parent' (Smithson and Stokoe 2005[72]) still routinely underpins understandings of the work-life concept and its policies. This applies to male workers' judgments of work-life balance in particular: men are likely to see work-life balance as about and for mothers and, correspondingly, to reject work-life balance as a framework for interpreting their own working lives (Collier 2013[73]). This rejection is likely to be intensified for working class men, for whom money concerns and not just time shape their everyday lives, but working class men too seldom feature in research into work-life balance.

An expanded vision of work-life balance must link to an extension in the type of initiatives that are badged as promoting 'work-life balance'. Extending the remit of work-life has the potential to incorporate a more diverse workforce and, in so doing, mainstream work-life balance policies more successfully. A raft of work-life measures must include, but not be restricted to, the familiar 'family-friendly' initiatives developed to make more time available for caring via flexible working and leaves. Crucially, money-based programmes, such as living wage guarantees and support for housing and caring costs, are also vitally important if work-life balance policies are to ease the work-life imbalances of the working classes too.

§17.07 CONCLUSION: HOLISTIC WORK-LIFE BALANCE ACADEMIC AND POLICY AGENDAS

This chapter has argued that the study of work-life balance has too narrowly focused on the working lives of time-squeezed middle class workers. To fix this significant drawback, multiple indicators of work-life im/balance are required, including but not restricted to having 'enough time'. A re-envisaged framework of work-life imbalance will still recognize those time-squeezed executives wishing for more time to spend on themselves and with their families and friends. But the framework will also now acknowledge, rather than render invisible, the imbalance experienced by financially constrained employees who wish for more hours at work to boost their take-home pay. It will incorporate too the intense problems faced by those who are dual-imbalanced because they are working multiple jobs and yet still are financially insecure.

Widening out the conceptualization of work-life to make it more holistic and inclusive can help defend the study of work-life balance against the common criticism that it, and its associated polices, are solely for women with dependent children (Eikhof

71. Ellen E. Kossek and Alyssa Friede, *The Business Case: Managerial Perspectives on Work and the Family*, in Pitt-Catsouphes M, Kossek EE and Sweet S (eds) *The Work-Family Handbook: Multi-disciplinary Perspectives, Methods, and Approaches*. Mahwah: Lawrence Erlbaum Associates Press, 611–28 (2006).
72. Janet Smithson and Elizabeth H. Stokoe, 'Discourses of Work–Life Balance: Negotiating 'Genderblind' Terms in Organizations', *Gender, Work & Organization*, 12, 2, 147–168 (2005).
73. Richard Collier, 'Rethinking Men and Masculinities in the Contemporary Legal Profession: The Example of Fatherhood, Transnational Business Masculinities and Work-Life Balance in Large Law Firms', *Nevada Law Journal*, 13, 2, 101–130 (2013).

et al. 2007[74]), and I would stress, for financially comfortable mothers. Work-life balance must be gender- and class-mainstreamed if it is to be valuable as an academic concept and a policy action framework. It must pertain to men, of all classes, too. Unfortunately, encouraging men to take-up even limited family support policies (such as paternity and parental leaves, as well as work reduced hours) has been one of the least successful of work-life strategies in most, perhaps all, countries (Vandello et al. 2013[75]). Men in senior posts have been targeted more effectively than working class men. This is valuable because those men can also 'set an example' as role models to other men (Smithson et al. 2004[76]). Yet working class men are not totally hostile to innovative policies that might support their work-lives, as qualitative research in England by the author shows (Fox et al. 2009[77]). But a sticking point for many working class men is that the financial wellbeing of their families depends on the men working long hours and in jobs whose workplace cultures do not encourage 'men like them' to do anything non-standard. Work must pay, and pay enough to securely support a balanced work-life. As Kossek et al. (2010[78]) argued too, what is needed for effective work-life balancing programmes is not just 'structural support' (policies), but structural support underpinned by 'cultural work–life support': informal workplace cultures in which provisioning for work-life balance is established, and where opportunities are visible, accessible and mainstreamed for all groups of worker.

If we are really serious about promoting work-life balance then we need opportunities to rethink normalized workplace structures, cultures and practices. If it is to assist here, the study of work-life balance must become about more than just the time problems of squeezed middle class workers. A more inclusive work-life framework is necessary for the analysis of all workers' lives. It is time for researchers, employers, worker representatives, campaigning groups and policy makers to work together to co-produce a new more holistic and inclusive work-life balance vision for further debate and policy development.

REFERENCES

Adam, B. (1990). *Time and Social Theory*. Cambridge: Polity Press.

Adam, B. (1995). *Timewatch. The Social Analysis of Time*. Cambridge: Polity.

74. Doris R. Eikhof, Chris Warhurst and Axel Haunschild, *Introduction*: 'What Work? What Life? What Balance? Critical Reflections on the Work-life Balance Debate', *Employee Relations*, 29, 4, 325–333 (2017).
75. Jospeh Vandello, Vanessa E. Hettinger, Jennifer K. Bosson and Jasmine Siddiqi, 'When Equal Isn't Really Equal: The Masculine Dilemma of Seeking Work Flexibility', *Journal of Social Issues* 69, 2, 303–321 (2013).
76. Janet Smithson, Suzan Lewis, Cary Cooper and Jackie Dyer, 'Flexible Working and the Gender Pay Gap in the Accountancy Profession', *Work, Employment and Society*, 18, 1, 115–135 (2004).
77. Elizabeth Fox, Gillian Pascall and Tracey Warren, 'Work-Family Policies, Participation and Practices: Fathers and Childcare in Europe', *Community, Work and Family*, 12, 3, 313–326 (2009).
78. Ellen E. Kossek, Suzan Lewis and Leslie B. Hammer, 'Work–Life Initiatives and Organizational Change: Overcoming Mixed Messages to Move from the Margin to the Mainstream', *Human Relations*, 63, 1, 3–19 (2010).

Alexander, C. and Haley-Lock, A. (2015). 'Underwork, Work-Hour Insecurity, and A New Approach to Wage and Hour Regulation', *Industrial Relations*, 54, 4, 695–716.

Bain, P., Watson, A., Mulvey, G., Taylor, P. and Gall, G. (2002). 'Taylorism, Targets and the Pursuit of Quantity and Quality by Call Centre Management', *New Technology, Work and Employment*, 17, 3, 170–185.

BBC (2013). 'Amazon, the truth Behind the Click', *BBC Panorama*, 29 November.

Becker, G. (1985). 'A Theory of the Allocation of Time', *Economic Journal*, 75, 493–517.

Bell, D.N.F and Blanchflower, D.G. (2013). 'Underemployment in the UK Revisited', *National Institute Economic Review*, 224: F8-F22.

Bianchi, S., Robinson, J. and Milkie, M. (2006). *The Changing Rhythms of American Family Life*, New York: Russell Sage.

Bittman, M. and Wajcman, J. (2000). 'The Rush Hour: The Character of Leisure Time and Gender Equity', *Social Forces*, 79, 1, 165–89.

Bryson, V. (2007). *Gender and the Politics of Time: Feminist Theory and Contemporary Debates*, Bristol: The Policy Press.

Chatzitheochari, S. and Arber, S. (2012). 'Class, Gender and Time Poverty: A Time-Use Analysis of British Workers' Free Time Resources', *The British Journal of Sociology*, 63, 3, 451–471.

Collier, R. (2013). 'Rethinking Men and Masculinities in the Contemporary Legal Profession: The Example of Fatherhood, Transnational Business Masculinities and Work-Life Balance in Large Law Firms', *Nevada Law Journal*, 13, 2, 101–130.

Collier, R. (2015). 'Naming Men as Men in Corporate Legal Practice: Gender and the Idea of "Virtually 24/7 Commitment" in Law', *Fordham Law Review*, 83, 5.

Crompton, R. and Lyonette, C. (2008). 'Mothers' Employment, Work-life Conflict, Careers and Class' in J. Scott, S. Dex, H. Joshi (eds) *Women and Employment. Changing Lives and New Challenges*, Cheltenham: Edward Elgar.

Den Dulk, L., Groeneveld, S,. Ollier-Malaterre, A. and Valcour, M. (2013). 'National Context in Work-Life Research: A Multi-Level Cross National Analysis of the Adoption of Work-Life Arrangements in Europe', *European Management Journal* 31, 5, 478–494.

Durkheim, E. (1965). *The Elementary Forms of Religious Life*, New York: Free Press (first published in 1912).

Eikhof, D.R., Warhurst, C. and Haunschild, A. (2007). 'Introduction: What Work? What Life? What Balance? Critical Reflections on the Work-life Balance Debate', *Employee Relations*, 29, 4, 325–333.

Elias, N. (1992). *Time. An Essay*. Oxford: Blackwell.

Epstein, C.F. and Kalleberg, A.L. (2001). 'Time and the Sociology of Work. Issues and Implications', *Work and Occupations*, 28, 1, 5–16.

Eurofound (2016). *Sixth European Working Conditions Survey – Overview Report*, Luxembourg: Publications Office of the EU.

Fagan, C. (2003). *Working-Time Preferences and Work-Life Balance in the EU: Some Policy Considerations for Enhancing the Quality of Life*, Luxembourg: Office of Official Publications of the European Communities.

Fagan, C., Lyonette, C., Smith, M. and Saldaña-Tejeda, A. (2012). *The Influence of Working Time Arrangements on Work-Life Integration or 'Balance': A Review of the International Evidence*, Geneva: ILO.

Fagan, C., McDowell, L., Perrons, D., Ray, K. and Ward, K. (2008). 'Class Differences in Mothers' Work Schedules and Assessments of Their "Work-life Balance" in Dual-Earner Couples in Britain' in J. Scott, S. Dex, H. Joshi (eds) *Women and Employment. Changing Lives and New Challenges*, Cheltenham: Edward Elgar.

Fox, E., Pascall, G. and Warren, T. (2009). 'Work-Family Policies, Participation and Practices: Fathers and Childcare in Europe', *Community, Work and Family*, 12, 3, 313–326.

Garhammer, M. (1998). 'Time Poverty in Modern Germany', *Society and Leisure*, 21, 327–352.

Garthwaite, K. (2016). *Hunger Pains. Life Inside Foodbank Britain*, Bristol: Policy Press.

Gershuny, J. (2000). *Changing Times – Work and Leisure in Postindustrial Society*, Oxford: Oxford University Press.

Golden, L. (2009). 'Brief History of Long Work Time and the Contemporary Sources of Overwork', *Journal of Business Ethics*, 84, 2, 217–227.

Golden, L. (2015). 'Irregular Work Scheduling and Its Consequences', *Economic Policy Institute, Briefing Paper* #394, 9 April 2015.

Guardian, the (2016). 'Mike Ashley Running Sports Direct Like "Victorian Workhouse"', 22 July.

Hacker, J.S., Rehm, P. and Schlesinger, M. (2013). 'The Insecure American: Economic Experiences, Financial Worries, and Policy Attitudes', *Politics*, 11, 1, 23–49.

Hammermesh, D.S. and Lee, J. (2007). 'Stressed Out on Four Continents: Time Crunch or Yuppie Kvetch?', *Review of Economics and Statistics*, 89, 2, 374–383.

Hills, J., Cunliffe, J., Gambaro, L. and Obolenskaya, P. (2013). *Winners and Losers in the Crisis: The Changing Anatomy of Economic Inequality in the UK 2007-2010 Social Policy in a Cold Climate Research Report*, SPCCRR02. London: LSE.

Hochschild, A.R. (1997). *The Time Bind. When Work Becomes Home and Home Becomes Work*, New York: Henry Holt and Company.

Jacobs, J.A. and Gerson, K. (2001). 'Overworked Individuals or Overworked Families? Exploring Trends in Work, Leisure and Family Time', *Work and Occupations*, 28, 1, 40–63.

Kilkey, M., Perrons, D. and Plomien, A. with Hondagneu-Sotelo and Ramirez, H. (2013). *Gender, Migration and Domestic Work: Masculinities, Male Labour and Fathering in the UK and USA*, London: Palgrave Macmillan.

Kossek, E.E., Lewis, S. and Hammer, L. (2010). 'Work-Life Initiatives and Organizational Change: Overcoming Mixed Messages to Move from the Margin to the Mainstream', *Human Relations*, 63: 1–17.

Kossek, E.E. and Friede, A. (2006). 'The Business Case: Managerial Perspectives on Work and the Family' in Pitt-Catsouphes M, Kossek EE and Sweet S (eds) *The Work-Family Handbook: Multi- disciplinary Perspectives, Methods, and Approaches*. Mahwah: Lawrence Erlbaum Associates Press, 611–28.

Kossek, E.E., Lewis, S., and Hammer, L.B. (2010). 'Work–Life Initiatives and Organizational Change: Overcoming Mixed Messages to Move from the Margin to the Mainstream', *Human Relations*, 63, 1, 3–19.

Lautsch, B.A and Scully, M.A. (2007). 'Restructuring Time: Implications of Work-Hours Reductions for the Working Class', *Human Relations*, 60, 5, 719–743.

Lesnard, L. (2008). 'Off-scheduling Within Dual-Earner Couples: An Unequal and Negative Externality for Family Time', *American Journal of Science*, 114, 2, 466.

Lewis, S., Anderson, D., Lyonette, C., Payne, N. and Wood, S. (2016). 'Public Sector Austerity Cuts in Britain and the Changing Discourse of Work-Life Balance', *Work, Employment and Society*, OI: 10.1177/0950017016638994.

Lewis, S., Gambles, R., & Rapoport, R. (2007). 'The Constraints of a "Work-life Balance" Approach: An International Perspective', *International Journal of Human Resource Management*, 18, 3, 360–373.

Lutz, H. (2016) (ed.). *Migration and Domestic Work: A European Perspective on a Global Theme*, New York: Routledge.

Marx, K. (1971). *Preface to a Contribution to the Critique of Political Economy*, Various prints (first published in 1859).

McCarthy, A., Darcy, C. and Grady, G. (2010). 'Work-Life Balance Policy and Practice: Understanding Line Manager Attitudes and Behaviors', *Human Resource Management Review*, 20, 2, 158–167.

Nowotny, H. (2005). *Time: the Modern and Postmodern experience*, Cambridge: Polity Press.

O'Hara, M. (2015). *Austerity Bites: A Journey to the Sharp End of Cuts in the UK*, Bristol: Policy Press.

Presser, H.B. (1995). 'Job, Family and Gender: Determinants of Non-standard Work Schedules Among Employed Americans in 1991', *Demography*, 32, 4, 577–598.

Presser, H.B. (2006). 'Employment in a 24/7 Economy: Challenges for the Family', in D. Perrons, C. Fagan, L. McDowell, K. Ray, and K. Ward (eds) *Gender Divisions and Working Time in the New Economy. Changing Patterns of Work, Care and Public Policy in Europe and North America*. Cheltenham: Edward Elgar.

Reisch, L.A. (2001). 'Time and Wealth. The Role of Time and Temporalities for Sustainable Patterns of Consumption', *Time and Society*, 10, 367–385.

Resolution Foundation (2016). *Under New Management: Options for Supporting 'Just Managing' Families at the Autumn Statement*, London: RF, http://www.resolutionfoundation.org/wp-content/uploads/2016/11/Under-new-management.pdf.

Roberts, K. (2002). 'Are Long or Unsocial Hours of Work Bad for Leisure?', in G. Crow. and S. Heath (eds) *Social Conceptions of Time: Structure and Process in Work and Everyday Life*, London: Palgrave.

Robinson, J.P and Godbey, G. (1997). *Time for Life. The Surprising Ways Americans Use Their Time*, Pennsylvania University Park: Pennsylvania State University Press.

Schor, J. (1991). *The Overworked American: The Unexpected Decline of Leisure*. New York: Basic Books.

Schor, J. (2010). *Plenitude: The New Economics of True Wealth*, New York: Penguin.

Shildrick, T. and MacDonald, R. (2013). 'Poverty Talk: How People Experiencing Poverty Deny Their Poverty and Why They Blame "the Poor"', *The Sociological Review*, 61, 2, 285–303.

Sirianni, C. and Negrey, C. (2000). 'Working Time as Gendered Time', *Feminist Economics*, 6, 1, 59–76.

Smithson, J. and Stokoe, E.H. (2005). 'Discourses of Work–Life Balance: Negotiating "Genderblind" Terms in Organizations', *Gender, Work & Organization*, 12, 2, 147–168.

Smithson, J., Lewis, S., Cooper, C. and Dyer, J. (2004). 'Flexible Working and the Gender Pay Gap in the Accountancy Profession', *Work, Employment and Society*, 18, 1, 115–135.

Southerton, D. (2006). 'Analysing the Temporal Organization of Daily Life: Social Constraints, Practices and Their Allocation', *Sociology*, 40, 3, 435–454.

Sullivan, O. (2008). 'Busyness, Status Distinction and Consumption Strategies of the Income Rich, Time Poor', *Time and Society*, 17, 1, 5–26.

Thompson, E.P. (1967). 'Time, Work-Discipline and Industrial Capitalism', *Past and Present: A Journal of Scientific History*, 38, 56–176.

Vandello, J.A., Hettinger, V.E., Bosson, J.K. and Siddiqi, J. (2013). 'When Equal Isn't Really Equal: The Masculine Dilemma of Seeking Work Flexibility', *Journal of Social Issues* 69, 2, 303–321.

Veblen, T. (1963). *The Theory of the Leisure Class,* London: New English Library Limited (published originally in 1899).

Wajcman, J. (2015). *Pressed for Time: The Acceleration of Life in Digital Capitalism*, Chicago: University of Chicago Press.

Warren, T. (2003). 'Class- and Gender-Based Working Time? Time Poverty and the Division of Domestic Labour', *Sociology*, 37, 4, 733–754.

Warren, T. (2015a). 'Work-Life Balance/Imbalance: The Dominance of the Middle Class and the Neglect of the Working Class', *British Journal of Sociology*, 66, 4, 691–717.

Warren, T. (2015b). 'Work-Time Underemployment and Financial Hardship: Class Inequalities and Recession in the UK', *Work, Employment and Society*, 29, 2, 191–212.

Warren, T. and Lyonette, C. (2015). 'The Quality of Part-Time work in Britain' in F. Green, A. Felstead, and D. Gallie (eds). *Unequal Britain at Work: The Evolution and Distribution of Intrinsic Job Quality in Britain*, Oxford: Oxford University Press.

BCLR - BULLETIN OF COMPARATIVE LABOUR RELATIONS

Vol. Author/Title/Year/ISBN

1. Roger Blanpain, *Individual Employment Contracts: Collective Agreements,* 1970.
2. Roger Blanpain, *Social Planning,* 1971 (ISBN 90-312-0018-2).
3. Roger Blanpain, *Guaranteed Income Funds,* 1972 (ISBN 90-312-0019-0).
4. Roger Blanpain, *Employee Participation at the Level of the Enterprise,* 1973 (ISBN 90-312-0020-4).
5. Roger Blanpain, *Vastheid van Betrekking: Staking en Bezetting,* 1974.
6. Roger Blanpain, *Labour Law and Industrial Relations (International Bibliography),* 1975 (ISBN 90-312-0023-9).
7. Roger Blanpain, *Multinational Enterprises,* 1976 (ISBN 90-312-0024-7).
8. Roger Blanpain, *Worker's Participation in the European Company,* 1977 (ISBN 90-312-0044-1).
9. Roger Blanpain, *Women and Labour,* 1978 (ISBN 90-312-0077-8).
10. Roger Blanpain, *European Conference on Labour Law and Industrial Relations: Multinational Enterprises,* 1979 (ISBN 90-312-0091-3).
11. Roger Blanpain, *Job Security and Industrial Relations,* 1980 (ISBN 90-312-0147-2).
12. Roger Blanpain, Greg Bamber & Russell Lansbury, *Technological Change and Industrial Relations: An International Symposium,* 1983 (ISBN 90-312-0205-3).
13. Roger Blanpain, James Janssen van Raay & A. Moulty, *Worker's Participation in the European Community: The Fifth Directive,* 1984 (ISBN 90-654-4187-5).
14. Roger Blanpain, *Equality and Prohibition of Discrimination in Employment,* 1985 (ISBN 90-654-4215-4).
15. Roger Blanpain, *Restructuring Labour in the Enterprise: Law and Practice in France, F.R. of Germany, Italy, Sweden and the United Kingdom,* 1986 (ISBN 90-654-4283-9).
16. Roger Blanpain & E. Kassalow, *Unions and Industrial Relations: Recent Trends and Prospect: A Comparative Treatment,* 1987 (ISBN 90-654-4294-4).
17. Roger Blanpain & Marco Biagi, *Trade Union Democracy and Industrial Relations,* 1988 (ISBN 90-654-4394-0).
18. Roger Blanpain & Jelle Visser, *In Search of Inclusive Unionism,* 1990 (ISBN 90-654-4439-4).
19. Roger Blanpain, *Flexibility and Wages: A Comparative Treatment,* 1990 (ISBN 90-654-4461-0).

20. Roger Blanpain, Stephen Frenkel & Oliver Clarke, *Economic Restructuring and Industrial Relations in Industrialised Countries,* 1990 (ISBN 90-654-4488-2).
21. Roger Blanpain & Friedrich Fürstenberg, *Structure and Strategy in Industrial Relations,* 1991 (ISBN 90-654-4559-5).
22. Roger Blanpain, Amira Galin & Ozer Carmi, *Flexible Work Patterns and Their Impact on Industrial Relations,* 1991 (ISBN 90-654-4572-2).
23. Roger Blanpain, *Workers' Participation: Influence on Management Decision-Making by Labour in the Private Sector,* 1992 (ISBN 90-654-4600-1).
24. Roger Blanpain, Brian Brooks & Chris Engels, *Employed or Self-Employed,* 1992 (ISBN 90-654-4613-3).
25. Roger Blanpain & Tiziano Treu, *Industrial Relations Developments in the Telecommunications Industry,* 1993 (ISBN 90-654-4642-7).
26. Roger Blanpain & Marco Biagi, *Industrial Relations in Small and Medium Sized Enterprises,* 1993 (ISBN 90-654-4696-6).
27. Roger Blanpain & Marco Biagi, *Participative Management and Industrial Relations in a Worldwide Perspective,* 1993 (ISBN 90-654-4769-5).
28. Roger Blanpain, Jacques Rojot & Hoyt N. Wheeler, *Employee Rights and Industrial Justice,* 1994 (ISBN 90-654-4804-7).
29. Roger Blanpain & Ruth Ben-Israel, *Strikes and Lock-Outs in Industrialized Market Economies,* 1994 (ISBN 90-654-4841-1).
30. Roger Blanpain, Kazuo Sugeno & Yasuo Suwa, *The Harmonization of Working Life and Family Life,* 1995 (ISBN 90-411-0064-4).
31. Roger Blanpain & Laszio Nagy, *Labour Law and Industrial Relations in Central and Eastern Europe,* 1996 (ISBN 90-411-0298-1).
32. Roger Blanpain, *Labour Law and Industrial Relations in the European Union,* 1997 (ISBN 90-411-0527-1).
33. Taco Van Peijpe, *Employment Protection under Strain,* 1998 (ISBN 90-411-0528-8).
34. Roger Blanpain, Takashi Araki & Ryuichi Yamakawa, *The Process of Industrialization and the Role of Labour Law in Asia,* 1999 (ISBN 9-041-1104-7-X).
35. Roger Blanpain & Marco Biagi, *Non-standard Work and Industrial Relations,* 1999 (ISBN 90-411-1117-4).
36. Roger Blanpain, *Private Employment Agencies: The Impact of ILO Convention 181 (1997) and the Judgment of the European Court of Justice of 11 December 1997,* 1999 (ISBN 90-411-1118-2).
37. Roger Blanpain, *Multinational Enterprises and the Social Challenges of the XXIst Century: The ILO Declaration on Fundamental* Principles *at Work, Public and Private Corporate Codes of Conduct,* 2000 (ISBN 90-411-1280-4).
38. Roger Blanpain, Ryuichi Yamakawa & Takashi Araki, *Deregulation and Labour Law: In Search of a Labour Concept for the 21st Century,* 2000 (ISBN 90-411-1370-3).
39. Roger Blanpain, *The Council of Europe and the Social Challenges of the XXIst Century,* 2001 (ISBN 90-411-1543-9).

40. Roger Blanpain, *On-Line Rights for Employees in the Information Society, Use & Monitoring of E-Mail & Internet at Work*, 2002 (ISBN 90-411-1626-5).
41. Roger Blanpain, *The Evolving Employment Relationship and the New Economy: The Role of Labour Law & Industrial Relations*, 2001 (ISBN 90-411-1691-5).
42. Roger Blanpain, *Involvement of Employees in the European Union, Works Councils, Company Statute, Information and Consultation Rights*, 2002 (ISBN 90-411-1760-1).
43. Michele Colucci, *The Impact of the Internet and New Technologies on the Workplace: A Legal Analysis from a Comparative Point of View*, 2002 (ISBN 90-411-1824-1).
44. Roger Blanpain, *White Paper on the Labour Market in Italy: The Quality of European Industrial Relations and Changing Industrial Relations*, 2002 (ISBN 90-411-1841-1).
45. Roger Blanpain, Russell D. Lansbury & Young-Bum Park, *Impact of Globalisation on Employment Relations: A Comparison of the Automobile and Banking Industries in Australia and Korea*, 2002 (ISBN 90-411-1850-0).
46. Roger Blanpain & Antoine Jacobs, *Employee Rights in Bankruptcy:* A *Comparative-Law Assessment*, 2002 (ISBN 90-411-1942-6).
47. Roger Blanpain, Takashi Araki & Shinya Ouchi, *Corporate Restructuring and the Role of Labour Law*, 2003 (ISBN 90-411-1949-3).
48. Roger Blanpain, *Collective Bargaining, Discrimination, Social Security and European Integration*, 2003 (ISBN 90-411-2010-6).
49. Roger Blanpain & Luis Aparicio-Valdez, *Labour Relations in the Asia- Pacific Countries*, 2004 (ISBN 90-411-2239-7).
50. Roger Blanpain & Ronnie Graham, *Temporary Agency Work and the Information Society*, 2004 (ISBN 90-411-2252-4).
51. Roger Blanpain, *The Actors of Collective Bargaining: A World Report*, 2004 (ISBN 90-411-2253-2).
52. Roger Blanpain & Michele Colucci, *The Globalisation of Labour Standards: The Soft Law Track*, 2004 (ISBN 90-411-2303-2).
53. Roger Blanpain, Takashi Araki & Shinya Ouchi, *Labour Law in Motion: Diversification of the Labour Force & Terms and Conditions of Employment*, 2005 (ISBN 90-411-2315-6).
54. Roger Blanpain, *Smoking and the Workplace*, 2005 (ISBN 90-411-2325-3).
55. Roger Blanpain, *Confronting Globalization: The Quest for a Social Agenda*, 2005 (ISBN 90-411-2381-4).
56. Roger Blanpain, Thomas Blanke & Edgar Rose, *Collective Bargaining Wages in Comparative Perspective: Germany, France, the Netherlands, Sweden and the United Kingdom*, 2005 (ISBN 90-411-2388-1).
57. Roger Blanpain & Anne Numhauser-Henning, *Women in Academia & Equality Law: Aiming High - Falling Short?*, 2006 (ISBN 978-90-411-2427-6).
58. Roger Blanpain, *Freedom of Services in the European Union: Labour and Social Security Law: The Bolkestein Initiative*, 2006 (ISBN 978-90-411-2453-5).
59. Roger Blanpain, Frans Pennings & Nurhan Sural, *Flexibilisation and Modernisation of the Turkish Labour Market*, 2006 (ISBN 978-90-411-2490-X).

60. Roger Blanpain & Boel Flodgren, *Corporate and Employment Perspectives in a Global Business Environment*, 2006 (ISBN 978-90-411-2537-X).
61. Roger Blanpain, Shinya Ouchi & Takashi Araki, *Decentralizing Industrial Relations and The Role of Labor Unions and Employee Representatives,* 2007 (ISBN 978-90-411-2583-3).
62. Roger Blanpain, *European Framework Agreements and Telework: Law and Practice: A European and Comparative Study,* 2007 (ISBN 978-90-411-2560-4).
63. Roger Blanpain, Jim Kitay, Leanne Cutcher & Nick Wailes, *Globalization and Employment Relations in Retail Banking,* 2007 (ISBN 978-90-411-2620-1).
64. Roger Blanpain, Russell Lansbury, Jim Kitay, Nick Wailes & Anja Kirsch, *Globalization and Employment Relations in the Auto Assembly Industry:* A *Study of Seven Countries,* 2008 (ISBN 978-90-411-2698-6).
65. Roger Blanpain & Michele Tiraboschi, *The Global Labour Market: From Globalization to Flexicurity,* 2008 (ISBN 978-90-411-2722-8).
66. Roger Blanpain, Michele Colucci & Frank Hendrickx, *The Future of Sport in the European Union: Beyond the EU Reform Treaty and the White Paper,* 2008 (ISBN 978-90-411-2761-7).
67. Roger Blanpain, Linda Dickens, *Challenges in European Employment Relations: Employment Regulation, Trade Union Organization, Equality, Flexicurity, Training and New Approaches to Pay,* 2008 (ISBN 978-90-411-2771-6).
68. Roger Blanpain, Hiroya Nakakubo & Takashi Araki, *New Developments in Employment Discrimination Law, 2008* (ISBN 978-90-411-2782-2).
69. Roger Blanpain, Andrzej Marian wiątkowski, *The Laval and Viking Cases: Freedom of Services and Establishment v. Industrial Conflict in the European Economic Area and Russia,* 2009 (ISBN 978-90-411-2850-8).
70. Roger Blanpain, William Bromwich, Olga Rymkevich, Silvia Spattini, *The Modernization of Labour Law and Industrial Relations in a Comparative Perspective,* 2009 (ISBN 978-90-411-2865-2).
71. Roger Blanpain, Juan Pablo Landa & Brian Langille, *Employment Policies and Multilevel Governance,* 2009 (ISBN 978-90-411-2866-9).
72. Roger Blanpain, European Works Councils; *The European Directive 2009/ 38/EC of 6 May 2009, 2009* (ISBN 978-90-411-3208-6).
73. Roger Blanpain, William Bromwich, Olga Rymkevich & Silvia Spattini, *Labour Productivity, Investment in Human Capital and Youth Employment: Comparative Developments and Global Responses,* 2010 (ISBN 978-90-411-3249-9).
74. Greg J. Bamber & Philippe Pochet, *Regulating Employment Relations, Work and Labour Laws: International Comparisons between Key Countries,* 2010 (ISBN 978-90-411-3199-7). General Editor: Roger Blanpain.
75. Roger Blanpain, Desislava Nikolaeva Dimitrova, *Seafarers' Rights in the Globalized Maritime Industry,* 2010 (ISBN 978-90-411-3349-6).
76. Roger Blanpain, Hiroya Nakakubo & Takashi Araki, *Regulation of Fixed- Term Employment Contracts,* 2010 (ISBN 978-90-411-3356-4).

77. Roger Blanpain, William Bromwich, Olga Rymkevich & Iacopo Senatori, *Rethinking Corporate Governance*, 2011 (ISBN 978-90-411-3450-9).
78. Roger Blanpain & Frank Hendrickx, *Labour Law between Change and Tradition: Liber Amicorum Antoine Jacobs*, 2011 (ISBN 978-90-411-3424-0).
79. Roger Blanpain, Thomas Klebe, Marlene Schmidt & Bernd Waas, *Trade Union Rights at the Workplace*, 2012 (ISBN 978-90-411-3460-8).
80. Roger Blanpain, William Bromwich, Olga Rymkevich & Iacopo Senatori, *Labour Markets, Industrial Relations and Human Resources Management: From Recession to Recovery*, 2012 (ISBN 978-90-411-4004-3).
81. Roger Blanpain, Hiroya Nakakubo & Takashi Araki, *Systems of Employee Representation at the Enterprise: A Comparative Study*, 2012 (ISBN 978-90-411-4080-7).
82. Roger Blanpain & Frank Hendrickx, *Temporary Agency Work in the European Union and the United States*, 2013 (ISBN 978-90-411-4769-1).
83. Roger Blanpain, Toker Dereli, Y. Pınar Soykut-Sarıca & Aslı en-Tabaı, *Emerging Patterns of Work and Turkish Labour Market Challenges under Globalization: Readings on Labour and Employment Relations*, 2014 (ISBN 978-90-411-4983-1).
84. Roger Blanpain, Pablo Arellano Ortiz, Marius Olivier & Gijsbert Vonk, *Social Security and Migrant Workers: Selected Studies of Cross-border Social Security Mechanisms*, 2014 (ISBN 978-90-411-4770-7).
85. Roger Blanpain & Nikita Lyutov, *Workers' Representation in Central and Eastern Europe: Challenges and Opportunities for the Works Councils' System*, 2014 (ISBN 978-90-411-4746-2).
86. Roger Blanpain, Ulla Liukkunen & Chen Yifeng, *China and ILO Fundamental Principles and Rights at Works*, 2014 (ISBN 978-90-411-4984-8).
87. Roger Blanpain, *The Use of Languages and Employment Relations*, 2014 (ISBN 978-90-411-5606-8).
88. Roger Blanpain, Hiroya Nakakubo & Takashi Araki, *Protection of Employees' Personal Information and Privacy*, 2014 (ISBN 978-90-411-5608-2).
89. Roger Blanpain, Jan Wouters, Glenn Rayp, Laura Beke & Axel Marx, *Protecting Labour Rights in a Multi-polar Supply Chain and Mobile Global Economy*, 2015 (ISBN 978-90-411-5662-4).
90. Roger Blanpain & Stefania Marassi, *Globalization and Transnational Collective Labour Relations: International and European Framework Agreements at Company Level*, 2015 (ISBN 978-90-411-4748-6).
91. Roger Blanpain, Frank Hendrickx & Petra Herzfeld Olsson, *National Effects of the Implementation of EU Directives on Labour Migration from Third Countries*, 2016 (ISBN 978-90-411-6257-1).
92. Roger Blanpain, Frank Hendrickx & D'Arcy du Toit, *Labour Law and Social Progress: Holding the Line or Shifting the Boundaries?* 2016 (ISBN 978-90-411-6747-7).

93. Roger Blanpain & Frank Hendrickx, *Reasonable Accommodation in the Modern Workplace: Potential and Limits of the Integrative Logics of Labour Law*, 2016 (ISBN 978-90-411-6258-8).
94. Roger Blanpain, Frank Hendrickx & Bernd Waas, *New Forms of Employment in Europe*, 2016 (ISBN 978-90-411-6239-7).
95. Roger Blanpain, Frank Hendrickx, Hiroya Nakakubo & Takashi Araki, *The Notion of Employer in the Era of the Fissured Workplace: Should Labour Law Responsibilities Exceed the Boundary of the Legal Entity?*, 2017 (ISBN 978-90-411-8470-2).
96. Elena Sychenko, *Individual Labour Rights as Human Rights: The Contributions of the European Court of Human Rights to Worker's Rights Protection*, 2017 (ISBN 978-90-411-8629-4).
97. William Bromwich & Olga Rymkevich, *Improving Workplace Quality: New Perspectives and Challenges for Worker Well-Being*, 2017 (ISBN 978-90-411-8628-7).
98. Sarah De Groof, *Work-Life Balance in the Modern Workplace: Interdisciplinary Perspectives from Work-Family Research, Law and Policy*, 2017 (ISBN 978-90-411-8630-0).